OREMUS

A Lutheran Breviary

Compiled and Edited by
Rev. David A. Kind

+ In nomine Jesu +

CONTENTS

HOW TO USE THIS BOOK

What is a Breviary?

A breviary is a prayer book; not just any prayer book, but a prayer book containing everything that one needs to pray the church's traditional daily prayers. One could call these prayers liturgies, and they are indeed known by the name "The Liturgy of the Hours" (also "Daily Office," "Divine Office," or "Canonical Hours"); but they differ from the Divine liturgy of Sunday morning. These liturgies do not frame the celebration of the Lord's Supper, that highest of gifts from Christ to His Church. Rather they flow down from that liturgical mountain peak, like streams seeking the lower places, the daily routine and grind of life. Flowing with the words and prayers of Scripture these streams of devotion hallow those places where we dwell with our families, where our vocations are lived out among our neighbors, where our confession is called for, where our mettle is tested, and where our fragile faith faces the temptations of our world, of the devil and of the flesh. Some have spoken of the practice of praying these liturgies as the hallowing of time, and they are not wrong for doing so. But these ancient prayers do more than hallow time. They hallow daily life by keeping daily life near to its source, Jesus Christ.

How to Use this Prayer Book

The prayers of the breviary are made up of several parts, the chief of which are: the Ordinary, the Propers and the Psalter. The ordinary contains the parts of the liturgy that are constant (or nearly so). Here you will find the day's liturgies laid out for you in their bare form. The Propers contain the parts of the liturgy that change from season to season or from day to day. There are propers for each day of the Church Year (the *temporale*). There are also propers for the feasts and commemorations of the Church Year (the *sanctorale*). The Psalter contains the Psalms with their appropriate antiphons and the Canticles (which are prayed like Psalms in some of the day's liturgies) with their antiphons. You will use all three elements in each of the day's prayers, with the exception of Compline which rarely has propers.

First, determine what day it is in the church year. Begin with the season. Is it Advent, Lent, Easter? Have you just celebrated one of the Church's holidays? Are you well into the long season of Trinity? Then, determine the week and day. Is it Thursday in the Third Week of Advent or Monday in Quinquagesima? This will determine several propers in the liturgies, such which lessons are read, which hymns are sung, which antiphons and collects are chanted. Be sure to check the calendar to see if the day happens to be is a feast or a commemoration, which will change some of the day's propers.

The next consideration is the time of day. There are seven liturgies contained in this book, each corresponding with a particular hour of the day. The first liturgy of the day is Matins, to be prayed upon waking in the morning. This is followed by Lauds, another morning liturgy, usually prayed near sunrise. These two morning liturgies can be prayed consecutively. Lauds is followed by Terce which is prayed at 9:00 AM, the hour at which the Holy Spirit descended on Pentecost. At noon, the hour in which Christ was hung on the cross, one prays Sext. This in turn is followed by None (pronounced like "tone"). None is prayed at 3:00 PM, the hour at which Christ was removed from the Cross to be buried. Vespers is prayed in the evening, preferably at sunset. The final liturgy is Compline which is prayed immediately before going to bed. An eighth liturgy, Prime, is not included in this breviary as it falls between Lauds and Terce and would unnecessarily increase the amount of time devoted to prayer in the morning. Historically, this hour was added mainly to keep lazy monks from returning to bed.

This book is designed to be used with your Bible. The vast majority of Scripture Readings for the various hours, days and seasons are not included. You will need to read them from your own Bible. The Psalter and the Biblical Canticles are included in their entirety as they are pointed for chant.

Praying the Psalter

Since ancient times, the faithful people of God have prayed the Psalter. From the days of King David it has been the prayer book of the church. Portions of the Psalms were prayed daily in the Temple. They comforted the Israelites in exile and gave voice to their jubilation when they returned. Our Lord Himself prayed the Psalms, even while suffering crucifixion. Constantly found on the lips of the saints, the recitation of the Psalter connects us with them and the entire Church catholic in prayer.

The Psalms contain more than mere human sentiment and desire. They are, like the rest of the Holy Scriptures, the inspired Word of God. Yet they contain within them every sentiment that is truly human, and address every imaginable condition and need of mankind. They strengthen the weak, give help to the afflicted, hope to the forlorn, joy to the forgiven. At the heart of the Psalter one finds Christ. These prayers reveal Him and are prayed by Him. As such they build up the body of Christ, the Church (James 5:13, Colossians 3:16). They are timeless.

The foundation of the Canonical Hours is the praying the Psalter. Monks of the medieval era prayed the entire Psalter at least once each week. Some in the early church era prayed the entire Psalter daily! While greatly reduced in frequency from the use of the Medieval Church, the goal of this breviary is that the entire Psalter be prayed through every month or so, and that the Psalms would thus be gradually bound to one's heart and mind (Deuteronomy 11:18).

The schedule provided in the propers is based upon the weekly Psalter according to the Rule of St. Benedict. A few Psalms are recited daily, a few weekly, some every other week, some only once every four weeks. Monthly recitation of the entire Psalter is only achieved if one is praying all of the prayer offices every day. It is recognized that not many will do this. So one is free, of course, to adapt the Psalter to one's own devotional practice.

Chanting

Chant, like poetry, is a means of elevating human language above the common and mundane, and of hallowing it. The type of chant used throughout this book is Plainchant, commonly known as Gregorian Chant. Plainchant is one of the oldest and most beautiful forms of music in the church. Its roots are likely in the chants of the Old Testament synagogue and of the early Christian house church. It has been in use continuously since the sixth century AD, developing and expanding gradually throughout the middle ages. It is the church's chant *par excellance*.

For many, however, Gregorian Chant has been a treasure out of reach. This is due in part to the complexity of many of the traditional chants and in part to the traditional neumatic notation (consisting of various neumes of different shapes and a four line staff with a moveable clef) used in most sources for Plainchant.

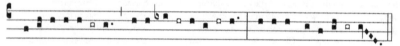

Tone 1D in neumatic notation

Because reading this notation is difficult for most and takes some effort to learn, Gregorian Chant has been an enigma for the modern musician, pastor, and layman. The musical notation has been modernized in this book in the hope that this beautiful music of the Church would become accessible to all.

Tone 1D in modern notation

Chant, even in modern notation, is neither limited by time signatures nor by conventional rhythmic notation. Plainchant should be sung freely, not allowing printed rhythms to enslave the music or musician. The text is the determinative factor in setting pace. While there are some notes that are given greater weight or length, these are not for the sake of musical rhythm but for the sake of the spoken phrase. Chant should sound like musical speech, not like the singing of a song. Without doubt there is a tune to some of the chants, but even when there is the text rules the tune, rather than the tune the text.

Please note that the chants in this volume may be sung starting on any desired pitch. The intervals between notes, rather than the starting pitch, are what determine the mode of the particular chant. If the music as printed is too high or too low for comfortable chanting, one may transpose the chants up or down as desired.

Psalm Tones

There are nine traditional Gregorian Psalm tones (Tones 1-8 plus the *Tonus Peregrinus*). Each of these is used in the Psalter. Each tone consists of several parts. The first group of notes is called the **Intonation**. For the Psalms, the intonation is only sung for the first verse. For the canticles and the *Miserere Mei* (Psalm 51) the intonation is sung for every verse. The second part is called the **Tenor**, also known as the Dominant or Reciting note. Several words are usually sung at this pitch. Good phrasing is important here that the music not become dull and monotonous. The *Liber Usualis* suggests: "There must be life and movement but no hurry." In very long phrases, the first part may be divided by a **Flex**, so named due to the lowering of pitch. The need for a Flex will not be printed in the tone or indicated in the Psalm text, but is left up to the discretion of the one chanting. Next comes the **Mediation**. This cadence is sung at the end the first half verse. The **Tenor** is then repeated, followed by the **Termination**, a final cadence ending the verse. Most Psalm tones have several different options for terminations. These are intended to make the transition from the antiphon to the Psalm Tone and back again to the antiphon.

Intonation Tenor   Mediation   Tenor   Termination

Pointing

Text which corresponds to chant is usually pointed, meaning that there are certain symbols in the text which indicate when the various parts of the tone are to be chanted. The words used for the intonation will always be in **CAPS**. The words following the intonation are to be sung on the Tenor note until a backslash / indicating the Mediation is seen. A pause is taken at the end of the half verse and is marked by an asterisk *. The next half verse is sung on the Tenor note until the backslash / is seen again, indicating the Termination. Because the English language is strongly accented (unlike Latin), additional hollow notes (which look like whole notes) are included in some of the chants. These notes are sung only when needed and are treated just like any other note when used (i.e. not like whole notes). If one were to chant Psalm 95 to Tone 1D (above) the first verse would look like this when pointed. Note that in this example the hollow notes are not needed:

OH COME, let us / sing to the Lord *
Let us shout joyfully to the Rock of / our salvation.

The Lectionary

Many lectionaries have been used over the history of the Christian Church. The lectionary included in this book is based on the historic Western (Roman) lectionary that dates back to at least the 8th century. A balance, however, has been struck between the use of this historic lectionary and the monastic practice of a *lectio continua*, or continuous reading of the Bible.

The Matins lectionary, containing the readings from the Holy Gospel, is based on the historic lectionary, which includes readings for most Wednesdays and Fridays, and occasionally for other weekdays as well. There have been, of course, many variants to this lectionary depending on time and locale, especially for weekday readings, but the editor has attempted to include what is thought to be the strongest and most fitting among them. Additional "alternative" Gospel readings are included in smaller print for those who wish for more variety during the week and for a more complete reading of the Gospels. These alternative readings are often parallel to or closely related to the historic lesson they would replace. The four Gospels are included in their entirety throughout the lectionary when including the alternate readings and the readings in the *sanctorale*.

The readings for Terce, Sext and None are the Epistles of the historic lectionary. If praying all three offices, the reading is either divided among them or may be replaced with a reading of one's choice rather than repeating it.

The lectionary for Lauds and Vespers follows a *lectio continua* principle, with selections from the books of the Old and New Testaments (excluding the Gospels and Psalms). These books are not arranged sequentially, but seasonally, and according to the ancient tradition.

There is no lectionary for Compline, which has two fixed readings.

The Body at Prayer

Prayer is more than act of the mind and voice. It involves the whole person, including one's body. To give order to the body's involvement in prayer, specific postures and bodily actions have evolved for various portions of the Divine Office. Chief among these are standing, sitting, kneeling and making the sign of the cross. Directions for some of these are included in the ordinary, but not for all. The making of the sign of the cross will always be indicated in the text with cross symbol ✠.

STAND　　　　　　　For the opening versicles of every office
　　　　　　　　　　During the *Venite* of Matins
　　　　　　　　　　During the psalmody (sitting is optional)
　　　　　　　　　　For the *gloria Patri* at the end of each Psalm or Canticle (if sitting previously)
　　　　　　　　　　During all hymns (sitting is optional)

	During the Gospel lesson at Matins
	During the *Te Deum* at Matins
	During the *Benedictus, Magnificat,* and *Nunc Dimittis* and their antiphons
	During and all of Compline except the *Confiteor*

SIT During the readings at Lauds and Vespers
During the responsories
During the homily at Matins

BOW During the first half of every *gloria Patri* or "Glory be..." (if already standing)
During the *Venite* at the words "Oh come, let us worship and bow down"
During the *Te Deum* at the words "holy, holy, holy"
During the *Magnificat* at the words "holy is His name"

KNEEL During the *Te Deum* beginning at the words "We therefore pray You to help Your servants..."
During the prayers at Lauds and Vespers beginning with the *Kyrie,*
During the *Confiteor* at Compline.
Please note that there is no kneeling during the Eastertide.

Leading the Church's Prayer

The Divine Office is ordinarily led by the clergy when prayed publicly by the Church. But because the Divine Office is not a sacramental rite, lay people also may lead the service, and are encouraged to do so, when there is no ordained pastor present. In the household, the father will ordinarily lead the prayers. He is free, of course, to delegate portions of the liturgies, especially readings and prayers to other members of the family as he sees fit. In cases where the father is not present, the mother, an elder relative, or an older child may lead the prayers. In a mixed company of adults outside of the home it is best to have a male lead the prayers when no pastor is available.

Enjoying Christian Freedom

Having been freed by Christ from the burden of the Law, one is free to tailor one's daily prayers as one sees fit. One should not feel obliged to follow these rubrics or liturgies slavishly. The liturgies are one collection of many of the Church's historic and living prayers. The rubrics are given as a guide in following the historic practices of the Church at prayer, and to lend order and reverence where needed. But one is free to make use of this book and the many resources contained herein as one sees fit. Please do so remembering, that while all things are lawful to us, not all things are profitable.

Whether you diligently pray the seven hours every day, or pray Lauds and Vespers, or just make use of Matins and Compline, or whatever other combination one might choose, it is my fervent prayer that you will be enriched in your devotion and faith by Christ through His words and through the preaching, poetry, and prayers of His faithful servants contained in these pages.

THE CALENDAR

Feasts of our Lord are in bold type. Other feasts are in regular type. Commemorations are in italics.

November

30	St. Andrew the Apostle

December

4	*John of Damascus*
6	*Nicholas of Myra*
7	*Ambrose of Milan*
13	*Lucia*
20	*Sebastian*
21	St. Thomas the Apostle
24	Eve of the Nativity of Our Lord
25	**The Nativity of Our Lord**
26	St. Stephen
27	St. John the Evangelist

28	Holy Innocents
31	*Sylvester*

January

1	**The Circumcision of our Lord**
2	*Wilhelm Löhe*
6	**The Epiphany of our Lord**
14	*Hilary of Poitiers*
17	*Antony of Egypt*
18	The Confession of St. Peter
24	St. Timothy
25	The Conversion of St. Paul
26	St. Titus
27	*John Chrysostom*

February

2	**The Presentation of our Lord**
14	*Valentine*
18	*Martin Luther*
23	*Polycarp of Smyrna*
24	St. Matthias the Apostle

March

7	*Perpetua & Felicitas*
12	*Gregory the Great of Rome*
17	*Patrick of Ireland*
18	*Cyril of Jerusalem*
19	St. Joseph, Guardian of our Lord
21	*Benedict of Nursia*
25	The Annunciation of the BVM

April

4	*Isidore of Seville*
6	*Martin Chemnitz*
11	*Leo the Great of Rome*
20	*Johannes Bugenhagen*
21	*Anselm of Canterbury*
24	*Johann Walter*
25	St. Mark the Evangelist

May

1	Sts. Phillip & James, Apostles
2	*Athanasius of Alexandria*
5	*Frederick the Wise of Saxony*
7	*C.F.W. Walther*
9	*Gregory of Nazianzus*
11	*Cyril & Methodius*
21	*Constantine the Great*
25	*Bede the Venerable*
27	*Augustine of Canterbury*
31	The Visitation of the BVM

June

1	*Justin*
5	*Boniface of Mainz*
9	*Columba of Iona*
11	St. Barnabas
14	*Basil the Great of Caesarea*
18	*Ephrem the Syrian*
24	The Nativity of St. John the Baptist

25	*The Presentation of the Augsburg Confession*
27	*Cyril of Alexandria*
28	*Irenaeus of Lyons*
29	Sts. Peter & Paul the Apostles

July

19	*Macrina the Younger*
22	St. Mary Magdalene
25	St. James the Elder the Apostle
28	*Johann Sebastian Bach*
31	*Peter Chrysologus*

August

10	Lawrence of Rome
15	The Blessed Virgin Mary (BVM)
17	*Johann Gerhard*
19	*Bernard of Clairvaux*
24	St. Bartholomew the Apostle
27	*Monica*
28	*Augustine of Hippo*
29	*The Beheading of St. John the Baptist*
31	*Aidan & Cuthbert*

September

14	Holy Cross
16	*Cyprian of Carthage*
21	St. Matthew the Apostle
29	St. Michael & All Angels
30	*Jerome of Jerusalem*

October

1	*Remigius of Rheims*
17	*Ignatius of Antioch*
18	St. Luke, Evangelist
23	St. James the Just
26	*Alfred the Great*
28	Sts. Simon & Jude the Apostles
31	Reformation

November

1	All Saints
2	Faithful Departed
11	*Martin of Tours*
17	*Gregory Thaumaturgus*
22	*Cecelia*
23	*Clement of Rome*

Ember & Rogation Days

Ember days and Rogation days are days of fasting and prayer. Ember days were originally tied to the agricultural cycles in Italy when fasting and prayers were offered to implore the Lord's blessings upon the crops and the harvest. Over time the focus became broader: that of seeking the Lord's blessing upon all people in their vocations, especially upon those who are preparing for ordination. Ember days take place during the weeks of Guadete, Invocavit, Pentecost, and the week after Holy Cross Day (September 14). One may observe ember days by fasting and saying collects for the Lord's blessing upon the fruits of the earth, those preparing for or serving in the Holy Ministry, and all according to their vocation. Rogation days fall on the weekdays of Rogate week before Ascension. It is customary on these days to fast, pray the Litany, and seek the Lord's protection and blessing of the local congregation and of fields and crops.

Grant, I implore You, Almighty and Merciful God, that speaking with understanding and good will, and in plainness, I may be found worthy to be heard by You; for I need Your help in all things; so that by the gift of Your grace, I may be enabled not unworthily to sing the words of Your Majesty, through our Lord, Jesus Christ. Amen.

Bede the Venerable

MATINS
Prayer at the Beginning of the Day

℣: O Lord, open ✠ my lips.

℟: And my mouth shall show forth Your praise.

Psalm 51:15

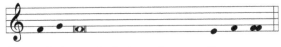

℣: ✠ Make haste, O God, to de - liv - er me.

℟: Make haste to help me, O Lord.

Psalm 70:1

All: Glory be to the Father and to the Son and to the Holy Spir - it;

As it was in the beginning, is now, and will be forever. A - men.

Al - le - lu - ia.

From Septuagesima through Holy Saturday the Alleluia is replaced with the following:

Praise to You, O Christ, King of eternal glo-ry.

1

Invitatory - *Adoremus Dominum*   *Seasonal inviatories as specified in the propers*   *Tone 6*

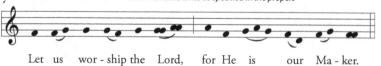

Let us wor - ship the Lord,   for He is   our Ma - ker.

Psalm: 95 - *Venite exultemus*   *Tone 6*

The Venite may also be chanted to a simple tone, as provided in the Psalter.

Oh come, let us sing to the Lord! Let us shout joy - ful - ly

to the Rock of our sal - va - tion.   Let us come be - fore His

pre-sence with thanks-giv - ing;   Let us shout joy- ful - ly   to

Him with psalms.   For the Lord is the great God,   And the great

King a- bove all   gods.   In His hand are the deep plac - es of

the earth;   The heights of the hills are His al - so.   The sea

is His, for He made it;   And His hands formed the dry land.

Oh come, let us wor-ship   and bow down;   Let us kneel be-

fore the Lord our Ma - ker.   For He is   our God,   And we

2

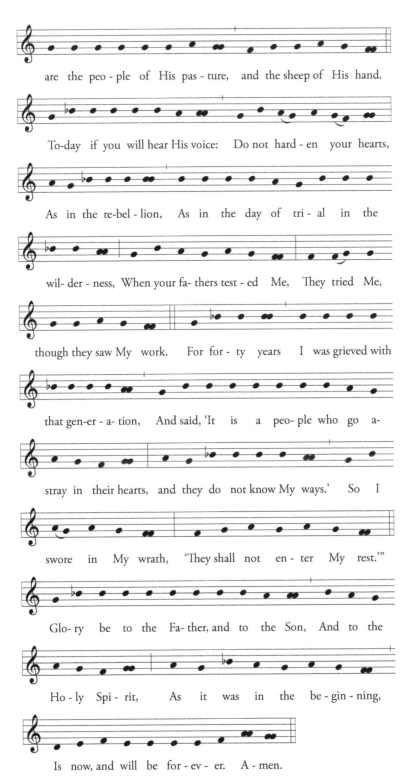

are the peo-ple of His pas-ture, and the sheep of His hand.

To-day if you will hear His voice: Do not hard-en your hearts,

As in the re-bel-lion, As in the day of tri-al in the

wil-der-ness, When your fa-thers test-ed Me, They tried Me,

though they saw My work. For for-ty years I was grieved with

that gen-er-a-tion, And said, 'It is a peo-ple who go a-

stray in their hearts, and they do not know My ways.' So I

swore in My wrath, 'They shall not en-ter My rest.'"

Glo-ry be to the Fa-ther, and to the Son, And to the

Ho-ly Spi-rit, As it was in the be-gin-ning,

Is now, and will be for-ev-er. A-men.

Hymn, Psalmody, Lesson and Homily *As specified in the propers.*

Responsory *To be sung on ferial weekdays*

℣: Christ, Son of the liv - ing God, have mer - cy up - on us.
℟: Christ, Son of the liv - ing God, have mer - cy up - on us.

℣: Who sits at the right hand of the Fa - ther,
℟: Christ ...

℣: Glo-ry be to the Fa - ther, and to the Son, and to the Ho-ly Spi - rit.
℟: Christ ...

℣: Arise, O Christ, for our / help.
℟: And redeem us for Your mercy's / sake. *Psalm 44:26*

Canticle - *Te Deum laudamus* *To be sung on Sundays and festival days*

We praise You O God, we ac-know-ledge You to be the Lord.

All the earth now wor-ships You, the Fa - ther ev - er - last - ing.

To you all an-gels cry a- loud, the hea-vens and all the pow'rs there-in.

To You cher - u- bim and ser - a - phim con-tin- ual - ly do cry:

4

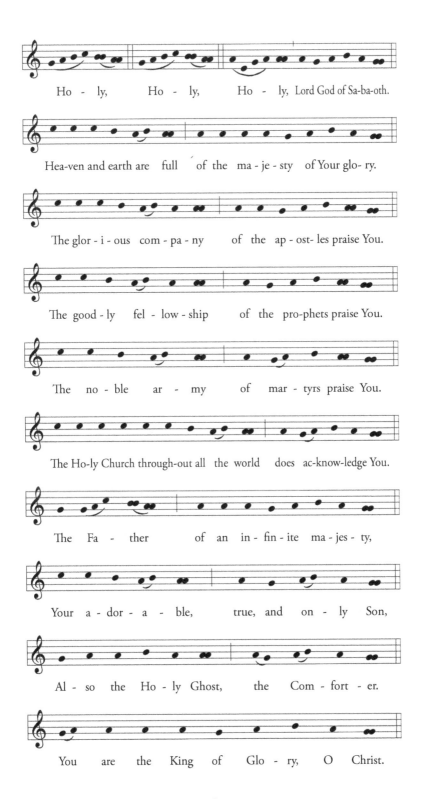

Ho - ly, Ho - ly, Ho - ly, Lord God of Sa-ba-oth.

Hea-ven and earth are full of the ma - je - sty of Your glo- ry.

The glor - i - ous com - pa - ny of the ap - ost- les praise You.

The good - ly fel - low - ship of the pro-phets praise You.

The no - ble ar - my of mar - tyrs praise You.

The Ho-ly Church through-out all the world does ac-know-ledge You.

The Fa - ther of an in - fin - ite ma - jes - ty,

Your a - dor - a - ble, true, and on - ly Son,

Al - so the Ho - ly Ghost, the Com - fort - er.

You are the King of Glo - ry, O Christ.

You are the ev - er - last - ing Son of the Fa - ther.

When You took up - on Your-self to de - liv - er man

You humb- led Your- self to be born of a vir - gin.

When You had ov - er - come the sharp - ness of death,

You o-pened the King-dom of Heav- en to all be - liev - ers.

You sit at the right hand of God In the glo-ry of the Fa-ther.

We be - lieve that You will come To be our judge.

We there - fore pray You to help Your ser - vants

Whom You have re - deemed with Your pre - cious blood.

Make them to be num-bered with Your saints In glo-ry ev - er - last - ing.

If Matins is to be followed immediately by Lauds, the office concludes here.

Collects

℣: O Lord, hear my prayer.

℟: And let my cry come to You.

Psalm 102:1

℣: Let us pray.

The collect specified in the propers is prayed first. Other prayers or collects may be added, including prayers for:

Sunday: The local parish
Monday: One's vocation, fellow workers, family and friends
Tuesday: Enemies, schismatics and heathen
Wednesday: The impenitent and those who neglect their faith

Thursday: The Church, her institutions, pastors and teachers
Friday: The suffering, sick, persecuted and dying
Saturday: The nation, rulers and world

Conclude with one of the following collects:

We thank you, heavenly Father, through Jesus Christ, Your dear Son, that You have kept us this night from harm and danger; and we pray that You would keep us this day also from sin and every evil, that all our doings and life may please You. For into Your hands we commend ourselves, our bodies and souls, and all things. Let Your holy angel be with us, that the wicked foe may have no power over us.

Martin Luther

OR

Send forth, we pray You, O Lord, Your light into our hearts; that we may perceive the light of Your commandments, and, walking in Your way, may fall into no error, through Jesus Christ, our Lord, who lives and reigns with You and the Holy Spirit, one God, now and forever.

Gelasian Sacramentary

OR

O God, who divides the day from the night, separate our deeds from the gloom of darkness, that ever meditating on that which is holy, we may continually live in Your light, through Jesus Christ, our Lord, who lives and reigns with You and the Holy Spirit, one God, now and forever.

Leonine Sacramentary

OR

O Merciful Lord God, Heavenly Father, I give You most high laud, praise and thanks, that You have preserved me under Your protection, both this night and all the times and days of my life up to now, and has allowed me to live until this present hour; and I heartily implore You that You will condescend to receive me this day, and for the rest of my life, into Your good keeping, ruling and governing me with Your Holy Spirit, that all manner of darkness and evil may be utterly chased and driven out of my heart; and that I may walk in the light of Your truth, to Your glory and praise, and to the help and furtherance of my neighbor; through Jesus Christ, Your Son, our Lord, who lives and reigns with You and the Holy Spirit, one God, now and forever. *Primer of Henry VIII*

OR

O almighty and eternal God, direct, sanctify and govern our hearts and bodies in the ways of Your laws, and in the works of Your commandments; that, through Your mighty protection, now and always, we may be preserved in body and soul; through Your Son, Jesus Christ our Lord, who lives and reigns with You and the Holy Spirit, one God, now and forever. *Sarum Breviary*

R⁄: A - men.

Benedicamus

V⁄:   Let   us   bless   the   Lord.

R⁄: Thanks be   to   God.

If led by a pastor the following benediction may be said:

V⁄: The Almighty and mer-   ci - ful Lord,   the Fa- ther,

the   Son,   and the Holy Spirit, bless ✠ and pre - serve us.

R⁄: A - men.

LAUDS
Prayer in the Morning

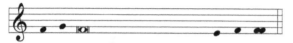

℣: ✠ Make haste, O God, to de - liv - er me.

℟: Make haste to help me, O Lord.

Psalm 70:1

All: Glory be to the Father and to the Son and to the Holy Spir - it;

As it was in the beginning, is now, and will be forever. A - men.

Al - le - lu - ia.

From Septuagesima through Holy Saturday the Alleluia is replaced with the following:

Praise to You, O Christ, King of eternal glo-ry.

Psalmody and Chapter *As specified in the propers*

Hymn - *Splendor paternae gloria* *Or as specified in the propers.*
Additional morning hymns may be found beginning on p.652

1. O splen- dor of God's glo - ry bright, Who bring- est forth
2. Come, ve - ry Sun of truth and love, Come in Thy ra-
3. Like-wise to Thee our prayers as - cend, Fa - ther of glo-

the light from Light;   O Light of Light, light's Foun-tain-spring;
diance from a - bove,   And shed the Ho - ly Spi - rit's ray
ry with- out end,   Fa - ther of sov'- reign grace, for power

O Day, our days en - light - en - ing;
On all we think or do to - day.
To con - quer in temp - ta - tion's hour,

4. Teach us to walk with all our might;
   Beat back the devil's threat'ning spite;
   Turn all to good that seems most ill;
   Help us our calling to fulfill;

5. Direct and govern heart and mind,
   With body chaste and disciplined;
   Let faith her eager fires renew,
   And hate the false and love the true.

6. On Christ the true Bread let us feed;
   Let faith to us be drink indeed,
   And let us taste with joyfulness
   The Spirit's temperate excess.

7. O joyful be the livelong day,
   Our thoughts as pure as morning ray,
   Our faith like noonday's glowing height
   Our souls undimmed by shades of night.

8. The dawn begins to speed her way,
   Let the true Dawn Himself display,
   The Son with God the Father One,
   And God the Father in the Son. Amen.

Ambrose of Milan

Verse *Or as specified in the propers, and chanted to this tone*

℣: At daybreak we were filled with Your mer- / cy.
   ℟: We rejoiced and were delight- / ed.   *Liturgical text*

Canticle - *Benedictus* *Seasonal antiphons and chant tones as specified in the propers* Tone 4E

Antiphon - *Benedictus Dominus*

Bless - éd   is the Lord God of Is - ra - el;   who has vis - it-

ed   and re - deemed us.   *Luke 1:68*

11

Canticle

✠ BLESSÉD is the Lord God / of Israel; *
   For He has visited and / redeemed His people.

AND HAS raised up a horn of sal- / vation for us *
   In the house of / His servant David

AS HE spoke by the mouth of His / holy prophets, *
   Who have been / since the world began,

THAT WE should be saved from / our enemies *
   And from the hand / of all who hate us

TO PERform the mercy promised / to our fathers, *
   And to remember / His holy covenant.

THE OATH which he swore to our fa- / ther Abraham *
   To grant us that we, being delivered from the / hand of our enemies

MIGHT SERVE / Him without fear *
   In holiness and righteousness before Him all / the days of our life

AND YOU, child, will be called the prophet / of the Highest; *
   For you will go before the face of the Lord / to prepare His ways

TO GIVE knowledge of salvation / to His people *
   By the / remission of their sins,

THROUGH THE tender mer- / cy of our God,*
   With which the Dayspring from on high / has visited us

TO GIVE light to those who sit in darkness and the / shadow of death *
   And to guide our feet in- / to the way of peace.

GLORY be to the Father, / and to the Son *
   and to / the Holy Spirit

AS IT was in / the beginning *
   Is now and will be / forever. Amen.

Luke 1: 68-79

Kyrie *On rogation days before Ascension the Litany is said in place of the Kyrie and Lord's Prayer.*

All: Lord,   have   mer - cy;
      Christ, have   mer - cy;
      Lord,   have   mer - cy;

Lord's Prayer

℣: Our Fa - ther * who art in heaven, hallowed be Thy name, Thy kingdom come, Thy will be done on earth as it is in heaven. Give us this day our daily bread; and forgive us our trespasses as we forgive those who trespass against us, and lead us not into / temptation.

℟: But deliver us from ✠ / e - vil.

Preces   *Said during Advent and from Septuagesima through Passiontide*

℣: I said; O Lord be merciful / to me;
℟: Heal my soul, for I have sinned a- / gainst You.   *Psalm 41:4*

℣: Return, O Lord, / how long?
℟: And have compassion on Your / servants.   *Psalm 90:13*

℣: Let Your mercy, O Lord, be up- / on us;
℟: According as we hope / in You.   *Psalm 33:22*

℣: Let Your priests be clothed with right- / eous-ness;
℟: And let Your saints shout / for joy.   *Psalm 132:9*

℣: O Lord, save our / rulers;
℟: May the King hear us when / we call.   *Psalm 20:9*

℣: Save Your people, and bless Your inher- / itance;
℟: Shepherd them also, and bear them up for- / ever.   *Psalm 28:9*

℣: Remember Your congre- / gation;
℟: Which You have purchased / of old.   *Psalm 74:2*

℣: Peace be within / Your walls;
℟: And prosperity within Your pal- / aces.   *Psalm 122:7*

℣: Let us pray for our absent brothers and / sisters;
℟: O our God, save Your servants that trust / in You.   *Psalm 86:2*

℣: Let us pray for the broken-hearted and the / captives
℟: Redeem Israel, O God, out of all his / troubles.   *Psalm 25:22*

℣: Send them help from the Sanctu- / ary;
℟: And strengthen them out of / Zion.   *Psalm 20:2*

℣: Restore us, O God / of hosts;
℟: Cause Your face to shine and we shall / be saved.   *Psalm 80:7*

℣: Arise, O Christ, for / our help;
℟: And redeem us, for Your mer- / cies' sake.

Psalm 44:26

℣: Give peace in our days,/ O Lord:
℟: Because there is none other that fights for us, except You, / our God.

℣: O Lord, let there be peace in / Your strength:
℟: And abundance in Your / towers.

Collects

℣: O Lord, hear my prayer.
℟: And let my cry come to You.

Psalm 102:1

℣: Let us pray.

The collect specified in the propers is prayed first. Other prayers or collects may be added, including prayers for:

Sunday: The local parish	Thursday: The Church, her institutions, pastors and teachers
Monday: One's vocation, fellow workers, family and friends	Friday: The suffering, sick, persecuted and dying
Tuesday: Enemies, schismatics and heathen	Saturday: The nation, rulers and world
Wednesday: The impenitent and those who neglect their faith	

Conclude with one of the following collects:

O everlasting Jesus, who in the early morning gave Yourself over to be reviled and scoffed at by Your enemies, visit us at this hour, we pray, with Your grace and mercy that throughout the day we may find peace and joy in all that serves to Your praise and glory, who lives and reigns with the Father and the Holy Spirit, ever one God, world without end.

Sarum Breviary

OR

O Lord, God Almighty, You have brought us to the beginning of this day, save us today by Your power, that we may not fall into sin this day, but that all our thoughts, words, and works may be directed to the fulfillment of Your will, through Jesus Christ, Your Son, our Lord, who lives and reigns with You and the Holy Spirit, one God, now and forever.

Gelasian Sacramentary

OR

O Lord, our Heavenly Father, Almighty and Everlasting God, You have safely brought us to the beginning of this day: defend us in the same with Your mighty power; and grant that this day we fall into no sin, neither run into any kind of danger, but that all our doings, being ordered by Your governance, may be righteous in Your sight; through Jesus Christ, Your Son, our Lord, who lives and reigns with You and the Holy Spirit, one God, now and forever.

Sarum Breviary

OR

Grant us, O Lord, to pass this day in gladness and peace, without stumbling or stain, that reaching the evening victorious over all temptation, we may praise You, eternal God, who is blessèd, and governs all things throughout the ages.

Mozarabic Breviary

OR

O Eternal and Merciful God, You have commanded Your people in Your Law to offer you a burnt offering every morning to praise and thank You for Your merciful protection: therefore I too would bring to You my offering of praise, the fruit of my lips, and magnify Your holy name. For by Your grace and mercy You have kept me this night from all evil and harm in body and soul, and have graciously protected me. If you had not been my shield and my help, many calamities would have engulfed me, and I could not have risen in health and safety. Therefore I thank You for Your protection.

But I continue to call to You from the depths of my heart, and my supplication ascends to You in the early hour. Early do I seek Your countenance and pray You to safeguard me and mine from the wiles and power of the devil, from sin and disgrace and all wickedness. Visit me in this early hour with Your grace, as without You I can do nothing, and grant that this day I may begin all my work in Your name and end it joyfully, to the glory of Your divine majesty and the good of my neighbor. Preserve my soul, mind, reason, senses, and thoughts, all that I do or leave undone, that the prince of darkness may do me no injury. Safeguard me against the destruction that lays waste at noonday. Defend me against my enemies that neither secretly nor openly they harm or injure me with their craft and cunning, violence or malice.

O God, Father and Lord of my life, shield me from all impurity and disorderly conduct. Keep me form all intemperance and unchastity, and turn from me shameless thoughts. Help me by Your grace to pluck out the eye that offends me and cast it away, and renounce all wicked and impure desires of the heart. Grant whatever is pleasing to You and useful to me, that I may serve You in true faith. Look upon me with the eyes of Your mercy, O Savior of the world, and enlighten my heart and eyes, that I may walk in the light of Your grace, which rises above me, and never loose You, the Eternal Light. *Johann Habermann*

OR

O God, the author of light, and the discoverer of all brightness, enlighten, we implore You, the darkness of our souls, and confirm Your servants with Your morning blessing; through Jesus Christ, Your Son, our Lord, who lives and reigns with You and the Holy Spirit, one God, now and forever. *Mozarabic Breviary*

OR

O Merciful Lord God, Heavenly Father, I give You most high laud, praise and thanks, that You have preserved me under Your protection, both this night and all the times and days of my life up to now, and has allowed me to live until this present hour; and I heartily implore You that You will condescend to receive me this day, and for the rest of my life, into Your good keeping, ruling and governing me with Your Holy Spirit, that all manner of darkness and evil may be utterly chased and driven out of my heart; and that I may walk in the light of Your truth, to Your glory and praise, and to the help and furtherance of my neighbor; through Jesus Christ, Your Son, our Lord, who lives and reigns with You and the Holy Spirit, one God, now and forever. *Primer of Henry VIII*

℟: A - men.

Benedicamus

℣: Let us bless the Lord.

℟: Thanks be to God.

If led by a pastor the following benediction may be said:

℣: The Almighty and mer- ci - ful Lord, the Fa- ther, the Son, and the Holy Spirit, bless ✠ and pre - serve us.

℟: A - men.

TERCE
Prayer at Nine O'clock a.m.

℣: ✠ Make haste, O God, to de - liv - er me.

℟: Make haste to help me, O Lord.

Psalm 70:1

All: Glory be to the Father and to the Son and to the Holy Spir - it;

As it was in the beginning, is now, and will be forever. A - men.

Al - le - lu - ia.

From Septuagesima through Holy Saturday the Alleluia is replaced with the following:

Praise to You, O Christ, King of eternal glo - ry.

Hymn at Terce - *Nunc Sancte nobis Spiritus*

1. Come Ho - ly Ghost, in es - sence One, with God the Fa -
2. May lips, tongue, mind, heart, strength pro-claim the hon - or of
3. O Fa - ther this we ask be done through Je - sus Christ

ther and the Son. Deign to de - scend u - pon us now
Thy ho - ly name. The fire of love to us im - part,
Thine on - ly Son, who with the Par - a - clete and Thee

17

Thy grace u - pon our souls pour out.
And kin - dle ev' - ry hu - man heart.
doth live and reign e - ter - nal - ly.　　　A - men.

Ambrose of Milan

Psalmody　*The following are split into three parts, sharing a single antiphon that is said before and after the psalmody.*

Sunday: 119a　　　　　　Wednesday: 119d　　　　　Friday: 119f
Monday: 119b　　　　　　Thursday: 119e　　　　　　Saturday: 119g
Tuesday: 119c

Chapter　*As specified in the propers*

Responsory and Verse　*Seasonal responsories as specified in the propers.*

℣: In- cline my heart, O　Lord　　to Your test - i - mo - nies.
℟: In-cline my heart, O　Lord　　to Your test - i - mo - nies.

℣: Turn my eyes from van-i - ty　　and re- vive me in Your way.
℟: Incline...

℣: Glo - ry be to the Fa-ther, and to the Son, and to the Ho-ly Spi - rit.
℟: Incline...

Psalm 119:36-37

℣: You have been my help; Do not leave / me
℟: Do not forsake me, O God of my salva- / tion.

Psalm 27:9

Collect

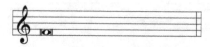

℣: O Lord, hear my prayer,
℟: And let my cry come to You.

Psalm 102:1

℣: Let us pray.

O God, almighty Father, we humbly implore Your Divine Majesty that, as You strengthened your apostles at the third hour by the visitation of Your Holy Spirit, so You will deign to enlighten and guard our hearts and bodies by His coming; through the merits of Jesus Christ our Lord, who lives and reigns with you and the same Holy Spirit, one God, now and forever.   *Ambrosian Missal*

OR

O Lord, Jesus Christ, Son of the Living God, who at the third hour of the day was led forth to the pain of the cross for the salvation of the whole world; we humbly implore You, that by virtue of Your most sacred Passion, You would blot out all our sins, and mercifully bring us to that eternal glory, where You live and reign with the Father and the Holy Spirit, one God, now and forever.   *Sarum Breviary*

OR

O Almighty God, You have brought me, after the darkness of the night, to the third hour of this day; preserve me this day in every hour and in every moment of time; and, of Your great goodness, grant that I may continue safe and unharmed in soul and in body throughout the same, through our Lord, Jesus Chris who lives and reigns with You and the Holy Spirit, one God, now and forever.   *Sarum Breviary*

OR

O Almighty God, who has granted to us, Your servants, regeneration by water and the Holy Spirit, and has given to us the forgiveness of sins; strengthen us, we implore You, O Lord, with the Holy Spirit the Comforter, and daily increase in us Your manifold gifts of grace; the Spirit of Wisdom and Understanding; the Spirit of Counsel and Spiritual Strength; the Spirit of Knowledge and True Godliness; and fill us, O Lord, with the Spirit of Your most Holy Fear: through Him who has sent down the Spirit upon His Church, Jesus Christ, our Lord and Savior, who lives and reigns with You and the same Spirit, one God, now and forever.

Book of Common Prayer

℟: A - men.

Benedicamus

℣: Let us bless the Lord.

℟: Thanks be to God.

SEXT
Prayer at Noon

℣: ✠ Make haste, O God, to de - liv - er me.

℟: Make haste to help me, O Lord.

Psalm 70:1

All: Glory be to the Father and to the Son and to the Holy Spir - it;

As it was in the beginning, is now, and will be forever. A - men.

Al - le - lu - ia.

From Septuagesima through Holy Saturday the Alleluia is replaced with the following:

Praise to You, O Christ, King of eternal glo-ry.

Hymn - *Rector potens, verax Deus*

1. O God of Truth, O Lord of might, Who or - ders time
2. Ex - tin - guish Thou each sin - ful fire, And ban - ish ev' -
3. O Fa - ther this we ask be done, through Je - sus Christ

and change a - right, And sends the ear - ly morn- ing ray
ry ill de - sire; And while Thou keep'st the bo - dy whole,
Thine on - ly Son, Who with the Ho - ly Ghost and Thee

20

And lights the glow of per - fect day;
Shed forth Thy peace up - on the soul.
Doth live and reign e - ter - nal - ly.   A - men.

Ambrose of Milan

Psalmody *The following are split into three parts, sharing a single antiphon that is said before and after the psalmody.*

Sunday: 119a   Wednesday: 119d   Friday: 119f
Monday: 119b   Thursday: 119e   Saturday: 119g
Tuesday: 119c

Chapter *As specified in the propers*

Responsory and Verse *Seasonal responsories as specified in the propers..*

℣: For - ev - er,   O   Lord,   Your word is sett - led in hea-ven.
℟: For - ev - er,   O   Lord,   Your word is sett - led in hea-ven.

℣: Your faith - ful - ness to all gen - er - a - tions.
℟: Forever...

℣: Glo-ry be to the Fa - ther, and to the Son, and to the Ho-ly Spi - rit.
℟: Forever...

Psalm 119:89-90

℣: The Lord is my Shepherd, I shall not / want.
   ℟: He makes me to lie down in green pas- / tures.

Psalm 23:1-2

Collect

℣: O Lord, hear my prayer,
   ℟: And let my cry come to You.

Psalm 102:1

℣: Let us pray.

O most gracious Jesus, our Lord and our God, who, at this hour bore our sins in Your own body on the tree that we being dead to sin might live to righteousness, have mercy on us, we implore You, both now and at the hour of our death; and grant to us, Your humble servants, with all other Christians who devoutly remember Your blessed Passion, a godly and peaceful life in this present world and through Your grace eternal glory in the life to come, where You live and reign with the Father and the Holy Spirit, one God, now and forever.

John Cosin

OR

O Lord, Jesus Christ, Son of the Living God, who at the sixth hour of the day ascended the cross of pain on Golgatha with great tumult; upon which, thirsting for our salvation, You permitted gall and vinegar to be given You to drink, we Your suppliants implore You that You would kindle and enflame our hearts with love of Your Passion, and make us continually find our delight in You alone, our crucified Lord, who lives and reigns with the Father and the Holy Spirit, one God, now and forever.

Sarum Breviary

OR

We humbly implore Your holy and terrible Name, O Lord Almighty, who at the sixth hour of the day willed Your most glorious Son, our Lord, to ascend the cross to deliver us from the power of the most wicked enemy; grant, we pray You, that redeemed by this His cross, we may at all times serve You righteously without offense, through the fame our Lord Jesus Christ, who lives and reigns with You and the Holy Spirit, one God, now and forever.

Gallican Psalter

OR

O Lord Jesus Christ, who at the Sixth Hour of the day was lifted up on the cross of suffering for the salvation of the world, and on it spilled forth Your precious Blood for the remission of our sins; we humbly beseech You, that through the merits of Your Passion and wounds, we, after death, may be found worthy to enter rejoicing into the gate of Paradise, where You live and reign with the Father and the Holy Spirit, one God, now and forever.

Sarum Breviary

℟: A - men.

Benedicamus

℣: Let us bless the Lord.

℟: Thanks be to God.

NONE

Prayer at Three O-Clock p.m.

℣: ✠ Make haste, O God, to de - liv - er me.

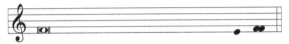

℟: Make haste to help me, O Lord.

Psalm 70:1

All: Glory be to the Father and to the Son and to the Holy Spir - it;

As it was in the beginning, is now, and will be forever. A - men.

Al - le - lu - ia.

From Septuagesima through Holy Saturday the Alleluia is replaced with the following:

Praise to You, O Christ, King of eternal glo-ry.

Hymn at None - *Rerum Deus, tenax vigor*

1. God of cre - a - tion, wond-rous Might, E - ter - nal pow'r
2. Shed light up - on our fad - ing day, That in our lives
3. O Fa - ther this we ask be done, Through Je - sus Christ

that all a - dore. Thou rul'st the chang-ing day and night,
no dusk may be. So death shall bring us to the ray
Thine on - ly Son, Who with the Ho - ly Ghost and Thee,

23

Thy - self un - chang-ing ev - er - more.
Of heav'n-ly glo - ry, Lord, with Thee.
Doth live and reign e - ter - nal - ly.　　　A - men.

Ambrose of Milan

Psalmody　*The following are split into three parts, sharing a single antiphon that is said before and after the psalmody.*

Sunday: 119a	Wednesday: 119d	Friday: 119f
Monday: 119b	Thursday: 119e	Saturday: 119g
Tuesday: 119c		

Chapter　*As specified in the propers*

Responsory and Verse　*Seasonal responsories as specified in the propers.*

℣: I cry out with my whole heart; hear me, O Lord.
℟: I cry out with my whole heart; hear me, O Lord.

℣: I will keep Your stat - utes.
℟: I cry out...

℣: Glo-ry be to the Fa - ther, and to the Son, and to the Ho-ly Spi - rit.
℟: I cry out...

Psalm 119:145

℣: Cleanse me from my secret faults, O / Lord;
℟: Keep back Your servant also from presumptous / sins.

Psalm 19:12-13

Collect

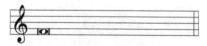

℣: O Lord, hear my prayer,
℟: And let my cry come to You.

Psalm 102:1

℣: Let us pray.

O Lord Jesus Christ, Son of the living God, who at the ninth hour of the day with hands extended on the cross and Your head bowed in death, delivered up Your Spirit to God the Father, and who by the key of Your death unlocked the door of Heaven; grant, we implore You, that in the hour of death our souls may rise to You who are the true Paradise, who live and reign with the Father and the Holy Spirit, one God, now and forever.

Sarum Breviary

OR

O Lord Jesus Christ, who, while hanging on the cross at the ninth hour, opened Paradise to the penitent thief who confessed Your name; we humbly beg You that You will cause us, who confess our sins, to enter with joy the portals of Heaven, where You live and reign with the Father and the Holy Spirit, one God, now and forever.   *Ambrosian Missal*

OR

O Lord Jesus Christ, Son of the Living God, who for the salvation of mankind was made to drink gall and vinegar on the cross, then You, all things being finished, expiring on that Cross, committed Your Spirit into the hand of the Father; so I commend my spirit, at the hour of my death, into the hands of Your pity, that You may receive it in peace and join it to the choirs of Your elect, where You live and reign with the Father and the Holy Spirit, one God, now and forever.   *Sarum Breviary*

OR

Hear us, O Lord, and remember now the hour in which You commended Your blessed Spirit into the hands of Your heavenly Father, when with a torn body and a broken heart You showed forth Your mercy by dying to deliver us from eternal death, and so assist us by Your most precious death, that, dying to the world, we may live to You, and that at the hour of our departure from this mortal life we may be received into Your everlasting kingdom, there to reign with You, forever and ever.   *Book of Common Prayer*

℟: A - men.

Benedicamus

℣:   Let   us   bless   the   Lord.

℟: Thanks be   to   God.

VESPERS
Prayer in the Evening

℣: ✠ Make haste, O God, to de - liv - er me.

℟: Make haste to help me, O Lord.

Psalm 70:1

All: Glory be to the Father and to the Son and to the Holy Spir - it;

As it was in the beginning, is now, and will be forever. A - men.

Al - le - lu - ia.

From Septuagesima through Holy Saturday the Alleluia is replaced with the following:

Praise to You, O Christ, King of eternal glo-ry.

Psalmody and Chapter *As specified in the propers*

Hymn - *Lucis Creator optime* *Or as specified in the propers.*
Additional evening hymns may be found beginning on p.652.

1.	O blest Cre- a - tor of the light,	Who mak'st the day
2.	Whose wis-dom joined in meet ar - ray	The morn and eve,
3.	Lest sunk in sin, and whelmed with strife,	They lose the gift

with ra - diance bright, And o'er the form - ing world didst call
and named them Day; Night comes with all its dark-ling fears;
of end - less life; While think-ing but the thoughts of time,

The light from cha - os first of all;
Re - gard Thy peo- ple's prayers and tears.
They weave new chains of woe and crime.

4. But grant them grace that they may strain
The heavenly gate and prize to gain;
Each harmful lure aside to cast,
And purge away each error past.

5. O Father, this we ask be done,
Through Jesus Christ, Thine only Son;
Who, with the Holy Ghost and Thee,
Doth live and reign eternally. Amen.

Gregory I

Verse *Or as specified in the propers, and chanted to this tone*

℣: Let my prayer be set before You as in- / cense
℟: The lifting up of my hands as the evening sacri- / fice.

Psalm 141:2

Canticle - *Magnificat* *Seasonal antiphons and chant tones as specified in the propers*   Tone 5

Antiphon - *Exsultavit spiritus meus*

My spi - rit has re - joiced in God my Sav - ior.   *Luke 1:46*

Canticle

✠ MY SOUL magnifies / the Lord, *
  And my spirit has rejoiced in / God my Savior.

FOR HE has regarded the lowly state of His / maidservant. *
  For behold, henceforth all generations will / call me blessèd:

HE WHO is mighty has done great / things for me, *
  And / holy is His Name.

AND HIS mercy is on those who / fear Him*
  From generation to / generation.

HE HAS shown strength with / His arm, *
  He has scattered the proud in the imagi- / nation of their hearts.

HE HAS put down the mighty from / their thrones, *
  And exalt- / ed the lowly.

HE HAS filled the hungry with / good things, *
  And the rich He has sent / away empty.

HE HAS helped His servant / Israel *
  In remembrance / of His mercy,

AS HE spoke to our / fathers, *
  To Abraham and his / seed forever.

GLORY be to the Father, and / to the Son *
  and to the / Holy Spirit

AS IT was in the be- / ginning *
  Is now and will be for / ever. Amen.

Luke 1:46-55

Kyrie *On rogation days before Ascension the Litany is said in place of the Kyrie and Lord's Prayer.*

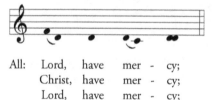

All: Lord,   have   mer - cy;
      Christ, have   mer - cy;
      Lord,   have   mer - cy;

Lord's Prayer

℣:   Our Fa - ther * who art in heaven, hallowed be Thy name, Thy kingdom come, Thy will be done on earth as it is in heaven. Give us this day our daily bread; and forgive us our trespasses as we forgive those who trespass against us, and lead us not into / temptation.

℟: But deliver us from ✠ / e - vil.

Preces *Said during Advent and from Septuagesima through Passiontide*

℣: I said; O Lord be merciful / to me;
   ℟: Heal my soul, for I have sinned a- / gainst You.   *Psalm 41:4*

℣: Return, O Lord, / how long?
   ℟: And have compassion on Your / servants.   *Psalm 90:13*

℣: Let Your mercy, O Lord, be up- / on us;
   ℟: According as we hope / in You.   *Psalm 33:22*

℣: Let Your priests be clothed with right- / eous-ness;
   ℟: And let Your saints shout / for joy.   *Psalm 132:9*

℣: O Lord, save our / rulers;
   ℟: May the King hear us when / we call.   *Psalm 20:9*

℣: Save Your people, and bless Your inher- / itance;
   ℟: Shepherd them also, and bear them up for- / ever.   *Psalm 28:9*

℣: Remember Your congre- / gation;
   ℟: Which You have purchased / of old.   *Psalm 74:2*

℣: Peace be within / Your walls;
   ℟: And prosperity within Your pal- / aces.   *Psalm 122:7*

℣: Let us pray for our absent brothers and / sisters;
   ℟: O our God, save Your servants that trust / in You.   *Psalm 86:2*

℣: Let us pray for the broken-hearted and the / captives
   ℟: Redeem Israel, O God, out of all his / troubles.   *Psalm 25:22*

℣: Send them help from the Sanctu- / ary;
   ℟: And strengthen them out of / Zion.   *Psalm 20:2*

℣: Restore us, O God / of hosts;
   ℟: Cause Your face to shine and we shall / be saved.   *Psalm 80:7*

℣: Arise, O Christ, for / our help;
   ℟: And redeem us, for Your mer- / cies' sake.   *Psalm 44:26*

℣: Give peace in our days, / O Lord:
   ℟: Because there is none other that fights for us, except You, / our God.

℣: O Lord, let there be peace in / Your strength:
   ℟: And abundance in Your / towers.

Collects

℣: O Lord, hear my prayer,
   ℟: And let my cry come to You.   *Psalm 102:1*

℣: Let us pray.

The collect specified in the propers is prayed first. Other prayers or collects may be added, including prayers for:

Sunday: The local parish

Monday: One's vocation, fellow workers, family and friends

Tuesday: Enemies, schismatics and heathen

Wednesday: The impenitent and those who neglect their faith

Thursday: The Church, her institutions, pastors and teachers

Friday: The suffering, sick, persecuted and dying

Saturday: The nation, rulers and world

Conclude with one of the following collects:

O Lord, God Almighty, who has commanded us to call the evening, the morning, and the noonday one day; and has made the sun to know its going down: dispel, we implore You, the darkness from our hearts, that by Your light we may know You to be the true God and eternal Light, through Jesus Christ our Lord, who lives and reigns with You and the Holy Spirit, one God, now and forever.

Gelasian Sacramentary

OR

O Lord, when the darkness covers us, let Your righteousness dawn upon our souls, that we, who now prayerfully render thanks to You after the labors of another day are done, may also come before Your face in the morning to pay You the vows of thanksgiving, through Jesus Christ, our Lord, who lives and reigns with You and the Holy Spirit, one God, now and forever. *Gelasian Sacramentary*

OR

O God, from whom come all holy desires, all good counsels, and all just works; give to us, Your servants, that peace which the world cannot give, that our hearts may be set to obey Your commandments, and also that we, being defended from the fear of our enemies, may live in peace and quietness; through Jesus Christ, Your Son, our Lord, who lives and reigns with You and the Holy Spirit, one God, now and forever. *Gelasian Sacramentary*

OR

O Lord, our heavenly Father, Almighty and Everlasting God, by whose providence both day and night are governed; grant, we implore You, as You have preserved us this day by Your goodness, so also this night to shadow us under the blessed wing of Your protection, and to cover us with Your heavenly mercy, that neither the princes of darkness may have any power over us, nor the works of darkness overwhelm us; but that we, being armed with Your defence, may be preserved from all adversities that may hurt the body, and from all wicked thoughts which may assault and defile the soul; through Jesus Christ, Your Son, our Lord, who lives and reigns with You and the Holy Spirit, one God, now and forever. *John Cosin*

OR

Lord, merciful God, Holy Father, in the daytime I cry to You with my voice, in my distress I call upon You, and at evening I remember Your goodness and mercy which You have wrought for me. And I especially magnify You now, that purely out of fatherly grace and mercy, without any merit or worthiness on my part, You have preserved me this day from all harm and danger and kept me from sudden death. Therefore I now and at all times render to You praise and thanksgiving, and pray You, for the sake of the bitter sufferings of Jesus Christ, to forgive me wherever I have sinned against You this day.

Mercifully protect me during the night against my adversary, the devil, and against the fears and terrors of the night. Let me rest without anxiety and worry, and may the eyes of my faith always behold the luster of Your countenance, even during the shades of night. For You are that shining and true light, which dispels all darkness that surrounds us. You, O Lord, are ever with me. You are my rock, and my fortress, and my deliverer, my strength, in whom I will trust, my buckler, the horn of my salvation, and my high tower.

Lord, my God, at evening I lift up my hands to You. Come to me as the latter rains that make the earth fruitful. Abide with us, for the day is far spent and in the darkness there is none to defend us except You alone, our God. Hasten to uphold us. Defend us this night, lest our souls be overcome with evil. Awaken us again in due time, and make us to hear joy and pace, for we love Your word and Your testimonies, which are the delight of our souls. May our ears be saved from all messages of sorrow, and all anguish be turned form our souls; for You can prosper all who live, and fill my life with Your blessing; in Jesus Christ, our Lord. Amen.　　　　　　　　　*Johann Habermann*

OR

Ah, sweet Jesus, pierce the marrow of my soul with the healing shafts of Your love, that it may truly burn, and melt, and languish, with the desire only for You; that it may desire to be dissolved and be with You; let it hunger only for the bread of life; let it thirst for You, the spring and fountain of eternal light, the stream of true pleasure; let it always desire You, seek You, and find You, and sweetly rest in You, who lives and reigns with the Father and the Holy Spirit, one God, now and forever.　　　　　　　　　*Bonaventure*

℟: A - men.

Benedicamus

℣: Let us bless the Lord.

℟: Thanks be to God.

If led by a pastor the following benediction may be said:

℣: The Almighty and mer- ci - ful Lord, the Fa- ther,

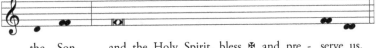

the Son, and the Holy Spirit, bless ✠ and pre - serve us.

℟: A - men.

COMPLINE
Prayer at the End of the Day

℣: The Lord Almighty grant us a qui-et night and peace at the last.

℟: A - men.

Short Lesson: I Peter 5:8-11

Be sober, be vigilant; because your adversary the devil walks about like a roaring lion, seeking whom he may devour. Resist him, steadfast in the faith, knowing that the same sufferings are experienced by your brotherhood in the world. But may the God of all grace, who called us to His eternal glory by Christ Jesus, after you have suffered a while, perfect, establish, strengthen, and settle you. To Him be the glory and the dominion forever and ever. Amen.

℣: Our help is in the name of / the Lord.
℟: Who made heaven / and earth.

Confiteor

Silence for examination of conscience

℣: I confess to God Almighty, before the whole company of heaven and to you my brothers and sisters, that I have sinned exceedingly in thought, word, and deed by my fault, by my own fault, by my own most grievous fault; wherefore, I pray God Almighty to have mercy on me. Amen.

℟: May almighty God have mercy on you, forgive you all your sins, and bring you to life everlasting. Amen.

I confess to God Almighty, before the whole company of heaven and to you father (or pastor), that I have sinned exceedingly in thought, word, and deed by my fault, by my own fault, by my own most grievous fault; wherefore, I pray God Almighty to have mercy on me. Amen.

℣: May almighty God have mercy on you, forgive you all your sins, and bring you to life everlasting.
℟: Amen.

℣: May the almighty and merciful Lord grant us pardon, ✠ absolution and remission of all our sins.
℟: Amen.

If not led by a pastor the following is said by all instead of the above:

I confess to God Almighty, before the whole company of heaven and to you my brothers and sisters, that I have sinned exceedingly in thought, word, and deed by my fault, by my own fault, by my own most grievous fault; wherefore, I pray God Almighty to have mercy on me. Amen.

May almighty God have mercy on us, forgive us all our sins, and bring us to life everlasting. Amen.

℣: ✠ Convert us, O / God our Savior.

℟: And turn away Your / anger from us.

℣: ✠ Make haste, O God, to de - liv - er me.

℟: Make haste to help me, O Lord. *Psalm 70:1*

All: Glory be to the Father and to the Son and to the Holy Spir - it;

As it was in the beginning, is now, and will be forever. A - men.

Al - le - lu - ia.

From Septuagesima through Holy Saturday the Alleluia is replaced with the following:

Praise to You, O Christ, King of eternal glo-ry.

Psalm

Sunday: 4	Monday: 6	Tuesday: 13	Wednesday: 91
Thursday: 134	Friday: 139a	Saturday: 139b	

Hymn - *Te lucis ante terminum*

1. Be - fore the end - ing of the day, Cre - a - tor of
2. From e - vil dreams de - fend our sight, From all the ter-
3. O Fa - ther this we ask be done, Through Je - sus Christ,

the world we pray! Thy grace and peace to us al - low
rors of the night, From all de - lud - ing thoughts that creep
Thine on - ly Son, Who with the Ho - ly Ghost and Thee,

And be our guard and keep - er now.
On heed- less minds dis - armed by sleep
Doth live and reign e - ter - nal - ly. A - men.

Ambrose of Milan

Chapter: Jeremiah 14:7-9

O Lord, though our iniquities testify against us, do it for Your name's sake; for our backslidings are many, we have sinned against You. O the Hope of Israel, his Savior in time of trouble, why should You be like a stranger in the land, and like a traveler who turns aside to tarry for a night? Why should You be like a man astonished, like a mighty one who cannot save? Yet You, O Lord, are in our midst, and we are called by Your name; do not leave us!

℣: Lord have mer - cy up - on us.

℟: Thanks be to God.

Responsory and Verse

℣: In - to your hands, O Lord, I com - mend my spi - rit.
℟: In-to your hands, O Lord, I com - mend my spi - rit.

℣: You have re-deemed us, O Lord, God of truth.
℟: In-to ...

℣: Glo-ry be to the Fa-ther, and to the Son, and to the Ho-ly Spi-rit.
℟: In-to ...

Psalm 31:5

℣: Keep us, O Lord, as the apple of Your / eye.
℟: Hide us under the shadow of Your / wings.

Psalm 17:8

Antiphon - *Salva nos, Domine*

Guide us wak-ing O Lord, and guard us sleep-ing

that a-wake we may watch with Christ, and a-sleep we may rest in peace.

Canticle - *Nunc Dimittis*

Tone 3a

✠ LORD, NOW You are letting Your / servant go in peace; *
According / to Your word;

FOR MY eyes have seen / Your salvation *
Which you have prepared before the face of / all peoples,

A LIGHT to bring revelation / to the Gentiles, *
And the glory of Your people / Israel.

GLORY be to the Father / and to the Son *
and to the / Holy Spirit;

AS IT was in / the beginning, *
Is now and will be for- / ever. Amen.

Luke 2:29-32

Preces *Said only during Advent and from Septuagesima through Passiontide.*

All: Lord, have mer- cy; Christ, have mer- cy; Lord have mer - cy.

℣: Our Fa - ther * who art in heaven, hallowed be Thy name, Thy kingdom come, Thy will be done on earth as it is in heaven. Give us this day our daily bread; and forgive us our trespasses as we forgive those who trespass against us, and lead us not into / temptation.

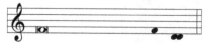

℞: But deliver us from ✠ / e - vil.

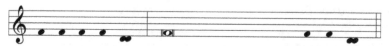

℣: I be-lieve in God * the Father Almighty, Maker of heaven and earth. And in Jesus Christ, His only Son, our Lord, who was conceived by the Holy Ghost, born of the Virgin Mary, suffered under Pontius Pilate, was crucified, dead, and buried; He descended into hell; the third day He rose again from the dead; He ascended into heaven, and sitteth at the right hand of God the Father Almighty; from thence He shall come to judge the quick and the dead. I believe in the Holy Ghost; the holy Christian Church, the communion of saints; the forgiveness of sins; the resurrection of / the body.

℞: And the ✠ life everlasting. / Amen.

℣: Blessed are You, O Lord God of our / fathers.
℞: And praiseworthy and glorious for- / ever.

℣: Let us bless the Father and the Son and the Holy / Spirit.
℞: Let us praise and magnify Him for- / ever.

℣: Blessed are You, O Lord, in the firmament of / heaven.
℞: And praiseworthy, and glorious, and magnified for- / ever.

℣: May the Almighty and merciful Lord bless us and / keep us.
℞: Amen.

℣: Grant, O Lord, / this night.
℞: To keep us with- / out sin.

℣: Have mercy on us, / O Lord.
℞: Have mercy / on us.

℣: Let Your mercy, O Lord, be up- / on us.
℞: As we have hoped / in You.

Collect

℣: O Lord, hear my prayer

℟: And let my cry come unto You.

℣: Let us pray.

Visit this house, O Lord, and drive far from it all the snares of the enemy: let Your holy angels dwell here, that we may rest in peace; and let Your blessing be always upon us, through Jesus Christ our Lord.

Missal of Pius V

OR

We thank you heavenly Father, through Jesus Christ, Your dear Son, that you have graciously kept us this day; and we pray you that You would forgive us all our sins where we have done wrong, and graciously keep us this night. For into Your hands we commend ourselves, our bodies and souls and all things. Let Your holy angel be with us, that the wicked Foe may have no power over us.

Martin Luther

OR

O Lord Jesus Christ, Son of the living God, Who at the sad hour of compline rested in the sepulchre, and thereby sanctified the grave to be a bed of hope to Your people; make us so to abound in sorrow for our sins, which were the cause of Your Passion, that when our bodies lie in the dust our souls may live with You.

Sarum Breviary

OR

Be present, O merciful God, and protect us through the silent hours of this night, so that we who are fatigued by the changes and chances of this fleeting world, may rest upon Your eternal changelessness; through Jesus Christ our Lord, who lives and reigns with You and the Holy Spirit, one God, now and forever.

Ambrosian Missal

OR

Look down, O Lord, from Your Heavenly Throne, illuminate the darkness of this night with Your celestial brightness, and from the sons of Light banish the deeds of darkness; through Jesus Christ our Lord, who lives and reigns with You and the Holy Spirit, one God, now and forever.

Ambrosian Missal

OR

Lighten our darkness, we implore You, O Lord; and by Your great mercy defend us from all perils and dangers of this night; for the love of Your only Son, our Savior Jesus Christ, who lives and reigns with You and the Holy Spirit, one God, now and forever.

Ambrosian Missal

OR

O Lord God, the Ruler and Protector of all men, who has divided the light from the darkness: I beseech You with the prayer of faith, that through the darkness of the coming night, Your right hand may protect me, and that I may rise again with joy in the light of the morning, through our Lord Jesus Christ, who lives and reigns with You and the Holy Spirit, one God, now and forever.

Sarum Breviary

OR

O God our Father, You invite us to pray, and grant what we ask when we ask according to your will. Hear me as I tremble in this darkness, and stretch forth Your hand to me. Shine your light before me and recall me from my wanderings. With you as my Guide, restore me to myself and to you.

Augustine of Hippo

OR

Watch, O Lord, with those who wake, or watch, or weep tonight, and give Your angels charge over those who sleep. Tend Your sick ones, O Lord Christ. Rest Your weary ones. Bless Your dying ones. Soothe Your suffering ones. Pity Your afflicted ones. Shield Your joyous ones; and all for Your love's sake.

Augustine of Hippo

OR

O Lord God, the Life of mortals, the Light of the faithful, the Strength of those who labor, the Repose of the dead; grant us a night free from all disturbance; that after a period of quite slumber, we may, by Your bounty, at the return of light, be endowed with activity from the Holy Spirit, and enabled in peace to render You thanks.

Mozarabic Breviary

OR

May Your holy angels, O Christ, son of the living God, tend our sleep, our rest, our bright bed. Let them reveal godly visions to us in our sleep, O High Prince of the universe, O great and mysterious King. May no demons, no evil, no injury or terrifying dreams disturb our rest, our prompt and swift repose. May our waking, our work, and our living be holy; our sleep, our rest, without hinderance or harm.

An early Irish prayer

OR

Enlighten our night, we implore You, Almighty Lord, and cause us, Your servants, ever to sleep to sin: so that awake to the virtues of the angels, and safe from every evil, we may by Your help be worthy to attain to the clear day through our Lord Jesus Christ.

Gallican Psalter

℟: A - men.

Benedicamus

℣: Let us bless the Lord.

℟: Thanks be to God.

If led by a pastor the following benediction may be said:

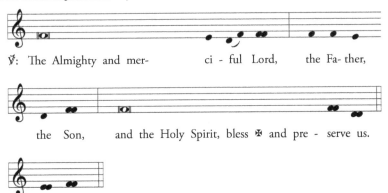

℣: The Almighty and mer-   ci - ful Lord,   the Fa- ther,

the   Son,   and the Holy Spirit, bless ✠ and pre - serve us.

℟: A - men.

O Liberator of Souls, Redeemer of the world, Jesus Christ, the Lord, King Eternal and Immortal: I make supplication and implore Your infinite goodness: that of Your great mercy by the Psalms, which I unworthy and a sinner, sing before You, You would free my soul from the power of sin, turn my heart from every evil way, from all wicked and perfidious thoughts, release my soul from the slavery of sin, drive far away all carnal concupiscence, loose me from every snare of Satan and his wicked ministers visible and invisible, who seek after my soul: protect me from these and all other evils, Almighty Lord. Amen. *Gallican Psalter*

THE PSALTER

PSALM 1

Tone 8G

Antiphon - *Beatus vir, qui in lege*

Bless-èd is the man who med - i - tates on the law of the Lord.

Psalm - *Beatus vir qui non abiit*

BLESSÈD is the man who walks
not in the counsel of the un- / godly *
   Nor stands in the path of sinners,
   nor sits in the seat / of the scornful;

But his delight is in the law of / the LORD *
   And in His law he
   medi- / tates day and night

He shall be like a tree planted
by the rivers of / water *
   That brings forth its fruit / in due season,

Whose leaf also shall not / wither; *
   And whatever he / does shall prosper.

The ungodly are / not so *
   But are like chaff which
   the / wind drives away.

Therefore the ungodly shall
not stand in the / judgment, *
   Nor sinners in the
   congregation / of the righteous.

For the LORD knows the way of the / righteous, *
   But the way of the ungod- / ly shall perish.

Glory be to the Father, and / to the Son, *
   And to the / Holy Spirit

As it was in the be- / ginning *
   Is now and will be for- / ever. Amen.

PSALM 2

Tone 8G

Antiphon - *Servite Domino in timore*

Serve the Lord with fear and re - joice with trem-bl-ing.

Psalm - *Quare fremuerunt gentes*

WHY DO the na- / tions rage *
   And the people / plot a vain thing?

The kings of the earth set themselves
and the rulers take counsel to- / gether, *
   Against the LORD and against
   His A- / nointed saying,

"Let us break Their bonds in / pieces *
   And cast a- / way their cords from us"

He who sits in the heavens / shall laugh; *
   The Lord shall hold them / in derision.

Then He shall speak to them in / His wrath, *
    And distress them in His / deep displeasure:

"Yet I have set My King
on My holy hill of / Zion." *
    "I will / declare the decree:

The Lord has / said to me, *
    'You are My Son, today
    I / have begotten You.

Ask of Me, and I will give You the
nations for Your in- / heritance, *
    And the ends of the
    earth for / Your possession.

You shall break them with a rod of / iron; *
    You shall dash them in
    pieces like a / potter's vessel.'"

Now therefore, be wise, / O kings; *
    Be instructed, you / judges of the earth.

Serve the Lord / with fear *
    And re- / joice with trembling.

Kiss the Son, lest He be / angry *
    And you / perish in the way,

When His wrath is kindled but a / little. *
    Blessèd are all those
    who / put their trust in Him.

Glory be to the Father, and / to the Son, *
    And to the / Holy Spirit

As it was in the be- / ginning *
    Is now and will be for- / ever. Amen.

PSALM 3

Tone 8c

Antiphon - *Ego dormivi*

I lay down and slept; and I a-woke, for the Lord sus-tained me.

Psalm - *Domine, quid multiplicati*

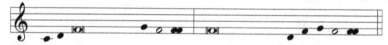

LORD, HOW they have
increased who / trouble me! *
    Many are they who rise / up against me.

Many are they who say / of me, *
    "There is no / help for him in God."

But You, O Lord, are a / shield for me, *
    My glory and the One / who
    lifts up my head.

I cried to the Lord with / my voice, *
    And He heard me / from His holy hill.

I lay down / and slept; *
    I awoke, for the / Lord sustained me.

I will not be afraid of ten thousands
of people who have set themselves
against me all / around. *
    Arise O Lord; / save me, O my God!

For You have struck all my
enemies on the / cheekbone; *
    You have broken the teeth of / the ungodly.

Salvation belongs to / the Lord. *
    Your blessing is up- / on Your people.

Glory be to the Father and / to the Son *
    and to the / Holy Spirit;

As it was in the be- / ginning *
    Is now and will be for- / ever. Amen.

Antiphon - *Misereri mihi Domine*

Have mer - cy   on   me,   O   Lord,   and   hear   my   prayer.

Psalm - *Cum invocarem*

HEAR ME when I call, O
God of my / righteousness! *
  You have relieved me
  when / I was in distress;

Have mercy / on me *
  And / hear my pray-er.

How long, O you sons of men,
will you turn my glory / to shame? *
  How long will you love
  worthlessness / and seek falsehood?

But know that the LORD has set apart
for Himself him who is / godly; *
  The LORD will hear / when I call to Him.

Be angry, and do / not sin *
  Meditate within your heart
  on your / bed, and be still.

Offer the sacrifices of righteousness,
and put your trust / in the LORD. *
  There are many who say, "Who
  will / show us any good?"

LORD, lift up the light of Your
countenance up- / on us. *
  You have put / gladness in my heart,

More than in the / season *
  That their / grain and wine increased.

I will both lie down in peace, / and sleep; *
  For you alone, O LORD,
  make me / dwell in safety.

Glory be to the Father and / to the Son *
  and to the / Holy Spirit;

As it was in the be- / ginning *
  Is now and will be for- / ever. Amen.

Antiphon - *Intende voci orationis*

Give heed   to   the   voice   of   my   cry,   my   King   and   my   God.

Psalm - *Verba mea auribus percipe*

GIVE EAR to my words, / O LORD *
  Consider my / meditation.

Give heed to the voice of / my cry, *
  My / King and my God,

For to You I / will pray. *
 My voice You shall hear
 in / the morning, O LORD;

In the morning I will direct it
to You, and I will / look up. *
 For You are not a God who
 takes pleasure / in wickedness,

Nor shall evil / dwell with You. *
 The boastful shall / not stand in Your sight;

You hate all workers of in- / iquity. *
 You shall destroy
 those / who speak falsehood;

The LORD abhors the bloodthirsty
and de- / ceitful man. *
 But as for me, I will come into Your
 house in the multitude / of Your mercy;

In fear of You I will / worship *
 Toward Your / holy temple.

Lead me, O LORD, in Your righteousness
because of my / enemies; *
 Make Your way / straight before my face.

For there is no faithfulness in / their mouth *
 Their inward part / is destruction;

Their throat is an open tomb;
they flatter with / their tongue. *
 Pronounce them / guilty, O God!

Let them fall by their own counsels; cast them
out in the multitude of their trans- / gressions, *
 For they have re- / belled against You.

But let all those rejoice who
put their trust / in You; *
 Let them ever shout for joy because
 You defend them; let those also who
 love Your name be / joyful in You.

For You, O LORD, will bless the / righteous; *
 With favor You will surround
 him / as with a shield.

Glory be to the Father, and / to the Son, *
 And to the / Holy Spirit

As it was in the be- / ginning *
 Is now and will be for- / ever. Amen.

PSALM 6

Tone 8G

Antiphon - *Salvum me fac Domine*

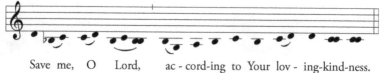

Save me, O Lord, ac - cord-ing to Your lov - ing-kind-ness.

Psalm - *Domine, ne in furore... miserere*

O LORD, do not rebuke me in Your / anger, *
 Nor chasten me in your / hot displeasure.

Have mercy on me, O LORD, for I / am weak; *
 O LORD, heal me, for my / bones are troubled.

My soul also is greatly / troubled; *
 But / You, O LORD, how long?

Return, O LORD, de- / liver me! *
 Oh, save me / for Your mercies' sake!

For in death there is no remembrance / of You; *
 In the grave / who will give You thanks?

I am weary with my groaning;
all night I make my / bed swim; *
 I drench my / couch with my tears.

My eye wastes away because / of grief; *
 It grows old because of / all my enemies.

Depart from me, all you workers of in- / iquity; *
    For the Lord has heard
    the voice / of my weeping

The Lord has heard my suppli- / cation; *
    The Lord / will receive my prayer.

Let all my enemies be
ashamed and greatly / troubled; *
    Let them turn back and
    be / ashamed suddenly.

Glory be to the Father and / to the Son *
    and to the / Holy Spirit;

As it was in the be- / ginning *
    Is now and will be for- / ever. Amen.

PSALM 7

Tone 8G

Antiphon - *Nequando rapiat*

Save me lest they tear my soul like a li - on;

while there is none to re - deem me or to save me.

Psalm - *Domine, Deus meus*

O LORD my God, in You have I put / my trust; *
    Save me from all those who
    persecute me; / and deliver me,

Lest they tear me like a / lion, *
    Rending me in pieces, while
    there is none / to deliver.

O Lord my God, if I have / done this: *
    If there is iniqui- / ty in my hands,

If I have repaid evil to him
who was at / peace with me, *
    Or have plundered my
    ene- / my without cause,

Let the enemy pursue me and overtake me;
yes, let him trample my life to / the earth, *
    And lay my / honor in the dust.

Arise, O Lord, in Your / anger; *
    Lift Yourself up because
    of the rage / of my enemies,

And awake for me to the judgment
You have com- / manded! *
    So the congregation of the
    peoples / shall surround You;

For their sakes, therefore, return / on high. *
    The Lord shall / judge the peoples;

Judge me, O Lord, according
to my / righteousness, *
    And according to my integri- / ty within me.

O let the wickedness of the wicked come
to an end, but establish / the just; *
    For the righteous God / tests
    the hearts and minds.

My defense is / of God, *
    Who saves the / upright in heart.

God is a / just judge, *
    And God is angry with
    the / wicked ev'ry day.

If he does not turn back,
He will sharpen / His sword; *
    He bends His bow and / makes it ready.

He also prepares for Himself
instruments / of death; *
    He makes His arrows / into fi'-ry shafts.

Behold, the wicked travails with in- / iquity, *
    Conceives trouble and / brings forth falsehood.

He made a pit and dug / it out, *
    And has fallen into
    the / ditch which he made.

His trouble shall return upon his / own head, *
    And his violent dealing shall
    come down / on his own crown.

I will praise the LORD according
to His / righteousness, *
    And will sing praise to the
    name / of the LORD Most High.

Glory be to the Father, and / to the Son, *
    And to the / Holy Spirit

As it was in the be- / ginning *
    Is now and will be for- / ever. Amen.

PSALM 8

Antiphon - *Quam admirabile*

How   ex - cel - lent   is   Your name, in   all   the earth!

Psalm - *Domine Dominus noster*

O LORD, our Lord, how excellent
is Your / name in all the earth, *
    You who set Your glory a- / bove the heavens!

Out of the mouth of babes and
infants / You have ordained strength, *
    Because of Your enemies, that You
    may silence the enemy and / the avenger.

When I consider Your heavens,
the work / of Your fingers, *
    The moon and the stars
    which / You have ordained,

What is man that You are / mindful of him,*
    And the son of man that / You visit him?

For You have made him a
little lower / than the angels, *
    And You have crowned him
    with glo- / ry and honor.

You have made him to have dominion
over the / works of Your hands; *
    You have put all things / under his feet,

All / sheep and oxen *
    Even the / beasts of the field,

The birds of the air and the / fish of the sea *
    That pass through the / path of the seas

- / O LORD, our Lord, *
    How excellent is Your / name in all the earth!

Glory be to the / Father, and to the Son, *
    And to the / Holy Spirit

As it was in / the beginning *
    Is now and will be for- / ever. Amen.

PSALM 9

Antiphon - *Exsurge, Domine*

A - rise, O Lord, do not let man pre - vail.

Psalm - *Confitebor tibi... in toto corde*

I WILL praise You, O
LORD, / with my whole heart; *
   I will tell of all Your / marvelous works.

I will be / glad and rejoice in You; *
   I will sing praise to
   Your / name, O Most High.

When my / enemies turn back, *
   They shall fall and perish / at Your presence.

For You have maintained
my / right and my cause; *
   You sat on the throne
   judging / in righteousness.

You have rebuked the nations,
You / have destroyed the wicked; *
   You have blotted out their
   name forev- / er and ever.

O enemy, destructions are / finished forever! *
   And you have destroyed cities;
   even their me- / mory has perished.

But the LORD shall en- / dure forever;*
   He has prepared His / throne for judgment.

He shall judge the / world in righteousness, *
   And He shall administer judgment
   for the peo- / ples in uprightness.

The LORD also will be a
refuge / for the oppressed, *
   A refuge in / times of trouble.

And those who know Your name
will / put their trust in You; *
   For You, LORD, have not
   forsaken / those who seek You.

Sing praises to the LORD, who / dwells in Zion! *
   Declare His deeds a- / mong the people.

When He avenges blood, / He remembers them; *
   He does not forget the cry / of the humble.

Have mercy / on me, O LORD! *
   Consider my trouble from those who hate me,
   You who lift me up / from the gates of death,

That I may tell of all Your praise in
the gates of the / daughter of Zion. *
   I will rejoice in / Your salvation.

The nations have sunk down
in the / pit which they made; *
   In the net which they hid,
   their / own foot is caught.

The LORD is known by the
judgment / He executes; *
   The wicked is snared in
   the work / of his own hands.

The wicked shall / be turned into hell,*
   And all the nations / that forget God.

For the needy shall not always / be forgotten; *
   The expectation of the poor
   shall not per- / ish forever.

Arise, O LORD, do / not let man prevail; *
   Let the nations be / judged in Your sight.

Put / them in fear, O LORD, *
   That the nations may know
   themselves / to be but men.

Glory be to the / Father, and to the Son, *
   And to the / Holy Spirit

As it was in / the beginning *
   Is now and will be for- / ever. Amen.

Antiphon - *Ut quid, Domine?*

Why do You stand a - far off, O Lord?

Psalm 10 - *Ut quid, Domine?*

WHY DO You stand afar off, / O Lord? *
　　Why do You hide Yourself
　　in times / of trouble?

The wicked in his pride persecutes / the poor; *
　　Let them be caught in the
　　plots which / they have devised.

For the wicked boasts of his heart's / desire; *
　　He blesses the greedy and
　　renoun- / ces the Lord.

The wicked in his proud countenance
does not / seek God; *
　　God is in / none of his thoughts.

His ways are always / prospering; *
　　Your judgments are far above,
　　out of his sight; as for all his
　　enemies, he / sneers at them.

He has said in his heart,
"I shall not / be moved; *
　　I shall never be in / adversity."

His mouth is full of cursing
and deceit and op- / pression; *
　　Under his tongue is trouble and / iniquity.

He sits in the lurking places of the / villages; *
　　In the secret places he murders the innocent;
　　his eyes are secretly fixed on / the helpless.

He lies in wait secretly, as a lion in his
den; he lies in wait to catch / the poor; *
　　He catches the poor when
　　he draws him in- / to his net.

So he crouches, he / lies low, *
　　That the helpless may / fall by his strength.

He has said in / his heart, *
　　"God has forgotten; He hides
　　His face; He will ne- / ver see it."

Arise, O Lord! O God, lift up / Your hand! *
　　Do not forget / the humble.

Why do the wicked re- / nounce God? *
　　He has said in his heart, "You
　　will not require / an account."

But You have seen it, for you observe trouble
and grief, to repay it by / Your hand. *
　　The helpless commits himself to You;
　　You are the helper of / the fatherless.

Break the arm of the wicked and the / evil man; *
　　Seek out his wickedness
　　until / You find none.

The Lord is King forever and / ever; *
　　The nations have perished out / of His land.

Lord, You have heard the desire of the / humble; *
　　You will prepare their heart; You
　　will cause / Your ear to hear.

To do justice to the fatherless
and the / oppressed, *
　　That the man of the earth
　　may / oppress no more.

Glory be to the Father, and / to the Son, *
　　And to the Ho- / ly Spirit

As it was in the be- / ginning *
　　Is now and will be forev- / er. Amen.

PSALM 11

Antiphon - *Justus Dominus*

The LORD is right - eous; He loves right- eous - ness.

Psalm - *In Domino confido*

IN THE LORD / I put my trust; *
  How can you say to my soul, "Flee
    as a bird / to your mountain"?

For look! The wicked bend their bow, they
make ready their / arrow on the string, *
  That they may shoot secretly
    at the / upright in heart.

If the foun- / dations are destroyed, *
  What can / the righteous do?

The LORD is in His holy temple,
the LORD's throne / is in heaven; *
  His eyes behold, His eyelids
    test / the sons of men.

The LORD / tests the righteous, *
  But the wicked and the one who
    loves vio- / lence His soul hates.

Upon the wicked He will rain coals, fire
and brimstone / and a burning wind; *
  This shall be the por- / tion of their cup.

For the LORD is righteous, /
He loves righteousness, *
  His countenance be- / holds the upright.

Glory be to the / Father, and to the Son, *
  And to the / Holy Spirit

As it was in / the beginning *
  Is now and will be for- / ever. Amen.

PSALM 12

Antiphon - *Tu Domine servabis nos*

You, O Lord, shall keep us, You shall pre - serve us for - ev - er.

Psalm - *Salvum me fac Domine*

HELP, LORD, for the godly man / ceases! *
  For the faithful disappear
    from among / the sons of men.

They speak idly everyone with his / neighbor; *
  With flattering lips and
    a dou- / ble heart they speak.

May the LORD cut off all flatter- / ing lips, *
  And the / tongue that speaks proud things,

Who have said, "With our tongue we
will prevail; our lips are / our own; *
  Who / is lord over us?"

For the oppression of the poor, for the sighing
of the needy, now I will arise, says / the Lord; *
    I will set him in the
    safety / for which he yearns.

The words of the Lord are / pure words, *
    Like silver tried in a furnace of
    earth, pu- / rified seven times.

You shall keep them, / O Lord, *
    You shall preserve them from
    this genera- / tion forever.

The wicked prowl on / ev'ry side, *
    When vileness is exalted
    among / the sons of men.

Glory be to the Father, and / to the Son, *
    And to the / Holy Spirit

As it was in the be- / ginning *
    Is now and will be for- / ever. Amen.

PSALM 13

Antiphon - *Convertere exaudi me*

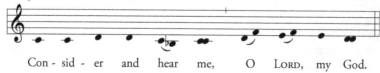

Con - sid - er and hear me, O Lord, my God.

Psalm - *Usquequo, Domine?*

HOW LONG, O Lord?
Will you forget me for- / ever? *
    How long will You / hide your face from me?

How long shall I take counsel in / my soul, *
    Having sorrow in / my heart daily?

How long will my enemy be exalted / over me? *
    Consider and hear me, / O Lord my God;

Enlighten my eyes, lest I
sleep the sleep / of death; *
    Lest my enemy say, "I have
    pre- / vailed against him";

Lest those who trouble me
rejoice when I / am moved. *
    But I have trusted / in Your mercy;

My heart shall rejoice in Your
salvation. I will sing to / the Lord, *
    Because he has dealt bounti- / fully with me.

Glory be to the Father, and / to the Son, *
    And to the / Holy Spirit

As it was in the be- / ginning *
    Is now and will be for- / ever. Amen.

PSALM 14

Antiphon - *Dominus de coelo*

The Lord looks down from hea-ven up - on the child- ren of men.

Psalm - *Dixit insipiens... sepulchrum*

THE FOOL has said in his
heart, "There is / no God." *
    They are corrupt, they have
    done abominable works, there
    is none / who does good.

The LORD looks down from heaven
upon the children / of men *
    To see if there are any who
    understand, / who seek God.

They have all turned aside, they
have together become / corrupt; *
    There is none who does good, / no, not one.

Have all the workers of
iniquity no / knowledge, *
    Who eat my people up as bread,
    and do not / call on the Lord?

There they are in / great fear, *
    For God is with the generation
    of / the righteous.

You shame the counsel of / the poor,*
    But the Lord is / his refuge.

Oh, that the salvation of Israel
would come out of / Zion! *
    When the Lord brings back the
    captivity of His people, let Jacob
    rejoice and Isra- / el be glad.

Glory be to the Father, and / to the Son, *
    And to the Ho- / ly Spirit

As it was in the be- / ginning *
    Is now and will be forev- / er. Amen.

PSALM 15

Antiphon - *Qui operatur*

He who works right-eous-ness may a- bide in Your ho-ly hill, O Lord.

Psalm - *Domine, quis habitabit*

LORD, WHO may abide in Your / tabernacle? *
    Who may dwell in Your holy / hill?

He who / walks uprightly *
    And works righteousness,
    and speaks the truth in his / heart;

He who does not / backbite with his tongue, *
    Nor does evil to his neighbor, nor does
    he take up a reproach against his / friend;

In whose eyes a vile person is despised, but
he honors / those who fear the LORD; *
    He who swears to his own
    hurt and does not / change;

He who does not put out his money / at usury *
    Nor does he take a bribe
    against the inno- / cent.

He / who does these things *
    Shall never be / moved.

Glory be to the Father, / and to the Son, *
    And to the Holy Spi- / rit

As it was in / the beginning *
    Is now and will be forever. / Amen.

PSALM 16

Antiphon - *Conserva me, Domine*

Pre - serve me, O God, for in You I put my trust.

Psalm - *Conserva me, Domine*

PRESERVE / me, O- God, *
  For in You / I put my trust.

O my soul, you have / said to the LORD, *
  "You are my Lord, my goodness
  is nothing / apart from You"

And to the saints / who are on the earth, *
  They are the excellent ones, in
  whom is / all my delight."

Their sorrows shall be multiplied
who hasten after / another god; *
  Their drink offerings of blood I will not
  offer, nor take up their / names on my lips.

You, O LORD, are the portion of
my inheri- / tance and my cup; *
  You / maintain my lot.

The lines have fallen to me in / pleasant places; *
  Yes, I have a good / inheritance.

I will bless the LORD who
has / given me counsel; *
  My heart also instructs
  me in / the night seasons.

I have set the LORD / always before me; *
  Because He is at my right
  hand I / shall not be moved.

Therefore my heart is glad,
and my / glory rejoices; *
  My flesh also / will rest in hope.

For You will not leave my / soul in Sheol, *
  Nor will You allow Your
  Holy One to / see corruption.

You will show / me the path of life; *
  In Your presence is fullness of joy; at
  Your right hand are pleasures / forevermore.

Glory be to the / Father, and to the Son, *
  And to the / Holy Spirit

As it was in / the beginning *
  Is now and will be for- / ever. Amen.

PSALM 17

Antiphon - *Inclina, Domine*

In - cline Your ear to me, O Lord, and hear my speech.

Psalm - *Exaudi, Domine*

HEAR A just cause, O LORD, / attend to my cry; *
  Give ear to my prayer that
  is not / from deceitful lips.

Let my vindication come / from Your presence; *
  Let Your eyes look on the
  things / that are upright.

You have tested my heart; You have
visited / me in the night; *
   You have tried me and found
   nothing; I have purposed that
   my mouth / shall not transgress.

Con- / cerning the works of men, *
   By the word of Your lips, I have kept
   myself from the paths of / the destroyer.

Uphold my / steps in Your paths, *
   That my foot- / steps may not slip.

I have called upon You, for
You will / hear me, O God; *
   Incline Your ear to / me, and hear my speech.

Show Your marvelous
lovingkindness / by Your right hand, *
   O You who save those who trust in You
   from those who rise / up against them.

Keep me as the / apple of Your eye; *
   Hide me under the sha- / dow of Your wings.

From the wicked / who oppress me, *
   From my deadly enemies / who surround me.

They have / closed up their fat hearts; *
   With their mouths / they speak proudly.

They have now surrounded / us in our steps; *
   They have set their eyes,
   crouching / down to the earth,

Like a lion that is eager / to tear his prey, *
   And as a young lion lurking in / secret places.

Arise, O Lord, con- / front him, cast him down; *
   Deliver my life from the
   wick- / ed with Your sword,

With Your hand from men, O Lord,
from men of the world who have
their / portion in this life, *
   And whose belly You fill
   with Your / hidden treasure.

They are satis- / fied with children, *
   And leave the rest of their
   sub- / stance for their babes.

As for me, I will see Your / face in righteousness; *
   I shall be satisfied when
   I awake / in Your likeness.

Glory be to the / Father, and to the Son, *
   And to the / Holy Spirit

As it was in / the beginning *
   Is now and will be for- / ever. Amen.

PSALM 18a (1-24)

Tone 6

Antiphon - *Diligam te...virtus mea*

I   will   love   You,   O   Lord,   my   strength.

Psalm - *Diligam te, Domine*

I WILL love / You, O Lord, my strength. *
   The Lord is my rock and my
   fortress and / my deliverer;

My God, my strength, in / whom I will trust; *
   My shield and the horn of my
   salvation, / and my stronghold.

I will call upon the Lord,
who is / worthy to be praised; *
   So shall I be saved / from my enemies.

The pangs of / death encompassed me, *
   And the floods of ungodliness / made me afraid.

The sorrows of Sheol / surrounded me; *
   The snares of / death confronted me.

In my distress I called upon the
Lord, and / cried unto my God; *
    He heard my voice from His temple, and my
    cry came before Him, / even to His ears.

Then the earth / shook and trembled; *
    The foundations of the hills also quaked
    and were shaken, because / He was angry.

Smoke went up from His nostrils, and
devouring / fire from His mouth; *
    Coals were / kindled by it.

He bowed the heavens / also, and came down *
    With darkness / under His feet.

And He rode upon a / cherub, and flew; *
    He flew upon the / wings of the wind.

He made darkness / His secret place; *
    His canopy around Him was dark
    waters and thick / clouds of the skies.

From the / brightness before Him, *
    His thick clouds passed with
    hailstones / and coals of fire.

The Lord also thundered / in the heavens, *
    And the Most High uttered His
    voice, hailstones / and coals of fire.

He sent out His arrows and / scattered the foe, *
    Lightnings in abundance,
    and / He vanquished them.

Then the channels of waters were seen, and the
foundations of the / world were uncovered *
    At Your rebuke, O Lord, at the
    blast of the breath / of Your nostrils.

He sent from a- / bove, He took me; *
    He drew me out of / many waters.

He delivered me from my strong
enemy, from / those who hated me, *
    For they / were too strong for me.

They confronted me in the day / of calamity, *
    But the Lord / was my support.

He also brought me out / into a broad place; *
    He delivered me because He / delighted in me.

The Lord rewarded me
according / to my righteousness; *
    According to the cleanness of my
    hands He has / recompensed me.

For I have kept the / ways of the Lord, *
    And have not wickedly / departed from God.

For all His judgments / were before me, *
    And I did not put away His / statutes from me.

I was also / blameless before Him, *
    And I kept myself from / my iniquity.

Therefore the Lord has recompensed me
according / to my righteousness, *
    According to the cleanness
    of my / hands in His sight.

Glory be to the Father, / and to the Son, *
    And to the / Holy Spirit

As it was in / the beginning *
    Is now and will be / forever. Amen.

PSALM 18b (25-50)

Tone 7b

Antiphon - *Vivit Dominus*

The Lord lives, and bless-èd is the God of my sal - va - tion.

Psalm - *Cum sancto sanctus*

WITH THE merciful You
will / show Yourself merciful; *
    With a blameless man You
    will / show Yourself blameless;

With the pure You will / show Yourself pure; *
    And with the devious You
    will / show Yourself shrewd.

For You will save the / humble people, *
    But will / bring down haughty looks.

For / You will light my lamp; *
    The LORD my God will
    en- / lighten my darkness.

For by You I can / run against a troop, *
    And by my God I can leap / over a wall.

As for God, His / way is perfect; *
    The word of the LORD is proven; He
    is a shield to / all who trust in Him.

For who is / God, except the LORD? *
    And who is a rock, / except our God?

It is God who / arms me with strength, *
    And makes / my way perfect.

He makes my feet / like the feet of deer, *
    And sets me / on my high places.

He teaches my / hands to make war, *
    So that my arms can / bend a bow of bronze.

You have also given me the
shield of / Your salvation; *
    Your right hand has held me up,
    Your gentle- / ness has made me great.

You enlarged my / path under me; *
    So that my / feet did not slip.

I have pursued my enemies
and / overtaken them; *
    Neither did I turn back
    again till / they were destroyed.

I have wounded them, so that
they were not / able to rise; *
    They have fallen / under my feet.

For You have armed me with
strength / for the battle; *
    You have subdued under me
    those who rose / up against me.

You have also given me
the / necks of my enemies, *
    So that I destroyed those / who hated me.

They cried out, but there
was / none to save them, *
    Even to the LORD, but
    He / did not answer them.

Then I beat them as fine
as the / dust before the wind; *
    I cast them out like / dirt in the streets.

You have delivered me from
the strivings / of the people, *
    You have made me the head of the nations;
    a people I have not / known shall serve me.

As soon as they hear of me / they obey me; *
    The foreigners / submit to me.

The / foreigners fade away, *
    And come frightened / from their hideouts.

The LORD lives! / Blessèd be my Rock! *
    Let the God of my salvation / be exalted.

It is / God who avenges me, *
    And subdues the / peoples under me;

He delivers me / from my enemies. *
    You also lift me up above those
    who rise against me; You have
    delivered me from the / violent man.

Therefore I will give thanks to
You, O LORD, a- / mong the Gentiles, *
    And sing / praises to Your name.

Great deliverance He gives to His king,
and shows mercy to / His anointed, *
    To David and his descendants / forevermore.

Glory be to the / Father, and to the Son, *
    And to the / Holy Spirit

As it was in / the beginning *
    Is now and will be for- / ever. Amen.

PSALM 19

Antiphon - *Justitiae Domini rectae*

The stat-utes of the LORD are right, re-joic-ing the heart.

Psalm - *Coeli enarrant*

THE HEAvens declare the / glory of God; *
   And the firmament shows His / handiwork.

Day unto / day utters speech, *
   And night unto night re- / veals knowledge.

There is no / speech nor language *
   Where their voice / is not heard.

Their line has gone / out through all the earth, *
   And their words to the end / of the world.

In them He has set a taber- / nacle for the sun, *
   Which is like a bridegroom
   coming out of / his chamber,

And rejoices like a strong / man to run its race. *
   Its rising is from one end / of heaven,

And its circuit / to the other end; *
   And there is nothing hidden / from its heat.

The law of the LORD is
perfect, con- / verting the soul; *
   The testimony of the LORD is
   sure, making wise / the simple;

The statutes of the LORD are
right, re- / joicing the heart; *
   The commandment of the LORD
   is pure, enlighten- / ing the eyes;

The fear of the LORD is
clean, endur- / ing forever; *
   The judgments of the LORD are
   true and righteous al- / together.

More to be desired are they than
gold, / yea, than much fine gold; *
   Sweeter also than honey
   and the / honeycomb.

Moreover by them / Your servant is warned, *
   And in keeping them there is / great reward.

Who can under- / stand his errors? *
   Cleanse me from / secret faults.

Keep back Your servant
also / from presumptuous sins; *
   Let them not have dominion / over me.

Then I / shall be blameless, *
   And I shall be innocent
   of great / transgression.

Let the words of my mouth and the meditation
of my heart be accepta- / ble in Your sight, *
   O LORD, my strength and my / Redeemer.

Glory be to the / Father, and to the Son, *
   And to the Ho- / ly Spirit

As it was in / the beginning *
   Is now and will be forev- / er. Amen.

PSALM 20

Antiphon - *Exaudiat te Dominus*

May the LORD ans-wer you in the day of trou-ble.

Psalm - *Exaudiat te Dominus*

MAY THE LORD answer you
in the day of / trouble; *
    May the name of the God
    of Ja- / cob defend you;

May He send you help from the sanctu- / ary, *
    And strengthen you / out of Zion;

May He remember all your / offerings, *
    And accept / your burnt sacrifice.

May He grant you according
to your / heart's desire, *
    And fulfill / all your purpose.

We will rejoice in your sal- / vation, *
    And in the name of our God
    we will set / up our banners!

May the LORD fulfill all your pe- / titions. *
    Now I know that the
    LORD saves / His anointed;

He will answer him from His holy / heaven *
    With the saving strength / of His right hand.

Some trust in chariots, and some in / horses; *
    But we will remember the
    name / of the LORD our God.

They have bowed down and / fallen; *
    But we have risen / and stand upright.

- / Save, LORD! *
    May the King answer / us when we call.

Glory be to the Father, and / to the Son, *
    And to the / Holy Spirit

As it was in the be- / ginning *
    Is now and will be for- / ever. Amen.

PSALM 21

Tone 8G

Antiphon - *Domine, in virtute tua*

The king shall have joy in Your strength, O LORD.

Psalm - *Domine, in virtute tua*

THE KING shall have joy in
Your strength, / O LORD; *
    And in Your salvation how
    greatly / shall he rejoice!

You have given him his / heart's desire, *
    And have not withheld
    the re- / quest of his lips.

For You meet him with the
blessings of / goodness; *
    You set a crown of pure / gold upon his head.

He asked life from You, and You gave it / to him *
    Length of days forev- / er and ever.

His glory is great in Your sal- / vation; *
    Honor and majesty You
    have / placed upon him.

For You have made him most blessèd for- / ever; *
    You have made him exceedingly
    glad / with Your presence.

For the king trusts / in the LORD, *
 And through the mercy of the
 Most High / he shall not be moved.

Your hand will find all Your / enemies; *
 Your right hand will find / those who hate You.

You shall make them as a fiery
oven in the time of Your / anger; *
 The LORD shall swallow them up in His
 wrath, and the fire / shall devour them.

Their offspring You shall
destroy from / the earth, *
 And their descendants from
 a- / mong the sons of men.

For they intended evil a- / gainst You; *
 They devised a plot which they
 are not / able to perform.

Therefore You will make them / turn their back; *
 You will make ready Your arrows
 on Your string / t'ward their faces.

Be exalted, O LORD, in Your / own strength! *
 We will / sing and praise Your power.

Glory be to the Father, and / to the Son, *
 And to the / Holy Spirit

As it was in the be- / ginning *
 Is now and will be for- / ever. Amen.

PSALM 22

Tone 2

Antiphon - *Ne discedas a me*

Do not for-sake me, O Lord, for trou-ble is near, and there is none to help.

Psalm - *Deus, Deus meus*

MY GOD, My God, why
have You for- / saken Me? *
 Why are You so far from helping Me,
 and from the words of / My groaning?

O My God, I cry in the daytime,
but You do / not hear; *
 And in the night season, and am / not silent.

But You are / holy, *
 Enthroned in the praises / of Israel.

Our fathers trusted / in You; *
 They trusted, and You de- / livered them.

They cried to You, and were de- / livered; *
 They trusted in You, and were / not ashamed.

But I am a worm, and / no man; *
 A reproach of men, and
 despised by / the people.

All those who see Me ridi- / cule Me; *
 They shoot out the lip, they
 shake the / head, saying,

"He trusted in the LORD, let Him / rescue Him; *
 Let Him deliver Him, since
 He / delights in Him!"

But You are He who took
Me out of / the womb; *
 You made Me trust while
 on / My mother's breasts.

I was cast upon You / from birth. *
 From My mother's womb
 You have / been My God.

Be not far from Me, for trouble / is near; *
 For there / is none to help.

Many bulls have sur- / rounded Me; *
 Strong bulls of Bashan have / encircled Me.

They gape at Me with / their mouths, *
  Like a raging and / roaring lion.

I am poured out like / water, *
  And all My bones / are out of joint;

My heart is / like wax; *
  It has melted / within Me.

My strength is dried up like a potsherd,
and My tongue clings to / My jaws; *
  You have brought Me to / the dust of death.

For dogs have sur- / rounded Me; *
  The congregation of the
  wicked has / enclosed Me.

They pierced My hands and / My feet; *
  I can count / all My bones.

They look and stare at Me. They divide
My garments a- / mong them, *
  And for My clothing / they cast lots.

But You, O Lord, do not be far / from Me; *
  O My Strength, hasten / to help Me!

Deliver Me from / the sword, *
  My precious life from the power / of the dog.

Save Me from the / lion's mouth *
  And from the horns of the / wild oxen!

You have answered Me. I will declare
Your name to My / brethren; *
  In the midst of the assembly
  I / will praise You.

You who fear the Lord, / praise Him! *
  All you descendants of
  Jacob, glor- / ify Him,

And fear Him, all you offspring of / Israel! *
  For He has not despised nor
  abhorred the affliction of the / afflicted;

Nor has He hidden His / face from Him; *
  But when He cried to / Him, He heard.

My praise shall be of You in
the great as- / sembly; *
  I will pay My vows before
  those / who fear Him.

The poor shall eat and be satisfied; those
who seek Him will praise / the Lord. *
  Let your heart live / forever!

All the ends of / the world *
  Shall remember and / turn to the Lord,

And all the families of the / nations *
  Shall worship / before You.

For the kingdom is / the Lord's, *
  And He rules over / the nations.

All the prosperous of the earth
shall eat and / worship; *
  All those who go down to the
  dust shall bow / before Him,

Even he who cannot keep himself / alive.*
  A posterity / shall serve Him.

It will be recounted of the Lord
to the next generation, they will
come and declare His righteousness
to a people who will / be born, *
  That He / has done this.

Glory be to the Father, and / to the Son, *
  And to the Ho- / ly Spirit

As it was in the be- / ginning *
  Is now and will be forev- / er. Amen.

PSALM 23

Antiphon - *In loco pascuae*

The Lord makes me to lie down in green pas - tures.

Psalm - *Dominus regit me*

THE LORD / is my shepherd; *
  - / I shall not want.

He makes me to lie down / in green pastures; *
  He leads me beside / the still waters.

- / He restores my soul; *
  He leads me in the paths of
  righteousness / for His name's sake.

Yea, though I walk through the valley of
the shadow of death, I will / fear no evil; *
  For You are with me; Your rod
  and Your / staff, they comfort me.

You prepare a table before me
in the presence / of my enemies; *
  You anoint my head with
  oil; my / cup runs over.

Surely goodness and mercy shall
follow me all the / days of my life; *
  And I will dwell in the
  house of the / LORD forever.

Glory be to the / Father, and to the Son, *
  And to the / Holy Spirit

As it was in / the beginning *
  Is now and will be for- / ever. Amen.

PSALM 24

Antiphon - *Innocens manibus*

He who has clean hands and a pure heart

may as - cend in - to the hill of the LORD.

Psalm - *Domini est terra*

THE EARTH is the LORD's, and / all its fullness, *
  The world and / those who dwell therein.

For He has founded / it upon the seas, *
  And established it / upon the waters.

Who may ascend into the / hill of the LORD? *
  Or who may / stand in His holy place?

He who has clean hands / and a pure heart, *
  Who has not lifted up his soul to
  an idol, / nor sworn deceitfully.

He shall receive / blessing from the LORD, *
  And righteousness from
  the God / of his salvation.

This is Jacob, the generation
of / those who seek Him, *
  - / Who seek Your face—.

Lift up your heads, O you gates!
And be lifted up, you / everlasting doors! *
  And the King of / glory shall come in.

Who is this / King of glory? *
 The LORD strong and mighty,
 the LORD / mighty in battle.

Lift up your heads, O you gates!
Lift up, you / everlasting doors! *
 And the King of / glory shall come in.

Who is this / King of glory? *
 The LORD of hosts, He is / the King of glory.

Glory be to the Father, / and to the Son, *
 And to / the Holy Spirit

As it was in / the beginning *
 Is now and will be / forever. Amen.

PSALM 25

Antiphon - *Deus meus, in te confido*

O my God, I trust in You; let me not be a-shamed.

Psalm - *Ad te, Domine, levavi*

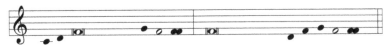

TO YOU, O LORD, I lift up / my soul. *
 O my God, I trust in You;
 let / me not be ashamed;

Let not my enemies triumph / over me.*
 Indeed, let no one who
 waits on / You be ashamed;

Let those be / ashamed *
 Who deal treacherous- / ly without cause.

Show me Your / ways, O LORD; *
 - / Teach me Your paths.

Lead me in Your truth and / teach me,*
 For You are the God of my
 salvation; on You I / wait all the day.

Remember, O LORD, Your tender / mercies *
 And Your lovingkindnesses,
 for / they are from of old.

Do not remember the sins of / my youth,*
 Nor / my transgressions;

According to Your mercy re- / member me,*
 For Your / goodness' sake, O LORD.

Good and upright / is the LORD; *
 Therefore He teaches / sinners in the way.

The humble He guides in / justice, *
 And the humble He / teaches His way.

All the paths of the LORD are mercy / and truth, *
 To such as keep His covenant
 and His / testimonies.

For Your name's sake, / O LORD, *
 Pardon my iniquity, / for it is great.

Who is the man that / fears the LORD? *
 Him shall He teach in the / way He chooses.

He himself shall dwell in pros- / perity,*
 And his descendants
 shall in- / herit the earth.

The secret of the LORD is
with those who / fear Him, *
 And He will show / them His covenant.

My eyes are ever / t'ward the LORD, *
 For He shall pluck my feet / out of the net.

Turn Yourself to me, and have mercy / on me, *
 For I am desolate / and afflicted.

The troubles of my heart have / enlarged; *
 Bring me out of / my distresses!

Look on my affliction and / my pain,*
 And for- / give all my sins.

Consider my enemies, for they are / many;*
 And they hate me with / cruel hatred.

Keep my soul, and de- / liver me; *
    Let me not be ashamed,
    for I / put my trust in You.

Let integrity and uprightness pre- / serve me, *
    For / I wait for You.

Redeem Israel, / O God, *
    Out of / all their troubles!

Glory be to the Father, and / to the Son, *
    And to the / Holy Spirit

As it was in the be- / ginning *
    Is now and will be for- / ever. Amen.

PSALM 26

Antiphon - *Misericordia tua Domine*

Your lov - ing - kind - ness, O Lord, is be - fore my eyes, and I have walked in Your truth.

Psalm - *Judica me, Domine*

VINDIcate me, O LORD, for
I have walked in / my integrity. *
    I have also trusted in the
    LORD; / I shall not slip.

Examine me, O / LORD, and prove me; *
    Try my / mind and my heart.

For Your lovingkindness / is before my eyes, *
    And I / have walked in Your truth.

I have not sat with i- / dolatrous mortals, *
    Nor will I go in / with hypocrites.

I have hated the assembly of / evildoers, *
    And will not sit / with the wicked.

I will wash my / hands in innocence; *
    So I will go about Your / altar, O LORD,

That I may proclaim with
the / voice of thanksgiving, *
    And tell of all / Your wondrous works.

LORD, I have loved the
habi- / tation of Your house, *
    And the place where / Your glory dwells.

Do not gather my / soul with sinners, *
    Nor my life with / bloodthirsty men,

In whose hands is a / sinister scheme, *
    And whose right / hand is full of bribes.

But as for me, I will walk in / my integrity; *
    Redeem me and be mer- / ciful to me.

My foot stands / in an even place; *
    In the congregations I / will bless the LORD.

Glory be to the / Father, and to the Son, *
    And to the / Holy Spirit

As it was in / the beginning *
    Is now and will be for- / ever. Amen.

PSALM 27

Antiphon - *Illuminatio mea*

My light and my sal - va - tion is the LORD.

Psalm - *Dominus illuminatio*

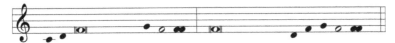

THE LORD is my light and
my salvation; whom shall / I fear? *
   The LORD is the strength of my
   life; of whom shall / I be afraid?

When the wicked came a- / gainst me *
   To / eat up my flesh,

My enemies / and foes, *
   They / stumbled and fell.

Though an army may encamp a- / gainst me, *
   My / heart shall not fear;

Though war should rise a- / gainst me, *
   In this I / will be confident.

One thing I have desired of
the LORD, that will / I seek: *
   That I may dwell in the house
   of the LORD all the / days of my life,

To behold the beauty of / the LORD, *
   And to inquire / in His temple.

For in the time of trouble He
shall hide me in His pa- / vilion; *
   In the secret place of His
   tabernacle / He shall hide me;

He shall set me high upon / a rock. *
   And now my head shall be lifted up
   above my enemies / all around me;

Therefore I will offer sacrifices
of joy in His taber- / nacle; *
   I will sing, yes, I will
   sing / praises to the LORD.

Hear, O LORD, when I cry with / my voice! *
   Have mercy also upon / me, and answer me.

When You said, "Seek / My face," *
   My heart said to You,
   "Your / face, LORD, I will seek."

Do not hide Your / face from me; *
   Do not turn Your servant a- / way in anger;

You have been / my help; *
   Do not leave me nor forsake
   me, O God of / my salvation.

When my father and my mother for- / sake me, *
   Then the LORD / will take care of me.

Teach me Your way, / O LORD, *
   And lead me in a smooth
   path, because / of my enemies.

Do not deliver me to the will of my adversaries;
for false witnesses have risen a- / gainst me, *
   And such as / breathe out violence.

I would have lost heart, unless I had believed
that I would see the goodness of / the LORD *
   In the land / of the living.

Wait on the LORD; Be of good / courage, *
   And He shall strengthen your
   heart; wait, I / say, on the LORD!

Glory be to the Father, and / to the Son, *
   And to the / Holy Spirit

As it was in the be- / ginning *
   Is now and will be for- / ever. Amen.

PSALM 28

Antiphon - *Dominus fortitudo*

The LORD is the sav - ing strength of His an - oint-ed.

Psalm - *Ad te, Domine clamabo*

TO YOU I will cry, O LORD my
Rock: do not be / silent to me, *
    Lest, if You are silent to me, I become
    like those who / go down to the pit.

Hear the voice of my
supplications / when I cry to You, *
    When I lift up my hands
    toward Your / holy sanctuary.

Do not take me away / with the wicked *
    And with the workers / of iniquity,

Who speak peace / to their neighbors, *
    But e- / vil is in their hearts.

Give them ac- / cording to their deeds, *
    And according to the
    wickedness / of their endeavors;

Give them according to the / work of their hands; *
    Render to / them what they deserve.

Because they do not regard the works of the
LORD, nor the opera- / tion of His hands, *
    He shall destroy / them and not build them up.

Bles- / sèd be the LORD, *
    Because He has heard the
    voice of / my supplications!

The LORD is my / strength and my shield; *
    My heart trusted in / Him, and I am helped;

Therefore my heart great- / ly rejoices, *
    And with my / song I will praise Him.

The / LORD is their strength, *
    And He is the saving refuge / of His anointed.

Save Your people, and bless / Your inheritance; *
    Shepherd them also, and
    bear / them up forever.

Glory be to the Father, / and to the Son, *
    And to / the Holy Spirit

As it was in / the beginning *
    Is now and will be / forever. Amen.

PSALM 29

Antiphon - *Deus majestatis*

The God of glo - ry thun-ders; give glo - ry to His name.

Psalm - *Afferte Domino*

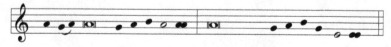

GIVE UNto the LORD, / O you mighty ones, *
    Give unto the / LORD glory and strength.

Give unto the LORD the glory / due to His name; *
    Worship the LORD in the / beauty of holiness.

The voice of the LORD is over the
waters; the God of / glory thunders; *
   The LORD is ov- / er many waters.

The voice of the / LORD is powerful; *
   The voice of the LORD / is full of majesty.

The voice of the LORD / breaks the cedars, *
   Yes, the LORD splinters
   the / cedars of Lebanon.

He makes them also / skip like a calf, *
   Lebanon and Sirion / like a young wild ox.

The voice of the LORD divides the flames of fire.
The voice of the LORD / shakes the wilderness; *
   The LORD shakes the wil- / derness of Kadesh.

The voice of the LORD makes the deer
give birth, and strips / the forests bare; *
   And in His temple
   everyone / speaks of His glory.

The LORD sat / enthroned at the Flood, *
   And the LORD sits / as King forever.

The LORD will give strength / to His people; *
   The LORD will bless / His people with peace.

Glory be to the Father, / and to the Son, *
   And to / the Holy Spirit

As it was in / the beginning *
   Is now and will be / forever. Amen.

PSALM 30

Tone 8G

Antiphon - *Exaltabo te, Domine*

I will ex- tol You, O LORD, for You have lift - ed me up.

Psalm - *Exaltabo te, Domine*

I WILL extol You, O Lord, for
You have lifted / me up, *
   And have not let my foes / rejoice over me.

O Lord my God, I cried out / to You, *
   - / And You healed me.

O Lord, You brought my
soul up from / the grave; *
   You have kept me alive, that I
   should not / go down to the pit.

Sing praise to the Lord, you / saints of His, *
   And give thanks at the
   remembrance / of His holy name.

For His anger is but for a / moment, *
   His / favor is for life;

Weeping may endure for / a night, *
   But joy comes / in the morning.

Now in my prosperity / I said, *
   "I shall / never be moved."

Lord, by Your / favor *
   You have made my / mountain stand strong;

You hid / Your face, *
   And / I was troubled.

I cried out to You, / O Lord; *
   And to the Lord I made / supplication:

"What profit is there in / my blood, *
   When I / go down to the pit?

Will the dust / praise You? *
   Will / it declare Your truth?

Hear, O Lord, and have mercy / on me; *
   Lord, / be my helper!"

You have turned for me my
mourning into / dancing; *
    You have put off my sackcloth
    and clothed / me with gladness,

To the end that my glory may sing
praise to You and not be / silent. *
    O Lᴏʀᴅ my God, I will
    give thanks to / You forever.

Glory be to the Father, and / to the Son, *
    And to the / Holy Spirit

As it was in the be- / ginning *
    Is now and will be for- / ever. Amen.

PSALM 31

Antiphon - *In tua justitia*

In Your right - eous - ness, de - liv - er me, O Lᴏʀᴅ.

Psalm - *In te, Domine, speravi*

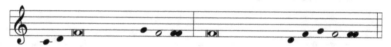

IN YOU, O Lᴏʀᴅ, I put my trust;
let me never be / ashamed; *
    Deliver me / in Your righteousness.

Bow down Your / ear to me, *
    Deli- / ver me speedily;

Be my rock of refuge, a fortress
of defense to / save me. *
    For You are my rock / and my fortress;

Therefore, for Your / name's sake, *
    Lead / me and guide me.

Pull me out of the net which they
have secretly / laid for me, *
    For / You are my strength.

Into Your hand I commit my / spirit; *
    You have redeemed me, /
    O Lᴏʀᴅ God of truth.

I have / hated those *
    Who regard / useless idols;

But I trust / in the Lᴏʀᴅ. *
    I will be glad and rejoice / in Your mercy,

For You have considered my / trouble; *
    You have known my soul / in adversities,

And have not shut me up into
the hand of the / enemy; *
    You have set my feet / in a wide place.

Have mercy on me, O Lᴏʀᴅ, for I am in
trouble; my eye wastes away / with grief, *
    Yes, my soul / and my body!

For my life is spent / with grief, *
    And my / years with sighing;

My strength fails because of my in- / iquity, *
    And / my bones waste away.

I am a reproach among all my enemies,
but especially among my / neighbors, *
    And am repulsive to / my acquaintances;

Those who see me outside / flee from me. *
    I am forgotten like a / dead
    man, out of mind;

I am like a broken / vessel. *
    For I hear the slander of many;
    fear / is on every side;

While they take counsel together a- / gainst me, *
    They scheme to / take away my life.

But as for me, I trust in You,
O Lord; I say, "You are / my God." *
　　My / times are in Your hand;

Deliver me from the hand of my / enemies, *
　　And from those who / persecute me.

Make Your face shine upon Your servant;
save me for Your / mercies' sake. *
　　Do not let me be ashamed,
　　O Lord, for I have / called upon You;

Let the wicked be ashamed;
let them be silent in / the grave. *
　　Let the lying lips be / put to silence,

Which speak inso- / lent things *
　　Proudly and contemptuously
　　a- / gainst the righteous.

Oh, how great is Your / goodness, *
　　Which You have laid up
　　for / those who fear You,

Which You have prepared for
those who / trust in You *
　　In the presence / of the sons of men!

You shall hide them in the
secret place of Your / presence *
　　From / the plots of man;

You shall keep them secretly in a pa- / vilion *
　　From / the strife of tongues.

Blessèd / be the Lord, *
　　For He has shown me His
　　marvelous kindness in / a strong city!

For I said in / my haste, *
　　"I am cut off / from before Your eyes";

Nevertheless You heard the
voice of my suppli- / cations *
　　When / I cried out to You.

Oh, love the Lord, all you / His saints! *
　　For the Lord preserves the faithful,
　　and fully repays / the proud person.

Be of good courage, and He
shall strengthen / your heart, *
　　All you who / hope in the Lord.

Glory be to the Father, and / to the Son, *
　　And to the / Holy Spirit

As it was in the be- / ginning *
　　Is now and will be for- / ever. Amen.

PSALM 32

Antiphon - *Exsultate justi*

Re-joice, you right-eous, and be ex - ult - ed   you up-right in heart.

Psalm - *Beati quorum*

BLESSÈD is he whose
transgression / is forgiven, *
　　Whose / sin is covered.

Blessèd is the man to whom the
Lord does not im- / pute iniquity, *
　　And in whose spirit / there is no deceit.

When / I kept silent, *
　　My bones grew old through
　　my groaning / all the day long.

For day and night Your hand
was / heavy upon me; *
　　My vitality was turned into
　　the / drought of summer.

I acknowledged / my sin to You, *
    And my iniquity I / have not hidden.

I said, "I will confess my
trans- / gressions to the LORD," *
    And You forgave the in- / iquity of my sin.

For this cause everyone who
is godly / shall pray to You *
    In a time when / You may be found;

Surely in a / flood of great waters *
    They shall / not come near him.

You are my hiding place; You
shall pre- / serve me from trouble; *
    You shall surround me
    with / songs of deliverance.

I will instruct you and teach
you in the / way you should go; *
    I will / guide you with My eye.

Do not be like the / horse or like the mule,*
    Which have no / understanding,

Which must be harnessed with / bit and bridle, *
    Else they will / not come near you.

Many sorrows shall be / to the wicked;*
    But he who trusts in the
    LORD, mercy / shall surround him.

Be glad in the LORD and
re- / joice, you righteous; *
    And shout for joy, all you / upright in heart!

Glory be to the / Father, and to the Son, *
    And to the / Holy Spirit

As it was in / the beginning *
    Is now and will be for- / ever. Amen.

PSALM 33

Tone 7a

Antiphon - *Exsultate justi*

Re-joice, you right-eous, and be ex - ult - ed you up-right in heart.

Psalm - *Exsultate, justi*

REJOICE in the LORD, / O you righteous! *
    For praise from the upright / is beautiful.

Praise the / LORD with the harp; *
    Make melody to Him with
    an / instrument of ten strings.

Sing to / Him a new song; *
    Play skillfully / with a shout of joy.

For the / word of the LORD is right, *
    And all His / work is done in truth.

He loves righteous- / ness and justice; *
    The earth is full of
    the / goodness of the LORD.

By the word of the / LORD the heavens were made, *
    And all the host of them
    by the / breath of His mouth.

He gathers the waters of the
sea to- / gether as a heap; *
    He lays up the / deep in storehouses.

Let all the / earth fear the LORD; *
    Let all the inhabitants of the
    world / stand in awe of Him.

For He / spoke, and it was done; *
    He commanded, / and it stood fast.

The LORD brings the counsel
of the / nations to nothing; *
    He makes the plans of
    the peoples / of no effect.

The counsel of the LORD / stands forever, *
    The plans of His heart to all / generations.

Blessèd is the nation whose / God is the LORD, *
    The people He has chosen
    as His / own inheritance.

The LORD / looks from heaven; *
    He sees / all the sons of men.

From the place / of His dwelling *
    He looks on all the
    in- / habitants of the earth;

He fashions their hearts / individually; *
    He con- / siders all their works.

No king is saved by the multitude / of an army; *
    A mighty man is not
    de- / livered by great strength.

A horse is a vain / hope for safety; *
    Neither shall it deliver
    any / by its great strength.

Behold, the eye of the LORD
is on / those who fear Him, *
    On those who / hope in His mercy,

To de- / liver their soul from death, *
    And to keep them a- / live in famine.

Our soul / waits for the LORD; *
    He is our / help and our shield.

For our / heart shall rejoice in Him, *
    Because we have trusted / in His holy name.

Let Your mercy, O LORD, / be upon us,*
    Just / as we hope in You.

Glory be to the / Father, and to the Son, *
    And to the / Holy Spirit

As it was in / the beginning *
    Is now and will be for- / ever. Amen.

PSALM 34

Tone 3a

Antiphon - *Immittet Angelus Domini*

The an - gel of the LORD en - camps all a - round

those who fear Him, and de - liv - ers them.

Psalm - *Benedicam Dominum*

I WILL bless the / LORD at all times; *
    His praise shall continually
    be / in my mouth.

My soul shall make its / boast in the LORD; *
    The humble shall hear of it / and be glad.

Oh, magni- / fy the LORD with me, *
    And let us exalt His name / together.

I sought the LORD, / and He heard me, *
    And delivered me / from all my fears.

They looked to / Him and were radiant, *
    And their faces / were not ashamed.

This poor man cried out,
and / the LORD heard him, *
    And saved him out of all / his troubles.

The angel of the LORD encamps
all around / those who fear Him, *
   And / delivers them.

Oh, taste and / see that the LORD is good; *
   Blessèd is the man who / trusts in Him!

Oh, fear the / LORD, you His saints! *
   There is no want to those / who fear Him.

The young lions lack and / suffer hunger; *
   But those who seek the LORD
   shall not lack an- / y good thing.

Come, you children, / listen to me; *
   I will teach you the fear / of the LORD.

Who is the man / who desires life, *
   And loves many days,
   that he / may see good?

Keep your / tongue from evil, *
   And your lips from speak- / ing deceit.

Depart from / evil and do good; *
   Seek peace and / pursue it.

The eyes of the LORD are / on the righteous, *
   And His ears are open / to their cry.

The face of the LORD is against
those / who do evil, *
   To cut off the remembrance
   of them / from the earth.

The righteous cry out, / and the LORD hears, *
   And delivers them out of all / their troubles.

The LORD is near to those
who / have a broken heart, *
   And saves such as have a con- / trite spirit.

Many are the afflictions / of the righteous, *
   But the LORD delivers him out / of them all.

He / guards all his bones; *
   Not one of them / is broken.

Evil shall / slay the wicked, *
   And those who hate the
   righteous shall / be condemned.

The LORD redeems the soul / of His servants, *
   And none of those who trust
   in Him shall / be condemned.

Glory be to the / Father, and to the Son, *
   And to the Ho- / ly Spirit

As it was in / the beginning *
   Is now and will be forev- / er. Amen.

PSALM 35

Tone 1a

Antiphon - *Expugna, Domine*

Fight a - gainst those who fight a - gainst me, O LORD.

Psalm - *Judica, Domine*

PLEAD MY / cause, O- LORD, *
   With / those who strive with me;

- / Fight against those *
   Who / fight against me.

Take hold of / shield and buckler, *
   And stand / up for my help.

Also / draw out the spear, *
   And stop those / who pursue me.

- / Say to my soul, *
   "I am / your salvation."

Let those be put to shame and brought
to dishonor who / seek after my life; *
   Let those be turned back and brought
   to confusion / who plot my hurt.

Let them be like / chaff before the wind, *
    And let the angel of / the LORD chase them.

Let their way be / dark and slippery, *
    And let the angel of the / LORD pursue them.

For without cause they have hidden
their net for / me in a pit, *
    Which they have dug
    without / cause for my life.

Let destruction come upon him
unexpectedly, and let his net that
he has / hidden catch himself; *
    Into that very destruc- / tion let him fall.

And my soul shall be / joyful in the LORD; *
    It shall rejoice in / His salvation.

All / my bones shall say, *
    "LORD, / who is like You,

Delivering the poor from him
who / is too strong for him, *
    Yes, the poor and the needy
    from / him who plunders him?"

Fierce / witnesses rise up; *
    They ask me things / that I do not know.

They reward me / evil for good, *
    To the / sorrow of my soul.

But as for me, when they were
sick, my cloth- / ing was sackcloth; *
    I humbled myself with fasting; and my
    prayer would return / to my own heart.

I paced about as though he
were my / friend or brother; *
    I bowed down heavily, as one
    who mourns / for his mother.

But in my adversi- / ty they rejoiced *
    And gath- / ered together;

Attackers gathered against me,
and I / did not know it; *
    They tore at / me and did not cease; *

With ungodly / mockers at feasts *
    They gnashed at / me with their teeth.

Lord, how / long will You look on? *
    Rescue me from their destructions,
    my precious life / from the lions.

I will give You thanks in the / great assembly; *
    I will praise You among / many people.

Let them not rejoice over me who
are wrongfully / my enemies; *
    Nor let them wink with the
    eye who hate / me without a cause.

For they / do not speak peace, *
    But they devise deceitful matters
    against the qui- / et ones in the land.

They also opened their mouth
wide a- / gainst me and said, *
    "Aha, aha! Our / eyes have seen it."

This You / have seen, O LORD; *
    Do / not keep silence.

O Lord, do not be far from me. Stir up
Yourself, and awake to my / vindication, *
    To my cause, my / God and my Lord.

Vindicate me, O LORD my God,
according / to Your righteousness; *
    And let them not / rejoice over me.

Let them not say in their hearts,
"Ah, so / we would have it!" *
    Let them not say, "We
    have / swallowed him up."

Let them be ashamed and brought
to mutu- / al confusion *
    Who / rejoice at my hurt;

Let them be clothed with shame / and dishonor *
    Who exalt them- / selves against me.

Let them shout for / joy and be glad, *
    Who favor / my righteous cause;

And let them say continually,
"Let the / LORD be magnified, *
    Who has pleasure in the
    prosperity / of His servant."

And my tongue shall
speak / of Your righteousness *
    And of Your praise / all the day long.

Glory be to the / Father, and to the Son, *
    And to the / Holy Spirit

As it was in / the beginning *
    Is now and will be for- / ever. Amen.

PSALM 36

Antiphon - *Domine, in caelo*

Your mer - cy, O Lord, is in the heav - ens.

Psalm - *Dixit injustus*

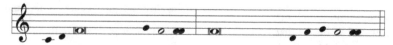

AN ORacle within my heart concerning
the transgression of the / wicked: *
   There is no fear of / God before his eyes.

For he flatters himself in his / own eyes, *
   When he finds out his
   iniquity / and when he hates.

The words of his mouth are
wickedness and / deceit; *
   He has ceased to be wise / and to do good.

He devises wickedness on his bed; he
sets himself in a way that is / not good; *
   He does not / abhor evil.

Your mercy, O Lord, is in the / heavens; *
   Your faithfulness / reaches to the clouds.

Your righteousness is like the great / mountains; *
   Your judgments / are a great deep;

O Lord, You preserve man / and beast. *
   How precious is Your
   loving- / kindness, O God!

Therefore the children of men put / their trust *
   Under the sha- / dow of Your wings.

They are abundantly satisfied
with the fullness of / Your house, *
   And You give them drink from
   the river / of Your pleasures.

For with You is the fountain / of life; *
   In Your / light we see light.

Oh, continue Your lovingkindness
to those who / know You, *
   And Your righteousness to
   the / upright in heart.

Let not the foot of pride come a- / gainst me, *
   And let not the hand of
   the wicked / drive me away.

There the workers of iniquity have / fallen; *
   They have been cast down
   and are not / able to rise.

Glory be to the Father, and / to the Son, *
   And to the / Holy Spirit

As it was in the be- / ginning *
   Is now and will be / forever. Amen.

PSALM 37a (1-22)

Antiphon - *Noli aemulari*

Do not fret be-cause of him who does e - vil and pros-pers.

Psalm - *Noli aemulari*

DO NOT fret because of / evildoers, *
    Nor be envious of the workers / of iniquity.

For they shall soon be cut / down like the grass, *
    And wither / as the green herb.

Trust in the / LORD, and do good; *
    Dwell in the land, and
    feed on / His faithfulness.

Delight yourself / also in the LORD, *
    And He shall give you
    the de- / sires of your heart.

Commit / your way to the LORD, *
    Trust also in Him, and He
    shall / bring it to pass.

He shall bring forth your /
righteousness as the light, *
    And your justice / as the noonday.

Rest in the LORD, and wait / patiently for Him; *
    Do not fret because of him who prospers
    in his way, because of the man who
    brings wick- / ed schemes to pass.

Cease from anger, and forsake wrath;
do not fret - it / only causes harm. *
    For evildoers / shall be cut off;

But those who / wait on the LORD, *
    They shall in- / herit the earth.

For yet a little while and the
wicked / shall be no more; *
    Indeed, you will look carefully
    for his place, but it / shall be no more.

But the meek shall in- / herit the earth, *
    And shall delight themselves
    in the a- / bundance of peace.

The wicked / plots against the just, *
    And gnashes / at him with his teeth.

The / Lord laughs at him, *
    For He sees that his / day is coming.

The / wicked have drawn the sword *
    And / have bent their bow,

To cast down the / poor and needy, *
    To slay those who are of / upright conduct.

Their sword shall / enter their own heart, *
    And their bows / shall be broken.

A little that a / righteous man has *
    Is better than the riches of / many wicked.

For the arms of the wicked / shall be broken, *
    But the LORD up- / holds the righteous.

The LORD knows the / days of the upright, *
    And their inheritance shall / be forever.

They shall not be a- / shamed in the evil time, *
    And in the days of famine
    they / shall be satisfied.

But the wick- / ed shall perish; *
    And the / enemies of the LORD,

Like the splendor of the
mea- / dows, shall vanish. *
    Into smoke they shall / vanish away.

The wicked borrows and / does not repay, *
    But the righteous shows / mercy and gives.

For those blessed by Him
shall in- / herit the earth, *
    But those cursed by Him / shall be cut off.

Glory be to the / Father, and to the Son, *
    And to the / Holy Spirit

As it was in / the beginning *
    Is now and will be for- / ever. Amen.

PSALM 37b (23-40)

Antiphon - *Custodi innocentiam*

Guard the in - no - cent man and look to jus - tice.

Psalm - *A Domino gressus*

THE STEPS of a good man
are ordered by / the LORD, *
    And He de- / lights in his way.

Though he fall, he shall not
be utterly / cast down; *
    For the LORD up- / holds him with His hand.

I have been young, and now / am old; *
    Yet I have not seen the righteous forsaken,
    nor his de- / scendants begging bread.

He is ever merciful, / and lends; *
    And his de- / scendants are blessèd.

Depart from evil, and / do good; *
    And dwell / forevermore.

For the LORD loves / justice, *
    And does not / forsake His saints;

They are preserved for- / ever, *
    But the descendants of the
    wicked / shall be cut off.

The righteous shall inherit / the land, *
    And dwell in / it forever.

The mouth of the righteous speaks / wisdom, *
    And his tongue / talks of justice.

The law of his God is in / his heart; *
    None of / his steps shall slide.

The wicked watches the / righteous, *
    And / seeks to slay him.

The LORD will not leave him in / his hand, *
    Nor condemn him / when he is judged.

Wait on the LORD, and keep / His way, *
    And He shall exalt you to in- / herit the land;

When the wicked are / cut off, *
    - / You shall see it.

I have seen the wicked in / great pow'r, *
    And spreading himself
    like a / native green tree.

Yet he passed away, and behold, he / was no more; *
    Indeed I sought him, but
    he / could not be found.

Mark the blameless man,
and observe the / upright; *
    For the future of / that man is peace.

But the transgressors shall be
destroyed to- / gether; *
    The future of the wicked / shall be cut off.

But the salvation of the
righteous is / from the LORD; *
    He is their strength in the / time of trouble.

And the LORD shall help
them and de- / liver them; *
    He shall deliver them from the wicked, and
    save them, be- / cause they trust in Him.

Glory be to the Father, and / to the Son, *
    And to the / Holy Spirit

As it was in the be- / ginning *
    Is now and will be for- / ever. Amen.

Antiphon - *Ne in ira tua*

Do not chast - en   me   in   Your an - ger,   O   Lord.

Psalm - *Domine, ne in furore*

O LORD, do not re- / buke me in Your wrath, *
  Nor chasten me in Your / hot displeasure!

For Your arrows / pierce me deeply, *
  And Your hand / presses me down.

There is no soundness in my
flesh because / of Your anger, *
  Nor any health in my
  bones be- / cause of my sin.

For my iniquities have / gone over my head; *
  Like a heavy burden they
  are too / heavy for me.

My wounds are / foul and festering *
  Because / of my foolishness.

I am troubled, I am / bowed down greatly; *
  I go mourning / all the day long.

For my loins are full of / inflammation, *
  And there is no sound- / ness in my flesh.

I am feeble and se- / verely broken; *
  I groan because of the tur- / moil of my heart.

Lord, all my desire / is before You; *
  And my sighing is not / hidden from You.

My heart pants, / my strength fails me; *
  As for the light of my eyes,
  it al- / so has gone from me.

My loved ones and my friends
stand a- / loof from my plague, *
  And my relatives / stand afar off.

Those also who seek my life / lay snares for me; *
  Those who seek my hurt speak of
  destruction, and plan deception /
  all the day long.

But I, like a / deaf man, do not hear; *
  And I am like a mute who
  does not / open his mouth.

Thus I am like a / man who does not hear, *
  And in whose / mouth is no response.

For in You, / O LORD, I hope; *
  You will hear, / O Lord my God.

For I said, "Hear me, lest they / rejoice over me, *
  Lest, when my foot slips, they
  exalt them- / selves against me."

For I am / ready to fall, *
  And my sorrow is continual- / ly before me.

For I will declare / my iniquity; *
  I will be in anguish / over my sin.

But my enemies are
vigorous, / and they are strong; *
  And those who hate me
  wrongfully / have multiplied.

Those also who render / evil for good, *
  They are my adversaries, because
  I / follow what is good.

Do not for- / sake me, O LORD; *
  O my God, / be not far from me!

Make / haste to help me, *
  O Lord, / my salvation!

Glory be to the Father, / and to the Son, *
  And to the / Holy Spirit

As it was in / the beginning *
  Is now and will be / forever. Amen.

PSALM 39

Antiphon - *Amove, Domine*

O Lord, re - move Your plague from me.

Psalm - *Dixi, custodiam*

I SAID, "I will guard / my ways, *
    Lest I / sin with my tongue;

I will restrain my mouth with a / muzzle, *
    While the wicked / are before me."

I was mute with silence, I held
my peace even / from good; *
    And my sor- / row was stirred up.

My heart was hot with- / in me; *
    While I was musing, / the fire burned.

Then I spoke with / my tongue: *
    "LORD, make me / to know my end,

And what is the measure of / my days, *
    That I may know / how frail I am.

Indeed, You have made my
days as / handbreadths, *
    And my age is as no- / thing before You;

Certainly every man at his
best state is but / vapor. *
    Surely every man walks
    about / like a shadow;

Surely they busy themselves / in vain; *
    He heaps up riches, and does
    not know / who will gather them.

"And now, Lord, what do I / wait for? *
    My / hope is in You.

Deliver me from all my trans- / gressions; *
    Do not make me the reproach / of the foolish.

I was mute, I did not open / my mouth, *
    Because it was / You who did it.

Remove Your plague / from me; *
    I am consumed by the / blow of Your hand.

When with rebukes You correct man for iniquity,
You make his beauty melt away / like a moth; *
    Surely every / man is vapor.

"Hear my prayer, / O LORD, *
    And / give ear to my cry;

Do not be silent at my tears;
for I am a stranger / with You, *
    A sojourner, as / all my fathers were.

Remove Your gaze from me,
that I may re- / gain strength, *
    Before I go away / and am no more."

Glory be to the Father, and / to the Son, *
    And to the / Holy Spirit

As it was in the be- / ginning *
    Is now and will be for- / ever. Amen.

PSALM 40

Antiphon - *Respexit me*

The Lord looked down on me and heard my plea.

Psalm - *Exspectans exspectavi*

I WAITed patiently for / the LORD; *
   And He inclined to me / and heard my cry.

He also brought me up out of a horri- / ble pit, *
   Out / of the miry clay,

And set my feet upon / a rock, *
   And es - / tablished my steps.

He has put a new song in / my mouth *
   - / Praise to our God;

Many will see it / and fear, *
   And / will trust in the LORD.

Blessèd is that man who
makes the LORD / his trust, *
   And does not respect the proud,
   nor such as / turn aside to lies.

Many, O LORD my God,
are Your wonder- / ful works *
   - / Which You have done;

And Your thoughts / t'ward us *
   Cannot be recounted to / You in order;

If I would declare and speak / of them, *
   They are more than / can be numbered.

Sacrifice and offering You did not / desire; *
   My ears / You have opened.

Burnt offering and sin offering
You did not / require. *
   Then I said, / "Behold, I come;

In the scroll of the book it is written
of me. I delight to do / Your will, *
   O my God, And Your
   law / is within my heart."

I have proclaimed the good news
of righteousness in the great as- / sembly; *
   Indeed, I do not restrain my
   lips, O LORD, / You Yourself know.

I have not hidden Your
righteousness within / my heart; *
   I have declared Your faithfulness
   and / Your salvation;

I have not concealed Your loving- / kindness *
   And Your truth from the / great assembly.

Do not withhold Your tender
mercies from me, / O LORD; *
   Let Your lovingkindness and
   Your truth continual- / ly preserve me.

For innumerable evils have surrounded
me; my iniquities have over- / taken me, *
   So that I am not / able to look up;

They are more than the hairs of / my head; *
   Therefore / my heart fails me.

Be pleased, O LORD, to de- / liver me; *
   O LORD, make / haste to help me!

Let them be ashamed and
brought to mutual con- / fusion *
   Who seek / to destroy my life;

Let them be driven backward
and brought to dis- / honor *
   Who / wish me evil.

Let them be confounded
because of / their shame, *
   Who say to me, / "Aha, aha!"

Let all those who seek You
rejoice and be glad / in You; *
   Let such as love Your salvation say
   continually, "The / LORD be magnified!"

But I am poor and / needy; *
   Yet the LORD / thinks upon me.

You are my help and my de- / liverer; *
   Do not / delay, O my God.

Glory be to the Father, and / to the Son, *
   And to the / Holy Spirit

As it was in the be- / ginning *
   Is now and will be for- / ever. Amen.

Antiphon - *Suscepisti me Domine*

You have up - held me, O Lord, and have set me be - fore Your face for - ev - er.

Psalm - *Beatus qui intelligit*

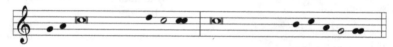

BLESSÈD is he who considers / the poor; *
  The LORD will deliver him
  in / time of trouble.

The LORD will preserve him and keep him alive,
and he will be blessed on / the earth; *
  You will not deliver him
  to the will / of his enemies.

The LORD will strengthen him
on his bed of / illness; *
  You will sustain him / on his sickbed.

I said, "LORD, be merciful / to me; *
  Heal my soul, for I
  have / sinned against You."

My enemies speak evil / of me: *
  "When will he die, and / his name perish?"

And if he comes to see me, he / speaks lies; *
  His heart gathers iniquity to itself;
  when he goes / out, he tells it.

All who hate me whisper together a- / gainst me; *
  Against me they / devise my hurt.

"An evil disease," they say, / "clings to him. *
  And now that he lies down,
  he will / rise up no more."

Even my own familiar friend
in whom I / trusted, *
  Who ate my bread, has lifted
  up his / heel against me.

But You, O LORD, be merciful
to me, and / raise me up, *
  That I / may repay them.

By this I know that You are
well / pleased with me, *
  Because my enemy does
  not / triumph over me.

As for me, You uphold me in my in- / tegrity, *
  And set me before Your / face forever.

Blessèd be the LORD God of Israel from everlasting to ever- / lasting! *
  A- / men and Amen.

Glory be to the Father, and / to the Son, *
  And to the / Holy Spirit

As it was in the be- / ginning *
  Is now and will be for- / ever. Amen.

PSALM 42

Antiphon - *Sitivit anima mea*

My soul thirsts for God, for the liv - ing God.

Psalm - *Quemadmodum*

AS THE deer pants / for the water brooks, *
So pants my soul / for You, O God.

My soul thirsts for God, / for the living God. *
When shall I come and ap- / pear before God?

My tears have been my / food day and night, *
While they continually say to
me, / "Where is your God?"

When I remember these things,
I pour out my / soul within me. *
For I used to go with / the multitude;

I went with them to the house of
God, with the / voice of joy and praise, *
With a multitude that kept / a pilgrim feast.

Why are you / cast down, O my soul? *
And why are you disquiet- / ed within me?

Hope in God, for I / shall yet praise Him *
For the help of / His countenance.

O my God, my soul is cast / down within me; *
Therefore I will remember You from
the land of the Jordan, and from the
heights of Hermon, from / the Hill Mizar.

Deep calls unto deep at the
noise / of Your waterfalls; *
All Your waves and billows
have / gone over me.

The LORD will command His
lovingkindness / in the daytime, *
And in the night His song shall be with
me; a prayer to the / God of my life.

I will say to God my Rock,
"Why have / You forgotten me? *
Why do I go mourning because
of the oppression of / the enemy?"

As with a breaking of my bones,
My ene- / mies reproach me, *
While they say to me all
day long, / "Where is your God?"

Why are you / cast down, O my soul? *
And why are you disquiet- / ed within me?

Hope in God; for I / shall yet praise Him,*
The help of my counten- / ance and my God.

Glory be to the / Father, and to the Son, *
And to the / Holy Spirit

As it was in / the beginning *
Is now and will be for- / ever. Amen.

PSALM 43

Antiphon - *Salutare vultus mei*

You are the help of my coun - ten - ance, my God.

Psalm - *Judica me, Deus*

VINDIcate me, O God, and plead
my cause against an un- / godly nation; *
    Oh, deliver me from the
    deceit- / ful and unjust man!

For You are the God of my strength;
why / do You cast me off? *
    Why do I go mourning because
    of the oppression / of the enemy?

Oh, send out Your light and Your
truth! / Let them lead me; *
    Let them bring me to Your holy
    hill and to Your / tabernacle.

Then I will go to the / altar of God, *
    To God / my exceeding joy;

And on the harp I will praise
You, / O God, my God. *
    Why are you cast down, O my soul?
    And why are you disquiet- / ed within me?

Hope in God; For I / shall yet praise Him, *
    The help of my counten- / ance and my God.

Glory be to the Father, / and to the Son, *
    And to the / Holy Spirit

As it was in / the beginning *
    Is now and will be / forever. Amen.

PSALM 44

Tone 2

Antiphon - *Salvasti nos*

You have saved us, O Lord, and we will praise your name for - ev - er.

Psalm - *Deus, auribus*

WE HAVE heard with our ears, / O God, *
    Our fathers / have told us,

The deeds You did in / their days, *
    In / days of old:

You drove out the nations with
Your hand, but them You / planted; *
    You afflicted the peoples, and / cast them out.

For they did not gain possession of
the land by their / own sword, *
    Nor did their own / arm save them;

But it was Your right hand, Your arm,
and the light of Your / countenance, *
    Because You / favored them.

You are my King, / O God; *
    Command victories / for Jacob.

Through You we will push down our / enemies; *
    Through Your name we will trample
    those who rise up / against us.

For I will not trust in / my bow, *
    Nor shall my / sword save me.

But You have saved us from our / enemies, *
    And have put to shame those / who hated us.

In God we boast all / day long, *
    And praise Your name / forever.

But You have cast us off and put us / to shame, *
    And You do not go out with / our armies.

You make us turn back from the / enemy, *
  And those who hate us have
    taken spoil / for themselves.

You have given us up like
sheep intended / for food, *
  And have scattered us among / the nations.

You sell Your people for next to / nothing, *
  And are not enriched / by selling them.

You make us a reproach to our / neighbors, *
  A scorn and a derision to those all / around us.

You make us a byword among the / nations, *
  A shaking of the head among / the peoples.

My dishonor is continually be- / fore me, *
  And the shame of my face / has covered me,

Because of the voice of him
who reproaches and / reviles, *
  Because of the enemy and the / avenger.

All this has come upon us; but
we have not for- / gotten You, *
  Nor have we dealt falsely with / Your covenant.

Our heart has not / turned back, *
  Nor have our steps departed / from Your way;

But You have severely broken
us in the place of / jackals, *
  And covered us with the sha- / dow of death.

If we had forgotten the name of / our God, *
  Or stretched out our
    hands to / a foreign god,

Would not God search / this out? *
  For He knows the secrets / of the heart.

Yet for Your sake we are killed all / day long; *
  We are accounted as sheep for / the slaughter.

Awake! Why do You sleep, / O Lord? *
  Arise! Do not cast us off / forever.

Why do You hide / Your face, *
  And forget our affliction and our / oppression?

For our soul is bowed down to / the dust; *
  Our body clings / to the ground.

Arise for / our help, *
  And redeem us for / Your mercies' sake.

Glory be to the Father, and / to the Son, *
  And to the Ho- / ly Spirit

As it was in the be- / ginning *
  Is now and will be forev- / er. Amen.

PSALM 45

Antiphon - *Speciousus forma*

You are fair - er   than the sons of men;   grace is poured up - on Your lips.

Psalm - *Eructavit cor meum*

MY HEART is overflowing with a good theme;
I recite my composition con- / cerning the King; *
  My tongue is the pen of a / ready writer.

You are fairer / than the sons of men; *
  Grace is poured upon Your lips;
    therefore God has blessed / You forever.

Gird Your sword upon
Your thigh, / O Mighty One, *
  With Your glory / and Your majesty.

And in Your majesty ride prosperously because
of truth, humility, / and righteousness; *
  And Your right hand shall
    teach / You awesome things.

Your arrows are sharp in the
heart of the / King's enemies; *
 The peo- / ples fall under You.

Your throne, O God, is for- / ever and ever; *
 A scepter of righteousness is the
 scepter / of Your kingdom.

You love righteousness / and hate wickedness; *
 Therefore God, Your God, has
 anointed You with the oil of
 gladness more than / Your companions.

All Your garments are scented
with myrrh and / aloes and cassia, *
 Out of the ivory palaces, by
 which / they have made You glad.

Kings' daughters are among
Your / hon'rable women; *
 At Your right hand stands the
 queen in / gold from Ophir.

Listen, O daughter,
consider / and incline your ear; *
 Forget your own people
 also, / and your father's house;

So the King will greatly de- / sire your beauty; *
Because He is your / Lord, worship Him.

And the daughter of Tyre will / come with a gift; *
 The rich among the
 people will / seek your favor.

The royal daughter is all glorious within the
palace; Her clothing is / woven with gold. *
 She shall be brought to the
 King in robes of / many colors;

The virgins, her companions / who follow her, *
 Shall / be brought to You.

With gladness and
rejoicing / they shall be brought; *
 They shall enter / the King's palace.

Instead of Your fathers / shall be Your sons, *
 Whom You shall make
 prin- / ces in all the earth.

I will make Your name to be
remembered in all / generations; *
 Therefore the people shall
 praise You forev- / er and ever.

Glory be to the / Father, and to the Son, *
 And to the / Holy Spirit

As it was in / the beginning *
 Is now and will be for- / ever. Amen.

PSALM 46

Antiphon - *Adjutor in tribulationibus*

A   help   in   trou - ble   is   our   God.

Psalm - *Deus noster refugium*

GOD IS our / refuge and strength, *
 A very present / help in trouble.

Therefore we will not fear even
though the / earth be removed, *
 And though the mountains be
 carried into the / midst of the sea;

Though its waters roar / and be troubled, *
 Though the mountains
 shake / with its swelling.

There is a river whose streams
shall make glad the / city of God, *
 The holy place of the
 tabernacle / of the Most High.

82

God is in the midst of
her, / she shall not be moved; *
  God shall help her,
  just at / the break of dawn.

The nations raged, the / kingdoms were moved; *
  He uttered His voice, / the earth melted.

The LORD of / hosts is with us; *
  The God of Jacob / is our refuge.

Come, behold the / works of the LORD, *
  Who has made deso- / lations in the earth.

He makes wars cease to the end of the earth;
  He breaks the bow and / cuts the spear in two; *
  He burns the char- / iot in the fire.

Be still, and / know that I am God; *
  I will be exalted among the nations,
  I will be exalt- / ed in the earth!

The LORD of / hosts is with us; *
  The God of Jacob / is our refuge.

Glory be to the / Father, and to the Son, *
  And to the / Holy Spirit

As it was in / the beginning *
  Is now and will be for- / ever. Amen.

PSALM 47

Antiphon - *Jubilate Deo*

Shout   to   God   with   the   voice   of   tri - umph!

Psalm - *Omnes gentes, plaudite*

OH, CLAP your hands, / all you peoples! *
  Shout to God with the / voice of triumph!

For the LORD Most / High is awesome; *
  He is a great King / over all the earth.

He will subdue the / peoples under us, *
  And the nations / under our feet.

He will choose our in- / heritance for us, *
  The excellence of / Jacob whom He loves.

God has gone / up with a shout, *
  The LORD with the / sound of a trumpet.

Sing praises to / God, sing praises! *
  Sing praises to our / King, sing praises!

For God is the / King of all the earth; *
  Sing praises with / understanding.

God reigns / over the nations; *
  God sits on / His holy throne.

The princes of the people have gathered together,
  the people of the / God of Abraham. *
  For the shields of the earth belong
  to God; He is / greatly exalted.

Glory be to the / Father, and to the Son, *
  And to the / Holy Spirit

As it was in / the beginning *
  Is now and will be for- / ever. Amen.

PSALM 48

Antiphon - *Magnus Dominus*

Great is the Lord, and great-ly to be praised in the ci - ty of our God.

Psalm - *Magnus Dominus*

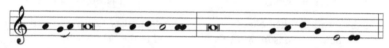

GREAT IS the LORD, and / greatly to be praised *
  In the city of our God, in / His holy mountain.

Beautiful in elevation, the joy of
the whole earth, / is Mount Zion *
  On the sides of the north,
  the ci- / ty of the great King.

God is / in her palaces; *
  He is / known as her refuge.

For behold, the / kings assembled, *
  They / passed by together.

They saw it, and / so they marveled; *
  They were troubled, / they hastened away.

Fear / took hold of them there, *
  And pain, as of a / woman in birth pangs,

As when You break the / ships of Tarshish *
  - / With an east-- wind.

As we have heard, / so we have seen *
  In the ci- / ty of the LORD of hosts,

In the ci- / ty of our God: *
  God will esta- / blish it forever.

We have thought, O God,
on Your / lovingkindness, *
  In the / midst of Your temple.

According to Your name, O God, so
is Your praise to the / ends of the earth; *
  Your right hand is / full of righteousness.

Let Mount Zion rejoice, let the
daughters of / Judah be glad, *
  Be- / cause of Your judgments.

Walk about Zion, and go / all around her. *
  - / Count her tow-- ers;

Mark well her bulwarks; Consi- / der her palaces; *
  That you may tell it to
  the gen- / eration following.

For this is God, our God forev- / er and ever; *
  He will be our / guide even to death.

Glory be to the Father, / and to the Son, *
  And to / the Holy Spirit

As it was in / the beginning *
  Is now and will be / forever. Amen.

PSALM 49

Antiphon - *Ne timueris*

Fear not; the glo-ry of the rich shall not de-scend in-to the grave with him.

Psalm - *Audite haec, omnes*

HEAR THIS, all / peoples; *
　Give ear, all inhabi- / tants of the world,

Both low / and high, *
　Rich and / poor together.

My mouth shall speak / wisdom, *
　And the meditation of my
　heart shall give / understanding.

I will incline my ear to a / proverb; *
　I will disclose my dark / saying on the harp.

Why should I fear in the days of / evil,*
　When the iniquity at my / heels surrounds me?

Those who trust in / their wealth *
　And boast in the multitude / of their riches,

None of them can by any
means redeem his / brother, *
　Nor give to God a / ransom for him

For the redemption of their souls is costly,
and it shall cease for- / ever *
　That he should continue to live
　eternally, / and not see the Pit.

For he sees wise / men die; *
　Likewise the fool and the senseless person
　perish, and leave their / wealth to others.

Their inner thought is that their houses
will last forever, their dwelling places
to all gener- / ations; *
　They call their lands af- / ter their own names.

Nevertheless man, though
in honor, does not / remain; *
　He is like the / beasts that perish.

This is the way of those who are / foolish,*
　And of their posterity who
　ap- / prove their sayings.

Like sheep they are laid / in the grave;*
　Death shall feed on them; the upright shall
　have dominion over them / in the morning;

And their beauty shall be
consumed / in the grave, *
　Far / from their dwelling.

But God will redeem my soul
from the power / of the grave, *
　For He / shall receive me.

Do not be afraid when one be- / comes rich, *
　When the glory of his / house is increased;

For when he dies he shall carry nothing / away; *
　His glory shall not / descend after him.

Though while he lives he blesses / himself *
　(For men will praise you when
　you do / well for yourself),

He shall go to the generation of his / fathers; *
　They shall / never see light.

A man who is in honor,
yet does not / understand, *
　Is like the / beasts that perish.

Glory be to the Father, and / to the Son, *
　And to the / Holy Spirit

As it was in the be- / ginning *
　Is now and will be for- / ever. Amen.

Antiphon - *Intelligite*

Con - sid - er this, you who for - get God.

Psalm - *Deus Deorum*

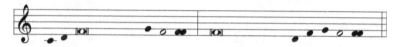

THE MIGHty One, God the Lord, has / spoken *
  And called the earth from the
  rising of the sun / to its going down.

Out of Zion, the perfection of
beauty, God will / shine forth. *
  Our God shall come,
  and shall / not keep silent;

A fire shall devour be- / fore Him, *
  And it shall be very
  tempestuous / all around Him.

He shall call to the heavens from
above, and / to the earth, *
  That He may / judge His people:

"Gather My saints together / to Me, *
  Those who have made a
  covenant with / Me by sacrifice."

Let the heavens declare His / righteousness, *
  For / God Himself is Judge.

"Hear, O My people, and I / will speak, *
  O Israel, and I will testify against
  you; / I am God, your God!

I will not rebuke you for your sacri- / fices *
  Or your burnt offerings, which
  are continual- / ly before Me.

I will not take a bull from / your house,*
  Nor goats / out of your folds.

For every beast of the forest / is Mine, *
  And the cattle / on a thousand hills.

I know all the birds of the / mountains,*
  And the wild beasts / of the field are Mine.

"If I were hungry, I would not / tell you; *
  For the world is Mine, and / all its fullness.

Will I eat the / flesh of bulls, *
  Or / drink the blood of goats?

Offer to God thanks- / giving, *
  And pay your vows / to the Most High.

Call upon Me in the day of / trouble; *
  I will deliver you, and you shall / glorify Me."

But to the wicked God says: "What
right have you to declare My / statutes,*
  Or take My coven- / ant in your mouth,

Seeing you hate in- / struction *
  And cast My / words behind you?

When you saw a thief, you consented / with him, *
  And have been a partaker / with adulterers.

You give your mouth to / evil, *
  And your / tongue frames deceit.

You sit and speak against your / brother; *
  You slander / your own mother's son.

These things you have done, and I kept silent;
You thought that I was altogether / like you; *
  But I will rebuke you, and set
  them in order / before your eyes.

"Now consider this, you who for- / get God,*
  Lest I tear you in pieces,
  and there be none / to deliver:

Whoever offers praise glori- / fies Me;*
  And to him who orders his conduct aright
  I will show the sal- / vation of God."

Glory be to the Father, and / to the Son, *
  And to the / Holy Spirit

As it was in the be- / ginning *
  Is now and will be for- / ever. Amen.

PSALM 51

Antiphon - *Amplius lava me*

Wash me thor-ough-ly, O Lord, from my in - i - qui - ty.

Psalm - *Miserere mei, Deus, secundum*

HAVE MERcy up- / on me, O God *
 According to Your / loving kindness

According to the multitude
of Your / tender mercies *
 Blot out / my transgressions

Wash me thoroughly from / my iniquity *
 And / cleanse me from my sin

For I acknowledge / my transgressions, *
 And my sin is / ever before me.

Against You, You / only, have I sinned, *
 And done this / evil in your sight

That You may be found / just when You speak, *
 And / blameless when You judge.

Behold, I was brought forth / in iniquity,*
 And in sin my / mother conceived me

Behold, You desire truth / in the inward parts, *
 And in the hidden part You will
 make me / to know wisdom.

Purge me with hyssop, and / I shall be clean *
 Wash me and I shall be / whiter than snow

Make me to hear / joy and gladness, *
 That the bones which You
 have / broken may rejoice.

Hide Your / face from my sins, *
 And blot out all / my iniquities.

Create in me a / clean heart, O God, *
 And renew a steadfast / spirit within me.

Do not cast me away / from Your presence, *
 And do not take Your Holy / Spirit from me.

Restore to me the joy of / Your salvation, *
 And uphold me with / Your free Spirit.

Then I will teach trans- / gressors Your ways, *
 And sinners shall be con- / verted to You.

Deliver me from blood- / guiltiness, O God,*
 The God of / my salvation

And my / tongue shall sing aloud *
 Of / Your righteousness

O Lord / open my lips, *
 And my mouth / shall show forth Your praise.

For You do not desire sacrifice,
or else / I would give it; *
 You do not delight in / burnt offering

The sacrifices of God are a / broken spirit, *
 A broken and a contrite heart.
 These, O God, / You will not despise.

Do good in Your good / pleasure to Zion; *
 Build the walls / of Jerusalem

Then You shall be pleased with the
sacrifices / of righteousness *
 With burnt offering and
 whole / burnt offering

Then they / shall offer bulls *
 - / On Your altar.

Glory be to the / Father and to the Son *
 and to the / Holy Spirit;

As it was in / the beginning *
 Is now and will be for- / ever. Amen.

PSALM 52

Antiphon - *Expectabo nomen tuum*

I will wait on Your name, for it is good be - fore Your saints.

Psalm - *Quid gloriaris?*

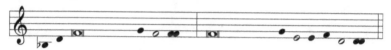

WHY DO you boast in evil, O / mighty man? *
   The goodness of God endures / continually.

Your tongue devises de- / struction, *
   Like a sharp razor, work- / ing deceitfully.

You love evil more / than good, *
   Lying rather than / speaking righteousness.

You love all de- / vouring words, *
   You / deceitful tongue.

God shall likewise destroy you for- / ever; *
   He shall / take you away,

And pluck you out of your / dwelling place, *
   And uproot you from the land / of the living.

The righteous also shall / see and fear, *
   And shall laugh / at him, saying,

"Here is the man who did
not make God / his strength, *
   But trusted in the abundance
   of his riches, and strengthened
   himself / in his wickedness."

But I am like a green olive
tree in the / house of God; *
   I trust in the mercy of God
   forev- / er and ever.

I will praise You forever,
because You have / done it; *
   And in the presence of Your saints I
   will wait on Your name, / for it is good.

Glory be to the Father, and / to the Son, *
   And to the / Holy Spirit

As it was in the be- / ginning *
   Is now and will be for- / ever. Amen.

PSALM 53

Antiphon - *Quis dabit ex Sion*

Oh, that the sal-va-tion of Is - ra - el would come out of Zi - on!

APsalm - *Dixit insipiens*

THE FOOL has said in / his heart, *
   - / "There is no God."

They are corrupt, and have
done abominable in- / iquity; *
   There is / none who does good.

God looks down from heaven
upon the children / of men, *
 To see if there are any who
 under- / stand, who seek God.

Every one of them has turned aside;
they have together become / corrupt; *
 There is none who does / good, no, not one.

Have the workers of iniquity no / knowledge, *
 Who eat up my people as they eat
 bread, and do not / call upon God?

There they are in / great fear *
 - / Where no fear was,

For God has scattered the bones
of him who encamps a- / gainst you; *
 You have put them to shame,
 because God / has despised them.

Oh, that the salvation of Israel
would come out of / Zion! *
 When God brings back the captivity of His
 people, let Jacob rejoice and Is- / rael be glad.

Glory be to the Father, and / to the Son, *
 And to the / Holy Spirit

As it was in the be- / ginning *
 Is now and will be for- / ever. Amen.

PSALM 54

Antiphon - *Deus adjuvat me*

God is my help-er; the Lord is with those who up-hold my life.

Psalm - *Deus, in nomine*

SAVE ME, O God, by / Your name, *
 And vindicate / me by Your strength.

Hear my prayer, / O God; *
 Give ear to the / words of my mouth.

For strangers have risen up against me,
and oppressors have sought after / my life; *
 They have not set / God before them.

Behold, God is my / helper; *
 The Lord is with those / who uphold my life.

He will repay my enemies for their / evil. *
 Cut them / off in Your truth.

I will freely sacrifice / to You; *
 I will praise Your name,
 O LORD, / for it is good.

For He has delivered me out of all / trouble; *
 And my eye has seen its
 desire upon / my enemies.

Glory be to the Father, and / to the Son, *
 And to the / Holy Spirit

As it was in the be- / ginning *
 Is now and will be for- / ever. Amen.

Antiphon - *Dominus redemit*

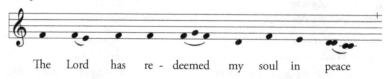

The Lord has re - deemed my soul in peace

from the bat - tle that was a - gainst me.

Psalm - *Exaudi, Deus*

GIVE EAR to my prayer, / O God, *
    And do not hide Yourself
    from my / supplication.

Attend to me, and / hear me; *
    I am restless in my
    complaint, / and moan noisily,

Because of the voice of the / enemy, *
    Because of the oppression / of the wicked;

For they bring down trouble up- / on me, *
    And in / wrath they hate me.

My heart is severely pained with- / in me,*
    And the terrors of death
    have fal- / len upon me.

Fearfulness and trembling
have come up- / on me, *
    And horror has / overwhelmed me.

So I said, "Oh, that I had wings / like a dove! *
    I would fly a- / way and be at rest.

Indeed, I would wander / far off, *
    And remain / in the wilderness.

I would hasten my / escape *
    From the windy / storm and tempest."

Destroy, O Lord, and divide / their tongues,*
    For I have seen violence and strife / in the city.

Day and night they go around it on / its walls; *
    Iniquity and trouble are also / in the midst of it.

Destruction is in / its midst; *
    Oppression and deceit do
    not de- / part from its streets.

For it is not an enemy who re- / proaches me; *
    Then / I could bear it.

Nor is it one who hates me who
has exalted himself a- / gainst me; *
    Then / I could hide from him.

But it was you, a man my / equal, *
    My companion and / my acquaintance.

We took sweet counsel to- / gether, *
    And walked to the
    house / of God in the throng.

Let death seize them; let them
go down alive in- / to hell, *
    For wickedness is in their
    dwellings / and among them.

As for me, I will call up- / on God, *
    And the / LORD shall save me.

Evening and morning and at
noon I will pray, and / cry aloud, *
    And / He shall hear my voice.

He has redeemed my soul in peace
from the battle that was a- / gainst me, *
    For there were ma- / ny against me.

God will hear, and afflict them,
even He who abides from / of old. *
    Because they do not change,
    therefore they / do not fear God.

He has put forth his hands against
those who were at peace / with him; *
    He has bro- / ken his covenant.

The words of his mouth were smoother
than butter, but war was in / his heart; *
    His words were softer than oil,
    yet / they were drawn swords.

Cast your burden on the LORD,
and He shall sus- / tain you; *
    He shall never permit the
    right- / eous to be moved.

But You, O God, shall bring / them down *
    To the pit / of destruction;

Bloodthirsty and deceitful men shall
not live out half / their days; *
    But / I will trust in You.

Glory be to the Father, and / to the Son, *
    And to the / Holy Spirit

As it was in the be- / ginning *
    Is now and will be for- / ever. Amen.

PSALM 56

Antiphon - *In Deo speravi*

In God   I have put my trust; I will not fear what man can do to me.

Psalm - *Miserere mei, Deus, quoniam*

BE MERciful to me, O God,
for man would / swallow me up; *
    Fighting all day / he oppresses me.

My enemies would / hound me all day, *
    For there are many who fight
    against / me, O Most High.

When- / ever I am afraid, *
    - / I will trust in You.

In God (I will praise His word), In God
I have put my trust; / I will not fear. *
    What can / flesh do to me?

All / day they twist my words; *
    All their thoughts are against / me for evil.

They gather together, they
hide, / they mark my steps, *
    When they lie in / wait for my life.

Shall they escape / by iniquity? *
    In anger cast down the / peoples, O God!

You number my wanderings;
put my tears in- / to Your bottle; *
    Are they / not in Your book?

When I cry out to You, then
my / enemies will turn back; *
    This I know, because / God is for me.

In God / (I will praise His word), *
    In the LORD / (I will praise His word),

In God I have put my trust; I / will not be afraid. *
    What can / man do to me?

Vows made to You are
binding / upon me, O God; *
    I will render / praises to You,

For You have delivered my soul from death.
Have You not kept my / feet from falling, *
 That I may walk before God
 in the light / of the living?

Glory be to the / Father, and to the Son, *
 And to the / Holy Spirit

As it was in / the beginning *
 Is now and will be for- / ever. Amen.

PSALM 57

Antiphon - *Miserere mei, Deus, miserere*

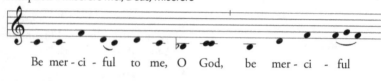

Be mer - ci - ful to me, O God, be mer - ci - ful

to me! For my soul trusts in You.

Psalm - *Miserere mei, Deus, miserere*

BE MERciful to me, O God, be merciful / to me! *
 For / my soul trusts in You;

And in the shadow of Your
wings I will make my / refuge, *
 Until these calami- / ties have passed by.

I will cry out to God / Most High, *
 To God who performs / all things for me.

He shall send from heaven and save me; He
reproaches the one who would swallow / me up. *
 God shall send forth
 His / mercy and His truth.

My soul is among / lions; *
 I lie among the sons of
 men / who are set on fire,

Whose teeth are spears and / arrows, *
 And their / tongue a sharp sword.

Be exalted, O God, above the / heavens; *
 Let Your glory be a- / bove all the earth.

They have prepared a net for / my steps; *
 My / soul is bowed down;

They have dug a pit be- / fore me; *
 Into the midst of it they
 them- / selves have fallen.

My heart is steadfast, O God,
my heart is / steadfast; *
 I will / sing and give praise.

Awake, my glory! Awake, / lute and harp!*
 I will a- / waken the dawn.

I will praise You, O Lord, among the / peoples; *
 I will sing to You a- / mong the nations.

For Your mercy reaches unto the / heavens, *
 And Your truth / unto the clouds.

Be exalted, O God, above the / heavens; *
 Let Your glory be a- / bove all the earth.

Glory be to the Father, and / to the Son, *
 And to the / Holy Spirit

As it was in the be- / ginning *
 Is now and will be for- / ever. Amen.

PSALM 58

Antiphon - *Vere est Deus iudicans*

Sure - ly He is God who jud - ges in the earth.

Psalm - *Si vere utique*

DO YOU indeed speak
righteousness, / you silent ones? *
   Do you judge uprightly, / you sons of men?

No, in / heart you work wickedness; *
   You weigh out the violence
   of your / hands in the earth.

The wicked are e- / stranged from the womb; *
   They go astray as soon as
   they are / born, speaking lies.

Their poison is like the poison / of a serpent; *
   They are like the deaf
   cobra / that stops its ear,

Which will not heed the / voice of charmers, *
   Charming ev- / er so skillfully.

Break their teeth / in their mouth, O God! *
   Break out the fangs of the
   young / lions, O LORD!

Let them flow away as waters
which / run continually; *
   When he bends his bow, let his
   arrows be as if / cut in pieces.

Let them be like a snail which
melts / away as it goes, *
   Like a stillborn child of a woman,
   that they / may not see the sun.

Before your pots can feel the burning thorns,
He shall take them away as / with a whirlwind, *
   As in His living / and burning wrath.

The righteous shall rejoice
when he / sees the vengeance; *
   He shall wash his feet in
   the blood / of the wicked,

So that men will say, "Surely there
is a reward / for the righteous; *
   Surely He is God who judg- / es in the earth."

Glory be to the / Father, and to the Son, *
   And to the / Holy Spirit

As it was in / the beginning *
   Is now and will be for- / ever. Amen.

PSALM 59

Antiphon - *Deus meus*

My God, Your mer - cy shall come to meet me.

Psalm - *Eripe me de inimicis*

DELIVer me from my / enemies, O my God; *
Defend me from those
who rise up / against me.

Deliver me from the workers / of iniquity, *
And save me from blood- / thirsty men.

For look, they lie in / wait for my life; *
The mighty gather / against me,

Not for my transgression
nor for / my sin, O LORD. *
They run and prepare themselves
through no / fault of mine.

Awake to / help me, and behold! *
You therefore, O LORD God
of hosts, the God / of Israel,

Awake to punish / all the nations; *
Do not be merciful to
any wicked / transgressors.

At / evening they return, *
They growl like a dog, and
go all around / the city.

Indeed, they belch with their
mouth; / swords are in their lips; *
For they / say, "Who hears?"

But You, O / LORD, shall laugh at them; *
You shall have all the nations in / derision.

I will wait for You, / O You his Strength; *
For God is / my defense;

My God of mercy shall / come to meet me;*
God shall let me see my
desire on my / enemies.

Do not slay them, lest my / people forget; *
Scatter them by Your power, and
bring them down, O / Lord our shield.

For the sin of their mouth
and the / words of their lips, *
Let them even be taken in their pride, and
for the cursing and lying / which they speak.

Consume them in wrath, consume
them, that / they may not be; *
And let them know that God rules
in Jacob to the ends / of the earth.

And at evening they
return, / they growl like a dog, *
And go all around / the city.

They wander / up and down for food, *
And howl if they are not / satisfied.

But I will / sing of Your power; *
Yes, I will sing aloud of
Your mercy in / the morning;

For You have / been my defense *
And refuge in the day of / my trouble.

To You, O my Strength, I / will sing praises; *
For God is my defense, my God / of mercy.

Glory be to the / Father, and to the Son, *
And to the Ho - / ly Spirit

As it was in / the beginning *
Is now and will be forev- / er. Amen.

PSALM 60

Antiphon - *Da nobis auxilium*

Give us help from trou-ble, O Lord,   for the help of man is use-less.

Psalm - *Deus, repulisti nos*

O GOD, You have cast us off;
You have broken / us down; *
   You have been displeased;
   Oh, restore / us again!

You have made the earth
tremble; You have / broken it; *
   Heal its breaches, for it / is shaking.

You have shown Your people / hard things; *
   You have made us drink
   the wine of / confusion.

You have given a banner to those who / fear You, *
   That it may be displayed
   because / of the truth.

That Your beloved may be de- / livered,*
   Save with Your right hand, / and hear me.

God has spoken in His / holiness: *
   "I will rejoice; I will divide Shechem and
   measure out the Valley / of Succoth.

Gilead is Mine, and Manasseh / is Mine; *
   Ephraim also is the helmet for
   My head; Judah is My / lawgiver.

Moab is My washpot; Over
Edom I will cast / My shoe; *
   I shout in triumph over / Philistia."

Who will bring me to the strong / city?*
   Who will lead me / to Edom?

Is it not You, O God, who cast / us off?*
   And You, O God, who did
   not go out with / our armies?

Give us help from / trouble, *
   For the help of man / is useless.

Through God we will do / valiantly, *
   For it is He who shall
   tread down / our enemies.

Glory be to the Father, and / to the Son, *
   And to the Ho- / ly Spirit

As it was in the be- / ginning *
   Is now and will be forev- / er. Amen.

PSALM 61

Antiphon - *Rex nobis sedebit*

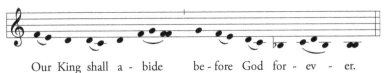

Our King shall a - bide   be - fore God for - ev - er.

Psalm - *Exaudi, Deus deprecationem meam*

HEAR MY cry, / O God; *
   At- / tend to my prayer.

From the end of the earth I will cry / to You, *
   When my heart / is overwhelmed;

Lead me to the rock that is higher / than I. *
   For You have been a shelter for me,
   a strong tower / from the enemy.

I will abide in Your tabernacle for- / ever; *
  I will trust in the shel- / ter of Your wings.

For You, O God, have heard / my vows; *
  You have given me the heritage
  of / those who fear Your name.

You will prolong the / king's life, *
  His years as many / generations.

He shall abide before God for- / ever. *
  Oh, prepare mercy and truth,
  which / may preserve him!

So I will sing praise to Your name for- / ever, *
  That I may dail- / y perform my vows.

Glory be to the Father, and / to the Son, *
  And to the / Holy Spirit

As it was in the be- / ginning *
  Is now and will be for -/ ever. Amen.

PSALM 62

Tone 4a

Antiphon - *In Deo salutare meum*

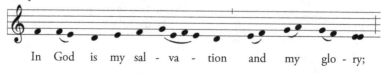

In God is my sal - va - tion and my glo - ry;

and my ref - uge, is in God.

Psalm - *Nonne Deo?*

TRULY my soul si- / lently waits for God; *
  From Him / comes my salvation.

He only is my rock and / my salvation; *
  He is my defense; I
  shall / not be greatly moved.

How long will / you attack a man? *
  You shall be slain, all of you,
  like a leaning wall / and a tott'ring fence.

They only consult to cast him
down from his / high position; *
  - / They delight in lies;

They / bless with their mouth, *
  But / they curse inwardly.

My soul, wait silently / for God alone,*
  For my expec- / tation is from Him.

He only is my rock and / my salvation; *
  He is my defense; / I shall not be moved.

In God is my salvation / and my glory; *
  The rock of my strength,
  and my / refuge, is in God.

Trust in Him at all times, you people;
pour out your / heart before Him;*
  God / is a refuge for us.

Surely men of low degree / are a vapor, *
  Men of high / degree are a lie;

If they / are weighed on the scales, *
  They are altogether / lighter than vapor.

Do not trust in oppression,
nor vainly / hope in robbery; *
  If riches increase, do
  not / set your heart on them.

God has spoken once, twice / I have heard this: *
  That / power belongs to God.

Also to You, O Lord, / belongs mercy; *
  For You render to each
  one / according to his work.

Glory be to the Father, / and to the Son, *
  And to / the Holy Spirit

As it was in / the beginning *
  Is now and will be / forever. Amen.

PSALM 63

Antiphon - *Benedicam te in vita mea*

I will bless You while I live, O Lord;
I will lift up my hands in Your name.

Psalm - *Deus, Deus meus*

O GOD, / You are my God; *
  Early / will I seek You;

My soul thirsts for You; / My flesh longs for You *
  In a dry and thirsty land
  where there / is no water.

So I have looked for You in the / sanctuary, *
  To see Your power / and Your glory.

Because Your lovingkindness is / better than life, *
  My / lips shall praise You.

Thus I will / bless You while I live; *
  I will lift up my / hands in Your name.

My soul shall be satisfied as
with / marrow and fatness, *
  And my mouth shall
  praise You / with joyful lips.

When I remember / You on my bed, *
  I meditate on You / in the night watches.

Because / You have been my help, *
  Therefore in the shadow of
  Your wings / I will rejoice.

My soul follows / close behind You; *
  Your right / hand upholds me.

But those who seek my / life, to destroy it, *
  Shall go into the lower / parts of the earth.

They shall / fall by the sword; *
  They shall be a / portion for jackals.

But the king shall rejoice in God;
everyone who swears by / Him shall glory; *
  But the mouth of those who
  speak / lies shall be stopped.

Glory be to the / Father, and to the Son, *
  And to the / Holy Spirit

As it was in / the beginning *
  Is now and will be for- / ever. Amen.

PSALM 64

Antiphon - *Laetabitur justus*

The right-eous shall be glad in the Lord, and shall trust in Him.

Psalm - *Exaudi, Deus*

HEAR MY voice, O God, in / my meditation; *
Preserve my life from fear / of the enemy.

Hide me from the secret plots / of the wicked, *
From the rebellion of the
workers / of iniquity,

Who sharpen / their tongue like a sword, *
And bend their bows to shoot
their / arrows - bitter words,

That they may shoot in secret / at the blameless; *
Suddenly they shoot at him / and do not fear.

They encourage themselves in an / evil matter; *
They talk of laying snares secretly;
they say, / "Who will see them?"

They devise iniquities: "We have
per- / fected a shrewd scheme." *
Both the inward thought and
the / heart of man are deep.

But God shall shoot at them / with an arrow; *
Suddenly they / shall be wounded.

So He will make them
stumble / over their own tongue; *
All who see them / shall flee away.

All men shall fear, And shall
de- / clare the work of God; *
For they shall wisely con- / sider His doing.

The righteous shall be glad
in the LORD, / and trust in Him. *
And all the upright in / heart shall glory.

Glory be to the / Father, and to the Son, *
And to the / Holy Spirit

As it was in / the beginning *
Is now and will be for- / ever. Amen.

PSALM 65

Antiphon - *Te decet hymnus*

Praise is a - wait - ing You, O God, in Zi - on.

Psalm - *Te decet hymnus*

PRAISE IS awaiting You, O God, in / Zion; *
And to You the / vow shall be performed.

O You who / hear prayer, *
To You / all flesh will come.

Iniquities prevail a- / gainst me; *
  As for our transgressions, You
  will provide a- / tonement for them.

Blessèd is the man You choose,
and cause to ap- / proach You, *
  That he may / dwell in Your courts.

We shall be satisfied with the
goodness of / Your house, *
  Of Your / holy temple.

By awesome deeds in
righteousness You will / answer us, *
  O God of / our salvation,

You who are the confidence of
all the ends of / the earth, *
  And / of the far off seas;

Who established the
mountains by / His strength, *
  Being / clothed with power;

You who still the noise of / the seas, *
  The noise of their waves, and
  the tumult / of the peoples.

They also who dwell in the farthest
parts are afraid of / Your signs;*
  You make the outgoings of the
  morning and / evening rejoice.

You visit the earth and / water it, *
  You greatly enrich it; the
  river of God is / full of water;

You provide / their grain, *
  For so You / have prepared it.

You water its ridges a- / bundantly, *
  You set- / tle its furrows;

You make it soft with / showers, *
  - / You bless its growth.

You crown the year with Your / goodness, *
  And Your paths drip / with abundance.

They drop on the pastures of the / wilderness, *
  And the little hills re- / joice on ev'ry side.

The pastures are clothed with flocks;
the valleys also are covered / with grain; *
  They shout for / joy, they also sing.

Glory be to the Father, and / to the Son, *
  And to the / Holy Spirit

As it was in the be- / ginning *
  Is now and will be for- / ever. Amen.

PSALM 66

Antiphon - *Videte opera Domini*

Come and see the works of God, and make the voice of His praise to be heard.

Psalm - *Jubilate Deo*

MAKE A joyful shout to God, / all the earth! *
Sing out the honor of His name;
make / His praise glorious.

Say to God, "How awesome are / Your works! *
Through the greatness of Your power Your
enemies shall submit / themselves to You.

All the earth shall worship
You and sing praises / to You; *
They shall sing / praises to Your name."

Come and see the works / of God; *
He is awesome in His doing
toward / the sons of men.

He turned the sea into dry land;
They went through the river / on foot. *
Therefore we / will rejoice in Him.

He rules by His power forever;
His eyes observe the / nations; *
Do not let the rebellious / exalt themselves.

Oh, bless our God, you / peoples! *
And make the voice of
His / praise to be heard,

Who keeps our soul among the / living,*
And does not allow our / feet to be moved.

For You, O God, have / tested us; *
You have refined us as sil- / ver is refined.

You brought us into / the net; *
You laid afflic- / tion on our backs.

You have caused men to ride over our heads;
we went through fire and through / water; *
But You brought us out to / rich fulfillment.

I will go into Your house with burnt / offerings; *
I will / pay You my vows,

Which my lips have / uttered *
And my mouth has spoken
when I / was in trouble.

I will offer You burnt sacrifices of fat
animals, with the sweet aroma / of rams;*
I will of- / fer bulls with goats.

Come and hear, all you who / fear God,*
And I will declare what
He has / done for my soul.

I cried to Him with / my mouth, *
And He was / extolled with my tongue.

If I regard iniquity in / my heart, *
The / Lord will not hear.

But certainly God has / heard me; *
He has attended to the / voice of my prayer.

Blessèd be God, Who has not
turned away / my prayer, *
Nor His / mercy from me!

Glory be to the Father, and / to the Son, *
And to the / Holy Spirit

As it was in the be- / ginning *
Is now and will be for- / ever. Amen.

PSALM 67

Antiphon - *Illumina Domine*

Cause Your face, O Lord, to shine up - on us.

Psalm - *Deus misereatur*

GOD BE merciful to / us and bless us, *
And cause His face to / shine upon us.

That Your way / may be known on earth, *
Your salvation a- / mong all nations.

Let the peoples / praise You, O God; *
Let all the / peoples praise You.

Oh, let the nations be / glad and sing for joy! *
For You shall judge the people righteously,
and govern the / nations on earth.

Let the peoples / praise You, O God; *
Let all the / peoples praise You.

Then the earth shall / yield her increase; *
God, our own / God, shall bless us.

- / God shall bless us, *
And all the ends of the / earth shall fear Him.

Glory be to the / Father, and to the Son, *
And to the / Holy Spirit

As it was in / the beginning *
Is now and will be for- / ever. Amen.

PSALM 68a (1-18) *Tone 7a*

Antiphon - *Exsurgat Deus*

Let God a - rise, let His en - e - mies be scat - tered.

Psalm - *Exsurgat Deus*

LET GOD arise, let His ene- / mies be scattered; *
Let those also who hate Him / flee before Him.

As smoke is driven away, / so drive them away; *
As wax melts before the fire, so let the
wicked perish at the / presence of God.

But let the righteous be glad;
let them re- / joice before God; *
Yes, let them rejoice / exceedingly.

Sing to God, sing / praises to His name; *
Extol Him who / rides on the clouds,

By / His name "the LORD," *
And re- / joice before Him.

A father of the fatherless, a
defen- / der of widows, *
Is God in His holy / habitation.

God sets the solitary in families; He brings out
those who are bound in- / to prosperity; *
But the rebellious dwell / in a dry land.

O God, when You went
out be- / fore Your people, *
When You marched / through the wilderness,

The earth shook; the heavens also
dropped rain at the / presence of God; *
Sinai itself was moved at the
presence of God, the / God of Israel.

You, O God, sent a plentiful rain,
whereby You confirmed / Your inheritance, *
When / it was weary.

Your congre- / gation dwelt in it; *
You, O God, provided from
Your / goodness for the poor.

101

The / Lord gave the word; *
   Great was the company of
   those / who proclaimed it:

"Kings of / armies flee, they flee, *
   And she who remains at
   home / divides the spoil.

Though you lie down among the
sheepfolds, You will be like the wings
of a dove cov- / ered with silver, *
   And her feathers / with yellow gold."

When the Almighty / scattered kings in it, *
   It was white as / snow in Zalmon.

A mountain of God is the
moun- / tain of Bashan; *
   A mountain of many peaks
   is the moun- / tain of Bashan.

Why do you fume with envy, you
mountains of many peaks? This is the
mountain which God de- / sires to dwell in; *
   Yes, the LORD will dwell in / it forever.

The chariots of God are twenty thousand,
even thou- / sands of thousands; *
   The Lord is among them as
   in Sinai, / in the Holy Place.

You have ascended on high, You
have led captivity captive; You have
received / gifts among men, *
   Even from the rebellious, that
   the LORD / God might dwell there.

Glory be to the / Father, and to the Son, *
   And to the / Holy Spirit

As it was in / the beginning *
   Is now and will be for- / ever. Amen.

PSALM 68b (19-35)

Tone 8G

Antiphon - *In ecclesiis benedicite*

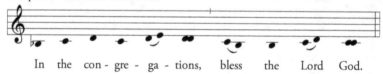

In the con - gre - ga - tions, bless the Lord God.

Psalm - *Benedíctus Dominus die quotídie*

BLESSÈD be the Lord, who
daily loads us with / benefits, *
   The God of / our salvation!

Our God is the God of sal- / vation; *
   And to God the Lord
   belong / escapes from death.

But God will wound the head of His / enemies, *
   The hairy scalp of the one who
   still goes on / in his trespasses.

The Lord said, "I will bring back from / Bashan, *
   I will bring them back
   from the / depths of the sea,

That your foot may crush them / in blood, *
   And the tongues of your dogs may
   have their portion / from your enemies."

They have seen Your procession, / O God, *
   The procession of my God,
   my King, into the / sanctuary.

The singers went before, the players
on instruments followed / after; *
   Among them were the
   maidens / playing timbrels.

Bless God in the congre- / gations, *
   The Lord, from the fountain / of Israel.

There is little Benjamin, their leader,
the princes of Judah and their / company, *
   The princes of Zebulun
   and the princes / of Naphtali.

Your God has commanded / your strength; *
   Strengthen, O God,
   what / You have done for us.

Because of Your temple at Je- / rusalem,*
   Kings will bring / presents to You.

Rebuke the beasts of / the reeds, *
   The herd of bulls with
   the calves / of the peoples,

Till everyone submits himself
with pieces of / silver. *
   Scatter the peoples / who delight in war.

Envoys will come out of / Egypt; *
   Ethiopia will quickly stretch
   out / her hands to God.

Sing to God, you kingdoms of / the earth; *
   Oh, sing / praises to the Lord,

To Him who rides on the heaven
of heavens, which were / of old! *
   Indeed, He sends out
   His voice, / a mighty voice. *

Ascribe strength / to God;
   His excellence is over Israel,
   and His / strength is in the clouds.

O God, You are more awesome than
Your holy places. The God of Israel is He
who gives strength and power to His / people. *
   - / Blessèd be God!

Glory be to the Father, and / to the Son, *
   And to the / Holy Spirit

As it was in the be- / ginning *
   Is now and will be for- / ever. Amen.

PSALM 69a (1-15)

Antiphon - *Salvum me fac Deus*

Save me, O God, for the wa - ters have come up to my neck.

Psalm - *Salvum me fac Deus*

SAVE ME, / O God! *
   For the waters have / come up to my neck.

I sink in deep mire, where there is no / standing; *
   I have come into deep waters,
   where the floods / overflow me.

I am weary with my crying; my throat / is dry; *
   My eyes fail while I / wait for my God.

Those who hate me without a cause
are more than the hairs of / my head; *
   They are mighty who would destroy
   me, being my en- / emies wrongfully;

Though I have stolen nothing,
I still must re- / store it.
   O God, You know my foolishness;
   and my sins are not / hidden from You.

Let not those who wait for You, O Lord
God of hosts, be ashamed because / of me; *
   Let not those who seek You be confounded
   because of me, O / God of Israel.

Because for Your sake I have borne / reproach; *
   Shame has / covered my face.

I have become a stranger to my / brothers,*
   And an alien to my / mother's children;

Because zeal for Your house has eaten / me up, *
   And the reproaches of those who
   reproach You have / fallen on me.

When I wept and chastened my soul with
fasting, that became my / reproach. *
   I also made sackcloth my garment;
   I became a / byword to them.

Those who sit in the gate speak a- / gainst me, *
   And I am the song / of the drunkards.

But as for me, my prayer is to You,
O Lord, in the accepta- / ble time; *
   O God, in the multitude of Your mercy,
   hear me in the truth of / Your salvation.

Deliver me out of the mire, and let me / not sink;
   Let me be delivered from those who
   hate me, and out of / the deep waters.

Let not the floodwater overflow me,
nor let the deep swallow / me up; *
   And let not the pit / shut its mouth on me.

Glory be to the Father, and / to the Son, *
   And to the / Holy Spirit

As it was in the be- / ginning *
   Is now and will be for- / ever. Amen.

PSALM 69b (16-36)

Antiphon - *Propter inimicos meos*

De - liv - er me be - cause of my en - e - mies, O Lord.

Psalm - *Exaudi me, Domine, quoniam benigna*

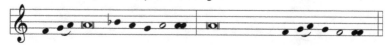

HEAR ME, O Lord, for Your
loving- / kindness is good; *
   Turn to me according to the
   multitude of Your / tender mercies.

And do not hide Your face / from Your servant, *
   For I am in trouble; / hear me speedily.

Draw near to my soul, / and redeem it;*
   Deliver me because / of my enemies.

You know my reproach,
my shame, and / my dishonor; *
   My adversaries are / all before You.

Reproach has / broken my heart, *
   And I am / full of heaviness;

I looked for someone to take
pity, / but there was none; *
   And for comforters, / but I found none.

They also gave me / gall for my food, *
   And for my thirst they
   gave me / vinegar to drink.

Let their table become a / snare before them, *
   And their well- / being a trap.

Let their eyes be darkened,
so / that they do not see; *
   And make their loins / shake continually.

Pour out Your indigna- / tion upon them, *
   And let Your wrathful
   an- / ger take hold of them.

Let their dwelling place / be desolate; *
   Let no one / live in their tents.

For they persecute the / ones You have struck, *
   And talk of the grief of
   those / You have wounded.

Add iniquity to / their iniquity, *
  And let them not come
  in- / to Your righteousness.

Let them be blotted out
of the book / of the living, *
  And not be written / with the righteous.

But I am / poor and sorrowful; *
  Let Your salvation, O
  God, / set me up on high.

I will praise the name of / God with a song, *
  And will magnify Him / with thanksgiving.

This also shall please the Lord / better than an ox *
  Or bull, / which has horns and hooves.

The humble shall see / this and be glad; *
  And you who seek God, / your hearts shall live.

For the / Lord hears the poor, *
  And does not de- / spise His prisoners.

Let heaven / and earth praise Him, *
  The seas and everything / that moves in them.

For God will save Zion and
build the ci- / ties of Judah, *
  That they may dwell there / and possess it.

Also, the descendants of
His servants / shall inherit it, *
  And those who love His
  name / shall dwell in it.

Glory be to the Father, / and to the Son, *
  And to the / Holy Spirit

As it was in / the beginning *
  Is now and will be / forever. Amen.

PSALM 70

Antiphon - *Adjutor meus*

The Lord is my help and my de - liv - er - er.

Psalm - *Deus, in adjutorium*

MAKE HASTE, O God, to de- / liver me! *
  Make haste to / help me, O Lord!

Let them be ashamed and
confounded who seek / my life; *
  Let them be turned back and
  confused who / desire my hurt.

Let them be turned back because of / their shame, *
  Who say, / "Aha, aha!"

Let all those who seek You
rejoice and be / glad in You; *
  And let those who love Your salvation
  say continually, "Let / God be magnified!"

But I am poor and / needy; *
  Make haste to / help me, O God!

You are my help and my de- / liverer;*
  O Lord, / do not delay.

Glory be to the Father, and / to the Son, *
  And to the / Holy Spirit

As it was in the be- / ginning *
  Is now and will be for- / ever. Amen.

Antiphon - *Justitiam tuam Deus*

Your right - eous - ness, O God, is ve - ry high.

Psalm - *In te, Domine, speravi*

IN YOU, O / LORD, I put my trust; *
    Let me never / be put to shame.

Deliver me in Your righteousness,
and / cause me to escape; *
    Incline Your ear to / me, and save me.

Be my strong refuge, to which
I may resort continually;
You have given the command- / ment to save me, *
    For You are my rock / and my fortress.

Deliver me, O my God, out
of the hand / of the wicked, *
    Out of the hand of the
    unright- / eous and cruel man.

For You are my / hope, O Lord God; *
    You are my / trust from my youth.

By You I have been upheld from birth; You are
He who took me out / of my mother's womb. *
    My praise shall be contin- / ually of You.

I have become as a / wonder to many, *
    But You are / my strong refuge.

Let my mouth / be filled with Your praise *
    And with Your / glory all the day.

Do not cast me off in the / time of old age; *
    Do not forsake me / when my strength fails.

For my enemies / speak against me; *
    And those who lie in wait for
    my life take coun- / sel together,

Saying, "God has forsaken
him; pur- / sue and take him, *
    For there is none / to deliver him."

O God, do / not be far from me; *
    O my God, make / haste to help me!

Let them be confounded and consumed
who are adver- / saries of my life; *
    Let them be covered with reproach
    and dishon- / or who seek my hurt.

But I will / hope continually, *
    And will praise You / yet more and more.

My mouth shall tell of Your righteousness
and Your sal- / vation all the day, *
    For I do not / know their limits.

I will go in the strength / of the Lord God; *
    I will make mention of Your
    righteousness, / of Yours only.

O God, You have / taught me from my youth; *
    And to this day I de- / clare
    Your wondrous works.

Now also when I am old / and grayheaded, *
    O God, do / not forsake me,

Until I declare Your strength
to this / generation, *
    Your power to everyone / who is to come.

Also Your righteousness, O / God, is very high, *
    You who have done great things;
    O God, / who is like You?

You, who have shown me
great and / severe troubles, *
    Shall revive me again, and bring me
    up again from the / depths of the earth.

You shall in- / crease my greatness, *
    And comfort / me on ev'ry side.

Also with the lute I will praise you
for Your faithful- / ness, O my God! *
  To You I will sing with the harp,
  O Holy / One of Israel.

My lips shall greatly rejoice / when I sing to You, *
  And my soul, / which You have redeemed.

My tongue also shall talk of Your
righteousness / all the day long; *
  For they are confounded, for they are
  brought to / shame who seek my hurt.

Glory be to the / Father, and to the Son, *
  And to the / Holy Spirit

As it was in / the beginning *
  Is now and will be for- / ever. Amen.

PSALM 72 Tone 1g

Antiphon - *Benedicentur in ipso*

Men shall be blessed in Him; all na-tions shall call Him bless-èd.

Psalm - *Deus, judicium*

GIVE THE king Your / judgments, O God, *
  And Your righteousness / to the king's Son.

He will judge Your / people with righteousness, *
  And Your / poor with justice.

The mountains will bring peace / to the people, *
  And the little / hills, by righteousness.

He will bring justice to the poor of the people;
He will save the children / of the needy, *
  And will break in pieces / the oppressor.

They shall fear You as long
as the / sun and moon endure, *
  Throughout all / generations.

He shall come down like rain
upon the grass / before mowing, *
  Like showers that / water the earth.

In His days the / righteous shall flourish, *
  And abundance of peace,
  until the / moon is no more.

He shall have dominion also / from sea to sea, *
  And from the River to the / ends of the earth.

Those who dwell in the
wilderness will / bow before Him, *
  And His ene- / mies will lick the dust.

The kings of Tarshish and of
the isles / will bring presents; *
  The kings of Sheba and Seba / will offer gifts.

Yes, all kings shall fall / down before Him; *
  All na- / tions shall serve Him.

For He will deliver the / needy when he cries, *
  The poor also, and him who / has no helper.

He will spare the / poor and needy, *
  And will save the souls / of the needy.

He will redeem their life from
oppress- / ion and violence; *
  And precious shall be
  their / blood in His sight.

And He shall live; and the gold
of Sheba will be / given to Him; *
  Prayer also will be made for Him
  continually, and daily / He shall be praised.

There will be an abundance of grain
in the earth, on the top of the mountains;
its fruit shall / wave like Lebanon; *
  And those of the city shall
  flourish like / grass of the earth.

His name shall en- / dure forever; *
His name shall continue as / long as the sun.

And men / shall be blessed in Him; *
All nations shall / call Him blessèd.

Blessèd be the LORD God, the / God of Israel, *
Who only / does wondrous things!

And blessèd be His glorious / name forever! *
And let the whole earth be filled
with His glory. / Amen and Amen.

Glory be to the / Father, and to the Son, *
And to the / Holy Spirit

As it was in / the beginning *
Is now and will be for- / ever. Amen.

PSALM 73

Antiphon - *Quam bonus Israel*

Tru-ly God is good to Is - ra - el, to such as are pure in heart.

Psalm - *Quam bonus Israel*

TRULY God is good to / Israel, *
To such / as are pure in heart.

But as for me, my feet had almost / stumbled; *
My steps / had nearly slipped.

For I was envious of the / boastful, *
When I saw the prosperity / of the wicked.

For there are no pangs in / their death, *
- / But their strength is firm.

They are not in trouble as / other men, *
Nor are they / plagued like other men.

Therefore pride serves as their / necklace; *
Violence covers them / like a garment.

Their eyes bulge with a- / bundance; *
They have more / than heart could wish.

They scoff and speak wickedly
concerning op- / pression; *
- / They speak loftily.

They set their mouth against the / heavens, *
And their / tongue walks through the earth.

Therefore his people re- / turn here, *
And waters of a full cup / are drained by them.

And they say, "How does / God know?*
And is there knowledge / in the Most High?"

Behold, these are the un- / godly, *
Who are always at ease;
they in- / crease in riches.

Surely I have cleansed my heart / in vain, *
And washed my / hands in innocence.

For all day long I have / been plagued,*
And chastened / ev'ry morning.

If I had said, "I will / speak thus," *
Behold, I would have been untrue
to the generation / of Your children.

When I thought how to under- / stand this, *
It was too / painful for me

Until I went into the sanctuary / of God; *
Then I / understood their end.

Surely You set them in slippery / places; *
You cast them down / to destruction.

Oh, how they are brought to
desolation, as in a / moment! *
They are utterly con- / sumed with terrors.

As a dream when one / awakes, *
   So, Lord, when You awake,
   You shall de- / spise their image.

Thus my heart / was grieved, *
   And I was / vexed in my mind.

I was so foolish and / ignorant; *
   I was like a / beast before You.

Nevertheless I am continually / with You; *
   You hold me / by my right hand.

You will guide me with Your / counsel, *
   And afterward receive / me to glory.

Whom have I in heaven / but You? *
   And there is none upon earth
   that I de- / sire besides You.

My flesh and my / heart fail; *
   But God is the strength of my
   heart and my por- / tion forever.

For indeed, those who are
far from You shall / perish; *
   You have destroyed all those
   who desert / You for harlotry.

But it is good for me to draw near to God;
I have put my trust in the / Lord God, *
   That I may de-/ clare all Your works.

Glory be to the Father, and / to the Son, *
   And to the / Holy Spirit

As it was in the be- / ginning *
   Is now and will be for- / ever. Amen.

PSALM 74

Antiphon - *Memor esto*

Re - mem - ber Your con - gre - ga - tion, O

Lord, which You have pur - chased of old.

Psalm - *Ut quid, Deus?*

O GOD, why have You cast us off for- / ever? *
   Why does Your anger smoke
   against the sheep / of Your pasture?

Remember Your congregation, which You
have purchased of old, the tribe of Your
inheritance, which You have / redeemed *
   This Mount Zion / where You have dwelt.

Lift up Your feet to the perpetual deso- / lations. *
   The enemy has damaged
   everything in the / sanctuary.

Your enemies roar in the midst
of Your / meeting place; *
   They set up their / banners for signs.

They seem like men who lift
up axes among the / thick trees. *
   And now they break down its carved work,
   all at once, with ax- / es and hammers.

They have set fire to Your sanctu- / ary; *
   They have defiled the dwelling place
   of Your / name to the ground.

They said in their hearts, "Let
us destroy them alto- / gether." *
   They have burned up all the
   meeting places of / God in the land.

We do not see our signs; There
is no longer any / prophet; *
   Nor is there any among
   us / who knows how long.

O God, how long will the adversary / reproach? *
   Will the enemy blaspheme
   Your / name forever?

Why do You withdraw Your
hand, even Your / right hand? *
   Take it out of Your bosom / and destroy them.

For God is my King from / of old, *
   Working salvation in the / midst of the earth.

You divided the sea by / Your strength;*
   You broke the heads of the
   sea serpents / in the waters.

You broke the heads of Leviathan in / pieces, *
   And gave him as food to the
   people inhabiting / the wilderness.

You broke open the fountain / and the flood; *
   You dried up / mighty rivers.

The day is Yours, the night also / is Yours; *
   You have prepared the / stars and the sun.

You have set all the borders / of the earth; *
   You have made sum- / mer and winter.

Remember this, that the enemy
has reproached, / O Lord, *
   And that a foolish people
   has / blasphemed Your name.

Oh, do not deliver the life of Your
turtledove to the / wild beast! *
   Do not forget the life of Your / poor forever.

Have respect to the / covenant; *
   For the dark places of the earth
   are full of the / haunts of cruelty.

Oh, do not let the oppressed return / ashamed! *
   Let the poor and / needy praise Your name.

Arise, O God, plead Your / own cause; *
   Remember how the foolish
   man reproach- / es You daily.

Do not forget the voice of Your / enemies; *
   The tumult of those who rise up
   against You increases / continually.

Glory be to the Father, and / to the Son, *
   And to the / Holy Spirit

As it was in the be- / ginning *
   Is now and will be for- / ever. Amen.

PSALM 75

Antiphon - *Invocabimus nomen tuum*

We will call up - on Your name, O Lord;

we will de - clare your won - drous works.

Psalm - *Confitebimur tibi*

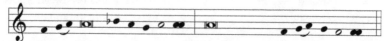

WE GIVE thanks to
You, / O God, we give thanks! *
   For Your wondrous works
   declare that / Your name is near.

When I / choose the proper time, *
   I will / judge uprightly.

The earth and all its inhabi- / tants are dissolved; *
   I set up its / pillars firmly.

I said to the boastful, do / not deal boastfully, *
   And to the wicked, do not / lift up the horn.

Do not lift / up your horn on high; *
   Do not speak / with a stiff neck.

For exaltation comes / neither from the east *
   Nor from the west / nor from the south.

But / God is the Judge: *
   He puts down one, and ex- / alts another.

For in the hand of the LORD / there is a cup, *
   And the wine is red; it is fully
   mixed, and / He pours it out;

Surely its dregs shall all the wicked
of the earth / drain and drink down. *
   But I will declare forever, I will
   sing praises to the / God of Jacob.

All the horns of the wicked I will / also cut off, *
   But the horns of the
   righteous shall / be exalted.

Glory be to the Father, / and to the Son, *
   And to the / Holy Spirit

As it was in / the beginning *
   Is now and will be / forever. Amen.

PSALM 76

Antiphon - *Notus in Judaea*

In Ju- dah God is known; His name is great in Is - ra - el.

Psalm - *Notus in Judaea*

IN JUdah God / is known; *
   His name is / great in Israel.

In Salem also is His taber- / nacle, *
   And His dwelling / place in Zion.

There He broke the arrows of / the bow, *
   The shield and / sword of battle.

You are more glorious and / excellent *
   Than the / mountains of prey.

The stouthearted were plundered;
they have sunk into / their sleep; *
   And none of the mighty men have
   found the / use of their hands.

At Your rebuke, O God of / Jacob, *
   Both the chariot and horse
   were cast in- / to a dead sleep.

You, Yourself, are to / be feared; *
   And who may stand in Your
   presence when once / You are angry?

You caused judgment to be heard from / heaven; *
   The earth / feared and was still,

When God arose to / judgment, *
   To deliver all the op- / pressed of the earth.

Surely the wrath of man shall / praise You; *
   With the remainder of
   wrath / You shall gird Yourself.

Make vows to the LORD
your God, and / pay them; *
    Let all who are around Him bring presents
    to Him / who ought to be feared.

He shall cut off the spirit of / princes;*
    He is awesome to the / kings of the earth.

Glory be to the Father, and / to the Son, *
    And to the / Holy Spirit

As it was in the be- / ginning *
    Is now and will be for- / ever. Amen.

PSALM 77

Tone 7c

Antiphon - *Voce mea ad Dominum*

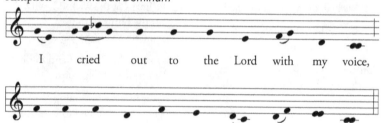

I cried out to the Lord with my voice,

and God will not for - get to be gra - cious.

Psalm - *Voce mea ad Dominum*

I CRIED out to God with my
voice, and / He gave ear to me. *
    In the day of my trouble / I sought the Lord;

My hand was stretched out
in the / night without ceasing; *
    My soul refused / to be comforted.

I remembered / God, and was troubled; *
    I complained, and my
    spirit / was overwhelmed.

You hold my / eyelids open; *
    I am so troubled / that I cannot speak.

I have considered / the days of old, *
    The years / of ancient times.

I call to remembrance my / song in the night; *
    I meditate within my heart,
    and my spirit makes / diligent search.

Will the Lord cast / off forever? *
    And will He be favor- / able no more?

Has His mercy / ceased forever? *
    Has His promise failed / forevermore?

Has God forgotten / to be gracious? *
    Has He in anger shut up
    His / tender mercies?

And I said, / "This is my anguish; *
    But I will remember the years of
    the right hand / of the Most High."

I will remember the / works of the LORD; *
    Surely I will remember Your / wonders of old.

I will also medi- / tate on all Your work,*
    And / talk of Your deeds.

Your way, O God, is in the / sanctuary; *
    Who is so great a / God as our God?

You are the God / who does wonders;*
    You have declared Your
    strength a- / mong the peoples.

You have with Your arm
re- / deemed Your people, *
    The sons of / Jacob and Joseph.

The waters saw You, O God; the
waters saw You, / they were afraid; *
   The depths / also trembled.

The clouds poured out water;
the / skies sent out a sound; *
   Your arrows / also flashed about.

The voice of Your thunder was in the
whirlwind; the lightnings / lit up the world; *
   The earth / trembled and shook.

Your way was in the sea,
Your path in / the great waters, *
   And Your / footsteps were not known.

You led Your / people like a flock *
   By the hand of / Moses and Aaron.

Glory be to the / Father, and to the Son, *
   And to the / Holy Spirit

As it was in / the beginning *
   Is now and will be for- / ever. Amen.

PSALM 78a (1-16) *Tone 5*

Antiphon - *Coram patribus*

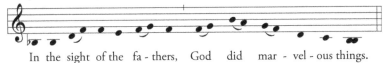

In the sight of the fa-thers, God did mar-vel-ous things.

Psalm - *Attendite, popule*

GIVE EAR, O my people, to / my law; *
   Incline your ears to the / words of my mouth.

I will open my mouth in a / parable; *
   I will utter dark / sayings of old,

Which we have / heard and known, *
   And our fa- / thers have told us.

We will not hide them from their / children, *
   Telling to the gener- / ation to come

The praises of the LORD, and / His strength *
   And His wonderful works / that He has done.

For He established a testimony in / Jacob, *
   And appointed a law / in Israel,

Which He commanded our / fathers, *
   That they should make them
   known / to their children;

That the generation to come might know
them, the children who / would be born, *
   That they may arise and declare
   them / to their children,

That they may set their hope in God,
and not forget the / works of God, *
   But keep / His commandments;

And may not be like their / fathers, *
   A stubborn and rebellious / generation,

A generation that did not set its / heart aright, *
   And whose spirit was / not faithful to God.

The children of Ephraim, being
armed and carry- / ing bows, *
   Turned back in the / day of battle.

They did not keep the covenant / of God; *
   They refused to / walk in His law,

And forgot / His works *
   And His wonders that / He had shown them.

Marvelous things He did in
the sight of their / fathers, *
   In the land of Egypt, in the / field of Zoan.

He divided the sea and
caused them to / pass through; *
   And He made the waters / stand up like a heap.

In the daytime also He led them / with the cloud, *
 And all the night / with a light of fire.

He split the rocks in the / wilderness, *
 And gave them drink in
 abun- / dance like the depths.

He also brought streams out / of the rock, *
 And caused waters to run / down like rivers.

Glory be to the Father, and / to the Son, *
 And to the / Holy Spirit

As it was in the be- / ginning *
 Is now and will be for- / ever. Amen.

PSALM 78b (17-39)

Antiphon - *Janus coeli*

The Lord o - pened the doors of hea - ven,
and rained down man - na on them to eat.

Psalm - *Et addiderunt ultra peccare*

BUT THEY sinned even more a- / gainst Him *
 By rebelling against the
 Most High in / the wilderness.

And they tested God in / their heart *
 By asking for the food of / their fancy.

Yes, they spoke a- / gainst God: *
 They said, "Can God prepare
 a table in / the wilderness?

Behold, He struck the rock, so that the waters
gushed out, and the streams / overflowed. *
 Can He give bread also? Can
 He provide meat for / His people?"

Therefore the LORD heard this and was furious;
so a fire was kindled against / Jacob, *
 And anger also came up a- / gainst Israel,

Because they did not believe / in God, *
 And did not trust in His salvation. Yet
 He had commanded the / clouds above, *

And opened the doors of heaven, and
rained down manna on them / to eat, *
 And given them of the bread / of heaven.

Men ate / angels' food; *
 He sent them food / to the full.

He caused an east wind to blow in the / heavens; *
 And by His power He
 brought in / the south wind.

He also rained meat on them / like the dust, *
 Feathered fowl like the sand / of the seas;

And He let them fall in the midst of / their camp, *
 All around / their dwellings.

So they ate and were / well filled, *
 For He gave them / their own desire.

They were not deprived of their craving;
but while their food was still in / their mouths, *
 The wrath of God came / against them,

And slew the stoutest / of them, *
 And struck down the choice men / of Israel.

In spite of this they / still sinned, *
And did not believe in His / wondrous works.

Therefore their days He consumed in fu- / tility, *
And their / years in fear.

When He slew them, then they / sought Him; *
And they returned and
sought ear- / nestly for God.

Then they remembered that God was / their rock, *
And the Most High God their / Redeemer.

Nevertheless they flattered
Him with / their mouth, *
And they lied to Him / with their tongue;

For their heart was not steadfast / with Him, *
Nor were they faithful in / His covenant.

But He, being full of compassion, forgave
their iniquity, and did not destroy them.
Yes, many a time He turned His anger / away, *
And did not stir up / all His wrath;

For He remembered that they were / but flesh, *
A breath that passes away
and does / not come again.

Glory be to the Father, and / to the Son, *
And to the Ho- / ly Spirit

As it was in the be- / ginning *
Is now and will be forev- / er. Amen.

PSALM 78c (40-72)

Tone 6

Antiphon - *Aedificavit Deus*

God built His sanc- tu - a - ry   like   the   heights.

Psalm - *Quotiens provocaverunt*

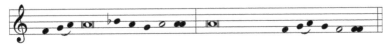

HOW OFten they provoked
Him / in the wilderness, *
And grieved Him / in the desert!

Yes, again and again / they tempted God, *
And limited the Holy One / of Israel.

They did not re- / member His power: *
The day when He redeemed
them from / the enemy,

When He worked His / signs in Egypt, *
And His wonders in the / field of Zoan;

Turned their / rivers into blood, *
And their streams, that / they could not drink.

He sent swarms of flies among
them, / which devoured them, *
And frogs, / which destroyed them.

He also gave their crops to the / caterpillar, *
And their labor / to the locust.

He destroyed / their vines with hail, *
And their syca- / more trees with frost.

He also gave up their / cattle to the hail, *
And their flocks to / fi'ry lightning.

He cast on them the fierceness of His
anger, wrath, indig- / nation, and trouble, *
By sending angels of
destruc- / tion among them.

He made a path for His anger; He
did not / spare their soul from death, *
But gave their life o- / ver to the plague,

And destroyed all the first- / born in Egypt, *
The first of their strength in / the tents of Ham.

But He made His own
people / go forth like sheep, *
And guided them in the
wil- / derness like a flock;

115

And He led them on safely,
so that / they did not fear; *
   But the sea overwhelmed / their enemies.

And He brought them to His / holy border, *
   This mountain which His
   right / hand had acquired.

He also drove out the nations before them,
allotted them an inheri- / tance by survey, *
   And made the tribes of
   Israel / dwell in their tents.

Yet they tested and
provoked / the Most High God, *
   And did not keep His / testimonies,

But turned back and acted
unfaithfully / like their fathers; *
   They were turned aside like / a deceitful bow.

For they provoked Him to
anger with / their high places, *
   And moved Him to jealousy
   with / their carved images.

When God heard this, / He was furious, *
   And greatly ab- / horred Israel,

So that He forsook the taberna -/ cle of Shiloh, *
   The tent He had / placed among men,

And delivered His strength in- / to captivity, *
   And His glory into the / enemy's hand.

He also gave His people / over to the sword, *
   And was furious with / His inheritance.

The fire con- / sumed their young men, *
   And their maidens were
   not giv- / en in marriage.

Their priests / fell by the sword, *
   And their widows made no / lamentation.

Then the Lord a- / woke as from sleep, *
   Like a mighty man who
   shouts / because of wine.

And He beat back / His enemies; *
   He put them to a perpet- / ual reproach.

Moreover He rejected the / tent of Joseph, *
   And did not choose the tribe / of Ephraim,

But chose the / tribe of Judah, *
   Mount / Zion which He loved.

And He built His sanctu- / ary like the heights, *
   Like the earth which He
   has estab- / lished forever.

He also chose Da- / vid His servant, *
   And took him / from the sheepfolds;

From following the ewes that had young He
brought him, to shepherd Ja- / cob His people, *
   And Israel His / inheritance.

So he shepherded them according
to the integri- / ty of his heart, *
   And guided them by the
   skillful- / ness of his hands.

Glory be to the Father, / and to the Son, *
   And to the / Holy Spirit

As it was in / the beginning *
   Is now and will be / forever. Amen.

PSALM 79

Tone 8G

Antiphon - *Adjuva nos, Deus*

Help us, O God of our sal- va - tion; and pro-vide a-tone-ment for our sins.

Psalm - *Deus, venerunt*

O GOD, the nations have come into Your inheritance; Your holy temple they have / defiled; *
They have laid Je- / rusalem in heaps.

The dead bodies of Your servants they have given as food for the birds of the / heavens, *
The flesh of Your saints to
the / beasts of the earth.

Their blood they have shed like water all around Je- / rusalem, *
And there was no / one to bury them.

We have become a reproach to our / neighbors, *
A scorn and derision to
those who / are around us.

How long, LORD? Will You be angry for- / ever? *
Will Your jealous- / y burn like fire?

Pour out Your wrath on the nations that do not / know You, *
And on the kingdoms that
do not / call on Your name.

For they have devoured / Jacob, *
And laid / waste his dwelling place.

Oh, do not remember former iniquities against us! Let Your tender mercies come speedily to / meet us, *
For we have / been brought very low.

Help us, O God of our salvation, for the glory of / Your name; *
And deliver us, and provide atonement
for our sins, / for Your name's sake!

Why should the na- / tions say, *
- / "Where is their God?"

Let there be known among the nations in / our sight *
The avenging of the blood of
Your servants / which has been shed.

Let the groaning of the prisoner come be- / fore You; *
According to the greatness of Your power
preserve those who are ap- / pointed to die;

And return to our neighbors sevenfold into their / bosom *
Their reproach with which they
have re- / proached You, O Lord.

So we, Your people and sheep of Your pasture, will give You thanks for- / ever; *
We will show forth Your
praise to all / generations.

Glory be to the Father, and / to the Son, *
And to the / Holy Spirit

As it was in the be- / ginning *
Is now and will be for- / ever. Amen.

PSALM 80

Tone 1a2

Antiphon - *Excita Domine*

Stir up Your strength, O Lord, and save us.

Psalm - *Qui Regis Israel*

GIVE EAR, O Shepherd of Israel, You who lead / Joseph like a flock; *
You who dwell between
the cher- / ubim, shine forth!*

Before Ephraim, Benjamin, / and Manasseh, *
Stir up Your strength, and / come and save us!

Restore us, O God; / cause Your face to shine, *
And / we shall be saved!

- / O LORD God of hosts, *
How long will You be angry
against the prayer / of Your people?

You have fed them / with the bread of tears, *
   And given them tears
   to drink / in great measure.

You have made us a strife / to our neighbors, *
   And our enemies / laugh among themselves.

Restore us, O God of
hosts; / cause Your face to shine, *
   And / we shall be saved!

You have brought a / vine out of Egypt; *
   You have cast out the nations, / and planted it.

You / prepared room for it, *
   And caused it to take deep
   root, / and it filled the land.

The hills were covered / with its shadow, *
   And the mighty / cedars with its boughs.

She sent out her / boughs to the Sea, *
   And her branches / to the River.

Why have You broken / down her hedges, *
   So that all who pass by
   the / way pluck her fruit?

The boar out of the / woods uproots it, *
   And the wild beast of the / field devours it.

Return, we beseech / You, O God of hosts; *
   Look down from heaven
   and see and / visit this vine

And the vineyard which Your
right / hand has planted, *
   And the branch that You
   made / strong for Yourself.

It is burned with fire, / it is cut down; *
   They perish at the
   rebuke / of Your countenance.

Let Your hand be upon the
man / of Your right hand, *
   Upon the son of man whom
   You made / strong for Yourself.

Then we will / not turn back from You; *
   Revive us, and we will / call upon Your name.

Restore us, O Lord God of
hosts; / cause Your face to shine, *
   And / we shall be saved!

Glory be to the / Father, and to the Son, *
   And to the / Holy Spirit

As it was in / the beginning *
   Is now and will be for- / ever. Amen.

PSALM 81

Tone 8G

Antiphon - *Ego sum Dominus*

I am the Lord your God, O Is - ra - el,

who brought you out of the land of E - gypt.

Psalm - *Exultate Deo*

SING Aloud to God / our strength; *
   Make a joyful shout to the / God of Jacob.

Raise a song and strike the / timbrel, *
   The pleasant / harp with the lute.

Blow the trumpet at the
time of the / New Moon, *
   At the full moon, on our / solemn feast day.

For this is a statute for / Israel, *
   A law of the / God of Jacob.

This He established in Joseph as a testi- / mony, *
   When He went throughout
   the land of Egypt, where I heard
   a language I / did not understand.

"I removed his shoulder from the / burden; *
   His hands were freed / from the baskets.

You called in trouble, and I delivered you;
I answered you in the secret place of / thunder; *
   I tested you at the wa- / ters of Meribah.

"Hear, O My people, and I will ad- / monish you! *
   O Israel, if you will / listen to Me!

There shall be no foreign god a- / mong you;*
   Nor shall you worship an- / y foreign god.

I am the LORD your God, who brought
you out of the land of / Egypt; *
   Open your mouth wide, and / I will fill it.

"But My people would not heed / My voice,*
   And Israel / would have none of Me.

So I gave them over to
their own / stubborn heart, *
   To walk in / their own counsels.

"Oh, that My people would listen / to Me, *
   That Israel would / walk in My ways!

I would soon subdue their / enemies, *
   And turn My hand against their / adversaries.

The haters of the LORD would
pretend submission / to Him, *
   But their fate would en- / dure forever.

He would have fed them also
with the finest / of wheat; *
   And with honey from the
   rock I would have / satisfied you."

Glory be to the Father, and / to the Son, *
   And to the / Holy Spirit

As it was in the be- / ginning *
   Is now and will be for- / ever. Amen.

PSALM 82

Tone 4a

Antiphon - *Surge Deus*

A - rise, O God and judge the earth;

For You shall in - her - it all na - tions.

Psalm - *Deus stetit*

GOD STANDS in the
congregation / of the mighty; *
   He / judges among the gods.

How long will you / judge unjustly, *
   And show partiali- / ty to the wicked?

Defend the / poor and fatherless; *
   Do justice to the af- / flicted and needy.

Deliver the / poor and needy; *
   Free them from the / hand of the wicked.

They do not know, nor do they
understand; they walk a- / bout in darkness; *
 All the foundations of the / earth are unstable.

I / said, "You are gods, *
 And all of you are
 child- / ren of the Most High.

But / you shall die like men, *
 And fall like / one of the princes."

Arise, O / God and judge the earth; *
 For You shall in- / herit all nations.

Glory be to the Father, / and to the Son, *
 And to / the Holy Spirit

As it was in / the beginning *
 Is now and will be / forever. Amen.

PSALM 83

Tone 1D

Antiphon - *Ne taceas, Deus*

Do not keep si-lent, O God, for Your en - e- mies have lift-ed up their head.

Psalm - *Deus, quis similis?*

DO NOT keep / silent, O God! *
 Do not hold Your peace,
 and do / not be still, O God!

For behold, Your enemies / make a tumult; *
 And those who hate You
 have / lifted up their head.

They have taken crafty
counsel a- / gainst Your people, *
 And consulted together
 a -/ gainst Your sheltered ones.

They have said, "Come, and let us
cut them off from be- / ing a nation, *
 That the name of Israel may
 be re- / membered no more."

For they have consulted
together / with one consent; *
 They form a confedera- / cy against You:

The tents of Edom / and the Ishmaelites; *
 Moab / and the Hagrites;

Gebal, Am- / mon, and Amalek; *
 Philistia with the in- / habitants of Tyre;

Assyria also / has joined with them; *
 They have helped the / children of Lot.

Deal with them / as with Midian, *
 As with Sisera, as with
 Jabin / at the Brook Kishon,

Who per- / ished at En Dor, *
 Who became as / refuse on the earth.

Make their nobles like Oreb / and like Ze-eb, *
 Yes, all their princes like
 Zebah / and Zalmunna,

Who said, "Let us / take for ourselves *
 The pastures of God for / a possession."

O my God, make them / like the whirling dust, *
 Like the / chaff before the wind!

As the / fire burns the woods, *
 And as the flame sets the / mountains on fire,

So pursue them / with Your tempest, *
 And frighten / them with Your storm.

Fill their / faces with shame, *
 That they may seek / Your name, O Lord.

Let them be confounded and
dis- / mayed forever; *
 Yes, let them be put to / shame and perish,

That they may know that You,
whose name a- / lone is the LORD, *
  Are the Most High / over all the earth.

Glory be to the / Father, and to the Son, *
And to the / Holy Spirit

As it was in / the beginning *
  Is now and will be for- / ever. Amen.

PSALM 84

Antiphon - *Beati qui habitant*

Bless - èd are those who dwell in Your house, O LORD.

Psalm - *Quam dilecta!*

HOW LOVEly is Your taber- / nacle, *
  - / O LORD of hosts!

My soul longs, yes, even faints
for the courts of / the LORD; *
  My heart and my flesh cry
  out / for the living God.

Even the sparrow has found / a home, *
  And the swallow a nest for herself,
  where / she may lay her young

Even Your altars, O LORD / of hosts, *
  My / King and my God.

Blessèd are those who dwell in / Your house; *
  They will / still be praising You.

Blessèd is the man whose strength is / in You, *
  Whose heart is / set on pilgrimage.

As they pass through the Valley
of Baca, they make it / a spring; *
  The rain also / covers it with pools.

They go from strength / to strength; *
  Each one appears before / God in Zion.

O LORD God of hosts, hear / my prayer;
  Give ear, O / God of Jacob!

O God, behold / our shield, *
  And look upon the face of / Your anointed.

For a day in Your courts is
better than a / thousand. *
  I would rather be a doorkeeper in
  the house of my God than
  dwell in the / tents of wickedness.

For the LORD God is a sun / and shield; *
  The LORD will give / grace and glory;

No good thing will He / withhold *
  From those who / walk uprightly.

O LORD / of hosts, *
  Blessèd is the / man who trusts in You!

Glory be to the Father, and / to the Son, *
And to the / Holy Spirit

As it was in the be- / ginning *
  Is now and will be for- / ever. Amen.

PSALM 85

Antiphon - *Benedixisti, Domine*

You have been fa - vor - a - ble   to Your land, O   Lord.

You have for - giv - en the in - i - qui - ty   of Your peo - ple.

Psalm - *Benedixisti, Domine*

LORD, YOU have been
favora- / ble to Your land; *
   You have brought back
   the captivi- / ty of Jacob.

You have forgiven the iniquity / of Your people; *
   You have / covered all their sin.

You have taken a- / way all Your wrath; *
   You have turned from
   the fierceness / of Your anger.

Restore us, O God of / our salvation, *
   And cause Your anger / t'ward us to cease.

Will You be angry with / us forever? *
   Will You prolong Your
   anger to all / generations?

Will You not re- / vive us again, *
   That Your people / may rejoice in You?

Show / us Your mercy, LORD, *
   And grant us / Your salvation.

I will hear what / God the LORD will speak, *
   For He will speak peace / to His people

- / And to His saints; *
   But let them not turn / back to folly.

Surely His salvation is near
to / those who fear Him, *
   That glory may / dwell in our land.

Mercy and truth have / met together; *
   Righteousness / and peace have kissed.

Truth shall / spring out of the earth, *
   And righteousness shall
   look / down from heaven.

Yes, the LORD will / give what is good; *
   And our land will / yield its increase.

Righteousness will / go before Him, *
   And shall make His foot- / steps our pathway.

Glory be to the / Father, and to the Son, *
   And to the / Holy Spirit

As it was in / the beginning *
   Is now and will be for- / ever. Amen.

PSALM 86

Antiphon - *Domine, da fortitudinem*

Lord,   give Your strength   to   Your   ser - vant,

and save the son of Your maid - ser - vant.

Psalm - *Inclina, Domine*

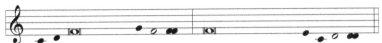

BOW DOWN Your ear, O Lord, / hear me; *
For I am poor / and needy.

Preserve my life, for I am / holy; *
You are my God; save Your
servant / who trusts in You!

Be merciful to me, O Lord, for I cry to You all
day long. Rejoice the soul of Your / servant, *
For to You, O Lord, I / lift up my soul.

For You, Lord, are good, and ready to / forgive, *
And abundant in mercy to
all those who call / upon You.

Give ear, O Lord, to / my prayer; *
And attend to the voice
of my sup- / plications.

In the day of my trouble I will call up- / on You, *
For You will / answer me.

Among the gods there is none like You, / O Lord; *
Nor are there any / works like Your works.

All nations whom You have made shall
come and worship before You, / O Lord, *
And shall glori- / fy Your name.

For You are great, and do / wondrous things; *
You a- / lone are God.

Teach me Your way, O Lord;
I will walk in / Your truth; *
Unite my heart to / fear Your name.

I will praise You, O Lord my
God, with / all my heart, *
And I will glorify Your name / forevermore.

For great is Your mercy / t'ward me, *
And You have delivered my
soul from the depths / of Sheol.

O God, the proud have risen against me, and
a mob of violent men have / sought my life, *
And have not set You / before them.

But You, O Lord, are a God full
of compassion, and / gracious, *
Longsuffering and abundant
in mer- / cy and truth.

Oh turn to me, and have mercy on me!
Give Your strength to Your / servant, *
And save the son of Your / maidservant.

Show me a sign for good, that those who
hate me may see it and be / ashamed, *
Because You, Lord have
helped me and / comforted me.

Glory be to the Father, and / to the Son, *
And to the Ho- / ly Spirit

As it was in the be- / ginning *
Is now and will be forev- / er. Amen.

PSALM 87

Tone 5

Antiphon - *Gloriosa dicta sunt*

Glor-ious things are spo-ken of You, O ci - ty of God!

Psalm - *Fundamenta ejus*

HIS FOUNdation is in the holy / mountains.
 The LORD loves the gates of Zion more
 than all the dwelling pla- / ces of Jacob.

Glorious things are spoken / of You, *
 O / city of God!

"I will make mention of / Rahab *
 And Babylon to / those who know Me;

Behold, O Philistia and Tyre, with Ethi- / opia: *
 'This / one was born there.'"

And of Zion it will be said, "This
one and that one were born / in her; *
 And the Most High
 Himself / shall establish her."

The LORD will record, when
He registers the / peoples: *
 "This / one was born there."

Both the singers and the
players on instru- / ments say, *
 "All my / springs are in you."

Glory be to the Father, and / to the Son, *
 And to the / Holy Spirit

As it was in the be- / ginning *
 Is now and will be for- / ever. Amen.

PSALM 88

Antiphon - *Intret oratio mea*

Let my prayer come be - fore You, O LORD.

Psalm - *Domine Deus*

O LORD, God of my sal- / vation, *
 I have cried out day and / night before You.

Let my prayer come be- / fore You; *
 Incline Your / ear to my cry.

For my soul is full of / troubles, *
 And my life draws / near to the grave.

I am counted with those
who go down to / the pit; *
 I am like a man who has no
 strength, a- / drift among the dead,

Like the slain who lie in the grave,
whom You remember / no more, *
 And who are / cut off from Your hand.

You have laid me in the / lowest pit, *
 In / darkness, in the depths.

Your wrath lies heavy up- / on me, *
 And You have afflicted
 me / with all Your waves.

You have put away my
acquaintances far / from me; *
 You have made me an
 abomi- / nation to them;

I am shut up, and I cannot / get out; *
   My eye wastes away because / of affliction.

Lord, I have called daily up- / on You; *
   I have stretched / out my hands to You.

Will You work wonders for / the dead? *
   Shall the dead a- / rise and praise You?

Shall Your lovingkindness be
declared in / the grave? *
   Or Your faithfulness in the
   place / of destruction?

Shall Your wonders be known in / the dark? *
And Your righteousness
in the land / of forgetfulness?

But to You I have cried out, / O Lord, *
And in the morning my
prayer / comes before You.

Lord, why do You cast off / my soul? *
   Why do You / hide Your face from me?

I have been afflicted and ready
to die from / my youth; *
   I suffer Your terrors; / I am distraught.

Your fierce wrath has gone / over me; *
   Your terrors / have cut me off.

They came around me all day long like / water; *
   They engulfed me / altogether.

Loved one and friend You have put far / from me, *
   And my acquaintances / into darkness.

Glory be to the Father, and / to the Son, *
   And to the / Holy Spirit

As it was in the be- / ginning *
   Is now and will be for- / ever. Amen.

PSALM 89a (1-18)

Tone 7a

Antiphon - *Misericordia et veritas*

Mer-cy and truth   shall go   be - fore Your face, O   Lord.

Psalm - *Misericordias Domini*

I WILL sing of the mercies of the / Lord forever; *
   With my mouth will I make known
   Your faithfulness to all / generations.

For I have said, mercy shall be built / up forever; *
   Your faithfulness You shall
   establish in the / very heavens.

I have made a covenant / with My chosen, *
   I have sworn to My / servant David:

Your seed I will estab- / lish forever, *
   And build up your throne to all / generations.

And the heavens will praise
Your / wonders, O Lord; *
   Your faithfulness also in
   the assem- / bly of the saints.

For who in the heavens can
be / compared to the Lord? *
   Who among the sons of the mighty
   can be li- / kened to the Lord?

God is greatly to be feared in
the as- / sembly of the saints, *
   And to be held in reverence
   by all / those around Him.

O Lord God of hosts, who is
mighty / like You, O Lord? *
   Your faithfulness al- / so surrounds You.

You rule the / raging of the sea; *
   When its waves / rise, You still them.

You have broken Rahab in
pieces, / as one who is slain; *
    You have scattered Your
    enemies / with Your mighty arm.

The heavens are Yours, the earth
also is Yours; the world and all its
fullness, / You have founded them. *
    The north and the south,
    You have / created them;

Tabor and Hermon re- / joice in Your name. *
    You have / a mighty arm;

- / Strong is Your hand, *
    And high / is Your right hand.

Righteousness and justice are
the foun- / dation of Your throne; *
    Mercy and truth / go before Your face.

Blessèd are the people
who / know the joyful sound! *
    They walk, O Lord, in the
    light / of Your countenance.

In Your name they re- / joice all day long, *
    And in Your righteousness they / are exalted.

For You are the / glory of their strength, *
    And in Your favor our horn / is exalted.

For our shield be- / longs to the Lord, *
    And our king to the Holy One / of Israel.

Glory be to the / Father, and to the Son, *
    And to the / Holy Spirit

As it was in / the beginning *
    Is now and will be for- / ever. Amen.

PSALM 89b (19-37)

Tone 2

Antiphon - *Ego autem primogenitum*

I will make him My first-born, high- er than the kings of the earth.

Psalm - *Tunc locutus*

THEN YOU spoke in a vision to Your
holy one, and said: I have given help
to one who is / mighty; *
    I have exalted one chosen from / the people.

I have found My servant / David; *
    With My holy oil I have / anointed him,

With whom My hand shall be est- / ablished; *
    Also My arm / shall strengthen him.

The enemy shall not out- / wit him, *
    Nor the son of wickedness / afflict him.

I will beat down his foes before / his face, *
    And plague those / who hate him.

But My faithfulness and My
mercy shall be / with him, *
    And in My name his horn shall be / exalted.

Also I will set his hand over / the sea, *
    And his right hand over / the rivers.

He shall cry to Me, You are my / Father, *
    My God, and the rock of my / salvation.

Also I will make him My / firstborn, *
    The highest of the / kings of the earth.

My mercy I will keep for him for- / ever, *
    And My covenant shall / stand firm with him.

His seed also I will make to endure for- / ever, *
    And his throne as the days / of heaven.

If his sons forsake My law and do
not walk in My / judgments, *
    If they break My statutes and
    do not keep My / commandments,

Then I will punish their
transgression / with the rod, *
And their ini- / quity with stripes.

Nevertheless My lovingkindness
I will not utterly take / from him, *
Nor allow My faithful- / ness to fail.

My covenant I will / not break, *
Nor alter the word that has
gone out / of My lips.

Once I have sworn by My / holiness; *
I will not lie / to David:

His seed shall endure for- / ever, *
And his throne as the sun / before Me;

It shall be established forever / like the moon, *
Even like the faithful wit- / ness in the sky.

Glory be to the Father, and / to the Son, *
And to the Ho- / ly Spirit

As it was in the be- / ginning *
Is now and will be forev- / er. Amen.

PSALM 89c (38-52)

Antiphon - *Recordare Domine*

Re-mem-ber, O   Lord, how I   bear in My bo-som the re-proach of all.

Psalm - *Tu autem reppulisti*

BUT YOU have cast off and / abhorred, *
You have been furious with / Your anointed.

You have renounced the
covenant of Your / servant; *
You have profaned his crown
by casting / it to the ground.

You have broken down all his / hedges; *
You have brought his strong- / holds to ruin.

All who pass by the way / plunder him; *
He is a reproach / to his neighbors.

You have exalted the right
hand of his adver- / saries; *
You have made all his / enemies rejoice.

You have also turned back
the edge of / his sword, *
And have not sustained him / in the battle.

You have made his / glory cease, *
And cast his throne / down to the ground.

The days of his youth You have / shortened;*
You have / covered him with shame.

How long, LORD? Will You
hide Yourself for- / ever? *
Will Your / wrath burn like fire?

Remember how short my / time is; *
For what futility have You
created all the / children of men?

What man can live and not / see death? *
Can he deliver his life
from the / power of the grave?

Lord, where are Your
former loving- / kindnesses, *
Which You swore to / David in Your truth?

Remember, Lord, the reproach of Your / servants *
How I bear in My bosom the
reproach of all the / many peoples,

127

With which Your enemies have reproached, / O Lord, *
    With which they have reproached
    the footsteps of / Your anointed.

Blessèd be the Lord for- / evermore! *
    A- / men and Amen.

Glory be to the Father, and / to the Son, *
    And to the / Holy Spirit

As it was in the be- / ginning *
    Is now and will be for- / ever. Amen.

PSALM 90

Tone 6

Antiphon - *Domine, Refugium*

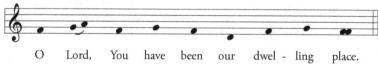

O Lord, You have been our dwel - ling place.

Psalm - *Domine, Refugium*

LORD, YOU have been / our dwelling place *
    In all / generations.

Before the mountains were brought forth, or
ever You had formed the / earth and the world, *
    Even from everlasting to
    ever- / lasting, You are God.

You turn man / to destruction, *
    And say, "Return, O / children of men."

For a thousand / years in Your sight *
    Are like yesterday when it is past,
    and like a / watch in the night.

You carry them a- / way like a flood; *
    They / are like a sleep.

In the morning they are like grass which grows up:
in the morning it flourish- / es and grows up; *
    In the evening it is cut / down and withers.

For we have been consumed / by Your anger, *
    And by Your wrath / we are terrified.

You have set our iniqui- / ties before You, *
    Our secret sins in the
    light / of Your countenance.

For all our days have passed
a- / way in Your wrath; *
    We finish / our years like a sigh.

The days of our lives are seventy years; and if
by reason of strength / they are eighty years, *
    Yet their boast is only labor and sorrow;
    for it is soon cut off, / and we fly away.

Who knows the power / of Your anger? *
    For as the fear of You, / so is Your wrath.

So teach us to / number our days, *
    That we may gain a / heart of wisdom.

Return, / O Lord! How long? *
    And have compassion / on Your servants.

Oh, satisfy us early / with Your mercy, *
    That we may rejoice and / be glad all our days!

Make us glad according to the days
in which You / have afflicted us, *
    And the years in which we / have seen evil.

Let Your work appear / to Your servants, *
    And Your glory / to their children.

And let the beauty of the
Lord our God / be upon us, *
    And establish the work of our hands for
    us; yes, establish the / work of our hands.

Glory be to the Father, / and to the Son, *
    And to the / Holy Spirit

As it was in / the beginning *
    Is now and will be / forever. Amen.

PSALM 91

Antiphon - *Misereri mihi Domine*

Have mer - cy   on   me,   O   Lord,   and   hear   my   prayer.

Psalm - *Qui habitat*

HE WHO dwells in the secret
place of the / Most High *
    Shall abide under the
    shadow of / the Almighty.

I will say of the LORD, He is
my refuge and my / fortress; *
    My God, in / Him I will trust.

Surely He shall deliver you
from the snare of the / fowler *
    And from the per- / ilous pestilence.

He shall cover you with His / feathers, *
    And under His wings you / shall take refuge;

His truth shall be your shield and / buckler. *
    You shall not be afraid of the terror by
    night, nor of the arrow / that flies by day,

Nor of the pestilence that walks in / darkness, *
    Nor of the destruction
    that lays / waste at noonday.

A thousand may fall at your side,
and ten thousand at your / right hand; *
    But it shall / not come near you.

Only with your eyes shall / you look, *
    And see the reward / of the wicked.

Because you have made the
LORD, who is my / refuge, *
    Even the Most / High, your dwelling place,

No evil shall be- / fall you, *
    Nor shall any plague
    come / near your dwelling;

For He shall give His angels charge / over you, *
    To keep / you in all your ways.

In their hands they shall bear / you up, *
    Lest you dash your / foot against a stone.

You shall tread upon the lion and the / cobra, *
    The young lion and the serpent
    you shall / trample underfoot.

Because he has set his love upon
Me, therefore I will de- / liver him; *
    I will set him on high,
    because / he has known My name.

He shall call upon Me, and I will / answer him; *
    I will be with / him in trouble;

I will deliver him and / honor him. *
    With long life I will satisfy him,
    and show him / My salvation.

Glory be to the Father and / to the Son *
    and to the / Holy Spirit;

As it was in the be- / ginning *
    Is now and will be for- / ever. Amen.

PSALM 92

Antiphon - *Quam magnificata sunt*

How great are Your works, O Lord.

Psalm - *Bonum Est Confiteri*

IT IS good to / give thanks to the LORD, *
  And to sing praises to
  Your / name, O Most High;

To declare Your lovingkindness / in the morning, *
  And Your faithful- / ness ev'ry night,

On an instru- / ment of ten strings, *
  On the lute, and on the
  harp, / with harmonious sound.

For You, LORD, have made
  me / glad through Your work; *
  I will triumph in the / works of Your hands.

O LORD, how / great are Your works! *
  Your / thoughts are very deep.

A senseless / man does not know, *
  Nor does a fool / understand this.

When the wicked / spring up like grass, *
  And when all the workers
  of in- / iquity flourish,

It is that they may be de- / stroyed forever. *
  But You, LORD, are on / high forevermore.

For behold, Your enemies, O LORD,
  for behold, Your ene- / mies shall perish; *
  All the workers of iniquity / shall be scattered.

But my horn You have exalted / like a wild ox; *
  I have been a- / nointed with fresh oil.

My eye also has seen my desire / on my enemies; *
  My ears hear my desire on the
  wicked who rise / up against me.

The righteous shall flourish / like a palm tree, *
  He shall grow like a / cedar in Lebanon.

Those who are planted in the / house of the LORD *
  Shall flourish in the / courts of our God.

They shall still bear / fruit in old age; *
  They shall be / fresh and flourishing,

To declare that the / LORD is upright; *
  He is my rock, and there
  is no un- / righteousness in Him.

Glory be to the / Father, and to the Son, *
  And to the / Holy Spirit

As it was in / the beginning *
  Is now and will be for- / ever. Amen.

PSALM 93

Antiphon - Dominus regnavit

The LORD reigns, He is clothed with ma - jes - ty.

Psalm - *Dominus regnavit*

THE LORD reigns, He
is / clothed with majesty; *
The LORD is clothed, He has
girded / Himself with strength.

Surely the world / is established, *
So that it / cannot be moved.

Your throne is es- / tablished from of old;*
You are from / everlasting.

The floods have / lifted up, O LORD, *
The floods have lift- / ed up their voice;

The floods have / lifted up their waves. *
The LORD on high is mightier
than the noise of many waters,
than the mighty / waves of the sea.

Your testimonies / are very sure; *
Holiness adorns Your house, O / LORD, forever.

Glory be to the Father, / and to the Son, *
And to the / Holy Spirit

As it was in / the beginning *
Is now and will be / forever. Amen.

PSALM 94

Antiphon - *Exaltare Domine*

Rise up, O Lord, who jud - ges the earth.

Psalm - *Deus ultionum*

O LORD God, to whom vengeance / belongs *
O God, to whom
vengeance / belongs, shine forth!

Rise up, O Judge of / the earth; *
Render punish- / ment to the proud.

LORD, how long will the / wicked, *
How long will the / wicked triumph?

They utter speech, and speak inso- / lent things; *
All the workers of
iniquity / boast in themselves.

They break in pieces Your people, / O LORD, *
And af- / flict Your heritage.

They slay the widow and the / stranger, *
And mur- / der the fatherless.

Yet they say, "The LORD does / not see, *
Nor does the God of Ja- / cob understand."

Understand, you senseless among the / people; *
And you fools, when / will you be wise?

He who planted the ear, shall He / not hear? *
He who formed the eye, / shall He not see?

He who instructs the nations,
shall He not / correct, *
He who teach- / es man knowledge?

The LORD knows the thoughts / of man, *
That / they are futile.

Blessèd is the man whom
You instruct, / O LORD, *
And teach / out of Your law,

131

That You may give him rest
from the days of ad- / versity, *
  Until the pit is dug / for the wicked.

For the Lord will not cast off His / people, *
  Nor will He forsake / His inheritance.

But judgment will return to / righteousness, *
  And all the upright in / heart will follow it.

Who will rise up for me against the evil- / doers? *
  Who will stand up for me
  against the workers / of iniquity?

Unless the Lord had been / my help, *
  My soul would soon
  have set- / tled in silence.

If I say, "My / foot slips," *
  Your mercy, O Lord, / will hold me up.

In the multitude of my anxieties with- / in me, *
  Your com- / forts delight my soul.

Shall the throne of in- / iquity, *
  Which devises evil by law,
  have / fellowship with You?

They gather together against
the life of the / righteous; *
  And condemn / innocent blood.

But the Lord has been my / defense, *
  And my God the rock / of my refuge.

He has brought on them their own iniquity, and
shall cut them off in their own / wickedness; *
  The Lord our / God shall cut them off.

Glory be to the Father, and / to the Son, *
  And to the / Holy Spirit

As it was in the be- / ginning *
  Is now and will be for- / ever. Amen.

PSALM 95   *Antiphon as specified in the ordinary for Matins*   *Tone 6*

Psalm - *Venite, exultemus*

OH COME, let us / sing to the Lord! *
  Let us shout joyfully to
  the Rock of / our salvation.

Let us come before His
presence / with thanksgiving; *
  Let us shout joyfully / to Him with psalms.

For the Lord / is the great God, *
  And the great King / above all gods.

In His hand are the deep / places of the earth; *
  The heights of the hills / are His also.

The sea is His, / for He made it; *
  And His hands / formed the dry land.

Oh come, let us / worship and bow down; *
  Let us kneel before the / Lord our Maker.

For / He is our God, *
  And we are the people of His
  pasture, and the / sheep of His hand.

Today if you / will hear His voice: *
  Do not / harden your hearts,

As in / the rebellion, *
  As in the day of trial in / the wilderness,

When your / fathers tested Me, *
  They tried Me, though / they saw My work.

For forty years I was grieved
with that / generation, *
  And said, 'It is a people who go
  astray in their hearts, and they
  do / not know My ways.'

So I / swore in My wrath, *
  "They shall not / enter My rest.'"

Glory be to the Father, / and to the Son, *
  And to the / Holy Spirit,

As it was in / the beginning, *
  Is now and will be / forever. Amen.

PSALM 96

Antiphon - *Cantate Domino et benedicite*

Sing   to   the   LORD   and   bless   His   name.

Psalm - *Cantate Domino... Cantate*

OH SING to the LORD a / new song! *
Sing to the LORD, / all the earth.

Sing to the LORD, bless / His name; *
Proclaim the good news of
His salvation from / day to day.

Declare His glory among the / nations, *
His wonders among / all peoples.

For the LORD is great and greatly / to be praised; *
He is to be feared / above all gods.

For all the gods of the peoples are / idols, *
But the LORD made / the heavens.

Honor and majesty are be- / fore Him;*
Strength and beauty are in His sanc- / tuary.

Give to the LORD, O families of the / peoples, *
Give to the LORD / glory and strength.

Give to the LORD the glory due / His name; *
Bring an offering, and come / into His courts.

Oh, worship the LORD in the beauty of / holiness! *
Tremble before Him, / all the earth.

Say among the nations, "The LORD
reigns; the world also is firmly
established, it shall / not be moved; *
He shall judge the peo- / ples righteously."

Let the heavens rejoice,
and let the / earth be glad; *
Let the sea roar, and all / its fullness;

Let the field be joyful, and all that is / in it.
Then all the trees of the woods
will rejoice be- / fore the LORD.

For He is coming, for he is
coming to / judge the earth. *
He shall judge the world with righteousness,
and the peo- / ples with His truth.

Glory be to the Father, and / to the Son, *
And to the Ho- / ly Spirit

As it was in the be- / ginning *
Is now and will be forev- / er. Amen.

PSALM 97

Antiphon - *Dominus regnavit*

The   LORD   reigns;   let   the   earth   re - joice.

Psalm - *Dominus regnavit*

THE LORD reigns; / let the earth rejoice; *
  Let the multi- / tude of isles be glad!

Clouds and dark- / ness surround Him; *
  Righteousness and justice are
  the foun- / dation of His throne.

A fire / goes before Him, *
  And burns up His en- / emies round about.

His / lightnings light the world; *
  The / earth sees and trembles.

The mountains melt like wax
at the / presence of the LORD, *
  At the presence of
  the / Lord of the whole earth.

The heavens de- / clare His righteousness, *
  And all the peo- / ples see His glory.

Let all be put to shame who serve
carved images, who / boast of idols. *
  Wor- / ship Him, all you gods.

Zion / hears and is glad, *
  And the daughters of Judah rejoice
  because of / Your judgments, O LORD.

For You, LORD, are most / high above the earth; *
  You are exalted / far above all gods.

You who love the LORD, hate evil!
He preserves the / souls of His saints; *
  He delivers them out of
  the / hand of the wicked.

Light is sown / for the righteous, *
  And gladness / for the upright in heart.

Rejoice in the / LORD, you righteous, *
  And give thanks at the
  remembrance / of His holy name.

Glory be to the / Father, and to the Son, *
  And to / the Holy Spirit

As it was in / the beginning *
  Is now and will be / forever. Amen.

PSALM 98

Tone 8G

Antiphon - *Jubilate in conspectu*

Shout joy - ful - ly   be - fore   the   LORD,   the   King.

Psalm - *Cantate Domino... Quia Mirabilia*

OH, SING to the LORD a / new song! *
  For He has / done mighty things;

His right hand and His / holy arm *
  Have gained / Him the victory.

The LORD has made known His sal- / vation; *
  His righteousness He has revealed
  in the sight / of the nations.

He has remembered His / mercy *
  And His faithfulness to the / house of Israel;

All the ends / of the earth *
  Have seen the salva- / tion of our God.

Shout joyfully to the LORD, / all the earth; *
  Break forth in song,
  rejoice, / and sing praises.

Sing to the LORD / with the harp, *
  With the harp and the / sound of a psalm.

With trumpets and sound of / a horn; *
  Shout joyfully be- / fore the LORD, the King.

Let the sea roar, and all its / fullness, *
  The world and / those who dwell in it.

Let the rivers clap their hands; let the
hills be joyful together be- / fore the LORD, *
  For He is coming / to judge the earth.

With righteousness He shall / judge the world, *
  And the peoples / with equity.

Glory be to the Father, and / to the Son, *
  And to the / Holy Spirit

As it was in the be- / ginning *
  Is now and will be for- / ever. Amen.

PSALM 99

Tone 6

Antiphon - *Exaltate Dominum Deum*

Ex - alt   the Lord our God, and wor- ship   at   His   ho - ly   hill.

Psalm - *Dominus Regnavit*

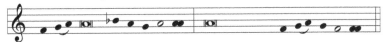

THE LORD reigns, let the / peoples tremble! *
  He dwells between the cherubim;
  let / the earth be moved!

The LORD is / great in Zion, *
  And He is high above / all the peoples.

Let them praise Your / great and awesome name *
  - / He is holy.

The King's strength also loves justice;
You have est- / ablished equity; *
  You have executed justice
  and righteous- / ness in Jacob.

Exalt the LORD our God, and
worship / at His footstool *
  - / He is holy.

Moses and Aaron were among
His priests, Samuel was among those
who / called upon His name; *
  They called upon the
  LORD, / and He answered them.

He spoke to them in the / cloudy pillar; *
  They kept His testimonies and
  the ordin- / ance He gave them.

You answered them, O LORD our God;
You were to them / God-Who-Forgives, *
  Though You took ven- / geance on their deeds.

Exalt the LORD our God, and
worship / at His holy hill; *
  For the LORD our / God is holy.

Glory be to the Father, / and to the Son, *
  And to the / Holy Spirit

As it was in / the beginning *
  Is now and will be / forever. Amen.

PSALM 100

Tone 4a

Antiphon - *Jubilate Deo*

Make a joy - ful shout to the LORD, all you lands!

Psalm - *Jubilate Deo*

MAKE A joyful shout to the / LORD, all you lands! *
  Serve the LORD with gladness; come
  before His / presence with singing. *

Know that the LORD, He is God; it is He
who has made us, and / not we ourselves; *
  We are His people and
  the / sheep of His pasture.

Enter into His gates with thanksgiving,
and into / His courts with praise. *
  Be thankful to / Him, and bless His name.

For the LORD is good; His mercy is / everlasting,*
  And His truth endures to / all generations.

Glory be to the Father, / and to the Son, *
  And to / the Holy Spirit

As it was in / the beginning *
  Is now and will be / forever. Amen.

PSALM 101

Tone 6

Antiphon - *Tibi Domine psallam*

To you, O Lord, I will be-have wise-ly in a per-fect way.

Psalm - *Misericordiam et judicium*

I WILL sing of mer- / cy and justice; *
  To You, O LORD, I / will sing praises.

I will behave wisely / in a perfect way. *
  Oh, when / will You come to me?

I will walk within my
house / with a perfect heart. *
  I will set nothing wicked / before my eyes;

I hate the work of those / who fall away; *
  It shall / not cling to me.

A perverse heart / shall depart from me; *
  I will / not know wickedness.

Whoever secretly slan- / ders his neighbor, *
  Him / I will destroy;

The one who has a haughty
look / and a proud heart, *
  Him I / will not endure.

My eyes shall be on the faithful of the
land, that / they may dwell with me; *
He who walks in a perfect
way, / he shall serve me.

He who works deceit shall
not / dwell within my house; *
He who tells lies shall not
continue / in my presence.

Early I will destroy all the / wicked of the land, *
That I may cut off all the evildoers
from the ci- / ty of the LORD.

Glory be to the Father, / and to the Son, *
And to the / Holy Spirit

As it was in / the beginning *
Is now and will be / forever. Amen.

PSALM 102

Antiphon - *Clamor meus Domine*

Let my cry come to You, O Lord; do not hide Your face from me.

Psalm - *Domine, exaudi... et clamor meus*

HEAR MY prayer, / O LORD, *
And let my / cry come to You.

Do not hide Your face from
me in the day of my / trouble; *
In- / cline Your ear to me;

In the day that / I call, *
An- / swer me speedily.

For my days are consumed / like smoke, *
And my bones are / burned like a hearth.

My heart is stricken and withered / like grass, *
So that I forget / to eat my bread.

Because of the sound of my / groaning *
My bones / cling to my skin.

I am like a pelican of the / wilderness; *
I am like an owl / of the desert.

I lie / awake, *
And am like a sparrow alone / on the housetop.

My enemies reproach me all / day long, *
Those who deride me
swear an / oath against me.

For I have eaten ashes / like bread, *
And mingled my / drink with weeping,

Because of Your indignation and / Your wrath; *
For You have lifted me up and / cast me away.

My days are like a shadow that / lengthens, *
And I wither / away like grass.

But You, O LORD, shall endure for- / ever, *
And the remembrance of
Your name to all / generations.

You will arise and have mercy on / Zion; *
For the time to favor her,
yes, / the set time, has come.

For Your servants take pleasure in / her stones, *
And show / favor to her dust.

So the nations shall fear the name of / the LORD, *
And all the kings of the / earth Your glory.

For the LORD shall build up / Zion; *
He shall appear / in His glory.

He shall regard the prayer of the / destitute, *
And shall / not despise their prayer.

This will be written for the generation / to come, *
  That a people yet to be
  created / may praise the Lord.

For He looked down from the
height of His sanctu- / ary; *
  From heaven the / Lord viewed the earth,

To hear the groaning of the / prisoner, *
  To release those ap- / pointed to death,

To declare the name of the Lord in / Zion, *
  And His praise / in Jerusalem,

When the peoples are gathered to- / gether, *
  And the kingdoms, / to serve the Lord.

He weakened my strength in / the way; *
  He / shortened my days.

I said, "O my God, do not take me
away in the midst of / my days; *
  Your years are throughout all / generations.

Of old You laid the foundation of / the earth, *
  And the heavens are the / work of Your hands.

They will perish, but You will / endure; *
  Yes, they will all grow old / like a garment;

Like a cloak You will / change them, *
  And / they will be changed.

But You are / the same, *
  And Your / years will have no end.

The children of Your servants will con- / tinue, *
  And their descendants will
  be esta- / blished before You.

Glory be to the Father, and / to the Son, *
  And to the / Holy Spirit

As it was in the be- / ginning *
  Is now and will be for- / ever. Amen.

PSALM 103

Tone 8G

Antiphon - *Benedic, anima mea*

Bless   the   Lord,   O   my   soul.

Psalm - *Benedic, anima mea*

BLESS THE Lord, O / my soul; *
  And all that is within
  me, / bless His holy name!

Bless the Lord, O / my soul, *
  And forget not / all His benefits:

Who forgives all your in- / iquities, *
  Who heals all / your diseases,

Who redeems your life from de- / struction,*
  Who crowns you with loving
  kindness and / tender mercies,

Who satisfies your mouth with / good things, *
  So that your youth is
  renewed / like the eagle's.

The Lord executes / righteousness *
  And justice for / all who are oppressed.

He made known His ways to / Moses, *
  His acts to the child- / ren of Israel.

The Lord is merciful and / gracious, *
  Slow to anger, and abound- / ing in mercy.

He will not always / strive with us, *
  Nor will He keep His an- / ger forever.

He has not dealt with us according to / our sins, *
   Nor punished us according to / our iniquities.

For as the heavens are high above / the earth, *
   So great is His mercy
   toward / those who fear Him;

As far as the east is from / the west, *
   So far has He removed our
   trans- / gressions from us.

As a father pities his / children, *
   So the LORD pities / those who fear Him.

For He knows / our frame; *
   He remembers / that we are dust.

As for man, his days are / like grass; *
   As a flower of the field, / so he flourishes.

For the wind passes over it, and it / is gone, *
   And its place re- / members it no more.

But the mercy of the LORD is from
everlasting to ever- / lasting *
   On / those who fear Him,

And His righteousness to children's / children, *
   To such as keep His covenant,
   and to those who remember His
   command- / ments to do them.

The LORD has established His throne in / heaven, *
   And His kingdom / rules over all.

Bless the LORD, you His angels,
who excel / in strength, *
   Who do His word, heeding
   the / voice of His word.

Bless the LORD, all you / His hosts, *
   You ministers of His, who / do His pleasure.

Bless the LORD, all His works,
in all places of His do- / minion. *
   Bless the / LORD, O my soul!

Glory be to the Father, and / to the Son, *
   And to the / Holy Spirit

As it was in the be- / ginning *
   Is now and will be for- / ever. Amen.

PSALM 104a (1-12)

Antiphon - *Domine Deus meus, magnificatus*

O   LORD,   my   God,   You   are   ve - ry   great.

Psalm - *Benedic, anima mea*

BLESS THE LORD, O / my soul! *
   O LORD my God, / You are very great:

You are clothed with honor and / majesty, *
   Who cover Yourself with
   light as / with a garment,

Who stretch out the heavens like a / curtain. *
   He lays the beams of His upper
   chambers / in the waters,

Who makes the clouds His / chariot, *
   Who walks on the / wings of the wind,

Who makes His angels / spirits, *
   His ministers / a flame of fire.

You who laid the foundations of / the earth, *
   So that it should not be / moved forever,

You covered it with the deep as with a / garment; *
   The waters stood a- / bove the mountains.

At Your rebuke / they fled; *
   At the voice of Your thunder
   they / hastened away.

They went up over the mountains;
they went down into the / valleys, *
   To the place which You / founded for them.

You have set a boundary that
they may not pass / over, *
   That they may not return to / cover the earth.

He sends the springs into the / valleys,*
   They / flow among the hills.

They give drink to every beast of / the field; *
   The wild / donkeys quench their thirst.

By them the birds of the
heavens have / their home; *
   They sing a- / mong the branches.

Glory be to the Father, and / to the Son, *
   And to the / Holy Spirit

As it was in the be- / ginning *
   Is now and will be for- / ever. Amen.

PSALM 104b (13-23)

Tone 8G

Antiphon - *De fructu operum*

The earth is sat - is - fied with the fruit of Your works, O LORD.

Psalm - *Qui inrigas montes*

HE WAters the hills from His upper / chambers; *
   The earth is satisfied with
   the / fruit of Your works.

He causes the grass to grow for the / cattle, *
   And vegetation for the / service of man,

That he may bring forth food from / the earth, *
   And wine that makes / glad the heart of man,

Oil to make his / face shine, *
   And bread which / strengthens man's heart.

The trees of the LORD are full / of sap, *
   The cedars of Lebanon / which He planted,

Where the birds make / their nests; *
   The stork has her home / in the fir trees.

The high hills are for the / wild goats;*
   The cliffs are a refuge for / the rock badgers.

He appointed the moon for / seasons; *
   The sun / knows its going down.

You make darkness, and it / is night, *
   In which all the beasts
   of the / forest creep about.

The young lions roar after / their prey,*
   And / seek their food from God.

When the sun rises, they gather to- / gether *
   And / lie down in their dens.

Man goes out to / his work *
   And to his labor un- / til the evening.

Glory be to the Father, and / to the Son, *
   And to the / Holy Spirit

As it was in the be- / ginning *
   Is now and will be for- / ever. Amen.

PSALM 104c (24-35)

Tone 1g

Antiphon - *Emittes spiritum tuum*

You send forth Your Spi - rit, they are cre - a - ted;

and You re - new the face of the earth.

Psalm - *Quam multa sunt opera*

O LORD, how manifold are Your works!
In wisdom / You have made them all. *
   The earth is full of / Your possessions

This / great and wide sea, *
   In which are innumerable teeming things
   living things / both small and great.

There the ships sail about;
there is / that Leviathan *
   Which You have / made to play there.

These / all wait for You, *
   That You may give them
   their food / in due season.

What You give / them they gather in; *
   You open Your hand, / they
   are filled with good.

You hide Your face, / they are troubled; *
   You take away their breath, they
   die and re- / turn to their dust.

You send forth Your Spirit, they / are created; *
   And You renew the / face of the earth.

May the glory of the LORD en- / dure forever; *
   May the LORD re- / joice in His works.

He looks on the earth, / and it trembles; *
   He touches the / hills, and they smoke.

I will sing to the LORD / as long as I live; *
   I will sing praise to my God
   while I / have my being.

May my meditation / be sweet to Him; *
   I will be / glad in the LORD.

May sinners be con- / sumed from the earth, *
   And the / wicked be no more.

Bless the / LORD, O my soul!
   - / Praise ye the LORD!

Glory be to the / Father, and to the Son, *
   And to the / Holy Spirit

As it was in / the beginning *
   Is now and will be for- / ever. Amen.

PSALM 105a (1-15)

Tone 5

Antiphon - *Memor fuit*

The Lord our God re-mem-bers His cov - e - nant for - e - ver.

141

Psalm - *Confitemini Domino invocavit*

OH, GIVE thanks to the LORD!
Call upon / His name; *
  Make known His deeds
  a- / mong the peoples!

Sing to Him, sing psalms / to Him; *
  Talk of / all His wondrous works!

Glory in His ho- / ly name; *
  Let the hearts of those
  re- / joice who seek the LORD!

Seek the LORD and / His strength; *
  Seek / His face evermore!

Remember His marvelous
works which He / has done, *
  His wonders, and the
  judg- / ments of His mouth,

O seed of Abraham His / servant, *
  You children of Jacob, / His chosen ones!

He is the LORD / our God; *
  His judgments / are in all the earth.

He remembers His covenant for- / ever, *
  The word which He commanded,
  for a thousand / generations,

The covenant which He made with / Abraham, *
  And His / oath to Isaac,

And confirmed it to Jacob for a / statute, *
  To Israel as an ever- / lasting covenant,

Saying, "To you I will give the land of / Canaan *
  As the allotment of / your inheritance,"

When they were few in / number, *
  Indeed very few, and / strangers in it.

When they went from one nation to an- / other, *
  From one kingdom to an- / other people,

He permitted no one to do / them wrong;*
  Yes, He rebuked / kings for their sakes,

Saying, "Do not touch My a- / nointed ones,*
  And do My / prophets no harm."

Glory be to the Father, and / to the Son, *
  And to the / Holy Spirit

As it was in the be- / ginning *
  Is now and will be for- / ever. Amen.

PSALM 105b (16-27)

Tone 7b

Antiphon - *Auxit Dominus populum*

The LORD in - creased His peo - ple great - ly,

and made them strong - er than their en - e - mies.

Psalm - *Et vocavit famem*

MOREOVer He called
for a / famine in the land; *
He destroyed all the pro- / vision of bread.

He sent a man before them --
Joseph -- who was / sold as a slave. *
They hurt his feet with
fetters, / he was laid in irons.

Until the time that / his word came to pass, *
The word of / the LORD tested him.

The king sent / and released him, *
The ruler of the people / let him go free.

He made him / lord of his house, *
And ruler of all / his possessions,

To bind his princes / at his pleasure, *
And teach his / elders wisdom.

Israel also came / into Egypt, *
And Jacob dwelt / in the land of Ham.

He increased His / people greatly, *
And made them stronger / than their enemies.

He turned their heart to / hate His people, *
To deal craftily / with His servants.

He sent Mo- / ses His servant, *
And Aaron whom / He had chosen.

They performed His / signs among them, *
And wonders / in the land of Ham.

Glory be to the / Father, and to the Son, *
And to the / Holy Spirit

As it was in / the beginning *
Is now and will be for- / ever. Amen.

PSALM 105c (28-45)

Tone 4a

Antiphon - *Eduxit Deus*

God brought out   His   peo - ple   with   joy,

and   His   cho - sen   ones   with   glad - ness.

Psalm - *Misit tenebras*

HE SENT darkness, / and made it dark; *
And they did not re- / bel against His word.

He turned their waters into
blood, / and killed their fish. *
Their land abounded with frogs,
even in the / chambers of their kings.

He spoke, and / there came swarms of flies, *
And lice in all / their territory.

He / gave them hail for rain, *
And flam- / ing fire in their land.

He struck their vines also, / and their fig trees, *
And splintered the trees of / their territory.

He spoke, and locusts came,
young locusts / without number, *
And ate up all the vegetation in their land,
and devoured / the fruit of their ground.

He also destroyed all the / firstborn in their land, *
The / first of all their strength.

He also brought them out with / silver and gold, *
And there was none
fee- / ble among His tribes.

143

Egypt was glad when / they departed, *
  For the fear of them had / fallen upon them.

He spread a cloud / for a covering, *
  And fire / to give light in the night.

The people asked, / and He brought quail, *
  And satisfied them with / the bread of heaven.

He opened the rock, and / water gushed out; *
  It ran in the dry pla- / ces like a river.

For He remembered His / holy promise, *
  And A- / braham His servant.

He brought out His / people with joy, *
  His cho- / sen ones with gladness.

He gave them the lands / of the Gentiles, *
  And they inherited the
  la- / bor of the nations,

That they might observe His
statutes / and keep His laws. *
  - / Praise- ye the LORD!

Glory be to the Father, / and to the Son, *
  And to / the Holy Spirit

As it was in / the beginning *
  Is now and will be / forever. Amen.

PSALM 106a (1-31)

Antiphon - *Salvavit eos Dominus*

The Lord saved them for His name's sake.

Psalm - *Confitemini Domino... quis loquetur*

PRAISE THE LORD! Oh, give
thanks to the LORD, for He / is good! *
  For His mercy en- / dures forever.

Who can utter the mighty acts / of the LORD? *
  Who can / declare all His praise?

Blessèd are those who keep / justice, *
  And he who does righteous- / ness at all times!

Remember me, O LORD, with the
favor You have toward Your / people; *
  Oh, visit me with Your salvation, that I
  may see the benefit / of Your chosen ones,

That I may rejoice in the
gladness of Your / nation, *
  That I may glory with / Your inheritance.

We have sinned with our / fathers, *
  We have committed iniquity,
  we / have done wickedly.

Our fathers in Egypt did not
understand Your / wonders; *
  They did not remember the
  multitude of Your mercies, but
  rebelled by the / sea, the Red Sea.

Nevertheless He saved them
for His / name's sake, *
  That He might make
  His / mighty power known.

He rebuked the Red Sea also, and it / dried up; *
  So He led them through the
  depths, as / through the wilderness.

He saved them from the hand
of him who / hated them, *
  And redeemed them from
  the hand / of the enemy.

The waters covered their / enemies; *
  There was not / one of them left.

Then they believed / His words; *
- / They sang His praise.

They soon forgot / His works; *
They did not wait / for His counsel,

But lusted exceedingly in the / wilderness, *
And tested God / in the desert.

And He gave them their / request, *
But sent leanness / into their soul.

When they envied Moses / in the camp,*
And Aaron / the saint of the LORD,

The earth opened up and swallowed / Dathan, *
And covered the faction / of Abiram.

A fire was kindled in their / company; *
The flame burned / up the wicked.

They made a calf in / Horeb, *
And worshiped the / molded image.

Thus they changed their glory into
the image of an ox that / eats grass. *
They forgot God their Savior, who
had done great / things in Egypt,

Wondrous works in the / land of Ham,*
Awesome things / by the Red Sea.

Therefore He said that He would
destroy them, had not Moses His chosen
one stood before Him / in the breach, *

To turn away His wrath,
lest / He destroy them.

Then they despised the / pleasant land;*
They did not / believe His word,

But complained in / their tents, *
And did not heed the / voice of the LORD.

Therefore He raised up His hand
in an oath a- / gainst them, *
To overthrow them / in the wilderness,

To overthrow their descendants
among the / nations, *
And to scatter / them in the lands.

They joined themselves also to Baal of / Peor, *
And ate sacrifices / made to the dead.

Thus they provoked Him to
anger with / their deeds, *
And the plague broke / out among them.

Then Phinehas stood up and in- / tervened, *
And / the plague was stopped.

And that was accounted to
him for / righteousness *
To all generations / forevermore.

Glory be to the Father, and / to the Son, *
And to the / Holy Spirit

As it was in the be- / ginning *
Is now and will be for- / ever. Amen.

PSALM 106b (32-48)

Antiphon - *Cum tribularentur*

The LORD re - gard - ed their af-flic-tion, When He heard their cry.

Psalm - *Et provocaverunt super aquam*

THEY ANgered Him also
at the / waters of strife, *
So that it went ill with
Moses on / account of them;

Because they rebelled a- / gainst His Spirit, *
So that he spoke rash- / ly with his lips.

They did not de- / stroy the peoples, *
    Concerning whom the
    Lord / had commanded them,

But they mingled / with the Gentiles *
    - / And learned their works; *

They served their idols, which
be- / came a snare to them. *
    They even sacrificed their sons
    and their daugh- / ters to demons,

And shed innocent blood, the blood
of their / sons and daughters, *
    Whom they sacrificed to the
    idols of Canaan; and the land
    was pol- / luted with blood.

Thus they were de- / filed by their own works, *
    And played the har- / lot by their own deeds.

Therefore the wrath of the Lord
was kindled a- / gainst His people, *
    So that He abhorred His / own inheritance.

And He gave them into the
hand / of the Gentiles, *
    And those who hated / them ruled over them.

Their enemies al- / so oppressed them,*
    And they were brought into
    subjection / under their hand.

Many times / He delivered them; *
    But they rebelled in their counsel,
    and were brought low for / their iniquity.

Nevertheless He regarded / their affliction, *
    - / When He heard their cry;

And for their sake He
remembered / His covenant, *
    And relented according to
    the multitude / of His mercies.

He also made them / to be pitied *
    By all those who carried them / away captive.

Save us, / O Lord our God, *
    And gather us from a- / mong the Gentiles,

To give thanks / to Your holy name, *
    To tri- / umph in Your praise.

Blessèd be the Lord / God of Israel *
    From everlasting to / everlasting!

And let / all the people say, *
    A- / men! Praise the Lord!

Glory be to the / Father, and to the Son, *
    And to the / Holy Spirit

As it was in / the beginning *
    Is now and will be for- / ever. Amen.

PSALM 107a (1-22)

Antiphon - *Clamaverunt ad Dominum*

They cried out to the Lord,   and He saved them from their dis-tress-es.

Psalm - *Confitemini Domino... dicant qui redempti*

OH, GIVE thanks to the Lord, / for He is good! *
    For His mercy en- / dures forever.

Let the redeemed of / the Lord say so, *
    Whom He has redeemed from
    the hand of / the enemy,

And gathered out of the lands,
from the / east and from the west, *
    From the north / and from the south.

They wandered in the
wilderness in a / desolate way; *
   They found no ci- / ty to dwell in.

Hun- / gry and thirsty, *
   Their soul / fainted in them.

Then they cried out to the
Lord / in their trouble, *
   And He delivered them
   out of / their distresses.

And He led them forth / by the right way, *
   That they might go to a
   city for / a dwelling place.

Oh, that men would give thanks
to the Lord / for His goodness, *
   And for His wonderful works
   to the / children of men!

For He satisfies / the longing soul, *
   And fills the hungry / soul with goodness.

Those who sat in darkness and
in the / shadow of death, *
   Bound in afflic- / tion and irons

Because they rebelled
a- / gainst the words of God, *
   And despised the counsel / of the Most High,

Therefore He brought down
their / heart with labor; *
   They fell down, and there / was none to help.

Then they cried out to
the Lord / in their trouble, *
   And He saved them out of / their distresses.

He brought them out of darkness
and the / shadow of death, *
   And broke their / chains in pieces.

Oh, that men would give thanks
to the Lord / for His goodness, *
   And for His wonderful works
   to the / children of men!

For He has broken / the gates of bronze, *
   And cut the bars / of iron in two.

Fools, because of / their transgression,*
   And because of their
   iniquities, / were afflicted.

Their soul abhorred all / manner of food, *
   And they drew near to / the gates of death.

Then they cried out to the
Lord / in their trouble, *
   And He saved them out of / their distresses.

He sent His / word and healed them, *
   And delivered them
   from / their destructions.

Oh, that men would give thanks
to the Lord / for His goodness, *
   And for His wonderful works
   to the / children of men!

Let them sacrifice the
sacrifices / of thanksgiving, *
   And declare His works / with rejoicing.

Glory be to the Father, / and to the Son, *
   And to the / Holy Spirit

As it was in / the beginning *
   Is now and will be / forever. Amen.

PSALM 107b (23-43)

Tone 8c

Antiphon - *Ipsi viderunt*

They see the works of the Lord, and His won - ders.

Psalm - *Qui descendunt in mare navibus*

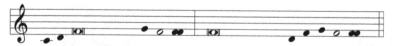

THOSE WHO go down to the sea / in ships, *
Who do business / on great waters,

They see the works of / the LORD, *
And His / wonders in the deep.

For He commands and raises the / stormy wind, *
Which lifts up the / waves of the sea.

They mount up to the / heavens, *
They go down a- / gain to the depths;

Their soul melts because of trouble. They reel
to and fro, and stagger like a / drunken man, *
And are / at their wits' end.

Then they cry out to the LORD in their / trouble, *
And He brings them out of / their distresses.

He calms / the storm, *
So that / its waves are still.

Then they are glad because they are / quiet; *
So He guides them to their / desired haven.

Oh, that men would give thanks
to the LORD for His / goodness, *
And for His wonderful works
to the / children of men!

Let them exalt Him also in
the assembly of the / people, *
And praise Him in the
company / of the elders.

He turns rivers into a / wilderness, *
And the watersprings / into dry ground;

A fruitful land into / barrenness, *
For the wickedness of / those who dwell in it.

He turns a wilderness into pools of / water, *
And dry land / into water-springs.

There He makes the hun- / gry dwell, *
That they may establish a
city / for a dwelling place,

And sow fields and plant / vineyards, *
That they may yield a / fruitful harvest.

He also blesses them, and
they multiply / greatly; *
And He does not let their / cattle decrease.

When they are diminished and / brought low *
Through oppression, afflic- / tion and sorrow,

He pours contempt on / princes, *
And causes them to wander in the
wilderness where / there is no way;

Yet He sets the poor on
high, far from af- / fliction, *
And makes their fami- / lies like a flock.

The righteous see it and / rejoice, *
And all ini- / quity stops its mouth.

Whoever is wise will observe / these things, *
And they will understand the
lovingkind- / ness of the LORD.

Glory be to the Father, and / to the Son, *
And to the / Holy Spirit

As it was in the be- / ginning *
Is now and will be for- / ever. Amen.

PSALM 108

Antiphon - *Exsurge Domine*

Rise up, O Lord, who jud - ges the earth.

Psalm - *Paratum cor meum*

O GOD, my heart is / steadfast; *
 I will sing and give praise,
  even / with my glory.

Awake, lute / and harp! *
 I will / awaken the dawn.

I will praise You, O LORD, among the / peoples, *
 And I will sing praises to
  You a- / mong the nations.

For Your mercy is great above the / heavens, *
 And Your truth / reaches to the clouds.

Be exalted, O God, above the heavens,
 and Your glory above / all the earth; *
  That Your beloved may / be delivered,

Save with Your right hand, and / hear me. *
 God has spoken / in His holiness:

"I will rejoice; I will divide / Shechem *
 And measure out the Val- / ley of Succoth.

Gilead is Mine; Manasseh / is Mine; *
 Ephraim also is the helmet for
  My head; Judah / is My lawgiver.

Moab is My washpot; over
 Edom I will cast / My shoe; *
  Over Philistia / I will triumph."

Who will bring me into the strong / city? *
 Who will lead / me to Edom?

Is it not You, O God, who cast / us off? *
 And You, O God, who did
  not go out / with our armies?

Give us help from / trouble, *
 For the help of / man is useless.

Through God we will do / valiantly, *
 For it is He who shall
  tread / down our enemies.

Glory be to the Father, and / to the Son, *
 And to the / Holy Spirit

As it was in the be- / ginning *
 Is now and will be for- / ever. Amen.

PSALM 109

Tone 1f

Antiphon - *Ne tacueris*

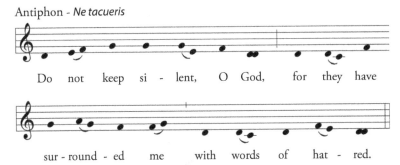

Do not keep si - lent, O God, for they have
sur - round - ed me with words of hat - red.

Psalm - *Deus, laudem*

DO NOT keep silent, O / God of my praise! *
  For the mouth of the wicked and the mouth
  of the deceitful have op- / ened against me;

They have spoken against me with a
lying tongue. They have also surrounded
me with / words of hatred,*
  And fought against / me without a cause.

In return for my love they are / my accusers, *
  But I give / myself to prayer.

Thus they have rewarded me / evil for good, *
  And hat- / red for my love.

Set a wicked / man over him, *
  And let an accuser stand / at his right hand.

When he is judged, let him / be found guilty, *
  And let his / prayer become sin.

- / Let his days be few, *
  And let another / take his office.

Let his / children be fatherless, *
  And his / wife a widow.

Let his children continually
be / vagabonds, and beg; *
  Let them seek their bread also
  from their de- / solate places.

Let the creditor seize / all that he has, *
  And let strangers plun- / der his labor.

Let there be none to extend / mercy to him, *
  Nor let there be any to favor
  his fa- / therless children.

Let his pos- / terity be cut off, *
  And in the generation following
  let their / name be blotted out.

Let the iniquity of his fathers be
re- / membered before the LORD, *
  And let not the sin of his
  moth- / er be blotted out.

Let them be continually / before the LORD, *
  That He may cut off the
  memory of / them from the earth;

Because he did not remember / to show mercy, *
  But persecuted the poor and needy man,
  that he might even slay the / broken in heart.

As he loved cursing, so / let it come to him; *
  As he did not delight in
  blessing, so let / it be far from him.

As he clothed himself with
cursing as / with his garment, *
  So let it enter his body like water,
  and like oil / into his bones.

Let it be to him like
the / garment which covers him, *
  And for a belt with which
  he girds himself / continually.

Let this be the LORD's reward to / my accusers, *
  And to those who speak
  evil a- / gainst my person.

But You, O God the Lord, deal
with me / for Your name's sake; *
  Because Your mercy is good, / deliver me.

For I am / poor and needy, *
  And my heart is wound- / ed within me.

I am gone like a shadow / when it lengthens; *
  I am shaken off / like a locust.

My knees are / weak through fasting, *
  And my flesh is feeble from / lack of fatness.

I also have become / a reproach to them;*
  When they look at
  me, / they shake their heads.

- / Help me, O LORD my God! *
  Oh, save me according / to Your mercy,

That they may know that / this is Your hand *
  That You, / LORD, have done it!

Let them / curse, but You bless; *
  When they arise, let them be ashamed,
  but let Your / servant rejoice.

Let my accusers / be clothed with shame, *
  And let them cover themselves with
  their own disgrace as / with a mantle.

I will greatly praise the / Lord with my mouth; *
  Yes, I will praise Him
  a- / mong the multitude.

For He shall stand at the
right / hand of the poor, *
  To save him from those / who condemn him.

Glory be to the / Father, and to the Son, *
  And to the / Holy Spirit

As it was in / the beginning *
  Is now and will be for- / ever. Amen.

PSALM 110

Tone 7c²

Antiphon - *Dixit Dominus*

The Lord said to my Lord, sit at My right hand.

Psalm - *Dixit Dominus*

THE LORD / said to my Lord, *
  Sit at My right hand, till I make
  Your / enemies Your footstool.

The Lord shall send the rod
of Your / strength out of Zion. *
  Rule in the midst of / Your enemies!

Your people shall be volunteers in the day
of Your power; in the beauties of holiness,
from the / womb of the morning,
  You have the / dew of Your youth.

The Lord has sworn / and will not relent, *
  "You are a priest forever according
  to the order / of Melchizedek."

The Lord is / at Your right hand; *
  He shall execute kings in
  the / day of His wrath.

He shall judge among the nations,
He shall fill the places / with dead bodies, *
  He shall execute the heads
  of / many countries.

He shall drink of the brook / by the wayside; *
  Therefore He shall / lift up the head.

Glory be to the / Father, and to the Son, *
  And to the / Holy Spirit

As it was in / the beginning *
  Is now and will be for- / ever. Amen.

PSALM 111

Tone 3b

Antiphon - *Magna opera Domini*

The works of the Lord are great,

stud - ied   by   all   who   have   plea - sure   in   them.

Psalm - *Confitebor tibi*

PRAISE THE LORD! I will praise
the LORD / with my whole heart, *
   In the assembly of the upright
   and in the con- / gregation.

The works / of the LORD are great, *
   Studied by all who have plea- / sure in them.

His work is honorable / and glorious,*
   And His righteousness endures / forever.

He has made His wonderful
works to / be remembered; *
   The LORD is gracious and full of / compassion.

He has given food to / those who fear Him; *
   He will ever be mindful of His / covenant.

He has declared to His people
the / power of His works, *
   In giving them the heritage of / the nations.

The works of His hands are veri- / ty and justice; *
   All His pre- / cepts are sure.

They stand fast for- / ever and ever, *
   And are done in truth and / uprightness.

He has sent redemption / to His people;*
   He has commanded His covenant / forever:

Holy and / awesome is His name. *
   The fear of the LORD is
   the beginning / of wisdom;

A good understanding have all those
who do / His commandments.*
   His praise endures / forever.

Glory be to the / Father, and to the Son, *
   And to the Ho- / ly Spirit

As it was in / the beginning *
   Is now and will be forev- / er. Amen.

PSALM 112

Tone 4g

Antiphon - *Qui timet Dominum*

He who fears the LORD will de - light in   His   com - mand-ments.

Psalm - *Beatus vir*

PRAISE THE LORD! Blessèd is
the / man who fears the LORD, *
   Who delights greatly in
   His command- / ments.

His descendants will be / mighty on earth; *
   The generation of the
   upright will be bles- / sed.

Wealth and riches / will be in his house, *
   And his righteousness endures forev- / er.

Unto the upright there
arises light / in the darkness; *
  He is gracious, and full of
  compassion, and right- / eous.

A good man deals / graciously and lends; *
  He will guide his affairs with discre- / tion.

Surely he will ne- / ver be shaken; *
  The righteous will be in
  everlasting remem- / brance.

He will not be afraid of / evil tidings; *
  His heart is steadfast, trusting in / the LORD.

His heart is established; he / will not be afraid, *
  Until he sees his desire upon his en- / emies.

He has / dispersed abroad, *
  He has given to the / poor;

His righteousness en- / dures forever; *
  His horn will be exalted with hon- / or.

The wicked will see it and be grieved;
he will gnash his / teeth and melt away; *
  The desire of the wicked shall per- / ish.

Glory be to the Father, / and to the Son, *
  And to the Holy Spi- / rit

As it was in / the beginning *
  Is now and will be forever. / Amen.

PSALM 113

Antiphon - *Sit nomen Domini*

Bless-èd be the name of the LORD for - ev - er - more.

Psalm - *Laudate, pueri*

PRAISE THE LORD! Praise,
O / servants of the LORD, *
  Praise the / name of the LORD!

Blessèd be the / name of the LORD *
  From this time forth / and forevermore!

From the rising of the sun / to its going down *
  The LORD's name / is to be praised.

The LORD is high a- / bove all nations, *
  His glory a- / bove the heavens.

Who is like the LORD our
God, / who dwells on high, *
  Who humbles Himself to behold the things
  that are in the / heavens and in the earth?

He raises the poor / out of the dust, *
  And lifts the needy / out of the ash heap,

That He may seat / him with princes *
  With the princes / of His people.

He grants the barren / woman a home, *
  Like a joyful mother
  of / children. Praise the LORD!

Glory be to the / Father and to the Son *
  and to the / Holy Spirit;

As it was in / the beginning *
  Is now and will be for- / ever. Amen.

PSALM 114

Antiphon - *A facie Domine*

Trem-ble, O earth, at the pre-sence of the Lord, the God of Ja-cob.

Psalm - *In exitu Israel*

WHEN Israel / went out of Egypt, *
The house of Jacob from a
people of / strange language,

Judah became / His sanctuary, *
And Israel His / dominion.

The / sea saw it and fled; *
Jor- / dan turned back.

The / mountains skipped like rams, *
The little / hills like lambs.

What ails you, / O sea, that you fled? *
O Jordan, / that you turned back?

O mountains, / that you skipped like rams? *
O little / hills, like lambs?

Tremble, O earth, at / the presence of the Lord, *
At the presence of the God / of Jacob,

Who turned the rock into / a pool of water, *
The flint into a fountain / of waters.

Glory be to the / Father, and to the Son, *
And to the Ho- / ly Spirit

As it was / in the beginning *
Is now and will be forev- / er. Amen.

PSALM 115

Antiphon - *Deus autem noster*

Our God is in hea - ven; He does what-ev-er He pleas - es.

Psalm - *Non nobis, Domine*

NOT unto us, / O Lord, not unto us, *
But to Your name / give glory,

Be / cause of Your mercy, *
Because / of Your truth.

Why / should the Gentiles say, *
So where / is their God?

But our / God is in heaven; *
He does whatever / He pleases.

Their idols / are silver and gold, *
The work / of men's hands.

They have mouths, / but they do not speak; *
Eyes they have, but they / do not see;

They have ears, / but they do not hear; *
Noses they have, but they / do not smell;

They have hands, but they do not handle; feet
they have, / but they do not walk; *
Nor do they mutter / through their throat.

Those who / make them are like them; *
So is everyone who / trusts in them.

O Isra- / el, trust in the LORD; *
He is their help / and their shield.

O house of Aa- / ron, trust in the LORD; *
He is their help / and their shield.

You who fear the / LORD, trust in the LORD; *
He is their help / and their shield.

The LORD has / been mindful of us; *
He / will bless us;

He will bless / the house of Israel; *
He will bless the house / of Aaron.

He will bless / those who fear the LORD, *
Both / small and great.

May the LORD give / you increase more and more, *
You and / your children.

May you / be blessed by the LORD, *
Who made / heaven and earth.

The heaven, even / the heavens, are the LORD's; *
But the earth He has given
to the / children of men.

The dead / do not praise the LORD, *
Nor any who go down in- / to silence.

But / we will bless the LORD *
From this time forth and
forevermore. / Praise the LORD!

Glory be to the / Father, and to the Son, *
And to the Ho- / ly Spirit

As it was / in the beginning *
Is now and will be forev- / er. Amen.

PSALM 116

Tone 1g³

Antiphon - *Inclinavit Dominus*

The   LORD   has   in - clined   His   ear   to   me.

Psalm - *Dilexi, quoniam*

I LOVE the LORD, / because He has heard *
My voice and my / supplications.

Because He has in- / clined His ear to me, *
Therefore I will call upon
Him as / long as I live.

The pains of death surrounded me, and
the pangs of Sheol / laid hold of me; *
I found trou- / ble and sorrow.

Then I called upon the / name of the LORD: *
O LORD, I implore You, de- / liver my soul!

Gracious is the / LORD, and righteous; *
Yes, our God / is merciful.

The LORD pre- / serves the simple; *
I was brought low, / and He saved me.

Return to your / rest, O my soul, *
For the LORD has dealt bounti- / fully with you.

For You have delivered / my soul from death, *
My eyes from tears, and
my / feet from falling.

I will / walk before the LORD *
In the land / of the living.

I believed, therefore I spoke,
"I am / greatly afflicted." *
I said in my haste, "All / men are liars."

What shall I / render to the LORD *
  For all His ben- / efits t'ward me?

I will take up the cup / of salvation, *
  And call upon the / name of the LORD.

I will pay my / vows to the LORD *
  Now in the presence of / all His people.

Precious in the sight of the
LORD is the / death of His saints. *
  O LORD, truly I / am Your servant;

I am Your servant, the
son / of Your maidservant; *
  You / have loosed my bonds.

I will offer to You the sacrifice / of thanksgiving, *
  And will call upon the / name of the LORD.

I will pay my / vows to the LORD *
  Now in the presence of / all His people,

In the courts / of the LORD's house, *
  In the midst of you, O
Jerusa- / lem. Praise the LORD!

Glory be to the / Father, and to the Son, *
  And to the / Holy Spirit

As it was in / the beginning *
  Is now and will be for- / ever. Amen.

PSALM 117

Tone 1g³

Antiphon - *Laudate Dominum omnes gentes*

Praise   the   LORD,   all   you   Gen - tiles.

Psalm - *Laudate Dominum omnes gentes*

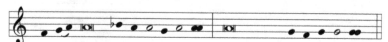

PRAISE THE LORD, / all you Gentiles! *
  Laud Him, / all you peoples!

For His merciful kind- / ness is great t'ward us, *
  And the truth of the LORD
  endures forev- / er. Praise the LORD!

Glory be to the / Father, and to the Son, *
  And to the / Holy Spirit

As it was in / the beginning *
  Is now and will be for- / ever. Amen.

PSALM 118a (1-13)

Tone 1g

Antiphon - *Non moriar sed vivam*

I shall not die but live,   and de- clare the works of the LORD.

Psalm - *Confitemini Domino... dicat nunc Israel*

OH, GIVE thanks to the LORD, / for He is good! *
For His mercy en- / dures forever.

Let / Israel now say, *
His mercy en- / dures forever.

Let the house of / Aaron now say,*
His mercy en- / dures forever.

Let those who / fear the LORD now say,*
His mercy en- / dures forever.

I called on the / LORD in distress; *
The LORD answered me and
set me / in a broad place.

The / LORD is on my side; *
I will not fear. What can / man do to me?

The LORD is for me among / those who help me; *
Therefore I shall see my
desire on / those who hate me.

It is better to / trust in the LORD *
Than to put con- / fidence in man.

It is better to / trust in the LORD *
Than to put confi- / dence in princes.

All na- / tions surrounded me, *
But in the name of the
LORD I / will destroy them.

They surrounded me, yes, / they surrounded me; *
But in the name of the
LORD I / will destroy them.

They surrounded me like bees; they were
quenched like / a fire of thorns; *
For in the name of the
LORD I / will destroy them.

You pushed me violently, / that I might fall,*
But / the LORD helped me.

Glory be to the / Father, and to the Son, *
And to the / Holy Spirit

As it was in / the beginning *
Is now and will be for- / ever. Amen.

PSALM 118b (14-28)

Tone 4a

Antiphon - *Fortitudo mea et laus*

The LORD is my strength and my song, and has be - come my sal-va- tion.

Psalm - *Fortitudo mea*

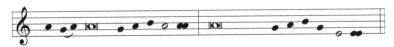

THE LORD / is my strength and song, *
And He has be- / come my salvation.

The voice of rejoicing / and salvation *
Is in the / tents of the righteous;

The right hand of the LORD does valiantly.
The right hand of the LORD / is exalted; *
The right hand of / the LORD does valiantly.

I / shall not die, but live, *
And de- / clare the works of the LORD.

The LORD has chastened / me severely, *
But He has not given / me over to death.

Open to me the gates of righteousness;
I / will go through them, *
- / And I will praise the LORD.

This is / the gate of the LORD, *
    Through which the / righteous shall enter.

I will praise You, for / You have answered me, *
    And have be- / come my salvation.

The stone which the build- / ers rejected *
    Has be- / come the chief cornerstone.

This was / the LORD's doing; *
    It is / marvelous in our eyes.

This is the day / the LORD has made; *
    We will rejoice / and be glad in it.

Save now, / I pray, O LORD; *
    O LORD, I pray, / send now prosperity.

Blessèd is he who comes
in the / name of the LORD! *

We have blessed you
from / the house of the LORD.

God is the LORD, and He has / given us light; *
    Bind the sacrifice with cords
    to the / horns of the altar.

You are my God, and / I will praise You; *
    You are my God, / I will exalt You.

Oh, give thanks to the LORD, / for He is good!*
    For His mercy / endures forever.

Glory be to the Father, / and to the Son, *
    And to / the Holy Spirit

As it was in / the beginning *
    Is now and will be / forever. Amen.

PSALM 119a (1-24)

Tone 5

Antiphon - *Tribue servo tuo*

Deal bount-i-ful - ly with Your ser-vant, that I may live, and keep Your Word.

Psalm - *Beati immaculati*

BLESSÈD are the undefiled / in the way, *
    Who walk in the / law of the LORD!

Blessèd are those who keep His testi- / monies, *
    Who seek Him / with the whole heart!

They also do no in- / iquity; *
    They / walk in His ways.

You have commanded us to
keep Your precepts dili- / gently. *
    Oh, that my ways were
    directed to / keep Your statutes!

Then I would not be / ashamed, *
    When I look into all / Your commandments.

I will praise You with uprightness / of heart, *
    When I learn Your / righteous judgments.

I will keep Your / statutes; *
    Oh, do not forsake / me utterly!

Glory be to the Father, and / to the Son, *
    And to the / Holy Spirit

As it was in the be- / ginning *
    Is now and will be for- / ever. Amen.

Psalm - *In quo corrigit?*

HOW CAN a young man cleanse / his way? *
By taking heed accord- / ing to Your word.

With my whole heart I have / sought You; *
Oh, let me not wander
from / Your commandments!

Your word I have hidden in / my heart, *
That I might not / sin against You!

Blessèd are You, / O LORD! *
Teach / me Your statutes!

With my lips I have / declared *
All the judg- / ments of Your mouth.

I have rejoiced in the way of Your testi- / monies, *
As much as / in all riches.

I will meditate on Your / precepts, *
And / contemplate Your ways.

I will delight myself in Your / statutes; *
I will / not forget Your word.

Glory be to the Father, and / to the Son, *
And to the / Holy Spirit

As it was in the be- / ginning *
Is now and will be for- / ever. Amen.

Psalm - *Retribue servo tuo*

DEAL BOUNTifully with Your / servant, *
That I may / live and keep Your word.

Open my eyes, that I / may see *
Wondrous / things from Your law.

I am a stranger in / the earth; *
Do not hide Your
com- / mandments from me.

My soul breaks with / longing *
For Your judg- / ments at all times.

You rebuke the proud, the / curséd, *
Who stray from / Your commandments.

Remove from me reproach and / contempt, *
For I have kept Your / testimonies.

Princes also sit and speak a- / gainst me, *
But Your servant meditates / on Your statutes.

Your testimonies also are my / delight *
- / And my counselors.

Glory be to the Father, and / to the Son, *
And to the / Holy Spirit

As it was in the be- / ginning *
Is now and will be for- / ever. Amen.

PSALM 119b (25-48)

Antiphon - *Deduc me, Domine*

Teach me, O Lord, the way of Your stat - utes

Psalm - *Adhaesit pavimento*

MY SOUL clings to / the dust; *
 Revive me accord- / ing to Your word.

I have declared my ways,
and You / answered me; *
 Teach me / Your statutes.

Make me understand the way of Your / precepts; *
 So shall I meditate on / Your wondrous works.

My soul melts from / heaviness; *
 Strengthen me accord- / ing to Your word.

Remove from me the way of / lying, *
 And grant me Your / law graciously.

I have chosen the way / of truth; *
 Your judgments I have laid / before me.

I cling to Your testi- / monies; *
 O Lord, do not put / me to shame!

I will run the course of Your com- / mandments, *
 For You shall / enlarge my heart.

Glory be to the Father, and / to the Son, *
 And to the Ho- / ly Spirit

As it was in the be- / ginning *
 Is now and will be forev- / er. Amen.

Psalm - *Legem pone*

TEACH ME, O Lord, the way of Your / statutes, *
 And I shall keep / it to the end.

Give me understanding, and
I shall keep / Your law; *
 Indeed, I shall observe it
 with / my whole heart.

Make me walk in the path
of Your com- / mandments, *
 For I / delight in it.

Incline my heart to Your testi- / monies,
 And not to cov- / etousness.

Turn away my eyes from
looking at / worthless things, *
 And revive / me in Your way.

Establish Your word to Your / servant, *
 Who is devoted / to fearing You.

Turn away my reproach which / I dread, *
 For Your judg- / ments are good.

Behold, I long for Your / precepts; *
 Revive me in / Your righteousness.

Glory be to the Father, and / to the Son, *
 And to the Ho- / ly Spirit

As it was in the be- / ginning *
 Is now and will be for- / ever. Amen.

Psalm - *Et veniat super me*

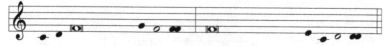

LET YOUR mercies come also to me, / O Lord *
 Your salvation accord- / ing to Your word.

So shall I have an answer for
him who re- / proaches me, *
 For I / trust in Your word.

And take not the word of truth
utterly out of / my mouth, *
    For I have hoped in Your ord- / inances.

So shall I keep Your law con- / tinually,*
    Forever / and ever.

And I will walk at / liberty, *
    For I seek / Your precepts.

I will speak of Your testimonies
also be- / fore kings, *
    And will / not be ashamed.

And I will delight myself in
Your com- / mandments, *
    Which / I have loved.

My hands also I will lift up to Your
commandments, which / I love, *
    And I will meditate on / Your statutes.

Glory be to the Father, and / to the Son, *
    And to the Ho- / ly Spirit

As it was in the be- / ginning *
    Is now and will be for- / ever. Amen.

PSALM 119c (49-72) Tone 4a

Antiphon - *Domine, vivifica me*

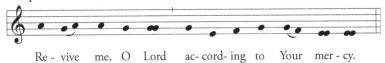

Re - vive   me, O Lord   ac- cord- ing to   Your   mer - cy.

Psalm - *Memor esto verbi tui*

REMEMber the word / to Your servant, *
    Upon which / You have caused me to hope.

This is my comfort in / my affliction, *
    For Your word / has given me life.

The proud have me in / great derision, *
    Yet I do not / turn aside from Your law.

I remembered Your judgments / of old, O Lord, *
    And / have comforted myself.

Indignation has / taken hold of me *
    Because of the wicked, / who forsake Your law.

Your statutes / have been my songs *
    In the house / of my pilgrimage.

I remember Your name / in the night, O Lord, *
    - / And I keep Your law.

This / has become mine, *
    Because / I kept Your precepts.

Glory be to the Father, / and to the Son, *
    And to / the Holy Spirit

As it was in / the beginning *
    Is now and will be / forever. Amen.

Psalm - *Portio mea, Domine*

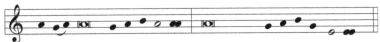

YOU ARE my / portion, O Lord; *
    I have said that / I would keep Your words.

I entreated Your favor / with my whole heart; *
    Be merciful to me ac- / cording to Your word.

I / thought about my ways, *
    And turned my feet to / Your testimonies.

I made haste, and / did not delay *
    To / keep Your commandments.

The cords of the wick- / ed have bound me, *
But I have not / forgotten Your law.

At midnight I will rise / to give thanks to You, *
Because of / Your righteous judgments.

I am a companion of / all who fear You, *
And of those / who keep Your precepts.

The earth, O Lord, is full / of Your mercy; *
- / Teach me Your statutes.

Glory be to the Father, / and to the Son, *
And to / the Holy Spirit

As it was in / the beginning *
Is now and will be / forever. Amen.

Psalm - *Bonitatem fecisti*

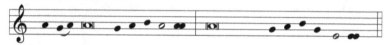

YOU HAVE dealt well
with Your / servant, O Lord, *
Ac- / cording to Your word.

Teach me good judg- / ment and knowledge, *
For I be- / lieve Your commandments.

Before I was afflicted / I went astray, *
But / now I keep Your word.

You are / good, and do good; *
- / Teach me Your statutes.

The proud have forged a / lie against me, *
But I will keep Your
pre- / cepts with my whole heart.

Their heart / is as fat as grease, *
But / I delight in Your law.

It is good for me that I have / been afflicted, *
That I / may learn Your statutes.

The law of Your mouth is / better to me *
Than thousands of coins / of gold and silver.

Glory be to the Father, / and to the Son, *
And to / the Holy Spirit

As it was in / the beginning *
Is now and will be / forever. Amen.

PSALM 119d (73-96)

Tone 8G

Antiphon - *Tuus sum ego*

I   am   Yours,   save   me,   O   Lord.

Psalm - *Manus tuae fecerunt me*

YOUR HANDS have made
me and / fashioned me; *
Give me understanding, that I
may learn / Your commandments.

Those who fear You will be
glad when they / see me, *
Because I have / hoped in Your word.

I know, O Lord, that Your judgments / are right, *
And that in faithfulness
You / have afflicted me.

Let, I pray, Your merciful
kindness be for my / comfort, *
According to Your word / to Your servant.

162

Let Your tender mercies come
to me, that I / may live; *
    For Your law / is my delight.

Let the proud be ashamed, for they
treated me wrongfully with / falsehood; *
    But I will meditate / on Your precepts.

Let those who fear You turn / to Me, *
    Those who know Your / testimonies.

Let my heart be blameless
regarding Your / statutes, *
    That I / may not be ashamed.

Glory be to the Father, and / to the Son, *
    And to the / Holy Spirit

As it was in the be- / ginning *
    Is now and will be for- / ever. Amen.

Psalm - *Deficit anima mea*

MY SOUL faints for Your sal- / vation,*
    But / I hope in Your word.

My eyes fail from searching / Your word, *
    Saying, "When / will You comfort me?"

For I have become like a wineskin / in smoke, *
    Yet I do not for- / get Your statutes.

How many are the days of Your / servant? *
    When will You execute judgment
    on those who / persecute me?

The proud have dug pits for me,
which is not according to / Your law. *
    All Your command- / ments are faithful;

They persecute me wrongfully; / help me! *
    They almost made an end of me on earth,
    but I did not for- / sake Your precepts.

Revive me according to Your loving- / kindness, *
    So that I may keep the
    testimon- / y of Your mouth.

Glory be to the Father, and / to the Son, *
    And to the / Holy Spirit

As it was in the be- / ginning *
    Is now and will be for- / ever. Amen.

Psalm - *In aeternum, Domine*

FOREVer, O Lord, Your
word is settled in / heaven. *
    Your faithfulness endures to all / generations;

You established the earth, and it / abides. *
    They continue this day according to Your
    ordinances, for all / are Your servants.

Unless Your law had been my / delight, *
    I would then have perished in / my affliction.

I will never forget Your / precepts, *
    For by them You have / given me life.

I am Yours, / save me; *
    For I have / sought Your precepts.

The wicked wait for me to de- / stroy me, *
    But I will consider Your / testimonies.

I have seen the consummation
of all per- / fection, *
    But Your commandment
    is / exceedingly broad.

Glory be to the Father, and / to the Son, *
    And to the / Holy Spirit

As it was in the be- / ginning *
    Is now and will be for- / ever. Amen.

PSALM 119e (97-120)

Antiphon - *Confirma me secundum verbum*

Up-hold me ac - cord - ing to Your Word, that I may live.

Psalm - *Quomodo dilexi!*

OH, HOW / I love Your law! *
  It is my medita- / tion all the day.

You, through Your commandments,
make me wiser / than my enemies; *
  For they are / ever with me.

I have more understanding
than / all my teachers, *
  For Your testimonies are my / meditation.

I understand more / than the ancients, *
  Because I / keep Your precepts.

I have restrained my feet from / every evil way, *
  That I / may keep Your word.

I have not departed / from Your judgments, *
  For You Your- / self have taught me.

How sweet are Your / words to my taste, *
  Sweeter than hon- / ey to my mouth!

Through Your precepts I get / understanding; *
  Therefore I hate / ev'-ry false way.

Glory be to the / Father, and to the Son, *
  And to the / Holy Spirit

As it was in / the beginning *
  Is now and will be for- / ever. Amen.

Psalm - *Lucerna pedibus meis*

YOUR WORD is a / lamp to my feet *
  And a / light to my path.

I have / sworn and confirmed *
  That I will keep Your / righteous judgments.

I am af- / flicted very much; *
  Revive me, O Lord,
  accord- / ing to Your word.

Accept, I pray, the freewill
offerings / of my mouth, O Lord, *
  And teach / me Your judgments.

My life is continual- / ly in my hand, *
  Yet I do not / forget Your law.

The wicked have / laid a snare for me, *
  Yet I have not strayed / from Your precepts.

Your testimonies I have taken
as a herit- / age forever, *
  For they are the rejoic- / ing of my heart.

I have inclined my heart
to per- / form Your statutes *
  Forever, / to the very end.

Glory be to the / Father, and to the Son, *
  And to the / Holy Spirit

As it was in / the beginning *
  Is now and will be for- / ever. Amen.

Psalm - *Iniquos odio habui*

I HATE the / doubleminded, *
 But / I love Your law.

You are my hiding / place and my shield; *
 I / hope in Your word.

Depart from me, you / evildoers, *
 For I will keep the
 command- / ments of my God!

Uphold me according to Your
 word, / that I may live; *
 And do not let me be
 a- / shamed of my hope.

Hold me up, / and I shall be safe, *
 And I shall observe Your
 stat- / utes continually.

You reject all those who
 stray / from Your statutes, *
 For their de- / ceit is falsehood.

You put away all the
 wicked / of the earth like dross; *
 Therefore I love Your / testimonies.

My flesh trem- / bles for fear of You, *
 And I am afraid / of Your judgments.

Glory be to the / Father, and to the Son, *
 And to the / Holy Spirit

As it was in / the beginning *
 Is now and will be for- / ever. Amen.

PSALM 119f (121-144)

Tone 5

Antiphon - *Faciem tuam, Domine*

Make Your face, O Lord, shine up - on Your ser- vant.

Psalm - *Feci judicium*

I HAVE done justice and / righteousness; *
 Do not leave me to / my oppressors.

Be surety for Your servant / for good; *
 Do not let the / proud oppress me.

My eyes fail from seeking Your sal- / vation *
 - / And Your righteous word.

Deal with Your servant
 according to Your / mercy, *
 And teach / me Your statutes.

I am Your servant; give me under- / standing, *
 That I may know Your / testimonies.

It is time for You to act, / O LORD, *
 For they have regarded / Your law as void.

Therefore I love Your com- / mandments *
 More than gold, / yes, than fine gold!

Therefore all Your precepts concerning
 all things I consider to / be right; *
 I hate / ev'-ry false way.

Glory be to the Father, and / to the Son, *
 And to the / Holy Spirit

As it was in the be- / ginning *
 Is now and will be for- / ever. Amen.

Psalm - *Mirabilia*

YOUR TESTimonies are / wonderful; *
 Therefore / my soul keeps them.

The entrance of Your words / gives light; *
 It gives understanding / to the simple.

I opened my mouth and / panted, *
 For I longed for / Your commandments.

Look upon me and be merciful / to me, *
 As Your custom is toward / those
 who love Your name.

Direct my steps by / Your word, *
 And let no iniquity have
 do- / minion over me.

Redeem me from the oppression / of man, *
 That I may / keep Your precepts.

Make Your face shine upon Your / servant, *
 And teach / me Your statutes.

Rivers of water run down from / my eyes, *
 Because men / do not keep Your law.

Glory be to the Father, and / to the Son, *
 And to the / Holy Spirit

As it was in the be- / ginning *
 Is now and will be for- / ever. Amen.

Psalm - *Justus es, Domine*

RIGHTEOUS are You, / O LORD, *
 And upright / are Your judgments.

Your testimonies, which
You have com- / manded, *
 Are righteous and / very faithful.

My zeal has con- / sumed me, *
 Because my enemies have
 for- / gotten Your words.

Your word is / very pure; *
 Therefore Your / servant loves it.

I am small and / despised, *
 Yet I do not for- / get Your precepts.

Your righteousness is an
everlasting / righteousness, *
 - / And Your law is truth.

Trouble and anguish have over- / taken me, *
 Yet Your commandments / are my delights.

The righteousness of Your
testimonies is ever- / lasting; *
 Give me understanding, / and I shall live.

Glory be to the Father, and / to the Son, *
 And to the / Holy Spirit

As it was in the be- / ginning *
 Is now and will be for- / ever. Amen.

PSALM 119g (145-176)

Tone 6

Antiphon - *Vivet anima mea*

Let my soul live, and it shall praise You.

Psalm - *Clamavi in toto corde meo*

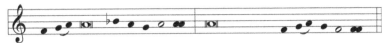

I CRY out with my whole
heart; / hear me, O LORD! *
  I will / keep Your statutes.

I / cry out to You; *
  Save me, and I will keep Your / testimonies.

I rise before the dawning / of the morning, *
  And cry for help; / I hope in Your word.

My eyes are awake through / the night watches, *
  That I may medi- / tate on Your word.

Hear my voice according
to Your / lovingkindness; *
  O LORD, revive me
  according / to Your justice.

They draw near who follow / after wickedness; *
  They are / far from Your law.

You / are near, O LORD, *
  And all Your / commandments are truth.

Concerning Your / testimonies, *
  I have known of old that You
  have founded / them forever.

Glory be to the Father, / and to the Son, *
  And to the / Holy Spirit

As it was in / the beginning *
  Is now and will be for- / ever. Amen.

Psalm - *Vide humilitatem*

CONSIDer my affliction / and deliver me, *
  For I do / not forget Your law.

Plead my cause / and redeem me; *
  Revive me ac- / cording to Your word.

Salvation is far / from the wicked, *
  For they do not / seek Your statutes.

Great are Your tender / mercies, O LORD; *
  Revive me according / to Your judgments.

Many are my persecutors / and my enemies, *
  Yet I do not turn from Your / testimonies.

I see the treacherous, and / am disgusted, *
  Because they / do not keep Your word.

Consider how I / love Your precepts; *
  Revive me, O LORD, according
  to Your / lovingkindness.

The entirety of / Your word is truth, *
  And every one of Your righteous
  judgments en- / dures forever.

Glory be to the Father, / and to the Son, *
  And to the / Holy Spirit

As it was in / the beginning *
  Is now and will be for- / ever. Amen.

Psalm - *Principes persecuti sunt*

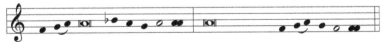

PRINCES persecute / me without a cause, *
  But my heart stands / in awe of Your word.

I re- / joice at Your word *
  As one who / finds great treasure.

I hate and / abhor lying, *
  - / But I love Your law.

Seven times a / day I praise You, *
  Because of Your / righteous judgments.

Great peace have / those who love Your law, *
  And nothing causes / them to stumble.

LORD, I hope for / Your salvation, *
  And I do / Your commandments.

My soul keeps Your / testimonies, *
  And I love / them exceedingly.

I keep Your precepts and Your / testimonies, *
  For all my ways / are before You.

Glory be to the Father, / and to the Son, *
  And to the / Holy Spirit

As it was in / the beginning *
  Is now and will be for- / ever. Amen.

Psalm - *Appropinquet deprecato*

LET MY cry come be- / fore You, O LORD; *
  Give me understanding
  ac- / cording to Your word.

Let my supplication / come before You; *
  Deliver me ac- / cording to Your word.

My / lips shall utter praise, *
  For You teach / me Your statutes.

My tongue shall / speak of Your word, *
  For all Your command- / ments
  are righteousness.

Let Your hand / become my help, *
  For I have chos- / en Your precepts.

I long for Your sal- / vation, O LORD, *
  And Your law / is my delight.

Let my soul live, and / it shall praise You; *
  And let Your / judgments help me.

I have gone astray / like a lost sheep; *
  Seek Your servant, for I do not
  forget / Your commandments.

Glory be to the Father, / and to the Son, *
  And to the / Holy Spirit

As it was in / the beginning *
  Is now and will be for- / ever. Amen.

PSALM 120

Tone 7b

Antiphon - *Clamavi, et Dominus*

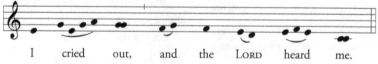

I   cried   out,   and   the   LORD   heard   me.

Psalm - *Ad Dominum clamavi*

IN MY distress / I cried to the LORD,*
  - / And He heard me.

Deliver my soul, O / LORD, from lying lips *
  And from / a deceitful tongue.

What shall be / given to you, *
  Or what shall be done
  to / you, you false tongue?

Sharp arrows / of the warrior, *
    With coals / of the broom tree!

Woe is me, that I / dwell in Meshech,*
    That I dwell among the / tents of Kedar!

My / soul has dwelt too long *
    With / one who hates peace.

- / I am for peace; *
    But when I speak, / they are for war.

Glory be to the / Father, and to the Son, *
    And to the / Holy Spirit

As it was in / the beginning *
    Is now and will be for- / ever. Amen.

PSALM 121 *Tone 1f*

Antiphon - *Auxilium meum a Domino*

My help comes from the LORD, who made hea-ven and earth.

Psalm - *Levavi oculos*

I WILL lift up my / eyes to the hills *
    From / whence comes my help?

My help / comes from the LORD, *
    Who made / heaven and earth.

He will not allow your / foot to be moved; *
    He who keeps you / will not slumber.

Behold, / He who keeps Israel *
    Shall neither / slumber nor sleep.

The LORD / is your keeper; *
    The LORD is your shade / at your right hand.

The sun shall not / strike you by day, *
    - / Nor the moon by night.

The LORD shall preserve you / from all evil; *
    He / shall preserve your soul.

The LORD shall preserve your
going out / and your coming in *
    From this time forth,
    and even / forevermore.

Glory be to the / Father, and to the Son, *
    And to the / Holy Spirit

As it was in / the beginning *
    Is now and will be for- / ever. Amen.

PSALM 122 *Tone 4g*

Antiphon - *Laetatus sum*

I was glad when they said this to me.

Psalm - *Laetatus sum*

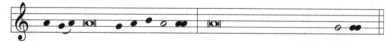

I WAS glad when / they said to me, *
    Let us go into the house of / the LORD.

Our feet have been standing within
your gates, / O Jerusalem! *
    Jerusalem is built as a city
    that is compact toge- / ther,

Where the tribes go up, the / tribes of the LORD, *
    To the Testimony of Israel, to give
    thanks to the name of the / LORD.

For thrones are set / there for judgment, *
    The thrones of the house of Da- / vid.

Pray for the peace / of Jerusalem: *
    May they prosper who love / you.

Peace be / within your walls, *
    Prosperity within your pal- / aces.

For the sake of my brethren / and companions, *
    I will now say, "Peace be within / you."

Because of the house of / the LORD our God *
    I will seek your / good.

Glory be to the Father, / and to the Son, *
    And to the Holy Spi- / rit

As it was in / the beginning *
    Is now and will be forever. / Amen.

PSALM 123

Tone 8G

Antiphon - *Qui habitas in caelis*

O You who dwell in the hea - vens, have mer-cy on us.

Psalm - *Ad te lavavi oculos meos*

UNTO You I lift up / my eyes, *
    O You who dwell / in the heavens.

Behold, as the eyes of servants look
to the hand of their / masters, *
    As the eyes of a maid to
    the hand / of her mistress,

So our eyes look to the LORD / our God, *
    Until He has / mercy on us.

Have mercy on us, O LORD, have mercy / on us! *
    For we are exceedingly / filled with contempt.

Our soul is exceedingly filled with
the scorn of those who are / at ease, *
    With the con- / tempt of the proud.

Glory be to the Father, and / to the Son, *
    And to the / Holy Spirit

As it was in the be- / ginning *
    Is now and will be for- / ever. Amen.

PSALM 124

Antiphon - *Adjutorium nostrum*

Our help is in the name of the LORD.

Psalm - *Nisi quia Dominus*

IF IT had not been the
LORD / who was on our side, *
  Let Israel now say: if it had not
  been the LORD who / was on our side,

When men rose up against us, then they
would have / swallowed us alive, *
  When their wrath was kind- / led against us;

Then the waters would have overwhelmed us,
the stream would have gone / over our soul; *
  Then the swollen waters would
  have gone / over our soul."

- / Blessèd be the LORD, *
  Who has not given us as / prey to their teeth.

Our soul has escaped as a bird
from the snare / of the fowlers; *
  The snare is broken, and / we have escaped.

Our help is in the / name of the LORD, *
  Who / made heav'n and earth.

Glory be to the / Father, and to the Son, *
  And to the / Holy Spirit

As it was in / the beginning *
  Is now and will be for- / ever. Amen.

PSALM 125

Antiphon - *In circuitu populi*

The LORD sur-rounds His peo- ple from this time forth and for-ev - er.

Psalm - *Qui confidunt*

THOSE WHO trust in the
LORD are / like Mount Zion, *
  Which cannot be moved,
  but a- / bides forever.

As the mountains sur- / round Jerusalem, *
  So the LORD surrounds His people
  from this time forth / and forever.

For the scepter of wickedness shall not rest
on the land allotted / to the righteous, *
  Lest the righteous reach out
  their hands / to iniquity.

Do good, O LORD, to / those who are good, *
  And to those who are
  up- / right in their hearts.

As for such as turn aside to their crooked
ways, the LORD shall lead them away
with the workers / of iniquity. *
  Peace be up- / on Israel!

Glory be to the / Father, and to the Son, *
  And to the / Holy Spirit

As it was in / the beginning *
  Is now and will be for- / ever. Amen.

PSALM 126

Antiphon - *Magnificavit Dominus*

The LORD has done great things for us, and we are glad.

Psalm 126 - *In convertendo*

WHEN THE LORD brought
back the captivi- / ty of Zion, *
  We / were like those who dream.

Then our mouth was / filled with laughter, *
  And our / tongue with singing.

Then they said a- / mong the nations, *
  "The LORD has done / great things for them."

The LORD has done / great things for us, *
  - / And we are glad.

Bring back our cap- / tivity, O LORD, *
  As the / streams in the South.

- / Those who sow in tears *
  - / Shall reap in joy.

He who continually / goes forth weeping, *
  Bearing / seed for sowing,

Shall doubtless come again / with rejoicing, *
  Bringing / his sheaves with him.

Glory be to the / Father, and to the Son, *
  And to the / Holy Spirit

As it was in / the beginning *
  Is now and will be for- / ever. Amen.

PSALM 127

Antiphon - *Dominus aedificet*

May the LORD build our house, and guard our ci - ty.

Psalm - *Nisi Dominus*

UNLESS the LORD builds / the house, *
  They labor in / vain who build it;

Unless the LORD guards the / city, *
  The watchman / stays awake in vain.

It is vain for you to rise up / early, *
  - / To sit up late,

To eat the bread of / sorrows; *
  For so He gives / His beloved sleep.

Behold, children are a heritage from / the LORD, *
  The fruit of the / womb is a reward.

Like arrows in the hand of a warrior,
so are the children of / one's youth. *
  Happy is the man who
  has his / quiver full of them;

They shall not be / ashamed, *
But shall speak with their
ene- / mies in the gate.

Glory be to the Father, and / to the Son, *
And to the / Holy Spirit,

As it was in the be- / ginning, *
Is now, and will be for- / ever. Amen.

PSALM 128

Tone 2

Antiphon - *Beati omnes*

Bless - èd is ev' - ry one who fears the LORD.

Psalm - *Beati omnes*

BLESSÈD is every one who fears / the LORD, *
Who walks / in His ways.

When you eat the labor of / your hands, *
You shall be happy, and
it shall / be well with you.

Your wife shall be like a fruitful vine
in the very heart of / your house, *
Your children like olive
plants all around / your table.

Behold, thus shall the man be
blessed who fears / the LORD. *
The LORD bless you out / of Zion,

And may you see the good of Je- / rusalem *
All the days / of your life.

Yes, may you see your children's / children. *
Peace be up- / on Israel!

Glory be to the Father, and / to the Son, *
And to the Ho- / ly Spirit

As it was in the be- / ginning *
Is now and will be forev- / er. Amen.

PSALM 129

Tone 8G

Antiphon - *Confundantur omnis*

Let all those be con-found - ed who hate Zi - on.

Psalm - *Saepe expugnaverunt*

MANY a time they have
afflicted me from / my youth,*
Let Is- / rael now say:

Many a time they have
afflicted me from / my youth; *
Yet they have not pre- / vailed against me.

The plowers plowed on / my back; *
  They / made their furrows long.

The LORD is / righteous; *
  He has cut in pieces the cords / of the wicked.

Let all those who hate / Zion *
  Be put to / shame and turned back.

Let them be as the grass on the / housetops, *
  Which withers be- / fore it grows up,

With which the reaper does not fill / his hand, *
  Nor he who / binds sheaves, his arms.

Neither let those who pass by them say,
  "the blessing of the LORD be up- / on you; *
  We bless you in the / name of the LORD!"

Glory be to the Father, and / to the Son, *
  And to the / Holy Spirit

As it was in the be- / ginning *
  Is now and will be for- / ever. Amen.

PSALM 130

Tone 8c

Antiphon - *De profundis*

Out of the depths I have cried to You, O LORD.

Psalm - *De profundis*

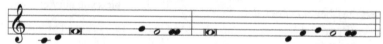

OUT OF the depths I have
cried to You, / O LORD; *
  - / Lord, hear my voice!

Let Your ears be at- / tentive *
  To the voice of my / supplications.

If You, LORD, should mark in- / iquities, *
  - / O Lord, who could stand?

But there is forgiveness / with You, *
  - / That You may be feared.

I wait for the LORD, my / soul waits, *
  And in His / word I do hope.

My soul waits for / the Lord *
  More than those who watch / for the morning

Yes, more than those who
watch for the / morning. *
  O Israel, / hope in the LORD;

For with the LORD there is / mercy, *
  And with Him is abun- / dant redemption.

And He shall redeem / Israel *
  From all / his iniquities.

Glory be to the Father, and / to the Son, *
  And to the / Holy Spirit

As it was in the be- / ginning *
  Is now and will be for- / ever. Amen.

PSALM 131

Tone 1g³

Antiphon - *Domine, non est exaltatum*

LORD, my heart is not haugh - ty.

Psalm - *Domine, non est*

LORD, MY heart / is not haughty, *
  Nor / my eyes lofty.

Neither do I concern myself / with great matters, *
  Nor with things too / profound for me.

Surely I have calmed and quieted my soul,
like a weaned child / with his mother; *
  Like a weaned child is my / soul within me.

O Israel, / hope in the LORD *
  From this time forth / and forever.

Glory be to the / Father, and to the Son, *
  And to the / Holy Spirit

As it was in / the beginning *
  Is now and will be for- / ever. Amen.

PSALM 132

Tone 3b

Antiphon - *Elegit Dominus Sion*

The LORD has cho - sen Zi - on   for   His   dwell - ing   place.

Psalm - *Memento, Domine*

LORD, REmember David
and all / his afflictions; *
  How he swore to the LORD, and
  vowed to the Mighty One / of Jacob:

Surely I will not go into
the / chamber of my house, *
  Or go up to the comfort / of my bed;

I will not give / sleep to my eyes *
  Or slumber to / my eyelids,

Until I find a / place for the LORD, *
  A dwelling place for the
  Mighty One / of Jacob.

Behold, we heard of / it in Ephrathah; *
  We found it in the fields / of the woods.

Let us go into His / tabernacle; *
  Let us worship at / His footstool.

Arise, O LORD, / to Your resting place, *
  You and the ark / of Your strength.

Let Your priests be / clothed with righteousness, *
  And let Your saints / shout for joy.

For Your / servant David's sake, *
  Do not turn away the face of Your / Anointed.

The LORD has sworn in / truth to David; *
  He will not / turn from it:

I will set upon your throne
the fruit / of your body. *
  If your sons will keep My / covenant

And My testimony which / I shall teach them, *
  Their sons also shall sit upon
  your throne for- / evermore.

For the LORD has / chosen Zion; *
  He has desired it for His / dwelling place:

"This is My resting / place forever; *
  Here I will dwell, for I have / desired it.

I will abundantly bless / her provision; *
  I will satisfy her / poor with bread.

I will also clothe her priests / with salvation, *
  And her saints shall shout a- / loud for joy.

There I will make the / horn of David grow; *
I will prepare a lamp for My / Anointed.

Glory be to the / Father, and to the Son, *
And to the Ho- / ly Spirit

His enemies / I will clothe with shame, *
But upon Himself His crown / shall flourish."

As it was in / the beginning *
Is now and will be forev- / er. Amen.

PSALM 133

Tone 1a

Antiphon - *Ecce, quam bonum*

Be - hold, how good and how plea - sant it is

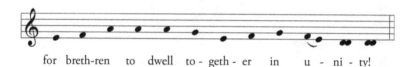

for breth-ren to dwell to - geth - er in u - ni - ty!

Psalm - *Ecce, quam bonum*

BEHOLD, how good and how / pleasant it is *
For brethren to dwell togeth- / er in unity!

It is like the precious oil upon the
head, / running down on the beard,*
  The beard of Aaron, running
  down on the edge / of his garments.

It is like the / dew of Hermon, *
Descending upon the moun- / tains of Zion;

For there the LORD command- / ed the blessing *
Life / forevermore.

Glory be to the / Father, and to the Son, *
And to the / Holy Spirit

As it was in / the beginning *
Is now and will be for- / ever. Amen.

PSALM 134

Tone 8G

Antiphon - *Misereri mihi Domine*

Have mer - cy on me, O Lord, and hear my prayer.

Psalm - *Ecce nunc*

BEHOLD, bless the LORD, all
you servants of / the LORD, *
  Who by night stand in
  the / house of the LORD!

Lift up your hands in the sanctu- / ary, *
 - / And bless the LORD.

176

The LORD who made heaven / and earth *
Bless / you from Zion!

Glory be to the Father, and / to the Son, *
and to the / Holy Spirit;

As it was in the be- / ginning *
Is now and will be for- / ever. Amen.

PSALM 135

Tone 2

Antiphon - *Laudate nomen Domini*

Praise the name of the LORD,   You who stand in the house of the LORD.

Psalm - *Laudate nomen*

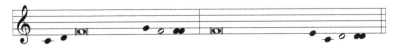

PRAISE THE LORD! Praise
the name of / the LORD; *
  Praise Him, O you servants / of the Lord!

You who stand in the house of / the LORD, *
  In the courts of the house / of our God,

Praise the LORD, for the LORD / is good; *
  Sing praises to His name, for it / is pleasant:

For the LORD has chosen Jacob for / Himself, *
  Israel for His spe- / cial treasure.

For I know that the LORD / is great, *
  And our Lord is / above all gods.

Whatever the LORD pleases / He does, *
  In heaven / and in earth,

In the seas and in all deep / places. *
  He causes the vapors to ascend
  from the ends / of the earth;

He makes lightning for / the rain; *
  He brings the wind out of / His treasuries.

He destroyed the firstborn of / Egypt, *
  Both / of man and beast.

He sent signs and wonders into
the midst of you, O / Egypt, *
  Upon Pharaoh and all / his servants.

He defeated many / nations *
  And / slew mighty kings

Sihon king of the Amorites,
Og king of / Bashan, *
  And all the kingdoms / of Canaan

And gave their land as a / heritage, *
  A heritage to Israel / His people.

Your name, O LORD, endures for- / ever, *
  Your fame, O LORD,
  throughout all gen- / erations.

For the LORD will judge His / people, *
  And He will have compassion on / His servants.

The idols of the nations are silver / and gold, *
  The work / of men's hands.

They have mouths, but they do / not speak; *
  Eyes they have, but / they do not see;

They have ears, but they do / not hear; *
  Nor is there any breath / in their mouths.

Those who make them are / like them; *
  So is everyone / who trusts in them.

Bless the LORD, O house of Is- / rael! *
  Bless the LORD, O house / of Aaron!

Bless the LORD, O house of / Levi! *
  You who fear the LORD, / bless the LORD!

Blessèd be the LORD out of / Zion, *
  Who dwells in Jerusalem! / Praise the LORD!

Glory be to the Father, and / to the Son, *
And to the Ho- / ly Spirit

As it was in the be- / ginning *
Is now and will be forev- / er. Amen.

PSALM 136a (1-9)

Tone 3g

Antiphon - *Confitemini Domino, quoniam*

Oh, give thanks to the LORD, for His mer - cy en-dures for- ev - er.

Psalm - *Confitemini Domino... confitemini Deo*

OH, GIVE thanks to the / LORD, for He is good! *
For His mercy en- / dures forever.

Oh, give thanks / to the God of gods! *
For His mercy en- / dures forever.

Oh, give thanks / to the Lord of lords! *
For His mercy en- / dures forever.

To Him who alone / does great wonders,*
For His mercy en- / dures forever.

To Him who by wisdom / made the heavens, *
For His mercy en- / dures forever.

To Him who laid out the earth a- / bove the waters, *
For His mercy en- / dures forever.

To Him / who made great lights, *
For His mercy en- / dures forever.

The sun / to rule by day, *
For His mercy en- / dures forever.

The moon and stars / to rule by night, *
For His mercy en- / dures forever.

Glory be to the / Father, and to the Son, *
And to the / Holy Spirit

As it was in / the beginning *
Is now and will be for- / ever. Amen.

PSALM 136b (10-26)

Tone 3g

Antiphon - *Confitemini Domino, quia*

Oh, give thanks to the LORD, who re-mem-bered us in our low - ly state.

Psalm - *Qui percussit Aegyptum*

TO HIM who struck Egypt / in their firstborn, *
For His mercy en- / dures forever.

And brought out Israel / from among them, *
For His mercy en- / dures forever.

With a strong hand,
and / with an outstretched arm, *
For His mercy en- / dures forever.

To Him who divided the / Red Sea in two, *
For His mercy en- / dures forever.

And made Israel pass / through the midst of it, *
  For His mercy en- / dures forever.

But overthrew Pharaoh and
his army / in the Red Sea, *
  For His mercy en- / dures forever.

To Him who led His
people / through the wilderness, *
  For His mercy en- / dures forever.

To Him who / struck down great kings,*
  For His mercy en- / dures forever.

And / slew famous kings, *
  For His mercy en- / dures forever.

Sihon / king of the Amorites, *
  For His mercy en- / dures forever.

And Og / king of Bashan, *
  For His mercy en- / dures forever.

And gave their / land as a heritage, *
  For His mercy en- / dures forever.

A heritage to / Israel His servant, *
  For His mercy en- / dures forever.

Who remembered us / in our lowly state,*
  For His mercy en- / dures forever.

And rescued us / from our enemies, *
  For His mercy en- / dures forever.

Who gives / food to all flesh, *
  For His mercy en- / dures forever.

Oh, give thanks to the / God of heaven!*
  For His mercy en- / dures forever.

Glory be to the / Father, and to the Son, *
  And to the / Holy Spirit

As it was in / the beginning *
  Is now and will be for- / ever. Amen.

PSALM 137

Antiphon - *Adhaereat lingua mea*

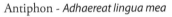

Let   my   tongue cling to   the   roof of   my mouth,

if I do not re - mem - ber you, Je - ru - sa - lem.

Psalm - *Super Flumina*

BY THE rivers of Babylon, there we sat down,
yea, we wept when we re- / membered Zion. *
  We hung our harps upon
  the willows in / the midst of it.

For there those who carried us
away captive asked / of us a song, *
  And those who plundered
  us re- / quested mirth,

Saying, "Sing us one of the / songs of Zion!" *
  How shall we sing the LORD's
  song in a / foreign land?

If I forget you, / O Jerusalem, *
  Let my right hand for- / get its skill!

If I do not remember you, let my tongue
cling to the / roof of my mouth *
  If I do not exalt Jerusalem
  above / my chief joy.

Remember, O LORD, against the / sons of Edom *
  The day of Jer- / usalem,

Who said, / "Raze it, raze it, *
  To its very / foundation!"

O daughter of Babylon,
who / are to be destroyed, *
    Happy the one who repays
    you as you / have served us!

Happy the one who / takes and dashes *
    Your little ones a- / gainst the rock!

Glory be to the / Father, and to the Son, *
    And to the Ho- / ly Spirit

As it was / in the beginning *
    Is now and will be forev- / er. Amen.

PSALM 138

Antiphon - *Confitebor nomine tuo*

I   will   praise   Your   name,   O   Lord,   for

Your   lov - ing - kind - ness   and   Your   truth.

Psalm - *Confitebor Tibi*

I WILL praise You with my / whole heart; *
    Before the gods I will sing / praises to You.

I will worship toward Your holy / temple, *
    - / And praise Your name

For Your lovingkindness and / Your truth; *
    For You have magnified
    Your / word above all Your name.

In the day when I cried out, You / answered me, *
    And made me bold with / strength in my soul.

All the kings of the earth
shall praise / You, O LORD, *
    When they hear the / words of Your mouth.

Yes, they shall sing of the ways of the
LORD, for great is the glory / of the LORD. *
    Though the / LORD is on high,

Yet He regards the / lowly; *
    But the proud He / knows from afar.

Though I walk in the midst of
trouble, You will re- / vive me; *
    You will stretch out Your hand
    against the wrath / of my enemies,

And Your right hand will / save me. *
    The LORD will perfect
    that / which concerns me;

Your mercy, O LORD, endures for- / ever; *
    Do not forsake the / works of Your hands.

Glory be to the Father, and / to the Son, *
    And to the / Holy Spirit

As it was in the be- / ginning *
    Is now and will be for- / ever. Amen.

PSALM 139a (1-12)

Antiphon - *Domine, probasti me*

O LORD, You have searched me and have known me.

Psalm - *Domine, probasti me*

O LORD, You have / searched
me and known me. *
  You know my sitting down /
  and my rising up;

You understand my / thought afar off. *
  You comprehend my path and my lying
  down, and are ac- / quainted with all my ways.

For there is not a / word on my tongue, *
  But behold, O LORD,
  You know / it altogether.

You have hedged me be- / hind and before, *
  And laid / Your hand upon me.

Such knowledge is too / wonderful for me; *
  It is high, I / cannot attain it.

Where can I go / from Your Spirit? *
  Or where can / I flee from Your presence?

If I ascend into / heaven, You are there; *
  If I make my bed in hell,
  / behold, You are there.

If I take the / wings of the morning, *
  And dwell in the utter- / most parts of the sea,

Even there Your / hand shall lead me,*
  And / Your right hand shall hold me.

If I say, "Surely the / darkness shall fall on me," *
  Even the night shall / be light about me;

Indeed, the darkness shall not hide from
You, but the night / shines as the day; *
  The darkness and the light /
  are both alike to You.

Glory be to the / Father, and to the Son, *
  And to / the Holy Spirit

As it was in / the beginning *
  Is now and will be / forever. Amen.

PSALM 139b (13-24)

Antiphon - *Mirabilia opera tua*

Mar - ve - lous are Your works, O Lord,

and that my soul knows ve - ry well.

Psalm - *Confitebor tibi quia*

FOR YOU formed / my inward parts; *
   You covered me in / my mother's womb.

I will praise You, for I am
fearfully and / wonderfully made; *
   Marvelous are Your works, and
   that my / soul knows very well.

My frame was not hidden from
You, when I was / made in secret, *
   And skillfully wrought in the
   lowest / parts of the earth.

Your eyes saw my
substance, / being yet unformed. *
   And in Your book they / all were written,

The days / fashioned for me, *
   When as yet there / were none of them.

How precious also are
Your / thoughts to me, O God! *
   How great is / the sum of them!

If I should count them, they would be
more in / number than the sand; *
   When I awake, I / am still with You.

Oh, that You would slay the / wicked, O God! *
   Depart from me, therefore,
   you / bloodthirsty men.

For they speak a- / gainst You wickedly;*
   Your enemies take / Your name in vain.

Do I not hate them, O / Lord, who hate You? *
   And do I not loathe those
   who rise / up against You?

I hate them with / perfect hatred; *
   I count them / my enemies.

Search me, O / God, and know my heart; *
   Try me, and know / my anxieties;

And see if there is any / wicked way in me, *
   And lead me in the way / everlasting.

Glory be to the Father, / and to the Son, *
   And to the / Holy Spirit

As it was / in the beginning *
   Is now and will be for- / ever. Amen.

PSALM 140

Antiphon - *Ne derelinquas me*

Do not for- sake   me,   O   Lord,   the strength of my   sal - va- tion.

Psalm - *Eripe me, Domine*

DELIVer me, O Lord, / from evil men; *
   Preserve / me from violent men,

Who plan evil / things in their hearts; *
   They continually gather / together for war.

They sharpen their tongues / like a serpent; *
   The poison of asps / is under their lips.

Keep me, O Lord, from
the hands / of the wicked; *
   Preserve / me from violent men,

Who have purposed to make / my steps stumble. *
   The proud have hidden
   a / snare for me, and cords;

182

They have spread a net / by the wayside; *
They / have set traps for me.

I said to the LORD: / "You are my God; *
Hear the voice of my / supplications, O LORD.

O God the Lord, the strength of / my salvation, *
You have covered my head
in / the day of battle.

Do not grant, O LORD,
the desires / of the wicked; *
Do not further his wicked
scheme, lest / they be exalted.

"As for the head of those / who surround me, *
Let the evil / of their lips cover them;

Let burning coals fall upon them;
let them be / cast into the fire, *

Into deep pits, that they / rise not up again.

Let not a slanderer be est- / ablished in the earth; *
Let evil hunt the violent
man / to overthrow him."

I know that the LORD will maintain
the cause of / the afflicted, *
And / justice for the poor.

Surely the righteous shall
give / thanks to Your name; *
The upright shall / dwell in Your presence.

Glory be to the Father, / and to the Son, *
And to / the Holy Spirit

As it was in / the beginning *
Is now and will be / forever. Amen.

PSALM 141

Antiphon - *Domine, clamavi*

O   LORD,   I   cry   out   to   you,   hear   me!

Psalm - *Domine, clamavi*

LORD, I cry out to You; make / haste to me! *
Give ear to my voice when / I cry out to You.

Let my prayer be set before You as / incense, *
The lifting up of my hands
as the / evening sacrifice.

Set a guard, O LORD, over / my mouth; *
Keep watch over the / door of my lips.

Do not incline my heart to any
evil thing, to practice wicked works
with men who work in- / iquity; *
And do not let me eat of / their delicacies.

Let the righteous strike me;
it shall be a / kindness. *
And let him rebuke me;
it shall be as / excellent oil;

Let my head not re- / fuse it. *
For still my prayer is against
the deeds / of the wicked.

Their judges are overthrown
by the sides / of the cliff, *
And they hear my words, / for they are sweet.

Our bones are scattered at
the mouth / of the grave, *
As when one plows and / breaks up the earth.

But my eyes are upon You, O / God the Lord; *
In You I take refuge; do
not leave / my soul destitute.

Keep me from the snares they have / laid for me, *
And from the traps of
the workers / of iniquity.

Let the wicked fall into their / own nets, *
   While I / escape safely.

Glory be to the Father, and / to the Son, *
   And to the / Holy Spirit

As it was in the be- / ginning *
   Is now and will be for- / ever. Amen.

PSALM 142

Tone 2

Antiphon - *Eripe me*

Res-cue me   from my en-e-mies, O Lord,   in You I take re-fuge.

Psalm - *Voce mea ad Dominum*

I CRY out to the LORD with / my voice; *
   With my voice to the LORD
   I make my sup- / plication.

I pour out my complaint be- / fore Him; *
   I declare before Him / my trouble.

When my spirit was overwhelmed with- / in me, *
   Then You / knew my path.

In the way in which / I walk *
   They have secretly set a / snare for me.

Look on my right hand / and see, *
   For there is no one who ac- / knowledges me;

Refuge has / failed me; *
   No one cares / for my soul.

I cried out to You, / O LORD: *
   I said, "You are my refuge, my
   portion in the land of / the living.

Attend to my cry, for I am brought / very low; *
   Deliver me from my persecutors,
   for they are strong- / er than I.

Bring my soul out of / prison, *
   That I may / praise Your name;

The righteous shall sur- / round me, *
   For You shall deal bountiful- / ly with me."

Glory be to the Father, and / to the Son, *
   And to the Ho- / ly Spirit

As it was in the be- / ginning *
   Is now and will be forev- / er. Amen.

PSALM 143

Tone 8G

Antiphon - *Propter nomen tuum*

For your name's sake, O Lord,   re-vive me in your right-eous-ness.

Psalm - *Domine, exaudi*

HEAR MY prayer, O LORD, give
ear to my suppli- / cations! *
   In Your faithfulness answer me,
   and / in Your righteousness.

Do not enter into judgment with Your / servant, *
   For in Your sight no one liv- / ing is righteous.

For the enemy has persecuted / my soul; *
   He has crushed / my life to the ground;

He has made me dwell in / darkness, *
   Like those who / have long been dead.

Therefore my spirit is
overwhelmed with- / in me; *
   My heart within / me is distressed.

I remember the days of old;
I meditate on all / Your works; *
   I muse on the / work of Your hands.

I spread out my / hands to You; *
   My soul longs for You / like a thirsty land.

Answer me speedily, O LORD; my / spirit fails! *
   Do not hide Your face from me, lest I be
   like those who go / down into the pit.

Cause me to hear Your
loving-kindness in the / morning, *
   For in / You do I trust;

Cause me to know the way
in which / I should walk, *
   For I lift / up my soul to You.

Deliver me, O LORD, from my / enemies; *
   In You / I take shelter.

Teach me to do Your will, for You are / my God; *
   Your Spirit is good. Lead me
   in the land / of uprightness.

Revive me, O LORD, for Your / name's sake! *
   For Your righteousness' sake
   bring my soul / out of trouble.

In Your mercy cut off my enemies, and destroy
all those who afflict / my soul; *
   For I / am Your servant.

Glory be to the Father, and / to the Son, *
   And to the / Holy Spirit

As it was in the be- / ginning *
   Is now and will be for- / ever. Amen.

PSALM 144

Antiphon - *Benedictus Dominus susceptor*

Bless-èd be the LORD, my help - er and my de - liv - er - er.

Psalm - *Benedictus Dominus*

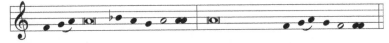

BLESSÈD be / the LORD my Rock, *
   Who trains my hands for war,
   and my fin- / gers for battle;

My lovingkindness / and my fortress, *
   My high tower and my / deliverer,

My shield and the One in whom / I take refuge, *
   Who subdues my / people under me.

LORD, what is man, that You
take / knowledge of him? *
   Or the son of man, that
   You are / mindful of him?

Man / is like a breath; *
His days are like a / passing shadow.

Bow down Your heavens,
O / Lord, and come down; *
Touch the mountains, / and
they shall smoke.

Flash forth lightning / and scatter them; *
Shoot out Your arrows / and destroy them.

Stretch out Your / hand from above; *
Rescue me and deliver
me out / of great waters,

From the hand of foreigners,
whose / mouth speaks vain words, *
And whose right hand is a
right / hand of falsehood.

I will sing a new / song to You, O God; *
On a harp of ten strings
I will sing / praises to You,

The One who gives sal- / vation to kings, *
Who delivers David His
servant / from the deadly sword.

Rescue me and deliver me from the hand of
foreigners, whose / mouth speaks lying words, *
And whose right hand is a
right / hand of falsehood.

That our sons may be as plants
grown / up in their youth; *
That our daughters may be as
pillars, sculptured / in palace style;

That our / barns may be full, *
Supplying all / kinds of produce;

That our sheep may / bring forth thousands*
And ten / thousands in our fields;

That our oxen may be well-laden; that there be
no breaking / in or going out;*
That there be no / outcry in our streets.

Happy are the people who / are in such a state; *
Happy are the people
whose / God is the Lord!

Glory be to the Father, / and to the Son, *
And to the / Holy Spirit

As it was in / the beginning *
Is now and will be for- / ever. Amen.

PSALM 145

Antiphon - *Magnus Dominus et laudabilis*

Great is the Lord, and great - ly to be praised;

and His great - ness is in - fin - ite.

Psalm - *Exaltabo te, Deus*

I WILL extol You, / my God, O King; *
And I will bless Your name fore- / ver and ever.

Every day / I will bless You, *
And I will praise Your
name fore- / ver and ever.

Great is the LORD, and / greatly to be praised; *
And His greatness / is unsearchable.

One generation shall praise
Your works / to another, *
And shall de- / clare Your mighty acts.

I will meditate on the glorious
splendor / of Your majesty, *
And / on Your wondrous works.

Men shall speak of the
might / of Your awesome acts, *
And I will de- / clare Your greatness.

They shall utter the memory
of / Your great goodness, *
And shall sing / of Your righteousness.

The LORD is gracious and full / of compassion, *
Slow to anger and / great in mercy.

The / LORD is good to all, *
And His tender mercies
are / over all His works.

All Your works shall / praise You, O LORD, *
And Your / saints shall bless You.

They shall speak of the glory / of Your kingdom, *
And / talk of Your power,

To make known to the sons
of / men His mighty acts, *
And the glorious majesty / of His kingdom.

Your kingdom is an ever- / lasting kingdom, *
And Your dominion endures
throughout all / generations.

The LORD up- / holds all who fall, *
And raises up / all who are bowed down.

The eyes of all look ex- / pectantly to You,*
And You give them their food / in due season.

You / open Your hand *
And satisfy the desire of / every living thing.

The LORD is righteous / in all His ways,*
Gra- / cious in all His works.

The LORD is near to all who / call upon Him,*
To all who call / upon Him in truth.

He will fulfill the desire
of / those who fear Him; *
He also will hear their / cry and save them.

The LORD preserves / all who love Him,*
But all the wick- / ed He will destroy.

My mouth shall speak the / praise of the LORD, *
And all flesh shall bless His
holy name fore- / ver and ever.

Glory be to the / Father, and to the Son, *
And to the / Holy Spirit

As it was in / the beginning *
Is now and will be for- / ever. Amen.

PSALM 146

Antiphon - *Lauda anima mea*

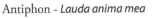

Praise the LORD, O my soul, who rais - es

the fal - len and loves the right - eous.

Psalm - *Lauda, anima mea*

PRAISE THE LORD! Praise the LORD, O my
soul! While I live / I will praise the LORD; *
  I will sing praises to my
  God while / I have my being.

Do not put your / trust in princes, *
  Nor in a son of man,
  in / whom there is no help.

His spirit departs, he re- / turns to his earth; *
  In that very day / his plans perish.

Happy is he who has the
God of / Jacob for his help, *
  Whose hope is / in the LORD his God,

Who made / heaven and earth, *
  The sea, and all / that is in them;

Who keeps / truth forever, *
  Who executes justice / for the oppressed,

Who gives food / to the hungry. *
  The LORD gives freedom / to the prisoners.

The LORD opens the / eyes of the blind; *
  The LORD raises those / who are bowed down;

The LORD / loves the righteous. *
  The LORD watches o- / ver the strangers;

He relieves the father- / less and widow; *
  But the way of the wicked
  He / turns upside down.

The LORD shall / reign forever *
  Your God, O Zion, to all
  gener- / ations. Praise the LORD!

Glory be to the Father, / and to the Son, *
  And to the / Holy Spirit

As it was in / the beginning *
  Is now and will be for- / ever. Amen.

PSALM 147a (1-11)

Tone 8c

Antiphon - *Deo nostro jucunda*

It   is   pleas - ant   to   praise   our   God.

Psalm - *Laudate Dominum quoniam bonum*

PRAISE THE LORD! For it is
good to sing praises to / our God; *
  For it is pleasant, and / praise is beautiful.

The LORD builds up Je- / rusalem; *
  He gathers together the out- / casts of Israel.

He heals the broken / hearted *
  And / binds up their wounds.

He counts the number / of the stars; *
  He calls / them all by name.

Great is our Lord, and mighty / in power; *
  His understanding / is infinite.

The LORD lifts up the / humble; *
  He casts the wicked / down to the ground.

Sing to the LORD with thanks- / giving; *
  Sing praises on the / harp to our God,

Who covers the heavens with clouds,
who prepares rain / for the earth, *
  Who makes grass to grow / on the mountains.

He gives to the beast / its food, *
And to the young / ravens that cry.

He does not delight in the
strength / of the horse; *
He takes no pleasure in the / legs of a man.

The LORD takes pleasure in those who / fear Him, *
In those who hope / in His mercy.

Glory be to the Father, and / to the Son, *
And to the / Holy Spirit

As it was in the be- / ginning *
Is now and will be for- / ever. Amen.

PSALM 147b (12-20)

Tone 1g³

Antiphon - *Lauda Jerusalem*

Praise the LORD, O Je - ru - sa - lem.

Psalm - *Lauda Jerusalem*

PRAISE THE LORD, / O Jerusalem! *
Praise your / God, O Zion!

For He has strengthened the / bars of your gates; *
He has blessed your / children within you.

He makes / peace in your borders, *
And fills you with / the finest wheat.

He sends out His com- / mand to the earth;*
His word runs / very swiftly.

He / gives snow like wool; *
He scatters the / frost like ashes;

He casts out His / hail like morsels; *
Who can stand / before His cold?

He sends out His / word and melts them; *
He causes His wind to blow,
and / the waters flow.

He declares His / word to Jacob, *
His statutes and His judgments / to Israel.

He has not dealt thus with / any nation; *
And as for His judgments, they have
not known / them. Praise the LORD!

Glory be to the / Father, and to the Son, *
And to the / Holy Spirit

As it was in / the beginning *
Is now and will be for- / ever. Amen.

PSALM 148

Tone 1g

Antiphon - *Laudate Dominum de caelis*

Praise the LORD from the heav - ens.

Psalm - *Laudate Dominum de caelis*

PRAISE THE LORD! Praise
the LORD / from the heavens; *
  Praise / Him in the heights!

Praise Him, / all His angels; *
  Praise / Him, all His hosts!

Praise / Him, sun and moon; *
  Praise Him, / all you stars of light!

Praise Him, you hea- / vens of heavens, *
  And you waters a- / bove the heavens!

Let them praise the / name of the LORD, *
  For He commanded and they / were created.

He also established them fore- / ver and ever; *
  He made a decree which shall / not pass away.

Praise the / LORD from the earth, *
  You great sea crea- / tures and all the depths;

Fire and / hail, snow and clouds; *
  Stormy wind, ful- / filling His word;

Moun- / tains and all hills; *
  Fruitful trees / and all cedars;

Beasts / and all cattle; *
  Creeping / things and flying fowl;

Kings of the earth / and all peoples; *
  Princes and all / judges of the earth;

Both young / men and maidens; *
  Old / men and children.

Let them praise the / name of the LORD,*
  For His name alone / is exalted;

His glory is above the / earth and heaven. *
  And He has exalted the horn / of His people,

The praise of all His saints --
of the child- / ren of Israel, *
  A people near / to Him. Praise the LORD!

Glory be to the Father, / and to the Son, *
  And to the / Holy Spirit

As it was in / the beginning *
  Is now and will be for- / ever. Amen.

PSALM 149

Tone 8c

Antiphon - *Filii Sion*

Let the child-ren of Zi - on   be joy - ful in their King.

Psalm - *Cantate Domino... laus eius*

PRAISE THE LORD! Sing
to the LORD a / new song, *
  And His praise in the as- / sembly of saints.

Let Israel rejoice in their / Maker; *
  Let the children of Zion
  be / joyful in their King.

Let them praise His name with / the dance; *
  Let them sing praises to Him
  with the / timbrel and harp.

For the LORD takes pleasure in His / people; *
  He will beautify the humble / with salvation.

Let the saints be joyful in / glory; *
Let them sing a- / loud on their beds.

Let the high praises of God be in / their mouth, *
And a two-edged / sword in their hand,

To execute vengeance on the / nations,*
And punishments / on the peoples;

To bind their kings / with chains, *
And their nobles with fet- / ters of iron;

To execute on them the written / judgment *
This honor have all / His
saints. Praise the LORD!

Glory be to the Father, and / to the Son, *
And to the / Holy Spirit

As it was in the be- / ginning *
Is now and will be for- / ever. Amen.

PSALM 150

Antiphon - *Omnis spiritus*

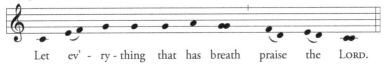

Let ev' - ry - thing that has breath praise the LORD.

Psalm - *Laudate Dominum in sanctis*

PRAISE THE LORD! Praise God in His / sanctuary; *
Praise Him in His / mighty firmament!

Praise Him / for His mighty acts; *
Praise Him according
to His / excellent greatness!

Praise Him with the / sound of the trumpet; *
Praise Him / with the lute and harp!

Praise Him with the / timbrel and dance; *
Praise Him with stringed /
instruments and flutes!

Praise Him / with loud cymbals; *
Praise Him with / clashing cymbals!

Let everything that has / breath praise the LORD. *
- / Praise you the LORD!

Glory be to the / Father, and to the Son, *
And to the / Holy Spirit

As it was in / the beginning *
Is now and will be for- / ever. Amen.

THE CANTICLES

CANTICLE 1

Antiphon - *Tres pueri*

The three young men were thrown in - to the fur - nace

by the king's or - der, they feared not the flames

but said: bless - èd be God! Al - le - lu - ia!

Canticle - *Benedicite omnia opera*

ALL YOU, works of the Lord, / bless the Lord! *
Praise and exalt Him above / all forever.

YOU HEAvens, / bless the Lord! *
You angels of the / Lord, bless the Lord!

ALL YOU waters that are above
the heavens, / bless the Lord! *
All you powers of the / Lord, bless the Lord!

YOU SUN and moon, / bless the Lord! *
You stars of / heaven, bless the Lord!

EV'RY shower and dew, / bless the Lord! *
All you / winds, bless the Lord!

YOU FIRE and heat, / bless the Lord! *
You winter and sum- / mer, bless the Lord!

YOU DEWS and storms
of snow, / bless the Lord! *
You frost and / cold, bless the Lord!

YOU ICE and snow, / bless the Lord! *
You nights and / days, bless the Lord!

YOU LIGHT and darkness, / bless the Lord! *
You lightnings and / clouds, bless the Lord!

LET THE earth, / bless the Lord! *
Praise and exalt Him above / all forever.

YOU MOUNtains and little
hills, / bless the Lord! *
You things that grow in
the / earth, bless the Lord!

YOU FOUNtains, / bless the Lord! *
You seas and / rivers, bless the Lord!

YOU WHALES and all that move
in the waters, / bless the Lord! *
All you birds of the / air, bless the Lord!

ALL YOU beasts and cattle, / bless the Lord! *
You children of / men, bless the Lord!

LET ISrael, / bless the Lord! *
Praise and exalt Him above / all forever.

YOU PRIESTS of the Lord, / bless the Lord! *
You servants of the / Lord, bless the Lord!

YOU SPIRits and souls of
the righteous, / bless the Lord! *
　　You holy men and humble
　　of / heart, bless the Lord!

HANAniah, Azaraiah, Mishael, / bless the Lord! *
　　Praise and exalt Him above / all forever.

LET US bless the Father, and
the Son, and the Holy / Spirit. *
　　Let us praise and exalt
　　Him above / all forever.

BLESSÈD are You, Lord, in
the firmament of / heaven. *
　　And above all to be praised
　　and glori- / fied forever.

GLORY be to the Father, and / to the Son, *
　　And to the / Holy Spirit

AS IT was in the be- / ginning *
　　Is now and will be for- / ever. Amen.
　　　　　　　　　　　　Apocryphal Daniel 3:35-66, 34

CANTICLE 2　　　　　　　　　　　　　　　*Tone 1f*

Antiphon - *Laudamus nomen tuum*

We　　praise　Your　glor - i - ous name,　　our　　God

Canticle - *Benedictus es, Dominus Deus Israel*

BLESSÈD are You, Lord / God of Israel, *
　　Our Father forev- / er and ever.

YOURS, O Lord, is the greatness,
the power / and the glory, *
　　The victory and / the majesty;

FOR ALL that is in heaven /
and in earth is Yours; *
　　Yours is the kingdom, O Lord, and
　　You are exalted as / head over all.

BOTH RICHes and / honor come from You, *
　　And You / reign over all.

IN YOUR hand is / power and might; *
　　In Your hand it is to make
　　great and / to give strength to all.

NOW THEREfore, our / God, we thank You *
　　And　praise / Your glorious name.

GLORY be to the / Father, and to the Son, *
　　And to the / Holy Spirit

AS IT was in / the beginning *
　　Is now and will be for- / ever. Amen.
　　　　　　　　　　　　I Chronicles 29:10-13

CANTICLE 3　　　　　　　　　　　　　　　*Tone 7a*

Antiphon - *Exaltate Regem*

Ex - tol　　　the ev - er - last - ing King　for　His　works.

Canticle - *Magnus es Domine*

BLESSÈD be God who / lives forever, *
And blessèd / be His kingdom.

FOR HE scourges, and has mercy; He leads
down to hell, / and brings up again; *
    Neither is there any
    who / can avoid His hand.

CONFESS Him before the Gentiles,
you child- / ren of Israel; *
    For He has scattered / us among them.

THERE DE- / clare His greatness, *
    And extol Him be- / fore the living;

FOR HE / is our Lord—, *
    And He is the God our / Father forever.

AND HE will scourge us for / our iniquities *
And will have / mercy again,

AND WILL gather us out / of all nations, *
    Among whom / he has scattered us.

IF YOU turn to Him with your whole
heart and / with your whole mind, *
    And deal upright- / ly before Him,

THEN HE / will turn to you, *
    And will not hide / His face from you.

THEREFORE see what / He will do with you; *
    And confess Him / with your whole mouth,

AND PRAISE / the Lord of might, *
    And extol the ev- / erlasting King.

IN THE land of my captivity / do I praise Him, *
    And declare His might and
    majesty to / a sinful nation.

O YOU sinners, turn and
do jus- / tice before Him, *
    Who can tell if He will accept
    you and have / mercy on you?

I WILL extol my God; and my soul
shall praise the / King of Heaven, *
    And shall rejoice / in His greatness.

LET ALL / men— speak—, *
    And let all praise Him for / His righteousness.

O JErusalem, the holy city, He will
scourge you / for your children's works, *
    And will have mercy again
    on the sons / of the righteous.

GIVE PRAISE / to the Lord—, *
    - / For He is good.

AND PRAISE the / everlasting King, *
    That His tabernacle may be
    built in you / again with joy.

AND LET Him make joyful there
in you those / who are captives, *
    And love in you forever
    those who / are miserable.

GLORY be to the / Father, and to the Son, *
    And to the / Holy Spirit

AS IT was in / the beginning *
    Is now and will be for- / ever. Amen.

Tobit 13:1-10

CANTICLE 4

Tone 4g

Antiphon - *Domine, magnus es tu*

O   Lord,   You   are   great   and   splen - did   in   Your strength.

Canticle - *Hymnum Cantamus Domino*

LET US sing a / hymn to the Lord. *
Let us sing to our God a new / song:

O LORD God, You are / great and glorious, *
Wonderful in strength, and invinci- / ble.

LET ALL / creatures serve You: *
For You spoke, and they were / made,

YOU SENT forth Your
Spirit, / and created them, *
And there is none that can resist Your / voice.

FOR THE mountains shall be moved
from their foundations / with the waters,*
The rocks shall melt as
wax at Your pre- / sence:

YET YOU / are merciful *
To all who fear / You.

WOE TO the nations that rise up
against my kindred! The Lord Almighty
will take ven- / geance upon them *
In the day of judg- / ment,

IN PUTting fire and / worms in their flesh; *
And they shall feel them, and weep forev- / er.

GLORY be to the Father, / and to the Son, *
And to the Holy / Spirit

AS IT was in / the beginning *
Is now and will be forever. / Amen.

Judith 16:13-15, 17

CANTICLE 5

Tone 4a

Antiphon - *Populus meus*

My peo-ple shall be sat- is- fied with My good-ness says the LORD.

Canticle - *Audite verbum Domini*

HEAR THE word of the / LORD, O nations, *
And declare it in / the isles afar off

AND SAY, "He who scattered
Israel / will gather him, *
And keep him as a / shepherd does his flock.

FOR THE LORD has / redeemed Jacob,*
And ransomed him from the
hand of / one stronger than he.

THEREFORE they shall come
and sing in the / height of Zion, *
Streaming to / the goodness of the LORD

FOR WHEAT and / new wine and oil, *
For the young of / the flock and the herd;

THEIR SOULS shall be
like a well / watered garden, *
And they shall sor- / row no more at all.

THEN SHALL the virgin
re- / joice in the dance, *
And the young men and / the old, together;

FOR I will turn their / mourning to joy, *
I will comfort them and make
them rejoice / rather than sorrow.

I WILL satiate the soul of
the priests / with abundance, *
And My people shall be satisfied
with / My goodness, says the LORD."

GLORY be to the Father, / and to the Son, *
And to / the Holy Spirit

AS IT was in / the beginning *
Is now and will be / forever. Amen.

Jeremiah 31:10-14

CANTICLE 6

Tone 5

Antiphon - *In Domino justificabitur*

In the LORD all the de - scen-dants of Is - ra - el

shall be jus - ti - fied and shall glo - ry.

Canticle - *Vere tu es Deus absconditus*

TRULY You are God, who hide / Yourself, *
O God of Isra- / el, the Savior!

THEY SHALL be ashamed and
also disgraced, / all of them; *
They shall go in confusion together,
who are mak- / ers of idols.

BUT ISrael shall be saved by the
LORD with an everlasting sal- / vation; *
You shall not be ashamed or
disgraced fore- / ver and ever.

FOR THUS says the LORD,
who created the / heavens, *
Who is God, who formed the earth and
made it, who / has established it,

WHO DID not create it in vain,
who formed it to be in- / habited: *
I am the LORD, and there / is no other.

I HAVE not spoken in / secret, *
In a dark / place of the earth;

I DID not say to the seed of
Jacob, "Seek Me / in vain;" *
I the LORD, speak righteousness,
I declare / things that are right.

ASSEMble yourselves and
come; draw near to- / gether, *
You who have escaped / from the nations.

THEY HAVE no knowledge, who carry
the wood of their carved / image *
And pray to a / god that cannot save.

TELL AND bring forth your case;
yes, let them take counsel to- / gether. *
Who has declared this from ancient time?
Who has / told it from that time?

HAVE NOT I, the LORD? And there
is no other God be- / sides Me, *
A just God and a Savior;
there is / none besides Me.

LOOK TO Me, and be saved,
all you ends of / the earth! *
For I am God and there / is no other.

I HAVE sworn by Myself; the word has gone
out of My mouth in / righteousness, *
And / shall not return,

THAT TO me every knee / shall bow, *
Every / tongue shall take an oath.

HE SHALL say, "Surely in the LORD
I have righteousness / and strength. *
  To Him men shall come, and all shall be
  ashamed who are in- / censed against Him.

IN THE LORD all the descendants of / Israel *
  Shall be justified, / and shall glory."

GLORY be to the Father, and / to the Son, *
  And to the / Holy Spirit

AS IT was in the be- / ginning *
  Is now and will be for- / ever. Amen.

Isaiah 45:15-25

CANTICLE 7

Tone 3a

Antiphon - *Ostende nobis*

Show us,　O　Lord,　the　light　of　Your　mer - cies.

Canticle - *Miserere Nostri, Deus Universi*

HAVE MERcy upon us, O Lord
God of all, / and behold us; *
  And send Your fear upon all the
  nations that do not seek / after You.

LIFT UP Your hand
against / the strange nations, *
  And let them / see Your power.

AS YOU were sanctified in / us before them: *
  So may You be magnified
  among them / before us.

AND LET them know You,
as / we have known You, *
  That there is no God but only / You, O God.

GLORIfy Your hand / and Your right arm, *
  That they may confess Your / wondrous works.

RAISE UP indignation, / and pour out wrath: *
  Take away the adversary,
  and destroy / the enemy.

MAKE THE time short,
remember / the covenant, *
  And let them declare
  Your won- / derful works.

LET HIM that escapes be
consumed / by the rage of the fire; *
  And let them perish that oppress / the people.

STRIKE THE heads of
the rulers / of the heathen, *
  That say, There is none o- / ther but us.

GATHER all the tribes of Ja- / cob together, *
  And inherit them, as from the / beginning.

O LORD, have mercy upon the
people who are / called by Your name, *
  And upon Israel, whom You
  have named / Your firstborn.

O BE merciful / to Jerusalem, *
  Your holy city, the place / of Your rest.

FILL ZIon with Your unspeaka- / ble oracles, *
  And Your people with / Your glory.

GLORY be to the / Father, and to the Son, *
  And to the Ho- / ly Spirit

AS IT was in / the beginning *
  Is now and will be forev- / er. Amen.

Ecclesiasticus 36:1-14

CANTICLE 8

Antiphon - *Tres pueri*

The three young men were thrown in - to the fur - nace

by the king's or - der, they feared not the flames

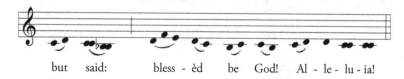

but said: bless - èd be God! Al - le - lu - ia!

Canticle - *Benedicite es, Dominus Deum Patrum*

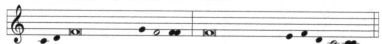

BLESSÈD are you, O
Lord God of our / fathers *
    And to be praised and
    exalted above / all forever.

AND BLESSèd is Your
glorious and / holy Name, *
    And to be praised and
    exalted above / all forever.

BLESSÈD are You in the
temple of Your holy / glory *
    And to be praised and
    glorified above / all forever.

BLESSÈD are You who beholds the
depths and sits upon the / cherubim, *
    And to be praised and
    exalted above / all forever.

BLESSÈD are You on the glorious
throne of Your / kingdom, *
    And to be praised and
    glorified above / all forever.

BLESSÈD are You in the
firmament of / heaven, *
    And above all to be praised
    and glori- / fied forever.

ALL YOU works of the Lord, / bless the Lord, *
    Praise and exalt Him above / all forever.

GLORY be to the Father, and / to the Son, *
    And to the / Holy Spirit

AS IT was in the be- / ginning *
    Is now and will be for- / ever. Amen.

Apocryphal Daniel 3:29-34

CANTICLE 9

Antiphon - *Conversus est*

Your an - ger, O LORD, is turned a- way, and You com- fort me.

Canticle - *Confitebor Tibi Domini*

O LORD, I will praise You;
though You were angry / with me, *
 Your anger is turned
 away, / and You comfort me.

BEHOLD, God is my sal- / vation, *
 I will trust and / not be afraid;

FOR THE LORD, the LORD is
my strength and / my song; *
 He also has become / my salvation.

THEREFORE with joy you will
draw water from the wells of salvation.
And that day you / will say: *
 "Praise the LORD, / call upon His name;

DECLARE His deeds among the / peoples, *
 Make mention that His name / is exalted.

SING TO the LORD, for He
has done excel- / lent things; *
 This is / known in all the earth.

CRY OUT and shout, O inhabitant of / Zion, *
 For great is the Holy One
 of Isra- / el in your midst!"

GLORY be to the Father, and / to the Son, *
 And to the / Holy Spirit

AS IT was in the be- / ginning *
 Is now and will be for- / ever. Amen.

Isaiah 12:1-6

CANTICLE 10   Tone 8G

Antiphon - *Corripes me Domine*

You will re - store me, O LORD, and make me live.

Canticle - *Ego Dixi*

I SAID, "In the prime of / my life *
 I shall go to the / gates of Sheol;

I AM deprived of the remainder of / my years." *
 I said, "I shall not see the LORD
 God in the land / of the living;

I SHALL observe man / no more *
 Among the inhabi- / tants of the world.

MY LIFE span / is gone, *
 Taken from me like / a shepherd's tent;

I HAVE cut off my life like a weaver.
He cuts me off / from the loom; *
 From day until night
 You / make an end of me.

I HAVE considered until / morning *
 Like a lion, so He / breaks all my bones; *

FROM DAY until night
You make an / end of me. *
 Like a crane or a swallow, so I
 chattered; / I mourned like a dove;

MY EYES fail from looking / upward. *
 O LORD, I am oppressed; / undertake for me!

WHAT SHALL / I say? *
 He has both spoken to me,
 and He Him- / self has done it.

I SHALL walk carefully / all my years *
 In the bitter- / ness of my soul.

199

O LORD, by these things men live; and
in all these things is the life of my spirit;
so You will restore me and make / me live. *
    Indeed it was for my own peace
    that I / had great bitterness;

BUT YOU have lovingly delivered my
soul from the pit of cor- / ruption, *
    For You have cast all
    my / sins behind Your back.

FOR SHEol cannot thank You,
death cannot / praise You; *
    Those who go down to the pit
    cannot / hope for Your truth.

THE LIVing, the living man,
he shall praise You, as I do / this day; *
    The father shall make known
    Your truth / to the children.

THE LORD was ready to / save me *
    Therefore we will sing my songs
    with stringed instruments all the days
    of our life in the / house of the LORD.

GLORY be to the Father, and / to the Son, *
    And to the / Holy Spirit

AS IT was in the be- / ginning *
    Is now and will be for- / ever. Amen.

Isaiah 38:10-20

CANTICLE 11

Tone 7a

Antiphon - *Exsultavit cor meum*

My heart re - joic-es in the LORD. He brings low and rais - es up.

Canticle - *Exultavit cor meum*

MY HEART rejoic- / es in the LORD; *
    My horn is exalt- / ed in the LORD.

I SMILE at / my enemies, *
    Because I rejoice in / Your salvation.

THERE IS none holy like the LORD,
for there is / none beside You, *
    Nor is there any / rock like our God.

TALK NO more so / very proudly; *
    Let no arrogance / come from your mouth,

FOR THE LORD is the / God of knowledge; *
    And by Him / actions are weighed.

THE BOWS of the mighty / men are broken, *
    And those who stumbled
    are / girded with strength.

THOSE WHO were full have
hired them- / selves out for bread, *
    And those who were hungry
    have / ceased to hunger.

EVEN the barren / has borne seven, *
    And she who has many
    children has / become feeble.

THE LORD kills / and makes alive; *
    He brings down to the / grave and brings up.

THE LORD makes / poor and makes rich; *
    He brings / low and lifts up.

HE RAISes the / poor from the dust *
    And lifts the beggar / from the ash heap,

TO SET them / among princes *
    And make them inherit the / throne of glory.

FOR THE pillars of the / earth are the LORD's, *
    And he has set the / world upon them.

HE WILL guard the feet of His saints, but the
wicked shall be si- / lent in darkness.*
    For by strength no / man shall prevail.

THE ADversaries of the LORD
shall be bro- / ken in pieces; *
  From heaven He will
  thun- / der against them.

THE LORD will judge the ends of the
earth. He will give / strength to His king *
  And exalt the horn of / His anointed.

GLORY be to the / Father, and to the Son, *
  And to the / Holy Spirit

AS IT was in / the beginning *
  Is now and will be for- / ever. Amen.

I Samuel 2:1-10

CANTICLE 12

Tone 4a

Antiphon - *Fortitudo mea*

The LORD is my strength and my song, and has be-come my sal - va - tion.

Canticle - *Cantemus Domino*

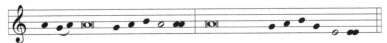

I WILL sing to the LORD, for He
has tri- / umphed gloriously! *
  The horse and its rider He
  has / thrown into the sea!

THE LORD is my / strength and my song, *
  And He has be- / come my salvation;

HE IS my God, and / I will praise Him; *
  My father's God, and / I will exalt Him.

THE LORD is a man of
war; the / LORD is His name. *
  Pharaoh's chariots and his
  army He has / cast into the sea;

HIS CHOSen captains also
are drowned / in the Red Sea. *
  The depths have covered them;
  they sank to the / bottom like a stone.

YOUR RIGHT hand, O LORD, has become
glorious in power; Your right hand, O LORD
has dashed the ene- / my in pieces. *
  And in the greatness of Your excellence You
  have overthrown those / who rose against you;

YOU SENT for them Your wrath which
consumed / them like stubble. *
  And with the blast of Your nostrils the
  waters were / gathered together;

THE FLOODS stood up- / right like a heap; *
  And the depths congealed
  in / the heart of the sea.

THE ENemy said, "I will
pursue, / I will overtake, *
  I will divide the spoil; my desire
  shall be / satisfied on them.

I WILL / draw my sword—, *
  My / hand shall destroy them."

YOU BLEW with Your
wind, the / sea covered them; *
  They sank like lead in / the mighty waters.

WHO IS like You, O LORD, / among the gods? *
  Who is like You, glorious in holiness,
  fearful in prais- / es, doing wonders?

YOU STRETCHED out Your right
hand; the / earth swallowed them. *
  You in Your mercy have led forth the
  people / whom You have redeemed;

YOU HAVE guided / them in Your strength *
  To Your ho- / ly habitation.

THE PEOple will hear / and be afraid; *
  Sorrow will take hold of
  the inhabi- / tants of Philistia.

THEN THE chiefs of Edom will be
dismayed; trembling will take hold
of the mighty / men of Moab; *
    All the inhabitants of / Canaan will melt away.

FEAR AND dread / will fall on them; *
    By the / greatness of Your arm

YOUR PEOple pass / over, O LORD, *
    Till the people pass over / whom
    You have purchased.

YOU WILL bring them in and plant them
in the mountain of / Your inheritance,*
    In the place, O LORD, which You
    have made / for Your own dwelling,

THE SANCtuary, O LORD, which
Your hands / have established. *
    The LORD shall reign for- / ever and ever.

FOR THE horses of Pharaoh went with his
chariots and his horsemen / into the sea,*
    And the LORD brought back the
    waters of / the sea upon them.

BUT THE children of Israel / went on dry land *
    In / the midst of the sea.

GLORY be to the Father, / and to the Son, *
    And to / the Holy Spirit

AS IT was in / the beginning *
    Is now and will be / forever. Amen.

Exodus 15:1-19

CANTICLE 13

Tone 1f

Antiphon - *Cum iratus fueris*

In   wrath,   O   Lord,   re - mem - ber   mer - cy.

Canticle - *Domine Audivi*

O LORD, I / have heard Your speech *
    - / And was afraid;

O LORD, / revive Your work *
    In the / midst of the years!

IN THE midst of the / years make it known; *
    In wrath re- / member mercy.

GOD CAME / forth from Teman, *
    The Holy One / from Mount Paran.

HIS GLOry co- / vered the heavens,*
    And the earth was / full of His praise.

HIS BRIGHTness / was like the light; *
    He had rays flash- / ing from His hand,

AND THERE His / power was hidden.*
    Before Him / went pestilence,

AND FEver / followed at His feet. *
    He stood and / measured the earth;

HE LOOKED and start- / led the nations.*
    And the everlasting
    mount- / ains were scattered,

THE PERpe- / tual hills bowed. *
    His ways are / everlasting.

I SAW the tents of Cushan / in affliction; *
    The curtains of the land of / Midian trembled.

O LORD, were You displeased / with the rivers, *
    Was Your anger against the rivers,
    was Your / wrath against the sea,

THAT YOU rode / on Your horses, *
    Your chariots / of salvation?

YOUR BOW was / made quite ready; *
    Oaths were sworn ov- / er Your arrows.

YOU DIvided the earth with rivers.
The mountains saw / You and trembled; *
    The overflowing of the / water passed by.

THE DEEP / uttered its voice, *
  And lifted / its hands on high.

THE SUN and moon stood
still in their / habitation; *
  At the light of Your arrows they went,
  at the shining of Your / glittering spear.

YOU MARCHED through
the land in / indignation; *
  You trampled the na- / tions in anger.

YOU WENT forth for the
salvation / of Your people, *
  For salvation with / Your Anointed.

YOU STRUCK the head from
the / house of the wicked. *
  By laying bare from found- / ation to neck.

YOU THRUST through with his own
arrows the head of his villages. They came
out like a whirlwind / to scatter me;
  Their rejoicing was like feasting
  on the / poor in secret.

YOU WALKED through the
sea / with Your horses, *
  Through the heap / of great waters.

WHEN I heard, my body trembled;
my lips quiv- / ered at the voice;
  Rottenness entered my bones;
  and I / trembled in myself,

THAT I might rest in the / day of trouble. *
  When he comes up to the people,
  He will invade / them with his troops.

THOUGH THE fig tree / may not blossom,*
  Nor fruit / be on the vines;

THOUGH THE labor of the / olive may fail, *
  And the / fields yield no food;

THOUGH THE flock be
cut / off from the fold, *
  And there be no / herd in the stalls

YET I will re- / joice in the LORD, *
  I will joy in the God of / my salvation.

THE LORD / God is my strength; *
  He will make my feet like deer's feet, and
  He will make me walk / on my high hills.

GLORY be to the / Father, and to the Son, *
  And to the / Holy Spirit

AS IT was in / the beginning *
  Is now and will be for- / ever. Amen.

Habakkuk 3:1-19

CANTICLE 14 Tone 5

Antiphon - *In servis suis*

The LORD will have com - pas - sion   on   His   ser - vants

He will pro - vide a-tone-ment   for His land and for His peo-ple.

Canticle - *Audite, caeli* (shorter version)

GIVE EAR, O heavens, and I / will speak; *
  And hear, O earth, the / words of my mouth.

LET MY teaching drop as / the rain, *
  My / speech as the dew,

AS RAINdrops on the tender herb,
and as showers on / the grass. *
    For I proclaim the / name of the LORD:

ASCRIBE greatness to our God.
He is the Rock. His work is / perfect; *
    For all His / ways are justice,

A GOD of truth and without in- / justice; *
    Righteous and / upright is He.

FOR THE LORD's portion is His / people; *
    Jacob is the place of / His in-heritance.

FOR THE LORD will judge His / people *
    And have compassion / on His servants,

WHEN HE sees that their power / is gone, *
    And there is no one
    re- / maining, bond or free.

HE WILL say: I, even I / am He, *
    And there is no / God besides me;

I KILL and I make / alive, *
    I / wound and I heal;

NOR IS there any who can
deliver from / my hand.*
    For I lift My hand to heaven
    and say, I / live forever,

REJOICE, O Gentiles, with His / people; *
    For He will avenge the
    blood / of His servants,

AND RENder vengeance to His adver- / saries; *
    He will provide atonement
    for His land / and His people.

GLORY be to the Father, and / to the Son, *
    And to the / Holy Spirit

AS IT was in the be- / ginning *
    Is now and will be for- / ever. Amen.
                                    Deuteronomy 32:1-4, 9, 36, 39-40, 43

SEASONAL PSALM ANTIPHONS
Arranged by season and tone

ADVENT

Ecce veniet desideratus Tone 1

Be - hold, He is com - ing, the De - sired of the Na-

tions, and the house of the Lord will be filled with glo - ry.

Haggai 2:8 (Septuagint)

Ecce in nubibus caeli Tone 1

Be- hold in the clouds of heav - en the Lord shall come

with great pow - er. Al - le - lu - ia!

Matthew 24:30

In tuo adventu Tone 1

En - light - en us, O Lord, by Your com - ing. *Liturgical text*

Multiplicabitur ejus Tone 1

Of the in - crease of His go - vern - ment and peace

there will be no end.

Isaiah 9:7

205

Erunt prava in directa

Tone 1

The crook-ed plac-es shall be made straight, and the rough

plac-es plain. Come, O Lord, and do not de-lay.

Al - le - lu - ia.

Isaiah 40:4

De Sion veniet Dominus

Tone 1

From Zi-on the Lord al-migh-ty will come, to

save His peo-ple.

Liturgical text

Juste et pie vivamus

Tone 2

Let us live so-ber-ly and right-eous-ly, look-ing for

the bles-sed hope and the ad-vent of the Lord.

Titus 2:12-13

Constantes estote

Tone 2

Stand firm, and you will see the sal-va-tion of

the Lord, who is with you.

206

II Chronicles 20:17

Omnipotens sermo tuus — Tone 2

Your al-migh-ty Word, O Lord, will come from hea-ven's
roy-al throne. Al-le-lu-ia!

Wisdom 18:15

Ecce Dominus noster — Tone 3

Be-hold, our Lord shall come with pow-er, to en-light-en the eyes of His ser-vants. Al-le-lu-ia!

Liturgical text

Dominus legifer noster — Tone 3

The Lord, our Law-giv-er, the Lord, our King, will come Him-self, and will save us.

Isaiah 33:22

Ego Dominus prope — Tone 3

I, the Lord, bring My right-eous-ness near, it shall not be far off; and My sal-va-tion shall not lin-ger.

Isaiah 46:13

Tuam Domine — *Tone 4*

Stir up Your strength, O Lord, and come to save us. *Psalm 80:2*

Ecce veniet Dominus — *Tone 4*

Be - hold, the Lord will come, prince of the kings of the earth!

Bles - sed are those who are read - y to meet Him. *Liturgical text*

Rorate caeli desuper — *Tone 4*

Rain down, you heav-ens, from a - bove, and let the clouds rain down

the Right-eous One; let the earth be o - pened, and bring forth

the Sa - vior. *Isaiah 45:8*

Veni Domine, et noli tardare — *Tone 4*

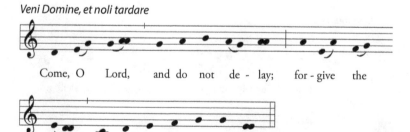

Come, O Lord, and do not de - lay; for - give the

sins of Your peo - ple Is - ra - el. *Liturgical text on Daniel 9:19*

Ecce Dominus veniet

Tone 5

Be - hold, the Lord shall come, and all His saints with Him,

and there shall be a great light in that day. Al - le - lu - ia!

Zechariah 14:5, 7

Ecce virgo

Tone 5

Be - hold, the vir - gin shall con-ceive and bear a Son,

and shall call His name Im - man- u - el.

Isaiah 7:14

Ecce jam venit

Tone 5

Be - hold, now has come the full - ness of time, in which

God has sent His Son in - to the world.

Liturgical text on Galatians 4:4

Miserere Mei

Tone 6

Have mer- cy on me, O Lord.

Orietur in diebus   Tone 6

In His days   the   right - eous shall   flour - ish,   and a-

bun-dance of   peace,   and all kings shall fall   down be-

fore   Him;   all   na - tions shall   serve   Him.   *Psalm 72:7, 11*

Ecce apparebit Dominus   Tone 7

Be -hold, the   Lord   will   come   and will not dis - ap - point;

if   He   tar - ries,   wait   for Him,   be - cause He   will   come,

and   will   not   tar - ry.   Al - le - lu - ia!   *Liturgical text on Habakkuk 2:3*

Jerusalem gaude   Tone 7

Re- joice, Je - ru - sa - lem,   with   great   joy!   For   your

Sa - vior   will come   to   you. Al - le - lu - ia!

Liturgical text on Zechariah 9:9

Nox precessit — Tone 7

The night is far spent, but the day is at hand. Let us cast off the works of dark - ness, and let us put on the ar - mor of light.

Romans 13:12

Sit nomen Domini — Tone 7

Bles - sed be the name of God for - e - ver and e - ver.

Daniel 2:20

Omnes sitientes — Tone 8

All you who thirst, come to the wa - ters; Seek the Lord while He may be found.

Al - le - lu - ia!

Isaiah 55:1, 6

Veni et libera nos — Tone 8

Come and de - liv - er us, O Lord, our God.

Liturgical text

Jucundare filia Sion — *Tone 8*

Be glad, O daugh-ter of Zi - on,

re-joice great-ly, O daugh-ter of Je-ru - sa - lem. Al - le - lu - ia! *Zephaniah 3:14*

Dabo in Sion — *Tone 8*

I will give sal - va - tion in Zi - on, and in Je-

ru - sa - lem My glo - ry. Al - le - lu - ia!

Liturgical text on Isaiah 46:13

Convertere Domine — *Tone 8*

Turn to us, O Lord, at last, and come

to Your ser - vants with - out de - lay. *Liturgical text*

Nolite timere — *Tone 8*

Do not be a - fraid; for in a short time our

212

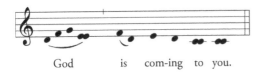

God   is   com-ing   to   you.   *Liturgical text*

Nos qui vivimus   *Tone P*

We   who   live,   let   us   bless   the   Lord.   *Psalm 115:18 (113:26 Vulgate)*

LENT

Circumdantes circumdederunt me   *Tone 1*

They sur-round-ed me, they sur-round-ed me;   but   in   the   name   of   the

Lord   I   will   be   a - venged   on   them.   *Psalm 118:11*

Reges terrae   *Tone 1*

Kings of   the   earth   and   all   peop - les,   praise   the   Lord.   *Psalm 148:11*

Amen, amen, dico vobis   *Tone 1*

A- men, a - men   I   say   to   you,   if   an - y - one   keeps

My   word   he   shall   ne - ver   see   death.   *John 8:51*

Qui non colligit mecum — Tone 1

He who does not ga - ther with Me scat - ters; and He who is not with Me is a - gainst Me.

Luke 11:23

Factus est adjutor meus — Tone 1

The Lord my God, is be - come my help - er.

Psalm 30:10

Dominus Deus auxiliator meus — Tone 2

The Lord God will help Me; and there-fore I will not be dis-graced.

Isaiah 50:7

Ipsi vero — Tone 2

Those who seek my life, to de - stroy it, shall go in-to the low - er parts of the earth.

Psalm 63:9

O Domine, salvum me fac — Tone 2

O Lord, save now; O Lord,

send now pros - per - i - ty.

Psalm 118:25

Domine, vim patior

Tone 3

Lord, I am op-pressed; an-swer for me; for I know

not what to say to my en - e - mies.

Liturgical text on Isaiah 38:14

Fac benigne in bona voluntate

Tone 3

Do good in Your good plea - sure; and build the

walls, O Lord, of Je - ru - sa - lem.

Psalm 51:18

Confundantur qui me persequuntur

Tone 4

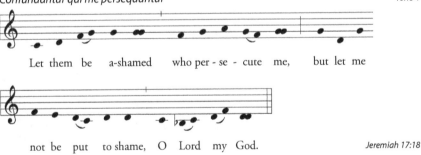

Let them be a-shamed who per - se - cute me, but let me

not be put to shame, O Lord my God.

Jeremiah 17:18

Invocabo nomen tuum — Tone 4

I will call u - pon Your name, O Lord; do not turn

Your face from my cry.

Liturgical text

Judicasti Domine — Tone 4

You have judged, O Lord, the cause of my soul; You are

the de - fen - der of my life, O Lord, my God.

Lamentations 3:58

Popule meus — Tone 4

O My peo - ple, what have I done to you, or how

have I mo - les - ted you? An - swer Me.

Micah 6:3

Fac Domine judicum — Tone 5

Do jus - tice, Lord, for those who suf - fer wrong,

and de - stroy the way of sin - ners.

Psalm 146:7, 9

Non in solo pane — *Tone 5*

Man shall not live by bread a - lone, but by eve - ry word that pro - ceeds from the mouth of God. *Matthew 4:4*

Dominum deum tuum adorabis — *Tone 6*

You shall wor - ship the Lord your God, and Him on - ly you shall serve. *Matthew 4:10*

Tunc acceptabis — *Tone 7*

Then You shall be pleased with the sac - ri - fi - ces of right- eous - ness, if You hide Your face from my sins. *Psalm 51:19, 9*

Omnes inimici mei — *Tone 7*

All my en - e - mies have heard of my troub-le, O Lord; they are glad that You have done it. *Lamentations 1:21*

217

In tribulatione invocavi Domine

Tone 7

In dis - tress, I called up - on the Lord; and He an-swered

me and set me in a broad place.

Psalm 118:5

Vide Domine

Tone 7

See, O Lord, and con-si - der be-cause of my e - ne - mies;

de - li - ver me speed - i - ly. *Liturgical text on Lamentations 1:11 and Psalm 69:18*

Inundaverunt aquae

Tone 8

The wa - ters flowed o - ver my head; I said, "I am cut off!"

I will call on Your name, O Lord God. *Lamentations 3:54*

Judica causam meam

Tone 8

Judge my cause, O Lord; de - fend me, for

You are pow - er - ful.

Liturgical text

Labia insurgentium — Tone 8

Be-hold, O Lord, the lips of my en - e - mies, and their schemes.

Liturgical text on Lamentations 3:61-63

Labia mea laudabunt — Tone 8

My lips shall praise You in my life, O my God. *Psalm 62: 3-4*

Dextera Domini — Tone 8

The right hand of the Lord does val - iant - ly. The right

hand of the Lord is ex - alt - ed. *Psalm 118:15-16*

Potens es, Domine — Tone 8

You are a - ble, O Lord, to de - liv - er us from the strong

hand; to lib - er - ate us, O our God.

Liturgical text on Daniel 3:17

In matutinis, Domine — Tone P

In the night watch-es, O Lord, I med - i - tate on You. *Psalm 63:6*

EASTERTIDE

Al - le - lu - ia, al - le - lu - ia, al - le - lu - ia.

Al - le - lu - ia, al - le - lu - ia, al - le - lu - ia.

Al - le - lu - ia, al - le - lu - ia, al - le - lu - ia.

Al - le - lu - ia, al - le - lu - ia, al - le - lu - ia.

Al - le - lu - ia, al - le - lu - ia, al - le - lu - ia.

Al - le - lu - ia, al - le - lu - ia, al - le - lu - ia.

Al - le - lu - ia, al - le - lu - ia, al - le - lu - ia.

Al - le - lu - ia, al - le - lu - ia, al - le - lu - ia.

Al - le - lu - ia, al - le - lu - ia, al - le - lu - ia.

Al - le - lu - ia, al - le - lu - ia, al - le - lu - ia.

Al - le - lu - ia, al - le - lu - ia, al - le - lu - ia.

Al - le - lu - ia, al - le - lu - ia, al - le - lu - ia.

Al - le - lu - ia, al - le - lu - ia, al - le - lu - ia.

Al - le - lu - ia, al - le - lu - ia, al - le - lu - ia.

Al - le - lu - ia, al - le - lu - ia, al - le - lu - ia.

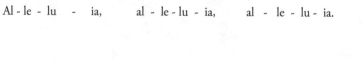

Al - le - lu - ia, al - le - lu - ia, al - le - lu - ia.

Al - le - lu - ia, al - le - lu - ia, al - le - lu - ia.

Al- le - lu - ia, al - le - lu- ia, al - le - lu - ia.

Al - le - lu - ia, al - le - lu - ia, al - le - lu - ia.

Al - le - lu - ia, al - le - lu - ia, al - le - lu - ia.

Tone P

Al - le - lu - ia, al - le - lu - ia, al - le - lu - ia.

AD TE LEVAVI
The First Week in Advent

AT MATINS

Invitatory - *Regem venturum* *Tone 6*

The Lord, the King, is com-ing. O come, let us wor-ship Him!

Hymn - *Veni redemptor gentium*

1. Sav-ior of the na-tions, come, Vir-gin's Son, make here Thy home,

Mar-vel now, O heav'n and earth, That the Lord chose such a birth.

2. Not by human flesh and blood,
By the Spirit of our God,
Was the Word of God made flesh
Woman's blossom, pure and fresh.

3. Though the Virgin was with Child,
Chastity proved undefiled!
By Thy strength divine, O Lord,
Help our frail flesh afford.

4. Thus proceeds the Lord of all,
From His pure and royal hall;
God is He, and yet true man,
His heroic course began.

5. From the Father forth He came,
And returned unto the same,
Down to hell He went alone,
And again to God's high throne!

6. Thou, the Father's equal, win
Vict'ry in the flesh o'er sin,
By Thy strength divine, O Lord,
Help our frail flesh afford.

7. Lord, Thy manger is so bright,
Night sends forth a novel light;
Darkness must not enter there,
Faith abides in light fore'er.

8. Praise to God the Father sing,
Praise to God the Son, our King,
Praise to God the Spirit be
Ever and eternally. *Ambrose of Milan, 340-397*

Psalmody

Sunday: 21, 22, 23	Wednesday: 30, 31, 32	Friday: 37a, 37b, 38
Monday: 24, 25, 26	Thursday: 33, 34, 35	Saturday: 39, 40, 41
Tuesday: 27, 28, 29		

Lesson

Sunday, Monday and Tuesday: Matthew 21:1-9

Monday: Mark 11:1-13
Tuesday: Luke 19:28-40

Wednesday and Thursday: Matthew 3:1-6

Thursday: Mark 1:1-6

Friday and Saturday: Luke 3:7-14

Saturday: Luke 3:15-20

Homily

Sunday - Martin Luther

He "comes." Without a doubt you do not come to Him and bring Him to you; He is too high and too far from you. With all your effort, work and labor you cannot come to Him, lest you boast as though you had received Him by your own merit and worthiness. No, dear friend, all merit and worthiness is out of the question, and there is nothing but demerit and unworthiness on your side, nothing but grace and mercy on His. The poor and the rich here come together, as Proverbs 22:2 says.

By this are condemned all those infamous doctrines of free will, which come from the pope, universities and monasteries. For all their teaching consists in that we are to begin and lay the first stone. We should by the power of free will seek God, come to Him, run after Him and acquire His grace. Beware, beware of this poison! It is nothing but the doctrine of devils, by which all the world is betrayed. Before you can cry to God and seek Him God must come to you and must have found you, as Paul says, Romans 10:14-15: "How then shall they call on Him in whom they have not believed? And how shall they believe in Him whom they have not heard? And how shall they hear without a preacher, and how shall they preach except they be sent?" God must lay the first stone and begin with you, if you are to seek Him and pray to Him. He is present when you begin to seek. If He were not you could not accomplish anything but mere sin, and the greater the sin, the greater and holier the work you will attempt, and you will become a hardened hypocrite.

Church Postil for the First Sunday in Advent

Monday - Jerome of Jerusalem

The Coming of Christ is the Salvation of the world. Hence there follows: "Blessed is He who comes in the name of the Lord." The Savior also confirms this Himself in His Gospel, saying: "I have come in My Father's name, and you do not receive Me; if another comes in his own name, him you will receive."

And through what follows, "Hosanna in the highest," it is distinctly indicated that the Coming of Christ is for salvation, not of men alone, but of the whole world; joining the things of earth to those that are above; so "that at the name of Jesus every knee should bow, of those in heaven, and of those on earth, and of those under the earth." Amen.

The Meaning of the [Palm Sunday] Gospel

Tuesday - Bernard of Clairvaux

What does it mean that He should come to us; and why rather have we not gone to Him? For it is we who were in need, and it is not usual for the rich to come seeking the poor, that is, if they still desire to retain their own superiority. And in truth, brethren, it was more fitting that we should go to Him, but against this was a twofold barrier, our eyes were dim and groping, and He "inhabits light inaccessible;" and, lying paralyzed upon our poor beds, we could not ascend to that divine sublimity. And so the Most Benign Savior, the Physician of our souls, comes down from His Glory, tempering the brightness of His Splendor to our infirm sight. He veiled Himself, as it were in a lantern, in that glorious, that most pure and stainless Body which He put on; this Body that is the swift and shining cloud upon which, as the Prophet had foretold, the Lord would ascend that He might enter into Egypt.

The Advent of the Lord and Its Six Circumstances (Homily 1)

Wednesday - Johann Gerhard

The very foundation and principle of a holy life is godly sorrow for sin. For where there is true penitence there is forgiveness of sin; where there is forgiveness of sin there is the grace of God; where the grace of God is there is Christ; where Christ is there is Christ's merit; where Christ's merit is there is satisfaction for sin; where there is satisfaction there is justification; where there is justification there is a glad and quiet conscience; where there is peace of conscience there is the Holy Spirit; where the Holy Spirit is present there is the ever blessed Trinity; and where the Holy Trinity is there is life eternal. Therefore where there is true penitence there is life eternal. And hence where there is no true penitence there is neither forgiveness of sins, nor the grace of God, nor Christ, nor His merit, nor satisfaction for sin, nor justification, nor peace of conscience, nor the Holy Spirit, nor the blessed Trinity, nor eternal life. Why therefore do we delay repentance? Why put it off until tomorrow! Neither tomorrow nor true repentance is in our own power. For we must render an account at the final judgment, not only for tomorrow, but for today as well. That tomorrow shall come is not certain, but that everlasting destruction shall overtake the impenitent is certain. God has promised grace to the penitent soul, but He does not promise a tomorrow.

Sacred Meditation 3

Thursday - John Chrysostom

The Jews were senseless, and had never any feeling of their own sins, but while they were justly accountable for the worst evils, they were justifying themselves in every respect; and this more than anything caused their destruction and led them away from the faith. Paul reproved them for this, saying, "For they, being ignorant of God's righteousness, and seeking to establish their own righteousness, have not submitted to the righteousness of God." And again, "What shall we say then? That Gentiles, who did not pursue righteousness have attained to righteousness, even the righteousness of faith; but Israel, pursuing the law of righteousness, has not attained to the law of righteousness. Why? Because they did not seek it by faith, but as it were, by the works of the law."

Because their ignorance was the cause of their afflictions John came, and for no other reason than that he might awaken them to the knowledge of their sins. Even his clothing revealed this purpose, for it signified confession and repentance. His preaching too showed this purpose. For he didn't proclaim anything else but that they should bring forth fruits worthy of repentance. And because they would not turn from their sins, they turned their backs on Christ, as Paul has declared. For to consider their sins would awaken a desire for forgiveness, and the Redeemer would be sought after. John came to bring this about, to exhort them to penance, not that they might be punished, but that they might, becoming humbler through repentance, and by accusing themselves, hurry to seek pardon.

Homily 10 on the Gospel of Matthew

Friday - Augustine of Hippo

But we, dearly beloved, do we come of Abraham's race, or was Abraham in any sense our father according to the flesh? The flesh of the Jews draws its origin from his flesh, not so the flesh of Christians. We have come of other nations, and yet, by imitating him, we have become the children of Abraham... We then have become Abraham's seed by the grace of God. It was not of Abraham's flesh that God made any co-heirs with him. He disinherited the former, He adopted the latter; and from that olive tree whose root is in the patriarchs, He cut off the proud natural branches, and grafted in the lowly wild olive. And so, when the Jews came to John to be baptized, he broke out upon them, and addressed them, "O generation of vipers." Very greatly indeed did they boast of the loftiness of their origin, but he called them a generation of vipers, not even of human beings, but of vipers. He saw the form of men, but detected the poison. Yet they had come to be changed, because at all events to be baptized; and he said to them, "Brood of vipers! Who warned you to flee from the wrath to come? Therefore bear fruits worthy of repentance, and do not think to say to yourselves, 'We have Abraham as our father.' For I say to you that God is able to raise up children to Abraham from these stones." If you don't bring forth fruits worthy of repentance, do not flatter yourselves about having a lineage. God is able to condemn you without depriving Abraham of children. For He has a way to raise up children to Abraham. Those who imitate his faith will be made his children. "God is able to raise up children to Abraham from these stones." Such are we. In our parents we were stones, when we worshipped stones for our god. Of such stones God has created a family to Abraham.   *Tractate 42 on the Gospel of John*

Saturday - Gregory of Nazianzus

What is swifter than mercy? The disciples seek the flames of Sodom for those who drive Jesus away, but He disparages revenge. Peter cuts off the ear of Malchus, one of those who insulted Him, but Jesus restores it. And what of him who asks whether he must forgive a brother seven times if he has trespassed, is he not condemned for his niggardliness, for to the seven is added seventy times seven? What of the debtor in the Gospel who will not forgive as he has been forgiven? Is it not more bitterly exacted of him for this...?

Having so many examples let us imitate the mercy of God. Let us not desire to learn for ourselves how great an evil retaliation for sin is. You see the way goodness proceeds. First it makes laws, then it commands, threatens, reproaches, holds out warnings, restrains, threatens again, and only when forced to do so strikes the blow, but this little by little, opening the way to amendment. Let us then not strike suddenly (for it is not safe to do so), but being self-restrained in our fear let us conquer by mercy, and make them our debtors by our kindness, tormenting them by their conscience rather than by anger.   *Epistle 77*

Collect

Stir up, we pray You, Your power, O Lord, and come, that by Your protection we may be rescued from the threatening perils of our sins and saved by Your mighty deliverance; who lives and reigns with the Father and the Holy Spirit, one God, now and forever.   *Gregorian Sacramentary*

AT LAUDS

Psalmody

Sunday: 67, C1, 5	Wednesday: 64, C4, 65	Friday: 76, C5, 92
Monday: 63, C2, 36	Thursday: 88, C6, 90	Saturday: 143, C7, 148
Tuesday: 43, C3, 57		

Lesson

Sunday: Isaiah 1:1-9	Wednesday: Isaiah 4:1-6	Friday: Isaiah 6:1-13
Monday: Isaiah 1:21-31	Thursday: Isaiah 5:8-17	Saturday: Isaiah 8:11-18
Tuesday: Isaiah 2:10-22		

Hymn - *Vox clara ecce intonat*

1. A thrill - ing voice by Jor - dan rings, Re - buk - ing guilt
2. Now let each tor - pid soul a - rise, That sunk in guilt
3. The Lamb de-scends from heav'n a - bove To par - don sin

and dark-some things: Vain dreams of sin and vis - ions fly;
and wound-ed lies; See! the new Star's re - ful - gent ray
with fre - est love: For such in - dul - gent mer - cy shown

Christ in His might shines forth on high.
Shall chase dis - ease and sin a - way.
With tear - ful joy our thanks we own.

4. That when again He shines revealed,
   And trembling worlds to terror yield.
   He give not sin its just reward,
   But in His love protect and guard.

5. To God the Father glory be
   And to the Son be victory,
   And to the Spirit praise is owed
   From age to age eternally. Amen.

anonymous, 6th c.

Verse

℣: The voice of one crying in the wilderness: Prepare the way of the / Lord.
℟: Make His paths / straight.

Mark 1:3

Antiphon to the Benedictus - *De caelo veniet*

Tone 7a

The Lord and Ru - ler, comes from Hea - ven; and

in His hand are ho - nor and do - min - ion.

Liturgical text

✠ BLESSÉD is the Lord / God of Israel; *

For He has visited and re- / deemed His people. etc.

Collect

O King, whom our hearts desire, Lord Jesus Christ, come, we implore You, cleanse us as a furnace of fire from the dross of our sins, and make us like gold that is pure and like silver that is without alloy; inflame our hearts by Your inspiration that they may seek You unceasingly; so may we ardently desire You, and eagerly pant to be united with You, who lives and reigns with the Father and the Holy Spirit, one God, now and forever.

Mozarabic Breviary

AT TERCE, SEXT AND NONE

Chapter

Sunday, Monday and Tuesday: Romans 13:11-14
Wednesday and Thursday: James 5:7-8
Friday and Saturday: Titus 2:1-10

Responsory and Verse at Terce

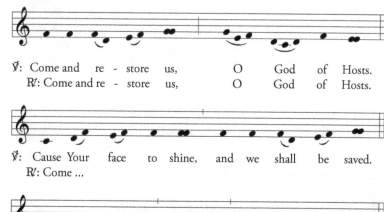

℣: Come and re - store us,   O   God   of   Hosts.
℟: Come and re - store us,   O   God   of   Hosts.

℣: Cause Your face to shine, and we shall be saved.
℟: Come ...

℣: Glo-ry be to the Fa - ther, and to the Son, and to the Ho - ly Spi - rit.
℟: Come ...

Psalm 80:7

℣: The nations shall fear Your name, / O Lord,
℟: And all the kings of the earth Your / glory.

Psalm 102:15

Responsory and Verse at Sext

℣: Show us, O Lord, Your mer - cy.
℟: Show us, O Lord, Your mer - cy.

℣: And grant us Your sal - va - tion.
℟: Show...

℣: Glo-ry be to the Fa - ther, and to the Son, and to the Ho - ly Spi - rit.
℟: Show...

Psalm 85:7

℣: Remember us, O Lord, as You favor Your peo- / ple.
℟: Visit us with Your salva- / tion.

Psalm 106:4

Responsory and Verse at None

℣: O - ver you, Je - ru - sa - lem, the Lord will a - rise.
℟: O - ver you, Je - ru - sa - lem, the Lord will a - rise.

℣: And His glo - ry will be seen up - on you.
℟: Over...

℣: Glo-ry be to the Fa - ther, and to the Son, and to the Ho - ly Spi - rit.
℟: Over...

Isaiah 60:2

℣: Come, O Lord, and do not de- / lay.
℟: Loosen the bonds of Your people's / sins.

Liturgical Text

AT VESPERS

Psalmody

Sunday: 110, 111, 112, 113   Wednesday: 123, 124, 125   Friday: 129, 130, 131, 132
Monday: 114, 115, 116, 117   Thursday: 126, 127, 128   Saturday: 133, 135, 136a
Tuesday: 120, 121, 122

Lesson

Sunday: Isaiah 1:10-20   Wednesday: Isaiah 5:1-7   Friday: Isaiah 7:1-14
Monday: Isaiah 2:1-9   Thursday: Isaiah 5:18-25   Saturday: Isaiah 10:15-23
Tuesday: Isaiah 3:1-12

Hymn - *Creator alme siderum*

1. Cre - a - tor of the star - ry height, Thy peo - ple's ev-
2. Thou, sorrow-ing at the help - less cry Of all cre - a-
3. When earth was near its eve - ning hour, Thou didst, in love's

er - last - ing Light, Je - su, Re - deem - er of us all,
tion doomed to die, Didst save our lost and guil - ty race
re- deem - ing power, Like bride-groom from his cham - ber come

Hear Thou Thy ser - vants when they call.
By heal - ing gifts of heav'n-ly grace.
Forth from a Vir - gin mo - ther's womb.

4. At Thy great Name, exalted now,
All knees in lowly homage bow;
All things in Heav'n and earth adore,
And own Thee King for evermore.

5. To Thee, O Holy One, we pray,
Our Judge in that tremendous day,
Ward off, while yet we dwell below,
The weapons of our crafty foe.

6. To God the Father, God the Son,
And God the Spirit, Three in One,
Praise, honor, might, and glory be
From age to age eternally. Amen.

anonymous, 9th c.

Verse

℣: Rain down, you heavens, from above, and let the skies pour down the Righteous / One.
℟: Let the earth open her womb and bring forth Salva- / tion.

Isaiah 45:8

Antiphon to the Magnificat - *Veni, Domine, visitare*

Come, O Lord, vis - it us in peace. That we may

re - joice be - fore You with a loy - al heart.

I Chronicles 29:9

✠ MY SOUL / magnifies the Lord, *
And my spirit has rejoiced in / God my Savior. etc.

Collect

Lord God, heavenly Father, we thank You, we bless and praise You forever, that You sent Your Son to rule over us poor sinners, who for our transgressions have justly deserved to remain in the bondage of sin and Satan, and gave us in Him a meek and righteous King, who by His death became our Savior from sin and eternal death: We implore You so to enlighten, govern and direct us by Your Holy Spirit, that we may always remain faithful to this righteous King and Savior, and not, after the manner of the world, be offended by His humble form and despised word, but, firmly believing in Him, obtain eternal salvation; through the same, Your beloved Son, Jesus Christ, our Lord, who lives and reigns with You and the Holy Spirit, one God, now and forever. *Veit Dietrich*

POPULUS ZION
The Second Week in Advent

AT MATINS

Invitatory *As during the week of Ad Te Levavi, p.225*

Hymn

1. Lo! He comes with clouds de - scend - ing,
Once for fa - vored sin - ners slain;
Thou-sand thou - sand saints at - tend - ing
Swell the tri - umph of His train:
Al - le - lu - ia, al - le - lu - ia, al - le-
lu - ia! God ap - pears on earth to reign.

2. Every eye shall now behold Him
Robed in dreadful majesty;
Those who set at naught and sold Him,
Pierced and nailed Him to the tree,
Deeply wailing, deeply
wailing, deeply wailing,
Shall the true Messiah see!

3. Those dear tokens of His passion,
Still His dazzling body bears,
Cause of endless exultation
To His ransomed worshippers.
With what rapture, with what
rapture, with what rapture,
Gaze we on those sacred scars!

4. Yea, Amen! Let all adore Thee,
   High on Thine eternal throne;
   Savior, take the power and glory;
   Claim the Kingdom for Thine own.
   O come quickly! O come
      quickly! O come quickly!
   Alleluia! Come, Lord, come!   *Charles Wesley, 1765*

Psalmody

Sunday: 42, 44, 45	Wednesday: 53, 55, 56	Friday: 61, 62, 66
Monday: 46, 47, 48	Thursday: 58, 59, 60	Saturday: 68a, 68b, 69a
Tuesday: 49, 50, 52		

Lesson

Sunday, Monday and Tuesday: Luke 21:25-38
Monday: Luke 21:5-19
Tuesday: Matthew 24:29-36

Wednesday and Thursday: Matthew 11:11-19
Thursday: Luke 7:24-35

Friday and Saturday: Luke 17:20-24
Saturday: Mark 13:19-23

Homily

Sunday - Martin Luther

Here you may say, who can lift up his head in the face of such terrible wrath and judgment? If the whole world is filled with fear at that day, and lets its head and countenance fall out of terror and anxiety, how shall we look up and lift up our heads, which evidently means, how shall we manifest any joy in and longing for these signs? In answer I would say that all this is spoken only to those who are truly Christians and not to heathen and Jews. True Christians are so afflicted with all manner of temptations and persecutions that in this life they are miserable. Therefore they wait and long and pray for redemption from sin and all evil; as we also pray in the Lord's Prayer, "Thy kingdom come," and "Deliver us from evil." If we are true Christians we will earnestly and heartily join in this prayer. If we do not so pray, we are not yet true Christians.

If we pray rightly, our condition must truly be such that, however terrible these signs may be, we will look up to them with joy and earnest desire, as Christ admonishes: "When these things begin to come to pass, look up." He does not say, Be filled with fear or drop your heads; for that for which we have been so earnestly praying is coming. If we really wish to be freed from sin and death and hell, we must look forward to this coming of the Lord with joy and pleasure.

Church Postil for the Second Sunday in Advent

Monday - Theophylactus of Bulgaria

For since He had foretold that there would be commotions, and wars, and changes in the elements, as well as in other things, lest some should fear that Christianity itself would be destroyed, He goes on to say: Heaven and earth shall pass away, but My words shall not pass away, as though saying: should all else be brought to nothing, My Faith shall not fail. In this He shows that He places the Church above every other creature; though all other creatures shall suffer change, the church of the faithful and the promises of the Gospel shall remain.

From the Catena Aurea of Thomas Aquinas

Tuesday - Ephrem the Syrian

But what shall we do, I ask you, when God comes down in anger and dreadful wrath and sits on the Throne of His Glory and summons all the earth to Himself, from the rising of the sun to the setting of it, and all the ends of the earth, so that He may judge His people and render to each according to his works? Oh, Woe! Woe! What kind of people shall we be then? In what state of mind shall we be, when naked and fearful we will appear there, delivered to that dread tribunal? Woe! Woe! Woe is me! Where now is the pride of the flesh? Where now is vain and useless beauty? Where, all human delight? Where then, shameless and impudent boldness? Where the delight of sin, sordid and unclean? What then of those who wallow in the wickedness of lust, of "what is shameful?" Where then will they be who worship with drum and wine and dance, but have not considered the works of the Lord? What then of those who have passed their lives in sloth and disorder? Where then will be the enticements of pleasure? All these things will have passed away, and like a little cloud will have been dissolved.

Where then shall avarice be, the desire of earthly possessions, from which arises hardness of heart? Where the monstrous pride that disposes all things, and thinks to itself that it alone exists? Where now the vain and fleeting success and glory of men? Where then human might? Where now is the tyrant? Where the king? Where the prince? Where the leader? Where the magistrate? Where are those that reveled in luxury, who gloried in the multitude of their riches and despised God? In that moment, look up; they will be struck dumb, they will be utterly confused and shaken. Fear will seize them; their pains as of a woman in labor. With a vehement wind You shall break them in pieces.

Where then will be the wisdom of the wise? Where all their vain cleverness? Woe! Woe! They are terrified; "They reel to and fro, and stagger like a drunken man, and are at their wits' end." Where now the learned? Where the scribe? Where the recruiting officer of this foolish world? My brother, what shall we be then, and in what state of soul, as we render an account of all things that we have done, big and small, even to the least; for even an idle word we will render an account to the Just Judge? What must we do that in that hour we may find mercy before Him?

And with what joy will we be filled if we are directed to the right hand of the King? What must we be like when the just embrace us there? When, I repeat, they will embrace thee there, Abraham, Isaac, Jacob, Moses, Noah, Job, Daniel, the holy prophets, the apostles, the martyrs, who all were pleasing to God in the days of the flesh? And whoever you have heard of, and whose life you have admired, and whom you now wish to look upon, they will come to you, and embrace you, rejoicing in your salvation. So what manner of men must we be? Of what sort shall be that unspeakable delight which we are to receive when the King will joyfully say to those who will be on His right hand: "Come, you blessed of My Father, inherit the kingdom prepared for you from the foundation of the world." *On Patience, the Second Coming, and the Last Judgment*

Wednesday - Martin Luther

John was to be a witness, testifying and preaching to the Jews about Him who is the Light and Life of mankind. He does not say that John instructed the people about his strict ascetic life, about drinking only water, wearing a garment of camel's hair, and subsisting on wild honey and locusts - all this perhaps with a view to organizing a new sect, calling upon all to emulate his example as a means of attaining salvation. If he had done this, he might have attracted the people to his person and become the founder of a new doctrine and sect. No; far from this! He comes as a witness; it is his office to point to Christ and to testify that He is the Lamb of God. In accordance with this mission, he directs all, even his own disciples, away from himself and toward Christ the Lord. It is as if he wanted to say: "I am not Christ, I am not the Light, I cannot illumine you, nor can I give you life. I must witness and preach about Christ, not about my camelskin or any other phase of my ascetic life. However, by means of my distasteful appearance I want to urge and arouse you to pay better attention to me as I testify of Christ, the Life and the Light of mankind. He was God and

Creator of heaven and earth from eternity, and now He has assumed human nature and is dwelling in your midst. He is the Bridegroom. His is the Bride." *Sermons on the Gospel of John*

Thursday - Anonymous

Our eternal salvation, the never-failing Light of the world.
Light everlasting and our true redemption.
Moved with compassion to see the human race perish by its idolatry, offered to its very tempter.
Not leaving Your high throne above,
You descended to these depths of our misery.
Then, by Your gracious love, assuming our human nature,
You saved all on earth that was lost.
Giving joy to this world.
Come, O Christ, purify our souls and bodies.
And make them Your own pure abode.
Justify us by Your first coming.
And in Your second, deliver us;
That when the day of great light comes, and you judge all things,
We may be adorned with a spotless robe, and may follow Your footsteps where ever they are seen.
Amen. *Prose from an eleventh century Roman-French Missal*

Friday - Cyril of Alexandria

But He will descend from heaven in the latter times of the world, neither obscurely nor secretly, but with divine glory, and as dwelling in light which no man can approach. This He declared saying that His coming will be like lightning. He was truly born in the flesh of a woman to fulfill the dispensation for our sakes. And for this reason He emptied Himself and made Himself poor, and no longer showed Himself in the glory of the Godhead. The times themselves and the necessity to give grace summoned Him to this humiliation. But after His resurrection from the dead - having ascended into heaven, and seated with God the Father - He will descend again, not with His glory hidden, not in the weakness of human nature, but in the majesty of the Father, with the companies of the angels guarding Him and standing before Him as God and Lord of all. He will come, therefore, as the lightning, and not secretly. *Homily 117 on Luke*

Saturday - Ambrose of Milan

There will be various signs in the sun, and in the moon, and in the stars. These signs are expressed more clearly in Matthew: "then," says He, "the sun will be darkened, and the moon will not give its light; the stars will fall from heaven." For the many falling away from Christianity, the brightness of faith will be dimmed by the cloud of apostasy; since the heavenly Sun grows dim, or shines in greater splendor, according to my faith. As when many together look at the rays of the earthly sun, it will seem dim or bright according to the eye of the beholder, so does the light of the Spirit fill each one according to the measure of his faith. And as the moon in its monthly eclipse disappears from view, by reason of the earth coming between it and the sun, so likewise the Holy Church, when the vices of flesh stand in the way of the celestial light, can no longer borrow the splendor of His divine light from the Sun of Christ. And in the persecutions it was invariably the love of this life that kept out the light of the Divine Sun.
Homily on the Gospel for the First Sunday in Advent

Collect:

Stir up our hearts, O Lord, to prepare the way of Your Only-begotten Son, so that by His coming we may be enabled to serve You with pure minds, who lives and reigns with You and the Holy Spirit, one God, now and forever.   *Gelasian Sacramentary*

AT LAUDS

Psalmody

Sunday: 3, C8, 51   Wednesday: 8, C11, 20   Friday: 146, C13, 15
Monday: 118a, C9, 118b   Thursday: 18a, C12, 18b   Saturday: 149, C14, 150
Tuesday: 1, C10, 2

Lesson

Sunday: Isaiah 11:1-10   Wednesday: Isaiah 16:1-8   Friday: Isaiah 22:20-25
Monday: Isaiah 12:1-6   Thursday: Isaiah 19:1-10   Saturday: Isaiah 25:1-9
Tuesday: Isaiah 14:1-11

Hymn, Verse and Antiphon to the Benedictus   *As during the week of Ad Te Levavi, p.229*

Collect

O Lord God, Father Almighty, purify the recesses of our heart, and mercifully wash away the stain of our sins; and grant, O Lord, that, cleansed from our sins by Your merciful blessing, we may await in confidence the dread and terrible coming of our Lord Jesus Christ, who lives and reigns with You and the Holy Spirit, one God, now and forever.   *Gallican Sacramentary*

AT TERCE, SEXT AND NONE

Chapter

Sunday, Monday and Tuesday: Romans 15:4-13
Wednesday and Thursday: Malachi 3:1-6
Friday and Saturday: II Corinthians 3:18-4:5

Responsories and Verses   *As during the week of Ad Te Levavi, p.230*

AT VESPERS

Psalmody

Sunday: 136b, 137, 138   Wednesday: 9, 10, 11   Friday: 17, 147a, 147b
Monday: 140, 141, 142   Thursday: 12, 13, 14, 16   Saturday: 19, 54, 77
Tuesday: 144, 145, 7

Lesson

Hymn, Verse and Antiphon to the Magnificat *As during the week of Ad Te Levavi, p.232*

Collect

Lord God, heavenly Father, by Your Son You have revealed to us that heaven and earth shall pass away, that our bodies shall rise again, and that we all shall appear before the judgment seat: we beseech You to keep us in Your Word by Your Holy Spirit; establish us in the true faith, graciously defend us from sin and preserve us in all temptations, that our hearts may not be weighed down with carousing, drunkenness, and cares of this life, but that we may always watch and pray and, trusting fully in Your grace, await with joy the glorious coming of Your Son, and at last obtain eternal salvation; through the same, Your beloved Son, Jesus Christ, our Lord, who lives and reigns with You and the Holy Spirit, one God, now and forever.

Veit Dietrich

GAUDETE
The Third Week in Advent

AT MATINS

Invitatory   *As during the week of Ad Te Levavi, p.225*

Hymn - *Jordanis oras praevia*

1. On Jor-dan's bank the Bap-tist's cry An-nounc-es that the Lord is nigh;

A-wake, and hear-ken, for he brings Glad tid-ings from the King of kings.

2. Then cleansed be ev'ry breast from sin
Make straight the way for God within.
And let us all our hearts prepare
For Christ to come and enter there.

3. We hail Thee as our Savior, Lord,
Our Refuge and our great Reward.
Without Thy grace we waste away
Like flowers that wither and decay.

4. Lay on the sick Thy healing hand
And make the fallen strong to stand;
Show us the glory of Thy face
Till beauty springs in every place.

5. All praise, Eternal Son, to Thee,
Whose advent sets Thy people free,
Whom with the Father we adore,
And Holy Spirit, evermore.

Charles Coffin, 1736

Psalmody

Sunday: 69b, 70, 71
Monday: 72, 73, 74
Tuesday: 78a, 78b, 78c

Wednesday: 75, 79, 80
Thursday: 81, 82, 83

Friday: 84, 86, 87, 93
Saturday: 85, 89a, 89b

Lesson

Sunday, Monday and Tuesday: Matthew 11:2-10
Monday: Luke 7:18-23
Tuesday: Luke 1:1-25

Wednesday and Thursday: Luke 1:26-38
Thursday: Luke 9:7-11

Friday : Luke 1:39-56
Saturday: Luke 3:1-6

Homily

Sunday - Martin Luther

This sending of his disciples is nothing else but John saying: Certainly I myself know that He is the true Christ, as I have been preaching about Him, but the people do not believe it yet. And since I am now in prison and must quit preaching, they won't regard my testimony about Him. Now go to Him yourselves so that you may be assured of this, and that my preaching to you not be wasted. Hear from His own lips, in order that from now on you may divorce yourselves from me and from all that is Jewish, and cling to this Man alone, upon whom your and the whole world's salvation depends. This is the ultimate purpose of the message of John to Christ, that his disciples might see and hear Him themselves, learn to know Him, and so believe in Him and be saved.

Well, what does Christ say to this message? He doesn't say "Yes" or "No" when they ask Him whether He was the one. Rather He points them to the public testimony of His works and says: Here you see, hear and comprehend that I am He. Just as Isaiah and other prophets have prophesied that Christ would heal the lame, give the blind their sight, etc., now you see it with your own eyes, and have no further need of instruction nor answer, if you will but rightly receive this.

This is a precious, beautiful sermon concerning Christ. It embraces everything that can be preached about Him - what kind of a king He is and what kind of a kingdom He has. His is a kingdom to which the blind, the lame, the leprous, the deaf, the dead, and especially poor sinners and all who are wretched, needy and worthless belong. And in it they find comfort and help. We should diligently mark this sermon about Christ and His kingdom, and always proclaim that Christ has such a kingdom, and is such a King, and is willing to help wretched, poor people, in body and soul, when the whole world and all that is in it can offer no help whatsoever. There has never been such a skillful Doctor before, who could restore sight to the blind, cleanse the lepers, etc.; just as there has never been a preacher who could preach the gospel to the poor, that is, who could truly comfort sad, wretched, anguished consciences, and cause timid hearts, filled with sadness and sorrow, to rejoice and be glad. *House Postil for the Third Sunday of Advent*

Monday - Hilary of Poitiers

And when the Lord had revealed Himself in wonders, namely in the blind seeing, the lame walking, in lepers being cleansed, the deaf hearing, the dumb speaking, in the dead rising again, and in the preaching of the Gospel to the poor, He says: "blessed is he who is not offended because of Me." Was there anything in what Christ had done which might scandalize John? Far from it. For in the whole course of his mission and teaching he had had nothing to say opposed to Him.

But the force and significance of the preceding sentence must be carefully pondered; namely, that which is preached to the poor; that is, they who have laid down their lives, who have taken up the cross and followed after, who have become humble in spirit, for these a kingdom is prepared in heaven. Therefore because this universality of suffering was to be fulfilled in Christ Himself, and because His cross would become a stumbling block to many, He now declares that they are blessed to whom His cross, His death, His burial, will offer no trial of faith. *Homily on the Gospel*

Tuesday - Johann Gerhard

When the Lord God prepared to announce to His people in the Old Testament the approaching Babylonian Captivity and the merciful deliverance from it, He gave them a great prophet and wondrous man, Jeremiah, who in the first chapter of his prophecy wrote of himself: "Now the word of the Lord came to me saying, Before I formed you in the womb I knew you, and before you were born I consecrated you; I appointed you a prophet to the nations." Likewise, the Lord God sent a great prophet at the beginning of the New Testament when He prepared to announce the coming of the salvation from the hellish power and prison by the Messiah, of which the deliverance from the Babylonian captivity by Cyrus was a type, as the captivity was also a prophetic picture of the destruction of the Jewish nation. This great prophet was John, who was filled with the Holy Spirit while still in his mother's womb and in this way consecrated to his holy and lofty office. Of him Christ said that he was a burning and shining light. He burned with a consuming love for Christ and with fiery zeal against the wicked. He shone also by the example of his holy life and by the brightness of his heavenly teaching. This burning and shining light was kindled in the Jewish land before the Sun of Righteousness arose and the day dawned from on high, before the promised Messiah appeared as the beautiful morning star shines bright and clear before the rising of the sun... of whom Christ the eternal Truth testified that among those born of women there has risen no one greater than John the Baptist.

Sermon on the Nativity of John the Baptist

Wednesday - Tertullian of Carthage

Isaiah foretells that it is fitting for Him to be called Immanuel... "Now," they say, "that Christ of yours, who is come, wasn't called by that name..." But we, on the contrary, think they ought to be admonished to remember the context of this passage. For attached to it is the interpretation of Immanuel - "God with us" - in order that you may consider not only how the name sounds, but its sense too. For the Hebrew sound, which is Immanuel, has an interpretation, which is, God with us. Ask, then, whether this saying, "God with us" (which is Immanuel), has been commonly applied to Christ ever since His light has dawned, and I think you won't be able to deny it. For those Jews who believe in Christ, ever since their believing on Him, whenever they shall wish to say Immanuel, do signify that God is with us: and thus it is agreed that He who was always predicted as Emmanuel is already come, because that which Immanuel signifies is come - that is, "God with us."

"But again," they say, "nature does not allow a 'virgin' to be a parent; and yet the prophet must be believed." And rightly so; for he spoke of faith in an incredible thing, saying that it was to be a sign. "Therefore," he says, "a sign will be given to you. Behold, the virgin shall conceive and bear a Son." But a sign from God would not have been recognized as a sign unless it consisted in some portentous novelty. In a word, if, when you are eager to topple someone's belief in this divine prediction or to convert the simple, you have the audacity to lie, as if the Scripture contained the announcement that not "a virgin," but "a young female," was to conceive and bring forth; you are refuted by the simple fact that a daily occurrence - that is, the pregnancy and childbearing of a young female - cannot possibly be seen as a sign. So then, the setting before us of a virgin-mother is rightly believed to be a sign.

An Answer to the Jews 9

Thursday - Gregory Thaumaturgas

Most of the holy fathers, and patriarchs, and prophets desired to see Him, and to be eye-witnesses of Him, but did not get to. And some of them by visions saw Him in type, and darkly; others, again, were privileged to hear the divine voice through the medium of the cloud, and were favored with sights of holy angels; but to Mary the pure virgin alone did the archangel Gabriel manifest himself luminously, bringing her the glad address, "Hail, highly favored one!" And thus she received the word. And in the due time, according to the natural course of the body, she brought forth the priceless pearl. Come, then, you too, dearly beloved, and let us chant the melody which has been taught us by the inspired harp of David, and say, "Arise, O Lord, to Your resting place, You and the ark of Your strength." For the holy Virgin is truly an ark, wrought with gold both within and without, that has received the whole treasury of the sanctuary. "Arise, O Lord, to Your resting place." Arise, O Lord, out of the bosom of the Father, in order that You may raise up the fallen race of the first-formed man.

First Homily on the Annunciation

Friday - Gregory Thaumaturgus

Christ, the Redeemer of our race, the Savior of all nature, the spiritual Adam who has healed the injury of the creature of earth, comes forth from Your holy womb. "Blessed are you among women, and blessed is the fruit of your womb." For He who bears all blessings for us is manifested as your fruit. This we read in the clear words of her who was barren; but yet more clearly did the holy Virgin herself express this again when she presented to God the song replete with thanksgiving, and acceptance, and divine knowledge; announcing ancient things together with what was new; proclaiming along with things which were of old, things also which belong to the consummation of the ages; and summing up in a short discourse the mysteries of Christ...

The whole mystery of salvation is comprehended in these few words. For, in order to save the race of men and to fulfill the covenant that was made with our father, Christ has once "bowed down the heavens and come down." And thus He shows Himself to us in a manner in which we are capable of receiving Him, in order that we might have power to see Him, to handle Him, and to hear Him when He speaks. And on this account God the Word deemed it proper to take upon Himself flesh and perfect humanity by a woman, the holy Virgin; and He was born a man, in order that He might discharge our debt and fulfil even in Himself the ordinances of the covenant made with Abraham.

Second Homily on the Annunciation

Saturday - Gregory I of Rome

What is meant by valleys but the humble, and by the hills and mountains but the proud? At the coming of the Redeemer therefore, the valleys will be filled, the mountains and hills brought low, according to His Word: Whoever exalts himself will be humbled, and he who humbles himself will be exalted. The valley that is filled in grows, the mountain and hill that is brought low diminishes, because in the faith of the Mediator of God and of men, the Man Jesus Christ, the Gentiles will receive the fullness of grace, and Judea, through the error of her pride which has caused her to be puffed up, will be brought low. Every valley will be filled, because the hearts of the humble will be replenished by the teachings of sacred truth with the gift of virtues... But as water falls away from the mountain, so the words of truth forsake the mind of the proud. But springs well up in the valleys because the minds of the humble accept the words of prophecy. *Sermon for the Vigil of the Fourth Sunday of Advent*

Collect

Lord, we pray You, give ear to our prayers, and lighten the darkness of our hearts by Your gracious visitation; who lives and reigns with the Father and the Holy Spirit, one God, now and forever.

Gelasian Sacramentary

AT LAUDS

Psalmody

Sunday: 67, C1, 5	Wednesday: 64, C4, 65	Friday: 76, C5, 92
Monday: 63, C2, 36	Thursday: 88, C6, 90	Saturday: 143, C7, 148
Tuesday: 43, C3, 57		

Lesson

Sunday: Isaiah 26:7-15	Wednesday: Isaiah 35:1-10	Friday: Isaiah 41:1-7
Monday: Isaiah 28:16-19	Thursday: Isaiah 40:9-11	Saturday: Isaiah 42:1-13
Tuesday: Isaiah 30:18-29		

Hymn and Verse *As during the week of Ad Te Levavi, p.229*

Antiphon to the Benedictus - *Super solium David* Tone 8G

Up - on the throne of Da - vid, and ov - er his king-dom, He will sit for - ev - er and ev - er. Al - le - lu - ia.

Isaiah 9:7

✠ BLESSÉD is the Lord God of / Israel; *
For He has visited and re- / deemed His people. etc.

Collect

O Lord Jesus Christ, who, having assumed human nature and having become the Savior of the human race, was given as a light to the nations; open the eyes of the hearts of those who believe in You, and mercifully set them free from their prison who are bound in the fetters of unbelief; and whom You see captive in prison and in the darkness of ignorance, enlighten, we beseech You, by the splendor of the knowledge of You, who lives and reigns with the Father and the Holy Spirit, one God, now and forever. *Mozarabic Breviary*

AT TERCE, SEXT AND NONE

Chapter

Sunday, Monday and Tuesday: I Corinthians 4:1-5
Wednesday and Thursday: Isaiah 7:10-14
Friday: Isaiah 11:1-5
Saturday: II Thessalonians 2:1-8

Responsories and Verses *As during the week of Ad Te Levavi, p.230*

AT VESPERS

Psalmody

Sunday: 110, 111, 112, 113   Wednesday: 123, 124, 125   Friday: 129, 130, 131, 132
Monday: 114, 115, 116, 117   Thursday: 126, 127, 128   Saturday: 133, 135, 136a
Tuesday: 120, 121, 122

Lesson

Sunday: Isaiah 27:1-6
Monday: Isaiah 29:17-24
Tuesday: Isaiah 34:1-8

Wednesday: Isaiah 40:1-8
Thursday: Isaiah 40:12-31

Friday: Isaiah 41:8-14
Saturday: Isaiah 43:1-13

Hymn and Verse   *As during the week of Ad Te Levavi, p.232*

Antiphon to the Magnificat - *Ante me non est*   *Tone 1f*

Be-fore Me there was no god; and there will be none

af - ter Me. To Me ev' - ry knee shall bow

and ev' - ry tongue shall con - fess.   *Isaiah 45:21b, 23b*

✠ MY SOUL / magnifies the Lord, *
And my spirit has rejoiced in / God my Savior. etc.

Antiphons for December 17-23 are found under Advent IV

Collect

Lord God, heavenly Father, You gave Your Son, our Lord Jesus Christ, to become Man and to come into the world that He might destroy the works of the devil, deliver us poor offenders from sin and death, and give us everlasting life; we beseech You so to rule and govern our hearts by Your Holy Spirit that we may always be found among the faithful followers of Your Son, Jesus Christ, and by faith in Him obtain eternal salvation; through the same, Your beloved Son, Jesus Christ, our Lord, who lives and reigns with You and the Holy Spirit, one God, now and forever.   *Veit Dietrich*

RORATE COELI
The Fourth Week in Advent

AT MATINS

Invitatory   *As during the week of Ad Te Levavi, p.225*

Hymn

1. O come, O come, Em - man - u - el, And ran-som cap-tive Is - ra - el,

That mourns in lone-ly ex - ile here, Un- til the Son of God ap-pear.

Re-joice! Re-joice! Em - man - u - el Shall come to thee, O Is - ra - el.

2. O come, Thou wisdom from on high,
Who orders all things mightily;
To us the path of knowledge show
And teach us in her ways to go.
Rejoice...

3. O come, O come, Thou Lord of might,
Who to Thy tribes on Sinai's height
In ancient times didst give the law
In cloud and majesty and awe.
Rejoice...

4. O come, Thou Rod of Jesse's stem
From ev'ry foe deliver them
That trust Thy mighty pow'r to save,
And give them vict'ry o'er the grave.
Rejoice...

5. O come, Thou Key of David, come,
And open wide our heav'nly home;
Make safe the way that leads on high,
And close the path to misery.
Rejoice...

6. O come, Thou Dayspring, come and cheer
Our spirits by Thine advent here;
Disperse the gloomy clouds of night,
And death's dark shadows put to flight.
Rejoice...

7. O come, Desire of nations, bind
All people in one heart and mind;
Bid Thou our sad divisions cease,
And be Thyself our King of Peace.
Rejoice...

Anonymous Versification of the O Antiphons, c.12th cent.

Psalmody

Sunday: 89c, 94, 96
Monday: 97, 98, 99, 100
Tuesday: 101, 102, 103

Wednesday: 104a, 104b, 104c
Thursday: 105a, 105b, 105c

Friday: 106a, 106b, 107a
Saturday: 107b, 108, 109

Lesson

Sunday, Monday and Tuesday: John 1:19-28

Monday: Mark 1:7-8
Tuesday: Mark 1:9-11

Wednesday and Thursday: Matthew 3:7-12

Friday : John 1:15-18

Christmas Eve: Matthew 1:18-25

Homily

Sunday - Gregory I of Rome

You know, dearest brethren, that the Only-Begotten Son is called the Word of the Father, as John testifies when he says: In the beginning was the Word, and the Word was with God, and the Word was God. From your own speech you are aware that the voice first sounds and then the word is heard. John accordingly declares that he is a Voice, because he precedes the Word. Going before the coming Lord, he is called a voice, because through his ministry the Word of the Lord is heard by men. He also cries out in the desert, because he is announcing to the lost and unhappy Judea the consolation of her Redeemer. He goes on to say what he cries out: Make straight the way of the Lord, as the prophet Isaiah says. The way of the Lord to the heart is made straight when His words of truth are received with humility. The way of the Lord to the heart is made straight when our life is lived in harmony with His teachings. Hence was it written: If any one loves Me, he will keep My Word, and My Father will love him and We will come to him, and make our home with him. *Homily 7 on the Gospels*

Monday - Augustine of Hippo

He said: "I am the voice of one crying the wilderness." What does the voice cry out? "Prepare the way of the Lord; make His paths straight." Doesn't it seem to you that it is the office of the Herald to cry out: stand aside, make way? Except that where a Herald says, "make way," John says, "come." A Herald sweeps men from before the path of the Judge; but John calls us to the Judge. Rather John calls us near to the Lowly One, lest we feel the power of the Mighty Judge. "I am the voice of one crying in the wilderness." He did not say: I am John, I am Elijah, I am the Prophet. But what did he say? "I am the voice of one crying in the wilderness. Prepare the way of the Lord." I am prophecy itself. *Tract 4 in John's Gospel*

Tuesday - Gregory I of Rome

Announcing the mystery of our redemption, John declares that it is already among men, and unknown to them; because the Lord, appearing in the flesh, was visible in His Body but invisible in Majesty. Of whom he also says, "He who comes after me, is preferred before me." For, "is preferred before me," is said to indicate who was before me... For He that was born of a mother in time was Begotten of the Father before all time.

He then teaches us by his own humility the reverence due Him by saying, "whose sandal strap I am not worthy to loose." It was a custom of the ancients that if a man was not willing to retain the woman who was his wife, that he should untie the shoes of the one who came by right of kinship to claim her as bride. How has Christ appeared among men, but as the Bridegroom of the Church? John also says of Him, "He that has the Bride is the Bridegroom." But as men believed that John was the Christ, which he denied, he rightly makes it clear that he is unworthy to untie His shoes. It is as if he were openly to say, "I am not worthy to uncover the feet of the Redeemer. And the title of Bridegroom, which is not mine, I will not usurp."

This may be understood in yet another way. Who doesn't know that sandals are made from the skins of dead animals? In His incarnation the Lord appears among men, as though shod; because over His Divinity, He has put on the mortal covering of our corruptibility... The straps of His sandal are therefore the seals of a mystery. John was not worthy to loose His sandal because he was unable to search into the mystery of His incarnation.

Homily 7 on the Gospels

Wednesday - Tertullian of Carthage

Freely promising grace, which in the last times God was intending to pour as a flood of light on the world through His Spirit, He commanded that the baptism of repentance lead the way. He did so to prepare those whom He was calling through grace to inherit the promise made to Abraham, by means of the sign and seal of repentance. John is not silent, but says, "Repent, for now salvation is coming to the nations" - that is, the Lord who is bringing salvation according to God's promise. John, as His forerunner, directed to Him the repentance which he preached. This was preached to purge men's minds, that whatever defilement deep-seated error had imparted, whatever contamination ignorance had bred in the heart of man, repentance should sweep, scrape away, and cast out the door; and thus cleanse and prepare the home of the heart for the Holy Spirit.

On Repentance

Thursday - Hippolytus of Rome

We who know the way God works adore His mercy, because He has come, not to judge, but to save the world. For this reason John, the forerunner of the Lord... cried out and spoke to those who came to be baptized by him, "O Brood of Vipers," why do you look so earnestly at me? I am not the Christ. I am the servant, not the lord; I am the subject, not the king; I am the sheep, not the shepherd; I am a man, not God. By my birth I loosed the barrenness of my mother; I did not make virginity barren. I was brought up from beneath; I did not come down from above. I bound the tongue of my father; I did not unfold divine grace. I was known by my mother; I was not announced by a star. I am worthless, and the least; but after me there comes One who is before me - after me indeed in time, but before by reason of the inaccessible and unspeakable light of divinity. "He who is coming after me is mightier than I, whose sandals I am not worthy to carry. He will baptize you with the Holy Spirit and fire." I am subject to authority, but He has authority Himself. I am bound by sins, but He is the Remover of sins. I apply the Law, but He brings grace to light. I teach as a slave, but He judges as the Master. I have the earth as my couch, but He possesses heaven. I baptize with the baptism of repentance, but He confers the gift of adoption. "He will baptize you with the Holy Spirit and fire." Why do you give attention to me? I am not the Christ.

Homily on the Holy Theophany

Friday - Martin Luther

"Behold the Lamb of God, who takes away the sin of the world." This is the chief article of our Christian doctrine; on it our faith is founded. It is necessary that we know this Lamb well - His person, His function, and His office. We must know that He is the bearer of sin, not only of ours but of that of the entire world. These are, to be sure, brief words; but they are terse and comprehensive, including almost everything recorded about Christ's deeds for us, as for example, His birth, His suffering, death, and resurrection. The fact that St. John calls Him the Lamb of God implies that He was sent by God and not chosen by man.

Now another testimony of Christ's divinity is added; for John declares that Christ existed before him... In the beginning of John's Gospel you heard the evangelist describe John the Baptist as a witness to the Lamb, testifying that He is very God and God's Son, but also true man, because God had become man. Later on the Lamb let Himself be slaughtered and sacrificed for us; He bore the sins of the whole world. This sermon and testimony of John regarding the Lamb that bears the sin of the world is to endure until the end of the world.

Sermon 13 on the Gospel of John

Christmas Eve, December 24th - Johann Gerhard

It is proper also to observe that Christ is called the First-born, not that Mary may later have had more children; rather in keeping with the mode of the holy language [Greek], He is called the First-born who is born first, no matter whether He later had other brothers or not. Christ is the only-begotten Son of His heavenly Father, who was sired by Him in eternity; that's why He through this eternal birth possesses from the Father all heavenly gifts and treasures. But it pleased Him that He also wanted to be the first-born Son of Mary; and thus He also for a second time had the right to the heavenly treasures, just as in the Old Testament the first-born possessed the kingdom and the priesthood. The one right to the heavenly treasures He kept for Himself, but the other He gave to us as His brothers and sisters, as is written about this in Rev. 1:5, that He is the first-born who has made us into kings and priests before God and His Father. If a rich brother can bequeath the inheritance of the father's treasures to his brothers and sisters, how much more will not this our wealthy Brother, who is Lord of heaven and earth, be able to give us the kingdom of His treasures which He has won for us through His birth in poverty, through His holy life and through His bitter death! By grace He wants to do this. *Sermon on Holy Christmas Day I*

Collects

Through December 23rd

Stir up, O Lord, we pray You, Your power, and come and help us with Your great might, that by Your grace whatever is hindered by our sins may be quickly accomplished through Your mercy and satisfaction; who lives and reigns with the Father and the Holy Spirit, one God, now and forever.

Gelasian Sacramentary

December 24th

O Jesus, almighty Son of God, mercifully come and save Your people on the day of Your nativity; and deign in Your compassion to deliver us from all the anxieties and fears of this present age; who lives and reigns with the Father and the Holy Spirit, one God, now and forever.

Ambrosian Missal

AT LAUDS

Psalmody

Sunday: 3, C8, 51
Monday: 118a, C9, 118b
Tuesday: 1, C10, 2

Wednesday: 8, C11, 20
Thursday: 18a, C12, 18b

Friday: 146, C13, 15
Saturday: 149, C14, 150

Lesson

Sunday: Isaiah 43:25-44:8
Monday: Isaiah 45:1-8
Tuesday: Isaiah 51:1-8

Wednesday: Isaiah 60:1-9
Thursday: Isaiah 62:1-12

Friday: Isaiah 64:1-8
Saturday: Isaiah 66:10-24

Hymn and Verse   *As during the week of Ad Te Levavi, p.229, through December 23rd.*

December 24th

℣: Tomorrow the iniquity of the world shall be blotted / out.
R℣: And the Savior of the world shall rule over / us.

Liturgical text

Antiphon to the Benedictus - *Consolamini, consolamini* Tone 2

Be com-fort- ed, be com- fort - ed, My peo - ple, says your God. *Isaiah 40:1*

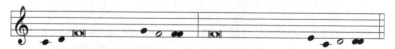

✠ BLESSÉD is the Lord God of Is-/ rael; *
For He has visited and redeemed / His people. etc.

Collect

O God, whose nature and property is goodness, and with whom there is no change, be propitious to our prayers, and show to Your Church Your mercy, which we confess; show to Your people the wonderful mystery of Your only-begotten Son; that what You have promised according to the Word of Your Gospel may be fulfilled by all nations coming to faith, and that the testimony of truth may be verified by the completion of adoption; through Christ our Lord, who lives and reigns with You and the Holy Spirit, one God, now and forever. *Gallican Missal*

December 24th:

O merciful and most loving God, by whose will and bounteous grace our Lord Jesus Christ humbled Himself that He might exalt the whole human race, and came down to what was lowest the He might raise up the humble; who being God, did become man, born of a Virgin, that He might re-form in man the heavenly image that had been corrupted; grant that these, Your people, may cling to You, and that they, whom You have redeemed by Your bounteous grace, may ever please You in devout service, through the same, Jesus Christ, Your Son, our Lord, who lives and reigns with You and the Holy Spirit, one God, now and forever. *Gallican Missal*

AT TERCE, SEXT AND NONE

Chapter

Sunday, Monday and Tuesday: Philippians 4:4-7
Wednesday and Thursday: II Peter 3:8-10
Friday: James 4:17-5:8
December 24th: Romans 1:1-6

Responsories and Verses *As during the week of Ad Te Levavi, p.230*

AT VESPERS

Psalmody

Sunday: 136b, 137, 138
Monday: 140, 141, 142
Tuesday: 144, 145, 7

Wednesday: 9, 10, 11
Thursday: 12, 13, 14, 16

Friday: 17, 147a, 147b
Saturday: 19, 54, 77

Lesson

Sunday: Isaiah 44:21-28
Monday: Isaiah 49:1-13
Tuesday: Isaiah 55:1-11

Wednesday: Isaiah 61:1-11
Thursday: Isaiah 63:15-19

Friday: Isaiah 65:17-25
December 24: Isaiah 9:2-7

Hymn and Verse   *As during the week of Ad Te Levavi, p.232, through December 23rd.*

December 24th - *Von Himmel Hoch*

1. From heav'n a - bove to earth I come To
bear good news to ev - 'ry home; Glad ti - dings of great
joy I bring, Where - of I now will say and sing:

2. To you this night is born a child
Of Mary chosen virgin mild;
This little child of lowly birth,
Shall be the joy of all the earth.

3. This is the Christ, our God and Lord,
Who in all need shall aid afford;
He will Himself your Savior be
From all your sins to set you free.

4. He will on you the gifts bestow
Prepared by God for all below,
That in His kingdom, bright and fair,
You may with us His glory share.

5. These are the tokens ye shall mark:
The swaddling-clothes and manger dark;
There ye shall find the Infant laid
By whom the heavens and earth were made.

6. Now let us all with gladsome cheer
Go with the shepherds and draw near
To see the precious Gift of God,
Who hath His own dear Son bestowed.

7. Give heed, my heart, lift up thine eyes!
What is it in yon manger lies?
Who is this child, so young and fair?
The blessèd Christ-child lieth there.

8. Welcome to earth, Thou noble Guest,
Through whom the sinful world is blest!
Thou com'st to share my misery;
What thanks shall I return to Thee?

9. Ah, Lord, who hast created all,
How weak are Thou, how poor and small,
That Thou dost choose Thine infant bed
Where humble cattle lately fed!

10. Were earth a thousand times as fair,
    Beset with gold and jewels rare,
    It yet were far too poor to be
    A narrow cradle, Lord, for Thee.

11. For velvets soft and silken stuff
    Thou has but hay and straw so rough,
    Whereon Thou, King, so rich and great,
    As 'twere Thy heaven, art throned in state.

12. And thus, dear Lord, it pleaseth Thee
    To make this truth quite plain to me,
    That all the world's wealth, honor, might,
    Are naught and worthless in Thy sight.

13. Ah, dearest Jesus, holy Child,
    Make Thee a bed, soft, undefiled,
    Within my heart, that it may be
    A quiet chamber kept for Thee.

14. My heart for very joy doth leap,
    My lips no more can silence keep;
    I, too, must sing with joyful tongue
    That sweetest ancient cradle-song:

15. Glory to God in highest heaven,
    Who unto us His Son hath given!
    While angels sing with pious mirth
    A glad new year to all the earth.

Martin Luther, 1524

Antiphon to the Magnificat:

December 17 - *O Sapientia*   Tone 2

O   Wis - dom   who pro-ceeds from the mouth of the Most

High,   reach-ing   from be - gin - ning to   end,   or - der-

ing   all things might - i - ly   and   sweet - ly;   Come,   and

teach   us   the   way of   pru - dence.

Liturgical text on Ecclesiasticus 24:3, Wisdom 8:1

✠ MY SOUL magnifies / the Lord, *
    And my spirit has rejoiced in God / my Savior. etc.

December 18 - *O Adonai*

O   A - do - na - i   and Ru - ler of the house of Is - ra-

el,   who ap-peared to Mo - ses   in   the   fire   of   the burn - ing

bush,   and on Mount Si - nai   gave him Your   Law:

Come,   and   with   an   out-stretched arm re - deem   us.

Liturgical text on Exodus 3:2, Nehemiah 9:13

December 19 - *O radix Jesse*   Tone 2

O   Root   of   Jes - se,   who stands as   a   sign   of   the   peo-

ple,   be - fore whom kings shall keep   si - lence,   and to

whom all   na - tions shall   have   re - course: Come,   and

save   us,   and   do   not   de - lay.

Liturgical text on Isaiah 11:10, 52:15

December 20 - *O clavis David*   Tone 2

O Key of Da - vid and Scep-ter of the house of Is - ra - el,

who o - pens and no man clos - es;   who clos - es

and no man o - pens: Come, and lead the

cap - tive from the pris - on house,   who sits in dark-

ness and in the sha-dow of death.   *Liturgical text on Isaiah 22:22, 42:7*

December 21 - *O Oriens*   Tone 2

O Day - spring, Splen - dor of E - ter - nal Light

and Sun of Jus - tice: Come, and en - light - en

those who sit in dark - ness   and in the sha-dow of death.
Liturgical text on Zechariah 6:12 (Vulgate), Luke 2:78-79

December 22 - *O Rex gentium*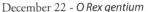 Tone 2

O King of Na - tions, and their De - sired One; the Cor-

ner - stone who makes of both one: Come, and

save man, whom You have formed out of dust.

Liturgical text on Jeremiah 10:7, Haggai 2:7, Isaiah 28:16

December 23 - *O Emmanuel* Tone 2

O Em - man - u - el, our King and Law - giv - er, Ex-

pec - ta - tion of the na - tions and their Sa - vior:

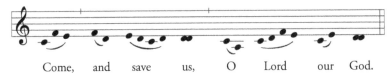

Come, and save us, O Lord our God.

Liturgical text on Isaiah 7:14, 33:22

December 24th - *Cum ortus fuerit* Tone 8G

When the sun shall have ris - en in the hea-vens, you shall see the

King of Kings: Com - ing from the Fa - ther,

255

as   a   Bride-groom from his   cham - ber.   *Liturgical text*

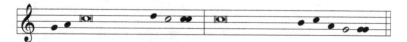

✠ MY SOUL magnifies / the Lord, *
And my spirit has rejoiced in / God my Savior. etc.

Collect

Lord God, heavenly Father, it is good and right that we should give thanks to You, that You have given us a glorious baptism like that of John the Baptist, and that therein You have promised us the forgiveness of sins, the Holy Spirit, and everlasting life through Your Son, Jesus Christ; we beseech You, by Your grace and mercy preserve us in such faith, that we never doubt Your promise, but be comforted by our baptism in all temptations; and grant us Your Holy Spirit that we may renounce sin, and ever continue in the righteousness bestowed on us in baptism, until, by Your grace, we obtain our eternal salvation; through the same, Your beloved Son, Jesus Christ, our Lord, who lives and reigns with You and the Holy Spirit, one God, now and forever.

Veit Dietrich

December 24th

O God, who has made this holy night to shine with the brightness of the true Light, grant, we pray you, that, as we have known on earth the mysteries of that Light, we may also come to the fullness of its joys in heaven; through the same Jesus Christ, Your Son, our Lord, who lives and reigns with You and the Holy Spirit, one God, now and forever.   *Gelasian Sacramentary*

CHRISTMASTIDE
December 25 - January 5

AT MATINS

Invitatory - *Christus natus est* Tone 6

Christ is born to us. O come, let us wor-ship Him!

Hymn - *Gelobet Seist Du, Jesu Christ*

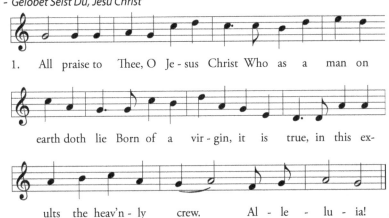

1. All praise to Thee, O Je-sus Christ Who as a man on earth doth lie Born of a vir-gin, it is true, in this ex-ults the heav'n-ly crew. Al - le - lu - ia!

2. The Father's one begotten Son
In manger low has made his cot,
In our poor dying flesh and blood
Doth mask itself the endless Good.
Alleluia!

3. Whom all the world could not enwrap,
Now lies helpless in Mary's lap.
A little child He's now become,
Who everything upholds alone.
Alleluia!

4. In Him th'eternal light breaks through
He gives the world a glory new;
A great light shines amid the night,
And makes us children of the light.
Alleluia!

5. The Father's Son, so God by name,
A guest into our world He came,
And leads us from the vale of tears;
He in His palace makes us heirs.
Alleluia!

6. Poor to the earth He cometh thus,
Such pity doth He take on us,
And makes us rich in heaven above,
And like the angels of His love.
Alleluia!

7. All this for us did Jesus do,
That His great love he might thus show.
Let Christendom rejoice therefore,
And give Him thanks forevermore.
Alleluia!

Based on Latin sequence, 11th cent
German, st. 1, 1370; Martin Luther, st. 2-7, 1524

Psalmody

Dec. 25: 2, 19, 72	Dec. 29: 30, 31, 32	Jan. 2: 42, 44, 45
Dec. 26: 21,22, 23	Dec. 30: 33, 34, 35	Jan. 3: 46, 47, 48
Dec. 27: 24, 25, 26	Dec. 31: 37a, 37b, 38	Jan. 4: 49, 50, 52
Dec. 28: 27, 28, 29	Jan. 1: 39, 40, 41	Jan. 5: 53, 55, 56

Lesson

The Nativity of Our Lord, December 25, 29-31: Luke 2:1-14
St. Stephen, December 26: Matthew 23:34-39
St. John the Evangelist, December 27: John 1:1-14
Holy Innocents, December 28: Matthew 2:13-23

December 29: Luke 2:15-20
December 30: Matthew 1:1-17
December 31: Luke 3:23-38

January 1-5: Luke 2:21

January 2: Luke 2:22-35
January 3: Luke 2:36-38
January 4: Luke 2:39-40
January 5: Matthew 1:18-21

Homily

The Nativity of Our Lord, December 25 - Leo I of Rome

Our Savior, dearly Beloved, was born this day. Let us rejoice. Sadness is not proper on the birthday of Life Itself. Life, by having dispelled the fear of death, fills us with gladness because of our own promised immortality. No one is excluded from sharing in this cheerfulness. The reason for our joy is common to all men. Our Lord, the Conqueror of sin and death, finding no one free from guilt, came that He might bring deliverance to all.

Let saints exult, for the palm of victory lies within their reach. Let sinners rejoice, for they have been called to pardon. Let the heathens take heart, for they have been called to life. The Son of God, in the fullness of time, as the unsearchable depths of divine wisdom has ordained, has taken upon Himself our human nature, so that the inventor of death, the devil, would be himself overcome through the very nature which he had overcome.

Sermon 21

St. Stephen, December 26 - Augustine of Hippo

In case you should say it's too much to expect of you to imitate your Lord, though "He suffered for you, leaving you an example, so that you might follow in His footsteps," take a look at Stephen, your fellow servant. He was a human being like you. He was born of the same sinful lump as you. He was redeemed with the same price as you were too. He was a deacon. He used to read the gospel, which you also read or hear. There he found it written, "Love your enemies." He learned the lesson he read there, he carried it out in practice. When he was being murdered by the Jews under a hail of rocks, not only did he not utter any threats against them, but over and above that he prayed for pardon for those who were stoning him. Kneeling down, you see, he began praying, and said: "Lord, do not hold this sin against them." They were stoning him, he was praying for them; they were pursuing him with rage, he was peaceably following Christ. They were blinded by their malice; for him the heavens were opened, he saw the Son of God, and he was enlightened by wisdom. They were hurling stones, he was shooting prayers ahead, as though he were saying, "Lord, if you kill these enemies now, whom will you later on make into friends?"

Sermon 382

St. John the Evangelist, December 27 - Cyril of Alexandria

Is it not wicked and shocking to try to take away from God the Word His birth from a woman according to the flesh? For how could His body possibly give life to us if were not the very own body of Him who is Life? And how could it be that the "blood of Jesus cleanses us from all sin" if it was really only that of an ordinary man subject to sin? And how has "God the Father sent his Son born of a woman, born subject to the law?" Or how has "He condemned sin in the flesh?" To condemn sin does not belong to someone with a nature like ours, under the tyranny of sin, an ordinary man. But insofar as it became the body of the one who knew no transgression, how rightly it could shake off the tyranny of sin to enjoy all the personal riches of the Word who is ineffably united with it in a manner beyond all description. Thus it is a holy and life-giving thing, full of divine energy. And we too are transformed in Christ as first-fruits, to be above corruption and sin. What the blessed Paul says is true: "Just as we bore the image of the earthly, so shall we bear the image of the heavenly," that is to say, of Christ. Christ is understood as the Heavenly Man, not as if He brought down His flesh from on high and out of heaven, but because the Word who is God came down from out of heaven and entered our likeness, that is to say submitted to birth from a woman according to the flesh, while ever remaining what He was, that is one from on high, from heaven, superior to all things as God even with the flesh. This is what the divine John says about Him somewhere: "He who comes from above is above all." He remained Lord of all things even when He came, for the economy, in the form of a slave, and this is why the mystery of Christ is truly wonderful. Indeed God the Father said to the Jews through one of the prophets: "Look on this you scoffers, be struck with wonder and disappear, for I am doing a work in your days, a work in which you will not believe even if one were to explain it to you." Indeed the mystery of Christ runs the risk of being disbelieved precisely because it is so incredibly wonderful. For God was in humanity. He who was above all creation was in our human condition; the invisible one was made visible in the flesh; He who is from the heavens and from on high was in the likeness of earthly things. The immaterial one could be touched; He who is free in His own nature came in the form of a slave; He who blesses all creation came to be accursed; He who is all righteousness was numbered among transgressors; life itself came in the appearance of death. All this followed because the body which tasted death belonged to no other but to Him who is the Son by nature. *On the Unity of Christ*

Holy Innocents, December 28 - Leo I of Rome

When the wise men had worshipped the Lord and completed all their devotion, in accordance with the warning given them in a dream, they do not go back the same way they had come. It was appropriate for them, now that they believed in Christ, to no longer walk the paths of their former way of life, but to take a new path and refrain from the wandering they had left behind. They also foiled the plots of Herod in this way, who, under the guise of homage, was arranging for a godless plot against the Infant Jesus.

Because his machinations were overthrown, the king's wrath rages even more. Reckoning from the time which the wise men had indicated, he pours out his cruel rage on all the little boys at Bethlehem. In a wide-scale slaughter he massacres the infants of that entire city, infants who would pass over into eternal glory, thinking that if he kills every single boy there he would kill Christ too.

But He who was postponing the shedding of His blood for the world's redemption until another time, was carried and brought into Egypt by the aid of His parents. He was going back, of course, to the ancient cradle of the Hebrew nation. By the power of a greater providence He arranged for the reign of the true Joseph. Coming from heaven as the Bread of Life and Food of Reason, He dispelled that famine - more dreadful than any other kind of hunger - by which the minds of the Egyptians were suffering: the lack of truth. Without that journey, the symbolism of that One Victim would not have been complete; for it is there, in the slaying of the lamb, that the saving sign of the Cross and the Passover of the Lord had first been prefigured.   *Sermon 33*

December 29 - John Chrysostom

I behold a new and wondrous mystery. My ears resound to the Shepherd's song, piping no soft melody, but chanting full forth a heavenly hymn. The angels sing. The archangels blend their voices in harmony. The cherubim hymn their joyful praise. The seraphim exalt His glory. All join to praise this holy feast, beholding the Godhead here on earth, and man in heaven. He who is above, now dwells here below for our redemption; and he that was lowly is by divine mercy raised.

Bethlehem this day resembles heaven; hearing from the stars the singing of angelic voices; and in place of the sun, enfolds within itself on every side, the Sun of Justice. And don't ask how: for where God wills, the order of nature yields. For He willed, He had the power, He descended, He redeemed; all things move in obedience to God. This day He who is, is Born; and He who is, becomes what He was not. For when He was God, He became man; yet not departing from the Godhead that is His. Nor yet by any loss of divinity did He become man, nor through the increase did He become God from man; but being the Word He became flesh, His nature, because of impassibility, remaining unchanged.   *Homily on Christmas Morning*

December 30 - Ephrem the Syrian

Blessed be that Child who gladdened Bethlehem today! Blessed be the Babe who made manhood young again today! Blessed be the Fruit, who lowered Himself to our famished state! Blessed be the Good One, who suddenly enriched our poverty and supplied our needs! Blessed be He whose tender mercies made Him condescend to visit our infirmities!

Praise to the Fountain that was sent for our propitiation. Praise be to Him who made void the Sabbath by fulfilling it! Praise too to Him who rebuked the leprosy and it remained not, whom the fever saw and fled! Praise to the Merciful, who bore our toil! Glory to Thy coming, which quickened the sons of men!

Glory to Him, who came to us by His First-born! Glory to the Silence, that spake by His Voice. Glory to the One on high, who was seen by His Dayspring! Glory to the Spiritual, who was pleased to have a Body, that in it His virtue might be felt, and He might by that Body show mercy on His household's bodies!

Glory to that Hidden One, whose Son is made manifest! Glory to that Living One, whose Son was made to die! Glory to that Great One, whose Son descended and was small! Glory to the Power who did confine His greatness by a form, His unseen nature by a shape!   *Hymn 2 on the Nativity*

December 31 - Bede the Venerable

So that the authority of one angel might not seem insufficient, when one from among them had announced the mystery of the nativity, "suddenly there was with the angel a multitude of the heavenly host." It is fitting that the approaching choir of angels be called the "heavenly army," which now humbly comes to adore that "Leader who is mighty in battle;" who has appeared to break down the gates of Hell; who alone, in Power and with heavenly might, has cast down those hostile powers whom man himself was powerless to overcome however much he strove or desired. Since both God and man is truly born, then rightly is peace proclaimed to men, and glory to God. Hence there follows: "Glory to God in the highest, and on earth peace, good will toward men!" Upon the announcement of one angel, one messenger, that God was born in the flesh, suddenly the multitude of the heavenly host break forth in praise of their Creator. May this example inspire us to greater devotion to Christ, so that, as often as one of the brethren gives forth a word of sacred praise, or we in our hearts should recall the things of holy love, we may immediately give praise to God, with voice, with deed, and in our hearts.

Homily on Luke 2

The Circumcision of our Lord, January 1 - Martin Luther

Personally, He had no need of circumcision, as little as He needed to obey His mother, or even to die on the cross! He had both right and authority not to be subjected to the Law; He did it for our sakes. But we needed a sinless one to keep the Law in our stead and thus appease the wrath of God, otherwise we would be under the curse of the Law forever. That's why He put Himself under the Law, and with His merit and work earned freedom for us from the Law, as St. Paul says in Galatians 4:4-5: "But when the fullness of time had come, God sent forth His Son, born of a woman, born under the law, to redeem those who were under the law, that we might receive the adoption as sons." The fact that He placed Himself under the Law was not done for His sake, for He had satisfied all righteousness and holiness required by the Law without such obedience. But He came under the Law for our sakes; and the victory and righteousness He attained there was granted to us, as He states, "Whoever believes on Me," him will neither circumcision nor law bind any longer, for, although I was not beholden to them, nonetheless I subjected myself under their demands and satisfied them; and by so doing, both circumcision and the Law have become subject to Me, their Lord who has exhausted their power. Therefore, whoever clings to Me in true faith I will assist in being made free from both the Law's and circumcision's burden so that he will not come under judgment.

First Sermon for New Year's Day

January 2 - John Chrysostom

So many are the wonders wrought by this Name! If you say with faith: In the Name of the Father, and of the Son, and of the Holy Ghost, you have done what is asked. See what great things you have done; for you have created within you a man, a new man, as well as the other effects of baptism. So likewise in commanding the sick this is a name of power. For this reason the devil, envying the honor given to us, has brought in the use of the name of angels. These are incantations of the demons. Even if it should be an angel, even an archangel, or even the very Cherubim, do not stand for it. For these very Powers will not hear, but turn away, when they have seen that it is but an affront to the Lord.

I have honored you, He says, and I have said, "Call upon Me;" and do you offend Him with dishonor? If you chant this hymn with praise, you will put to flight both demons and infirmities; and if you don't banish sickness, this happens not from lack of power, but because it is not expedient for you.

"According to Your name, so is Your praise." By this Name the whole world was changed, tyranny was laid low, the devil trod under foot, the heavens thrown open. What do I say: the heavens? We by this Name are born again. If this has happened to us, we are already glorified! This Name makes both martyrs and confessors; let us hold fast to it, as to a great gift, that we may live in glory, and that we may be pleasing to God, and be held worthy of the good things that are promised to those who love Him in grace and generosity of heart, through Jesus Christ our Lord, to whom be honor and glory, now and forever. Amen.

Homily 9 on Colossians 3:17

January 3 - Bernard of Clairvaux

The name of Jesus is not light alone, it is also food. Are you not strengthened as often as you recall it? What so fills the heart of him who meditates upon it? What so refreshes the tired senses, strengthens virtue, nourishes good and worthy habits, fosters pure affections? Dry indeed is all food of the soul, if it is not dipped in this oil; tasteless, if unseasoned by this salt. If you write anything, that which you write has no flavor unless I perceive there the name of Jesus. Should there be discussion, or if we converse together, for me it is again without flavor, unless I hear there the name of Jesus. Jesus is sweet upon the tongue, melody to the ear, and joy in the heart.   *On the Canticles*

January 4 - Martin Luther

Whoever esteems this child as Savior does God the greatest and highest honor, as Christ Himself says in John 5:23, "that all should honor the Son just as they honor the Father. He who does not honor the Son does not honor the Father who sent Him." If you receive Christ as your Savior, God is well-disposed toward you and no wrath is in Him. If God is well-disposed towards you, how can it harm you that the whole world rages against you? But if you do not esteem the Son as your Savior but seek after another helper, or think that your sins are greater than this child can rescue you from, you do God the greatest dishonor and make your salvation most uncertain. For God nowhere says that your good works should be your Savior. But when you believe on the Son, you have taken God captive in His promise. For He has named His Son to be the whole world's Savior.

That is the significance of the name Jesus, which was given to the Child, first by the angel before His conception, and then afterward by His mother at the time of His circumcision on the eighth day. As we have heard, that name serves for this purpose, that whoever believes that after this life there is another life might know where to find eternal life, namely, in this Child alone who is called Jesus, that is, Savior, and there is none other.   *Second Sermon for New Year's Day*

January 5 - Johann Gerhard

O Blessed Jesus, be Thou indeed a Jesus to me; for Thy holy name's sake have compassion on me! My life condemns me, but the name of Jesus will save me. For Thy name's sake deal with me according to Thy name; and since Thou are a true and great Savior, Thou wilt surely regard with mercy those who are real and great sinners. Have mercy upon me, O blessed Jesus, in the day of mercy, so as not to condemn me in the day of judgment. If Thou wilt receive me within the bosom of Thy compassion Thou wilt not on my account be the more straitened; if Thou wilt bestow upon me some crumbs of Thy goodness Thou wilt not, on that account, be the poorer. For me Thou art born, for me Thou art circumcised, to me also Thou art Jesus. How sweet and delightful is the name of Jesus! For what is Jesus but Savior? And what real harm can befall the saved? What beyond salvation can we either seek or expect? Receive me, O Lord Jesus, into the number of Thy children, so that with them I may praise Thy holy and saving name.   *Sacred Meditation 4*

Collects

December 25-31

Grant, we pray You, Almighty God, that the new birth of Your only-begotten Son in the flesh may set us free, who are held under the old bondage, under the yoke of sin; through the same Jesus Christ, Your Son, our Lord, who lives and reigns with You and the Holy Spirit, one God, now and forever.

Gelasian Sacramentary

January 1

O Lord God, who for our sakes has made Your blessèd Son, our Savior, subject to the Law and has caused Him to endure the circumcision of the flesh, grant us the true circumcision of the Spirit that our hearts may be pure from all sinful desires and lusts; through the same Jesus Christ, Your Son, our Lord, who lives and reigns with You and the Holy Spirit, one God, now and forever.

Gregorian Sacramentary

January 2-5

Almighty and Everlasting God, direct our actions according to Your good pleasure, that in the name of Your beloved Son we may be made to abound in good works; through the same Jesus Christ, Your Son, our Lord, who lives and reigns with You and the Holy Spirit, one God, now and forever.

Gelasian Sacramentary

AT LAUDS

Psalmody

Dec. 25: 45, C1, 98	Dec. 29: 64, C5, 65	Jan. 2: 3, C2, 51
Dec. 26: 67, C2, 5	Dec. 30: 88, C6, 90	Jan. 3: 118a, C3, 118b
Dec. 27: 63, C3, 36	Dec. 31: 76, C7, 92	Jan. 4: 1, C4, 2
Dec. 28: 43, C4, 57	Jan. 1: 143, C1, 148	Jan. 5: 8, C5, 20

Lesson

Dec. 25: Titus 2:11-14	Dec. 29: Romans 7:1-12	Jan. 2: Romans 12:9-21
Dec. 26: Romans 1:8-17	Dec. 30: Romans 9:1-5	Jan. 3: Romans 13:11-14
Dec. 27: Romans 3:1-8	Dec. 31: Romans 10:11-17	Jan. 4: Romans 15:1-6
Dec. 28: Romans 5:1-11	Jan. 1: Romans 11:25-36	Jan. 5: Romans 16:17-20

Hymn - *A solis ortus cardine*

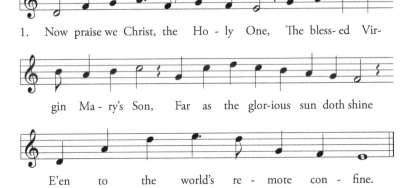

1. Now praise we Christ, the Ho - ly One, The bless- ed Vir-gin Ma - ry's Son, Far as the glor-ious sun doth shine E'en to the world's re - mote con - fine.

2. He who Himself all things did make
A servant's form vouchsafed to take
That He as man mankind might win
And save His creatures from their sin.

3. The grace and pow'r of God the Lord
Upon the mother was outpoured;
A virgin pure and undefiled
In wondrous wise conceived a child.

4. The holy maid became the home
And temple of the living God,
And she, who knew not man, was blest
With God's own Word made manifest.

5. The noble mother bore a Son -
For so did Gabriel's promise run, -
Whom John confessed and leaped with joy
Ere yet his mother knew her boy.

6. Upon a manger filled with hay
In poverty content He lay;
With milk was fed the Lord of all,
Who feeds the ravens when they call.

7. The heavenly choirs rejoice and raise
Their voice to God in songs of praise.
To humble shepherds is proclaimed
The Shepherd who the world hath framed.

8. All honor unto Christ be paid,
Pure Offspring of the favored maid,
With Father and with Holy Ghost
Till time in endless time be lost.

Coelius Sedulius, c. 450
German Version, Martin Luther, 1424

Verse

December 25

℣: The Lord has made known. Allelu- / ia.
℟: His salvation. Allelu- / ia.

Psalm 98:2

December 26-January 1

℣: The Word became flesh. Allelu- / ia.
℟: And dwelt among us. Allelu- / ia.

John 1:14

January 2-5

℣: Our help is in the name of the / Lord.
℟: Who made heaven and / earth.

Psalm 124:8

Antiphon to the Benedictus

December 25-31 - *Gloria in excelsis*

Tone 8G

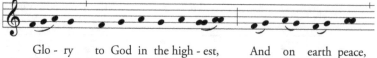

Glo - ry to God in the high - est, And on earth peace,

good will toward men. Al - le - lu - ia! Al - le - lu - ia!

Luke 2:14

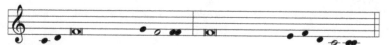

✠ BLESSÉD is the Lord God of / Israel; *
For He has visited and re- / deemed His people. etc.

January 1-5 - *Dedit se*

He gave him-self to de - liv - er His peo - ple, And to ob-

tain an ev - er - last - ing name. Al - le - lu - ia.

Liturgical text

Collect

December 25-31

Grant unto us, O Almighty God, that He whom You send for the world's salvation on this holy day, whereupon the heavens are renewed in light, may ever rise in our hearts and renew them; through the same, Jesus Christ, Your Son, our Lord, who lives and reigns with You and the Holy Spirit, one God, now and forever.

Gregorian Sacramentary

January 1

Almighty and Everlasting God, from whom comes down every good and perfect gift; we give thanks to You for all Your benefits, temporal and spiritual, bestowed upon us in the past year, and we beseech You of Your goodness, grant us a favorable and joyful year, defend us from all dangers and adversities, and send upon us the fullness of Your blessing; through Jesus Christ, Your Son, our Lord, who lives and reigns with You and the Holy Spirit, one God, now and forever.

Ober-Lausaitz Agenda, 1695

January 2-5

O Christ, You are the Star of truth that rises out of Jacob, and the man that springs from Israel. In the new Star You show Yourself as God, and, lying in the crib God and Man, we confess You to be the one Christ. In Your great mercy, grant us the grace of seeing You, and show us the radiant sign of Your light, whereby all the darkness of our sins may be put to flight; so that we who now languish with the desire of seeing You, may be refreshed with the enjoyment of that blissful vision, who lives and reigns with the Father and the Holy Spirit, one God, now and forever.

Mozarabic Breviary

AT TERCE, SEXT AND NONE

Chapter

December 25, 29-31: Hebrews 1:1-12
St. Stephen, December 26: Acts 6:8-15; 7:55-60; 8:2
St. John the Evangelist, December 27: I John 1:1-10
Holy Innocents, December 28: Revelation 14:1-5
January 1-5: Galatians 3:23-29

Responsory and Verse at Terce:

℣: The Word be-came flesh. Al - le - lu - ia. Al - le - lu - ia.
℟: The Word be-came flesh. Al - le - lu - ia. Al - le - lu - ia.

℣: And dwelt a - mong us. Al - le - lu - ia. Al - le - lu - ia.
℟: The Word...

℣: Glo-ry be to the Fa-ther, and to the Son, and to the Ho-ly Spi - rit.
℟: The Word...

John 1:14

℣: He shall cry to Me. Allelu- / ia.
℟: You are My Father. Allelu- / ia.

Responsory and Verse at Sext:

℣: The Lord has made known. Al - le - lu - ia. Al - le - lu - ia.
℟: The Lord has made known. Al - le - lu - ia. Al - le - lu - ia.

℣: His sal - va - tion. Al - le - lu - ia. Al - le - lu - ia.
℟: The Lord...

℣: Glo-ry be to the Fa-ther, and to the Son, and to the Ho-ly Spi - rit.
℟:: The Lord...

Psalm 98:2

℣: All the ends of the earth have seen. Allelu- / ia.
℟: The salvation of our God. Allelu- / ia.

Psalm 98:3

Responsory and Verse at None:

℣: All the ends of the earth have seen. Al - le - lu - ia. Al - le - lu - ia.
℟: All the ends of the earth have seen. Al - le - lu - ia. Al - le - lu - ia.

℣: The sal - va - tion of our God. Al - le - lu - ia. Al - le - lu - ia.
℟: All the ends...

℣: Glo-ry be to the Fa-ther, and to the Son, and to the Ho-ly Spi - rit.
℞: All the ends...

Psalm 98:3

℣: The Word became flesh. Allelu- / ia.
℞: And dwelt among us. Allelu- / ia.

John 1:14

AT VESPERS

Psalmody

Dec. 25: 85, 93, 96
Dec. 26: 110, 111, 112, 113
Dec. 27: 114, 115, 116, 117
Dec. 28: 120, 121, 122

Dec. 29: 123, 124, 125
Dec. 30: 126, 127, 128
Dec. 31: 129, 130, 131, 132
Jan. 1: 133, 135, 136a

Jan. 2: 136b, 137, 138
Jan. 3: 140, 141, 142
Jan. 4: 144, 145, 7
Jan. 5: 9, 10, 11

Lesson

Dec. 25: Isaiah 40:1-8; 52:1-10
Dec. 26: Romans 2:1-16
Dec. 27: Romans 3:27-4:8
Dec. 28: Romans 6:1-11

Dec. 29: Romans 8:1-11
Dec. 30: Romans 9:6-16
Dec. 31: Romans 11:11-24
Jan. 1: Romans 12:1-8

Jan. 2: Romans 13:1-10
Jan. 3: Romans 14:1-13
Jan. 4: Romans 15:7-13
Jan. 5: Romans 16:25-27

Hymn - *Jesu Redemptor Omnium*

1. Je - su, Re - deem - er   of man-kind,   Be - got- ten ere
2. O   Fa - ther's Light   and   splen-dor true,   Man's ev - er - last-
3. Re - call, Cre - a - tor   of the earth,   That long a - go

the light   first shined,   Of God the   Fa - ther Al - migh - ty
ing hope   are   You,   At - tend the prayer Your ser- vants raise
at   Your   own   birth   Our hu - man flesh You did as - sume

E - qual   in   glor - ious   ma - jes - ty.
Through-out the   world   by   night and day.
From Vir - gin   Ma - ry's   sac- red womb.

4. This present day does testify,
As year by year it cycles by,
That from the Father forth You came
Into our world to bless and save.

5. The earth, the sea, the stars, the sky,
and all that under heaven does lie,
The Author of salvation greet,
With hymns and canticles repleat.

6. And we, who by that sacred stream,
Of Your pure blood have been made clean,
Tribute to You by hymn we bring.
On this Your blest nativity.

7. O Jesu, glory, thanks and praise,
To You, the Virgin-born, we raise,
Whom with the Father we adore
And loving Spirit evermore. Amen.

Latin Office Hymn, c.6th cent

Verse

December 25

℣: The Lord has made known. Allelu- / ia. *
℟: His salvation. Allelu- / ia.

Psalm 98:2

December 26-January 1

℣: The Word became flesh. Allelu- / ia. *
℟: And dwelt among us. Allelu- / ia.

John 1:14

January 2-5

℣: Blessèd be the name of the Lord, Allelu- / ia. *
℟: From this time forth and forevermore! Allelu- / ia.

Psalm 113:2

Antiphon to the Magnificat

December 25-31 - *Hodie Christus natus est*   Tone 1g

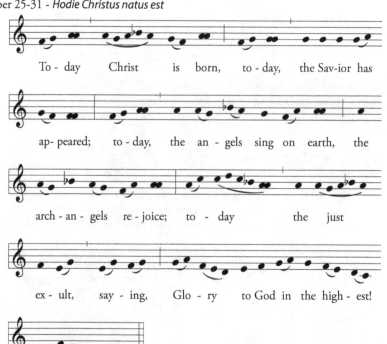

To - day   Christ   is   born, to - day, the Sav-ior has ap- peared; to - day, the an - gels sing on earth, the arch - an - gels re - joice; to - day the just ex - ult, say - ing, Glo - ry to God in the high - est! Al - le - lu - ia!

Liturgical text

268

✠ MY SOUL / magnifies the Lord, *
And my spirit has rejoiced in / God my Savior. etc.

January 1-5 - *Vocabis nomen ejus*   Tone 1g

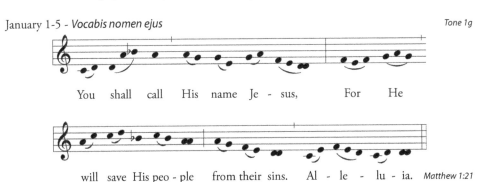

You shall call His name Je - sus,   For   He

will save His peo - ple   from their sins.   Al - le - lu - ia. *Matthew 1:21*

Collect

December 25-31

Lord God, heavenly Father, we give thanks to You that of Your mercy and compassion You caused Your Son to become incarnate, and through Him redeemed us from sin and everlasting death; we beseech You, enlighten our hearts by Your Holy Spirit that we may ever be thankful for such grace, and comfort ourselves thereby in all tribulation and temptation, and at last obtain eternal salvation; through the same Jesus Christ, Your Son, our Lord, who lives and reigns with You and the Holy Spirit, one God, now and forever.

Veit Dietrich

January 1:

O Almighty and Everlasting God, mercifully direct our ways that we may walk in Your Law, and be made to abound in good works; through Jesus Christ, Your Son, our Lord, who lives and reigns with You and the Holy Spirit, one God, now and forever.   *Veit Dietrich*

January 2-5:

O Lord God, heavenly Father, You allowed Your dear Son, Jesus Christ, to become a stranger and a sojourner in Egypt for our sakes, and led Him safely home to His fatherland; mercifully grant that we poor sinners, who are strangers and sojourners in this perilous world, may soon be called home to our true fatherland, the kingdom of heaven, where we shall live in eternal joy and glory, through the same Jesus Christ, Your Son, our Lord, who lives and reigns with You and the Holy Spirit, one God, now and forever.   *Veit Dietrich*

EPIPHANY

And the days after Epiphany that fall within the same week

*The opening versicles, invitatory, Venite, and hymn are omitted on the
Feast of the Epiphany. The office is begun directly with the Psalmody.*

AT MATINS

Invitatory - *Christus apparuit*

Tone 6

Christ has ap - peared to us, O come, let us wor-ship Him!

Hymn - *Wie schön leuchtet der Morgenstern*

1. How love - ly shines the Morn-ing Star! The na - tions see

and hail a - far The light in Ju - dah shin - ing.

Thou Da-vid's Son of Ja - cob's race, My Bride-groom and

my King of Grace, For Thee my heart is pin - ing.

Low - ly, Ho - ly, Great and glor-ious, Thou vic-tor-ious Prince of

gra - ces, Fill - ing all the heav'n - ly plac - es.

2. O highest joy by mortals won,
   True Son of God and Mary's Son,
   Thou high-born King of ages!
   Thou art my heart's most beauteous Flower,
   And Thy blest Gospel's saving power
   My raptured soul engages.
   Thou mine, I Thine; Sing hosanna!
   Heavenly manna Tasting, eating,
   Whilst Thy love in songs repeating.

3. Now richly to my waiting heart,
   O Thou, my God, deign to impart
   The grace of love undying.
   In Thy blest body let me be,
   E'en as the branch is in the tree,
   Thy life my life supplying.
   Sighing, Crying. For the savor
   Of Thy favor; Resting never,
   Till I rest in Thee forever.

4. A pledge of peace from God I see
   When Thy pure eyes are turned to me
   To show me Thy good pleasure.
   Jesus, Thy Spirit and Thy Word,
   Thy body and Thy blood, afford
   My soul its dearest treasure.
   Keep me Kindly In Thy favor,
   O my Savior! Thou wilt cheer me;
   Thy Word calls me to draw near Thee.

5. Thou, mighty Father, in Thy Son
   Didst love me ere Thou hadst begun
   This ancient world's foundation.
   Thy Son hath made a friend of me,
   And when in spirit Him I see,
   I joy in tribulation.
   What bliss Is this! He that liveth
   To me giveth Life forever;
   Nothing me from Him can sever.

6. Lift up the voice and strike the string.
   Let all glad sounds of music ring
   In God's high praises blended.
   Christ will be with me all the way,
   Today, tomorrow, every day,
   Till traveling days be ended.
   Sing out, Ring out Triumph glorious,
   O victorious, Chosen nation;
   Praise the God of your salvation.

7. Oh, joy to know that Thou, my Friend,
   Art Lord, Beginning without end,
   The First and Last, Eternal!
   And Thou at length--O glorious grace!--
   Wilt take me to that holy place,
   The home of joys supernal.
   Amen, Amen! Come and meet me!
   Quickly greet me! With deep yearning,
   Lord, I look for Thy returning.

Philipp Nicolai, 1597

Psalmody

Sunday: 69b, 70, 71   Wednesday: 75, 79, 80   Friday: 84, 86, 87, 93
Monday: 72, 73, 74   Thursday: 81, 82, 83   Saturday: 85, 89a, 89b
Tuesday: 78a, 78b, 78c

Lesson: Matthew 2:1-12

Homily

The Epiphany of Our Lord, January 6 - Ambrose of Milan

Can anyone say that the Lord is made known to us by signs of little import, when the Magi come and adore Him, the angels serve Him, and the martyrs confess Him? He comes forth from a womb, but He shines like lightning from above; He lies in an earthly resting place, but round about Him is the brightness of heaven. The espoused has brought forth; but a Virgin has conceived. A wife has conceived; but a Virgin has given birth.

There is another mystery here of no small significance, which the holy Matthew makes known... Now to this little Child, whom you will consider as an ordinary child if you do not believe, the wise men from the East now come, following on so long a journey. And falling down they adored Him and call Him King, and profess that He will rise from the dead; and they do this by offering Him from their treasures, gold, frankincense, and myrrh.

What are these gifts, offered in true faith? Gold, as to a King; incense, as to God; myrrh, for the dead. For one is the token of the dignity of a king; the other the symbol of divine majesty; the third is a service of honor to a Body that is to be buried, which does not destroy the body of the dead, but preserves it. We who read and hear these things, let us also offer similar gifts from our treasures. For we have treasures in earthen vessels. If you consider that which you are as being not from yourself, but from Christ; how much more ought you to consider that which you own as being not yours, but Christ's?

The Magi therefore offer Him gifts from their treasures. Do you want to know how precious their reward was? The Star is seen by them; where by Herod it is not seen; it is seen again where Christ is, and shows them the way. Therefore this Star is the way, and the way is Christ; for in the mystery of the Incarnation Christ is a star. "A star shall come out of Jacob; a Scepter shall rise out of Israel." Where Christ is, the star is. For He Himself is the bright and morning star. He shows us Himself therefore by His own light. *On Luke 2*

Monday - John Chrysostom

Let us now see, after the star had come to rest and after the journey of the Magi, what wondrous dignity accompanies the Newborn King. For immediately the Magi, falling down before the Lord, adore Him Newly-born and lying in a manger, and offering gifts they venerate the Infancy of a weeping Babe. With the eyes of their body they saw one thing, with the eyes of the mind another. The lowliness of the assumed body is before their eyes, yet the glory of the Divinity is not hidden. It is a Child that is adored, and together with it the unspeakable mystery of the divine condescension! For our sake that invisible and eternal nature has not disdained to take to Itself the infirmities of our flesh.

The Son of God, who is the God of all things is born a Man in body. He who holds the heavens in His hand permits Himself to be placed in a crib. He whom the world cannot contain is confined in a manger; He is heard in the voice of a wailing Infant, at whose voice in the hour of His passion the whole earth trembled. The Magi, seeing a Child, profess that this is the Lord of Glory, the Lord of Majesty, whom Isaiah has shown was both Child and God, and King Eternal, saying: "For unto us a Child is born, unto us a Son is given; and the government will be upon His shoulder. And His name will be called Wonderful, Counselor, Mighty God, Everlasting Father, Prince of Peace."

To Him the Magi offer gifts, that is: gold, frankincense and myrrh; as the Holy Spirit had in time past testified concerning them: "all those from Sheba shall come; they shall bring gold and incense, and they shall proclaim the praises of the Lord." This prophecy is clearly fulfilled by the Magi, who both announce the salvation of the Lord, born Christ the Son of God, and by their gifts proclaim Him Christ and God, and King of Man. For by gold the power of a king is signified, by frankincense the honor of God, by myrrh the burial of the body; and so they offer Him gold as King, frankincense as God, myrrh as Man. *Homily 1 on Matthew*

Tuesday - Leo I of Rome

Rejoice in the Lord, dearly Beloved, again I say rejoice. In the short space of time after the celebration of Christ's birth, the feast of His manifestation to the world has dawned. On this day the world recognizes the One whom the virgin bore on that day. For the Word that was made flesh has so ordered the beginnings of His life as man that the newborn Jesus is made visible to those who believe in Him, and remains hidden from those seeking to destroy Him.

Then indeed the heavens proclaimed the glory of God, and the sound of truth went forth into all the earth, when the hosts of heaven appeared to the shepherds heralding the birth of the Savior, and when the star that went before them led the Magi to adore Him. From the rising of the sun to its setting, the birth of the true King shone forth; when the kingdoms of the East learned the truth through the Magi, and it did not remain hidden from the Roman empire.

Even the cruelty of Herod, who wanted to destroy the suspected King at His birth, unwittingly served the purposes of God. Intent upon his horrid crime, he pursues a Child unknown to him with the indiscriminate slaughter of the infants. As he does so, the report becomes more widely known and spreads everywhere, declaring the birth of the Lord which had been announced in the heavens. Both the strangeness of the heavenly sign, and the godlessness of this blood-drenched persecutor caused the report to be passed on more eagerly and more carefully.

Then also the Savior was taken down even to Egypt, so that a people given over to error from ancient times should now be marked out, through a secret grace, as being near to salvation. That nation which had not yet cast their ancient superstitions from its heart would receive Truth as its guest.

Sermon 32

Wednesday - Martin Luther

It was His purpose to let Himself be found not at Jerusalem, but at Bethlehem. Bethlehem was not far at all from Jerusalem; nevertheless, God did not want to give recognition to Jerusalem nor allow the Governor of His people to be born in her, purposing thereby to reject false trust in the saints and teaching us that true holiness exists neither in the temple nor in spiritual ceremonies, but in Himself. This is what the story teaches us. Let's look now at Micah's prophecy, "But you, Bethlehem Ephrathah, though you are little among the thousands of Judah, yet out of you shall come forth to Me the One to be ruler in Israel."

This is a gladsome text, which not only testifies that Christ has come, but also teaches us why we should esteem and cling to Him, and what kind of a King and Lord He is. He should be a Lord of God's people, says the prophet, yet be born at Bethlehem and be the most despised man on earth. It is contradictory and shocking that a poor beggar, born in a lowly, poor place should be a ruler and Lord of the people in Israel. The world looks at the matter like this: The one who is to be a king and lord must have money, possessions, land, people, and power. But here the situation is: Bethlehem is small and poor, and yet out of Bethlehem comes a great, mighty King and Lord.

First Sermon for Epiphany

Thursday - Ambrose of Milan

Who are these Magi if not, as history tells us, men descended from Balaam by whom it was foretold that "a Star will rise out of Jacob." They are no less the heirs of his faith than heirs of his blood. He beheld the Star in spirit; they saw it with their eyes and believed. They beheld a new star, which had not been seen by a creature of this world. They beheld a new creation, and they sought, not only on earth, but in heaven, for the friendship of the New Man. For Moses had prophetically declared, "a Star shall rise out of Jacob and a Man shall spring up from Israel." And they understood that this was the Star, which meant both God and Man. And they adored a Child. They would not have adored if they had believed He was only a Child.

On Luke

Friday - Leo I of Rome

Herod, hearing that a King of the Jews had been born, grew afraid at the thought of a possible successor. Plotting death for the Author of Salvation, he makes false promises of coming to pay homage to Him. How happy he would have been if he had but imitated the faith of the Magi, if he had but turned into an act of religion the treachery he was planning. O blind impiety of senseless envy! Do you propose in your madness to defeat the divine will? The Lord of the world does not seek an earthly kingdom but bestows an eternal one. Why are you trying to overthrow the unchangeable order of what has been decreed? Why are you trying to outdo the crimes of others?

Christ's death does not belong to your time. Before that the Gospel must be established, the kingdom of heaven preached, the sick healed, miracles performed. Why, when the deed is to be done by another, do you wish it to be your crime? Why, since you will not get what you want from your misdeed, do you hurl yourself alone into the guilt of having willed it? You will gain nothing by your plotting. You accomplish nothing. He who was born of His own will will die by the power of His own choosing.

Sermon 31

Saturday - John Chrysostom

The Magi being warned return home another way, frustrating the cruelty of the tyrant. And thus the Child born King is, by the magi, made known to men. And the treachery of the tyrant Herod is brought to nothing. Isaiah had of old made prophecy that Our Lord and Savior as a Child would triumph this way, and in the very beginning of His infancy: "For before the Child knows to call his father and mother, the strength of Damascus, and the spoils of Samaria shall be taken away before the king of the Assyrians." The gold that was offered by the Magi, and which the Son of God born a Child has received is interpreted as "the strength of Damascus." "The spoils of Samaria" are the Magi themselves, whom He has drawn out of the error of the superstitions of Samaria, that is, the worship of idols; and who because of their false religion were formerly the spoil of the devil, now through the knowledge of Christ have become the spoil of God. The kings of the Assyrians means Herod, or at any event the devil. Against him the Magi stood forth as adversaries by adoring the Son of God, our Lord and Savior, who is blessed forever and ever. Amen.

Homily 1 on Matthew

Collect

O God, who by the leading of a star manifested Your only-begotten Son to the Gentiles, mercifully grant that we, who know You now by faith, may after this life have the fruition of Your glorious Godhead, through the same Jesus Christ, Your Son, our Lord, who lives and reigns with You and the Holy Spirit, one God, now and forever.

Gelasian Sacramentary

AT LAUDS

Psalmody

Sunday: 67, C1, 5	Wednesday: 64, C4, 65	Friday: 76, C5, 92
Monday: 63, C2, 36	Thursday: 88, C6, 90	Saturday: 143, C7, 148
Tuesday: 43, C3, 57		

Lesson

Jan. 6: I Corinthians 1:1-1-9	Wednesday: I Corinthians 7:10-16	Friday: I Corinthians 14:1-12
Monday: I Corinthians 2:1-10	Thursday: I Corinthians 9:13-23	Saturday: I Corinthians 15:20-28
Tuesday: I Corinthians 5:1-8		

Hymn - *O sola magnarum urbium*

1. O more than migh-ty   ci - ties known, Dear Beth - le - hem,
2. And fair - er, bright - er, than the sun   Did shine that beaut-
3. The Wise Men, see - ing Him, so fair,   Bow low be - fore

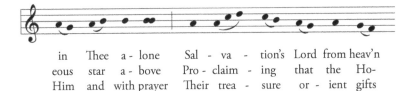

in	Thee	a - lone	Sal - va - tion's	Lord from heav'n
eous	star	a - bove	Pro - claim - ing	that the Ho-
Him	and	with prayer	Their trea - sure	or - ient gifts

took birth   In hu-man form up- on the earth.
ly   God   Had come to earth with flesh and blood.
un - fold   Of in-cense, myrrh, and ro-yal gold.

4. The fragrant incense which they bring,
The gold, proclaim Him God and King;
The bitter spicy dust of myrrh
Foreshadows His new sepulcher.

5. All glory, Lord to Thee we pay
For Thine Epiphany today;
Whom with the Father we adore,
And Holy Spirit evermore. Amen.

Aurelius Prudentius, 348-c.413

Verse

℣: Worship the Lord, allelu- / ia.
℟: All you His angels. Allelu- / ia.

Psalm 148:2

Antiphon to the Benedictus

Tone 4a

We have seen His star in the East, And have come

to wor - ship the Lord.

Matthew 2:2

✠ BLESSÉD is the Lord God / of Israel; *
For He has visited and / redeemed His people. etc.

Collect

O Lord Jesus Christ, who, when the Magi were questioned by Herod, enlightened them with the announcement of Your truth by showing Yourself to be the King of kings, whom they declared by saying that they had seen Your sign, the bright Star that gives light to the whole world; we implore and beseech You, that You grant to Your Church the light she so desires of Your vision. Show Yourself also, in her, as the Star prized by all; so that, when questioned by our enemy, we may so boldly confess Your mysteries, that we may shine for all eternity in the mansion of eternal light; for You live and reign with the Father and the Holy Spirit, one God, now and forever. *Spanish Gothic Breviary*

AT TERCE, SEXT AND NONE

Chapter: Isaiah 60:1-6

AT VESPERS

Psalmody

Sunday: 110, 111, 112, 113	Wednesday: 123, 124, 125	Friday: 129, 130, 131, 132
Monday: 114, 115, 116, 117	Thursday: 126, 127, 128	Saturday: 133, 135, 136a
Tuesday: 120, 121, 122		

Lesson

Jan. 6: I Corinthians 1:18-25	Wednesday: I Corinthians 8:1-13	Friday: I Corinthians 14:26-40
Monday: I Corinthians 3:1-11	Thursday: I Corinthians 12:12-27	Saturday: I Corinthians 16:1-14
Tuesday: I Corinthians 7:1-9		

Hymn - *Hostia Herodes impie*

1.   The star pro-claims the King is here; But, Her-od, why this sense-less fear?

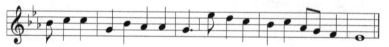

He takes no realms of earth a - way Who gives the realms of heav'n-ly day.

2. The wiser Magi see from far
   And follow on His guiding star;
   And led by light, to light they press
   And by their gifts their God confess.

3. Within the Jordan's crystal flood
   In meekness stands the Lamb of God
   And, sinless, sanctifies the wave,
   Mankind from sin to cleanse and save.

4. At Cana first His power is shown;
   His might the blushing waters own
   And, changing as He speaks the word,
   Flow wine, obedient to their Lord.

5. All glory, Jesus, be to Thee
   For this Thy glad Epiphany;
   Whom with the Father we adore
   And Holy Spirit evermore.

Coelius Sedulius, c. 450

Verse

℣: The Kings of Tarshish and of the Isles shall offer / gifts.
℟: The kings of Sheba and Seba will bring tri- / bute.   *Psalm 72:10*

Antiphon to the Magnificat - *Lux de luce*   *Tone 8c*

O   Light   of Light, You have ap-peared, O   Christ.   To   You

the Ma - gi of - fer gifts, al - le- lu- ia, al - le - lu-

ia, al - le - lu - ia.

Liturgical text

✠ MY SOUL magnifies / the Lord, *
And my spirit has rejoiced in / God my Savior.   etc.

Collect

Lord God, heavenly Father, You have given us the light of Your holy word, the guiding star that leads us to the Christ-child; send Your Holy Spirit into our hearts, we implore You, that we may receive this light and make use of it for our salvation, and that we, like the wise men, when they were seeking the star, may not be afraid because of any hardship or peril, but put all our trust in Your only-begotten Son as our only Savior, devote our earthly possessions to the advancement of Your kingdom, and in all things serve Him, Your only-begotten Son, Jesus Christ, our Lord, who lives and reigns with You and the Holy Spirit, one God, now and forever.   *Veit Dietrich*

THE FIRST WEEK
AFTER EPIPHANY

AT MATINS

Hymn - *Within the Father's House*

1. With-in the Fa-ther's house The Son hath found His home,

And to His Tem-ple sud-den-ly The Lord of Life hath come.

2. The doctors of the Law
Gaze on the wondrous Child
And marvel at His gracious words
Of wisdom undefiled.

3. Yet not to them is giv'n
The mighty truth to know,
To lift the earthly veil which hides
Incarnate God below.

4. The secret of the Lord
Escapes each human eye,
And faithful pondering hearts await
The full epiphany.

5. Lord, visit Thou our souls
And teach us by Thy grace,
Each dim revealing of Thyself
With loving awe to trace.

6. Till from our darkened sight
The clouds shall pass away
And on the cleansèd soul shall burst
The everlasting day,

7. Till we behold Thy face
And know as we are known
Thee, Father, Son and Holy Ghost,
Coequal Three in One.

James R. Woodford, 1863

The Baptism of Our Lord, January 13 - *Christ unser Herr zum Jordan kam*

1. To Jor-dan when our Lord had gone, His Fa-ther's pleas-ure will-ing;

He took His bap-tism of Saint John, All right-eous-ness ful-fill-ing.

There He did con-se-crate a bath To wash a-way trans-

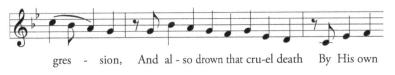

gres - sion, And al - so drown that cru-el death By His own

blood and pas - sion; New life for us cre - a - ting.

2. So hear ye all and well receive
   What God does call baptism
   And what a Christian should believe
   To shun error and schism
   Water indeed, not water mere
   In it can do His pleasure,
   His holy Word is also there
   With Spirit rich, unmeasured;
   He is the One baptizing.

3. This clearly He to us hath shown
   By Word, nor less by vision.
   On Jordan's banks was clearly heard
   The Father's voice from heaven:
   He said, This is My own dear Son,
   In whom I'm well contented;
   Hear Him! Oh hear Him everyone!
   To save you I have sent Him,
   Hear and believe His teaching.

4. In Jordan's water God's own Son
   In sinless manhood bending,
   The Holy Ghost from heaven's throne,
   In dove-like form descending.
   This truth must never be denied,
   Our faith should never waiver,
   That all Three Persons do preside
   At Baptism's holy laver,
   And dwell with each believer.

5. To His disciples Jesus said:
   Go forth, teach every nation,
   That, lost in sin, all must repent,
   And flee from condemnation.
   He who believes and is baptized
   Is thereby blest forever;
   Is from that hour a new-born man,
   And thenceforth dying never,
   The kingdom shall inherit.

6. But he who in this has no faith,
   Abides in his trespasses
   And is condemned to endless death
   Deep down in Hell's abysses.
   False holiness avails him not,
   Nor aught which he is doing;
   His in-born sin brings all to naught,
   And maketh sure his ruin;
   Himself he cannot rescue.

7. The eye but water doth behold,
   As from man's hand it floweth;
   But inward faith the power untold
   Of Jesus Christ's blood knoweth.
   Faith sees therein a crimson flood,
   With Christ's blood dyed and blended,
   Which sins of all kinds doth forgive,
   Inherited from Adam,
   And our own sinful doings.

Martin Luther, 1524

Psalmody

Sunday: 89c, 94, 96   Wednesday: 104a, 104b, 104c   Friday: 106a, 106b, 107a
Monday: 97, 98, 99, 100   Thursday: 105a, 105b, 105c   Saturday: 107b, 108, 109
Tuesday: 101, 102, 103

Lesson

The Baptism of Our Lord, January 13: Matthew 3:13-17
Sunday, Monday and Tuesday: Luke 2:41-52
Wednesday and Thursday: John 1:29-34
Thursday: Luke 3:21-22

Friday and Saturday: Matthew 4:12-17
Saturday: Mark 1:12-15

Homily

The Baptism of Our Lord, January 13 - Hippolytus of Rome

The Father of immortality sent the immortal Son and Word into the world, who came to man in order to wash him with water and the Spirit; and He, begetting us again to incorruption of soul and body, breathed into us the breath (spirit) of life, and gave us an incorruptible array. If, therefore, man has become immortal, he will also be divine. And if he is made divine by water and the Holy Spirit after the regeneration of the washing he is also found to be joint-heir with Christ after the resurrection of the dead. This is why I preach this way: Come, all you kindreds of the nations, to the immortality of Baptism. I bring good tidings of life to you who linger in the darkness of ignorance. Come into liberty from slavery, into a kingdom from tyranny, into incorruption from corruption. And how, one says, shall we come? How? By water and the Holy Ghost. This is the water in conjunction with the Spirit, by which Paradise is watered, by which the earth is enriched, by which plants grow, by which animals multiply, and (to sum up the whole thing in a single word) by which man is begotten again and endowed with life, in which also Christ was baptized, and in which the Spirit descended in the form of a dove.

This is the Spirit that at the beginning "moved upon the face of the waters;" by whom the world moves; by whom creation exists, and all things have life; who also worked mightily in the prophets, and descended in flight upon Christ. This is the Spirit that was given to the apostles in the form of fiery tongues. This is the Spirit that David sought when he said, "Create in me a clean heart, O God, and renew a right spirit within me." Of this Spirit Gabriel also spoke to the Virgin, "The Holy Ghost shall come upon thee, and the power of the Highest shall overshadow thee." By this Spirit Peter spoke that blessed word, "You are the Christ, the Son of the living God." By this Spirit the rock of the Church was established. This is the Spirit, the Comforter, that is sent for Your sake, that He may show You to be the Son of God.

Come then, be begotten again, O man, into the adoption of God... For he who comes down in faith to the washing of regeneration, and renounces the devil, and joins himself to Christ; who denies the enemy, and makes the confession that Christ is God; who puts off the bondage, and puts on the adoption, - he comes up from the baptism brilliant as the sun, flashing forth the beams of righteousness, and, which is truly the main thing, he returns a son of God and joint-heir with Christ. To Him be the glory and the power, together with His most holy, and good, and quickening Spirit, now and ever, and to all the ages of the ages. Amen.   *Discourse on the Holy Theophany*

Sunday - Origen of Alexandria

"And seeking Him," says the Evangelist, "they found Him in the Temple." Not anywhere, but in the temple. And not simply in the temple, but in the midst of the doctors, hearing them and asking them questions. So seek Him yourself in the temple of God: seek Him in the Church: seek Him among the teachers who are in the temple, and who do not depart from it. If you so seek Him you will find Him. Further, if anyone calls himself a teacher, and does not have Jesus with him, he is a teacher in name only, and with such a one Jesus the Word of God, and His Wisdom, cannot be found.   *The Child Jesus in the Temple*

Monday - Theophylactus of Bulgaria

Not that as He grew He became more wise, but that He unveiled His wisdom gradually. He did this in speaking with the Scribes, asking them questions with regard to the Law; to the astonishment of all who heard Him. You see how it was that He advanced in wisdom, in that His wisdom began to be known by many, and they wondered at Him. The progress then of His wisdom consists in the manner of its being shown. Note how the Evangelist interprets what is meant here by advancing in wisdom, for he adds immediately: "and stature;" for the increase in age is, he says, itself the growth of wisdom. *from the Catena Aurea*

Tuesday - Martin Luther

"His mother kept all these sayings in her heart." This is also given for our admonition, in order that we may endeavor to keep the Word of God in our hearts as the Blessed Virgin did, who, seeing she had erred and lacked understanding, became all the more diligent to keep in her heart all she heard from Christ. She supplies another example, that above all things we should hold to the Word and not let it go out of our hearts, but constantly use it, learn to gain strength from it, find comfort in it, and increase in it, as is indeed necessary for all of us. *Sermon for the First Sunday After Epiphany*

Wednesday - Gregory Thaumaturgas

When I [John] baptize others, I baptize into Your name, in order that they may believe on You, who comes with glory; but when I baptize You, of whom should I make mention? And into whose name should I baptize You? Into that of the Father? But You have the Father altogether in Yourself, and You are altogether in the Father. Or into that of the Son? But beside You there is no other Son of God by nature. Or into that of the Holy Spirit? But He is always together with You, as being of one substance, and of one will, and of one judgment, and of one power, and of one honor with You; and He receives, along with You, the same adoration from all. For this reason, O Lord, You baptize me, if You please; baptize me, the Baptist. Regenerate one whom You caused to be generated. Extend Your dread right hand, which You have prepared for Yourself, and crown my head with Your touch, in order that I may run the course before Your kingdom, crowned like a forerunner, and diligently announce the good tidings to the sinners addressing them with this earnest call: "Behold the Lamb of God, that takes away the sin of the world!" O Jordan, accompany me in the joyous choir, and leap with me, and stir your waters rhythmically, as in the movements of the dance; for your Maker stands by you in the body. Once of old you saw Israel pass through you, and you divided your floods, and waited in expectation of the passage of the people; but now divide yourself more decidedly, and flow more easily, and embrace the stainless limbs of Him who at that ancient time conveyed the Jews through you. O mountains and hills, O valleys and torrents, O seas and rivers, bless the Lord who has come upon the river Jordan; for through these streams He transmits sanctification to all streams. *Homily on the Holy Theophany*

Thursday - Martin Luther

As an example to us, and for our consolation, the sinless Son of God was baptized and did something He was not obligated to do. We poor, miserable and corrupt as we are, never do more than we have to, and are guilty of even neglecting to do what is our duty to do, in open rebellion against God. Remember that Christ, the Son of God, who instituted holy Baptism, was Himself baptized. He commands that baptism be given in the Church, and that all who desire to be saved should be baptized.

Certainly the devil has polluted and blinded the hell-bound people who despise Baptism or speak blasphemously against it, so that they don't see what is happening in this text. If the Son of God was baptized, why would you hesitate to have yourself or your children baptized? Why should you be so proud, yes, so blind and foolish, as to despise this holy and saving command? Even if Baptism were worthless and accomplished nothing, shouldn't we be eager to be baptized out of mere reverence for the Son of God, who was also baptized?

But we also learn from this event what the benefits of Baptism are. We see how God in heaven reveals His mercy at the Baptism of His Son. The heavens, which had been firmly closed, are now opened, as the Evangelist relates. A window is opened through which we can look and see that there is no barrier between God and us. The Father lets his voice be heard, the Son sanctifies baptism with His body, and the Holy Spirit descends in the form of a dove. Tell me, is this not a most glorious revelation and a sure sign that God is pleased with Baptism, and that He is present in it? *House Postil for Epiphany*

Friday - John Chrysostom

Implying that they did not of themselves seek and find, but that God showed Himself to them from above, he said to them, "Light is sprung up;" that is, the light of itself sprang up and shone forth; it was not that they first ran to the light. For in truth the condition of men was at the worst before Christ's coming. Since they more than "walked in darkness;" they "sat in darkness;" a kind of sign that they did not even hope to be delivered. For like people who don't even know where to put a step forward, so they sat, overtaken by darkness, not even being able to stand any more. *Homily 14 on Matthew 4*

Saturday - Martin Luther

When Christ became man and began His preaching ministry, then heaven was opened. Beginning with that time, it is open and remains open. It has never again been closed since Christ's Baptism in the Jordan; and it will never again be closed, hidden though this sight is from the physical eye. When heaven is open and God the Father addresses us, we note this with our spiritual sight only. Before the advent of Christ heaven was closed, and the devil had full sway; but in and through Christ the heaven stands open again... When you are baptized, partake of Holy Communion, receive absolution, or listen to a sermon, heaven is open, and we hear the voice of the Heavenly Father; all these works descend upon us from the open heaven above us. God converses with us, governs us, provides for us; and Christ hovers over us - but invisibly. And even though there were clouds above us as impervious as iron or steel, obstructing our view of heaven; this would not matter. Still we hear God speaking to us from heaven; we call and cry to Him, and He answers us. Heaven is open, as St. Stephen saw it open; and we hear God when He addresses us in Baptism, in Holy Communion, in confession, and in His Word as it proceeds from the mouth of the men who proclaim His message to the people. *Sermon 15 on the Gospel of John*

Collects

Through January 12

O God, who by the leading of a star manifested Your only-begotten Son to the Gentiles, mercifully grant that we, who know You now by faith, may after this life have the fruition of Your glorious Godhead, through the same Jesus Christ, Your Son, our Lord, who lives and reigns with You and the Holy Spirit, one God, now and forever. *Gelasian Sacramentary*

January 13:

O God, whose Only-Begotten Son appeared in the substance of our flesh; grant, we beseech You, that we may be inwardly reformed by Him, whom we confess to have outwardly taken our flesh on Himself, who lives and reigns with You and the Holy Spirit, one God, now and forever. *Gelasian Sacramentary*

After January 13:

O Lord, we pray You mercifully to receive the prayers of Your people who call upon You; and grant that they may both perceive and know what things they ought to do and also may have grace and power to faithfully do them; through Jesus Christ, Your Son, our Lord, who lives and reigns with You and the Holy Spirit, one God, now and forever. *Gelasian Sacramentary*

AT LAUDS

Psalmody

Sunday: 3, C8, 51
Monday: 118a, C9, 118b
Tuesday: 1, C10, 2

Wednesday: 8, C11, 20
Thursday: 18a, C12, 18b

Friday: 146, C13, 15
Saturday: 149, C14, 150

Lesson

Jan. 6: II Corinthians 1:1-11
Monday: II Corinthians 4:16-5:8
Tuesday: II Corinthians 8:1-9

Wednesday: II Corinthians 10:1-6
Thursday: II Corinthians 11:1-4, 12-15

Friday: Galatians 1:1-10
Saturday: Galatians 1:1-24

Collect

O God, who in all Your works are rich in mercy; Father of glory, who set Your Son as a light to the Gentiles, that He might preach redemption to the captives and give sight to the blind; O You, who through Christ are abundant in mercy, grant us the remission of our sins, and fellowship through faith with the saints, through the same Jesus Christ, Your Son, our Lord, who lives and reigns with You and the Holy Spirit, one God, now and forever. *Gallican Sacramentary*

AT TERCE, SEXT AND NONE

Chapter

Sunday, Monday and Tuesday: Romans 12:1-5
Wednesday and Thursday: Romans 6:12-18
Friday and Saturday: Romans 2:11-16

AT VESPERS

Psalmody

Sunday: 136b, 137, 138
Monday: 140, 141, 142
Tuesday: 144, 145, 7

Wednesday: 9, 10, 11
Thursday: 12, 13, 14, 16

Friday: 17, 147a, 147b
Saturday: 19, 54, 77

Lesson

Collect

Lord God, heavenly Father, who in mercy has established the Christian home among us: we implore You so to rule and direct our hearts, that we may be good examples to children and servants, and not offend them by word or deed, but faithfully teach them to love Your Church and to hear Your blessèd word. Give them Your Spirit and grace, that this seed may bring forth good fruit, so that our home life may redound to Your glory, honor and praise, to our own improvement and welfare, and give offense to no one; through the same, Your beloved Son, Jesus Christ our Lord, who lives and reigns with You and the Holy Spirit, one God, now and forever.   *Veit Dietrich*

THE SECOND WEEK
AFTER EPIPHANY

AT MATINS

Hymn - *Herr Christ, der einig Gotts Sohn*

1. The on - ly Son from heav-en,   Fore-told by   an - cient seers,

By God the Fa- ther giv - en,   In   hu - man form ap - pears.

No sphere His light con - fin - ing,   No star   so   bright- ly

shin - ing   As   He   our   Morn - ing   Star.

2. O time of God appointed,
O bright and holy morn!
He comes, the King anointed,
The Christ, the Virgin-born,
Grim death to vanquish for us,
To open heav''n before us
And bring us life again.

3. O Lord, our hearts awaken
To know and love Thee more,
In faith to stand unshaken,
In spirit to adore,
That we still heavenward hasting,
Yet here Thy joy foretasting,
May reap its fullness there.

4. O Father, here before Thee,
With God the Holy Ghost,
And Jesus, we adore Thee,
Thou Pride of angel-host:
Before Thee mortals lowly
Cry, "Holy, Holy, Holy,
One God in Persons Three!

Elizabeth Cruciger, 1524

Psalmody

Sunday: 21, 22, 23
Monday: 24, 25, 26
Tuesday: 27, 28, 29

Wednesday: 30, 31, 32
Thursday: 33, 34, 35

Friday: 37a, 37b, 38
Saturday: 39, 40, 41

Lesson

Sunday, Monday and Tuesday: John 2:1-11
Wednesday: Mark 1:40-45
Thursday: Luke 4:14-22
Friday: Mark 6:1-6
Saturday: Luke 13:10-17

Homily

Sunday - Bede the Venerable

That He condescended, according to the Gospels, to come to the wedding feast, truly confirms the faith of those who believe. Furthermore it shows how reprehensible is the false teaching of those who slander marriage. For if there were evil in the unstained bridal bed, and in nuptials chastely celebrated, the Lord would not have come to them. But because conjugal chastity is good... He is invited to the celebration of a wedding, and honors it by the presence of His holiness. *Homily on the Gospel*

Monday - Martin Luther

That there are six waterpots signifies the labor and toil which those who deal in works undergo in such purification; for the heart finds no rest in them, since the Sabbath, the seventh day, is wanting, in which we rest from our works and let God work in us. For there are six workdays, in which God created heaven and earth, and commanded us to labor. The seventh day is the day of rest, in which we are not to toil in the works of the Law, but let God work in us by faith, while we remain quiet and enjoy a holiday from the labors of the Law.

The water in the pots is the contents and substance of the Law by which the conscience is governed, and is graven in letters as in the waterpots of stone... Then comes the consoling Gospel and turns the water into wine. For when the heart hears that Christ fulfils the Law for us and takes our sin upon Himself, it no longer cares that impossible things are demanded by the Law, that we must despair of rendering them, and must give up our good works. Yes, it is an excellent thing, and delectable, that the Law is so deep and high, so holy and righteous and good, and demands things so great; and it is loved and praised for making so many and such great demands. This is because in Christ the heart now has all that the Law demands, and it would be sorry indeed if it demanded less. Behold the Law is delightful now and easy which before was disagreeable, difficult and impossible; for it lives in the heart by the Spirit. Water is no longer in the pots, it has turned to wine, it is passed to the guest, it is consumed, and has made the heart glad.

Church Postil for the Second Sunday after Epiphany

Tuesday - Augustine of Hippo

Our Lord, as God, did not have a mother. As man He had a mother. The miracle He was about to perform, He would perform through His divinity, not through His human weakness. His mother sought a miracle. But He, not acknowledging human bonds when being about to do a divine work, said: "Woman, what does your concern have to do with Me?" as if to say: That which in Me works wonders, My divinity, you did not give birth to. She is called woman because she is of the feminine sex, not because of any corruption of integrity. But because you have borne My humanity I will acknowledge you when this same humanity is hanging from the cross. So He adds: "My hour is not yet come," as though to say: when this weak body, which you have brought forth, has begun to hang upon the cross, there I will acknowledge you. For when He was about to die, before she died, and rise again, before her death, He commended His mother to His disciple. *Tractate 8 in John*

Wednesday - Paschasius Radbertus

However great our sinfulness, each one of us can be healed by God every day. We have only to worship Him with humility and love, and wherever we are to say with faith: Lord, if You want to You can make me clean. It is by believing from the heart that we are justified, so we must make our petitions with the utmost confidence, and without the slightest doubt of God's power. If we pray with a faith springing from love, God's will need be in no doubt. He will be ready and able to save us by an all-powerful command. He immediately answered the leper's request, saying: I do want to. Indeed, no sooner had the leper begun to pray with faith than the Savior's hand began to cure him of his leprosy.

This leper is an excellent teacher of the right way to make petitions. He did not doubt the Lord's willingness through disbelief in His compassion, but neither did he take it for granted, for he knew the depths of his own sinfulness. Yet because he acknowledged that the Lord was able to cleanse him if He wished, we praise this declaration of firm faith just as we praise the Lord's mighty power. For obtaining a favor from God rightly depends as much on having a real living faith as on the exercise of the Creator's power and mercy. If faith is weak it must be strengthened, for only then will it succeed in obtaining health of body or soul. The Apostle's words, purifying their hearts by faith referred, surely, to strong faith like this. And so, if the hearts of believers are purified by faith, we must give thought to this virtue of faith, for, as the Apostle says, Anyone who doubts is like a wave in the sea.

A faith shown to be living by its love, steadfast by its perseverance, patient by its endurance of delay, humble by its confession, strong by its confidence, reverent by its way of presenting petitions, and discerning with regard to their content--such a faith may be certain that in every place it will hear the Lord saying: I do want to.

Pondering this wonderful reply, let us put the words together in their proper sequence. The leper began: Lord, if you want to, and the Savior said: I do want to. The leper continued: You can make me clean, and the Lord spoke His powerful word of command: Be clean. All that the sinner's true confession maintained with faith, love and power immediately conferred. And in case the gravity of one's sins should make anyone despair, another Evangelist says this man who was cured had been completely covered with leprosy. For all have sinned and forfeited the glory of God. Since, as we rightly believe, God's power is operative everywhere, we ought to believe the same of His will, for His will is that all should be saved and come to the knowledge of the truth.

Commentary on Matthew

Thursday - Cyril of Alexandria

"The Spirit of the Lord is upon me." He is God by nature, the only Son, the holy of holies who sanctifies all creation. He has His being from the holy Father and sends the Spirit, who proceeds from Him, into the heavenly powers and also on those who saw Him when He appeared on earth. How then can He be sanctified? He exists as God and as man; as God He gives His Spirit to creation, and as man He receives the same Spirit from His God and Father. This we call his anointing.

The passage also explains the reason for the Incarnation. After saying what He has received from the Father, He adds: "because He has sent me to bring good news to the poor, to heal the brokenhearted, to proclaim release to the captives, and recovery of sight to the blind, to proclaim the day of retribution." These are some of the marvelous things accomplished during the sojourn of the only Son on earth. In order to reclaim the region under heaven and return those who dwelled all over the world to God the Father, to transform everything into something better, and, as it were, to renew the face of the earth, He took the form of a servant, though He was Lord of all.

Commentary on Isaiah

Friday - Baldwin of Forde

God can do all things for those who believe. For those who do not believe, this is not the case. The benefits of God are sometimes hindered by the sin of unfaithfulness, so that in a certain way God is said not to be able to do something because He is prevented from doing it by obstinate unfaithfulness. Thus it is written in the Gospel of Mark that Jesus went to His own country and could not do any miracles there, except to cure a few sick people by laying His hands on them; and He was amazed at their lack of belief. It says "He could not" because it was their sins that kept the grace of God away from them, just as Jeremiah says: "Our sins have kept good away from us." And it is said "he was amazed" because He shows us something that should amaze us: that it was because they were so unbelieving that He could not do any signs there.

The Commendation of Faith

Saturday - Irenaeus of Lyons

It is clear, therefore that Christ loosed and vivified those who believe in Him as Abraham did, and that He did nothing contrary to the Law when He healed on the Sabbath day. The Law did not prohibit men from being healed on the Sabbaths; it even circumcised them on that day, and gave command that the Offices should be performed by priests for the people. It did not forbid the healing even of dumb animals… For the Law commanded them to abstain from every self-serving work, that is, from all grasping after wealth which is had by trading and by other worldly business. Rather it exhorted them to attend to the exercises of the soul, which consist in reflection, and to doing beneficial works for their neighbors' good. And therefore the Lord reproved those who unjustly blamed Him for having healed on the Sabbath days. For He did not make void, but fulfilled the Law…

Against Heresies, Book 4

Collect

Almighty and everlasting God, who governs all things in heaven and earth, mercifully hear the supplications of Your people and grant us Your peace all the days of our life; through Jesus Christ, Your Son, our Lord, who lives and reigns with You and the Holy Spirit, one God, now and forever.

Gelasian Sacramentary

AT LAUDS

Psalmody

Sunday: 67, C1, 5
Monday: 63, C2, 36
Tuesday: 43, C3, 57

Wednesday: 64, C4, 65
Thursday: 88, C6, 90

Friday: 76, C5, 92
Saturday: 143, C7, 148

Lesson

Sunday: Galatians 3:1-9
Monday: Galatians 4:1-7
Tuesday: Galatians 5:1-15

Wednesday: Ephesians 1:1-14
Thursday: Ephesians 2:11-18

Friday: Ephesians 4:7-16
Saturday: Ephesians 6:1-9

Collect

Lord God, heavenly Father, from whom without ceasing we receive exceedingly abundantly all good gifts and by whom we are guarded daily from every evil: Grant us we beseech You by Your Spirit that we in true faith may acknowledge this Your goodness with our whole heart and may now and evermore thank and praise Your loving-kindness and tender mercy; through Jesus Christ Your Son our Lord, who lives and reigns with You and the Holy Spirit, one God, now and forever.

Martin Luther, 1529

AT TERCE, SEXT AND NONE

Chapter

Sunday, Monday and Tuesday: Romans 12:6-16a
Wednesday and Thursday: Colossians 1:25-28
Friday and Saturday: I Timothy 4:9-16

AT VESPERS

Psalmody

Sunday: 110, 111, 112, 113	Wednesday: 123, 124, 125	Friday: 129, 130, 131, 132
Monday: 114, 115, 116, 117	Thursday: 126, 127, 128	Saturday: 133, 135, 136a
Tuesday: 120, 121, 122		

Lesson

Sunday: Galatians 3:10-14	Wednesday: Ephesians 2:1-10	Friday: Ephesians 5:22-33
Monday: Galatians 4:8-20	Thursday: Ephesians 2:19-22	Saturday: Philippians 1:12-26
Tuesday: Galatians 6:11-18		

Collect

Lord God, heavenly Father, we thank You, that of Your grace You have instituted holy matrimony, in which You keep us from unchastity, and other offenses: we implore You to send Your blessing upon every husband and wife, that they may not provoke each other to anger and strife, but live peaceably together in love and godliness, receive Your gracious help in all temptations, and raise their children in accordance with Your will; grant unto us all to walk before You in purity and holiness, to put all our trust in You, and lead such lives on earth, that in the world to come we may have everlasting life, through the same, Your beloved Son, Jesus Christ our Lord, who lives and reigns with You and the Holy Spirit, one God, now and forever. *Veit Dietrich*

THE THIRD WEEK
AFTER EPIPHANY

AT MATINS

Hymn - *O Jesu Christe, Wahres Licht*

1. O Christ, our true and on - ly Light, En - light- en those who sit in night; Let those a - far now hear Thy voice, And in Thy fold with us re - joice.

2. Fill with the radiance of Thy grace
The souls now lost in error's maze,
And all whom in their secret minds
Some dark delusion haunts and blinds.

3. And all who else have strayed from Thee,
O gently seek! Thy healing be
To every wounded conscience given,
And let them also share Thy heaven.

4. O make the deaf to hear Thy Word,
And teach the dumb to speak, dear Lord,
Who dare not yet the faith avow,
Though secretly they hold it now.

5. Shine on the darkened and the cold,
Recall the wanderers from Thy fold,
Unite all those who walk apart,
Confirm the weak and doubting heart.

6. So they with us may evermore
Such grace with wondering thanks adore,
And endless praise to Thee be given
By all the Church in earth and heaven.

Johann Heermann, 1630

Psalmody

Sunday: 42, 44, 45
Monday: 46, 47, 48
Tuesday: 49, 50, 52

Wednesday: 53, 55, 56
Thursday: 58, 59, 60

Friday: 61, 62, 66
Saturday: 68a, 68b, 69a

Lesson

Sunday, Monday and Tuesday: Matthew 8:1-13
Monday: Luke 5:12-16
Tuesday: Luke 7:1-10

Wednesday and Thursday: Matthew 4:23-25
Thursday: Mark 1:35-39

Friday and Saturday: Luke 19:12-26

Saturday: Matthew 25:14-30

Homily

Sunday - Origen of Alexandria

Let us consider here, beloved Brethren, if there is any who has the taint of leprosy in his soul, or the contamination of guilt in his heart. If he has, let him at once worship God and say, "Lord, if You are willing, You can make me clean." Long ago You cleansed Naaman who committed many crimes, and You have had compassion throughout the ages on an immeasurable number of others who have implored You. "You," therefore, "if You are willing, You can make me clean." And the Lord, swiftly stretching forth the hand of His mercy, will say, "I am willing; be cleansed," as Jesus says it to the one cleansed of leprosy.

The Lord had compassion on this man who believed in Him, who trusted in His power. To him Jesus said: you have believed, you are healed; you have hoped, you are made clean. Do not forget what you were, nor what you are now made into. Do not cease to give thanks, nor cease to confess the Lord. Beloved, we must also do this, as often as He has delivered us from some peril, or comforted us in some grief, or infirmity, or sickness, or from any difficulty whatsoever. Let us not be ungrateful, nor forgetful of our Benefactor, but speedily render thanks to Him; and let us offer a gift according to our means, to show Him honor. *The Healing of the Leper*

Monday - John Chrysostom

"Lord, if You are willing, You can make me clean." He did not doubt that the will of God is disposed to every good action when saying "if You are willing." This does not imply doubt on the part of the leper, but rather the expression of his mind regarding Christ's judgment. For since Christ is good, He does not will to bestow that which is harmful, even though He be asked. Neither is wholeness of body profitable to everyone. Since, therefore, he did not know whether this healing was beneficial for him or not, he was unsure as to the divine will, although knowing it to be disposed to every good. For to believe good of the divine mercy is the sign of a believing man; but to know the judgements of the divine mercy is beyond the power either of man or of faith. It is clear that not even the Apostle knew this, when he three times implored the Lord that the thorn in the flesh, the messenger of Satan, might depart from him; which had been given to him lest he be exalted, and because of which it was said to him, "My grace is sufficient for you, for My strength is made perfect in weakness."

It is as if the leper said, I believe that whatever is good, You will it. But I do not know if what I seek is good for me. But this I clearly do not doubt, but rather believe: that if this is good for me, You will it also. The words of the leper therefore show him to be uncertain not of the mercy of God, but of the judgements of the divine mercy. *Sermon 21 on Matthew 8*

Tuesday - Augustine of Hippo

We have heard, as the Gospel was being read, the praise of our faith as manifested in humility. For when the Lord Jesus promised that He would go to the centurion's house to heal his servant, he answered, "I am not worthy that You should come under my roof. But only speak a word, and my servant will be healed." By calling himself unworthy, he showed himself worthy for Christ to come not into his house, but into his heart. Nor would he have said this with so great faith and humility, had he not borne Him in his heart already, of whose coming into his house he was afraid...

The centurion's faith is praised for its humility. For he said, "I am not worthy that You should come under my roof." And the Lord said, "Assuredly I say to you, I have not found such great faith, not even in Israel;" according to the flesh that is. For he too was, without a doubt, an Israelite according to the spirit... We can only measure the faith of men as men are able to judge it. But He

291

who saw the inward parts, He whom no man can deceive, gave His testimony to this man's faith, hearing words of lowliness, and pronouncing a sentence of healing.

But from where did he get such confidence? "I also," he said, "am a man under authority, having soldiers under me. And I say to this one, 'Go,' and he goes; and to another, 'Come,' and he comes; and to my servant, 'Do this,' and he does it." I am an authority to those who are placed under me, and am myself under those in authority over me. If I, a man under the authority of others, have the power of commanding, what power must You have, whom all powers serve?

Sermon 12 on Matthew 8

Wednesday - John Chrysostom

When, therefore He had called the disciples, then He begins to work miracles in their presence, by His deeds confirming the words of John concerning Him. And He continually visited their synagogues, even by this teaching them that He was not some sort of adversary of God and a deceiver, but that He had come in accordance with the Father.

And while visiting them, He did not just preach, but also performed miracles. And He did this because whenever God does anything strange or surprising, and any new polity is introduced, He is wont to work miracles, as pledges of His power, which He gives to those who are to receive His laws. Thus, for instance, when He was about to make man, He created a whole world, and then gave him that law which he had in Paradise. And when He was to give laws to Noah, He again showed forth great miracles, in that He reduced the whole creation again to its basic elements, and made that terrifying sea prevail for a full year; and in that, in the midst of so great a tempest, He preserved that righteous man. And in the time of Abraham too He granted many signs; such as his victory in the war, the plague upon Pharaoh, his deliverance from dangers. And when about to legislate for the Jews, He showed forth those marvelous and great phenomenon, and then gave the law. Just so in this case also, being about to introduce a certain high polity, and to tell what they had never heard, He confirms what He says by the display of miracles. Thus, because the kingdom He was preaching did not appear by the things that are visible, He makes it, though invisible, manifest.

Homily 14 on Matthew

Thursday - John Chrysostom

Now then, let us too follow Him; for we also have many diseases of our soul, and these especially He would gladly heal.

...Let us therefore come to Him, and let us ask nothing pertaining to this life, but rather remission of sins. For indeed He gives it even now, if we are in earnest. Since as then "His fame went throughout all Syria," so now into the whole world. And they indeed ran together on hearing that He healed possessed people. And you, having much more and greater experience of His power, will you not rouse yourself and run? But whereas they left both country, and friends, and relatives; will you not endure so little as to leave your house for the sake of drawing near and obtaining far greater things?

...Let us therefore now also draw nigh unto Him; let us entreat Him that He would brace our paralyzed soul, and leaving all things that pertain to this life, let us take account only of things spiritual.

Homily 14 on Matthew

Friday - Augustine of Hippo

In the Gospel, you have heard both the reward of the good servants and the punishment of the bad. The fault of that servant who was reproved and severely punished was this and only this: that he would not put to use what he had received. He preserved it intact, but his master was looking for a profit from it. God is greedy for our salvation. If such condemnation befalls the servant who did not use what he had received, what should they who lose it expect? We therefore are dispensers. We expend, but you receive. We expect a profit on your part - living good lives - for that is the profit from our dispensing. Do not think that you are free from the obligation of dispensing. Of course, you cannot dispense your gifts from this higher station of ours [the Office of the Ministry], but you can dispense them in whatever station you happen to be. When Christ is attacked, defend Him. Give an answer to those who complain. Rebuke blasphemers, but keep yourselves far from any fellowship with them. If in this way you gain anyone, you are putting your gifts to use.

Sermon 94

Saturday - Ambrose of Milan

We [bishops and priests] are stewards of the heavenly mysteries. We are ministers, but not all alike. "But," it says, "as the Lord gave to each one, I planted, Apollos watered, but God gave the increase." Let each one then strive that he may be able to receive a reward according to his labor. "For we are God's fellow workers," as the Apostle said; "we are God's field, God's building." Blessed therefore is he who sees such interest on his principal; blessed too is he who beholds the fruit of his work; blessed again is he "who builds on the foundation of faith with gold, silver, precious stones."

You who hear or read these words are all things to us. You are the interest of the money-lender, - the interest gained on speech, not on money; you are the return given to the farmer; you are the gold, the silver, the precious stones of the builder. In your merits lie the chief results of the labors of the priest; in your souls shines forth the fruit of a bishop's work; in your progress glitters the gold of the Lord; the silver is increased if you hold fast the divine words. "The words of the Lord are pure words, like silver tried in a furnace of earth, purified seven times." You therefore will make the lender rich, the farmer abound in produce; you will prove the master-builder skilful. I do not speak boastfully; for I do not desire so much my own advantage as yours.

Oh that I might safely say of you at that time: "Lord, you delivered to me five talents; look, I have gained five more talents besides them," and that I might show the precious talents of your virtues! "For we have this treasure in earthen vessels." These are the talents which the Lord bids us to trade with spiritually, or the two coins of the New and the Old Testament which that Samaritan in the Gospel left for the man robbed by the thieves for the purpose of healing his wounds.

Neither do I, my brethren, long for this with greedy desires, so that I may be set over many things; the reward I get from knowing of your advance is enough for me. Oh that I may not be found unworthy of that which I have received! Let those things which are too great for me be assigned to better men. I demand them not! Yet may You say, O Lord: "I wish to give to this last man the same as to you." Let the man that deserves it receive authority over ten cities… It is enough for me that I am not thrust out into the outer darkness, as he was who hid the talent entrusted to him in the earth, so to speak, of his own flesh.

Exposition of the Christian Faith

Collect

Almighty and everlasting God, mercifully look upon our infirmities, and in all our dangers and needs stretch forth the right hand of Your majesty to help and defend us; through Jesus Christ, Your Son, our Lord, who lives and reigns with You and the Holy Spirit, one God, now and forever.

Gelasian Sacramentary

AT LAUDS

Psalmody

Sunday: 3, C8, 51
Monday: 118a, C9, 118b
Tuesday: 1, C10, 2

Wednesday: 8, C11, 20
Thursday: 18a, C12, 18b

Friday: 146, C13, 5
Saturday: 149, C14, 150

Lesson

Sunday: Philippians 1:27-30
Monday: Philippians 2:12-18
Tuesday: Philippians 4:1-7

Wednesday: Colossians 1:1-8
Thursday: Colossians 1:19-29

Friday: Colossians 3:12-4:1
Saturday: I Thessalonians 1:1-10

Collect

Almighty and Ever-living God, who has given to all who believe exceedingly great and precious promises: grant us so perfectly, and without any doubt, to believe in Your Son Jesus Christ, that our faith in Your sight may never be reproved; hear us, O Lord, through the same, our Savior, Jesus Christ, who lives and reigns with You and the Holy Spirit, one God, now and forever.

Book of Common Prayer, 1549

AT TERCE, SEXT AND NONE

Chapter

Sunday, Monday and Tuesday: Romans 12:16b-21
Wednesday and Thursday: I Timothy 1:15-17
Friday and Saturday: I Corinthians 7:1b-9

AT VESPERS

Psalmody

Sunday: 136b, 137, 138
Monday: 140, 141, 142
Tuesday: 144, 145, 7

Wednesday: 9, 10, 11
Thursday: 12, 13, 14, 16

Friday: 17, 147a, 147b
Saturday: 19, 54, 77

Lesson

Sunday: Philippians 2:1-11
Monday: Philippians 3:12-21
Tuesday: Philippians 4:8-13

Wednesday: Colossians 1:9-18
Thursday: Colossians 2:11-19

Friday: Colossians 4:2-6
Saturday: I Thessalonians 2:1-12

Collect

O almighty and everlasting God, mercifully look upon our infirmities, and in all dangers and necessities stretch forth Your mighty hand, to defend us against our enemies, through Jesus Christ, Your Son, our Lord, who lives and reigns with You and the Holy Spirit, one God, now and forever.

Veit Dietrich

THE FOURTH WEEK
AFTER EPIPHANY

AT MATINS

Hymn - *Wär' Gott nicht mit us diese Zeit*

1. If God had not been on our side And had not come to aid us,

The foes with all their pow'r and pride Would sure-ly have dis- mayed us;

For we, His flock, would have to fear The threat of men both

far and near Who rise in might a - gainst us.

2. Their furious wrath, did God permit,
   Would surely have consumed us
   And as a deep and yawning pit
   Wisht life and limb entomed us.
   Like men o'er whom dark waters roll
   Their wrath would have engulfed our soul
   And, like a flood, o'erwhelmed us.

3. Blest be the Lord, who foiled their threat
   That they could not devour us;
   Our souls, like birds, escaped their net,
   They could not overpower us.
   The snare is broken - we are free!
   Our help is ever, Lord, in Thee,
   Who madest earth and heaven.

Martin Luther, 1524

Psalmody

Sunday: 69b, 70, 71
Monday: 72, 73, 74
Tuesday: 78a, 78b, 78c

Wednesday: 75, 79, 80
Thursday: 81, 82, 83

Friday: 84, 86, 87, 93
Saturday: 85, 89a, 89b

Lesson

Sunday, Monday and Tuesday: Matthew 8:23-27
Monday: Mark 4:35-41
Tuesday: Luke 8:22-26

Wednesday and Thursday: Luke 8:26-34
Thursday: Matthew 8:28-34

Friday and Saturday: Luke 8:35-39
Saturday: Luke 8:16-18

Homily

Sunday - Origen of Alexandria

They wondered therefore, saying: "What kind of man is this?" They say this… not questioning but affirming that He is such that the sea and the winds obey Him. What manner of man is this? As much as to say: how great, how strong, how wonderful… He commands the sea, and it does not disobey; He speaks to the winds, and to the storm, and behold! they are still; He commands every creature, and they don't move beyond what He commands. Only the race of men, which alone has the honor of being made in His likeness, to whom speech and understanding has been given, only these, only men, resist; they alone do not obey Him; they alone despise Him. And for this reason they alone will be condemned at the judgement and punished by His justice; in this they are lower than the mute animals, or than the things of the world that are without sense or without feeling.

They wonder at Him because He restrained the sea, and quieted the winds. Let us wonder at Him too, when He shows kindness and generosity towards us; when He comes down to deliver us from dangers; when He delivers from many trials and pains, when He rescues us from the snares of our enemies. Let us wonder, and wondering give thanks; let us be responsive to His grace, and being obedient, let us also fear Him, and fearing Him, let us love Him, so that we become heirs of eternal love.

They wondered, saying: "What kind of man is this?" He appears as man, but as God He shows forth His power. For while we see that He is of our flesh, He manifests signs and wonders that are above the power of all flesh. As man He sleeps, as God He commands the winds and the seas. He rests in the little ship, yet where He wills, all creatures bow down before His Majesty, Jesus Christ our Lord, who with the Father and the Holy Ghost, lives and reigns world without end. Amen.

The Testing of the Apostles

Monday - Cyril of Alexandria

The sea is for us a figure of the visible world, and the Church is the little ship, and the rowers are the just, who because they have received the faith have Christ always present with them. And it is often assailed by violent storms, and the waves of many persecutions beat against the little ark, and countless trials agitate it, and the cruelty of unclean spirits rages against it, and fills it with the fear of death.

But Christ is among His chosen servants, and while in His holy wisdom He permits that they suffer persecution, He seems to sleep. But when the storm is at its fiercest, and those in the ark can endure no more, then we should cry out: "Awake! Why do You sleep, O Lord?" Without delay He will awaken, and take away all your fear. He will reprove those that afflict us, and change our mourning into joy, unfolding to us a shining and untroubled sky. For He does not turn His face away from those who trust in Him, who lives and reigns with the Father and the Holy Spirit world without end. Amen.

Homily on the Gospel

Tuesday - Martin Luther

This Gospel, as a narrative, gives us an example of faith and unbelief, in order that we may learn how mighty the power of faith is, and that it of necessity has to do with great and terrible things and that it accomplishes nothing but wonders; and that on the other hand unbelief is so fainthearted, shamefaced and trembling with fear that it can do nothing whatever. An illustration of this we see in the experience of the disciples, which shows the real state of their hearts. First, as they in company with Christ entered the ship, all was calm and they experienced nothing unusual, and had anyone asked them then if they believed, they would have answered, Yes. But they were not conscious of how their hearts trusted in the calm sea and the signs of fair weather, and that thus their faith was founded upon what their natural eyes saw. But when the tempest comes and the waves fill the boat, their faith vanishes; because the calm and peace in which they trusted took wings and flew away, therefore they fly with the calm and peace, and nothing is left but unbelief.

But what is this unbelief able to do? It sees nothing but what it experiences. It does not experience life, salvation and safety; but instead the waves coming into the boat and the sea threatening them with death and every danger. And because they experience these things and give heed to them and turn not their fear from them, trembling and despair cannot be suppressed. Yea, the more they see and experience it the harder death and despair torment them and every moment threaten to devour them...

But had they had faith, it would have driven the wind and the waves of the sea out of their minds, and pictured before their eyes in place of the wind and tempest the power and grace of God, promised in His Word, as though anchored to an immovable rock and would not float on the water, and as though the sun shined brightly and all was calm and no storm was raging. For it is the great characteristic and power of faith to see what is not visible, and not to see what is visible, yea, that which at the time drives and oppresses us; just as unbelief can see only what is visible and can not in the least cleave to what is invisible.

Church Postil for Epiphany 4

Wednesday - Irenaeus of Lyons

Even the demons exclaimed on seeing the Son: "We know who You are, the Holy One of God." And the devil, looking at Him and tempting Him, said: "If You are the Son of God;" - all thus truly seeing and speaking of the Son and the Father, but in unbelief. For it was proper all should testify to the truth, and that it should become a judgment: for the salvation of those who believe, but for the condemnation of those who do not believe, that all should be fairly judged. And [it was proper] that faith in the Father and Son should be approved by all, both from those belonging to it because they are its friends, and by those having no connection with it because they are its enemies. For that evidence is true, and cannot be denied, which elicits even from its adversaries striking testimonies on its behalf; they having been convinced about it by their own plain contemplation of it, and bearing testimony to it and declaring it.

Against All Heresies Book 4

Thursday - Augustine of Hippo

James says openly in his epistle: "Do you not know that friendship with the world is enmity with God?" You have heard. Do you wish to not be an enemy of God? Then don't be a friend of this world; for if you are a friend of this world, you will be an enemy of God. For a wife cannot be an adulteress unless she is also an enemy of her own husband; so a soul which is an adulteress through its love of worldly things, cannot but be an enemy to God. It fears, but does not love. It fears punishment, but is not delighted with righteousness. All lovers of the world, therefore, are enemies of God.

Sermon on Psalm 92

Friday - Eusebius of Caesarea

Just as in this life, with winter passing, and the springtime following, the sun pours out its warm rays and awakens to life the seeds long since buried in the earth, which, shedding their husks come forth in new and varied forms, so the glorious coming of the Only Begotten of God, pouring forth His life-giving rays upon the new world, brings to the light seeds long buried throughout the whole earth, that is, those now sleeping in the dust of earth, and [they come forth] with bodies more perfect than before, and, death having now been overthrown, the life of this new world will reign forevermore.

from the Catena Aurea of Thomas Aquinas

Saturday - Archelaus of Carchar

If indeed He blinded the thoughts of unbelievers He blinded them for a good purpose: so that they might look with new sight on what is good. For he did not say that He blinded their soul, but, rather the thoughts of those who do not believe. And the meaning is something like this: "Blind the lewd thoughts of the lewd man, and he is saved. Blind the grasping and rapacious thought of the robber, and he is saved." But if you won't understand it this way, then there is yet another interpretation. The sun too blinds those whose sight is dim, and they whose eyes are diseased are hurt by the light and blinded. It's not that the sun's nature is to blind, but that the substance of the eyes is incapable of seeing. In a similar way unbelievers being diseased in their heart cannot look upon the radiance of the Godhead. He did not say, "He has blinded their thoughts so that they should not hear the Gospel;" but, that the light of the glory of the Gospel of our Lord Jesus Christ should not shine upon them. To hear the Gospel is permitted to everyone: but the glory of the Gospel is reserved for Christ's true children alone. Therefore the Lord spoke in parables to those who could not hear; but to the Disciples He explained the parables in private. The brightness of the glory is for those who have been enlightened, the blinding for those in unbelief.

Disputation with Manes

Collect

Almighty God, because You know that we are set among so many and great dangers that by reason of the weakness of our fallen nature we cannot always stand upright, grant us Your strength and protection to support us in all dangers and carry us through all temptations, through Jesus Christ, Your Son, our Lord, who lives and reigns with You and the Holy Spirit, one God, now and forever.

Gelasian Sacramentary

AT LAUDS

Psalmody

Sunday: 67, C1, 5	Wednesday: 64, C4, 65	Friday: 76, C5, 92
Monday: 63, C2, 36	Thursday: 88, C6, 90	Saturday: 143, C7, 148
Tuesday: 43, C3, 57		

Lesson

Sunday: I Thessalonians 3:11-4:8	Wednesday: I Timothy 1:1-11	Friday: I Timothy 3:1-13
Monday: II Thessalonians 1:1-12	Thursday: I Timothy 2:1-7	Saturday: I Timothy 6:3-10
Tuesday: II Thessalonians 2:13-17		

Collect

Almighty God, whom to know is everlasting life: grant us perfectly to know Your Son Jesus Christ to be the Way, the Truth and the Life; that following His steps we may steadfastly walk in the way that leads to eternal life; through the same, Jesus Christ, Your Son, our Lord, who lives and reigns with You and the Holy Spirit, one God, now and forever.

Book of Common Prayer, 1549

AT TERCE, SEXT AND NONE

Chapter

Sunday, Monday and Tuesday: Romans 13:8-10
Wednesday and Thursday: Romans 5:18-21
Friday and Saturday: Colossians 4:2-6

AT VESPERS

Psalmody

Sunday: 110, 111, 112, 113   Wednesday: 123, 124, 125   Friday: 129, 130, 131, 132
Monday: 114, 115, 116, 117   Thursday: 126, 127, 128   Saturday: 133, 135, 136a
Tuesday: 120, 121, 122

Lesson

Sunday: I Thessalonians 5:12-24   Wednesday: I Timothy 1:12-17   Friday: I Timothy 3:16-4:10
Monday: II Thessalonians 2:1-12   Thursday: I Timothy 2:8-15   Saturday: I Timothy 6:11-16
Tuesday: II Thessalonians 3:1-5

Collect

Lord God, heavenly Father, who in Your divine wisdom and fatherly goodness makes Your children to bear the cross, and sends diverse afflictions upon us to subdue the flesh and to quicken our hearts unto faith, hope and unceasing prayer: We beseech You to have mercy upon us, and graciously deliver us out of our trials and afflictions, so that we may perceive Your grace and fatherly help, and with all saints forever praise and worship You, through Your dear Son, Jesus Christ our Lord, who lives and reigns with You and the Holy Spirit, one God, now and forever.   *Veit Dietrich*

THE FIFTH WEEK
AFTER EPIPHANY

AT MATINS

Hymn - *Brich auf und werde lichte*

1.   A - rise and shine in splen-dor,   Let night to   day   sur - ren - der;

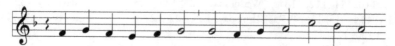

Thy Light is draw-ing near.   A - bove thee day   is   beam - ing,

In match-less beau-ty gleam-ing; The glo - ry of the Lord is here.

2. See earth in darkness lying,
The heathen nations dying
In hopeless gloom and night.
To thee the Lord of heaven -
Thy life, thy hope - hath given
Great glory, honor, and delight.

3. The world's remotest races,
Upon whose weary faces
The sun looks from the sky,
Shall run with zeal untiring,
With joy thy Light desiring
That breaks upon them from on high.

4. Lift up thine eyes in wonder;
See, nations gather yonder,
They all come unto thee.
The world has heard thy story,
Thy sons come to thy glory,
And daughters haste thy Light to see.

5. There are glad delegations
From Ephah and far nations
And clouds from Midian;
With gold shall Sheba cheer thee
And incense; all that near thee
Shall sing thy praise, O chosen one!

6. Thy heart will leap for gladness
When from the realms of sadness
They come o'er land and sea.
Thine eyes will wake from slumber
When people without number
Come thronging from afar to thee.

Martin Opitz, 1628

Psalmody

Sunday: 89c, 94, 96
Monday: 97, 98, 99, 100
Tuesday: 101, 102, 103

Wednesday: 104a, 104b, 104c
Thursday: 105a, 105b, 105c

Friday: 106a, 106b, 107a
Saturday: 107b, 108, 109

Lesson

Sunday, Monday and Tuesday: Matthew 13:24-30
Wednesday and Thursday: Mark 2:13-17
Thursday: Matthew 9:9-13
Friday and Saturday: Luke 4:31-37
Saturday: Mark 1:21-34

Homily

Sunday - John Chrysostom

The Lord forbade [the removal of the tares] for two reasons. First, that the wheat not be injured; second, because whoever has a disease that is not cured will not escape punishment. If you want to see them punished without harming the wheat, then you must wait for the due time. What else does He mean when He says lest you uproot the wheat also together with it, unless that if you take up arms and kill heretics, what will happen is that many of the sanctified will fall with them. And it is even likely that many from among the tares will be converted into wheat. So if you uproot them now, you will also destroy the wheat they would become, should they be converted. He did not, however, forbid us to reprove heretics, to silence their mouths, to restrict their liberty of speech, to scatter their assemblies; but He did forbid us to kill them.

But see His gentleness and patience. He not alone forbids, but He also gives His reasons. What if the tares continue till the end? Then He says I will say to the reapers, gather up first the tares, and bind them into bundles to burn. He recalls to their minds the words of John speaking of Him as the Judge, and says: we must spare the tares as long as they stand close to the wheat in the field, for it is possible that they too may become wheat. But when they have been cut down, and have not profited from the patience of the Lord, then must they receive their inevitable punishment.

Sermon on Matthew 13

Monday - Jerome of Jerusalem

But this seems to be contrary to the precept: "Put away the evil one from among yourselves." For if we are forbidden to uproot, and if we are to wait in patience until the harvest time, how then are we to cast out certain persons from among us? But between the true wheat and the tares, while the latter is still green, and the stalk not yet come into ear, there is a great similarity, and little or no difference between them so as to tell one from the other. The Lord therefore warns us that in the beginning we are not to be too ready to deliver judgement, where anything is uncertain; but that we leave judgement to God, so that when the day of the Judge shall come, He shall exclude the wicked from the company of the blessed, not on the mere suspicion of having committed an offense, but because of manifest guilt. *Excerpt from the Catena Aurea of Thomas Aquinas*

Tuesday - Martin Luther

But Christ says here, at harvest time My workers will gather the tares and tie them in bundles, just as a farmer gathers tares and bundles them, indicating they are ready to be burned. In like manner, the angels of God will separate the tares from the wheat and tie them into bundles, that is, they will condemn the evildoers to eternal death and unending fire. You who murder heretics ought to be praying for these poor people, that they might be converted and not be judged and condemned in this fashion. What you are doing is rushing in and condemning them before the time.

This is the other reason why Christ does not want the tares eliminated by the sword, for they are already condemned to be burned. As St. Paul says, a heretic has a distorted mind and stands self-condemned. A man should be moved to pity such a person rather than to desire to kill him. This is the way for God-fearing preachers and Christians to act. The ungodly and the hypocrites can do nothing else but slay and kill, just like the pope, Müntzer, and the fanatics.

Sermon on the Gospel for Epiphany 5, 1528

Wednesday - An Ancient Homily

Our people seemed to be abandoned by God, but now that we have believed, we have become more numerous than those who seemed to have God. Again another passage of scripture says: "I did not come to call the righteous, but sinners to repentance." This means that He must save those who are perishing. For it is truly a great and marvelous thing, to strengthen not what is standing, but what is fallen. So it was that Christ willed to save what was perishing. And He has saved many, coming and calling us while we were already perishing. *(traditionally ascribed to Clement of Rome), c. 120*

Thursday - Jerome of Jerusalem

There are two ways of interpreting the saying "I did not come to call the righteous, but sinners." The first is by analogy with the accompanying phrase: "Those who are well have no need of a physician, but those who are sick." The other way is to put a more literal construction on the statement, like this: Since no one is perfectly righteous, Christ has not come to call those who are not there, but the multitude of sinners who are there, with whom the world is filled, remembering the Psalm which says, "Help, Lord, for the godly man ceases!" *Against the Pelagians*

Friday - Cyril of Alexandria

The bystanders, witnesses of such great deeds, were astonished at the power of His Word. He performed miracles, without offering up a prayer, asking no one else at all for the power to accomplish them. Since He is the living and active Word of God the father, by whom all things exist, and in whom all things are, in His own person He crushed Satan and closed the profane mouth of impure demons. *Homily 12 on Luke*

Saturday - Ambrose of Milan

He describes the works of divine healing begun on the sabbath day, to show from the outset that the new creation began where the old creation ceased. He showed us that the Son of God is not under the law but above the law, and that the law will not be destroyed but fulfilled. For the world was not made through the law but by the Word, as we read: "By the Word of the Lord were the heavens established." Thus the law is not destroyed but fulfilled, so that the renewal of humankind, already in error, may occur. The apostle too says, "Stripping yourselves of the old man, put on the new, who was created according to Christ." He began properly on the sabbath, that He may show Himself as Creator. He completed the work that He had already begun by weaving together works with works. *Exposition of the Gospel of Luke*

Collect

O Lord, we pray You, keep Your Church and household continually in Your true religion that they who lean on the hope of Your heavenly grace may evermore be defended by Your might power; through Jesus Christ, Your Son, our Lord, who lives and reigns with You and the Holy Spirit, one God, now and forever. *Gelasian Sacramentary*

AT LAUDS

Psalmody

Sunday: 3, C8, 51
Monday: 118a, C9, 118b
Tuesday: 1, C10, 2

Wednesday: 8, C11, 20
Thursday: 18a, C12, 18b

Friday: 146, C13, 5
Saturday: 149, C14, 150

Lesson

Sunday: II Timothy 1:1-12
Monday: II Timothy 3:1-9
Tuesday: II Timothy 4:1-8

Wednesday: Titus 2:15-3:11
Thursday: Hebrews 1:1-4

Friday: Hebrews 2:1-9
Saturday: Hebrews 3:12-19

Collect

Almighty and Everlasting God, who by Your Son has promised us forgiveness of sins and everlasting life: we beseech You so to rule and govern our hearts by Your Holy Spirit, that in our daily need, and especially in all time of temptation, we may seek help from Him, and by a true and lively faith in Your Word obtain the same; through the same, Jesus Christ, Your Son, our Lord, who lives and reigns with You and the Holy Spirit, one God, now and forever.

Saxon Kirchenordnung (Duke Henry), 1539

AT TERCE, SEXT AND NONE

Chapter

Sunday, Monday and Tuesday: Colossians 3:12-17
Wednesday and Thursday: I Corinthians 1:26-31
Friday and Saturday: Romans 5:1-5a

AT VESPERS

Psalmody

Sunday: 136b, 137, 138
Monday: 140, 141, 142
Tuesday: 144, 145, 7

Wednesday: 9, 10, 11
Thursday: 12, 13, 14, 16

Friday: 17, 147a, 147b
Saturday: 19, 54, 77

Lesson

Sunday: II Timothy 2:1-13
Monday: II Timothy 3:10-17
Tuesday: Titus 1:1-9

Wednesday: Philemon 1-16
Thursday: Hebrews 1:5-14

Friday: Hebrews 3:1-11
Saturday: Hebrews 4:1-10

Collect

Lord God, heavenly Father, we thank You that You have sown the good seed, Your holy Word, in our hearts: we pray You that by Your Holy Spirit You will cause this seed to grow and bring forth fruit, and defend us from the enemy, that he may not sow tares therein. Keep us from carnal security, help us in all temptations, and give us at last eternal salvation; through Your beloved Son, who lives and reigns with You and the Holy Spirit, one God, now and forever.

Veit Dietrich

THE WEEK OF THE TRANSFIGURATION OF OUR LORD

AT MATINS

Hymn - *Caelestis formam gloriae*

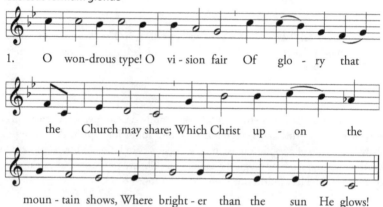

1. O won-drous type! O vi-sion fair Of glo-ry that

the Church may share; Which Christ up - on the

moun - tain shows, Where bright - er than the sun He glows!

2. With Moses and Elijah nigh
Th'incarnate Lord holds converse high;
And from the cloud the Holy One
Bears record to the only Son.

3. With shining face and bright array,
Christ deigns to manifest today
What glory shall be theirs above
Who joy in God with perfect love.

4. And faithful hearts are raised on high
By this great vision's mystery;
For which in joyful strains we raise
The voice of prayer, the hymn of praise.

5. O Father, with th'eternal Son,
And Holy Spirit, ever One,
Vouchsafe to bring us by Thy grace
To see Thy glory face to face.

Anonymous, Sarum Breviary, 1495

Psalmody

Sunday: 21, 22, 23
Monday: 24, 25, 26
Tuesday: 27, 28, 29

Wednesday: 30, 31, 32
Thursday: 33, 34, 35

Friday: 37a, 37b, 38
Saturday: 39, 40, 41

Lesson

Sunday, Monday and Tuesday: Matthew 17:1-9

Monday: Mark 9:2-10
Tuesday: Luke 9:28-36

Wednesday, Thursday, Friday and Saturday: Matthew 13:31-35

Thursday: Luke 13:18-21
Friday: Matthew 16:24-28
Saturday: Mark 8:34-9:1

Homily

Sunday - John Chrysostom

There was smoke and steam as from a furnace; here is transcendent light, and a Voice... And what did this Voice say? "This is My beloved Son." If He is beloved, do not be afraid, Peter. You should now know both of His power and His majesty, and be confident of His resurrection; but since you do not know these things, then at least take courage from the Voice of His Father. For if the Father is all powerful, so too is the Son. So don't be afraid of dangers. But if this won't reassure you, remember this at least: that He is His Son, and His Beloved! For, He says: "This is My beloved Son." If He is His beloved, don't be afraid. For no one casts off the one he loves. So don't be troubled; however much you love Him, you do not love Him as much as His own Father loves Him.

"In whom I am well pleased." He not only loves Him because He has begotten Him, but because He is equal to Him in all things, and because their will is one. Doubled then, no, tripled, is the basis of His love; because He is the Son, because He is the Beloved, and because in Him He is well pleased. And what does this mean: "In whom I am well pleased"? It is as if He said, in Whom I take My rest, in Whom I delight, Who is equal to Me in all things, Who is of one will with the Father, and while yet His Son, is One in all things with Him who has begotten Him. "Hear Him," He says. So that if He wills to be crucified, don't try to oppose Him. *Homily 56, The Transfiguration of Christ*

Monday - Ephrem the Syrian

[Moses and Elijah] gave thanks to Him that their own words had been fulfilled, and with them the words of all the prophets. They adored Him for the salvation He had wrought in the world for mankind, and because He had truly fulfilled the mystery which they had themselves foretold. The Prophets therefore were filled with joy, and the Apostles likewise, in their ascent of the mountain. The prophets rejoiced because they had seen His Humanity, which they had not known. And the Apostles rejoiced because they had seen the glory of the Divinity, which they had not known.

And when they heard the voice of the Father, giving testimony of the Son, they learned through this that which had been obscure to them until now: that the humanity had been assumed by Him. And together with His Father's Voice the glory of His own Body gave testimony to Him, shining resplendent because of that within Him which partakes of the Divinity, unchangeably and without confusion. And this was confirmed by three witnesses: by the Voice of the Father, and by the presence of Moses and Elijah, who stood by Him as servants. And they looked, the one upon the other, the Prophets upon the Apostles, the Apostles upon the Prophets. They looked upon each other, the Princes of the Old and the Princes of the New Testament. Moses the holy man looks upon Simon the sanctified. The servant of the Father looks upon the vicar of the Son...

The virgin of the old Testament looks upon the virgin of the New: Elijah looks upon John. He who had ascended into heaven in a fiery chariot looks upon him who had rested his head upon a Burning Breast. This mountain became a figure of the Church; and Jesus has united in Himself the two Testaments, which the Church receives, revealing to us that He is the Giver of both. The one received His divine secrets; the other has proclaimed the visible glory of His works. *On the Transfiguration of Our Lord*

Tuesday - Leo I of Rome

The apostle Peter, stirred by the revelation of these mysteries, rejecting the things of this world just as he scorned earthly matters, was seized by some sort of ecstasy in his desire for eternal things, and was filled with the joy of the whole vision, and wanted to dwell there with Jesus where His revealed glory brought delight. And so he says: "Lord, it is good for us to be here; if You wish, let us make here three tabernacles: one for You, one for Moses, and one for Elijah." But the Lord did not reply to this suggestion; implying that what Peter wanted was not only base but contrary to the divine purpose, for the world could only be saved by the death of Christ. The Lord's attitude in this is a challenge to the faith of believers, reminding us that although we should not doubt the promise of blessedness, we should understand that, amid the trials of this life, we must pray for perseverance before glory; for the joys of heaven cannot come before the times of trial. *Sermon 51*

Wednesday - Maximus of Turin

Rightly is the Lord compared to leaven, who since He appeared in the likeness of man, is become small in His lowliness, insignificant in His mortal weakness, yet within possesses such a power of wisdom that the whole world itself could scarcely contain all that He has taught, and who, since He began to diffuse Himself throughout the world by the power of His divinity, immediately drew into His own substance men of every race, that He might lay on all the yoke of His Holy Spirit, that is, that all Christians may become even as Christ is. For the Lord Jesus as Man, and He alone in this world, as a leaven hidden in the mass, makes it possible that all men be as He is. Whosoever therefore will adhere to the leaven of Christ, becomes a leaven himself, as profitable unto himself as he may be to all others; without fear for his own salvation, and a sure means of gaining others.

Homily 3

Thursday - Clement of Alexandria

For many reasons, then, the Scriptures hide the sense. First, so that we might become inquisitive, and be ever on the lookout to discover of the words of salvation. So it was not suitable for all to understand, so that they might not be harmed by taking the things declared for salvation by the Holy Spirit in another sense. For this reason the holy mysteries of the prophecies are veiled in parables - preserved for chosen men, selected to knowledge because of their faith.

The Stromata, Book 6, Chapter 15

Friday - Columban

Human life, fragile and marked for death, how many have you deceived, beguiled, and blinded? While in flight, you are nothing; while in sight, you are a shadow; while you rise up, you are but smoke. Every day you depart and every day you return; you depart in returning and you return in departing, different ending, same beginning, different pleasure, the same passing, sweet to the foolish and bitter to the wise. Those who love you do not know you, and those who condemn you really understand you. Thus you are not true but false; you present yourself as true but prove yourself false. What are you then, human life? You are the wayfaring of mortals and not their living; your beginning is in sin and in death your end. You would be true if the sin of the first human transgression had not cut you short so that you became unsteady and mortal and marked all who tread your way for death. And so you are the way that leads to life, but not life itself, for you are a true way, but not an open one; brief for some and long for others, broad for some and narrow for others, joyful for some and full of grief for others, but for each and every one, you hurry on and cannot be called back. A way is what you are, a way, but you are not evident to all. Though many see you, few understand that you are indeed a way. You are so cunning and alluring that it is given to few to know you as a way. Thus you are to be questioned and not believed or credited, you are to be traversed and not inhabited: wretched human life. For a road is to be walked on and not lived in, so that they who walk upon it may dwell finally in the land that is their home.

And so, mortal life, it is the foolish and the lost, spurned by those with sense and avoided by those to be saved, who dwell in you, who love you, and who believe in you... We should be careful therefore in case we are complacent on the way and fail to reach our true home. Indeed, there are many who are so at ease on this journey that they seem not so much to be wayfarers as to be already at home, and they travel unwillingly rather than freely toward a home that is for them already lost. These people have exhausted their home in the journey, and with a brief life have bought eternal death. Unfortunate creatures, they delight in their disastrous exchange. They have loved the transitory things of others and neglected their own eternal possessions... Let us be found faithful... so that we may be made inheritors in those things that are truly ours, by the gift of our Lord Jesus Christ, who lives and reigns from age to age. Amen.

Sermon 5

Saturday - Martin Luther

The holy Christian people are externally recognized by the holy possession of the sacred cross. They must endure every misfortune and persecution, all kinds of trials and evil from the devil, the world, and the flesh (as the Lord's Prayer indicates) by inward sadness, timidity, fear, outward poverty, contempt, illness, and weakness, in order to become like their head, Christ. And the only reason they must suffer is that they steadfastly adhere to Christ and God's word, enduring this for the sake of Christ, Matthew 5, "Blessed are you when men persecute you on my account." They must be pious, quiet, obedient, and prepared to serve the government and everybody with life and goods, doing no one any harm. No people on earth have to endure such bitter hate; they must be accounted worse than Jews, heathen, and Turks. In summary, they must be called heretics, knaves, and devils, the most pernicious people on earth, to the point where those who hang, drown, murder, torture, banish, and plague them to death are rendering God a service. No one has compassion on them; they are given myrrh and gall to drink when they thirst. And all of this is done not because they are adulterers, murderers, thieves, or rogues, but because they want to have none but Christ, and no other God. Wherever you see or hear this, you may know that the holy Christian church is there, as Christ says in Matthew 5, "Blessed are you when men revile you and utter all kinds of evil against you on my account. Rejoice and be glad, for your reward is great in heaven." This too is a holy possession whereby the Holy Spirit not only sanctifies his people, but also blesses them.

On the Councils and the Church

Collect

O God, who in the glorious transfiguration of Your only-begotten Son has confirmed the mysteries of the faith by the testimonies of the fathers, and who, in the voice that came from the bright cloud, did in a wonderful manner foreshow the adoption of sons, mercifully guarantee to make us coheirs with the King of His glory and bring us to the enjoyment of the same, through the same Jesus Christ, Your Son, our Lord, who lives and reigns with You and the Holy Spirit, one God, now and forever.

15th Century Roman Missal

AT LAUDS

Psalmody

Sunday: 67, C1, 5
Monday: 63, C2, 36
Tuesday: 43, C3, 57

Wednesday: 64, C4, 65
Thursday: 88, C6, 90

Friday: 76, C5, 92
Saturday: 143, C7, 148

Lesson

Sunday: Hebrews 5:1-11
Monday: Hebrews 6:11-20
Tuesday: Hebrews 7:20-28

Wednesday: Hebrews 9:16-28
Thursday: Hebrews 11:1-12

Friday: Hebrews 11:30-12:2
Saturday: Hebrews 13:1-6

Collect

Grant, we beseech You, Almighty God, that the brightness of Your glory may shine forth upon us, and that the light of Your light, by the illumination of the Holy Spirit may establish the hearts of all who have been born anew by Your grace, through Jesus Christ, Your Son, our Lord, who lives and reigns with You and the Holy Spirit, one God, now and forever.

Gregorian Sacramentary

AT TERCE, SEXT AND NONE

Chapter - II Peter 2:16b-21

AT VESPERS

Psalmody

Sunday: 110, 111, 112, 113   Wednesday: 123, 124, 125   Friday: 129, 130, 131, 132
Monday: 114, 115, 116, 117   Thursday: 126, 127, 128   Saturday: 133, 135, 136a
Tuesday: 120, 121, 122

Lesson

Sunday: Hebrews 5:12-6:10   Wednesday: Hebrews 10:1-18   Friday: Hebrews 12:12-24
Monday: Hebrews 7:1-19   Thursday: Hebrews 11:13-29   Saturday: Hebrews 13:7-17
Tuesday: Hebrews 8:1-7

Collect

O merciful and everlasting God, heavenly Father: We thank You that You have revealed to us the glory of Your Son, and let the light of Your Gospel shine upon us: we pray You, guide us by this light that we may walk diligently as Christians in all good works, ever be strengthened by Your grace, and conduct our lives in all godliness; through the same, Your beloved Son, Jesus Christ our Lord, who lives and reigns with You and the Holy Spirit, one God, now and forever.

Veit Dietrich

THE WEEK OF SEPTUAGESIMA

From Septuagesima through Holy Saturday, there are no alleluias said.

AT MATINS

Invitatory - *Prope est Dominus*   *Tone 6*

The Lord is near to all who call up-on Him, O come, let us wor-ship Him!

Hymn - *Es ist das heil uns kommen her*

1. Sal - va- tion un - to us has come By God's free grace and fa - vor

Good works can-not a - vert our doom; They help and save us nev - er

Faith looks to Je - sus Christ a - lone, Who did for all the

world a - tone; He is our one Re - deem - er.

2. What God did in His law demand
    No man to Him could render.
    Before this Judge all guilty stand;
    His law speaks curse in thunder.
    The law demands a perfect heart;
    We were defiled in ev'ry part,
    And lost was our condition.

3. False dreams deluded minds did fill,
    That God His law had given,
    As if to Him we could at will
    Earn grace and enter heaven.
    The law is but a mirror bright
    To bring the inbred sin to light
    That lurks within our nature.

4. From sin our flesh could not abstain,
    Sin held its sway unceasing;
    The task was useless and in vain,
    Our guilt was e'er increasing.
    None can remove sin's poisoned dart
    Or purify our guilty heart,
    So deep is our corruption.

5. Yet as the Law must be fulfilled
    Or we must die despairing,
    Christ came and hath God's anger stilled,
    Our human nature sharing.
    He hath for us the Law obeyed
    And thus the Father's vengeance stayed
    Which over us impended.

6. Since Christ hath full atonement made
   And brought to us salvation,
   Each Christian therefore may be glad
   And build on this foundation.
   Thy grace alone, dear Lord, I plead,
   Thy death is now my life indeed,
   For Thou hast paid my ranson.

7. Let me not doubt but trust in Thee,
   Thy Word cannot be broken;
   Thy call rings out, "Come unto Me!"
   No falsehood hast Thou spoken.
   Baptized into Thy precious name
   My faith cannot be put to shame,
   And I shall never perish.

8. The just is he - and he alone -
   Who by this faith is living,
   The faith that by good works is shown,
   To God the glory giving;
   Faith gives thee peace with God above,
   But thou thy neighbor, too, must love,
   If thou art new created.

9. The Law reveals the guilt of sin
   And makes men conscience-striken;
   The Gospel then doth enter in
   The sinful soul to quicken.
   Come to the cross, trust Christ and live;
   The Law no peace can ever give,
   No comfort and no blessing.

10. Faith clings to Jesus' cross alone
    And rests in Him unceasing;
    And by its fruits true faith is known,
    With love and hope increasing.
    Yet faith alone doth justify,
    Works serve thy neighbor and supply
    The proof that faith is living.

11. Hope waits for the accepted hour
    Till God give joy for mourning;
    When He displays His healing pow'r
    Thy sighs to songs are turning.
    Thy needs are known unto thy Lord,
    And He is faithful to His Word,
    This is our hope's foundation.

12. Though it may seem He hears thee not,
    Count not thyself forsaken;
    Thy wants are ne'er by Him forgot,
    Let this thy hope awaken;
    His Word is sure, here is thy stay,
    Though doubts may plague thee on thy way,
    Let not thy faith be shaken.

13. All blessing, honor, thanks and praise
    To Father, Son, and Spirit,
    The God who saved us by His grace -
    All glory to His merit!
    O Triune God in heaven above,
    Who hast revealed Thy saving love,
    Thy blessèd name be hallowed.

14. Thy kingdom come, Thy will be done
    In earth, as 'tis in heaven.
    Keep us in life, by grace lead on,
    Forgiving and forgiven.
    Save Thou us in temptation's hour,
    And from all ills; This the pow'r,
    And all the glory, Amen!

Paul Speratus, 1523

Psalmody

Sunday: 42, 44, 45   Wednesday: 53, 55, 56   Friday: 61, 62, 66
Monday: 46, 47, 48   Thursday: 58, 59, 60   Saturday: 68a, 68b, 69a
Tuesday: 49, 50, 52

Lesson

Sunday, Monday and Tuesday: Matthew 20:1-16
Wednesday and Thursday: Mark 9:30-37
Thursday: Luke 9:43-48

Friday and Saturday: Luke 9:51-56
Saturday: John 3:16-21

Homily

Sunday - Martin Luther

Now in this way Christ strikes a blow first against the presumption (as He also does in today's Epistle) of those who would storm their way into heaven by their good works; as the Jews did and wished to be next to God; as hitherto our own clergy have also done. These all labor for definite wages, that is, they take the law of God in no other sense than that they should fulfil it by certain defined works for a specified reward, and they never understand it correctly, and know not that before God all is pure grace. This signifies that they hire themselves out for wages, and agree with the householder for a penny a day; consequently their lives are bitter and they lead a career that is indeed hard.

Now when the Gospel comes and makes all alike, as Paul teaches in Romans 3:23, so that they who have done great works are no more than public sinners, and must also become sinners and tolerate the saying, "All have sinned," and that no one is justified before God by his works; then they look around and despise those who have done nothing at all, while their great worry and labor avail no more than such idleness and reckless living. Then they murmur against the householder, they imagine it is not right; they blaspheme the Gospel, and become hardened in their ways; then they lose the favor and grace of God, and are obliged to take their temporal reward and trot from Him with their penny and be condemned; for they served not for the sake of mercy but for the sake of reward, and they will receive that and nothing more, the others however must confess that they have merited neither the penny nor the grace, but more is given to them than they had ever thought was promised to them. These remained in grace and besides were saved, and besides this, here in time they had enough; for all depended upon the good pleasure of the householder. *Church Postil for Septuagesima*

Monday - John Chrysostom

The parable is directed to those who have embraced the way of virtue in their early youth, and to those who embraced it at a later age. To the former so that they might neither become proud nor scornful of those coming in later life, to the latter that they may learn that it is possible in a brief while to earn the whole wage. Because, prior to this, He had been speaking of great fervor, and of rejecting riches, and of contempt of the world. For this there was need for great courage of soul and for youthful fire. To kindle a flame of eager love, and form in them the will to endure, He showed that it is possible, even for these late comers, to receive the whole day's wage. But He does not say this, lest they be tempted to pride, but He shows that the whole wage comes from His own kindness and bounty, and that by His help they will not be lost, but will attain unspeakable joys. And this is mainly what He means to lay down for our instruction in this parable. *Homily 64 in Matthew*

Tuesday - Gregory I of Rome

Let everyone reflect on what he is doing, and consider whether he is laboring in the Lord's vineyard. No one who seeks his own will in this life has come to the Lord's vineyard. The Lord's laborers are those who think not of their own concerns but of the Lord's, who live lives of devotion with charitable zeal, who are intent on gaining souls, who hasten to bring others with them to life. One who lives for himself, nourished by the pleasures of his body, is rightly reproved as idle, since he is not striving for the fruit of good works. One who has neglected to live for God up to the last period of his life has stood idle, as it were, up to the eleventh hour. So it is aptly said to those who have stood lazily by up to the eleventh hour, "Why do you stand here all day idle?" meaning, "Even though you have not been willing to live for God in your childhood and young adulthood, at least come to your right mind in the final time of your life. Come to the ways of life, even though you will not labor much now, and are late."

Homily 11

Wednesday - Johann Gerhard

Consider, O man, the example of Christ. All the glory of heaven was at His command, nay more, He Himself alone is true Glory, and yet He casts away from Himself all worldly glory as worthless. And then He says: "Learn of Me, for I am meek and lowly in heart." He who truly loves Christ will imitate Him; and if Christ be precious to him, so will His humility also. Let the proud and haughty servant blush in confusion when he considers that the Lord of glory is so humble... True grace does not make one proud, but humble. You are not yet a partaker of the true grace of God, if you do not walk in humility of heart. The streams of divine grace flow downwards, not upwards. As nature's streams seek the lowlands, so those of divine grace flow down into lowly hearts... He who is lowly in his own eyes, is great in God's sight; he who is displeasing to himself, is pleasing to God.

Sacred Meditations 34

Thursday - Clement of Rome

Let us be humble and put away all pretension and arrogance and foolishness and anger, and let us do what is written. For the Holy Ghost says: "Let not the wise man glory in his wisdom, let not the mighty man glory in his might, nor let the rich man glory in his riches; but let him who glories glory in... the Lord," that he may seek Him out, and do judgment and righteousness. Above all, remember the words of the Lord Jesus which He uttered while teaching forbearance and patience. Have mercy, that you may receive mercy; forgive that it may be forgiven to you. As you judge, so shall you be judged. As you show kindness, so shall kindness be shown to you. With whatever measure you mete, it shall be measured back to you. With this commandment and these precepts let us strengthen one another, that we may walk in obedience to these holy words in all humility. For the holy Word says: "On whom shall I look, but on him who is meek and peaceable, and who trembles at My Word?"

Epistle to the Corinthians

Friday - Gregory of Nanzianus

We think it an important matter to get justice from those who have wronged us... but it is far more God-like to bear injustice. For the former course curbs wickedness, but the latter makes men good, which is much better and more perfect than merely being not wicked. Let us consider that the great pursuit of mercifulness is set before us, and let us forgive the wrongs done to us that we also may obtain forgiveness, and let us by kindness lay up a store of kindness...

What is swifter than Mercy? The disciples ask for flames of Sodom upon those who drive Jesus away, but He deprecates revenge. Peter cuts off the ear of Malchus... but Jesus restores it. And what of him who asks whether he must seven times forgive a brother if he has trespassed, is he not condemned for his niggardliness, for to the seven is added seventy times seven? What of the debtor in the gospel who will not forgive as he has been forgiven? Isn't it exacted more bitterly of him for this? And what says the pattern of prayer? Does it not desire that forgiveness be gained by forgiveness?

Having so many examples let us imitate the mercy of God, and don't desire to learn for yourself how great an evil the requital of sin is. You see the sequence of goodness: first it makes laws, then it commands, threatens, reproaches, holds out warnings, restrains, threatens again, and only when forced to do so strikes the blow, but this little by little, opening the way to amendment. Let us then not strike suddenly (for it is not safe to do so), but being self restrained in our fear let us conquer by mercy, and make them our debtors by our kindness, tormenting them by their conscience rather than by anger.

Epistle 77

Saturday - Tertullian of Carthage

The Creator, at the request of Elijah, inflicts the blow of fire from heaven in the case of that false prophet. I recognize in this the severity of the Judge. And I see, on the contrary, the severe rebuke of Christ on His disciples, when they were seeking to inflict a similar visitation on that obscure village of the Samaritans. The heretic [that is, Marcion, who taught the existence of two Gods: the wrathful Creator-God of the Old Testament and the merciful Savior-God of the New Testament], too, may discover that this gentleness of Christ was promised by the very same and most severe Judge. "He will not raise His voice, nor cause His voice to be heard in the street. A bruised reed He will not break, and smoking flax He will not quench." Being of such a character, He was of course much less disposed to burn men. For even at that time the Lord said to Elijah: "He was not in the fire, but in the still small voice."

Against Marcion

Collect

O Lord, we pray You favorably to hear the prayers of Your people that we, who are justly punished for our offenses, may be mercifully delivered by Your goodness, for the glory of Your name, through Jesus Christ, Your Son, our Lord, who lives and reigns with You and the Holy Spirit, one God, now and forever.

Gelasian Sacramentary

AT LAUDS

Psalmody

Sunday: 3, C8, 51
Monday: 118a, C9, 118b
Tuesday: 1, C10, 2

Wednesday: 8, C11, 20
Thursday: 18a, C12, 18b

Friday: 146, C13, 5
Saturday: 149, C14, 150

Lesson

Sunday: Genesis 1:1-25
Monday: Genesis 2:4-17
Tuesday: Genesis 3:1-24

Wednesday: Genesis 6:1-22
Thursday: Genesis 8:6-14

Friday: Genesis 9:8-17
Saturday: Genesis 12:1-7

Collect

O Lord God, heavenly Father, from whom without ceasing we receive exceeding abundantly all good gifts, and who daily of Your pure grace guards us against all evil: grant us, we beseech You, Your Holy Spirit, that acknowledging with our whole heart all Your goodness, we may now and evermore thank and praise Your loving kindness and tender mercy; through Jesus Christ, Your Son, our Lord, who lives and reigns with You and the Holy Spirit, one God, now and forever.

Brandenburg-Nuremberg Kirchenordnung, 1533

AT TERCE, SEXT AND NONE

Chapter

Sunday, Monday and Tuesday: I Corinthians 9:24-10:4
Wednesday and Thursday: Hebrews 4:11-16
Friday and Saturday: I Thessalonians 2:17-19a

AT VESPERS

Psalmody

Sunday: 136b, 137, 138
Monday: 140, 141, 142
Tuesday: 144, 145, 7

Wednesday: 9, 10, 11
Thursday: 12, 13, 14, 16

Friday: 17, 147a, 147b
Saturday: 19, 54, 77

Lesson

Sunday: Genesis 1:25-2:3
Monday: Genesis 2:18-25
Tuesday: Genesis 4:1-16

Wednesday: Genesis 7:1-12
Thursday: Genesis 8:15-22

Friday: Genesis 11:1-9
Saturday: Genesis 13:14-18

Collect

Lord God, heavenly Father, who through Your holy Word has called us into Your vineyard: send, we beseech You, Your Holy Spirit into our hearts, that we may labor faithfully in Your vineyard, shun sin and all offense, obediently keep Your Word and do Your will, and put our whole and only trust in Your grace, which You have bestowed upon us so plenteously through Your Son Jesus Christ, that we may obtain eternal salvation through Him, who lives and reigns with You and the Holy Spirit, one God, now and forever.
Veit Dietrich

THE WEEK OF SEXAGESIMA

AT MATINS

Invitatory   *As during the week of Septuagesima, p.309*

Hymn - *Es woll' uns Gott genädig sein*

1.   May God be-stow on   us   His grace, With bless-ings rich pro-

vide   us;   And may the bright-ness   of   His face

To   life e - ter - nal   guide   us That we His   sav-ing health may know,

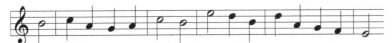

His grac-ious will and plea-sure, And al - so   to the hea-then show

Christ's rich-es with-out mea-sure   And un- to God con - vert them.

2. Thine over all shall be the praise
And thanks of every nation,
And all the world with joy shall raise
The voice of exaltation;
For Thou shalt judge the earth, O Lord,
Nor suffer sin to flourish;
Thy people's pasture is Thy Word
Their souls to feed and nourish,
In righteous paths to keep them.

3. Oh, let the people praise Thy worth,
In all good works increasing;
The land shall plenteous fruit bring forth,
Thy Word is rich in blessing.
May God the Father, God the Son,
And God the Spirit bless us!
Let all the world praise Him alone,
Let solemn awe possess us.
Now let our hearts say, Amen.

Martin Luther, 1524

Psalmody

Sunday: 69b, 70, 71
Monday: 72, 73, 74
Tuesday: 78a, 78b, 78c

Wednesday: 75, 79, 80
Thursday: 81, 82, 83

Friday: 84, 86, 87, 93
Saturday: 85, 89a, 89b

Lesson

Sunday, Monday and Tuesday: Luke 8:4-15
Monday: Matthew 13:1-9, 18-23
Tuesday: Mark 4:1-20

Wednesday and Thursday: Matthew 12:30-37
Thursday: Mark 3:28-30

Friday and Saturday: Luke 17:20-25
Saturday: Luke 17:26-37

Homily

Sunday - Athanasius of Alexandria

God, who is good, multiplied His loving-kindness toward us, not only when He granted the common salvation of us all through His Word, but now also, when enemies have persecuted us, and have sought to seize upon us. As the blessed Paul says somewhere when describing the incomprehensible riches of Christ: "But God, who is rich in mercy because of His great love with which He loved us, even when we were dead in trespasses, made us alive together with Christ." For the might of man and of all creatures is weak and poor; but the Might which is above man is uncreated, rich, incomprehensible, without beginning, and eternal. He does not have only one method of healing, but being rich, He works in many ways for our salvation by means of His Word. He is not restricted or hindered in His dealings toward us; but since He is abundantly rich, He varies Himself according to the individual capacity of each soul. For He is the Word and the Power and the Wisdom of God... He gives milk to those who have not yet attained to the perfect way... He is food such as they can take in to those who have advanced beyond childhood, but are still imperfect in their weakness... But as soon as a man begins to walk in the perfect way, he is no longer fed with the things mentioned before but has the Word for bread and Flesh for food...

Moreover, when the Word is sown it doesn't yield fruit uniformly in this human life, but richly and in variety; for it brings forth, some a hundred, and some sixty, and some thirty, as the Savior teaches - that blessed Sower of grace, and Bestower of the Spirit. And this is not doubtful or unprovable; but we can see the field which is sown by Him; for in the Church the Word is diverse and the produce rich... Nor is mercy confined to the perfect, but it is sent down also among those who occupy the middle and the third ranks, so that He might rescue all men to salvation.

Letter 10

Monday - Gregory of Nyssa

The good ground brings forth fruit in patience; because the good we do is worthless unless at the same time we patiently bear the evil-doing of our neighbor. And the higher anyone ascends in virtue, the harder this world will bear down on him; for the more the love of the heart turns from this present life, the more the opposition of this same world mounts up. So it is that we see so many strive after and do what is good; yet they sweat under the burden of afflictions. For though they have turned away from earthly things, they are still harassed with increasing tribulations. But, according to the word of the Lord, they will bring forth fruit in patience, and after their time of tribulation, they shall be received into rest above; because they have borne their cross in patience.

For the grapes must be treaded so that the preciousness of wine may flow. So must the virtue of the olive, pressed out by crushing, leave the husk and become the fatness of oil. So too is the grain, beaten out on the threshing floor, separated from the chaff, and being cleaned is brought into the barn. Whoever, then, wants to completely overcome his defects, must bear with pleasure the pain of being made clean; and the more he is purified now in the fire of tribulation, the more worthy he will be to appear at the judgement seat of God.

Homily on the Gospel

Tuesday - Johannes Tauler

There are some people who fall over themselves with enthusiasm as soon as they feel a pious desire to turn over a new leaf and live more virtuously. They become infatuated with their own devotion and eager to put it into practice. They never stop to wonder if they are taking on more than they can manage, or if they have been given the grace to keep it up. It is a mistake to embark on any new venture without first considering how we can carry it through. The first thing to do is always to have recourse to God. We must confide in Him and put our fervor and devotion in His hands. But no; these folk want to rush off by themselves and start all kinds of new practices; and it is this rashness which brings them to grief, because they are building on their own strength...

There is still a whole world inside you which will never be overcome without constant effort and care and the help of God. You have inside you many strong and cruel enemies to overcome; and to vanquish them is the labor of a lifetime.

The first of these is worldliness, which attacks you with spiritual pride. You want to be seen and noticed and respected; you want to look well in your habit and your demeanor; you want to impress people with your elegant conversation and manners, your friends, your family, your wealth, your rank and all the rest of it.

The second enemy is your own flesh, which attacks you with impurity of soul as well as body; for a man is guilty of this kind of sin whenever he seeks in any way at all to find his delight in outward things. There is need for constant vigilance against sinfulness of this kind. It may attack a man in various ways, both through the susceptibility of his own senses and through the seductiveness of things attractive to sense; or indeed through infatuated love for creatures of any kind, which a man may cherish in his heart and indulge in night and day. For just as your bodily nature can lead your body into impurity, so you can be led to purity by the inward purity of your spirit; and just as your spirit is nobler than your flesh, so also it is more liable to corruption.

Your third enemy is the devil himself. He attacks you with temptations to malevolence, hard thoughts, suspiciousness, rash judgments, hatred and spite. "Do you know what he did? Shall I tell you what he said to me?" you say, and tell the tale with a sour face, spiteful gestures and harsh words; you are determined to pay back the offender in any way you can. You may be quite sure that all this is the devil's work. If you want God to love you, you must renounce this sort of thing, for it is none other than [wickedness]. Be on a constant guard against these enemies in yourself, for truly they can kill [faith in Christ within] you. *Spiritual Conferences*

Wednesday - Johann Gerhard

The Sin against the Holy Ghost is an intentional denial of the evangelical truth, which has been acknowledged and approved by conscience, connected with a bold attack upon it, and voluntary blasphemy of it. For we must observe that this king of sin was proved against the Pharisees by Christ; for, although they were constrained by the force of the truth uttered by Him, and were convicted in their consciences by its illumination, yet they raged against Him by their wicked impiety, to such a degree that they blushed not to ascribe His doctrines and miracles to Satan. The epistle to the Hebrews thus describes those who sin against the Holy Ghost, that they, having been previously illuminated, have also tasted the heavenly gift and been made partakers of the Holy Ghost, have tasted also the good Word of God, and the powers of the world to come, yet afterwards fall away, and thus crucify to themselves afresh the Son of God, and put Him to an open shame; also that, by voluntary apostasy, they trample under foot the Son of God, and esteem His blood, by which they were sanctified, an unholy thing, and thus pay spite to the spirit of grace. *Loci Theologici*

Thursday - Cyprian of Carthage

The spouse of Christ cannot be adulterous; she is uncorrupted and pure. She knows one home; she guards with chaste modesty the sanctity of one couch. She keeps us for God. She appoints the sons whom she has born for the kingdom. Whoever is separated from the Church and is joined to an adulteress, is separated from the promises of the Church; nor can he who forsakes the Church of Christ attain to the rewards of Christ. He is a stranger; he is profane; he is an enemy. He can no longer have God for his Father, who has not the Church for his mother. If any one could escape who was outside the ark of Noah, then he also may escape who shall be outside of the Church. The Lord warns, saying, "He who is not with me is against me, and he who gathers not with me scatters." He who breaks the peace and the concord of Christ, does so in opposition to Christ; he who gathers elsewhere than the Church, scatters the Church of Christ.

On the Unity of the Church

Friday - Philip Melanchthon

The Gospel clearly teaches that the kingdom of Christ is spiritual. Christ sits at the right hand of the Father and intercedes for us, and gives the Holy Spirit and the remission of sins to the church, that is, to those who believe in Him and call upon God with confidence in Him that He will sanctify them, so that He may raise them up on the last day to eternal glory. In order that we may obtain these benefits, the ministry of the Gospel has been established, and through this men are called to the knowledge of Christ. And the Holy Spirit is efficacious through the Gospel. But meanwhile, before the last day, the church in this world suffers persecution, and there will be many evil men mixed in with the good in the church. This is the true and appropriate teaching of the church in regard to the kingdom of Christ and the Gospel.

The Jewish error of the Anabaptists must be rejected and condemned. They have the notion that the church before the last day will be some kind of civil and worldly state in which the godly will rule, and by force of arms destroy all the ungodly and occupy all the empires of the world... For this Jewish error for several reasons has this problem attached to it: it obscures and totally destroys spiritual consolations and does away with spiritual exercises, because human minds look only for those new worlds to rule, and they forget spiritual things and are burdened with despair when that hoped-for life of leisure about which they dream does not materialize.

Loci Communes

Saturday - Bonaventure

After Pilate had passed judgment to satisfy the desires of the wicked, those sacrilegious soldiers were not satisfied to crucify the Savior until they had heaped His soul full of mockery. The entire cohort assembled in the praetorium, stripped Him of His clothes, dressed Him in a scarlet tunic and placed a purple cloak around Him, a crown of thorns on His head and a reed in His right hand. They genuflected in mockery, gave Him blows, spat upon Him and struck that sacred head with the reed.

Attend now, O pride of human heart that flees from reproach and aspires after honors! Who is it who comes in the likeness of the King and yet is filled with the confusion of a despicable slave? He is your King and your God who is accounted as a leper and the last of men in order to snatch you from eternal confusion and to heal you from the disease of pride. Woe, therefore, and woe again to those who, after seeing this outstanding reflection of humility, are lifted on high in pride placing on display again the Son of God, who is all the more worthy of all honor from men because of how much humiliation He has endured for their sake.

The Tree of Life

Collect

O God, who sees that we put not our trust in anything that we do, mercifully grant that by Your power we may be defended against all adversity; through Jesus Christ, Your Son, our Lord, who lives and reigns with You and the Holy Spirit, one God, now and forever.

Gelasian Sacramentary

AT LAUDS

Psalmody

Sunday: 67, C1, 5
Monday: 63, C2, 36
Tuesday: 43, C3, 57

Wednesday: 64, C4, 65
Thursday: 88, C6, 90

Friday: 76, C5, 92
Saturday: 143, C7, 148

Lesson

Sunday: Genesis 14:13-20
Monday: Genesis 17:1-8
Tuesday: Genesis 18:9-15

Wednesday: Genesis 21:1-7
Thursday: Genesis 24:1-21

Friday: Genesis 25:19-26
Saturday: Genesis 27:1-29

Collect

Blessèd Lord, who has caused all Holy Scriptures to be written for our learning: grant that we may so hear them, read, mark, learn, and inwardly digest them, that by patience and comfort of Your Holy Word, we may embrace, and ever hold fast the blessèd hope of everlasting life, which You have given us in our Savior, Jesus Christ, who lives and reigns with You and the Holy Spirit, one God, now and forever.

Book of Common Prayer, 1549

AT TERCE, SEXT AND NONE

Chapter

Sunday, Monday and Tuesday: II Corinthians 11:19-12:9
Wednesday and Thursday: Hebrews 12:3-9
Friday and Saturday: I Thessalonians 2:13-19b

AT VESPERS

Psalmody

Sunday: 110, 111, 112, 113
Monday: 114, 115, 116, 117
Tuesday: 120, 121, 122

Wednesday: 123, 124, 125
Thursday: 126, 127, 128

Friday: 129, 130, 131, 132
Saturday: 133, 135, 136a

Lesson

Sunday: Genesis 15:1-6
Monday: Genesis 17:9-14
Tuesday: Genesis 19:15-28

Wednesday: Genesis 22:1-14
Thursday: Genesis 24:22-52

Friday: Genesis 25:27-26:5
Saturday: Genesis 28:10-22

Collect

Lord God, heavenly Father, we thank You, that through Your Son Jesus Christ You have sown Your Holy Word among us: We pray that You will prepare our hearts by Your Holy Spirit, that we may diligently and reverently hear Your Word, keep it in good hearts, and bring forth fruit with patience; and that we may not incline to sin, but subdue it by Your power, and in all persecutions comfort ourselves with Your grace and continual help, through Your beloved Son, Jesus Christ our Lord, who lives and reigns with You and the Holy Spirit, one God, now and forever. *Veit Dietrich*

THE WEEK OF QUINQUAGESIMA

AT MATINS

Invitatory *As during the week of Septuagesima, p.309*

Hymn - *Nun freut euch, liebe Christen g'mein*

1. Dear Chris-tians, one and all re-joice, With ex - ul - ta-tion spring - ing,

And, with u - nit - ed heart and voice And ho- ly rap- ture sing - ing,

Pro - claim the won- ders God hath done, How His right arm the

vic - t'ry won; Right dear - ly it hath cost Him.

2. Fast bound in Satan's chains I lay,
Death brooded darkly o'er me,
Sin was my torment night and day,
In sin my mother bore me;
Yea, deep and deeper still I fell,
Life had become a living hell,
So firmly sin possessed me.

3. My own good works availed me naught,
No merit they attaining;
Free will against God's judgment fought,
Dead to all good remaining
My fears increased till sheer despair
Left naught but death to be my share;
The pangs of hell I suffered.

4. But God beheld my wretched state
Before the world's foundation,
And, mindful of His mercies great,
He planned my soul's salvation.
A father's heart He turned to me,
Sought my redemption fervently:
He gave His dearest Treasure.

5. He spoke to His beloved Son:
'Tis time to have compassion.
Then go, bright Jewel of My crown,
And bring to men salvation;
From sin and sorrow set him free,
Slay bitter death for him that he
May live with Thee forever.

6. The Son obeyed His Father's will,
Was born of virgin mother,
And God's good pleasure to fulfill,
He came to be my Brother.
No garb of pomp or power He wore,
A servant's form, like mine, He bore.
To lead the devil captive.

7. To me He spake: Hold fast to Me,
I am thy Rock and Castle;
Thy Ransom I Myself will be,
For thee I strive and wrestle;
For I am with thee, I am thine,
And evermore thou shalt be Mine:
The Foe shall not divide us.

8. The Foe shall shed My precious blood,
   Me of My life bereaving.
   All this I suffer for thy good;
   Be steadfast and believing.
   Life shall from death the victory win,
   My innocence shall bear thy sin;
   So art thou blest forever.

9. Now to My Father I depart,
   The Holy Spirit sending
   And, heavenly wisdom to impart,
   My help to thee extending.
   He shall in trouble comfort thee,
   Teach thee to know and follow Me,
   And in all truth shall guide thee.

10. What I have done and taught, teach thou,
    My ways forsake thou never;
    So shall My kingdom flourish now
    And God be praised forever.
    Take heed lest men with base alloy
    The heavenly treasure should destroy;
    This counsel I bequeath thee.

Martin Luther, 1523

Psalmody

Sunday: 89c, 94, 96   Wednesday: 104a, 104b, 104c   Friday: 106a, 106b, 107a
Monday: 97, 98, 99, 100 Thursday: 105a, 105b, 105c   Saturday: 107b, 108, 109
Tuesday: 101, 102, 103

Lesson

Sunday, Monday and Tuesday: Luke 18:31-43
  Monday: Mark 10:32-34
  Tuesday: Mark 10:46-52

Ash Wednesday: Matthew 6:16-21
Thursday: Matthew 8:5-13
Friday: Matthew 5:43-6:6
Saturday: Mark 6:45-56

Homily

Sunday - Cyril of Alexandria

So that they might learn that He both foreknew His coming passion, and that He willingly went forth to meet it, when He could easily have avoided it, Our Blessed Lord shows what will come to pass. And He also needed to tell them that all these things had been foretold by the holy prophets, for God had willed that no one be scandalized when these things would come to pass. For beyond any doubt He was free to avoid the passion He had foreknown was to come. No one compelled Him. He suffered of His own free will, in the full knowledge that His passion would be salutary for the whole world. He suffered death, in His flesh. Overcoming corruption, He rose again; and by His resurrection from the dead, He poured His own life into the bodies of men; for in Him the whole nature of man is turned back toward immortality. *On the Gospel*

Monday - Martin Luther

These words were spoken by Christ on His last journey from Galilee to Jerusalem, where He was crucified. The Evangelist states three times that the disciples did not comprehend this prediction. They regarded His words as having some unusual and hidden meaning. They understood not a single word of these sayings. They were thinking: this man performs so many miracles, He raises the dead, He gives the blind their sight, and so on, so we must conclude that He will become a person of high position, for it is clear that God is with Him. Besides this, the Scriptures say that He shall have a glorious kingdom and exercise dominion over kings and princes on earth, while we, His servants, will also become princes and great lords. For who would want to harm such a Person, a man who overcomes death and cures all kinds of illnesses with a single word? If He wants, He can subjugate the heathen and put all His enemies under His feet. So they thought that God loves Him so much that He would not let any harm befall Him. His words about His sufferings and death surely must have another meaning. Such was the simplemindedness of the apostles.

God's works are indeed incomprehensible, if they are considered before they are accomplished. But as soon as they have been done they make perfect sense... So we must have faith in the Word of God. When God speaks He deals with things far beyond the power of human comprehension. So we should believe what He says. In due time we will experience that it is true and understand what it means.

I'll give you an example. The Word of God speaks of the resurrection of the dead, something our reason cannot understand. Those who are wise according to the world's way of thinking and interpret the Word of God according to their own reason think we are fools and laugh at us because we believe that there is another life after this life is ended. Again, reason will never comprehend how it is that God became man and was born of a virgin. The fact must be believed in faith until we enter into that other life, where we will see it all and say "now I understand and see that what I have believed is really true." Again, reason makes light of the fact that through Baptism with water the mercy and grace of God is conferred upon us without our merits, and that we have the forgiveness of our sins in holy absolution. It cannot understand how this is possible, and regards those who believe it as fools and simpletons...

Reason obstinately refuses to believe that through Baptism and faith in Christ we obtain salvation. It thinks the Word a silly thing and the one who preaches it a poor, miserable sinner. It thinks it ridiculous for a person to entrust his body and soul to faith. No matter how often and clearly the Word of God is preached to men, reason cannot and will not accept it. Reason has no faith. The world will therefore always regard the holy Gospel as a heresy and a demonic doctrine, which lures people away from the truth and prevents them from doing good works. This is the judgment of reason.

So let us learn to have a simple faith and say from our heart: What God says is true, whether my senses corroborate it or not. He is almighty. He can make His Word true. And although I do not fully understand it here on earth, I will grasp it all in the life to come.   *House Postil for Quinquagesima*

Tuesday - Gregory I of Rome

He who doesn't know the brightness of the eternal light is truly blind; but if he does believe in the Redeemer, he is sitting by the side of the road; and if he believes in Him but neglects to pray that he may receive the light eternal, and no longer prays, then is he a blind man sitting by the side of the road who does not beg. If, however, he has believed and has seen the blindness of his own heart and prays that he may receive the light of truth, then he is a blind man sitting by the side of the road begging.

Whoever, therefore, acknowledges the darkness of his own blindness; whoever sees within himself the need of the eternal light, let him cry out from the depth of his heart, let him cry out and say with the voice of his soul, "Jesus, Son of David, have mercy on me!"

But what is this added thing we hear concerning the blind man? "Then those who went before warned him that he should be quiet." Whom do they signify... if not the crowd of carnal desires, and the tumult of vices? Before Christ enters our hearts, these scatter our thoughts with their temptations, and confuse the pleas of the soul in prayer. For when we want to turn again to the Lord after we have committed many sins against Him, and while we struggle in prayer against these vices to which we have yielded, the images of sins we have committed often rise against us. They war against the fervor of our soul. They darken the spirit. They strive to silence the voice of our supplication. Those who went before rebuked him that he hold his peace, and so likewise the sins to which we have consented mock our pious aspirations by their evil memory… and bring confusion into our very prayer…

But let us hear what answer the blind man, who was about to be cured, made to this. The Gospel says: "but he cried out all the more, 'Son of David, have mercy on me!'" See how he whom the crowd rebukes, cries out more and more; and so the more we are tormented by the crowd of carnal thoughts within us, so much the more let us persevere in prayer.   *Homily on the Gospel*

Wednesday - Bernard of Clairvaux

Today, beloved, we enter the holy season of Lent, our Christian period of military service. In keeping it, we do not stand alone; we are united with all who hold the faith. Should not all Christians share the fast of Christ? Where the Head leads, should not the members follow? If from the Head we have received good things, shall we not also receive difficult things? Would we refuse the sorrowful, yet share the pleasant? If so, we prove ourselves unworthy to be joined to Him; for everything He suffers is for us. It is no great thing, surely, for a man to fast with Christ, when he looks to sit with Him at the Father's table; nor is it much for the member to suffer with the Head, seeing he stands to share His glory too.

Happy the member who cleaves to the Head through all, and follows Him wherever He goes; for otherwise, if he be parted or cut off from Him, he will lose the spirit of life…

Well, wholly well, is it for me to cleave to You, O glorious and ever-blessed Head, on Whom the angels yearn to look. Wherever You go, there will I follow You; if You pass through the fire, I will not be turned from You. I will fear no evil, for You are with me. You carry my griefs, and grieve for my sake; and through the narrow portal of the Passion You enter first, to make a wider passage for Your limbs that follow You.   *In Capite Jejunii*

Thursday - John Chrysostom

Don't merely ask what was said by the centurion, but note also his rank, and then you will see the man's excellency. Because I tell you the truth: great is the pride of those who are in positions of command, and not even in afflictions do they take lower ground. But this man does not even seek that He come bodily, neither did he bring the sick man to the Physician; a thing which did not imply lowly thoughts concerning Him, but rather suggested His divine dignity. And he said, "But only speak a word." And at the beginning he didn't even say "speak a word," but only described the affliction; for neither did he, in great humility, expect that Christ would immediately consent and ask about his house… Even when he said, "my servant lies sick," he did not add "speak," for fear that he might be unworthy to obtain the gift; but he merely made known the affliction. And not even when he saw the eagerness of Christ's response did he spring forward, but still continues to keep his own proper place to the end.

And if anyone should say, "Why didn't Christ honor him in return?" we say that He did indeed honor him in return and exceedingly so… by introducing him into His kingdom, and preferring him to the whole Jewish nation. For because he made himself out unworthy even to receive Christ into his house, he became worthy both of a kingdom, and of attaining to those good things which Abraham enjoyed… For it is clear that the centurion was not a Jew, both from his being a centurion and from the saying, "I have not found such great faith, not even in Israel." And it was a very great thing for a man who was not listed among the Jewish people to have so great a thought. For he did no less than think to himself, as it seems to me, that the armies of heaven, or that the diseases and death, and everything else, were subject to Him in the same way as his soldiers were to himself.

So He said: "For I also am a man under authority;" that is, You are God, and I man; I under authority, but You not under authority. If I, being a man, and under authority, can do so much, He can do far more, both as God, and as not being under authority. So He wants to convince Him with the strongest expression that he says this, not as one giving a similar example, but one far exceeding. For he said if I, being equal in honor to those whom I command, and under the authority of others, can by reason of the mere superiority of my rank do such great things - and no one contradicts me, but what I command is done through the various orders - You Yourself will be able to do much more.

And some actually read the place in this way, "For if I, being a man," and having inserted a pause they add, "having soldiers under authority under me." But take note how he signified that Christ is able both to overcome even death as a slave, and to command it as its master. For in saying, "come, and he comes," and "go, and he goes," he expresses this: "If You should command his end not to come upon him, it will not come." See how believing he was? For here is one revealing already that which would later be revealed to all: that He has power both of death and of life, and "leads down to the gates of hell, and brings up again…"

But having such great faith, he nevertheless still counted himself unworthy. Christ however, showing that he was worthy to have Him enter into his house, did much greater things, marveling at him, and proclaiming him, and giving more than he had asked. For he came seeking bodily health for his servant, but went away having received a kingdom. See how the saying had already been fulfilled, "Seek first the kingdom of God and His righteousness, and all these things shall be added to you." For because he showed forth great faith and lowliness of mind, He gave him both heaven and health.

And not by this alone did He honor him, but also by signifying upon whose casting out he is brought in. For from now on He proceeds to proclaim to all that salvation is by faith, not by works of the law. And this is why not to Jews only, but to Gentiles also the gift so given shall be proffered.

Homily 26 on Matthew

Friday - Peter Chrysologus

There are three things by which faith stands firm, devotion remains constant, and virtue endures. They are prayer, fasting and mercy. Prayer knocks at the door, fasting obtains, mercy receives. Prayer, mercy and fasting: these three are one, and they give life to each other.

Fasting is the soul of prayer, mercy is the lifeblood of fasting. Let no one try to separate them; they cannot be separated. If you have only one of them or not all together, you have nothing. So if you pray, fast; if you fast, show mercy; if you want your petition to be heard, hear the petition of others. If you do not close your ear to others you open God's ear to yourself.

When you fast, see the fasting of others. If you want God to know that you are hungry, know that another is hungry. If you hope for mercy, show mercy. If you look for kindness, show kindness. If you want to receive, give. If you ask for yourself what you deny to others, your asking is a mockery.

Let this be the pattern for all when they practice mercy: show mercy to others in the same way, with the same generosity, with the same promptness, as you want others to show mercy to you.

Therefore, let prayer, mercy and fasting be one single plea to God on our behalf, one speech in our defense, a threefold united prayer in our favor…

Fasting bears no fruit unless it is watered by mercy. Fasting dries up when mercy dries up. Mercy is to fasting as rain is to the earth. However much you may cultivate your heart, clear the soil of your nature, root out vices, sow virtues; if you do not release the springs of mercy, your fasting will bear no fruit.

When you fast, if your mercy is thin your harvest will be thin; when you fast, what you pour out in mercy overflows into your barn. Therefore, do not lose by saving, but gather in by scattering. Give to the poor and you give to yourself. You will not be allowed to keep what you have refused to give to others.

Sermon 43

Saturday - Aurelius Prudentius

Simon, whom men call Peter,
God's chief disciple,
Once as the sun was setting,
When the evening turns from gold to red,
Had pulled up his curved anchor,
Courting the breezes with his canvas
And wishing to sail across the sea.
But night brought up such a head-wind
As disturbed the waters from their depths
And tossed and shook the vessel.
The boatmen's cries of woe
And lamentation struck the skies
Amid the whistling in the ropes,
And they had no hope left
Of escaping speedy wreck and drowning,
When suddenly at some distance the company,
Whose perils had blanched their cheeks,
Saw Christ treading on the sea
Just as if He were walking
Over a dry shore on a firm path.
At this marvel
The rest of the men on board
Were struck dumb with fear;
Peter alone undismayed
Recognized the Lord
Of heaven and earth and of the pathless sea,
To whose omnipotence it belongs
To put the waters under his feet.
He stretched forth his hands in prayer,
Asking for the help he knew so well;

But Christ, beckoning calmly,
Bade him leap down from the ship.
Peter obeyed the command,
But scarce had he wetted
his soles on the surface of the water
when he felt his steps give way
and his feet slip and sink down.
God rebuked the mortal man
For the unsteadiness of his faith
And his want of strength
To tread on the waves
And follow Christ.
Then with his hand He raised his servant
And set him up and taught him
To walk on the heaving surface of the sea.
    In the same way I,
Passing the safe bounds of silence,
Am brought into anxious peril
By my restless tongue;
For I cannot, like the disciple Peter,
Place my trust both in merit and in faith,
But am such an one as manifold sins have
shipwrecked
And roll lightly over the waters...
I have no skill in handling my boat,
Unless Thou, O mighty Christ,
Reach forth thy hand
To aid me with thy divine power...

Against Symacchus 2: Preface

Collect

Sunday through Tuesday:

O Lord, we pray You, mercifully hear our prayers and, having set us free from the bonds of sin, defend us from all evil; through Jesus Christ, Your Son, our Lord, who lives and reigns with You and the Holy Spirit, one God, now and forever. *Gelasian Sacramentary*

Wednesday through Saturday:

Almighty and everlasting God, our Father, because You hate nothing that You have made and You forgive the sins of all those who are penitent, create and make in us new and contrite hearts, that we, lamenting our sins and acknowledging our wretchedness, may obtain from You, the God of all mercy, perfect remission and forgiveness; through Jesus Christ, Your Son, our Lord, who lives and reigns with You and the Holy Spirit, one God, now and forever. *Book of Common Prayer, 1549*

AT LAUDS

Psalmody

Sunday: 3, C8, 51	Wednesday: 8, C11, 20	Friday: 146, C13, 5
Monday: 118a, C9, 118b	Thursday: 18a, C12, 18b	Saturday: 149, C14, 150
Tuesday: 1, C10, 2		

Lesson

Sunday: Genesis 29:13-30	Wednesday: Genesis 39:1-23	Friday: Genesis 44:1-34
Monday: Genesis 33:1-11	Thursday: Genesis 41:14-45	Saturday: Genesis 46:1-7; 47:27-31
Tuesday: Genesis 37:1-11		

Collect

Almighty God, our Heavenly Father, who, of Your tender love towards us sinners, has given us Your Son, that believing on Him we might have everlasting life: grant us, we beseech You, Your Holy Spirit, that we may continue steadfast in this faith to the end, and may come to everlasting life, through Jesus Christ, Your Son, our Lord, who lives and reigns with You and the Holy Spirit, one God, now and forever. *Saxon Kirchenordnung (Duke Henry), 1539*

AT TERCE, SEXT AND NONE

Chapter

Sunday, Monday and Tuesday: I Corinthians 13:1-13	Friday: Isaiah 58:1-8
Wednesday: Joel 2:12-19	Saturday: Isaiah 58:9-14
Thursday: Isaiah 38:1-6	

AT VESPERS

Psalmody

Sunday: 136b, 137, 138	Wednesday: 9, 10, 11	Friday: 17, 147a, 147b
Monday: 140, 141, 142	Thursday: 12, 13, 14, 16	Saturday: 19, 54, 77
Tuesday: 144, 145, 7		

Lesson

Sunday: Genesis 32:1-32	Wednesday: Genesis 40:1-23	Friday: Genesis 45:1-15; 25-28
Monday: Genesis 35:1-29	Thursday: Genesis 42:1-28	Saturday: Genesis 50:15-26
Tuesday: Genesis 37:12-36		

Collect

Lord God, heavenly Father, who did manifest Yourself, with the Holy Ghost, in the fullness of grace at the baptism of Your dear Son, and with Your voice did direct us to Him who has borne our sins, that we might receive grace and the remission of sins: Keep us, we beseech You, in the true faith; and inasmuch as we have been baptized in accordance with Your command, and the example of Your dear Son, we pray You to strengthen our faith by Your Holy Spirit, and lead us to everlasting life and salvation; through Your beloved Son, Jesus Christ our Lord, who lives and reigns with You and the Holy Spirit, one God, now and forever. *Veit Dietrich*

INVOCAVIT
The First Week in Lent

AT MATINS

Invitatory *As during the week of Septuagesima, p.309*

Hymn - *Ein' feste Burg is unser Gott*

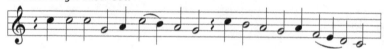

1. A migh-ty For-tress is our God, A trust-y Shield and Wea - pon;

He helps us free from ev' - ry need That hath us now o'er-tak - en.

The old ev - il Foe Now means dead - ly woe;

Deep guile and great might Are his dread arms in fight;

On Earth is not his e - qual.

2. With might of ours can naught be done,
Soon were our loss effected;
But for us fights the Valiant One,
Whom God Himself elected.
Ask ye, Who is this?
Jesus Christ it is.
Of Sabaoth Lord,
And there's none other God;
He holds the field forever.

3. Though devils all the world should fill,
All eager to devour us.
We tremble not, we fear no ill,
They shall not overpower us.
This world's prince may still
Scowl fierce as he will,
He can harm us none,
He's judged; the deed is done;
One little word can fell him.

328

4. The Word they still shall let remain
   Nor any thanks have for it;
   He's by our side upon the plain
   With His good gifts and Spirit.
   And take they our life,
   Goods, fame, child and wife,
   Let these all be gone,
   They yet have nothing won;
   The Kingdom our remaineth.   *Martin Luther, 1529*

Psalmody

Sunday: 21, 22, 23   Wednesday: 30, 31, 32   Friday: 37a, 37b, 38
Monday: 24, 25, 26   Thursday: 33, 34, 35   Saturday: 39, 40, 41
Tuesday: 27, 28, 29

Lesson

Sunday: Matthew 4:1-11
   Luke 4:1-13
Monday: Matthew 25:31-46
Tuesday: Matthew 21:10-17
Wednesday: Matthew 12:38-42
Thursday: Matthew 15:21-28
Friday: John 5:1-9
Saturday: Matthew 17:1-8

Homily

Sunday - Gregory I of Rome

We should keep in mind that temptation is accomplished in three stages: by suggestion, by delight, by consent. And when we are tempted we generally fall through pleasure or delight, and also by consent. Since we are begotten through the sin of the flesh, we bear within us that by which we now suffer conflict. But God who became incarnate in the womb of the Virgin came into this world without sin, and had no source of conflict within Him. He therefore could be tempted by suggestion; but the delight of sin could take no hold on his mind. And so all this diabolic temptation was from without, not from within.

But, dwelling on the sequence of the temptations, let us consider through what greatness we are delivered from temptation. Our ancient enemy set himself against the first man, our parent, with three temptations; for he tempted him by gluttony, by vanity, and by greed. And the devil defeated him by tempting him; for by consenting to the temptation he put himself under the devil's power.

He tempted him through gluttony when he placed before him the forbidden fruit of the tree, and persuaded him to eat it. He tempted him by vanity when he said: "You will be like God." And he tempted him from the heights of greed when he said: "knowing good and evil." ...In this the devil led our parent to pride, by provoking in him the greed of human grandeur.

But using the very means by which he laid low the first man, he himself succumbed to the Second Man. For he tempted Him by gluttony when he said: "Command that these stones become bread." He tempted Him by vanity when he said: "If you are the Son of God, throw Yourself down." By greed of dominion when he showed him all the kingdoms of the earth, and said: "All these things I will give You if You will fall down and worship me." But by these very means by which he gloried in defeating the First Man, he was overcome by the Second. And defeated he goes out of our hearts by the very way through which, once forcing an entrance, he held us in slavery.   *Sermon 16*

Monday - Cyprian of Carthage

What more could Christ declare to us? How could He more stimulate the works of our righteousness and mercy, than by saying that whatever is given to the needy and poor is given to Himself, and by saying that He is grieved when no supply is made for the needy and poor? So that he who in the Church is not moved by consideration for his brother, may yet be moved by contemplation of Christ; and he who does not think of his fellow servant in suffering and in poverty, may yet think of his Lord, who abides in that very man whom he is despising.

And therefore, dearest brethren, whose fear is inclined towards God, and who, having already despised and trampled the world under foot, have lifted up your mind to heavenly and divine things, let us with full faith, with devoted mind, with continual labor, give our obedience, to deserve well of the Lord. Let us give to Christ earthly garments, that we may receive heavenly raiment; let us give food and drink of this world, that we may come with Abraham, and Isaac, and Jacob to the heavenly banquet. That we may not reap little, let us sow abundantly. Let us, while there is time, think of our security and eternal salvation, according to the admonition of the Apostle Paul, who says: "Therefore, as we have opportunity, let us do good to all, especially to those who are of the household of faith. But let us not grow weary while doing good, for in due season we shall reap."

Treatise 8: On Works and Alms

Tuesday - Martin Luther

This is the way the Lord, our Ruler, establishes His kingdom, through the external oral Word which the Apostles preached and which now, by God's grace, we also preach, hear, accept, and believe… The Lord, our Ruler, establishes a strong and mighty kingdom that destroys the devil, pope and world. And this He does through the mouths of babes and sucklings, that is, the plain and simple who hold to the pure Word. For whoever wants to be in this kingdom and be saved, must turn and become like a child. As a child goes to school to learn the Our Father and the Creed, so we must also go to church to hear and learn the Gospel.

It is surely a strange and wondrous thing and a poor match in weapons… that the mouths of babes and sucklings should ordain such strength against emperors, kings, and potentates on earth and against the devil with all his hellish angels in the air. For all reason concludes that if one has powerful enemies and wants to defeat them, he must use a power that is greater than theirs, as Christ also testifies in the Gospel. Now, here are the strong and powerful enemies, the potentates on earth and the hellish enemy, whom one could hardly dent with a word. This is what human reason concludes; it cannot judge or conclude otherwise. But the mouths of babes and sucklings will do it, no matter how powerful and wicked the enemies may be. Precisely because the enemies boast of their power and might, God wants to destroy them with the mouths of babes and sucklings, as butter melts on the fire; or if they are not to be destroyed, in their great wisdom they should become children.

Therefore St. Paul says in I Corinthians 3:18: "If anyone among you seems to be wise in this age, let him become a fool that he may become wise." For whoever wants to be in this kingdom, as has been said, must become a child. Those who hold God's Word and desire His wisdom, let themselves be taught and learn, like pupils in school. Just as the Lord, our Ruler, becomes weak when He is born into the world, so He also begins His kingdom on earth in weakness. But on the Last Day he will appear as a powerful and great God. Now He founds His kingdom through the mouths of babes and sucklings; then He will be "revealed from heaven with His mighty angels in flaming fire." Now He addresses His enemies through the mouths of infants and sucklings, whom the world regards as fools; then He will address them differently, when He will wreak vengeance on those who do not know God and on those who are disobedient to His Gospel.

Commentary on Psalm 8

Wednesday - Cyprian the Poet

Then the Seer [Jonah] begins
Words prompted by the Spirit of the Lord:
"Lo! I your tempest am; I am the sum
Of the world's madness: 'tis in me" he says,
"That the sea rises, and the upper air
Down rushes; land in me is far, death near,
And hope in God is none! Come, headlong hurl
Your cause of bane: lighten your ship, and cast
This single mighty burden to the main,
A willing prey!" But they - all vainly! - strive
Homeward to turn their course; for helm refused
To suffer turning, and the yard's stiff poise
Willed not to change. At last unto the Lord
They cry: "For one soul's sake give us not o'er
Unto death's maw, nor let us be besprent
With righteous blood, if thus Thine own right hand
Leadeth." And from the eddy's depth a whale
Outrising on the spot, scaly with shells,
Unravelling his body's train, again urge
More near the waves, shocking the gleaming brine,
Seizing - at God's command - the prey; which, rolled
From the poop's summit prone, with slimy jaws
He sucked; and into his long belly sped
The living feast; and swallowed, with the man,

The rage of sky and main. The billowy waste
Grows level, and the ether's gloom dissolves;
The waves on this side, and the blasts on that,
Are to their friendly mood restored; and, where
The placid keel marks out a path secure,
White traces in the emerald furrow bloom.
The sailor then does to the reverend Lord
Of death make grateful offering of his fear;
Then enters friendly ports
Jonah the seer
The while is voyaging, in other craft
Embarked, and cleaving 'neath the lowest waves
A wave: his sails the intestines of the fish,
Inspired with breath ferine; himself, shut in;
By waters, yet untouched; in the sea's heart,
And yet beyond its reach; 'mid wrecks of fleets
Half-eaten, and men's carcasses dissolved
In putrid disintegrity: in life
Learning the process of his death; but still -
To be a sign hereafter of the Lord -
A witness was he
Not of destruction, but of death's repulse

A Strain of Jonah the Prophet, c. 400

Thursday - Thomas à Kempis,

Lord, I am not worthy of Your consolation or of any spiritual visitation. Therefore, You treat me justly when You leave me poor and desolate. For though I could shed a sea of tears, yet I should not be worthy of Your consolation. Hence I deserve only to be scourged and punished because I have offended You often and grievously, and have sinned greatly in many things. In all justice, therefore, I am not worthy of any consolation.

But You, O gracious and merciful God, who do not will that Your works should perish, deign to console Your servant beyond all his merit and above human measure, to show the riches of Your goodness toward the vessels of mercy. For Your consolations are not like the words of men.

The Imitation of Christ

Friday - John Chrysostom

What manner of cure is this? What mystery does it signify? These things, after all, are not written carelessly or without a purpose, but as figures and types to show in outline things to come... What is it then that they show in outline? A Baptism was about to be given, the greatest of gifts, having great power, a Baptism purging all sin and making men alive instead of dead...

He makes defilements of our bodies and infirmities of different kinds to be done away with by water. Because God, wanting to bring us nearer to faith in Baptism, no longer heals just defilements but disease too... And "an angel went down and stirred the waters," and endowed it with a healing power, so that the Jews might learn that the Lord of Angels could heal the diseases of the soul even more. Yet as it was not simply natural water here that healed, (for then this would have always taken place,) but water joined to the operation of the angel; so in our case, it is not merely the water that works, but when it has received the grace of the Spirit, then it puts away all our sins.

Around this pool "lay a great multitude of sick people, blind, lame, paralyzed, waiting for the moving of the water." Then his infirmity was a hinderance to the man who wanted to be healed, now all have the power to approach, for now it is not an angel that stirs, but the Lord of angels who works all. The sick man can no longer say, "I have no man;" he can not say, "while I am coming, another steps down before me;" for even though the whole world should come, the grace is not spent, the power is not exhausted, but remains just as great as it was before. Just as the sun's beams give light every day, yet are not exhausted, nor is their light made less by giving so abundantly; so, and much more so, the power of the Spirit is not in any way lessened by the quantity of those who enjoy it. And this miracle was done in order that men, learning that it is possible to heal the diseases of the body by water... might believe more easily that it can also heal the diseases of the soul.

Homily 36 on John

Saturday - Cyril of Alexandria

He goes up into a high mountain, taking with Him the three He had chosen from among them. There He is transfigured into a Being of wondrous glory, so that even His garments seemed to shine as though He were clothed with light. Then Moses and Elijah appear, standing beside Him, and speaking with Him of His death on the cross which was to take place in Jerusalem; speaking, that is, of the mystery of the plan of our redemption through His body and saving passion, which was to be accomplished on the cross.

For it was true that the Law of Moses and the words of the prophets had foreshadowed the mystery of Christ. The Law did this in types and figures as well as by its written Table. The prophets did it by foretelling at various times and in diverse ways that He would appear, and in our likeness, and would do so for the salvation of men and for their eternal life, He would not refuse the death of the cross. Therefore Moses and Elijah stood by and spoke with Him, and this was done to show that the Law and the Prophets were, so to speak, in attendance on our Lord Jesus Christ, making it plain that He was the Master of both the Law and the Prophets, and that He was proclaimed by them in unison. For what the Law declared, the Prophets confirmed.

Homily 9, On the Transfiguration of Our Lord

Collect

O Lord, mercifully hear our prayer and stretch forth the right hand of Your majesty to defend us from them that rise up against us; through Jesus Christ, Your Son, our Lord, who lives and reigns with You and the Holy Spirit, one God, now and forever. *Gelasian Sacramentary*

AT LAUDS

Psalmody

Sunday: 67, C1, 5	Wednesday: 64, C4, 65	Friday: 76, C5, 92
Monday: 63, C2, 36	Thursday: 88, C6, 90	Saturday: 143, C7, 148
Tuesday: 43, C3, 57		

Lesson

Sunday: Exodus 1:1-14	Wednesday: Exodus 7:1-25	Friday: Exodus 11:1-8
Monday: Exodus 2:11-25	Thursday: Exodus 9:1-35	Saturday: Exodus 12:31-51
Tuesday: Exodus 4:1-31		

Hymn - *Iam, Christe, sol iustitiae*

1. Now Christ, Thou Sun of right - eous - ness, Let dawn our dark-
2. Thou who dost give th'ac - cept - ed time, Give, too, a heart
3. Spare not, we pray, to send us here Some chast-'ning kind-

ened spi - rits bless: The light of grace to us re - store
that mourns for crime, Let those by mer - cy now be cured
ly but se - vere, So let Thy gift of pard-'ning grace

While day to earth re - turns once more.
Whom lov - ing - kind - ness long en - dured.
Our griev- ous sin - ful - ness ef - face.

4. Soon will that day, Thy day, appear
And all things with its brightness cheer:
We will rejoice in it, as we
Return thereby to grace, and Thee.

5. Let all the world from shore to shore
Thee, gracious Trinity, adore;
Right soon Thy loving pardon grant,
That we our new-made song may chant. Amen.

Anonymous, 10th c.

Verse

℣: He shall give His angels charge over / you.*
℟: To keep you in all your / ways.

Psalm 91:11

Antiphon to the Benedictus - *Generatio haec prava*   *Tone 8G*

A wick - ed and per-verse gen - er - a- tion seeks af - ter a sign,

And no sign shall be giv - en to it, ex - cept the

sign of the pro-phet Jon-ah.

✠ BLESSÉD is the Lord God of / Israel; *
For He has visited and re- / deemed His people. etc.

Collect

O Lord, who for our sake fasted forty days and forty nights; give us grace to use such abstinence, that, our flesh being subdued to the Spirit, we may ever follow Your godly example in righteousness, and true holiness, to Your honor and glory, who lives and reigns with the Father and the Holy Spirit, one God, now and forever.

Book of Common Prayer, 1549

AT TERCE, SEXT AND NONE

Chapter

Sunday: II Corinthians 6:1-10   Wednesday: I Kings 19:1-8   Friday: Ezekiel 18:20-28
Monday: Ezekiel 34:11-16   Thursday: Ezekiel 18:1-9   Saturday: I Thessalonians 5:14-24
Tuesday: Isaiah 55:6-11

Responsory and Verse at Terce:

℣:   He shall res - cue you from the snare of the fowl - er.
℟: He shall res - cue you from the snare of the fowl - er.

℣:   And from the sharp word.
℟: He shall rescue...

℣:   Glo-ry be to the Fa - ther, and to the Son, and to the Ho-ly Spi - rit.
℟: He shall rescue...

Psalm 91:3

℣: He shall cover you with His feath- / ers,
℟: And under His wings you shall take re- / fuge.

Psalm 91:4

Responsory and Verse at Sext:

℣: He shall co - ver you with His feath - ers.
℟: He shall co - ver you with His feath - ers.

℣: And un - der His wings you shall take re - fuge
℟: He shall cover...

℣: Glo-ry be to the Fa - ther, and to the Son, and to the Ho-ly Spi - rit.
℟: He shall cover...   *Psalm 91:4*

℣: His truth shall be your shield and buck- / ler.
℟: You shall not be afraid of the terror by / night.   *Psalm 91:5*

Responsory and Verse at None:

℣: His truth shall be your shield and buck - ler.
℟: His truth shall be your shield and buck - ler.

℣: You shall not be a - fraid of the ter - ror by night.
℟: His truth...

℣: Glo-ry be to the Fa - ther, and to the Son, and to the Ho-ly Spi - rit.
℟: His truth...   *Psalm 91:5*

℣: He shall give His angels charge over / you.*
℟: To keep you in all your / ways.   *Psalm 91:11*

AT VESPERS

Psalmody

Sunday: 110, 111, 112, 113   Wednesday: 123, 124, 125   Friday: 129, 130, 131, 132
Monday: 114, 115, 116, 117   Thursday: 126, 127, 128   Saturday: 133, 135, 136a
Tuesday: 120, 121, 122

Lesson

Sunday: Exodus 1:15-2:10   Wednesday: Exodus 8:1-32   Friday: Exodus 11:9-12:30
Monday: Exodus 3:1-22   Thursday: Exodus 10:1-29   Saturday: Exodus 13:17-14:31
Tuesday: Exodus 5:1-6:9

Hymn - *Audi benigne conditor*

1. O kind Cre - a - tor, bow Thine ear   To mark the cry,
2. Our hearts are o - pen, Lord, to Thee: Thou know-est our
3. Our sins are ma - ny, this we know;   Spare us, good Lord,

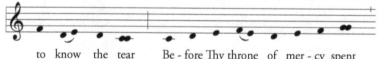

to know the tear   Be - fore Thy throne of mer - cy spent
in - fir - mi - ty;   Pour out on all who seek Thy face
Thy mer - cy show;   And for the hon - or of Thy name

In this Thy ho - ly   fast of Lent.
A - bun- dance of Thy   par - d'ning grace.
Our faint - ing souls to   life re - claim.

4. Give us the self-control that springs
From discipline of outward things,
That fasting inward secretly
The soul may purely dwell with Thee.

5. We pray Thee Blessèd Trinity,
One God, unchanging Unity,
That this our fast of forty days
May work our profit and Thy praise! Amen.

Gregory I, 540-604

Verse

℣: He shall give His angels charge over / you.*
℟: To keep you in all your / ways.

Psalm 91:11

Antiphon to the Magnificat - *Ecce nunc tempus*

Be - hold, now is the ac - cep - ted time; be - hold, now

is the day of sal- va - tion. Let us con- duct our - selves

as ser - vants of God in much pa - tience, in sleep-

less-ness, in fast - ings, and in sin - cere love.   *II Corinthians 6:2-3, 5-6*

✠ MY SOUL magnifies / the Lord, *
And my spirit has rejoiced in / God my Savior. etc.

Collect

Lord God, heavenly Father, inasmuch as the adversary continually afflicts us, and as a roaring lion walks about, seeking to devour us: We beseech You for the sake of the suffering and death of Your Son, Jesus Christ, to help us by the grace of Your Spirit, and to strengthen our hearts by Your word, that our enemy may not prevail over us, but that we may evermore abide in Your grace, and be preserved unto everlasting life; through the same, Your beloved Son, Jesus Christ, our Lord, who lives and reigns with You and the Holy Spirit, one God, now and forever.   *Veit Dietrich*

REMINISCERE
The Second Week in Lent

AT MATINS

Invitatory *As during the week of Septuagesima, p.309*

Hymn - *Wenn wir in Höchsten nöten sein*

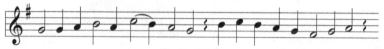

1. When in the hour of ut - most need We know not where to look for aid;

When days and nights of an-xious thought Nor help nor coun-sel yet have brought,

2. Then this our comfort is alone,
   That we may meet before Thy throne
   And cry, O faithful God to Thee
   For rescue from our misery;

3. To Thee may raise our hearts and eyes,
   Repenting sore with bitter sights,
   And seek Thy pardon for our sin
   And respite from our griefs within.

4. For Thou hast promised graciously
   To hear all those who cry to Thee
   Through Him whose name alone is great,
   Our Savior and our Advocate.

5. And thus we come, O God, today
   And all our woes before Thee lay;
   For sorely tried, cast down, we stand,
   Perplexed by fears on every hand.

6. Ah! Hide not for our sins Thy face,
   Absolve us through Thy boundless grace,
   Be with us in our anguish still,
   Free us at last from every ill,

7. That so with all our hearts we may
   To Thee our glad thanksgiving pay,
   Then walk obedient to Thy Word
   And now and ever praise Thee, Lord.

Paul Eber, 1560

Psalmody

Sunday: 42, 44, 45	Wednesday: 53, 55, 56	Friday: 61, 62, 66
Monday: 46, 47, 48	Thursday: 58, 59, 60	Saturday: 68a, 68b, 69a
Tuesday: 49, 50, 52		

Lesson

Sunday, Matthew 15:21-28
  Mark 7:24-30

Monday: John 8:21-29
Tuesday: Matthew 20:1-12
Wednesday: Matthew 20:17-28
  Mark 10:35-45

Thursday: Luke 16:19-31

Friday: Matthew 21:33-46
Mark 12:1-12 or Luke 20:9-19
Saturday: Luke 15:11-32

Homily

Sunday - Martin Luther

By this is set forth the condition of our heart in times of temptation; Christ here represents how it feels. It thinks there is nothing but no and yet that is not true. Therefore it must turn from this feeling and lay hold of and retain the deep spiritual yes under and above the no with a firm faith in God's Word, as this poor woman does, and say God is right in His judgment which He visits upon us; then we have triumphed and caught Christ in His own words. As for example when we feel in our conscience that God rebukes us as sinners and judges us unworthy of the kingdom of heaven, then we experience hell, and we think we are lost forever. Now whoever understands here the actions of this poor woman and catches God in his own judgment, and says: Lord, it is true, I am a sinner and not worthy of Your grace; but still You have promised sinners forgiveness, and You have come not to call the righteous, but, as St. Paul says in I Timothy 1:15, "to save sinners." Behold, then must God according to His own judgment have mercy on us.

King Manasseh did likewise in his penitence as his prayer proves; he conceded that God was right in His judgment and accused himself as a great sinner and yet he laid hold of the promised forgiveness of sins. David also does likewise in Psalm 51:4 and says: "Against You, You only, have I sinned, and done this evil in your sight, that You may be found just when You speak, and blame-less when You judge." For God's disfavor in every way visits us when we cannot agree with His judgment nor say yes and amen, when He considers and judges us to be sinners. If the condemned could do this, they would that very moment be saved. We say indeed with our mouth that we are sinners; but when God Himself says it in our hearts, then we are not sinners, and eagerly wish to be considered pious and free from that judgment. But it must be so; if God is to be righteous in His words that teach you are a sinner, then you may claim the rights of all sinners that God has given them, namely, the forgiveness of sins. Then you eat not only the crumbs under the table as the little dogs do; but you are also a child and have God as your portion according to the pleasure of your will.

This is the spiritual meaning of our Gospel and the Scriptural explanation of it. For what this poor woman experienced in the bodily affliction of her daughter, whom she miraculously caused to be restored to health again by her faith, that we also experience when we wish to be healed of our sins and of our spiritual diseases, which is truly a wicked devil possessing us; here she must become a dog and we become sinners and brands of hell, and then we have already recovered form our sickness and are saved.

Church Postil for Reminiscere Sunday

Monday - Ignatius of Antioch

Certain persons are ignorant and deny Him, or rather have been denied by Him. They are advocates of death rather than of the truth. They have not been persuaded by the prophecies nor by the law of Moses, nor even, thus far, by the Gospel, nor by our individual sufferings. For they have the same opinion concerning us too. For what good does it do me if a man praises me, but blasphemes my Lord and does not acknowledge that He is clothed in flesh? He who does not affirm this has denied Him completely, being himself a bearer of a corpse. But the names of these unbelievers, I have not thought fit to record in writing. No, far be it from me to even remember them until they repent in regard to the passion, which is our resurrection. Let no man deceive himself. Even the heavenly beings and the glory of the angels and the rulers visible and invisible will face judgment, unless they believe in the blood of Christ.

Epistle to the Smyrnæns

Tuesday - Gregory I of Rome

We may also see in these same varying hours the changing of the years in the life of every man. For the morning is the childhood of our reason. The third hour can be interpreted as adolescence, because while the heat of youth increases, it is as though the sun mounts higher in the sky. The sixth hour is young manhood, because as the sun is now as it were at its zenith, so now is the full strength of manhood attained. Mature age is signified by the ninth hour, in which the sun descends from its highest point, because in that age man already declines from the heat of youth. The eleventh hour is that time of life which is called senility or old age...

Because one man is called to the good life in boyhood, another in youth, another in manhood, another later in life, another in old age, the laborers are called at different hours to the Vineyard. Therefore, dearly beloved brethren, look to your manner of living, and see even now whether you are laborers of God. Let each one look to what he is doing, and let him consider whether or not he labors in the Vineyard of the Lord. For those that in this life seek the things that are their own, have not yet entered the Lord's Vineyard. For they work for the Lord who seek the Master's gain and not their own; who serve Him with the eagerness of love and the fervor of devotion; who are watchful to gain souls, and hurry to bring others with them to the true life. But he who lives for himself, who feeds on the pleasures of his own flesh, is rightly rebuked as idle, because he doesn't seek the fruit of divine labor.

He that has failed until his latest years to live for God, has truly been standing idle until the eleventh hour. And so it was rightly said to those who were inactive until the eleventh hour: "Why have you been standing here idle all day?" As if He said openly to them: If you have been unwilling to serve God in youth and in manhood, at least come to your senses in your old age. And though it is late come yet to the ways of true life, since there is little time left for you to work.

Homily for Septuagesima Sunday

Wednesday - Henry Suso

My child, I once read a saying in a book that I am just now beginning to understand. It is this: love makes unlike things alike. This is why Venus is painted blind and without eyes - because seeing with the eyes of love she loses the ability to see objectively. And though this is true of transitory love, it is much more so concerning spiritual love. It has stripped many noble and worthy people of their lofty position. Some, who were exalted rulers in Rome, gave it all up and became servants of poor people so that they would be like their beloved divine Child. And so, my child, give up the arrogance... and bow down today to the Child in His crib, in His abasement, that He might raise you to His eternal dignity. If you sow sparingly, you shall harvest poorly. But if you sow lavishly, you shall harvest in abundance. Act in your own interest and bow down to the feet of all men as though you were a doormat. A doormat does not get angry with anyone, no matter what is done to it, because it is a doormat.

True subordination in a person is a root of all virtue and happiness. From it there springs forth a meek calmness for true detachment from self with regard to things both insignificant and great. This causes pain: to have something to say but to remain silent, to receive insult and not to retaliate, as a capable and respected person to keep silent in front of a bungler of no repute. This is modeled on our noble Christ. What can be more useful to a person or give more praise to God?

The Exemplar: Little Book of Letters

Thursday - Clement of Alexandria

He is truly and properly rich who is rich in virtue, and is capable of making a holy and faithful use of any fortune. But he is spuriously rich who is rich according to the flesh, and turns life into outward possession, which is transitory and perishing, and now belongs to one, now to another, and in the end to nobody at all. Again, in the same way there is a genuine poor man, and another counterfeit and falsely called poor. He that is poor in spirit, and that is the right thing; and he that is poor in a worldly sense, which is a different thing. To him who is poor in worldly goods, but rich in vices, who is not poor in spirit and rich toward God, it is said: Abandon the alien possessions that are in your soul, that becoming pure in heart you may see God; which is another way of saying, Enter into the kingdom of heaven. And how can you abandon them? By selling them. What then? Are you to take money for things, effecting a mere exchange of riches by turning your possessions into money? Not at all. But in place of what was formerly inherent in your soul, which you desire to save, introduce other riches which deify and which minister everlasting life... for which there shall accrue to you endless reward and honor and salvation and everlasting immortality. In this way you rightly sell the possessions... which shut the heavens against you, by exchanging them for those which are able to save. Let the former be possessed by the carnally poor, who are destitute of the latter. But you, by receiving instead spiritual wealth, shall now have treasure in the heavens.   *On the Salvation of the Rich Man*

Friday - Cyril of Jerusalem

Believe in One Lord Jesus Christ, the Only-Begotten Son of God. For we say "One Lord Jesus Christ." That His Sonship may be "Only-begotten," we say "One." That you may not suppose there is another: we say "One." That you may not profanely diffuse the many names of His action among many sons, we say "One." For He is called a Door; but don't take the name literally for a thing of wood, but a spiritual, a living Door, differentiating those who enter in. He is called a Way, not one trod by feet, but leading to the Father in heaven. He is called a Sheep, not an irrational one, but the one which through its precious blood cleanses the world from its sins, which is led before the shearers, and knows when to be silent. This Sheep again is called a Shepherd, who says, I am the Good Shepherd: a Sheep because of His manhood, a Shepherd because of the loving-kindness of His Godhead. And would you know that there are rational sheep? The Saviour says to the Apostles, Behold, I send you as sheep in the midst of wolves. Again, He is called a Lion, not as a devourer of men, but indicating His kingly, steadfast, confident nature by the title. He is also called a Lion in opposition to our adversary, a lion who roars and devours those who have been deceived. For the Saviour came, not as having changed the gentleness of His own nature, but as the strong Lion of the tribe of Judah, saving those who believe, but treading down the adversary. He is called a Stone, not a lifeless stone, cut out by men's hands, but a chief corner-stone, on whom whoever believes will not be put to shame.

He is called Christ, not as having been anointed by men's hands, but eternally anointed by the Father to His High-Priesthood on behalf of men. He is called Dead, not as dwelling among the dead like those in Hades, but as being alone free among the dead. He is called Son of Man, not as having had His generation from earth, as we do, but as coming upon the clouds to judge both quick and dead. He is called Lord, not improperly as those who are called this among men, but as having a natural and eternal lordship. He is called Jesus, a fitting name, being called this on account of His salutary healing. He is called Son, not as advanced by adoption, but as naturally begotten. And many are the titles of our Savior; lest, therefore, His many names should make you think of many sons, and because of the errors of the heretics, who say that Christ is one, and Jesus another, and the Door another, and so on, the Faith secures you beforehand, saying well, In One Lord Jesus Christ. For though the titles are many, their subject is still one.   *10th Catechetical Lecture*

Saturday - Macarius Chrysocephalus

What choral dance and high festival is held in heaven, whenever there is someone that has become an exile and a fugitive from life under the Father, not knowing that those who put themselves far from Him shall perish; if he has squandered the gift, and substance, and inheritance of the Father; if there is someone whose faith has failed, and whose hope is spent, by rushing along with the Gentiles into the same extravagance of debauchery; and then, famished and destitute, and not even filled with what the swine eat, has risen up and come to his Father!

But the kind Father does not wait until the son comes to Him. For if he did not find Him gracious, perhaps he would never be able or dare to approach. This is why, when he was merely wishing, when he at once made a beginning, when he took the first step, while he was yet a great way off, his Father was moved with compassion, and ran, and fell upon his neck and kissed him. And then the son, taking courage, confessed what he had done.

For this reason the Father bestows on him the glory and honor that was due and proper, putting the best robe on him, the robe of immortality; and a ring, a royal signet and divine seal, the impress of consecration, signature of glory, pledge of testimony (for it is said, "He hath set to his seal that God is true,") and shoes, not those perishable ones which he who has set his foot on holy ground is commanded to take off, nor such as he who is sent to preach the kingdom of heaven is forbidden to put on, but such as do not wear out, and are suited for the journey to heaven, suitable and adorning the heavenly path, such as unwashed feet never put on, but those which are washed by our Teacher and Lord...

But whom Christ finds lost, because of sin committed since baptism, those Novatus, the enemy of God, resigns to destruction. So do not let us count any fault if we repent; guarding against falling, if we have fallen, let us retrace our steps. And while dreading to offend, after offending, let us avoid despair and be eager to be confirmed; and on sinking, let us make haste to rise up again. Let us obey the Lord, who calls to us, "Come to Me, all you who labor and are heavy laden, and I will give you rest" (Matthew 11:28). Let us employ the gift of reason and be prudent. Let us learn now to abstain from what is wicked, that we may not be forced to learn in the future. Let us employ life as a training school for what is good; and let us be roused to the hatred of sin. Let us carry a deep love for the Creator; let us cleave to Him with our whole heart; let us not wickedly waste the substance of reason, like the prodigal. Let us obtain the joy laid up, in which Paul exulting, exclaimed, "Who shall separate us from the love of Christ?" To Him belongs glory and honor, with the Father and the Holy Spirit, world without end. Amen.

Homily on Luke 15

Collect

O God, who sees that of ourselves we have no strength, keep us both outwardly and inwardly that we may be defended from all adversities which may happen to the body and from all evil thoughts which may assault and hurt the soul; through Jesus Christ, Your Son, our Lord, who lives and reigns with You and the Holy Spirit, one God, now and forever.

Gelasian Sacramentary

AT LAUDS

Psalmody

Sunday: 3, C8, 51	Wednesday: 8, C11, 20	Friday: 146, C13, 5
Monday: 118a, C9, 118b	Thursday: 18a, C12, 18b	Saturday: 149, C14, 150
Tuesday: 1, C10, 2		

Lesson

Sunday: Exodus 15:22-16:3	Wednesday: Exodus 25:1-22	Friday: Exodus 34:29-35
Monday: Exodus 18:13-27	Thursday: Exodus 33:7-23	Saturday: Leviticus 8:1-13,
Tuesday: Exodus 20:1-26		30-36; 10:1-4

Hymn and Verse   *As during the week of Invocavit, p.333*

Antiphon to the Benedictus - *Ecce ascendimus Jerosolymam*   *Tone 7a*

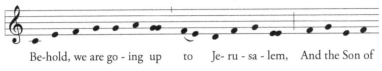

Be-hold, we are go - ing up   to   Je- ru - sa - lem,   And the Son of

Man   will   be   be-trayed   to   be   cru- ci - fied.   *Matthew 20:18*

✠ BLESSÉD is the Lord / God of Israel; *
For He has visited and re- / deemed His people. etc.

Collect

Grant us, we beseech You, O Lord, the assistance of Your grace; that while we diligently apply ourselves to fasting and prayer, we may be delivered by You from all enemies both of soul and body; through Jesus Christ, our Lord, who lives and reigns with You and the Holy Spirit, one God, now and forever.   *Roman Missal*

AT TERCE, SEXT AND NONE

Chapter

Sunday: I Thessalonians 4:1-7   Wednesday: Genesis 41:38-43   Friday: Genesis 37:3-11
Monday: Daniel 9:15-19   Thursday: Jeremiah 17:5-10   Saturday: Genesis 27:6-39
Tuesday: I Kings 17:8-16

Responsories and Verses   *As during the week of Invocavit, p.334*

AT VESPERS

Psalmody

Sunday: 136b, 137, 138   Wednesday: 9, 10, 11   Friday: 17, 147a, 147b
Monday: 140, 141, 142   Thursday: 12, 13, 14, 16   Saturday: 19, 54, 77
Tuesday: 144, 145, 7

Lesson

Sunday: Exodus 16:4-21	Wednesday: Exodus 31:12-32:35	Friday: Exodus 39:42-40:38
Monday: Exodus 19:1-24	Thursday: Exodus 34:1-28	Saturday: Leviticus 16:1-22
Tuesday: Exodus 24:1-18		

Hymn and Verse *As during the week of Invocavit, p.336*

Antiphon to the Magnificat - *Tradetur enim gentibus* Tone 1f

He will be de - liv - ered to the Gen-tiles, to be mocked

and to be scourged and to be cru- ci - fied. *Matthew 20:19*

✠ MY SOUL / magnifies the Lord, *
And my spirit has rejoiced in / God my Savior. etc.

Collect

Lord God, heavenly Father, grant us, we beseech You, by Your Holy Spirit, that He may strengthen our hearts and confirm our faith and hope in Your grace and mercy, so that, although we have reason to fear because of our conscience, our sin, and our unworthiness, we may nevertheless, with the woman of Canaan, hold fast to Your grace, and in every trial and temptation find You a very present help and refuge, through Your beloved Son, Jesus Christ, our Lord, who lives and reigns with You and the Holy Spirit, one God, now and forever. *Veit Dietrich*

OCULI
The Third Week in Lent

AT MATINS

Invitatory *As during the week of Septuagesima, p.309*

Hymn - *Mir nach, spricht Christus, unser Held*

1. Come fol-low Me, the Sav-ior spake, All in My way a - bid - ing;

De-ny your-selves, the world for-sake, O-bey My call and guid-ing.

Oh, bear the cross, what-e'er be-tide, Take My ex-am- ple for your guide.

2. I am the Light, I light the way,
   A godly life displaying;
   I bid you walk as in the day,
   I keep your feet from straying.
   I am the Way, and well I show
   How you must sojourn here below.

3. My heart abounds in lowliness,
   My soul with love is glowing,
   And gracious words my lips express,
   With meekness overflowing.
   My heart, My mind, My strength, My all,
   To God I yield, on Him I call.

4. I teach you how to shun and flee
   What harms your soul's salvation,
   Your heart from every guile to free,
   From sin and its temptation.
   I am the Refuge of the soul
   And lead you to your heavenly goal.

5. But if too hot you find the fray,
   I, at your side, stand ready;
   I fight myself, I lead the way,
   At all times firm and steady.
   A coward he who will not heed
   When the chief Captain takes the lead.

6. Who seeks to find his soul's welfare
   Without Me, he shall lose it;
   But who to lose it may appear,
   In God shall introduce it.
   Who bears no cross nor follows hard
   Deserves not Me nor My reward.

7. Then let us follow Christ, our Lord,
   And take the cross appointed
   And, firmly clinging to His Word,
   In suffering be undaunted.
   For who bears not the battle strain
   The crown of life shall not obtain.

Johann Scheffler, 1668

Psalmody

Lesson

Homily

Sunday - Bruno of Segni

Another Evangelist tells us what this means, saying: "But if I cast out demons by the Spirit of God," which is indeed true, and may not be doubted: "surely the kingdom of God has come upon you." For where the Spirit of God is, there also is the Kingdom of God. The Holy Spirit is called the Finger of God, because of the multiple division of graces. For in no part of the body do we find such division as in the fingers. And this is as if He had said, I cast out demons in the Spirit and Power of God; since they are subject to Me, since they are powerless to withstand Me, since I hold them tied and keep them bound.

"When a strong man, fully armed, guards his own palace, his goods are in peace. But when a stronger than he comes upon him and overcomes him, etc." For the devil was strong; but I am stronger. I have come into this world which he has held as though it were his own house; and the time draws near for the prince of this world to be cast forth. I have bound him; I have broken his armor; and I have delivered the unhappy people he held captive from his bondage. He is not there "with Me;" nor does he gather with Me; neither does he cast out devils together with Me; nor does he heal men, as I do; nor does he gather in the flocks, nor lead them to the living pastures, which I am doing. So what does he do? Do you want to hear? He scatters, he harries, he kills, he drags down to death and eternal damnation whomever he can. For this is the meaning of those words: "He who is not with Me is against Me, and he who does not gather with Me scatters."

The Kingdom of Evil

Monday - Origen of Alexandria

It is true that Jeremiah was not accepted in Anathoth, his native land; nor was Isaiah, whatever his native land was, nor the rest of the prophets. But it seems to me that the passage should be understood this way: we say that the native land of all the prophets was the people of the circumcision. This people received neither the prophets nor their prophecies. But, then, the Gentiles, who had been far from the prophets and had no knowledge of them, received the prophecy of Jesus Christ. So, "no prophet is accepted in his own country," that is, among the people of the Jews. We were foreign to the covenant and alien to the promises. But we received the prophets with all our hearts. We "have Moses and the prophets," who preached about Christ much more than they do. Since they did not receive Jesus, they did not receive those men, either, who proclaimed him.

This is why He adds something else to what He said. After "no prophet is accepted in his own country," He adds, "I tell you truly, many widows were in Israel in the days of Elijah, when the heaven was shut up three years and six months." What He is saying is this. Elijah was a prophet, and he was among the people of the Jews. But, when he was about to do something miraculous, although there were many widows in Israel, he left them and went "to a widow of Zarepeth of Sidonia" - that is, to a little Gentile woman. Elijah was revealing the form of a future reality. "It was not hunger for bread or thirst for water, but hunger for hearing the Word of God," that occupied the people of Israel...

Homily 33 on Luke

Tuesday - Callistus of Rome (attr.)

They are in error who think that the priests of the Lord, after a lapse, although they may have exhibited true repentance, are not capable of ministering to the Lord and engaging their honorable offices, though they may lead a good life thereafter and keep their priesthood correctly. And those who hold this opinion are not only in error, but also seem to dispute and act in opposition to the power of the keys committed to the Church, of which it is said: "and whatever you loose on earth will be loosed in heaven." And in short, this opinion either is not the Lord's, or it is true.

But be that as it may, we believe without hesitation, that both the priests of the Lord and other believers may return to their honors after a proper satisfaction for their error, as the Lord Himself testifies by His prophet: "Will they fall and not rise? Will one turn away and not return?" And in another passage the Lord says: "I have no pleasure in the death of the wicked, but that the wicked turn from his way and live." And the prophet David, on his repentance, said: "Restore to me the joy of Your salvation, and uphold me by Your generous Spirit." And he indeed, after his repentance, taught others also, and offered sacrifice to God, giving thereby an example to the teachers of the holy Church, that if they have fallen, and thereafter have exhibited a right repentance to God, they may do both things in like manner. For he taught when he said: "I will teach transgressors Your ways, and sinners shall be converted to You." And he offered sacrifice for himself, while he said: "The sacrifices of God are a broken spirit." For the prophet, seeing his own transgressions purged by repentance, had no doubt about healing those of others by preaching and by making offering to God. Thus the shedding of tears moves the mind's passions. And when the satisfaction is made good, the mind is turned aside from anger.

For how does that man think that mercy will be shown to himself, who does not forgive his neighbor? If offences abound, let mercy also abound; for with the Lord there is mercy, and with Him is plenteous redemption. In the Lord's hand there is abundance of all things because He is the Lord of powers and the King of glory. For the apostle says: "all have sinned and fall short of the glory of God, being justified freely by His grace through the redemption that is in Christ Jesus, whom God set forth as a propitiation by His blood, through faith, to demonstrate His righteousness, because in His forbearance God had passed over the sins that were previously committed, to demonstrate at the present time His righteousness, that He might be just and the justifier of the one who has faith in Jesus." And David says: "Blessed is he whose transgression is forgiven, whose sin is covered." Man, therefore, is cleansed of his sin, and rises again by the grace of God though he has fallen, and abides in his first position ... My brethren, shun not only the holding, but even the hearing, of the judgment that bans mercy; for better is mercy than all whole burnt-offerings and sacrifices.

Epistle to the Bishops of Gaul

Wednesday - Ignatius of Antioch

Do not be deceived by strange doctrines or by antiquated myths, since they are useless. For if we are still living in conformity with Judaism, we acknowledge that we have not received grace. For the most divine prophets lived in conformity with Christ Jesus. For this reason they were persecuted, though inspired by grace to convince the disobedient that there is one God who manifested Himself through Jesus Christ His Son, who is His Word which proceeded from silence and in every respect pleased Him who sent Him.

If, then, those who lived in antiquated customs came to newness of hope, no longer keeping the Sabbath but living in accordance with the Lord's Day, on which also our life arose through Him and His death (though some deny it), and by this mystery we received the power to believe, and for this reason we endure so that we may be recognized as disciples of Jesus Christ, our only teacher - how shall we be able to live apart from Him of whom even the prophets were disciples in the Spirit, Him whom they expected as their teacher? And therefore when He came, He whom they righteously awaited raised them from the dead.

Let us, then, not be insensible of His goodness, for if He imitated us in our actions we should no longer exist. For this reason we should become His disciples and learn to live in Christian fashion. Whoever is called by any name other than this does not belong to God. Therefore put aside the bad leaven, now antiquated and sour, and turn to the new leaven, which is Jesus Christ. Be salted with Him so that none of you may be spoiled, since you will be tested by your odor. It is absurd to talk of Jesus Christ and practice Judaism. For Christianity did not base its faith on Judaism, but Judaism on Christianity, in which "every language" believing in God was "brought together."

Epistle to the Magnesians

Thursday - Ambrose of Milan

Let us not, while we are grieving over the wounds of our sins, leave the physician, and while ministering to the sores of others, let our own go on increasing. The Physician is then asked for here. Do not fear because the Lord is great that perhaps He will not condescend to come to one who is sick, for He often comes to us from heaven; and is in the habit of visiting not only the rich but also the poor and the servants of the poor. And so now He comes when called upon to Peter's mother-in-law. "He stood over her and rebuked the fever, and it left her. And immediately she arose and served them." As He is worthy of being remembered, so too is He worthy of being longed for, worthy too of love for His condescension to every single matter which affects men and His marvellous acts. He does not hate to visit widows and to enter the tiny rooms of a poor cottage. As God He commands, as man He visits.

Thanks be to the Gospel, by means of which we also, who did not see Christ when He came into this world, seem to be with Him when we read His deeds; that as they, to whom He drew near, borrowed faith from Him, so may He, when we believe His deeds, draw near to us.

Do you see what kinds of healing are with Him? He commands the fever, He commands the unclean spirits, at another place He lays hands on them. He was in the habit of healing the sick, not only by word but also by touch. So you also, who burn with many desires, entranced either by someone's beauty or fortune, implore Christ. Call in the Physician, stretch forth your right hand to Him, let the hand of God touch your inmost being and let the grace of the heavenly Word enter the veins of your inward desires. Let God's right hand strike the secrets of your heart. He spreads clay on the eyes of some that they may see, and the Creator of all teaches us that we ought to be mindful of our own nature and to discern the vileness of our body; for no one can see divine things except one who because of the knowledge of his vileness cannot be puffed up. Another is commanded to show himself to the priest that he may be free forever from the scales of leprosy. For he alone can preserve his purity, both of body and soul, who knows how to show himself to that Priest, whom we have received as an Advocate for our sins, and to whom is plainly said: "You are a priest forever according to the order of Melchizedek."

Concerning Widows

Friday - Martin Luther

Look how gently the Lord deals with her! He does not break off talking to her but continues: "Dear daughter, it is true that I want you to give Me a drink; for I am physically fatigued. However, I am not merely interested in a drink for My body; I am looking for something else. I am seeking you Samaritans that you may hear Me." Now He begins to deliver an excellent sermon, saying: "If you knew the gift of God, and who it is who says to you, 'Give Me a drink,' you would have asked Him, and He would have given you living water."

"I would be happy to reverse the order and give you a drink. In fact, this is the reason for My presence here. I am asking for a drink to quench My physical thirst that I might have occasion to give you a drink. If you only realized what a gift is now to be found on earth, you would ask Me for it, and I would give you a drink that would taste better than this water. It is of the utmost importance to recognize this gift and to know Him who gives it." This is also our lament - and it will eternally remain so - that the schismatic spirits do not recognize the gift even when exhorted to do so; and the great multitude also despises this ineffably precious treasure and fails to recognize the Giver of this gift. In fact, we too, who claim to be saints, pay it no heed and do not fully appreciate the value of this treasure offered to us through the Gospel. My dear friend, how few there are among us who esteem this as a genuine treasure, as an eternal gem, as everlasting life! There must be some, however, who will hazard life and limb for it... Thus we find many who are willing to endure tortures because of it; they, too, will receive the drink...

Would to God that we could gradually train our hearts to believe that the preacher's words are God's Word and that the man addressing us is a scholar and a king. As a matter of fact, it is not an angel or a hundred thousand angels but the Divine Majesty Himself that is preaching there. To be sure, I do not hear this with my ears or see it with my eyes; all I hear is the voice of the preacher, or of my brother or father, and I behold only a man before me. But if I view the picture correctly I add that the voice and words of father or pastor are not his own words and doctrine but those of our Lord and God. It is not a prince, a king, or an archangel whom I hear; it is He who declares that He is able to dispense the water of eternal life. If we could believe this, we would be content indeed...

People generally think: "If I had an opportunity to hear God speak in person, I would run my feet bloody." This is why people in times past flocked to the Oak, to Aachen, and to the Grym Valley. Because the people believed that Mary would help them in these places, they all hurried there. If someone at that time had announced: "I know of a place in the world where God speaks and anyone can hear God there;" if I had gone there and seen and heard a poor pastor baptizing and preaching, and if I had been assured: "This is the place; here God is speaking through the voice of the preacher who brings God's Word" - I would have said: "Well, I have been duped! I see only a pastor." We should like to have God speak to us in His majesty. But I advise you not to run hither and yon for this...

My dear friend, regard it as a real treasure that God speaks into your physical ear. The only thing that detracts from this gift is our deficient knowledge of it. To be sure, I do hear the sermon; however, I am wont to ask: "Who is speaking?" The pastor? By no means! You do not hear the pastor. Of course, the voice is his, but the words he employs are truly spoken by my God. Therefore I must hold the Word of God in high esteem that I may become an apt pupil of the Word. If we looked upon it as the Word of God, we would be glad to go to church, to listen to the sermon, and to pay attention to the precious Word. There we would hear Christ say: "Give Me a drink."

4th Homily on the 4th Chapter of John

Saturday - Augustine of Hippo

What answer, then, did the Lord Jesus make? How answered Truth? How answered Wisdom? How answered that Righteousness against which a false accusation was ready? He did not say, don't stone her; lest He should seem to speak against the law. But God forbid that He should say, Let her be stoned; for He came not to lose what He had found, but to seek what was lost. So how did He answer? See how full it is of righteousness, how full of meekness and truth! "He who is without sin among you," He says, "let him throw a stone at her first." O answer of Wisdom! How He sent them to themselves! For outwardly they stood to accuse and censure, inwardly they did not examine themselves; they saw the adulteress, they did not look into themselves. Transgressors of the law, they wished the law to be fulfilled, and this by heedlessly accusing; not really fulfilling it, as if condemning adulteries by chastity. You have heard, O Jews, you have heard, O Pharisees, you have heard, O teachers of the law, the guardian of the law, but have not yet recognized Him as the Lawgiver. What else does He signify to you when He writes with His finger on the ground? For the law was written with the finger of God; but written on stone because of the hard-hearted. The Lord now wrote on the ground, because He was seeking fruit. You have heard then, Let the law be fulfilled, let the adulteress be stoned. But is it by punishing her that the law is to be fulfilled by those that ought to be punished? Let each of you consider himself, let him enter into himself, ascend the judgment-seat of his own mind, place himself at the bar of his own conscience, oblige himself to confess. For he knows what he is: for "what man knows the things of a man except the spirit of the man which is in him?" Each looking carefully into himself, finds himself a sinner. Yes, indeed. So, either let this woman go, or receive the penalty of the law together with her. Had He said, Do not let the adulteress be stoned, He would be proven unjust. Had He said, Let her be stoned, He would not appear gentle. Let Him say what was proper for Him to say, both the gentle and the just, "He who is without sin among you, let him throw a stone at her first." This is the voice of Justice: Let her, the sinner, be punished, but not by sinners: let the law be fulfilled, but not by the transgressors of the law. This certainly is the voice of justice. By this justice those men, looking into themselves and finding themselves guilty, were pierced through as if by an arrow and "went out one by one." The two were left alone, the wretched woman and Mercy. But the Lord, having struck them through with that arrow of justice, deigned not to heed their fall, but, turning His gaze away from them, "again He wrote with His finger on the ground."

But when that woman was left alone, and they were all gone out, He raised His eyes to the woman. We have heard the voice of justice, let us also hear the voice of clemency. For I suppose that woman was even more terrified when she had heard the Lord say, "He who is without sin among you, let him throw a stone at her first." But they, turning their thought to themselves, and by their very withdrawal having confessed concerning themselves, had left the woman with her great sin to Him who was without sin. And because she had heard this, "He who is without sin among you, let him throw a stone at her first," she expected to be punished by Him in whom sin could not be found. But He, who had driven back her adversaries with the tongue of justice, raising the eyes of clemency towards her, asked her, "Has no one condemned you?" She answered, "No one, Lord." And He said, "Neither do I condemn thee;" by whom, perhaps, you feared to be condemned, because in me you have not found sin. "Neither do I condemn you." What is this, O Lord? Do You therefore favor sins? Not so, evidently. Note what follows: "Go and sin no more." So the Lord also condemned, but condemned sins, not man. For if He were a patron of sin, He would say, Neither will I condemn you; go, live as you will: be secure in my deliverance; how ever much you want to sin, I will deliver you from all punishment, even of hell, and from the tormentors of the infernal world. This He did not say.

Tractate 33 on the Gospel of John

Collect

We pray You, Almighty God, look on the hearty desires of Your humble servants and stretch forth the right hand of Your majesty to be our defense against all our enemies; through Jesus Christ, Your Son, our Lord, who lives and reigns with You and the Holy Spirit, one God, now and forever.

Gregorian Sacramentary

AT LAUDS

Psalmody

Sunday: 67, C1, 5	Wednesday: 64, C4, 65	Friday: 76, C5, 92
Monday: 63, C2, 36	Thursday: 88, C6, 90	Saturday: 143, C7, 148
Tuesday: 43, C3, 57		

Lesson

Sunday: Leviticus 18:1-30	Wednesday: Numbers 6:13-27	Friday: Numbers 14:6-45
Monday: Leviticus 20:1-7	Thursday: Numbers 12:1-16	Saturday: Numbers 16:41-50
Tuesday: Leviticus 26:1-46		

Hymn and Verse *As during the week of Invocavit, p.333*

Antiphon to the Benedictus - *Si in digito* *Tone 3a*

If I cast out de - mons with the fing - er of God,

Sure - ly the king - dom of God has come up - on you. *Luke 11:20*

✠ BLESSÉD is the Lord God / of Israel; *
For He has visited and redeemed / His people. etc.

Collect

Almighty God, cast not away Your people who cry unto You in their tribulation; but for the glory of Your name, be pleased to save the afflicted; through Jesus Christ, our Lord, who lives and reigns with You and the Holy Spirit, one God, now and forever.

Gregorian Sacramentary

AT TERCE, SEXT AND NONE

Chapter

Sunday: Ephesians 5:1-9	Wednesday: Exodus 20:12-24	Friday: Numbers 20:2-13
Monday: II Kings 5:1-15	Thursday: Jeremiah 7:1-7	Saturday: Isaiah 1:16-20
Tuesday: II Kings 4:1-7		

Responsories and Verses *As during the week of Invocavit, p.334*

AT VESPERS

Psalmody

Sunday: 110, 111, 112, 113   Wednesday: 123, 124, 125   Friday: 129, 130, 131, 132
Monday: 114, 115, 116, 117   Thursday: 126, 127, 128   Saturday: 133, 135, 136a
Tuesday: 120, 121, 122

Lesson

Sunday: Leviticus 19:1-18, 26-37   Wednesday: Numbers 10:33-11:35   Friday: Numbers 16:1-40
Monday: Leviticus 23:1-44   Thursday: Numbers 13:1-4, 17-14:5   Saturday: Numbers 20:1-13, 22-29
Tuesday: Numbers 3:1-16

Hymn and Verse *As during the week of Invocavit, p.336*

Antiphon to the Magnificat - *Extollens quaedem mulier*   *Tone 8G*

A cer - tain wo - man from the crowd raised her voice and said to Him,

"Bless - ed is the womb that bore You, and the breasts which nursed You!"

But Je - sus said, "More than that, bless - ed are those who

hear the word of God and keep it!"   *Luke 11:27-28*

✠ MY SOUL magnifies / the Lord, *
And my spirit has rejoiced in / God my Savior. etc.

Collect

Lord God, heavenly Father, who has sent Your Son, our Lord Jesus Christ, to take upon Himself our flesh, that He might overcome the devil, and defend us poor sinners against the adversary: We give thanks to You for Your merciful help, and we implore You to attend us with Your grace in all temptations, to preserve us from carnal security, and by Your Holy Spirit to keep us in Your word and Your fear, that to the end we may be delivered from the enemy, and obtain eternal salvation, through the same, Your beloved Son, Jesus Christ, our Lord, who lives and reigns with You and the Holy Spirit, one God, now and forever.   *Veit Dietrich*

LAETARE

The Fourth Week in Lent

AT MATINS

Invitatory *As during the week of Septuagesima, p.309*

Hymn - *Jesu, Meine Freude*

1. Je - sus, price-less Trea- sure, Fount of pur - est plea-sure,

Tru - est Friend to me. Ah, how long in an - guish

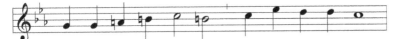

Shall my spir - it lan - guish, Yearn-ing, Lord, for Thee?

Thou art mine, O Lamb di - vine! I will suf - fer

naught to hide Thee, Naught I ask be - side Thee.

2. In Thine arms I rest me;
Foes who would molest me
Cannot reach me here.
Though the earth be shaking,
Every heart be quaking,
Jesus calms my fear.
Lightnings flash And thunders crash;
Yet, though sin and hell assail me,
Jesus will not fail me.

3. Satan, I defy thee;
Death, I now decry thee;
Fear, I bid thee cease.
World, thou shalt not harm me
Nor thy threats alarm me
While I sing of peace.
God's great power Guards every hour;
Earth and all its depths adore Him,
Silent bow before Him.

4. Hence, all earthly treasure!
Jesus is my Pleasure,
Jesus is my Choice.
Hence, all empty glory!
Naught to me thy story
Told with tempting voice.
Pain or loss, Or shame or cross,
Shall not from my Savior move me
Since He deigns to love me.

5. Evil world, I leave thee;
Thou canst not decieve me,
Thine appeal is vain.
Sin that once did blind me,
Get thee far behind me,
Come not forth again.
Past thy hour, O pride and power;
Sinful life, thy bonds I sever,
Leave thee now forever.

353

6. Hence, all fear and sadness!
    For the Lord of gladness,
    Jesus, enters in.
    Those who love the Father,
    Though the storms may gather,
    Still have peace within.
    Yea, whate'er I here must bear,
    Thou art still my purest Pleasure,
    Jesus, priceless Treasure. *Johann Franck, 1655*

Psalmody

Sunday: 89c, 94, 96   Wednesday: 104a, 104b, 104c   Friday: 106a, 106b, 107a
Monday: 97, 98, 99, 100   Thursday: 105a, 105b, 105c   Saturday: 107b, 108, 109
Tuesday: 101, 102, 103

Lesson

Sunday: John 6:1-14
Monday: John 2:13-25
Tuesday: John 7:14-30
Wednesday: John 9:1-38
Thursday: Luke 7:11-16
Friday: John 11:1-45
Saturday: John 8:12-20

Homily

Sunday - Martin Luther

Christians should recognize God's wonders and learn from them to rely on Him. Why would we even want to despair? The cherry tree doesn't, even though in winter it stands bare without leaves or fruit. It trusts the word God has spoken, bursts forth in summer and blossom, and relies on it! When summer comes it leafs out and blossoms. The field doesn't despair even though in winter it lies there, frozen and covered with snow, without a single blade of grass to be seen. We ought to learn from these everyday wonders to trust in God and not despair. Even though at times our situation seems poor, there is no need to worry; our needs will be provided if we but trust our God.

And what more is wanted? If our needs are met, and we're prevented from freezing to death or from starving, that's enough. If we have what we need, our hearts and bodies can be satisfied and we can be in good spirits and happy. On the other hand, when we have too much, greed and worry weigh down our hearts and bodies. Rather we should be content with what God provides, as we read in Psalm 145:16: "You open Your hand and satisfy the desire of every living thing," because we have all that we really need...

This miracle, then, has been written down for our good and to give us comfort, so that we might remember it and profess: I trust and am sure that my needs will be met, even if it might be in a meager way. For the Lord had but two fish and five loaves of barley bread, and with them He fed five thousand men, plus women and children, and everyone had enough. And what He did there He shows us year by year, day by day, with the trees, fields, meadows, lakes and streams, and all creatures, so that apples, pears, wheat, barley, grass, fish, and everything else needed to sustain life are produced. He does this so that we can believe that He will sustain us. It is His will that we will have enough to eat, be there but one fish multiplied to ten thousand, or one loaf to a hundred thousand. Therefore in poverty we must not be afraid but wait on His good will. *House Postil for Laetare Sunday*

Monday - Bernard of Clairvaux

There are four things to which we give allegiance in this life: the flesh, the world, the devil, and God. We serve the flesh by subjecting ourselves to the snares of gluttony and by yielding to the stings of lust. We serve the world by panting with swells of avarice and striving for the height of honor. We serve the devil by envying the successes of good people and by swelling up in a spirit of pride against God. We serve God by humbly devoting ourselves to works of piety, and by struggling against the powers on high through the power of the Spirit. Moreover, those four rulers have their particular gifts. The flesh bestows upon its recruits pleasure of brief duration; the world, a passing exaltation; the devil, endless captivity; God, boundless felicity. Only this last is of great value.

The Sentences, Second Series

Tuesday - Augustine of Hippo

What then is the doctrine of the Father, but the Father's Word? Therefore, Christ Himself is the doctrine of the Father, since He is the Word of the Father. But since the Word must belong to someone and not to no one, He called Himself "His doctrine," and also, "not His own," because He is the Word of the Father...

To speak briefly, beloved, it seems to me that when the Lord Jesus Christ said, "My doctrine is not Mine," He was saying, "I am not from Myself." For although we say and believe that the Son is equal to the Father, and that there is no diversity of nature and substance in them, that no interval of time has intervened between Him that begets and Him that is begotten, nevertheless we say these things, while keeping and guarding this, that the one is the Father, the other the Son. The one would not be a Father unless He had a Son, and the other would not be a Son unless He had a Father. Nonetheless, the Son is God from the Father, while the Father is God, but not from the Son... For the Lord Christ is called Light from Light. The Light then which is not from Light, and the equal Light which is from Light, are together one Light not two Lights...

"My doctrine," He says, "is not Mine, but His who sent Me." Let him who says he doesn't yet understand listen to counsel. Once this great and profound matter had been broached, the Lord Christ Himself certainly realized that not all would understand such a profound matter, and added some advice. Do you want to understand? Believe. For God has said by the prophet: "Unless you believe, you will not understand." What the Lord also added here is relevant too. "If anyone wants to do His will, he will know concerning the doctrine, whether it is from God or whether I speak on My own authority." What does this mean, "If anyone wants to do His will"? I have said, "if any one believes," and I gave this counsel: "If you have not understood," I said, "believe." For understanding is the reward of faith. So do not try to understand in order to believe, but believe that you may understand; because, "Unless you believe, you will not understand..." The Lord Himself openly says in another place: "This is the work of God, that you believe Him whom He sent."

Tractate 29 on the Gospel of John

Wednesday - John Chrysostom

The favors of God so far exceed human hope and expectation, that they are often not believed. For God has bestowed upon us such things as the mind of man never looked for, never thought of. It is for this reason that the Apostles spend so much discourse in securing a belief in the gifts that are granted us by God. For as men, upon receiving some great good, ask whether they are dreaming, as not believing it; so it is with respect to the gifts of God. What then was thought incredible? That those who were enemies, and sinners, neither justified by the law, nor by works, should immediately through faith alone be advanced to the highest favor.

Homily 4 on Timothy

Thursday - Gregory of Nyssa

Some one, perhaps, thinking of the decomposition of bodies, and judging the Deity by the measure of his own power, asserts that the idea of the resurrection is impossible... Let such a one, however, take as the first and greatest evidence of the truth concerning the resurrection the credibility of the herald who proclaims it. Now the faith of what is said derives its certainty from the result of the other predictions: for as the Divine Scripture delivers many and various statements, it is possible by examining how the rest of the statements stand in regard to truth and falsehood to survey also the doctrine concerning the resurrection in light of them.

...In what follows Christ ascends to higher wonders. For having set out on His way to the ruler of the synagogue's daughter, he voluntarily stopped in His way to make public the secret cure of the woman with an issue of blood, so that during this time death might overcome the sick girl. When, then, the soul had just been parted from the body, and those who were wailing over the sorrow were making a tumult with their mournful cries, He raises the damsel to life again, as if from sleep, by His word of command, leading human weakness... on to greater things.

Still in addition to these acts He exceeds them in wonder, and by an even more exalted act of power prepares for men the way of faith in the resurrection. The Scripture tells us of a city called Nain in Judea: a widow there had an only child - no longer a child in the sense of being among boys, but already passing from childhood to manhood as the narrative calls him "a young man." The story conveys a lot in a few words: the very recital of it is a real lamentation: the dead man's mother, it says, "was a widow." Do you see the weight of her misfortune, how the text briefly sets out the tragedy of her suffering? For what does the phrase mean? - that she had no more hope of bearing sons to cure the loss she had just sustained in him who had departed; for the woman was a widow: she had not in her power to look to another instead of to him who was gone; for he was her only child; and how great a grief is expressed here any one can easily see who is not an utter stranger to natural feeling. Him alone she had known in travail. Him alone she had nursed at her breast. He alone made her table cheerful. He alone was the cause of brightness in her home, in play, in work, in learning, in gaiety, at processions, at sports, at gatherings of youth. He alone was all that is sweet and precious in a mother's eyes. Now at the age of marriage, he was the stock of her race, the shoot of its succession, the staff of her old age. Moreover, even the added detail of his time of life is another lament: for he who speaks of him as "a young man" tells of the flower of his faded beauty, speaks of him as just covering his face with down, not yet with a full thick beard, but still bright with the beauty of his cheeks. So what do you think were his mother's sorrows over him? How would her heart be consumed as it were with a flame; how bitterly would she prolong her lament over him, embracing the corpse as it lay before her, lengthening out her mourning for him as far as possible, so as not to hasten the funeral of the dead, but to have her fill of sorrow! Nor does the narrative pass this by: for Jesus "when He saw her," it says, "had compassion;" "He came and touched the open coffin, and those who carried him stood still;" and He said to the dead, "Young man, I say to you, arise." "And He presented him to his mother" alive. Observe that it had not been a short time since the dead man had died, he was all but laid in the tomb! The miracle wrought by the Lord is greater, though the command is the same.

On the Making of Man

Friday - Ambrose of Milan

The Lord shows us in the Gospel... in what manner we shall rise again. "For He did not raise Lazarus alone, but the faith of all; and if you believe, as you read, your spirit also, which was dead, revives with Lazarus." For what does it mean, that the Lord went to the tomb and cried with a loud voice, "Lazarus, come forth," except that He would give us a visible proof and set before us an example of the future resurrection? Why did He cry with a loud voice, as though He were not willing to work in the Spirit or command in silence? He did this only that He might show what is written: "in a moment, in the twinkling of an eye, at the last trumpet... and the dead will be raised incorruptible." For the raising of the voice is like the peal of trumpets...

So, the dead man heard and came out from the tomb, bound hand and foot with grave cloths, and his face was bound with a napkin. Imagine, if you can, how he makes his way with closed eyes, directs his steps with bound feet, and moves with fastened limbs as though free. The bands remained on him but did not restrain him. His eyes were covered yet they saw. So the one rising again saw, was walking, was leaving the tomb. For at the power of the divine command, nature did not require its own functions, and brought to the extreme, no longer obeyed its own ways, but the divine will. The bands of death were burst before those of the grave. The power of moving was exercised before the means of moving were supplied.

If you marvel at this, consider who it was that gave the command, and cease to wonder: Jesus Christ, the Power of God, the Life, the Light, the Resurrection of the dead. The Power raised up him who was lying prostrate. The Life produced his steps. The Light drove away the darkness and restored his sight. The Resurrection renewed the gift of life.

Maybe it troubles you that the Jews took away the stone and loosened the grave cloths, and you may be worried about who will move the stone from your tomb. As though He Who could restore the Spirit could not remove the stone; or He Who made the bound to walk could not burst the bonds; or He Who had shed light upon the covered eyes could not uncover the face; or He Who could renew the course of nature could not cleave the stone! But, in order that they may believe their eyes who will not believe with their heart, they remove the stone, they see the corpse, they smell the stench, they loose the grave cloths. They can't deny that he is dead whom they see rising again. They see both the signs of death and the proofs of life. What if, while they are busied, they are converted by the very work they are doing? What if, while they hear, they believe their own ears? What if, while they see, they are taught by their own eyes? What if, while they loose the bonds, they free their own minds? What if, while Lazarus is being unbound, the people are set free, while they let Lazarus go, they themselves return to the Lord? For, finally, many who had come to Mary, seeing what had taken place, believed.
Book 2 on the Death of His Brother Satyrus

Saturday - John Chrysostom

He places Himself first; "I am One who bears witness of Myself." Here He shows His equality of honor, and that they gained nothing by saying that they knew God the Father, while they did not know Him. And He says that the cause of this ignorance was that they were not willing to know Him. Therefore He tells them that it is not possible to know the Father without knowing Him, that even so He might draw them to the knowledge of Him. For since they sought to get the knowledge of the Father apart from Him, He says, "You cannot know the Father without Me;" that they who blaspheme the Son, do not blaspheme the Son only, but Him that begot Him also.

This let us avoid, and glorify the Son. Had He not been of the same Nature, He would not have spoken this way. For had He merely taught, but been of different Substance, one might not have known Him, and yet have known the Father. And again, it could not have been that one who knew Him, would have altogether known the Father; for neither doth one who knows a man know an Angel. "Yes," reply some, "he that knows the creation, knows God." By no means. Many, or rather I should say, all men know the creation, (for they see it,) but they do not know God.

Let us then glorify the Son of God, not with this glory (of words) only, but that also which is by works. For the first without the last is nothing. "Behold," saith St. Paul, "Indeed you are called a Jew, and rest on the law, and make your boast in God - You, therefore, who teach another, do you not teach yourself? You who make your boast in the law, do you dishonor God through breaking the law?" Beware lest we also who make boast of the rightness of our faith dishonor God by not manifesting a life agreeable to the faith, causing Him to be blasphemed. For He would have the Christian to be the teacher of the world, its leaven, its salt, its light. And what is that light? It is a life which shines, and has in it no dark thing. Light is not useful to itself, nor leaven, nor salt, but shows its usefulness towards others, and so we are required to do good, not to ourselves only, but to others. For salt, if it does not salt, is not salt. Moreover another thing is evident, that if we be righteous, others shall certainly be so also; but as long as we are not righteous, we shall not be able to assist others.

Homily 52 on the Gospel of John

Collect

Grant, we pray You, Almighty God, that we, who for our evil deeds do worthily deserve to be punished, may be relieved by the comfort of Your grace; through Jesus Christ, Your Son, our Lord, who lives and reigns with You and the Holy Spirit, one God, now and forever.

Gelasian Sacramentary

AT LAUDS

Psalmody

Sunday: 3, C8, 51	Wednesday: 8, C11, 20	Friday: 146, C13, 5
Monday: 118a, C9, 118b	Thursday: 18a, C12, 18b	Saturday: 149, C14, 150
Tuesday: 1, C10, 2		

Lesson

Sunday: Numbers 21:4-35	Wednesday: Deuteronomy 4:1-31	Friday: Deuteronomy 18:15-22
Monday: Numbers 22:21-41	Thursday: Deuteronomy 6:1-25	Saturday: Deuteronomy 31:22-
Tuesday: Numbers 24:1-25		29; 34:1-12

Hymn and Verse *As during the week of Invocavit, p.333*

Antiphon to the Benedictus - *Qui sequitur me*   *Tone 3a*

He who fol - lows Me   shall not walk in   dark - ness,

But shall have the   light   of   life,   says   the   Lord.   *John 8:12*

✠ BLESSÉD is the Lord God / of Israel; *
For He has visited and redeemed / His people. etc.

Collect

Almighty God, our Heavenly Father, whose mercies are new to us every morning, and who, though we have in no way deserved Your goodness, abundantly provides for all our wants of body and soul: give us, we pray You, Your Holy Spirit, that we may heartily acknowledge Your merciful goodness toward us, give thanks for all Your benefits, and serve You in willing obedience, through Jesus Christ, Your Son, our Lord, who lives and reigns with You and the Holy Spirit, one God, now and forever.

Brandenburg-Nuremburg Kirchenordnung, 1533

AT TERCE, SEXT AND NONE

Chapter

Sunday: Galatians 4:21-31   Wednesday: Ezekiel 36:22-28   Friday: I Kings 17:17-24
Monday: I Kings 3:16-28   Thursday: II Kings 4:25-38   Saturday: Isaiah 49:8-15
Tuesday: Exodus 2:7-14

Responsories and Verses   *As during the week of Invocavit, p.334*

AT VESPERS

Psalmody

Sunday: 136b, 137, 138   Wednesday: 9, 10, 11   Friday: 17, 147a, 147b
Monday: 140, 141, 142   Thursday: 12, 13, 14, 16   Saturday: 19, 54, 77
Tuesday: 144, 145, 7

Lesson

Sunday: Numbers 22:1-20   Wednesday: Deuteronomy 5:1-33   Friday: Deuteronomy 28:58-
Monday: Numbers 23:1-30   Thursday: Deuteronomy 13:1-18   67; 30:15-20
Tuesday: Numbers 27:12-23   Saturday: Joshua 1:1-9

Hymn and Verse   *As during the week of Invocavit, p.336*

Antiphon to the Magnificat - *Solvite templum*   Tone 5

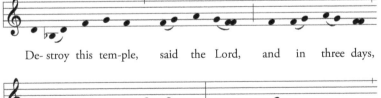

De- stroy this tem-ple, said the Lord, and in three days,

I will raise it up   He was speak - ing

359

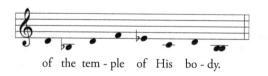

of the tem - ple of His bo - dy.

John 2:19, 21

✠ MY SOUL magnifies / the Lord, *
And my spirit has rejoiced in / God my Savior.. etc.

Collect

Lord God, heavenly Father, who by Your Son fed five thousand men in the desert with five loaves and two fishes: we implore You to abide graciously also with us in the fullness of Your blessing. Preserve us from avarice and the cares of this life, that we may seek first Your kingdom and Your righteousness, and in all things perceive Your fatherly goodness, through Jesus Christ, who lives and reigns with You and the Holy Spirit, one God, now and forever.   *Veit Dietrich*

JUDICA
The Fifth Week in Lent

AT MATINS

Invitatory *As during the week of Septuagesima, p.309*

Hymn - *Jesu, Deine Passion*

1. Je - sus I will pon - der now On Thy ho - ly Pas-sion;

With Thy Spi - rit me en - dow For such med - i - ta - tion.

Grant that I in love and faith May the im - age cher - ish

Of Thy suf-f'ring, pain, and death That I may not per - ish.

2. Make me see Thy great distress,
Anguish, and affliction,
Bonds and stripes and wretchedness
And Thy crucifixion;
Make me see how scourge and rod,
Spear and nails, did wound Thee,
How for man thou diedst, O God,
Who with thorns had crowned Thee.

3. Yet, O Lord, not thus alone
Make me see Thy Passion,
But its cause to me make known
And its termination.
Ah! I also and my sin
Wrought Thy deep affliction;
This indeed the cause hath been
Of Thy crucifixion.

4. Grant that I Thy Passion view
With repentant grieving
Nor Thee crucify anew
By unholy living.
How could I refuse to shun
Every sinful pleasure
Since for me God's only Son
Suffered without measure.

5. If my sins give me alarm
And my conscience grieve me,
Let Thy cross my fear disarm,
Peace of conscience give me.
Grant that I may trust in Thee
And Thy holy Passion.
If His Son so loveth me,
God must have compassion.

6. Grant that I may willingly
   Bear with Thee my crosses,
   Learning humbleness of Thee,
   Peace mid pain and losses.
   May I give Thee love for love!
   Hear me, O my Savior,
   That I may in heaven above
   Sing Thy praise forever.   *Sigismund von Birken, 1653*

Psalmody *The Gloria Patri is not said during Passiontide.*

Sunday: 21, 22, 23	Wednesday: 30, 31, 32	Friday: 37a, 37b, 38
Monday: 24, 25, 26	Thursday: 33, 34, 35	Saturday: 39, 40, 41
Tuesday: 27, 28, 29		

Lesson

Sunday: John 8:46-59
Monday: John 7:31-39
Tuesday: John 6:53-71
Wednesday: John 10:23-42
Thursday: Luke 7:36-50
Friday: John 11:46-57
Saturday: John 12:12-23

Homily

Sunday - Martin Luther

He does not say, before Abraham was, I was; but rather, before Abraham was, I am. This is an attribute that belongs to God alone, to be neither created nor made like Abraham or other creatures. It is God's nature to be neither created nor made, eternal in His essence, that is, to be I AM, without beginning or end. God was present at the beginning and His nature is to be eternal and without end.

This really made the Jews' guts churn, that Christ said He was God. They think it blasphemy against God and say, This is of the devil, that this individual, born a man, claims that he is God; and they become so enraged that they take up stones to kill Him.

For us, however, it is the highest consolation and proof to know that Christ is the true and eternal Son of God. This is the ground for Christ's Word being so mighty and for its being able to save everyone who believes it. Because He is the true and everlasting God, He is able also to give life and salvation to everyone that believes His Word and clings to it.

House Postil for Judica Sunday

Monday - Augustine of Hippo

If we thirst within, the Lord cries out to us to come and drink; and He says that when we have drunk, rivers of living water will flow from our belly. The belly of the inner man is the conscience of the heart. So once this water has been drunk, the cleansed conscience comes alive; and drinking deeply, it will have a fountain, or rather will be a fountain itself. What is the fountain? And what is the river that flows from the belly of the inner man? Kindness, by which a man considers the welfare of his neighbor. For if he imagines that what he drinks should satisfy only himself, there is no flow of living water from his belly; but if he hurries to think about the good of his neighbor, then, because it flows, he doesn't dry up. We will now see what those who believe in the Lord drink; because we are surely Christians, and if we believe, we drink. And every man should know in himself whether or not he drinks, and whether he lives by what he drinks; for the fountain does not forsake us if we do not forsake the fountain.

The evangelist explained… why the Lord had cried out, to what kind of drink He invites us, and what He poured out for those drinking, saying, "But this He spoke concerning the Spirit, whom those believing in Him would receive; for the Holy Spirit was not yet given, because Jesus was not yet glorified." What spirit is He talking about, if not the Holy Spirit?   *Tractate 32 on the Gospel of John*

Tuesday - Justin Martyr

When the one presiding has finished the prayers and the thanksgiving, everyone present consents and says "Amen," which in Hebrew means "So be it"… [T]hose whom we call deacons give each of those present a portion of the bread and wine mixed with water over which the thanks had been pronounced. And they carry a portion to those who are absent.

We call this food the Eucharist. No one is allowed to partake of it except those who believe that the things we teach are true, and who have also been washed with the washing that is for the forgiveness of sins, and unto regeneration, and who live as Christ has taught us. For we do not receive these things as common bread and common drink; but as Jesus Christ our Savior was made Flesh by the Word of God and took flesh and blood for our salvation, so also the food which is consecrated by the prayer of His words is the Flesh and Blood of Jesus who became Flesh and Blood, that our own flesh and blood may be transformed and nourished.   *The First Apology*

Wednesday - Anselm of Canterbury

God was not obliged to save mankind in this way, but human nature needed to make amends to God like this. God had no need to suffer so laboriously, but man needed to be reconciled thus. God did not need to humble Himself, but man needed this, so that he might be raised from the depths of hell. The Divine Nature did not need nor was it able to be humiliated and to labor. It was for the sake of human nature that all these things needed to be done, so that it might be restored to that for which it was made. But neither human nature nor anything that was not God could suffice for this. For man cannot be restored to that state in which he was first established unless he is made like the angels in whom there is no sin. And that could not be done unless he received forgiveness for all his sins, and that could not be unless he first made entire satisfaction.

To make such satisfaction it was necessary that the sinner, or someone for him, should give to God of his own something that he does not owe Him, and something more valuable than all that is not God. For to sin is to dishonor God, and this no man ought to do, even if it means that all that is other than God should perish. Immutable truth and plain reason then demand that whoever sins should give something better to God in return for the honor of which he has deprived Him, that is more than the supposed good for the sake of which he dishonored Him.

Human nature alone could not do this, nor could it be reconciled without the satisfaction of the debt, nor could the justice of God pass over the disorder of sin in His kingdom. The goodness of God came to help, and the Son of God assumed manhood in His own person, so that God and man should be one and the same person. He had what was above all beings that are other than God, and He took on Himself all the debt that sinners ought to pay, and this when He Himself owed nothing, so that He could pay the debt for the others who owed it and could not pay.

More precious is the life of that Man than all that is not God, and it is more than all the debt that sinners owe in order to make satisfaction for their sins. For His death was more than all that can be thought outside the person of God. It is clear that such a life is more good than all sins are bad. This Man, who was not obliged to die for a debt, because He was not a sinner, gave His life of His own accord to the Father, when He allowed His life to be taken from Him, for the sake of righteousness... Thus in Him human nature gave to God something it had of its own, willingly, and not because it was owed. So through Him human nature might be redeemed in the other men who had not that which would pay they debt that they owed.

Meditation on Human Redemption

Thursday - Ambrose of Milan

When the Lord asked him, "which of them will love him more," the Pharisee answered, "I suppose the one whom he forgave more." And the Lord replied: "You have rightly judged." The judgment of the Pharisee is praised, but his affection is blamed. He judges well concerning others, but doesn't believe that same judgment applies to himself.

So He said to Simon: "Do you see this woman? I entered your house; you gave Me no water for My feet, but she has washed My feet with her tears." We are all the one body of Christ, the head of which is God, and we are the members. Some are perhaps eyes, as the prophets; others teeth, as the apostles, who have passed the food of the Gospel preached into our breasts... And His hands are those who are seen to carry out good works. His belly are those who give nourishment to strengthen the poor. So also, some are His feet, and would that I might be worthy to be His heel! He pours water upon the feet of Christ, who forgives the very lowest their offences. And while delivering those of low estate, he is truly washing the feet of Christ.

And he who purifies his conscience from the defilement of sin pours water upon the feet of Christ, for Christ walks in the heart of each. Take heed, then, not to have your conscience polluted, and so begin to defile the feet of Christ. Take heed lest He find a thorn of wickedness in you, by which He may wound His heel as He walks in you. For this is why the Pharisee did not give water for the feet of Christ, because he did not have a soul pure from the filth of unbelief. For how could he who had not received the water of Christ cleanse his conscience? But the Church has both this water and tears. For faith which mourns over past sins is inclined to guard against fresh ones. Therefore, Simon the Pharisee, who had no water, also, of course, had no tears. For how could he have tears who had no penitence? He did not have tears because he didn't believe in Christ. For if he had had them he would have washed his eyes so that he might see Christ, whom, though he sat to eat with Him, he did not see. For had he seen Him, he would not have doubted His power.

The Pharisee had no hair, in that he couldn't recognize the Nazarite; the Church had hair, and she sought the Nazarite. Hair is considered superfluous to the body, but if it's anointed it provides a pleasant scent and an ornament for the head. But if hair is not anointed with oil it is a burden. Riches too are a burden if you don't know how to use them and don't sprinkle them with the scent of Christ. But if you nourish the poor, if you wash their wounds and wipe away their filth, you have indeed wiped the feet of Christ.

"You gave Me no kiss, but this woman has not ceased to kiss My feet since the time I came in." A kiss is the sign of love. How then can a Jew have a kiss, seeing he hasn't known peace and didn't receive peace from Christ when He said: "Peace I leave with you, My peace I give to you." The synagogue doesn't have a kiss, but the Church does, who waited for Him, who loved Him, who said: "Let Him kiss me with the kisses of His mouth." For by His kisses she wished to gradually quench the burning of that long desire, which had grown while waiting for the coming of the Lord, and to satisfy her thirst by this gift. And so the holy prophet says: "You open my lips, and my mouth shall show forth Your praise." He, then, who praises the Lord Jesus kisses Him; he who praises Him undoubtedly believes...

And the same Scripture teaches you... that he who receives the Spirit kisses Christ, where the holy prophet says: "I opened my mouth and drew in the Spirit." He, then, kisses Christ who confesses

Him: "For with the heart one believes unto righteousness, and with the mouth confession is made unto salvation." Again, he kisses the feet of Christ who, when reading the Gospel, recognizes the acts of the Lord Jesus and admires them with pious affection, and so piously he kisses, as it were, the footprints of the Lord Jesus as He walks. We kiss Christ, then, with the kiss of communion: "whoever reads, let him understand."

...But the Church does not stop kissing the feet of Christ, and therefore in the Song of Songs she desires not one but many kisses, and like Holy Mary she is intent upon all His sayings, and receives all His words when the Gospel or the Prophets are read, and "keeps all His sayings in her heart." So, then, the Church alone has kisses as a bride, for a kiss is as it were a pledge of nuptials and the privilege of marriage. How could the Jew, who does not believe in the Bridegroom, have kisses? How could the Jew have kisses, who does not know that the Bridegroom is come?

...The Church, then, both washes the feet of Christ and wipes them with her hair, and anoints them with oil, and pours ointment upon them, because not only does she care for the wounded and cherish the weary, but also sprinkles them with the sweet smell of grace; and pours forth the same grace not only on the rich and powerful, but also on men of lowly estate. She weighs all with equal balance, gathers all in the same bosom, and cherishes them in the same lap.

Christ died once, and was buried once, and nevertheless He wills that ointment should be poured on His feet daily. What, then, are those feet of Christ on which we pour ointment? The feet of Christ are those of whom He Himself says: "as you did it to one of the least of these, you did it to Me." These feet that woman in the Gospel refreshes, these feet she moistens with her tears; when sin is forgiven to the lowliest, guilt is washed away, and pardon granted. These feet he kisses, who loves even the lowest of the holy people. These feet he anoints with ointment, who imparts the kindness of his gentleness even to the weaker. In these the martyrs, in these the apostles, in these the Lord Jesus Himself declares that He is honored.

Letter 61, to His Sister

Friday - Augustine of Hippo

"Then the chief priests and the Pharisees gathered a council and said, 'What shall we do?'" But they did not say, Let us believe. For these abandoned men were more occupied in considering what evil they could do to bring about His ruin, than in consulting for their own preservation. And yet they were afraid, and took counsel of a sort together. They said, "What shall we do? For this Man works many signs. If we let Him alone like this, everyone will believe in Him, and the Romans will come and take away both our place and nation." They were afraid of losing their temporal possessions, and did not think of eternal life. And so they lost both. For the Romans, after our Lord's passion and entrance into glory, took from them both their place and nation, when they took the one by storm and exiled the other. And now they are pursued by the words, "But the sons of the kingdom will be cast out into outer darkness." But this was what they feared, that if all believed on Christ there would be no one left to defend the city of God and the temple against the Romans; just because they felt that Christ's teaching was directed against the temple itself and against the laws of their fathers.

"And one of them, Caiaphas, being high priest that year, said to them, 'You know nothing at all, nor do you consider that it is expedient for us that one man should die for the people, and not that the whole nation should perish.' Now this he did not say on his own authority; but being high priest that year he prophesied." We are taught here that the Spirit of prophecy used the agency even of wicked men to foretell the future; which, however, the evangelist attributes to the divine sacramental fact that he was pontiff, which is to say, the high priest.

Tractate 49 on John

Saturday - Bernard of Clairvaux

Watch with your mind, brethren, that the mysteries of this season may not pass away without profit. The blessing is plentiful. Provide clean receptacles; display devout souls, watchful senses, sober emotions, and chaste consciences for such great gifts of grace. In good truth, not only does your confession of faith admonish you to take care in this matter, but it is the practice of the universal Church, whose sons you are. For all Christians cultivate holiness in observance of these seven sacred days, display modesty, pursue humility, put on gravity, either according to or beyond what is usual, that they may in some way seem to suffer with Christ's suffering. For who is so impious as not to be sorrowful? Who so proud, as not to be humbled? Who so angry, as not to forgive? Who so luxurious, as not to abstain? Who so sensual, as not to practice self-restraint? Who so wicked, as not to repent during these days? And rightly so.

For the passion of the Lord is at hand, even now moving the earth, rending the rocks, and opening the tombs. Near also is His resurrection, in which you will celebrate a festival to the Most High, entering with enthusiasm and eagerness into the most glorious deeds which He has accomplished. Nothing better could be done in the world than that which was done by the Lord on these days. Nothing more useful or better could be recommended to the world, than that it should by perpetual ordinance celebrate year by year the memorial of these things with longing souls, and show forth the memory of His abundant sweetness...

Marvelous is Your passion, O Lord Jesus, which repelled the passions of all of us; made propitiation for our iniquities, and is found effectual for every one of our plagues. For what is there of death that is not destroyed by Your death?

Sermon 24, On the Passion of Our Lord

Collect

We pray You, Almighty God, mercifully look on Your people, that by Your great goodness they may be governed and preserved evermore both in body and soul; through Jesus Christ, Your Son, our Lord, who lives and reigns with You and the Holy Spirit, one God, now and forever.

Gelasian Sacramentary

AT LAUDS

Psalmody   *The Gloria Patri is not said during Passiontide.*

Sunday: 67, C1, 5	Wednesday: 64, C4, 65	Friday: 76, C5, 92
Monday: 63, C2, 36	Thursday: 88, C6, 90	Saturday: 143, C7, 148
Tuesday: 43, C3, 57		

Lesson

Sunday: Joshua 2:1-24	Wednesday: Judges 13:1-25	Friday: Ruth 1:1-22
Monday: Joshua 5:13-6:27	Thursday: Judges 15:1-20	Saturday: Jeremiah 1:1-19
Tuesday: Judges 2:1-23		

Hymn - *Luxtra sex qui jam peregit*

1. Now the thir - ty years ac-comp-lished Which on earth He willed
2. There the nails and spear He suf - fers, Vin - e - gar and gall,
3. Faith-ful Cross! a - bove all oth - er, One and on - ly no-

to see, Born for this, He meets His Pas - sion, Gives Him-
and reed; From His sac - red Bo - dy pierc - ed Blood and
ble Tree! None in fo - liage, none in blos - som, None in

self an Off - 'ring free; On the cross the Lamb is
Wa - ter both pro - ceed; Pre - cious flood, which all cre-
fruit thy peer may be; Sweet - est wood and sweet - est

lift - ed, There the Sac - ri - fice to be.
a - tion From the stain of sin hath freed.
i - ron! Sweet- est Weight is hung on thee!

4. Lofty tree, bend down thy branches,
To embrace thy sacred load;
Oh, relax the native tension
Of that all too rigid wood;
Gently, gently bear the members
Of thy dying King and God.

5. Tree, which solely wast found worthy
This world's Victim to sustain.
Harbor from the raging tempest!
Ark, that saved the world again!
Tree, with sacred blood anointed
Of the Lamb for sinners slain.

6. Praise and honor to the Father,
Praise and honor to the Son,
Praise and honor to the Spirit,
Ever Three and ever One,
One in might and One in glory,
While eternal ages run. Amen.

Venantius Fortunatus, 570

Verse

℣: Deliver me, O my God, out of the hand of the wick- / ed.
℟: Out of the hand of the unrighteous and cruel / man.

Psalm 71:4

Antiphon to the Benedictus - *Oves meae*

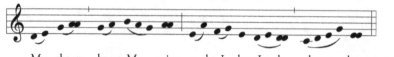

My sheep hear My voice; and I, the Lord, know them. *John 10:27*

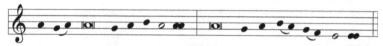

✠ BLESSÉD is the Lord God / of Israel; *
For He has visited and / redeemed His people. etc.

Collect

Give me, O Lord, a steadfast heart, which no unworthy affection may drag downwards; give me an unconquered heart, which no tribulation can wear out; give me an upright heart, which no unworthy purpose may tempt aside. Bestow upon me also, O Lord my God, understanding to know You, diligence to seek You, wisdom to find You, and a faithfulness that may finally embrace You, for You live and reign, one God, now and forever. *Thomas Aquinas*

AT TERCE, SEXT AND NONE

Chapter

Sunday: Hebrews 9:11-15 Wednesday: Leviticus 19:11-18 Friday: Jeremiah 17:13-18
Monday: Jonah 3:1-10 Thursday: Leviticus 19:11-18 Saturday: Zechariah 9:9-10
Tuesday: Jeremiah 18:18-23

Responsory and Verse at Terce

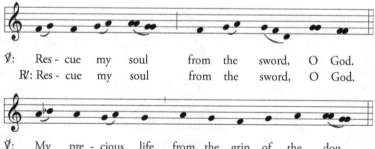

℣: Res - cue my soul from the sword, O God.
℟: Res - cue my soul from the sword, O God.

℣: My pre - cious life from the grip of the dog.
℟: Rescue my soul... *Psalm 22:20*

℣: Save me from the lion's mouth, O / Lord,
℟: And from the horns of the wild / bulls. *Psalm 22:21*

Responsory and Verse at Sext

℣: Save me, O Lord, from the li - on's mouth.
℟: Save me, O Lord, from the li - on's mouth.

℣: My wretch-ed life from the horns of the wild bulls.
℟: Save me...   *Psalm 22:21*

℣: Do not gather my soul with sinners, O / God.
℟: Nor my life with bloodthirsty / men.   *Psalm 26:9*

Responsory and Verse at None

℣: Do not ga - ther my soul with sin - ners, O God.
℟: Do not ga - ther my soul with sin - ners, O God.

℣: Nor my life with blood-thirs-ty men.
℟: Do not gather...   *Psalm 26:9*

℣: Deliver me, O Lord, from evil / men. *
℟: Preserve me from violent / men.   *Psalm 140:1*

AT VESPERS

Psalmody *The Gloria Patri is not said during Passiontide.*

Sunday: 110, 111, 112, 113   Wednesday: 123, 124, 125   Friday: 129, 130, 131, 132
Monday: 114, 115, 116, 117   Thursday: 126, 127, 128   Saturday: 133, 135, 136a
Tuesday: 120, 121, 122

Lesson

Sunday: Joshua 3:14-4:24   Wednesday: Judges 14:1-20   Friday: Ruth 4:1-22
Monday: Joshua 24:1-33   Thursday: Judges 16:1-31   Saturday: Jeremiah 7:1-34
Tuesday: Judges 7:1-25

Hymn - *Vexilla Regis Prodeunt*

1. The roy - al   ban - ners for - ward go;   The cross shines forth
2. Where deep for   us   the spear was   dyed,   Life's tor-rent rush-
3. Ful- filled is   all   that Da - vid told   In true pro- phet-

in   mys - tic   glow   Where He in   flesh, our flesh   was made,
ing from His   side,   To wash us   in   that pre - cious flood
ic   song of   old;   A-midst the na - tions, God,   saith he,

Our   sen -   tence bore, our   ran- som   paid;
Where min -   gled wa - ter flowed and   blood.
Hath   reigned   and   tri - umphed from the Tree.

4. O Tree of beauty, Tree of light,
   O Tree with royal purple dight,
   Elect, on whose triumphal breast
   Those holy limbs should find their rest;

6. O Cross, our one reliance, hail!
   So may thy power with us avail
   To give new virtue to the saint
   And pardon to the penitent.

5. On whose dear arms, so widely flung,
   The weight of this world's ransom hung
   The price of humankind to pay
   And spoil the spoiler of his prey

7. To Thee, eternal Three in One,
   Let homage meet by all be done
   Whom by the cross Thou dost restore,
   Preserve, and govern evermore. Amen.

Venantius Honorius Fortunatus, 569

Verse

℣: Deliver me, O my God, out of the hand of the wick- / ed. *
℟: Out of the hand of the unrighteous and cruel / man.

Psalm 71:4

Antiphon to the Magnificat - *Si quis sitit*   Tone 4E

If an - y - one thirsts, let him come to Me and drink;   and out of

His heart   will flow liv - ing wa-ters.

John 7:37-38

✠ MY SOUL / magnifies the Lord, *
And my spirit has rejoiced / in God my Savior.   etc.

Collect

Almighty and most Merciful God, who has appointed us to endure sufferings and death with our Lord Jesus Christ, before we enter with Him into eternal glory: grant us grace at all times to subject ourselves to Your holy will, and to continue steadfast in the true faith unto the end of our lives, and at all times to find peace and joy in the blessèd hope of the resurrection of the dead, and of the glory of the world to come, through Jesus Christ, Your Son, our Lord, who lives and reigns with You and the Holy Spirit, one God, now and forever.

Saxe-Coburg Kirchenordnung, 1626

PALMARUM
The Sixth Week in Lent

AT MATINS

Invitatory *As during the week of Septuagesima, p.309*

Hymn - *Gloria, laus et honor*

Refrain

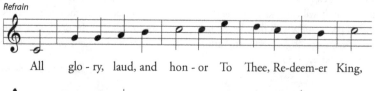

All glo - ry, laud, and hon - or To Thee, Re-deem-er King,

To whom the lips of chil-dren Made sweet ho-san- nas ring.

1. Thou art the King of Is - rael, Thou Da-vid's roy - al Son,

Refrain

Who in the Lord's name com-est, The King and Bless-ed One.

2. The company of angels
Are praising Thee on high,
And mortal men and all things
Created make reply.

3. The people of the Hebrews
With palms before Thee went;
Our prayer and praise and anthems
Before Thee we present.

4. To Thee, before Thy Passion,
They sang their hymns of praise;
To Thee, now high exalted,
Our melody we raise.

5. Thou didst accept their praises;
Accept the prayers we bring,
Who in all good delightest,
Thou good and gracious King.

Theodulph of Orleans, c. 820

Psalmody *The Gloria Patri is not said during Passiontide.*

Sunday: 42, 44, 45   Tuesday: 49, 50, 52
Monday: 46, 47, 48   Wednesday: 53, 55, 56

Lesson

Sunday: Matthew 21:1-9; The Passion According to St. Matthew (26:36-27:60) if not read previously at Mass
Monday: John 12:1-23
Tuesday: The Passion According to St. Mark (14:32-15:46)
Wednesday: The Passion According to St. Luke (22:1-23:56)

Homily

Sunday - Andrew of Crete

Let us go together to meet Christ on the Mount of Olives. Today He returns from Bethany and proceeds of His own free will toward His holy and blessed passion, to consummate the mystery of our salvation. He who came down from heaven to raise us from the depths of sin, to raise us with Himself, we are told in Scripture: "above every sovereignty, authority and power, and every other name that can be named," now comes of His own free will to make His journey to Jerusalem. He comes without pomp or ostentation. As the psalmist says: "He will not dispute or raise His voice to make it heard in the streets." He will be meek and humble, and He will make His entry in simplicity.

Let us run to accompany Him as He hastens toward His passion, and imitate those who met Him then, not by covering His path with garments, olive branches or palms, but by doing all we can to prostrate ourselves before Him by being humble and by trying to live as He would wish. Then we shall be able to receive the Word at His coming, and God, whom no limits can contain, will be within us.

In His humility Christ entered the dark regions of our fallen world and He is glad that He became so humble for our sake, glad that He came and lived among us and shared in our nature in order to raise us up again to Himself. And even though we are told that He has now ascended above the highest heavens - the proof surely of His power and godhead - His love for us will never rest until He has raised our earthbound nature from glory to glory, and made it one with His own in heaven.

So let us spread before His feet, not garments or soulless olive branches, which delight the eye for a few hours and then wither, but ourselves, clothed in His grace, or rather, clothed completely in Him. We who have been baptized into Christ must ourselves be the garments that we spread before Him. Now that the crimson stains of our sins have been washed away in the saving waters of Baptism and we have become white as pure wool, let us present the conqueror of death, not with mere branches of palms but with the real rewards of His victory. Let our souls take the place of the welcoming branches as we join today in the children's holy song: "Blessed is He who comes in the name of the Lord. Blessed is the King of Israel." *Sermon 9 for Palmarum*

Monday - Leo I of Rome

That He might release mankind from the chains of baneful deceit, he concealed the power of His majesty from the furious devil and put forward instead the weakness of our lowliness. Had this proud and cruel enemy known the plan of God's mercy, he would have strived to calm the spirits of the Jews with gentleness rather than inflame them with unjust hatred - in order to keep from losing the enslavement of his captives by persecuting the liberty of the One who owes him nothing.

And so he was tricked by his own wickedness. He inflicted torment on the Son of God, torment that was changed into a medicine for all the sons of men. He poured out that innocent blood which became the price and the cup for reconciling the world. Our Lord undertook what He had freely chosen. He suffered the impious hands of those who raged against Him. These, intent on their own crime, were yet serving the Redeemer's purpose.

So great was the tenderness of His love for His murderers, that from the cross He begged His Father not to avenge Him, but to pardon them, crying out: "Father, forgive them, for they know not what they do." Such was the power of His prayer that the preaching of Peter the apostle turned to repentance the hearts of many from among those who had cried, "His blood be on us and on our children." On a single day about three thousand Jews were baptized, and all were made one heart and one soul; ready to give their lives for Him for whose crucifixion they had clamored.

Sermon 62

Tuesday - Alexander of Alexandria

But now, after all this bondage to death and corruption of mankind, God has visited His creature which He formed after His own image and likeness; and this He has done that it might not forever be the sport of death. Therefore God sent down from heaven His incorporeal Son to take flesh upon Him in the Virgin's womb. And He was made man, just like you; to save lost man, and collect all His scattered members. For Christ, when He joined the manhood to His person, united that which, by the separation of the body, death had dispersed. Christ suffered that we should live forever.

For why else should Christ have died? Had He committed anything worthy of death? Why did He who was vested with glory clothe Himself in flesh? And since He was God, why did He become man? And since He reigned in heaven, why did He come down to earth, and become incarnate in the Virgin's womb? What necessity, I ask, impelled God to come down to earth, to assume flesh, to be wrapped in swaddling clothes in a manger-cradle, to be nourished with the milk from the breast, to receive baptism from a servant, to be lifted up upon the cross, to be interred in an earthly sepulchre, to rise again the third day from the dead?

What necessity, I say, impelled Him to this? It is sufficiently proven that He suffered shame for man's sake, to set him free from death... In truth He endured for our sakes sorrow, shame, torment, even death itself and burial...

Now, since You have come to earth, and have sought for the members of your fashioning, undertake for man who is Your own, receive that which is committed to You, recover Your image, Your Adam. Then the Lord, the third day after His death, rose again, thus bringing man to a knowledge of the Trinity. Then all the nations of the human race were saved by Christ. One submitted to judgment, and many thousands were absolved.

Epistle 5 on the Arian Heresy: On the Soul and Body and the Passion of the Lord

Wednesday - Melito of Sardis

The earth shook, and its foundations trembled; the sun fled away, and the elements turned back, and the day was changed into night; for they could not endure the sight of their Lord hanging on a tree. The whole creation was amazed, marveling and saying, "What new mystery, then, is this? The Judge is judged, and holds His peace; the Invisible One is seen, and is not ashamed; the Incomprehensible is laid hold upon, and is not indignant; the One who is without limits is circumscribed, and does not resist; the Impassible suffers and does not avenge; the Immortal dies, and answers not a word; the Celestial is laid in the grave, and endures it! What new mystery is this?" The whole creation, I say, was astonished; but when our Lord arose from the place of the dead, and trampled death under foot, and bound the strong one, and set man free, then the whole creation saw clearly that for man's sake the Judge was condemned, and the Invisible was seen, and the Illimitable was circumscribed, and the Impassible suffered, and the Immortal died, and the Celestial was laid in the grave. For our Lord, when He was born man, was condemned in order that He might show mercy, was bound in order that He might loose, was seized in order that He might release, suffered in order that he might send compassion, died in order that He might give life, was laid in the grave that He might raise from the dead.

On Soul and Body

Collects

Sunday

Almighty and Everlasting God, who has sent Your Son, our Savior Jesus Christ, to take on Him our flesh and to suffer death on the cross that all humanity should follow the example of His great humility, mercifully grant that we may both follow the example of His patience and also be made partakers of His resurrection; through the same Jesus Christ, Your Son, our Lord, who lives and reigns with You and the Holy Spirit, one God, now and forever. *Gelasian Sacramentary*

Monday

Grant, we pray you, Almighty God, that we, who amid so many adversities fail through our own infirmities, may be restored through the Passion and intercession of Your only-begotten Son, who lives and reigns with You and the Holy Spirit, one God, now and forever. *Gelasian Sacramentary*

Tuesday

Almighty and Everlasting God, grant us grace so to pass through this holy time of our Lord's Passion that we may obtain the pardon of our sins, through the same Jesus Christ, Your Son, our Lord, who lives and reigns with You and the Holy Spirit, one God, now and forever. *Gelasian Sacramentary*

Wednesday

Grant, we pray You, Almighty God, that we, who for our evil deeds are continually afflicted, may mercifully be relieved by the Passion of Your only-begotten Son, who lives and reigns with You and the Holy Spirit, one God, now and forever. *Gelasian Sacramentary*

AT LAUDS

Psalmody *The Gloria Patri is not said during Passiontide.*

Sunday: 3, C8, 51	Tuesday: 1, C10, 2
Monday: 118a, C9, 118b	Wednesday: 8, C11, 20

Lesson

Sunday: Jeremiah 11:1-23	Tuesday: Jeremiah 30:18-31:34
Monday: Jeremiah 23:1-32	Wednesday: Jeremiah 37:1-21

Hymn and Verse *As during the week of Judica, p. 365*

Antiphon to the Benedictus - *Benedictus qui venit* — Tone 4E

Bless - ed is He who comes in the name of the Lord!

Ho - san - na in the high-est! *Matthew 21:9*

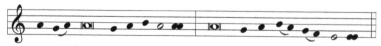

✠ BLESSÉD is the Lord God / of Israel; *
For He has visited and / redeemed His people. etc.

Collect

For all my sins and failures, I offer to You, most holy Father, the most perfect obedience of Your Son, who loved all men with perfect love. In His mouth was found no deceit. He did not deviate from Your law in His words or deeds. There was no corruption in His nature. To this mercy seat I flee in true faith, and through faith I draw from His wounds everything that is necessary for righteousness and salvation. Have mercy upon me, my God and Father, for You live and reign with Your Son and the Holy Spirit, one God, now and forever.   *Johann Gerhard*

AT TERCE, SEXT AND NONE

Chapter

Sunday: Philippians 2:5-11   Tuesday: Jeremiah 11:18-26
Monday: Isaiah 50:5-10   Wednesday: Isaiah 62:11-63:7

Responsories and Verses   *As during the week of Judica, p.366*

AT VESPERS

Psalmody   *The Gloria Patri is not said during Passiontide.*

Sunday: 136b, 137, 138   Tuesday: 144, 145, 7
Monday: 140, 141, 142   Wednesday: 9, 10, 11

Lesson

Sunday: Jeremiah 20:7-18   Tuesday: Jeremiah 33:10-26
Monday: Jeremiah 27:1-22   Wednesday: Jeremiah 38:1-23

Hymn and Verse   *As during the week of Judica, p.368*

Antiphon to the Magnificat - *Potestatem habeo*   *Tone 4E*

I have pow - er   to   lay down my life,   and   to

take   it   a - gain.

John 10:18

✠ MY SOUL / magnifies the Lord, *
And my spirit has rejoiced / in God my Savior.   etc.

Collect

Almighty and everlasting God, who has caused Your beloved Son to take our nature upon Himself, that He might give all mankind the example of humility and suffer death upon the cross for our sins: Mercifully grant us a believing knowledge of this, and, that following the example of His patience, we may be made partakers of the benefits of His sacred passion and death, through the same, Your beloved Son, Jesus Christ, our Lord, who lives and reigns with You and the Holy Spirit, one God, now and forever.   *Veit Dietrich*

HOLY TRIDUUM

Maundy Thursday, Good Friday and Holy Saturday

AT MATINS

Matins begins directly with the Psalmody.

Psalmody   *The Gloria Patri is not said during the Triduum.*

Maundy Thursday: Psalm 23, 140, 41
Good Friday: Psalm 2, 22, 27
Holy Saturday: Psalm 4, 15, 16

Lesson

Maundy Thursday: Lamentations 1:1-2:22; John 13:1-15
Good Friday: Lamentations 3:1-66; The Passion according to St. John (18:1-19:42)
Holy Saturday: Lamentations 4:1-5:22; Matthew 28:1-7

Homily

Maundy Thursday - Augustine of Hippo

Brethren, we have learned humility from the Highest; let us humbly do to one another what He, the Highest, did in His humility. Great is the commendation we have here of humility; and the brethren do this to one another in turn, even in the visible act itself, when they treat one another with hospitality; for the practice of such humility is usually revealed, and finds expression in the very deed that makes it discernible. And hence the apostle, when he would commend the well-deserving widow, says, "If she is hospitable, if she has washed the saints' feet." And wherever this is not the practice among the saints, what they do not do with the hand, they do in heart... But it is far better, and beyond all dispute more in accord with the truth, that it be should also be done with the hands; nor should the Christian think it beneath him to do what was done by Christ. For when the body is bent at a brother's feet, the feeling of such humility is either awakened in the heart itself, or is strengthened if already present.   *Tractate 58 on John*

Good Friday - Cyril of Jerusalem

Every deed of Christ is a cause of glory to the catholic church, but the greatest of all her glory is the cross... Wonder not that the whole world was ransomed; for it was no mere man, but the only begotten Son of God who died on its behalf. Moreover one man's sin, even Adam's, had power to bring death to the world; but if by the trespass of the one death reigned over the world, how shall not life much more reign by the righteousness of the One? And if because of the tree of food they were at that time cast out of paradise, shall not believers now enter into paradise more easily because of the Tree of Jesus? If the first man formed out of the earth brought in universal death, shall not He who formed him out of the earth bring in eternal life, being Himself the Life? ...

Let us not be ashamed of the cross of Christ, but rather glory in it... For it was not a mere man who died for us, as I said before, but the Son of God, God made man. Further; if the lamb under Moses drove the destroyer far away, did not much more the Lamb of God who takes away the sin of the world, deliver us from our sins? The blood of a silly sheep gave salvation; and shall not the blood of the Only-begotten much more save?   *Thirteenth Catechetical Lecture*

Holy Saturday - Amphilochius of Iconium

Death has seized our Lord Jesus Christ; but it shall not keep its hold on Life. It swallowed Him; it swallowed Him not knowing Him; but with Him, it will give up many. Of His own will He is now held. Tomorrow He will rise again, and hell shall be emptied. Yesterday on the cross, He darkened the sun's light, and behold in full day it was as night; today death has lost its dominion; suffering a kind of death itself. Yesterday the earth mourned, contemplating the evil hate of the Jews, and sadly clothed itself in a garment of darkness. Today, "the people who walked in darkness have seen a great light…"

O new and unheard of happening! He is stretched out upon a cross who by His Word "stretched out the heavens." He is held fast in bonds who has "set the sand a bound for the sea." He is given gall to drink who has given us wells of honey. He is crowned with thorns who has crowned the earth with flowers. With a reed they struck His head who of old struck Egypt with ten plagues, and submerged the head of Pharaoh in the waves. That countenance was spat upon at which the Cherubim dare not gaze. Yet, while suffering these things He prayed for His tormentors, saying: "Father forgive them for they know not what they do."

He overcame evil by goodness. Christ undertook the defense of those who put Him to death; eager to gather them into His net; annulling the charge, and pleading their ignorance. Mad the sport of their drunken frenzy, He submitted without bitterness. He suffered their drunkenness, and in His love for mankind called them to repentance. What more could He do?

Profiting nothing from that goodness, they enclose Him in a tomb whom creation cannot contain. They seal the tomb, safe-guarding our deliverance; and fearing He would rise again, they station soldiers to watch the sepulchre. Who has ever seen the dead placed under watch? Or rather, who has ever seen a dead body treated as an enemy? Who has ever seen one struck by death causing fear to those who have slain him? Who fears his enemy, once he has killed him? And who will not forget his enmity when sated by the death of his adversary?

Why do you still fear him, you Jews, Him whom you have done away with? Why do you dread Him whom you have slain? Why do you still dread Him who had gone forth from among the living? Why do you fear the dead? Why do you still fight with One whom you have crucified? His slaughter has made you safe; rest secure. If it is a mere man who has died, he will not rise again. If it is a mere man who has died, then there is no truth in those words of His: "Destroy this temple, and in three days I will raise it up."

If He was mere man, then death will keep Him. If He was a mere man, what need to seal His tomb; is it not useless? Wait till the third day, and see the disproof of His madness. Stop laboring in vain, and you will see what comes to pass. Stop raging against the truth. Don't try to wage war against God, inflicting wounds only on yourself. Quit offering insults to the Sun of justice; thinking you can put out its light. Cease, I say, and do not try to seal up the fountain of life.

Do not begin to make difficulties for yourself. Do not speak of guards. Have no traffic with corruption and the bribing of those who keep watch. Do not attempt what is foolish; nor spend what you have in impiety; nor imagine that you will defeat God. Do not give money to the soldiers, to say this and not that. Do not set a crowd to watch the tomb. Don't put your trust in armor. The resurrection will not be stopped by force of arms; nor impeded by seals; nor put down by soldiers; nor concealed by bribes. Rather it shall be believed in.

Did you not see Lazarus a little while ago throw off death as though it were a sleep? Have you not seen him come forth, clothed in his grave clothes, at the words: "Come forth"? Have you not seen the dead obedient to His voice when He commanded him come; and the binding sheet did not prevent him? Haven't you seen how His voice restored a man already dissolving in death? He who did that can also do this. He who raised His own servant, much more shall He Himself be raised up. He who gave life again to a body already corrupting shall not leave Himself in death.

Oration 5: For Holy Saturday

Collects

Maundy Thursday

O Lord God, who has left to us in a wonderful Sacrament a memorial of Your Passion, grant, we pray You, that we may so use this Sacrament of Your body and blood that the fruits of Your redemption may continually be revealed in us; You, who lives and reigns with the Father and the Holy Spirit, one God, now and forever.

Thomas Aquinas

Good Friday

Almighty and Everlasting God, who has willed that Your Son should bear for us the pains of the cross, that You might remove from us the power of the adversary; help us so to remember and give thanks for our Lords' passion that we may obtain remission of sin and redemption from everlasting death; *Silently:* through the same Jesus Christ, Your Son, our Lord, who lives and reigns with You and the Holy Spirit, one God, now and forever..

Gelasian Sacramentary

Holy Saturday

Grant, we pray You, Almighty God, that we who await the resurrection of Your Son with reverent expectation, may share in the glory of His resurrection; *Silently:* through the same Jesus Christ, Your Son, our Lord, who lives and reigns with You and the Holy Spirit, one God, now and forever.

Gelasian Sacramentary

AT LAUDS

Lauds begins directly with the Psalmody

Psalmody   *The Gloria Patri is not said during the Triduum.*

Maundy Thursday: Psalm 75, C12, Psalm 116
Good Friday: Psalm 38, C6, Psalm 40
Holy Saturday: Psalm 24, C10, Psalm 30

The lesson, hymn and verse are omitted.

Antiphon to the Benedictus

Maundy Thursday - *Traditor autem*   Tone 1g

His be - tray - er   had giv- en them a   sign, say- ing   "Whom-

ev - er   I   kiss,   He is the one.   Seize   Him.

Matthew 26:48

✠ BLESSÉD is the Lord / God of Israel; *
For He has visited and re- / deemed His people.   etc.

380

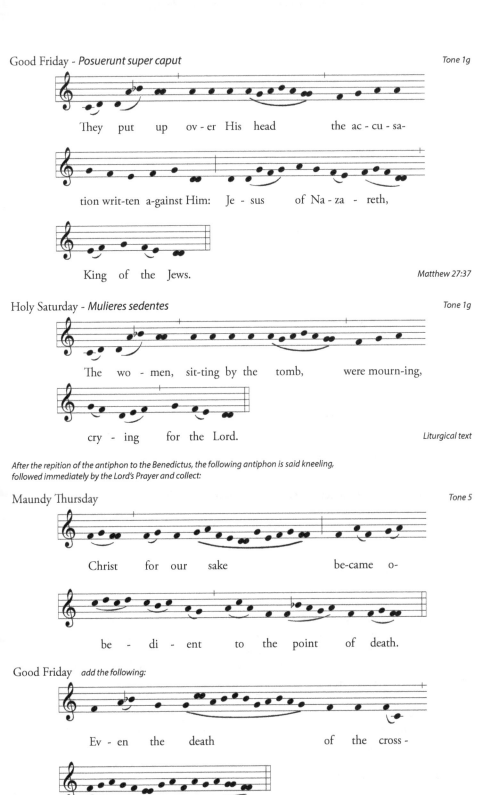

Good Friday - *Posuerunt super caput* · Tone 1g

They put up ov - er His head the ac - cu - sa-

tion writ-ten a-gainst Him: Je - sus of Na - za - reth,

King of the Jews. · *Matthew 27:37*

Holy Saturday - *Mulieres sedentes* · Tone 1g

The wo - men, sit-ting by the tomb, were mourn-ing,

cry - ing for the Lord. · *Liturgical text*

After the repition of the antiphon to the Benedictus, the following antiphon is said kneeling, followed immediately by the Lord's Prayer and collect:

Maundy Thursday · Tone 5

Christ for our sake be-came o-

be - di - ent to the point of death.

Good Friday *add the following:*

Ev - en the death of the cross -

381

Holy Saturday *add the following:*

There-fore God   has high-ly   ex- alt - ed   Him

and

giv - en   Him   the   name

which   is   a - bove   ev' - ry   name -

Philippians 2:8-9

Collect *The collect is recited without the introductory words "Let us pray." The termination is said silently.*

Maundy Thursday

O Lord Jesus Christ, we thank You, that of Your infinite mercy You have instituted this Your sacrament, in which we eat Your body and drink Your blood: Grant us, we beseech You, by Your Holy Spirit, that we may not receive this gift unworthily, but that we may confess our sins, remember Your agony and death, believe the forgiveness of sin, and day by day grow in faith and love, until we obtain eternal salvation through You,

Silently: who lives and reigns with the Father and the Holy Spirit, one true God, now and forever.

Veit Dietrich

Good Friday

Merciful and Everlasting God, who has not spared Your only Son, but delivered Him up for us all, that He might bear our sins upon the cross; grant that our hearts may be so fixed with steadfast faith in Him that we may not fear the power of any adversaries;

Silently: through the same Jesus Christ, Your Son, our Lord, who lives and reigns with You and the Holy Spirit, one God, now and forever.

Saxon Kirchenordnung, 1539

Holy Saturday

O Almighty God, grant that we, who in devout expectation look forward to the resurrection of Your Son, may enjoy the glory of that resurrection;

Silently: through the same Jesus Christ, Your Son, our Lord, who lives and reigns with You and the Holy Spirit, one God, now and forever.

Gelasian Sacramentary

After the collect, all rise and depart in silence.

AT TERCE, SEXT AND NONE

The little hours of Terce, Sext, and None, are said without candles or singing, and begin directly with the recitation of the Psalm which is said without an antiphon or the Gloria Patri. When the Psalmody is concluded, the following antiphon is said kneeling, followed immediately by the Lord's Prayer and collect:

Maundy Thursday

Christ for our sake became obedient to death.

Good Friday *add the following:*

Even to death on a cross.

Holy Saturday *add the following:*

Therefore God has highly exalted Him and given Him the name which is above every name.

Philippians 2:8-9

The collect is said without the introductory words "Let us pray." The termination is said silently. After the collect, all rise and depart in silence.

AT VESPERS

On Maundy Thursday, Vespers are not said by those attending the evening Divine Service of the Lord's Supper. On Good Friday, Vespers are not said by those attending the solemn afternoon liturgy. When Vespers are said, they are begun directly with the antiphon to the Psalm, and are said without lighted candles or singing.

Psalmody *The Gloria Patri is not said during the Triduum.*

Maundy Thursday: Psalm 55, 69 *(a & b as one Psalm),* 86
Good Friday: Psalm 64, 88, 94
Holy Saturday: Psalm 27, 54, 76

The lesson, hymn and verse are omitted.

Antiphon to the Magnificat - *Potestatem habeo*   Tone 4E

I   have   pow - er   to   lay down my life,   and   to

take   it   a - gain.   *John 10:18*

✠ MY SOUL / magnifies the Lord, *
   And my spirit has rejoiced / in God my Savior. etc.

After the repition of the antiphon to the Magnificat, the following antiphon is said kneeling, followed immediately by the Lord's Prayer and collect:

383

Maundy Thursday
Christ for our sake became obedient to death.

Good Friday *add the following:*
Even to death on a cross.

Holy Saturday *add the following:*
Therefore God has highly exalted Him and given Him the name which is above every name.

Philippians 2:8-9

Collect *The collect is said without the introductory words "Let us pray." The termination is said silently.*

Maundy Thursday:

Almighty God, we pray You, graciously to behold this Your family, for which our Lord Jesus Christ was contented to be betrayed and given up into the hands of wicked men and to suffer death upon the cross; *Silently:* through the same Jesus Christ, Your Son, our Lord, who lives and reigns with You and the Holy Spirit, one God, now and forever. *Gelasian Sacramentary*

Good Friday:

Almighty God, we pray You, graciously to behold this Your family, for which our Lord Jesus Christ was contented to be betrayed and given up into the hands of wicked men and to suffer death upon the cross; *Silently:* through the same Jesus Christ, Your Son, our Lord, who lives and reigns with You and the Holy Spirit, one God, now and forever. *Gelasian Sacramentary*

Holy Saturday:

O God, who enlightened this most holy night with the glory of the Lord's resurrection, preserve in all Your people the spirit of adoption which You have given, so that, renewed in body and soul, they may perform to You a pure service, *Silently:* through the same Jesus Christ, Your Son, our Lord, who lives and reigns with You and the Holy Spirit, one God, now and forever. *Gelasian Sacramentary*

After the collect, all rise and depart in silence.

AT COMPLINE

On Maundy Thursday Compline is said after the stripping of the altar, with candles extinguished and without singing.

On Good Friday Compline is said after the solemn afternoon liturgy, with candles extinguished and without singing. On Holy Saturday Compline is said only by those who are not taking part in the solemn Easter Vigil.

The Psalm and Nunc Dimittis are said without antiphons or the Gloria Patri.

After the Nunc Dimittis, the following antiphon is said kneeling except on Holy Saturday. It is followed immediately by the Lord's Prayer and collect:

Maundy Thursday
Christ for our sake became obedient to death.

Good Friday *add the following:*
Even to death on a cross.

Holy Saturday *add the following:*
Therefore God has highly exalted Him and given Him the name which is above every name.

Philippians 2:8-9

The collect is recited without the introductory words "Let us pray." The termination is said silently. After the collect, all rise and depart in silence.

EASTER WEEK

There is no kneeling throughout the Easter season, except where indicated
in the Invitatory Psalm, and in the hymn Te Deum.

AT MATINS

Invitatory for Eastertide - *Surrexit Dominus*   *Tone 6*

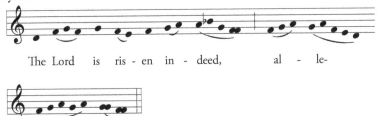

The Lord   is   ris - en   in - deed,   al   -   le-

lu   -   ia

Hymn - *Christ Lag in Todesbanden*

1.   Christ Je-sus lay in death's strong bands, For our of- fen - ses   giv - en;

But now at God's right hand He stands And brings us life from hea-ven;

There-fore let us joy - ful be   And sing to God right thank-ful-ly

Loud songs of   al - le - lu - ia!   Al - le - lu - ia!

2. No son of man could conquer Death,
    Such mischief sin had wrought us,
    For innocence dwelt not on earth,
    And therefore Death had brought us
    Into thraldom from of old
    And ever grew more strong and bold
    And kept us in his bondage. Alleluia!

3. But Jesus Christ, God's only Son,
    To our low state descended,
    The cause of Death He has undone,
    His pow'r forever ended,
    Ruined all his right and claim
    And left him nothing but the name -
    His sting is lost forever. Alleluia!

4. It was a strange and dreadful strife
   When Life and Death contended;
   The victory remained with Life,
   The reign of Death was ended;
   Holy Scripture plainly saith
   That Death is swallowed up by Death,
   His sting is lost forever. Alleluia!

5. Here the true Paschal Lamb we see,
   Whom God so freely gave us;
   He died on the accursed tree -
   So strong His love! - to save us.
   See, His blood doth mark our door;
   Faith points to it, Death passes o'er,
   And Satan cannot harm us. Alleluia!

6. So let us keep the festival
   Whereto the Lord invites us;
   Christ is Himself the Joy of all,
   The Sun that warms and lights us.
   By His grace He doth impart
   Eternal sunshine to the heart;
   The night of sin is ended. Alleluia!

7. Then let us feast this Easter Day (tide)
   On Christ, the Bread of heaven;
   The Word of Grace hath purged away
   The old and evil leaven.
   Christ alone our souls will feed,
   He is our meat and drink indeed;
   Faith lives upon no other. Alleluia!

Martin Luther, 1524

Psalmody

Sunday: 69b, 70, 71
Monday: 72, 73, 74
Tuesday: 78a, 78b, 78c

Wednesday: 75, 79, 80
Thursday: 81, 82, 83

Friday: 84, 86, 87, 93
Saturday: 85, 89a, 89b

Lesson

Sunday: Mark 16:1-8
Monday: Luke 24:13-35
Tuesday: Luke 24:36-47
Wednesday: John 21:1-14
Thursday: John 20:11-18
Friday: Matthew 28:16-20
Saturday: John 20:1-9

Homily

Sunday - John Chrysostom

If anyone be devout and a lover of God, enjoy this beautiful and radiant Feast of Feasts! If anyone is a wise servant, rejoice and enter into the joy of the Lord. If anyone is wearied in fasting, now receive your recompense.

If anyone has labored from the first hour, today receive your just reward. If anyone has come at the third hour, with thanksgiving keep the feast. If anyone has arrived at the sixth hour, have no misgivings; for you shall suffer no loss. If anyone delayed until the ninth hour, draw near without hesitation. If anyone has arrived even at the eleventh hour, do not fear on account of your delay. For the Lord is gracious and receives the last even as the first; He gives rest to the one that comes at the eleventh hour, just as to the one who has labored from the first. He has mercy upon the last, and cares for the first; to the one He gives, and to the other He is gracious. He both honors the work, and praises the intention.

Enter all of you, therefore, into the joy of our Lord, and whether first or last receive your reward. O rich and poor, one with another, dance for joy! O you ascetics and you negligent, celebrate the Day! You that have fasted and you that have disregarded the fast, rejoice today! The table is rich-laden; feast royally, all of you! The calf is fattened; let no one go hungry! Let all partake of the Feast of Faith. Let all receive the riches of goodness.

Let none lament their poverty, for the Universal Kingdom has been revealed. Let none mourn their transgressions, for Pardon has dawned from the tomb! Let no one fear Death, for the Savior's death has set us free!

He that was taken by Death has annihilated it! He descended into Hell, and took Hell captive! He embittered it when it tasted of His flesh! And anticipating this Isaiah exclaimed, "Hell was embittered when it encountered You in the lower regions." It was embittered, for it was abolished! It was embittered, for it was mocked! It was embittered, for it was purged! It was embittered, for it was destroyed! It was embittered, for it was bound in chains!

It took a body, and face to face met God! It took earth, and encountered Heaven! It took what it saw, but crumbled before what it had not seen!

"O Death, where is your sting? O Hell, where is your victory?" Christ is risen, and you are overthrown! Christ is risen, and the demons are fallen! Christ is risen, and the angels rejoice! Christ is risen, and Life reigns! Christ is risen, and not one dead remains in the tombs! For Christ being raised from the dead, has become the first-fruits of them that slept. To Him be glory and dominion through all the ages of ages!

Homily for Easter Day

Monday - Martin Luther

Let us not overlook the example contained in this Gospel which urges and admonishes us to speak and hear of Christ gladly, and to study the Scriptures and God's Word, though it may not always be understood and affect us as it ought. The Gospel also shows us the power, blessing and effect of the Word, if approached with a sincere heart.

For, in the first place, although these two disciples were yet filled with unbelief, He will not and cannot be separated from them, because they went their way discussing sorrowfully with one another about Christ, and questioning together almost without result. He at once drew near and went with them and soon touched their hearts and minds. He began a beautiful, masterly sermon, such as they had never heard before, concerning the very article of faith which caused them trouble and doubt. Then, in the second place, they immediately feel its power; their hearts are no longer heavy, slow, and cold to believe as before, but are moved and kindled, and enlightened and receive a new understanding, so that now they begin to know the Scriptures correctly, and what they had never understood before, becomes clear and manifest to their souls. Finally the mask and cover are taken away from their hearts and eyes, so that they no longer look upon Him as a guest and a stranger, but truly know Him and feel that He is no longer far from them, but at their side, and works certainty in their faith. Henceforth they no longer need bodily, visible revelations, but go forth at once to preach to others, and to strengthen and aid them against doubt and unbelief.

Therefore we should follow their example, and gladly hear the Word of God, without growing weary. For this is not only a needful practice for the strong and for the weak, for the wise and for the unwise, by which a knowledge of everything we need unto salvation is given - such study can never exhaust it - but it is also the punishment through which God wishes to work within our hearts, to give faith and the Holy Ghost, as St. Paul says in Romans 10:17: "Faith comes by hearing the Word of God." If man studies earnestly, even though the heart be cold and unwilling at first, if he only continues in the work, it will not be in vain, and the effect will be produced that the unwise and erring will be brought in and made better, the weak will be strengthened, and at last the heart will be kindled and enlightened, so that Christ is understood and known from the Scriptures.

Church Postil for Easter Monday

Tuesday - Augustine of Hippo

The Lord, as you have heard, appeared to His disciples after His resurrection and greeted them, saying: "Peace to you." This is truly peace. This is the salutation of Salvation; for salutation gets its name from salvation. And what could be better than that Salvation itself should greet mankind?

For Christ is our Salvation. For He is our Salvation who was wounded for us, and fastened with nails to the wood, and taken down from the wood, and laid in the tomb. But He rose from the tomb; and though His wounds were healed the scars remained. For He deemed it advantageous for His disciples that He keep His scars, to heal the wounds of their soul.

What wounds were these? The wounds of their unbelief. For He appeared before their eyes, showing them a true body; and they thought they saw a ghost. This is no minor wound of the soul. And those who continued in this wounded state have started a malignant heresy [Manichaenism]. And let's not think that because they were healed so quickly that the disciples weren't wounded.

Charitably consider that had they remained in this wounded state - thinking that His buried body had not risen, and that a spirit in the likeness of a body deceived their human eyes - had they remained in this belief (or rather, had they remained in this unbelief) we would be grieving, not for their wounds, but for their death! ...A serious wound; let the remedy of the scars appear! "Why are you troubled? And why do doubts arise in your hearts? Behold My hands and My feet," where I was fastened by the nails. "Handle Me and see." See what? "That a spirit does not have flesh and bones as you see I have. And when He had said this," it is written, "He showed them His hands and His feet."

"But while they still did not believe for joy, and marveled." They were now joyful, yet their hesitation remained. For something had taken place which was incredible; yet it had taken place. It doesn't seem incredible now that the body of Christ has risen from the tomb. The whole healed world believes it; and whoever doesn't believe it has not been healed. At that time it was incredible; and they were brought to believe not only through their eyes, but through their hands. That way faith might enter their heart by way of their senses, so that the faith entering their heart in this way might be preached throughout the world, to those who would neither see nor touch Him, and yet without hesitation would believe in Him.

"Have you," He says, "any food here?" How much the Good Builder adds to the confidence of our faith! He suffered no hunger, yet He asked for food. And He ate on this occasion not because of need. And then the Apostles acknowledge that His body is real; and the world acknowledges it from their preaching.

Sermon 116

Wednesday - John Chrysostom

As now in Springtime the earth brings forth roses and violets and other flowers, and the rains make the fields yet more lovely, you don't think that the rains cause the flowers to spring up, nor that the earth of its own power brings them forth. You know that it is by God's command that the seed produces. And in the beginning water also brought forth animals that moved; for the Scripture says: "Let the waters abound with an abundance of living creatures." And the command was fulfilled, and the lifeless substance brought forth living creatures. So now the waters bring forth, not reptiles, but divine spiritual gifts. The waters have brought forth fish that were dumb and without reason; now they bring forth spiritual fish endowed with reason; fish such as the Apostle caught: "Follow Me, and I will make you fishers of men" (Matthew 4:19). This is the fishing He spoke of. A new kind indeed; for those that want to fish draw fish out of the water, but we throw them into the water; and that is how we fish!

On the Pasch

Thursday - Proclus of Constantinople

Glorious is our Paschal Festival... The celebration of this week, or rather its joyfulness, is shared by such a multitude, that not only does man rejoice on earth, but even the powers of heaven are united with us in joyful celebration of Christ's Resurrection. For now the angels and the hosts of the archangels also keep holiday this day and stand waiting for the triumphant return from this earth of Christ Our Lord, who is the King of Heaven. And the multitude of the Blessed likewise rejoice, proclaiming Christ who was begotten before the day star rose. The earth rejoices, now washed by Divine blood. The sea rejoices, honored, as it was, by His Feet upon its waters. And ever more let each soul rejoice, who is born again of water and the Holy Ghost; and at last set free from the ancient curse!

With such great joy does Christ fill our hearts this day by His Resurrection, not only because He gives us the gladness of this day, but because He has also given us salvation through His Passion, immortality through His Death, healing for our wounds, and resurrection from our fall! And long ago, beloved, this Paschal mystery, begun in Egypt, was symbolically pointed out to us in the Old Law, in the sacrifice of the lamb. And now, in the Gospel, let us celebrate the Resurrection of the Lamb: our Pasch.

On the Holy Pasch

Friday - Bonaventure

The Lord appeared to the disciples also in Galilee and declared that all power in heaven and earth had been given to Him by the Father. In view of this He sent His disciples into the whole world to preach the Gospel to every creature, promising salvation to believers, threatening damnation to unbelievers. The Lord worked with them and confirmed the preaching by the signs that followed. So that in the power of the name of Jesus Christ they might have command over all creatures and all diseases. And thus it was to be manifest to the whole world that Jesus Christ, the Son of the mighty Father, lives and reigns like another Joseph and a true Savior not only of the land of Egypt, but also in every place where the eternal King has dominion. At the command of the God of heaven He has been led forth from the prison of death and the underworld. And shorn of the fleece of mortality, He exchanged the clothing of flesh for the glory of immortality. Like a true Moses drawn out of the waters of mortality, He undermined the power of Pharaoh. So exalted is His honor that at His name every knee should bend of those in heaven, on earth, and under the earth.

The Tree of Life

Saturday - Bernard of Clairvaux

The Lord did not defer His resurrection beyond the third day, that the prophet's saying might be verified, "After two days He will revive us; on the third day He will raise us up." It is entirely proper that the limbs should follow where the Head leads the way. He redeemed mankind upon the cross on the sixth day, the same in which He had created man in the beginning. The following day He kept His sabbath in the tomb, having finished the work that He had undertaken. But on the third, that is the first of days, then the New Man, the Conqueror of death, the First-fruits of them that sleep, appeared.

Likewise, let us who follow Him, while yet this day of our creation and redemption lasts, not stop repenting and carrying our cross, persevering in it even as He persevered with His, until the Spirit tells us that we may rest from our labors. Let us not listen to anyone, brethren, not to flesh and blood, nor to any spirit, that wants to persuade us to come down from the cross. Let us stay on the cross, let us die on the cross. Let it be the hands of others that remove us from there, not our own fickleness. Just men took down our Head; He graciously allows the holy angels to do that for us, that when the day of the cross has been bravely brought to its end, we may rest sweetly on the second day, that follows on our death, and sleep happily in our graves, looking for the blessed hope and the coming of the glory of God, who on the third day will raise our bodies at last, in the likeness of the body of His glory.

Eighth Sermon on the Holy Pasch

Collects

Sunday:

Almighty God, who through Your only-begotten Son, Jesus Christ, has overcome death and opened to us the gate of everlasting life, we humbly pray You that, as You put into our minds good desires, by Your continual help we may bring them to good effect; through the same Jesus Christ, Your Son, our Lord, who lives and reigns with You and the Holy Spirit, one God, now and forever.

Gelasian Sacramentary

Monday:

O God, whose blessèd Son manifested Himself to His disciples in the breaking of bread; open, we pray You, the eyes of our faith, that we may behold You in all Your works; through the same Jesus Christ, Your Son, our Lord, who lives and reigns with You and the Holy Spirit, one God, now and forever.

Book of Common Prayer, 1549

Tuesday:

O God, the Author of our freedom and of our salvation, hear the voices of Your people, and grant that those whom You have redeemed by the shedding of Your blood may both live by You, and enjoy perpetual safety in You, O Savior of the world, for You live and reign with the Father and the Holy Spirit, one God, now and forever.

Gothic Missal

Wednesday:

Grant, we beseech You, Almighty God, that we who celebrate the solemnities of the Lord's resurrection may by the renewal of the Holy Spirit rise again from the death of the soul; through Jesus Christ, Your Son, our Lord, who lives and reigns with You and the Holy Spirit, one God, now and forever.

Gelasian Sacramentary

Thursday:

O God, who in the Paschal Feast has bestowed restoration upon the world, continue unto Your people Your heavenly gift that they may both attain unto perfect freedom and advance unto eternal life; through Jesus Christ, Your Son, our Lord, who lives and reigns with You and the Holy Spirit, one God, now and forever.

Gregorian Sacramentary

Friday:

O almighty and eternal God, who through the resurrection of Your Son has sealed the covenant of man's reconciliation, grant unto us who joy in this, Your covenant, grace to show forth in our lives that which we profess with our lips; through the same Jesus Christ, Your Son, our Lord, who lives and reigns with You and the Holy Spirit, one God, now and forever.

Gregorian Sacramentary

Saturday:

Grant, we beseech You, Almighty God, that we who celebrate Your Paschal Feast, kindled with heavenly desires, may ever thirst for the Fountain of Life, Jesus Christ, Your Son, our Lord, who lives and reigns with You and the Holy Spirit, one God, now and forever.

Gregorian Sacramentary

AT LAUDS

Psalmody

Sunday: 67, C1, 5
Monday: 63, C2, 36
Tuesday: 43, C3, 57

Wednesday: 64, C4, 65
Thursday: 88, C6, 90

Friday: 76, C5, 92
Saturday: 143, C7, 148

Lesson

Sunday: Acts 1:1-3
Monday: Acts 1:9-26
Tuesday: Acts 2:22-47

Wednesday: Acts 4:1-37
Thursday: Acts 5:17-42

Friday: Acts 7:1-36
Saturday: Acts 7:51-60

Hymn - *Aurora lucis rutilat*

1. Light's glitt-'ring morn be-decks the sky, Heav'n thun-ders forth
2. While He, the King of glor-ious might, Treads down death's strength
3. Fast barred be - neath the stone of late In watch and ward

its vic-tor cry, The glad earth shouts its tri- umph high,
in death's de - spite, And tramp-ling hell by vic - tor's right
where sol-diers wait, Now shin - ing in tri - um- phant state,

and groan-ing hell makes wild rep - ly:
brings forth His sleep- ing Saints to light.
He ris - es Vic - tor from death's gate.

4. Hell's pains are loosed, and tears are fled;
Captivity is captive led;
The Angel, crowned with light, hath said,
"The Lord is risen from the dead."

5. Glory to God the Father be,
And to the resurrected Son,
And unto God the Paraclete,
While everlasting ages run. Amen.

Ambrose of Milan

Verse

℣: In Your resurrection, O Christ, allelu- / ia.
℟: Let heaven and earth rejoice, allelu- / ia.   *Liturgical text*

Antiphon to the Benedictus - *Stetit Jesus*   Tone 8G

Je - sus stood   in the midst of His dis - cip - les   and said

to them, "Peace to you."   Al - le - lu - ia   al - le - lu - ia!   *Luke 24:36*

✠ BLESSÉD is the Lord God of / Israel; *
For He has visited and re- / deemed His people.   etc.

Collect

Everlasting God, who by Your only-begotten Son has destroyed death, and by His resurrection has brought again innocence and eternal life, that we, being redeemed from the power of the devil, might live in Your kingdom; grant that we, with our whole hearts, may believe; and, in that faith abiding, evermore praise and thank You, through the same, Jesus Christ, our Lord. Amen.

Wilhelm Loehe, Seed-Grains of Prayer, 1854

AT TERCE, SEXT AND NONE

Chapter

Sunday: I Corinthians 5:6-8   Wednesday: Acts 3:12-15   Friday: I Peter 3:18-22
Monday: Acts 10:34-41   Thursday: Acts 8:26-40   Saturday: I Peter 2:1-10
Tuesday: Acts 13:26-33

Responsory and Verse at Terce

℣: The Lord is ris-en from the grave. Al - le - lu - ia, al - le - lu - ia.
℟: The Lord is ris-en from the grave. Al - le - lu - ia, al - le - lu - ia.

℣: Who hung up-on the tree for us.   Al - le - lu - ia, al - le - lu - ia.
℟: The Lord...

℣: Glo-ry be to the Fa-ther, and to the Son, and to the Ho-ly Spi - rit.
℟: The Lord...

Mark 16:6

℣: The Lord is risen indeed, allelu- / ia.
℟: And has appeared to Simon, allelu- / ia.

Luke 24:34

Responsory and Verse at Sext

℣: The Lord is ris - en in - deed. Al - le - lu - ia, al - le - lu - ia.
℟: The Lord is ris - en in - deed. Al - le - lu - ia, al - le - lu - ia.

℣: And has ap-peared to Si - mon. Al - le - lu - ia, al - le - lu - ia.
℟: The Lord...

℣: Glo-ry be to the Fa-ther, and to the Son, and to the Ho-ly Spi - rit.
℟: The Lord...

Luke 24:34

℣: The disciples rejoiced, allelu- / ia.
℟: When they saw the Lord, allelu- / ia.

John 20:20

Responsory and Verse at None

℣: The di - sci - ples re - joiced. Al - le - lu - ia, al - le - lu - ia.
℟: The di - sci - ples re - joiced. Al - le - lu - ia, al - le - lu - ia.

℣: When they saw the Lord. Al - le - lu - ia, al - le - lu - ia.
℟: The disciples...

℣: Glo-ry be to the Fa-ther, and to the Son, and to the Ho-ly Spi - rit.
℟: The disciples...

John 20:20

℣: Abide with us, Lord, allelu- / ia.

℟: For it is toward evening, allelu- / ia.

Luke 24:29

AT VESPERS

Psalmody

Sunday: 110, 111, 112, 113   Wednesday: 123, 124, 125   Friday: 129, 130, 131, 132
Monday: 114, 115, 116, 117   Thursday: 126, 127, 128   Saturday: 133, 135, 136a
Tuesday: 120, 121, 122

Lesson

Sunday: Acts 1:4-8   Wednesday: Acts 5:1-16   Friday: Acts 7:37-50
Monday: Acts 2:1-21   Thursday: Acts 6:1-15   Saturday: Acts 8:1-25
Tuesday: Acts 3:1-26

Hymn - *Ad cenem agni providi*

1. The Lamb's high ban - quet we a - wait, In snow-
2. Up - on the Al - tar of the Cross His Bo-
3. That Pas - chal Eve God's arm was bared, The de-

white robes of roy - al state, And now, the Red Sea's chan-
dy hath re - deemed our loss: And tas - ting of His rose-
vas - tat - ing An - gel spared: By strength of hand our hosts

nel past, To Christ our Prince we sing at last.
ate Blood, Our life is hid with Him in God.
went free From Pha - raoh's ruth - less ty - ran - ny.

4. Now Christ, our Paschal Lamb, is slain,
   The Lamb of God that knows no stain,
   The true Oblation offered here,
   Our own unleavened Bread sincere.

5. O Thou, from whom hell's monarch flies,
   O great, O very Sacrifice,
   Thy captive people are set free,
   And endless life restored in Thee.

6. For Christ, arising from the dead,
   From conquered hell victorious sped,
   And thrust the tyrant down to chains,
   And Paradise for man regains.

7. We pray Thee, King with glory decked,
   In this our Paschal joy, protect
   From all that death would fain effect
   Thy ransomed flock, Thine own elect.

8. To Thee who, dead, again dost live,
   All glory Lord, Thy people give;
   All glory, as is ever meet,
   To Father and to Paraclete. Amen.

Ambrosian Hymn, c. 6th c.

Verse

℣: Abide with us, Lord, allelu- / ia.

℟: For it is toward evening, allelu- / ia.

Luke 24:29

Antiphon to the Magnificat - *Videte manus meas*

Tone 8G

Be - hold My hands and My feet that it is I

My-self. Al - le - lu - ia al - le - lu - ia!

Luke 24:39

✠ MY SOUL magnifies / the Lord, *
And my spirit has rejoiced in / God my Savior. etc.

Collect

Almighty God, whose blessèd Son did on this day rise again for us, victorious over sin and the grave: grant that we, being risen with Him, may set our affection on things above, not on things on the earth; that when He who is our life shall appear, we may also appear with Him in glory; through the same, our Lord Jesus Christ.

Veit Dietrich

QUASIMODOGENITI

The Second Week of Easter

AT MATINS

Invitatory *As during the week of Easter, p.385*

Hymn - *O filii et filiae*

Al - le - lu - ia, al - le - lu - ia, al - le - lu - ia!

1. O Sons and daugh - ters of the King,
2. On the first morn - ing of the week,
3. An an - gel bade their sor - row flee

Whom heav'n - ly hosts in glo - ry sing,
Be - fore the day be - gan to break,
For thus he spake un - to the three,

To - day the grave has lost its sting! Al - le - lu - ia!
The Ma - rys went their Lord to seek. Al - le - lu - ia!
"Your Lord is gone to Gal - i - lee. Al - le - lu - ia!

Al - le - lu - ia, al - le - lu - ia, al - le - lu - ia!

4. That night the Apostles met in fear,
Amidst them came their Lord most dear
And said: "Peace be unto you here."
Alleluia!

5. When Thomas afterwards had heard
That Jesus had fulfilled His word,
He doubted if it were the Lord.
Alleluia!

6. "Thomas, behold My side," saith He,
"My hands, My feet, My body, see;
And doubt not, but believe in Me."
Alleluia!

7. No longer Thomas then denied;
He saw the feet, the hands, the side;
"Thou art my Lord and God," he cried.
Alleluia!

8. Blessèd are they that have not seen
And yet whose faith hath constant been,
In life eternal they shall reign.
Alleluia!

9. On this most holy day of days
To God your hearts and voices raise
In laud and jubilee and praise.
Alleluia!

10. And we with holy Church unite,
As evermore is just and right,
In glory to the King of light.
Alleluia!

attributed to Jean Tisserand, d.1494

Psalmody

Sunday: 89c, 94, 96	Wednesday: 104a, 104b, 104c	Friday: 106a, 106b, 107a
Monday: 97, 98, 99, 100	Thursday: 105a, 105b, 105c	Saturday: 107b, 108, 109
Tuesday: 101, 102, 103		

Lesson

Sunday & Monday: John 20:19-31
Tuesday: Mark 16:9-13
Wednesday: John 17:11-16
Thursday: Matthew 28:8-15
Friday: John 4:47-53
Saturday: John 6:1-3

Homily

Sunday - Bede the Venerable

When the Savior appears in the midst of the disciples, He immediately bestows on them the joys of peace. He now repeats in the fulfilled glory of His immortality, what He had committed to them as the special pledge of their salvation when He Himself was about to undergo His passion, saying to them: "Peace I leave with you, My peace I give to you."

In the same way, when He was born the angels whom the shepherds saw immediately proclaim the favor of this gift to men; praising God and saying, "Glory to God in the Highest, and on earth peace, goodwill toward men." The whole divine mission of our Redeemer in the flesh was to restore peace to the world. It was for this that He became man, for this He suffered, for this He rose from the dead; that by appeasing Him He might bring us back to the peace of God; we who by offending God have incurred His anger. And because of this rightly did the prophet speak of Him as "the Everlasting Father, the Prince of Peace."

Homily for the Vigil of Easter

Monday: Martin Luther

What are the means and process the Spirit employs to change and renew the heart? It is through preaching Jesus Christ the Lord, as Christ Himself says: "When the Helper comes, whom I shall send to you from the Father, the Spirit of truth who proceeds from the Father, He will testify of Me." As we have often heard, the Gospel is the message God would have preached world-wide, declaring to every individual that since no man can be made righteous through the Law, but must rather become more unrighteous, God sent His own beloved Son to shed His blood and die for our sins, from which sins we could not be released by our own effort.

It is not enough simply that Christ be preached; the Word must be believed. Therefore, God sends the Holy Spirit to impress the preaching upon the heart - to make it inhere and live therein. Unquestionably, Christ accomplished all - took away our sins and overcame every obstacle, enabling us to become, through Him, lords over all things. But the treasure lies in a heap; it is not everywhere distributed and applied. Before we can enjoy it, the Holy Spirit must come and communicate it to the heart, enabling us to believe and say, "I, too, am one who shall have the blessing." To everyone who hears is grace offered through the Gospel; to grace is he called, as Christ says, "Come to Me, all you who labor and are heavy laden, and I will give you rest."   *Church Postil for Pentecost*

Tuesday: Cyril of Jerusalem

But it is impossible, someone will say, that the dead should rise; and yet Elisha twice raised the dead - once when he was alive, and again when dead. Do we then believe that when Elisha was dead, a dead man who was cast upon him and touched him, arose; but Christ is not risen? But in that case the dead man who touched Elisha arose, while he who raised him remained dead. But in this case both the Dead of whom we speak Himself arose, and many dead were raised without having even touched Him. "For many bodies of the saints who had fallen asleep were raised; and coming out of the graves after His resurrection, they went into the holy city," evidently this city in which we now are [i.e., Jerusalem] "and appeared to many." So Elisha raised a dead man, but he did not conquer the world; Elisha raised a dead man, but devils are not driven away in the name of Elisha. We are not speaking evil of the Prophets, but we are celebrating their Master more highly...

How then did Jonah, who was three days and three nights in the belly of a whale, escape corruption? And, seeing that the nature of all men is such that we cannot live without breathing in air, how did he live without a breath of this air for three days? But the Jews make answer and say, The power of God descended with Jonah when he was tossed about in hell. So does the Lord give life to His own servant by sending His power with him, but is unable to grant it to Himself as well? If that is credible, this is credible too; if this is incredible, that also is incredible. For to me both are alike worthy of belief. I believe that Jonah was preserved, for "all things are possible with God;" I believe the Christ too was raised from the dead; for I have many testimonies of this, both from the Divine Scriptures, and from the operative power even now of Him who arose...

Since then we have these prophecies, let faith abide with us. Let them fall who fall through unbelief, since they so will; but you have taken your stand on the rock of the faith in the Resurrection. Let no heretic ever persuade you to speak evil of it.   *Fourteenth Catechetical Lecture*

Wednesday: Leo I of Rome

If without faltering we believe in our hearts what we confess with our lips, then have we in Christ been crucified, we have died with Him, we have been buried with Him, and have risen again with Him on the third day. Because of this the Apostle says: "If then you were raised with Christ, seek the things that are above, where Christ is, sitting at the right hand of God. Set your mind on things above, not on things on the earth. For you died, and your life is hidden with Christ in God."

So that the hearts of the faithful may know that they have the means by which (having put away the desires of the world) they may be raised to heavenly wisdom, the Lord promises us His own presence, saying: "Lo, I am with you always, even to the end of the age." For it was not without reason that the Holy Spirit said through the mouth of Isaiah: "Behold, the virgin shall be with child, and bear a Son, and they shall call His name Immanuel, which is translated, God with us." Jesus therefore fulfills the promise of His name. He who ascended to heaven does not abandon His adopted children. He who sits at the right hand of the Father dwells in His entire body. He strengthens to endurance those who dwell here below while inviting them to glory up above.

Let us not be led astray by vanities, nor falter when things are hard for us. In the one case deceit will flatter us, in the other our difficulties but grow worse. But since "The earth is full of the goodness of the Lord," everywhere the victory of the Lord is with us, that the word may be fulfilled that says: "Be of good cheer, I have overcome the world." Whether we are fighting the ambitions of the world, or the lusts of the flesh, or the darts of the heretics, we are always armed with the Lord's Cross. And if we in sincerity of truth keep from ourselves the leaven of our old wickedness, the Paschal feast will never end for us.

In all the changes of this life, which is filled with all sorts of trouble, we must remember what the Apostle teaches us: "Let this mind be in you which was also in Christ Jesus, who, being in the form of God, did not consider it robbery to be equal with God, but made Himself of no reputation, taking the form of a bondservant, and coming in the likeness of men. And being found in appearance as a man, he humbled Himself and became obedient to the point of death, even the death of the cross. Therefore God also has highly exalted Him and given Him the name which is above every name, that at the name of Jesus every knee should bow, of those in heaven, and of those on earth, and of those under the earth, and that every tongue should confess that Jesus Christ is Lord, to the glory of God the Father."

Imitate what He has done. Love what He has loved. And finding in you the grace of God, love your own nature again in Him. He did not lose His riches in poverty, nor His glory in lowliness, nor immortality in death. So you also, following in His footsteps, in these very footprints, scorn earthly things so that you may acquire what is heavenly.   *Sermon 72*

Thursday: Maximus of Turin

Most fittingly the world rejoices with great gladness upon this day; for with Christ returning from the dead the hope of resurrection has everywhere been awakened in the hearts of men. For it is only right that when the Lord of creation triumphs, the creatures He has made should also rejoice. This day the heavens rejoice, for now at last they see the earth, defiled by sin, made clean in the blood of the Lord. The multitudes of the hosts of heaven rejoice, for their king has overthrown in battle the hosts of the prince of evil. The sun rejoices, and now with unending thankfulness holds back by its joyful beams that woeful darkness that overshadowed it as Christ was dying. And together with them we too above all others must rejoice, for whom the only-begotten Son of God, who is also true God, clothed Himself in our flesh, that through that flesh He might come to the cross, by the cross suffer death, and through death despoil the kingdom of hell. Should we not rejoice; we whose sins the mystery of this new sacrament has taken away, to whom heaven is given, paradise restored?   *Sermon 39*

Friday: John Chrysostom

See how clearly the miracle took place. For the boy was not delivered from danger in some ordinary way, or by chance; but all of a sudden. And so it was apparent that his recovery was not due to natural causes, but to the action of Christ. For while drawing near to the very gate of death… all of a sudden he is delivered from his sickness; and this made the servants marvel. For they may have come, not simply to announce the good news, but also because they believed that Jesus' presence was no longer needed, and it was for this that they came to meet him; as they knew that he had gone to find Jesus.

Freed from fear, the ruler has glimpses of faith, and now wants to show that this had come about as a result of his journey, and not by chance. And so, after he had carefully learned all there was to learn, "he himself believed, and his whole household." And the testimony was very plain to see. For they who hadn't been present, and hadn't heard him speaking with Christ, and hadn't known when this had taken place, now learning from their master that this was the time, they had the most clear testimony to the power of Jesus, and because of this they believed.

What then do we learn from these things? Not to wait for signs and wonders; not to seek tokens of the divine power. For even now I see many show more love for God, who have received some consolation when a wife or child was sick. Yet even if our prayers are not heard, we should continue just the same to give praise and thanks to God. For this is the duty of good and devout servants. It is the way of steadfastness, of those who love the lord, to hasten to Him, not only when in affliction, but also when we are untroubled. For such things are the work of God's providence toward us, "For whom the Lord loves He chastens, and scourges every son whom He receives."

Homily 25 on the Gospel of John

Saturday: Gregory of Nazianzus

Yesterday I was crucified with Christ; today I am glorified with Him. Yesterday I died with Him; today I am given life with Him. Yesterday I was buried with Him; today I rise again with Him. Today let us offer Him who has suffered and who has risen for us - you think perhaps I was about to say gold, or silver, or precious things, or shining stones of rare price, the frail matter of this earth, which will remain here and of which the wicked and those who are slaves of earthly things and of the prince of this world posses the greatest part - rather, let us offer Him ourselves, which to God is the most precious and becoming of gifts. Let us offer to His image what is made in the image and likeness of this image. And let us recognize our own dignity. Let us give honor to Him in whose likeness we were made. Let us dwell upon the wonder of this mystery that we may understand for what Christ has died.

Let us become like Christ, since Christ became like us. Let us become gods because of Him, since He became man for us. He took upon Himself a low degree that He might give us a higher one. He became poor, that through His poverty we might become rich. He took upon Himself the form of a servant that we might be delivered from slavery. He was tempted that we might learn to overcome. He was despised that we might be given honor. He died that He might save us from death. He ascended to heaven that we who lie prone in sin may be lifted up to Him.

Let each one of you give all to Him; offer all to Him who gave Himself in exchange for us, as the price of our redemption. But should anyone come to understand this mystery in Christ, and that what He did He has done for him, he shall give nothing unless he gives his own self. *On the Holy Pasch*

Collect

Grant, we pray You, Almighty God, that we who have celebrated the solemnities of the Lord's resurrection may, by the help of Your grace, bring forth the fruits of it in our life and conversation; through the same Jesus Christ, Your Son, our Lord, who lives and reigns with You and the Holy Spirit, one God, now and forever. *Gelasian Sacramentary*

AT LAUDS

Psalmody

Sunday: 3, C8, 51	Wednesday: 8, C11, 20	Friday: 146, C13, 5
Monday: 118a, C9, 118b	Thursday: 18a, C12, 18b	Saturday: 149, C14, 150
Tuesday: 1, C10, 2		

Lesson

Sunday: Acts 8:26-40	Wednesday: Acts 12:1-24	Friday: Acts 15:1-35
Monday: Acts 9:31-43	Thursday: Acts 13:42-52	Saturday: Acts 16:11-40
Tuesday: Acts 10:24-48		

Hymn, Verse and Antiphon to the Benedictus *As during the week of Easter, p.391*

Collect

Gracious Lord, Jesus Christ, triumphant Easter King, we laud and magnify Your unspeakable love with which You greeted Your friends on the day of Your resurrection, and comforted their sorrowful hearts with mighty comfort. We pray You, be our companion also through the pilgrimage of this life. Be our guest in this home, and bless our bread. Be the treasure of our hearts, and enlighten them through the glory of Your saving word, that they glow with love and burn with faith. When our life's sun shall set, and the day of this world declines, abide with us in Your grace, and lead us from this vale of tears to the heavenly Jerusalem, that we may always behold You, in Your glory, together with the Father and the Holy Spirit, face to face. Amen.

Wilhelm Loehe, Seed-Grains of Prayer, 1854

AT TERCE, SEXT AND NONE

Chapter

Sunday and Monday: I John 5:4-10
Tuesday and Wednesday: Hebrews 13:17-21
Thursday, Friday and Saturday: I Timothy 6:17-21

Responsories and Verses *As during the week of Easter, p.392*

AT VESPERS

Psalmody

Sunday: 136b, 137, 138	Wednesday: 9, 10, 11	Friday: 17, 147a, 147b
Monday: 140, 141, 142	Thursday: 12, 13, 14, 16	Saturday: 19, 54, 77
Tuesday: 144, 145, 7		

Lesson

Sunday: Acts 9:1-30	Wednesday: Acts 12:25-13:41	Friday: Acts 15:36-16:10
Monday: Acts 10:1-23	Thursday: Acts 14:1-28	Saturday: Acts 17:1-15
Tuesday: Acts 11:1-30		

Hymn, Verse and Antiphon to the Magnificat *As during the week of Easter, p.394*

Collect

Lord God, heavenly Father, we thank You, that of Your ineffable grace, for the sake of Your Son, You have given us the holy Gospel, and have instituted the holy sacraments, that through the same we may have comfort and forgiveness of sin: We implore You, grant us Your Holy Spirit, that we may heartily believe Your Word; and through the holy Sacraments day by day establish our faith, until we at last obtain salvation; through Jesus Christ our Lord, who lives and reigns with You and the Holy Ghost, one true God, world without end.

Veit Dietrich

MISERICORDIAS DOMINI
The Third Week of Easter

AT MATINS

Invitatory   *As during the week of Easter, p.385*

Hymn - *The King of Love My Shepherd Is*

1. The King of love my Shep-herd is, Whose good-ness fail-eth nev-er; I noth-ing lack if I am His, And He is mine for-ev-er.

2. Where streams of living water flow,
My ransomed soul He leadeth,
And where the verdant pastures grow,
With food celestial feedeth.

3. Perverse and foolish oft I strayed,
But yet in love He sought me
And on His shoulder gently laid
And home, rejoicing, brought me.

4. In death's dark vale I fear no ill
With Thee, dear Lord, beside me;
Thy rod and staff my comfort still,
Thy cross before to guide me.

5. Thou spreadst a table in my sight,
Thine unction grace bestoweth;
And O what transport of delight
From Thy pure chalice floweth!

6. And so through all the length of days
Thy goodness faileth never.
Good Shepherd, may I sing Thy praise
Within Thy house forever.

Henry W. Baker, 1868

Psalmody

Sunday: 21, 22, 23
Monday: 24, 25, 26
Tuesday: 27, 28, 29

Wednesday: 30, 31, 32
Thursday: 33, 34, 35

Friday: 37a, 37b, 38
Saturday: 39, 40, 41

Lesson

Sunday, Monday and Tuesday: John 10:11-16
Tuesday: John 10:17-21

Wednesday: John 12:44-50

Thursday: Luke 24:1-12
Friday and Saturday: Matthew 9:14-17
Saturday: Mark 2:18-22

Homily

Sunday - Cyril of Alexandria

He shows how a shepherd may be proven good; and He teaches that he must be prepared to give up his life fighting for his sheep, which was fulfilled in Christ. For man has departed from the love of God and fallen into sin, and because of this was excluded from the divine abode of paradise. And when he was weakened by that disaster he yielded to the devil who was tempting him to sin, and to death following that sin. He became the prey of fierce and ravenous wolves. But after Christ was proclaimed as the true Shepherd of all men, He laid down His life for us, fighting for us against that pack of inhuman beasts. He bore the Cross for us that by His own death He might destroy death. He was condemned for us that He might deliver all of us from the sentence of punishment - the tyranny of sin being overthrown by our faith - fastening to the Cross the decree that stood against us, as it is written.

Therefore because the father of sin had shut the sheep up in hell, giving them to death to feed on, as is written in the Psalms, He died for us as truly Good, and truly our Shepherd, so that the dark shadow of death being driven away, He might join us to the company of the blessed in heaven; and in exchange for abodes that lie far in the depths of the pit and in the hidden places of the sea, grant us mansions in His Father's house above. Because of this He says to us in another place: "Do not fear, little flock, for it is your Father's good pleasure to give you the kingdom."

Homily on The Good Shepherd

Monday - John Chrysostom

It is a grave thing indeed to have the care of a church. It is a task that needs a measure of love and courage as great as that of which Christ spoke, so that a man may lay down his life for his flock, may never abandon them, and may boldly face the wolf. It is in this that the shepherd differs from the hireling. For the latter, indifferent to the sheep, is always looking out for his own safety; while the former, regardless of his own safety, seeks that of his sheep.

And having indicated to them the signs of the true shepherd, He tells them of two kinds of despoilers. One is the thief, who kills and steals. The other is not a destroyer himself, but should these things take place, he doesn't prevent them. By the one He refers to the followers of a certain [heretic]; by the other He exposes the teachers of the Jews, who had no concern for the sheep that were entrusted to them. And because of this Ezekiel reproached them, saying: "Woe to the shepherds of Israel who feed themselves! Should not the shepherds feed the flocks?" But they did the opposite; which is wickedness of the worst kind, and the cause of all other evils. And because of this He says: they have not led back those who strayed, nor sought those that were lost, nor bound up those that were broken, nor healed those that were sick, because they fed themselves and did not feed My sheep.

And Paul says this in other words too: "For all seek their own, not the things which are of Christ Jesus," and again: "Let no one seek his own, but each one the other's." From both kinds [of despoilers] Christ distinguishes Himself; from those that come to plunder by saying: "I have come that they may have life, and that they may have it more abundantly;" and from those who do not care whether the sheep are taken by the wolves, by not deserting them and by laying down His life that they may not perish. For when they sought to put Him to death, He neither stopped teaching nor betrayed those who believed in Him, but stood firm and chose to die.

Sermon 60, on the Gospel

Tuesday - Gregory I of Rome

Of these sheep He truly says later: "My sheep hear My voice, and I know them, and they follow Me, and I give them eternal life." And earlier He says concerning them: "If anyone enters by Me, he will be saved, and will go in and out and find pasture." He shall go in by faith, and go out by sight; from belief to contemplation; and pasture he shall find in the everlasting refreshment of the soul. His sheep therefore shall find pasture; for whoever follows him with a sincere heart is nourished on pastures of unfading greenness.

But what are the pastures of these sheep if not the hidden delights of the evergreen paradise? For the pastures of the elect are the ever present countenance of God, who while He is unfadingly contemplated by the soul, nourishes it without ceasing by the food of life eternal. In these pastures those who turned aside from the snares of earthly gratifications are satiated with the fullness of eternity. There shall be the singing choirs of angels; there the company of the citizens of heaven; there the sweet solemnity of the blessed returning from the weariness of this earthly pilgrimage. There shall be the far-seeing company of the prophets; the number of the Apostles who shall sit in judgment; there the uncountable host of triumphant martyrs. There the greater our joy shall be, the more we have suffered here below. There shall be the steadfast men, the strength of whose manhood the delights of this world could not soften; there the holy women who triumphed over the world… there the youths who here below in their lives surpassed their years; there the elders whom age had here enfeebled, yet they ceased not from works of virtue and mercy.

So let us seek this pasture where we shall share in the joy of so many friends. Let their joyfulness invite us to the feast. We know that if anywhere there should be a market-day, or people gathering together for the dedication of a church, for which word has been sent out, we would all hurry together to be there, and each in turn would be eager to be present for the solemn occasion, and would feel he had suffered a great loss if he did not share in this common rejoicing. Here it is the rejoicing of all the chosen people of heaven, all rejoicing with one another in their coming together, and yet we, lukewarm as we are toward that eternal love, having no burning desire for it, do not seek to be present at so great a solemnity. We deprive ourselves of everlasting blessedness, and we are happy!

Let us enkindle our soul as a light. Let faith grow fervent in what it has believed. Let our desires grow eager for the things of heaven; and thus to love is already to go there. Let no adversity turn us away from the joy of this inward fulfillment. For when any one has resolved to go to a chosen place, however rough the way, it does not alter his desire. Let no smiling good fortune entice us away; for he is a foolish traveler who, seeing a pleasant meadow on his way, forgets to go on in the way he was going.

Let the soul therefore long with desire for its heavenly home. Let it grasp at nothing in this world; for well we know that it will quickly let go. So, if we are truly sheep of the heavenly Shepherd, if we do not linger attached to the delights of the way, we shall be filled to satisfaction when we shall arrive in the eternal pastures; by the help of our Lord Jesus Christ who with the Father and the Holy Spirit lives and reigns world without end. Amen.　　*Sermon 14 for the Second Sunday after Easter*

Wednesday - Hilary of Poitiers

It was not the carnal body, which He had received by birth from the Virgin, that could make manifest to them the image and likeness of God. The human aspect which He wore could be no aid towards the mental vision of the incorporeal God. But God was recognized in Christ, by such as recognized Christ as the Son on the evidence of the powers of His Divine nature; and a recognition of God the Son produces a recognition of God the Father. For the Son is in such a sense the Image, as to be One in kind with the Father, and yet to indicate that the Father is His Origin. Other images, made of metals or colors or other materials by various arts, reproduce the appearance of the objects which they represent. Yet can lifeless copies be put on a level with their living originals? Painted or carved or molten effigies with the nature which they imitate? The Son is not the Image of the Father after such a fashion as this; He is the living Image of the Living. The Son that is born of the Father has a nature in no way different from His; and, because His nature is not different, He possesses the power of that nature which is the same as His own. The fact that He is the Image proves that God the Father is the Author of the birth of the Only-begotten, Who is Himself revealed as the Likeness and Image of the invisible God. And hence the likeness, which is joined in union with the Divine nature, is indelibly His, because the powers of that nature are inalienably His own.   *On the Trinity*

Thursday - Ambrose of Milan

There are some, dearly beloved, who seem to be seeking the Lord, but since they are lazy and strangers to virtue, they don't deserve to find Him; nor, when found, to see Him. What however were these holy women seeking at the tomb, if not the body of the Lord Jesus? And you, what is it you are seeking in the Church if not Jesus, that is, the Savior? But if you want to find Him, the sun being now risen, then come as these women came; that is, let there be no darkness of evil in your hearts; for the desires of the flesh and evil works are darkness. Those who have this kind of darkness in their hearts do not see the light and don't understand Christ; for Christ is the Light.

So drive the darkness from you; that is, all sinful desires, and all evil works, and provide yourselves with sweet spices, that is, earnest prayer, saying with the Psalmist: "Let my prayer be set before You as incense…"

Now since you are celebrating the holy Pasch, you should know, brethren, what the Pasch is. Pasch means the crossing-over; and so the festival is called by this name. For it was on this day that the Children of Israel crossed over out of Egypt, and the Son of God crossed over from this world to His Father. What does it profit you to celebrate the Pasch unless you imitate Him whom you worship; that is, unless you cross over from Egypt, that is, from the darkness of evildoing to the light of virtue, and from the love of this world to the love of your heavenly home?

For there are many who celebrate this holy festival and honor this solemnity, and yet do so unworthily because of their own wickedness; because they will not cross over from this world to their Father; they will not cross over from the desires of this world and from fleshly delights, to the love of heaven. O unhappy Christians, who still remain in Egypt, under the power of the devil, and taking delight in evil!

Because of these things I warn you, brethren, that you must celebrate the Pasch worthily, that is, that you cross over. Whomever among you are in sin, and celebrate this festival, let you cross over from evil doing to the life of virtue. Whomever among you are living justly, let you pass from virtue to virtue; so that there shall be none among you who has not crossed over.   *Sermon 34, On the Pasch*

Friday - Origen of Alexandria

"You send forth Your Spirit, they are created; and You renew the face of the earth;" which is clearly speaking of the Holy Spirit, who, after sinners and unworthy persons have been taken away and destroyed, creates for Himself a new people and renews the face of the earth, when, laying aside, through the grace of the Spirit, the old man with his deeds, they begin to walk in newness of life. And therefore the expression is correctly applied to the Holy Spirit, because He will take up His dwelling, not in all men, nor in those who are flesh, but in those whose land has been renewed. Lastly, for this reason the grace and revelation of the Holy Spirit was given by the imposition of the apostles' hands after Baptism. Our Savior also, after the resurrection, when old things had already passed away, and all things had become new, Himself a new man, and the first-born from the dead, His apostles also being renewed by faith in His resurrection, says, "Receive the Holy Spirit." This is doubtless what the Lord the Savior meant to convey in the Gospel, when He said that new wine cannot be put into old bottles, but commanded that the bottles should be made new, i.e., that men should walk in newness of life, that they might receive the new wine, i.e., the newness of grace of the Holy Spirit. In this manner, then, the working of the power of God the Father and of the Son is extended without distinction to every creature; but a share in the Holy Spirit we find possessed only by the saints.

On First Principles

Saturday - Gregory of Nyssa

In respect to what pertains to joy and happiness, today is more pleasant than the Last Day, since it will be necessary on the Last Day to see some weeping because their sins are uncovered. But today's joy admits of no sad faces. For the just man is joyful, and the man whose conscience is not clear hopes for forgiveness from his contrition and all grief sleeps today. For there is no one so overwhelmed with pain that he does not get relief from the splendor of the [Paschal] feast.

An Easter Homily

Collect

God, who by the humiliation of Your Son raised up the fallen world, grant to Your faithful ones perpetual gladness, and make those whom You have delivered from the danger of everlasting death partakers of Your eternal joys; through the same Jesus Christ, Your Son, our Lord, who lives and reigns with You and the Holy Spirit, one God, now and forever.

Gelasian Sacramentary

AT LAUDS

Psalmody

Sunday: 67, C1, 5	Wednesday: 64, C4, 65	Friday: 76, C5, 92
Monday: 63, C2, 36	Thursday: 88, C6, 90	Saturday: 143, C7, 148
Tuesday: 43, C3, 57		

Lesson

Sunday: Acts 17:16-34	Wednesday: Acts 21:37-22:29	Friday: Acts 26:1-32
Monday: Acts 19:1-20	Thursday: Acts 24:1-27	Saturday: Acts 27:39-28:10
Tuesday: Acts 20:1-38		

Hymn and Verse   *As during the week of Easter, p.391*

Antiphon to the Benedictus - *Euntes in mundum*   Tone 6

Go in - to the world, al - le - lu - ia; and teach all na-tions, al-

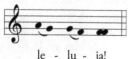

le - lu - ia!

Matthew 28:19

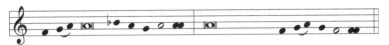

✠ BLESSÉD is the Lord / God of Israel; *
For He has visited and re- / deemed His people. etc.

Collect

O Life of the dying and Salvation of the sick, the only hope of the wretched, and the resurrection of the dead, who rose on the third day, joyful and free, having broken the bonds of death and hell: I beg You with heartfelt gratitude, most high God, to grant unto me in my weakness a part in the first resurrection by the remission of my sins, and a share with Your saints in the second resurrection which is without end, O Lord Jesus Christ. Amen.   *Nunnaminster Codex, 9th century*

AT TERCE, SEXT AND NONE

Chapter

Sunday and Monday: I Peter 2:21-25
Tuesday and Wednesday: I Peter 1:18-25
Thursday, Friday and Saturday: Romans 15:14-17

Responsories and Verses   *As during the week of Easter, p.392*

AT VESPERS

Psalmody

Sunday: 110, 111, 112, 113   Wednesday: 123, 124, 125   Friday: 129, 130, 131, 132
Monday: 114, 115, 116, 117   Thursday: 126, 127, 128   Saturday: 133, 135, 136a
Tuesday: 120, 121, 122

Lesson

Sunday: Acts 18:1-28   Wednesday: Acts 22:30-23:35   Friday: Acts 27:1-38
Monday: Acts 19:21-41   Thursday: Acts 25:1-27   Saturday: Acts 28:11-31
Tuesday: Acts 21:1-36

Hymn and Verse   *As during the week of Easter, p.394*

Antiphon to the Magnificat - *Pastor bonus*   *Tone 3a*

The Good Shep-herd   lays   down His life   for His

sheep, al - le - lu - ia!

John 10:11

✠ MY SOUL / magnifies the Lord, *
And my spirit has rejoiced in God / my Savior. etc.

Collect

Lord God, heavenly Father, who of Your fatherly goodness has been mindful of us poor, miserable sinners, and has given Your beloved Son to be our shepherd, not only to nourish us by His word, but also to defend us from sin, death, and the devil: we beseech You, grant us Your Holy Spirit, that, even as this Shepherd knows us and assists us in every affliction, we also may know Him, and, trusting in Him, seek help and comfort in Him, from our hearts obey His voice, and obtain eternal salvation, through the same, Your Son Jesus Christ, who lives and reigns with You and the Holy Spirit, one true God, world without end. Amen. *Veit Dietrich*

JUBILATE
The Fourth Week of Easter

AT MATINS

Invitatory *As during the week of Easter, p.385*

Hymn - Αισωμεν, πάνται λαοί

1. Come, you faith-ful raise the strain, Of tri - um-phant glad - ness;

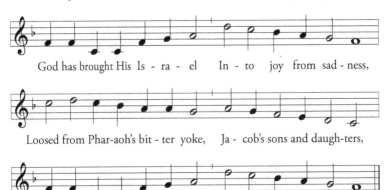

God has brought His Is - ra - el In - to joy from sad - ness,

Loosed from Phar-aoh's bit - ter yoke, Ja - cob's sons and daugh-ters,

Led them with un-moist-ened foot Through the Red Sea wa - ters.

2. This the spring of souls today;
   Christ has burst His prison
   And from three days' sleep in death
   As a sun has risen;
   All the winter of our sins,
   Long and dark, is flying
   From His light, to whom is given
   Laud and praise undying.

3. Now the queen of seasons bright
   With the day of splendor,
   With the royal feast of feasts
   Comes its joy to render;
   Comes to gladden faithful hearts
   Which with true affection
   Welcome in unwearied strain
   Jesus' resurrection!

4. For today among His own
   Christ appeared, bestowing
   His deep peace, which evermore
   Passes human knowing.
   Neither could the gates of death
   Nor the tomb's dark portal
   Nor the watchers nor the seal
   Hold Him as a mortal.

5. Alleluia! Now we cry
   To our King immortal,
   Who, triumphant, burst the bars
   Of the tomb's dark portal.
   Come, you faithful raise the strain
   Of triumphant gladness!
   God has brought His Israel
   Into joy from sadness!

John of Damascus, c.750

Psalmody

Sunday: 42, 44, 45
Monday: 46, 47, 48
Tuesday: 49, 50, 52

Wednesday: 53, 55, 56
Thursday: 58, 59, 60

Friday: 61, 62, 66
Saturday: 68a, 68b, 69a

Lesson

Sunday, Monday and Tuesday: John 16:16-23
Wednesday: John 14:15-21
Thursday: John 3:25-36
Friday and Saturday: John 12:46-50
Saturday: John 12:37-45

Homily

Sunday - Bede the Venerable

He speaks of the Holy Church as a woman, because of her fruitfulness in all good, and because she never ceases to bring forth children to God... For as the woman rejoices that a man is born into the world, so also the Church is filled with proper exultation at the birth of the Christian people into life eternal. Because of this birth she grieves now and is in labor, as a woman who brings forth in this present life. Nor should it seem strange to anyone that he who departs from the present life is said to be born. For just as he is said to be born who comes forth from his mother's womb into this light of ours, so also may he most justly be said to be born who, delivered of the bonds of the flesh, is uplifted to light eternal. For this reason it is the custom of the Church to call those days in which the passing of the martyrs and confessors of Christ is commemorated, not funeral celebrations, but birth festivals, or *natalitia...*

"Therefore you now have sorrow; but I will see you again and your heart will rejoice, and your joy no one will take from you." This is easily understood of the disciples; for they had to mourn over the slain and buried Christ. But after the glory of the resurrection, they were glad when they saw the Lord. And their joy no one takes from them; for though in the days that followed they suffered persecution and torment for Christ's name, yet they suffered these things gladly; for they were inflamed with the hope of resurrection and the hope of seeing Him. Indeed, they counted it all joy when they met with trials of every kind. For even when they were scourged by the chief priests, they went out, as it is written, "rejoicing that they were counted worthy to suffer shame for His name."

Their joy no one takes from them. By suffering such things for the sake of Christ they were counted worthy to reign with Christ forever. And the whole Church likewise, amid the trials and labors of this present life, goes steadily forward to the reward of eternal joy; as the Apostle bears witness, that: "We must through many tribulations enter the kingdom of God."

Homily 5 on the Gospel

Monday - Martin Luther

Now we must carefully consider this example. As it is here, so is it in temptation, and especially in the perils of death. Notice how God deals with the woman suffering in childbirth. There she is left alone in her pain by everybody, and no one can help her. Yea, nothing whatever is able to rescue her from her agony; that rests in the power of God alone. The midwife and others around her may indeed comfort her, but they cannot avoid the agony. She must go through it, and venture and freely hazard her life in it, not knowing whether she shall die or recover, because of the child. There she is truly in the perils of death and completely encompassed by death. This parable St. Paul also

410

uses in I Thessalonians 5:3, when he tells the Thessalonians how the day of judgment will suddenly fall upon them, just like the pangs of a woman in travail, and they will not be able to escape.

Just so it is also when the conscience is in agony or when one lies in the perils of death. Then neither reason nor anything else can help. No work, whether this or that. There is no comfort. You think you are forsaken by God and everybody; yea, you imagine how God and everything is against you. Then you must restrain yourself to quiet and cling only to God, who must deliver you. Besides Him nothing else, neither in heaven nor upon the earth, can deliver. The same God gives His help when He thinks it is time, as He does to the woman in travail. He gives her cheer when she no longer thinks of her pain; then joy and life are where death and all distress reigned before. In like manner God makes us happy, and give us peace and joy where before there were misery and all kinds of sorrow. Therefore, Christ here presents to us an example, and comforts us with it, in order that we may not despair in the time of death and temptation. It is as if He wanted to say to us: Dear man, when fear, sorrow, temptation and tribulation come, doubt not, despair not. It is only for a little time. When these are over, then follow their fruits, peace and joy.

2nd Church Postil for Misericordias Domini

Tuesday - Alcuin of York

"A little while, and you will not see Me," that is, for three days in which He lay in the sepulchre and again it will be another little while until you shall see Me, that is, these forty days, from His Passion to His Ascension, in which He frequently appeared to them. And so for that little while you shall see me; "for I go to the Father;" I shall not always remain bodily upon the earth, but shall, in this humanity I have assumed, ascend to heaven…

These words of Christ are meant for all the faithful, who amid the trials and afflictions of this present life strive to reach to the joy of heaven. But while the righteous now weep, the world rejoices; for it takes its joy in the present, having no hope of the joys of the life to come.

from the Catena Aurea of Thomas Aquinas

Wednesday - Polycarp of Smyrna

Now He that raised Him from the dead will raise us also, if we do His will and walk in His commandments and love the things which He loved, abstaining from all unrighteousness, covetousness, love of money, evil speaking, false witness; not rendering evil for evil or railing for railing, or blow for blow or cursing for cursing; but remembering the words which the Lord spoke, as He taught: "Judge not, that you be not judged." "Forgive, and you will be forgiven. Have mercy that you may receive mercy." "With what measure you use, it will be measured back to you." And again: "Blessed are the poor in spirit… and those who are persecuted for righteousness sake, for theirs is the kingdom of heaven."

These things, brethren, I write to you concerning righteousness, not because I took up this duty on my own, but because you invited me. For neither am I, nor is any one who is like me, able to follow the wisdom of the blessed and glorious Paul, who when he came among you taught face to face with the men of that day the word which concerns truth carefully and truly; who also, when he was absent, wrote a letter to you, into which if you look diligently, you will be able to be built up unto the faith given to you, which is the mother of us all, while hope follows after and love goes before - love toward God and Christ and toward our neighbor. For if any man is occupied with these, he has fulfilled the commandment of righteousness; for he who has love is far from all sin.

Letter to the Philippians

Thursday - Martin Luther

How necessary it was for John to point his disciples away from himself to Christ is very clear. For what benefit would it have been to them if they had depended a thousand times on John's piety and had not embraced Christ? Without Christ there is no help or remedy, no matter how pious men may be. So at the present day what benefit is it to the monks and nuns to observe the rules of St. Benedict, St. Bernard, St. Francis, St. Dominic and Augustine, if they do not embrace Christ and him only, and depart from their John? All Benedictines, Carthusians, Barefoot-Friars, Ecclesiasts, Augustinians, Carmelites, all monks and nuns are surely lost, as only Christians are saved. Whoever is not a Christian even John the Baptist cannot help, who indeed, according to Christ, was the greatest of all saints.

Church Postil for the Third Sunday of Advent

Friday - Martin Luther

It is true that Christ's office is to save, to free from sins, and to give eternal life. Thus Paul also correctly speaks of the Gospel as "the power of God for salvation to everyone who has faith." For those who receive Christ and believe His Word will truly obtain salvation. On that account the Scriptures also call Him the "Cornerstone" which sustains the whole weight of the building, on which the whole building rests, lest it fall. Those who do not receive Christ, however, and hate His Word—because they thrust away their own salvation, how can they escape destruction? Those who do not wish to lean on this stone, but audaciously go against Him, will either fall on this stone, or this stone will fall on them. So how can they fail to be injured?

For this reason Christ also says, John 12:47-48: "I did not come to judge the world but to save the world. He who rejects Me and does not receive My sayings has a judge; the Word that I have spoken will be his judge on the Last Day." The Word of the Gospel is indeed a scepter or a rod of salvation to all who believe. But those who reject it must perish, because they reject salvation. Nor is this the fault of the Word, which is holy and offers life, but their own fault. For they reject this salvation which is offered and lean rather on Law and sacrifices, like the Jews; on their vows and traditions, like the monks; on their divine services, like the self-righteous, who have assigned them to themselves. For why do they not humble themselves? Why do they not give honor to God? Why do they not confess that they are miserable sinners and embrace Christ? Then the Gospel would certainly be a rod of salvation and life for them.

The Interpretation of the Second Psalm

Saturday - Hippolytus of Rome

[The Word of God] casts away none of His servants, none does He despise as unworthy of His divine mysteries. ... He is compassionate to all, and desires to save all. He desires to reinstate all as sons of God, and to call all the saints into one perfect man. For there is one Son of God, through whom we too, being regenerated through the Holy Spirit, desire to become all as one perfect and heavenly man.

Although He was without flesh, the Son of God took on flesh from the Holy Virgin, like a bridegroom putting on a robe, which He wove for Himself in the sufferings of the cross, so that by uniting our mortal body to His own power, and mixing the corruptible with the incorruptible and the weak with the strong, He might save man who was perishing. The beam of the loom, therefore, is the suffering of the Lord which He endured on the cross: the warp on it is the power of the Holy Spirit; the woof is the holy flesh, woven by the Spirit; the thread is the grace which, through the love of Christ, binds and unites the two in one; the combs are the Word; the workers are the patriarchs and prophets, who weave the beautiful and perfect tunic of Christ, reaching to His feet; and the Word, passing through them like the combs, by their means finishes weaving whatever the Father wills.

On the Antichrist

Collect

Grant, we pray You, Almighty God, that we who have celebrated the solemnities of the Lord's resurrection may, by the help of Your grace, bring forth the fruits of it in our life and conversation; through the same Jesus Christ, Your Son, our Lord, who lives and reigns with You and the Holy Spirit, one God, now and forever. *Gelasian Sacramentary*

AT LAUDS

Psalmody

Sunday: 3, C8, 51	Wednesday: 8, C11, 20	Friday: 146, C13, 5
Monday: 118a, C9, 118b	Thursday: 18a, C12, 18b	Saturday: 149, C14, 150
Tuesday: 1, C10, 2		

Lesson

Sunday: Revelation 1:1-20	Wednesday: Revelation 7:1-17	Friday: Revelation 13:1-18
Monday: Revelation 3:1-22	Thursday: Revelation 10:1-11:19	Saturday: Revelation 15:1-16:21
Tuesday: Revelation 5:1-14		

Hymn and Verse *As during the week of Easter, p.391*

Antiphon to the Benedictus - *Cognoverunt Dominum*   *Tone 6*

The Lord was known to them, al - le - lu - ia,   in   the break-ing

of the bread,   al - le - lu - ia.   *Luke 24:35*

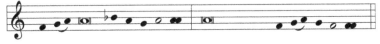

✠ BLESSÉD is the Lord / God of Israel; *
For He has visited and re- / deemed His people. etc.

Collect

Lord God, Heavenly Father, who for our sins gave Your only-begotten Son, and for our justification raised Him up from the dead; we beseech You in mercy to awaken our dead hearts to newness of life; and, with Christ, make us always to live by the power of the resurrection of Your Son, our Lord Jesus Christ, who lives and reigns with You and the Holy Spirit, face to face. Amen.

Wilhelm Loehe, Seed-Grains of Prayer, 1854

AT TERCE, SEXT AND NONE

Chapter

Sunday, Monday and Tuesday: I Peter 2:11-20
Wednesday and Thursday: I John 2:1-8
Friday and Saturday: Colossians 2:4-7

Responsories and Verses *As during the week of Easter, p.392*

AT VESPERS

Psalmody

Sunday: 136b, 137, 138	Wednesday: 9, 10, 11	Friday: 17, 147a, 147b
Monday: 140, 141, 142	Thursday: 12, 13, 14, 16	Saturday: 19, 54, 77
Tuesday: 144, 145, 7		

Lesson

Sunday: Revelation 2:1-29	Wednesday: Revelation 8:1-9:21	Friday: Revelation 14:1-20
Monday: Revelation 4:1-11	Thursday: Revelation 12:1-17	Saturday: Revelation 17:1-18
Tuesday: Revelation 6:1-17		

Hymn and Verse *As during the week of Easter, p.394*

Antiphon to the Magnificat - *Tristitia vestra*   Tone 6

Your sor - row,   al - le - lu - ia,   will be turned in - to joy,

al - le - lu - ia.   *John 16:20*

✠ MY SOUL / magnifies the Lord, *
And my spirit has rejoiced / in God my Savior. etc.

Collect

Lord God, heavenly Father, who of Your fatherly goodness suffers Your children to come under Your chastening rod here on earth, that we may be like unto Your only-begotten Son in suffering and hereafter in glory: We beseech You, comfort us in temptations and afflictions by Your Holy Spirit, that we may not fall into despair, but that we may continually trust in Your Son's promise, that our trials will endure but a little while, and will then be followed by eternal joy; that we thus, in patient hope, may overcome all evil, and at last obtain eternal salvation, through the same, Your Son, Jesus Christ, our Lord, who lives and reigns with You and the Holy Spirit, one true God, world without end. Amen.   *Veit Dietrich*

CANTATE

The Fifth Week of Easter

AT MATINS

Invitatory   *As during the week of Easter, p.385*

Hymn - *Nun freut euch, liebe Christen g'mein*

1. Dear Chris-tians, one and all re-joice, With ex - ul - ta-tion spring - ing,

And, with u - nit - ed heart and voice And ho- ly rap- ture sing - ing,

Pro - claim the won- ders God hath done, How His right arm the

vic - t'ry won; Right dear - ly it hath cost Him.

2. Fast bound in Satan's chains I lay,
Death brooded darkly o'er me,
Sin was my torment night and day,
In sin my mother bore me;
Yea, deep and deeper still I fell,
Life had become a living hell,
So firmly sin possessed me.

3. My own good works availed me naught,
No merit they attaining;
Free will against God's judgment fought,
Dead to all good remaining.
My fears increased till sheer despair
Left naught but death to be my share;
The pangs of hell I suffered.

4. But God beheld my wretched state
Before the world's foundation,
And, mindful of His mercies great,
He planned my soul's salvation.
A father's heart He turned to me,
Sought my redemption fervently:
He gave His dearest Treasure.

5. He spoke to His beloved Son:
'Tis time to have compassion.
Then go, bright Jewel of My crown,
And bring to men salvation;
From sin and sorrow set him free,
Slay bitter death for him that he
May live with Thee forever.

6. The Son obeyed His Father's will,
Was born of virgin mother,
And God's good pleasure to fulfill,
He came to be my Brother.
No garb of pomp or power He wore,
A servant's form, like mine, He bore,
To lead the devil captive.

7. To me He spake: Hold fast to Me,
I am thy Rock and Castle;
Thy Ransom I Myself will be,
For thee I strive and wrestle;
For I am with thee, I am thine,
And evermore thou shalt be Mine:
The Foe shall not divide us.

8. The Foe shall shed My precious blood,
Me of My life bereaving.
All this I suffer for thy good;
Be steadfast and believing.
Life shall from death the victory win,
My innocence shall bear thy sin;
So art thou blest forever.

9. Now to My Father I depart,
The Holy Spirit sending
And, heavenly wisdom to impart,
My help to thee extending.
He shall in trouble comfort thee,
Teach thee to know and follow Me,
And in all truth shall guide thee.

10. What I have done and taught, teach thou,
My ways forsake thou never;
So shall My kingdom flourish now
And God be praised forever.
Take heed lest men with base alloy
The heavenly treasure should destroy;
This counsel I bequeath thee.

Martin Luther, 1523

Psalmody

Sunday: 69b, 70, 71
Monday: 72, 73, 74
Tuesday: 78a, 78b, 78c

Wednesday: 75, 79, 80
Thursday: 81, 82, 83

Friday: 84, 86, 87, 93
Saturday: 85, 89a, 89b

Lesson

Sunday, Monday and Tuesday: John 16:5-15
Wednesday: John 3:22-29
Thursday: John 17:11b-26
Friday and Saturday: John 13:33-36

Homily

Sunday - Didymus the Blind

He said, therefore, "He will not speak on His own authority;" that is, not without Me, and without My and My Father's authority. Because He is not from Himself, but from the Father and Me. For His Being which is and which speaks proceeds to Him from the Father and from Me. "I speak the truth," that is, I inspire the things He utters, since He is the Spirit of Truth.

But to speak and pronounce in the Trinity is not to be understood after the manner of our nature, but after the manner of incorporeal natures, and especially that of the Trinity, which implants its will in the hearts of the believing, and of those who are worthy to receive it… For the Father to speak, and for the Son to hear, is but an indication of the unity of Nature of the Father and Son. The Holy Spirit likewise, who is the Spirit of Truth and the Spirit of Wisdom, cannot hear that which it did not know when the Son speaks; since He is that which is spoken by the Son, namely, the Truth proceeding from the Truth, the Comforter flowing forth from the Comforter, God the Spirit of Truth proceeding from God. Finally, so that no one separates Him from the will and the fellowship of the Father and the Son, it was written, "but whatever He hears He will speak."

On the Holy Spirit

Monday - Martin Luther

The Holy Spirit tells the world: You are all sinners; not one of you is just or wise, whether you live in Jerusalem or in Rome, whether you are of the higher or lower class. You must all learn true wisdom from Me or not one of you will be saved. If you despise My teachings, you will all go to hell, just as you are, with your entire bag of self-righteousness, of piety, and of good works...

This rebuke is no idle threat but a dread reality. Christ says: "He will convict the world of sin, and of righteousness, and of judgment." What will become of us if there is nothing but sin in the world, and no righteousness, no justice? This conviction of the Holy Spirit is a terrible shock to the world. We hear that we and all our good works are the devil's own, and that we cannot enter into the kingdom of God unless the Holy Spirit removes our sins, makes us righteous, and frees us from judgment...

What is sin? Is it to steal, to murder, to commit adultery, and such? Yes, these are sins; but they are not the most common or the most serious. Many have never committed these things that are clearly sins. But everyone is guilty of the chief sin, the sin of which the Holy Spirit convicts the world. If this weren't true, the Holy Spirit couldn't convict the whole world. Unbelief is the great sin of the world, the refusal to believe in Jesus Christ. And the world doesn't recognize this sin until the Holy spirit convicts people of it through His teaching. The world thinks sinful only those deeds which are contrary to the second table of the Law. It knows nothing of Christ, and much less is it aware of the sin of not believing in Him. And not just the world, but we find many Christians who do not consider unbelief a sin, much less an original sin. No one but the Holy Spirit can teach the world that unbelief is sin; He reproves all as sinners, no matter how some may attempt to cover up their faults by good works or to pass themselves off as pure under the tinsel of self-righteousness.

The Holy Spirit, therefore, preaches this truth that without exception all men are sinners and cannot of themselves believe in Christ. This is, of course, a strange sermon to the world. The world on its own is completely ignorant of the duty of having faith in Christ, the Son of Man. Men think that they have fulfilled their duty if they can say with the Pharisee that they are not murderers, not adulterers and not unjust. But the Holy Spirit teaches otherwise and tells man: I know that this one or that one may lead an outwardly upright life, but still the great sin of unbelief nestles deep down in the heart of every one. If we are not convicted of this sin by the Holy Spirit, we will never recognize it.

We must then conclude from this that every thing not done in faith is sin, whether it be monastic vows, or prayers, or fasting, and almsgiving. Wherever faith in Christ is lacking, there the Holy Spirit must come with His conviction. There is no other way to be relieved of this sin but to believe in Christ Jesus the Savior.

House Postil for Cantate

Tuesday - Martin Luther

Christ clearly says that we cannot become righteous by virtue of our own efforts, but only because "He went to the Father." Here we find true righteousness. The world knows nothing of it, since the writings of men do not allude to it at all. The wisdom of this world teaches that if we keep the ten commandments, observe the laws of the land, and lead an honest, upright life, we are surely good, just and honorable people. Here, however, we find nothing at all of this, nothing of our own works; Christ speaks only of what He does, of His work, that He goes to the Father and we see Him no more. This deed of Christ, and nothing else, is our righteousness.

If, then, we desire to be truly pious we must not rely on our works. It does nothing for us if we become monks and fast and watch and pray; but this counts for everything, that we want to be freed from our sins, and know and believe that Christ went to the Father on our behalf. What use is fasting, with prayers and good works if they are of no value at all? Good works are right and proper. We should not neglect them, because God has commanded them in the law. But they can never justify us or make us pleasing in God's sight. Christ's going to the Father is the one and only cause of our redemption and justification, and we must not look for another.

This going of Christ to the Father includes His suffering and cruel death on the cross, His ascension into heaven, and His sitting at the right hand of God. We do not see this, but we believe it, and this precious fact makes us just. We have no righteousness in ourselves, but Christ becomes our righteousness because He goes to the Father. To put it plainly, no one becomes righteous, blessed or free from sin, but by the sufferings, death and resurrection of Christ. Such force has the going of Christ to the Father... The world knows nothing of this. The Holy Spirit alone teaches it.

House Postil for Cantate

Wednesday - Ambrose of Milan

Moses was not the Bridegroom, for the word comes to him, "Take your sandals off your feet," to pay reverence to the Lord. Nor was Joshua the son of Nun the Bridegroom, for it was also said to him, "Take your sandal off your foot," lest some think him the Church's spouse because of the similarity of his name [Jesus, in Greek]. No one else is the Bridegroom but Christ alone, of whom St. John said: "He who has the bride is the bridegroom." They, therefore, take off their shoes, but His shoe cannot be loosed, even as St. John said: "I am not worthy to loose the strap of His sandal."

Christ alone, then, is the Bridegroom to whom His Bride the Church comes from the nations and gives herself in wedlock; previously poor and starving, but now rich with Christ's harvest; gathering in the hidden bosom of her mind handfuls of the rich crop and gleanings of the Word, so that she may nourish with fresh food her who is worn out, bereaved by the death of her son, and starving, even the mother of the dead people, leaving not the widow and destitute, while she seeks new children.

Only Christ is the Bridegroom. He doesn't grudge the sheaves of His harvest even to the synagogue. Oh that the synagogue had not of her own will shut herself out! She had sheaves that she might have gathered herself. But, her people being dead, like one bereaved by the death of her son she began to gather sheaves by which she might live by the hand of the Church. These sheaves those coming in joyfulness will carry, even as it is written: "Yet surely shall they come with rejoicing, bringing their sheaves with them."

Who, indeed, but Christ could dare to claim the Church as His bride, whom He alone, and no one else, has called from Lebanon, saying: "Come with me from Lebanon, my spouse, with me from Lebanon?" Or of whom else could the Church have said: "His mouth is most sweet, yes, he is altogether lovely?" And seeing that we started this discussion by speaking about the shoes of His feet, to whom else but the Word of God incarnate can those words apply? "His legs are pillars of marble set on bases of fine gold." For Christ alone walks in the souls and makes His path in the minds of His saints. In these, as upon bases of gold and foundations of precious stone, the heavenly Word has left His footprints indelibly impressed.

Exposition of the Christian Faith

Thursday - Ignatius of Antioch

I exhort you: be eager to do everything in God's harmony, with the bishop presiding in the place of God and the presbytery in the place of the council of the apostles and the deacons, most sweet to me, entrusted with the service of Jesus Christ - who before the ages was with the Father and was made manifest at the end. All of you, then, having received divine agreement in your convictions, admonish one another, and let no one view his neighbor in a merely human way; but constantly love one another in Jesus Christ. Let there be nothing in you that can divide you, but be united with the bishop and with those who preside, for an example and lesson of imperishability.

As, then, the Lord did nothing apart from the Father, either by Himself or through the apostles, since He was united with Him, so you must do nothing apart from the bishop and the presbyters. Do not try to make anything appear praiseworthy by yourselves, but let there be in common one prayer, one petition, one mind, one hope in love, in blameless joy - which is Christ Jesus, than whom nothing is better. All of you must run together as to the one temple of God, as to one sanctuary, to one Jesus Christ, who proceeded from the one Father and is with the one and departed to the one.

Letter to the Magnesians

Friday - Johann Gerhard

True and sincere love is an unfailing characteristic of the godly soul. There is no Christian without faith, and no faith without love. When the heart glows not with love, there can be no true and fervent faith. You can just as easily rob the sun of its light as separate love from faith. Love is an external exhibition of the real inward life of the Christian. The body without breath is dead, and so faith without love is dead. "Now if anyone does not have the Spirit of Christ, he is not His." And the man who does not exercise the gift of love, does not have the spirit of Christ, for the fruit of the spirit is love. A good tree is known by its fruits. Love is the bond of Christian perfection. As the members of the human body are joined together in a living organism through the spirit, that is, the soul, so all the members of the mystical body of Christ are united by the bond of love through the Holy Spirit... Let love move your heart to compassion and your hands to bountiful gifts; compassion alone is not enough, if it be unaccompanied with the gifts; nor will the gifts alone do, if your heart does not go with them. Faith receives all things from God; love, on the other hand, gives all its own to its neighbor. By faith we are made partakers of the divine nature, but God is love. Let no one think then that true faith dwells in the heart, whose love does not show itself in outward act. One who truly believes in Christ loves Him also, and thus loving Him, he will love his neighbor as well.

Sacred Meditation 36, On True Charity

Saturday - Melito of Sardis

The Lord clothed Himself with humanity, and with suffering on behalf of the suffering one, and bound on behalf of the one constrained, and judged on behalf of the one convicted, and buried on behalf of the one entombed, rose from the dead and cried aloud: "Who takes issue with Me? Let him stand before Me. I set free the condemned. I gave life to the dead. I raise up the entombed. Who will contradict Me?"

"It is I," says the Christ, "I am He who destroys death, and triumphs over the enemy, and crushes Hades, and binds the strong man, and bears humanity off to the heavenly heights. It is I," says the Christ.

"So come all families of people, adulterated with sin, and receive forgiveness of sins. For I am your freedom. I am the Passover of salvation. I am the Lamb slaughtered for you. I am your ransom. I am your life. I am your light. I am your salvation. I am your resurrection. I am your King. I shall raise you up by my right hand. I will lead you to the heights of heaven. There shall I show you the everlasting Father."

He it is who made the heaven and the earth, and formed humanity in the beginning, who was proclaimed through the law and the prophets, who took flesh from a virgin, who was hung on a tree, who was buried in earth, who was raised from the dead, and ascended to the heights of heaven, who sits at the right hand of the father, who has power to save all things, through whom the Father acted from the beginning and forever.

This is the Alpha and Omega, this is the beginning and the end, the ineffable beginning and the incomprehensible end. This is the Christ. This is the King. This is Jesus. This is the commander. This is the Lord. This is He who rose from the dead. This is He who sits at the right hand of the Father. He bears the Father and is borne by Him. To Him be the glory and the might forever. Amen.

On Pascha

Collect

O God, who makes the minds of the faithful to be of one will, grant to Your people that they may love what You command and desire what You promise, that among the many changes of this world our hearts may be fixed where true joys are to be found, through Jesus Christ, Your Son, our Lord, who lives and reigns with You and the Holy Spirit, one God, now and forever.

Gelasian Sacramentary

AT LAUDS

Psalmody

Sunday: 67, C1, 5	Wednesday: 64, C4, 65	Friday: 76, C5, 92
Monday: 63, C2, 36	Thursday: 88, C6, 90	Saturday: 143, C7, 148
Tuesday: 43, C3, 57		

Lesson

Sunday: Revelation 18:1-24	Wednesday: James 1:1-18	Friday: James 3:1-18
Monday: Revelation 20:1-15	Thursday: James 2:1-13	Saturday: James 4:11-5:6
Tuesday: Revelation 21:22-22:5		

Hymn and Verse *As during the week of Easter, p.391*

Antiphon to the Benedictus - *Pax vobis, ego sum*　　　　　　　*Tone 6*

Peace to you; it is I, al - le - lu - ia. Do not fear,

al - le - lu - ia.　　　　　*Liturgical text on John 20:19*

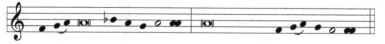

✠ BLESSÉD is the Lord / God of Israel; *
For He has visited and re- / deemed His people. etc.

Collect

O God, who by Your only-begotten Son has overcome death and opened to us the gate of everlasting life; bring us to the society of heavenly joys, that those who have been regenerated by Your Holy Spirit may be enabled by You to enter into Your Kingdom, through Your Son, who is risen from the dead, Jesus Christ our Lord. Amen.　　　　　*Gothic Missal*

AT TERCE, SEXT AND NONE

Chapter

Sunday and Monday: James 1:16-21
Tuesday through Saturday: I Thessalonians 5:5-11

Responsories and Verses *As during the week of Easter, p.392*

AT VESPERS

Psalmody

Sunday: 110, 111, 112, 113   Wednesday: 123, 124, 125   Friday: 129, 130, 131, 132
Monday: 114, 115, 116, 117   Thursday: 126, 127, 128   Saturday: 133, 135, 136a
Tuesday: 120, 121, 122

Lesson

Sunday: Revelation 19:1-21   Wednesday: James 1:19-27   Friday: James 4:1-10
Monday: Revelation 21:1-21   Thursday: James 2:14-26   Saturday: James 5:7-20
Tuesday: Revelation 22:6-21

Hymn and Verse   *As during the week of Easter, p.394*

Antiphon to the Magnificat - *Cum venerit Paraclitus*   *Tone 8G*

When the Pa - ra - clete, the Spi - rit of Truth, has come,

He will con - vict the world of sin, and of right-

eous - ness, and of judg - ment, al - le - lu - ia.   *John 16:8*

✠ MY SOUL magnifies / the Lord, *
And my spirit has rejoiced in / God my Savior. etc.

Collect

Lord God, heavenly Father, who through Your Son promised us Your Holy Spirit, that He should convince the world of sin, of righteousness, and of judgment: We beseech You, enlighten our hearts, that we may confess our sins, through faith in Christ obtain everlasting righteousness, and in all our trials and temptations retain this consolation, that Christ is Lord over the devil and death, and all things, and that He will graciously deliver us out of all our afflictions, and make us forever partakers of eternal salvation, through the same, Your Son, Jesus Christ, our Lord, who lives and reigns with You and the Holy Spirit, one true God, world without end. Amen.   *Veit Dietrich*

ROGATE
The Sixth Week of Easter

Propers for Sunday through Wednesday

AT MATINS

Invitatory *As during the week of Easter, p.385*

Hymn - *Vater unser im Himmelreich*

1. Our Fa-ther, Thou in heav'n a - bove, Who bid-dest us to

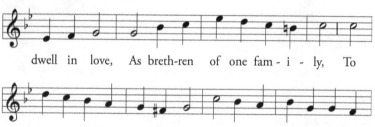

dwell in love, As breth-ren of one fam - i - ly, To

cry in ev' - ry need to Thee, Teach us no thought-less words to

say, But from our in - most heart to pray.

2. Thy name be hallowed. Help us, Lord,
   In purity to keep Thy Word,
   That to the glory of thy name
   We walk before Thee free from blame.
   Let no false doctrine us pervert;
   All poor, deluded souls convert.

3. Thy kingdom come. Thine let it be
   In time and in eternity.
   Let Thy good Spirit e'er be nigh
   Our hearts with graces to supply.
   Break Satan's power, defeat his rage;
   Preserve Thy Church from age to age.

4. Thy gracious will on earth be done
   As 'tis in heaven before Thy throne;
   Obedience in our weal and woe
   And patience in all grief bestow.
   Curb flesh and blood and every ill
   That sets itself against Thy will.

5. Give us this day our daily bread
   And let us all be clothed and fed.
   From war and strife be our Defense,
   From famine and from pestilence,
   That we may live in godly peace,
   Free from all care and avarice.

6. Forgive our sins, Lord, we implore,
   Remove from us their burden sore,
   As we their trespasses forgive
   Who by offenses us do grieve.
   Thus let us dwell in charity
   And serve our brother willingly.

7. Into temptation lead us not.
   When evil foes against us plot
   And vex our souls on every hand,
   Oh, give us strength that we may stand
   Firm in the faith, a well-armed host,
   Through comfort of the Holy Ghost!

8. From evil, Lord, deliver us;
The times and days are perilous.
Redeem us from eternal death,
And when we yield our dying breath,
Console us, grant us calm release,
And take our souls to Thee in peace.

9. Amen, that is, So shall it be.
Confirm our faith and hope in Thee
That we may doubt not, but believe
What here we ask we shall receive.
Thus in Thy name and at Thy word
We say: Amen. Oh, hear us, Lord!

Martin Luther, 1539

Psalmody

Sunday: Psalm 89c, 93, 94

Rogation Monday: Psalm 96, 97, 98

Rogation Tuesday: Psalm 99, 100, 101

Rogation Wednesday: Psalm 102, 103, 104a

Lesson

Sunday: John 16:23-33

Rogation Monday: Luke 11:5-13

Rogation Tuesday: Matthew 7:6-12

Rogation Wednesday: John 17:1-11a

Homily

Sunday - Basil the Great of Caesarea

We should give thanks to God for the good things He gives us, and not bear it with bad grace that He measures His giving. Should He grant us to be in union with Him: this we shall receive as a most perfect and joyful gift; should He delay this, let us suffer the loss in patience. For He disposes of our lives more perfectly than we could order them.

The halcyon is a sea bird which nests by the shore, laying its eggs in the sand, and bringing forth its young in the middle of winter; when the sea beats against the land in violent and frequent storms. But during the seven days while the halcyon broods: for it takes but seven days to hatch its young: all winds sink to rest, and the sea grows calm. And as it then is in need of food for its young ones, the most bountiful God grants this little creature another seven days of calm: that it may feed its young. Since all sailors know of this, they give this time the name of the halcyon days.

These things are ordered by the Providence of God for the creatures that are without reason, that you may be led to seek of God the things you need for your salvation. And when for this small bird He holds back the great and fearful sea, and bids it be calm in winter, what will He not do for you made in His own image? And if He should so tenderly cherish the halcyon, how much more will He not give you, when you call upon Him with all your Heart?

Let us then be resolved, Brethren, that as in our other needs so also in time of temptation, not to count on human expectations or seek help there, but let us send upwards our entreaties, and with sighs and tears, with earnest prayer, with long watching. And in this manner shall we obtain deliverance from our affliction; rejecting human help as vain, and keeping a firm hope in Him who alone has power to save us.

Sermon 9, On Prayer

Monday: Bede the Venerable

Let us pierce the ears of our benevolent Maker with our unwearying desire for eternal happiness, and let us not falter in what we have begun before He opens the gates, and we become worthy to be snatched from the prison of this death and to enter the gate of the heavenly fatherland. May no one delude himself in regard to his innocence; and may no one, trusting in his own actions, cease from his prayers as if he has no need of the mercy of the righteous Judge. Rather, even when someone recognizes that he has performed a good deed, since he does not know with what severity this may be judged let him with trembling cry out with the prophet, "Do not enter into judgment with your servant, because no one living will be justified in your sight;" and with blessed Job, "If I wish to declare myself righteous, my own mouth will condemn me; if I view myself as innocent, He will prove that I am evil." Let him be mindful always of the utterance of the apostle that "If we confess our sins, He is faithful and just to forgive us our sins and to cleanse us thoroughly from all iniquity; if we say that we have not sinned, we make Him a liar, and His word is not in us."

On the other hand, may no one in despair change his mind, and decide not to ask for pardon after he has reflected upon the nature and number of his sins. Let not the odiousness of the sight of his wounds, or the seriousness of his illness, prevent anyone from seeking salvation. Our Maker deigned to become our physician, to come to us Himself in the flesh, to take our infirmities upon Himself in order to heal them, to carry our sorrows in order to take them away: may these facts provide us with great confidence that we can obtain healing! He poured forth His blood on our behalf; He offered His death for our life. He showed that great remedy, repentance, for the great sins which have been committed... He loves to be asked so that He can give - He who, as a generous donor, raises up the minds of the needy to ask of Him, saying, "Everyone who asks receives, and the one who seeks finds, and to him who knocks it will be opened." Because the truth who made this promise cannot mislead, we must not doubt that those of us who ask receive, those of us who seek find, and to those of us who knock it will be opened. *Homily on the Greater Litanies*

Tuesday: Cyril of Alexandria

Perfect knowledge is knowledge that is true and undistorted, which stops itself from thinking or speaking perverse things, and that has a right belief in the Holy and Consubstantial Trinity. For although we now see through a glass dimly, and know only in part, as Paul tells us, as long as we hold carefully to that which we have been taught, and follow closely the mind of the holy and divinely revealed Scriptures, we will possess a knowledge that is not imperfect, and such as no one can have unless first enlightened by the Holy Spirit.

And regarding this the sainted Paul has given us the clearest testimony where he writes: "Grace to you, and peace from God our Father, and from the Lord Jesus Christ." As our Mediator and our High Priest and our Advocate, He intercedes with the Father for us. He is our assurance in the presence of the Father. So let us offer our prayers in Christ's Name. For in this way the Father will eagerly consent to them, and grant His graces to those who seek them, that receiving them we may rejoice. *On Confidence in Prayer*

Wednesday: Anglo-Saxon Homily

May we have this in our memory and set fast this example in our hearts so that we do not love worldly splendor or this world itself too much. This world is altogether decrepit, troubling, corruptible and unstable. And this world is completely transitory. Let us diligently consider and know concerning this whole world's commencement that when it was first formed it was full of beauty and was flourishing in itself with numerous pleasures. In that time, it was pleasant and wholesome to men upon earth, and there was upon the earth entire serenity, unbounded concord, and splendid youth. And this world was so fair and so delightful that it drew men to it by its beauty and fairness emanating from Almighty God. And when it was thus pleasant and appealing, it withered away in the hearts of Christ's faithful people, and is now blooming in our hearts as is appropriate.

Now there is lamentation and weeping on all sides. Now is mourning widespread and violation of peace. Now is everywhere evil and slaughter. Everywhere this world flees from us with great bitterness, and we follow it, as it flies from us, and desire it although it is passing away. Oh, we may hereby perceive that this world is illusory and transitory. Let us be mindful of this, while we may, so that we may diligently press on towards what is good. Let us obey our Lord faithfully. And let us give thanks to Him for all His gifts and for all His mercies, and for all His kindness and benefits which He has ever bestowed on us - the heavenly King that lives and reigns everlasting.

Blickling Homily for Rogation Wednesday

Collect

O God, from whom all good things come, grant to us, Your humble servants, that by Your holy inspiration we may think those things that are right and by Your merciful guiding may perform them, through Jesus Christ, Your Son, our Lord, who lives and reigns with You and the Holy Spirit, one God, now and forever.

Gelasian Sacramentary

AT LAUDS

Psalmody

Sunday: 3, C8, 51	Tuesday: 1, C10, 2
Monday: 118a, C9, 118b	Wednesday: 8, C11, 20

Lesson

Sunday: I Peter 1:1-21	Tuesday: I Peter 3:13-22
Monday: I Peter 2:11-25	Wednesday: I Peter 4:12-19

Hymn and Verse   *As during the week of Easter, p.391*

Antiphon to the Benedictus - *Petite, et accipietis*   Tone 8G

Ask, and it will be giv-en to you; seek, and you will find; knock, and it will be op-ened to you. al-le-lu-ia.

Matthew 7:7

✠ BLESSÉD is the Lord God of / Israel; *
For He has visited and re- / deemed His people. etc.

Collect

Be pleased, O Lord, to visit Your servants and Your handmaidens, who with humble faces ask the gifts of Your blessings; deliver them from the evil days and give them times of peace and the prize of the eternal reward; and as You once fed with the bread which You had blessed the multitude which had fasted for three days with You, so now deign to refresh us, for Your kingdom and dominion remain forever, world without end.

Pontifical of Egbert

AT TERCE, SEXT AND NONE

Chapter

Sunday: James 1:22-27　　　Tuesday: I Timothy 2:8-15
Monday: James 5:16-20　　　Wednesday: Ephesians 1:15-23

Responsories and Verses *As during the week of Easter, p.392*

AT VESPERS

Psalmody

Sunday: 136b, 137, 138　　　Tuesday: 144, 145, 7
Monday: 140, 141, 142　　　Wednesday: 9, 10, 11

Lesson

Sunday: I Peter 1:22-2:10　　　Tuesday: I Peter 4:1-11
Monday: I Peter 3:1-12　　　Wednesday: I Peter 5:1-14

Hymn and Verse *As during the week of Easter, p.394*

Antiphon to the Magnificat - *Usque modo non petistis*　　　　　*Tone 2*

Un - til　now　you　have asked no- thing　in　My　name.

Ask,　and you will re - ceive, al - le - lu - ia.　　*John 16:24*

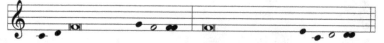

✠ MY SOUL magnifies / the Lord, *
And my spirit has rejoiced in God / my Savior.　etc.

Collect

Lord God, heavenly Father, who through Your Son promised us that whatsoever we ask in His name You will give us: We beseech You, keep us in Your word, and grant us Your Holy Spirit, that He may govern us according to Your will; protect us from the power of the devil, from false doctrine and worship; also defend our lives against all danger; grant us Your blessing and peace, that we may in all things perceive Your merciful help, and both now and forever praise and glorify You as our gracious Father, through our Lord Jesus Christ, Your Son, who lives and reigns with You and the Holy Spirit, one true God, world without end.　　　*Veit Dietrich*

ASCENSION

And the days after Ascension that fall in Rogate week

AT MATINS

Invitatory for Ascensiontide- *Christum ascendit*   *Tone 6*

Christ has as- cend - ed   to heav-en,   O come, let us wor-ship Him!

Hymn - *Auf Christi Himmelfahrt allein*

1. On Christ's as-cen-sion I now build The hope of mine as - cen - sion;

This hope a-lone has ev-er stilled All doubt and ap-pre - hen - sion;

For where the Head is, there full well   I   know His mem-bers

are   to dwell When Christ shall come and   call   them.

2. Since He returned to claim His throne,
Great gifts for men obtaining,
My heart shall rest in Him alone,
No other rest remaining;
For where My Treasure went before,
There all my thoughts shall ever soar
To still their deepest yearning.

3. Oh grant, dear Lord, this grace to me,
Recalling Thine ascension,
That I may ever walk with Thee,
Adorning Thy redemption;
And then, when all my days shall cease,
Let me depart in joy and peace
In answer to my pleading.

Josua Wagelin, 1636

Psalmody

Ascension Day: 104b, 105a, 105b
Friday: 106a, 106b, 107a
Saturday: 107b, 108, 109

Lesson

Ascension Day: Mark 16:14-20
Friday and Saturday: Luke 24:44-53

Homily

Thursday: Bernard of Clairvaux

"The One who descended is also the One who ascended" today "far above all the heavens, that He might fill all things." He had already proven that He was lord of all things on the earth and in the sea and in the lower regions; He had but to prove with similar but surely stronger arguments that He was also lord of the air and the heavens. The earth recognized her lord, because when He cried out in a loud voice: "Lazarus, come forth," at the sound of His mighty voice it restored the dead man. The sea recognized Him when it provided a firm footing for His steps, and the apostles thought He was a ghost. Even hell recognized Him when He shattered its bronze gates and iron bars and bound therein that insatiable murderer called the devil and Satan. Surely the one who raised the dead, cleansed lepers, gave sight to the blind and steadiness to the lame, and chased away all infirmities with a breath, was lord of all, and with the same hand He had used to shape things, He was reshaping what had become misshapen. Likewise when He predicted that a coin would be found right in the mouth of a fish, it was evident that He was lord of the sea and all things moving in it. He who put the powers of the air to public shame and nailed them to his cross had clearly received authority over the workshops of hell. It is it is "who went about doing good and healing all who were oppressed by the devil," who stood firm on level ground to teach the crowds and stood before the governor to endure blows to his face. All the while He was seen on earth and dwelt among humans He stood firm amidst many labors, working salvation throughout the earth.

Lord Jesus, to complete Your seamless garment, to bring the integrity of our faith to its wholeness, You, lord of the air, have only to ascend in open air, above all the heavens while Your disciples look on. This will prove that You are lord of the universe, because You fulfilled everything in all things. Accordingly, now it shall be Your due that at Your name every knee shall bend, in heaven, on earth, and in the lower regions, and every tongue shall confess that You are in glory and at the Father's right hand. In His right hand are delights for evermore. That is why the Apostle admonishes us to seek what is above, where Christ is, seated at the right hand of God. There surely is our treasure, Jesus Christ, "in whom are hidden all the treasures of wisdom and knowledge," in whom all the fullness of divinity resides bodily. *Sermon 2 for the Lord's Ascension*

Friday: Origen of Alexandria

In demonstrating the divinity of Jesus by using prophetic pronouncements about Him, we also give proof that the Scriptures which prophesy about Him are inspired and that those writings that announce His coming and His teaching speak with full power and authority; this is the reason they have won over the elect from among the nations. It must be admitted, however, that the divine quality of the prophetic statements and the spiritual character of the law of Moses came to light only with the coming of Jesus. Before Christ's advent it was hardly possible to present clear evidence that the old writings were inspired. But the coming of Jesus opened the eyes of readers who might have been skeptical about the divinity of the law and the prophets to the fact that these writings were indeed composed with the help of divine grace. Everyone who approaches the prophetic words attentively and diligently will experience a trace of divine enthusiasm in the very act of reading; the experience will convince him that what we believe to be God's words are not human writings. The light present in the law of Moses but previously hidden under a veil has begun to shine forth with the advent of Christ. The veil has been removed, and the good things whose shadow the letter displayed have gradually been raised to the status of knowledge. *On First Principles*

428

Saturday: Bruno of Segni

The Lord Jesus came to His disciples and found them sitting at supper; found them eating and drinking. He sat down with them. He ate, He drank with them; that He might show Himself to have assumed, not a phantasmal, but a true body, and might strengthen them by His Presence. He upbraided them for their unbelief; He confirmed them by His conversation. And eating together with them, He commanded them that they should not depart from Jerusalem, but wait for the promise of the Father. You, then, whoever you are, waiting for the promise of the Holy Spirit, do not depart from Jerusalem, do not forsake the Church, do not desert the companionship of the saints: there wait, there remain, because outside of the Church the Holy Spirit is given to none; and He leaves even those that have Him if they forsake it.

Sermon for Ascension Day

Collect

Grant, we pray You, Almighty God, that as we do believe Your only-begotten Son, our Lord Jesus Christ, to have ascended into the heavens, so may we also in heart and mind ascend there and with Him continually dwell, who lives and reigns with You and the Holy Spirit, one God, now and forever.

Gelasian Sacramentary

AT LAUDS

Psalmody

Thursday: Psalm 9, Canticle 5, Psalm 10
Friday: Psalm 11, Canticle 6, Psalm 12
Saturday: Psalm 13, Canticle 7, Psalm 150

Lesson

Thursday: II Peter 1:1-15
Friday: II Peter 2:4-22
Saturday: I John 1:1-10

Hymn - *Nobis, olympo redditus*

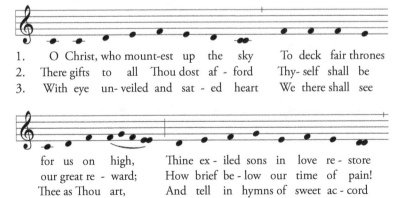

1. O Christ, who mount-est up the sky To deck fair thrones for us on high, Thine ex - iled sons in love re - store
2. There gifts to all Thou dost af - ford Thy- self shall be our great re - ward; How brief be - low our time of pain!
3. With eye un- veiled and sat - ed heart We there shall see Thee as Thou art, And tell in hymns of sweet ac - cord

Un - to their na - tive land once more.
How long our plea - sure shall re - main!
Our love and praise of Thee, O Lord.

4. Lest we be orphaned of Thy love
Send down from Thy high halls above
The Spirit of adoption sweet
Salvation's pledge, the Paraclete.

5. Jesu, to Thee our anthems tend
Who shalt be judge at time's last end;
To God the Father equal praise
And Holy Ghost through endless days. Amen.

Jean-Baptiste de Santeuil, 1686

Verse

℣: God has gone up with a shout, allelu- / ia.
℟: The Lord with the sound of a trumpet, allelu- / ia.

Psalm 47:5

Antiphon to the Benedictus *Ascendo ad Patrem*   *Tone 7a*

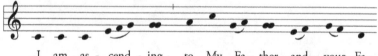

I am as - cend - ing to My Fa - ther and your Fa-

ther; to My God and your God, al - le - lu - ia.   *John 20:17*

✠ BLESSÉD is the Lord / God of Israel; *
For He has visited and re- / deemed His people. etc.

Collect

O God, who has gone up on high leading captivity captive, bestow on us the gifts of eternal peace; and as by ascending into heaven You have withdrawn Yourself corporeally from human sight, be graciously pleased to enter into our hearts, for You live and reign with the Father and the Holy Spirit, one God, now and forever.

Mozarabic Sacramentary

AT TERCE, SEXT AND NONE

Chapter

Ascension Day: Acts 1:1-11   Friday and Saturday: Acts 4:32-35

Responsory and Verse at Terce

℣: God has gone up with a shout. Al - le - lu - ia, al - le - lu - ia.
℟: God has gone up with a shout. Al - le - lu - ia, al - le - lu - ia.

℣: The Lord with the sound of a trum-pet. Al - le - lu- ia, al - le - lu - ia.
℟: God has gone up...

℣: Glo-ry be to the Fa-ther, and to the Son, and to the Ho-ly Spi - rit.
℟: God has gone up...

Psalm 47:5

℣: Christ ascended on high, allelu- / ia.
℟: He led captivity captive, allelu- / ia.

Ephesians 4:8

Responsory and Verse at Sext

℣: Christ as - cend - ed on high. Al - le - lu - ia, al - le - lu - ia.
℟: Christ as-cend- ed on high. Al - le - lu - ia, al - le - lu - ia.

℣: He led cap - ti - vi - ty cap-tive. Al - le - lu - ia, al - le - lu - ia.
℟: Christ ascended...

℣: Glo-ry be to the Fa-ther, and to the Son, and to the Ho-ly Spi - rit.
℟: Christ ascended...

Ephesians 4:8

℣: I am ascending to My Father and your Father, allelu- / ia.
℟: To My God and your God, allelu- / ia.

John 20:17

Responsory and Verse at None

℣: I am as-cend-ing to My Fa-ther and your Fa-ther.
℟: I am as-cend-ing to My Fa-ther and your Fa-ther.

Al - le - lu - ia, al - le - lu - ia.
Al - le - lu - ia, al - le - lu - ia.

℣: To My God and your God. Al - le - lu - ia, al - le - lu - ia.
℟: I am ascending...

℣: Glo-ry be to the Fa-ther, and to the Son, and to the Ho-ly Spi - rit.
℟:: I am ascending...

John 20:17

℣: The Lord has established, allelu- / ia.
℟: His throne in heaven, allelu- / ia.

Psalm 103:19

AT VESPERS

Psalmody

Thursday: 147b, 14, 15   Friday: 16, 17, 18a   Saturday: 18b, 19, 20

Lesson

Thursday: II Peter 1:16-2:3   Friday: II Peter 3:1-18   Saturday: I John 2:1-11

Hymn - *Jesu, nostra redemptio*

1. Je - su,   Re-demp-tion all   di - vine, Whom here we   love,
2. What love   of Thine was that, which led   To   take our   woes
3. To Thee   Hell's gate gave rea - dy   way, De - mand- ing   there

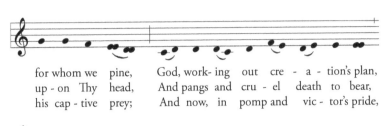

for whom we pine, God, work- ing out cre - a - tion's plan,
up - on Thy head, And pangs and cru - el death to bear,
his cap - tive prey; And now, in pomp and vic - tor's pride,

And, in the lat - ter time, made Man;
To ran - som us from death's des - pair.
Thou sit - test at the Fa - ther's side.

4. Let Thy true mercy move Thee still
To spare us, conquering all our ill;
And, granting what we ask, on high
With Thine own face to satisfy.

5. Be Thou our Joy and Thou our Guard,
Who art to be our great Reward;
Our glory and our boast in Thee
Forever and forever be.

6. All glory, Lord, to Thee we pay,
Ascending o'er the stars today;
All glory, as is ever meet,
To Father and to Paraclete. Amen.

Ambrosian Hymn, c. 7th c.

Verse

℣: The Lord has established, allelu- / ia.
℟: His throne in heaven, allelu- / ia.

Psalm 103:19

Antiphon to the Magnificat - *O Rex gloriae*   Tone 2

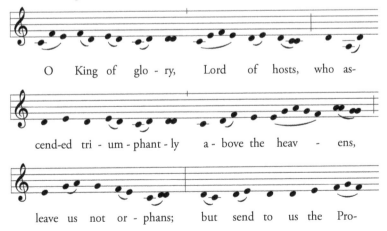

O King of glo - ry, Lord of hosts, who as-

cend-ed tri - um - phant - ly a - bove the heav - ens,

leave us not or - phans; but send to us the Pro-

433

mise   of the Fa - ther,   the Spi - rit   of truth, al - le - lu - ia.

Liturgical text

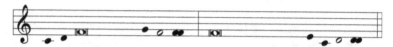

✠ MY SOUL magnifies / the Lord, *
And my spirit has rejoiced in God / my Savior.   etc.

Collect

O Jesus Christ, almighty Son of God, no longer in humiliation here on earth, but sitting at the right hand of Your Father, Lord over all things: We beseech You, send us Your Holy Spirit; give Your Church pious pastors, preserve Your word, control and restrain the devil and all who would oppress us: mightily uphold Your kingdom, until all Your enemies have been put under Your feet, that we may hold the victory over sin, death, and the devil, through You, who lives and reigns with God the Father and the Holy Spirit, one true God, world without end.   *Veit Dietrich*

EXAUDI
The Seventh Week of Easter

AT MATINS

Invitatory *As during the Ascension, p.427*

Hymn - *Komm, O Komm, Du Geist des Lebens*

1. Come, O come, Thou quick-'ning Spi-rit, God from all e - ter - ni - ty!

May Thy pow- er ne - ver fail us; Dwell with-in us con-stant-ly.

Then shall truth and life and light Ban-ish all the gloom of night.

2. Grant our hearts in fullest measure
Wisdom, counsel, purity,
That they ever may be seeking
Only that which pleaseth Thee.
Let Thy knowledge spread and grow,
Working error's overthrow.

3. Show us, Lord, the path of blessing;
When we trespass on our way,
Cast, O Lord, our sins behind Thee
And be with us day by day.
Should we stray, O Lord, recall;
Work repentance when we fall.

4. With our spirit bear Thou witness
That we are the sons of God
Who rely upon Him solely
When we pass beneath the rod;
For we know, as children should,
That the cross is for our good.

5. Prompt us, Lord, to come before Him
With a childlike heart to pray;
Sigh in us, O Holy Spirit,
When we know not what to say.
Then our prayer is not in vain,
And our faith new strength shall gain.

6. If our soul can find no comfort
And despondency grows strong
That the heart cries out in anguish:
"O my God, how long, how long?"
Comfort then the aching breast,
Grant us courage, patience, rest.

7. Holy Spirit, strong and mighty.
Thou who makest all things new,
Make Thy work within us perfect
And the evil Foe subdue.
Grant us weapons for the strife
And with victory crown our life.

8. Guard, O God, our faith forever;
Let not Satan, death, or shame
Ever part us from our Savior;
Lord our Refuge is Thy name.
Though our flesh cry ever: Nay!
Be Thy Word to us still Yea!

9. And when life's frail thread is breaking.
Then assure us more and more,
As the heirs of life unending,
Of the glory there in store,
Glory never yet expressed,
Glory of the saints at rest.

Heinrich Held, c.1664

Psalmody

Lesson

Sunday, Monday and Tuesday: John 15:26-16:4
Wednesday and Thursday: John 15:1-11
Thursday: John 15:12-17
Friday: John 12:44-50
Saturday: John 14:15-21

Homily

Sunday - Basil the Great of Caesarea

But when we speak of the plan of salvation for men, accomplished in God's goodness by our great God and Savior Jesus Christ, who would deny that it was all made possible through the grace of the Spirit? Whether you wish to examine the Old Testament - the blessings of the patriarchs, the help given through the law, the types, the prophecies, the victories in battle, the miracles performed through righteous men - or everything that happened since the Lord's coming in the flesh, it all comes to pass through the Holy Spirit. In the first place, the Lord was anointed with the Holy Spirit, who would henceforth be inseparably united to His very flesh, as it is written, "He on whom you see the Spirit descend and remain, this is He who... is My beloved Son," and "God anointed Jesus of Nazareth with the Holy Spirit." After His baptism, the Holy Spirit was present in every action He performed. He was there when the Lord was tempted by the devil: "Jesus was led up by the Spirit into the wilderness to be tempted." The Spirit was united with Jesus when He performed miracles: "But if it is by the Spirit of God that I cast out demons..." Nor did the Spirit leave Him after His resurrection from the dead. When the Lord renewed mankind by breathing into His Apostles' faces, (thus restoring the grace which Adam had lost, which God breathed into him in the beginning) what did He say? "Receive the Holy Spirit. If you forgive the sins of any, they are forgiven; if you retain the sins of any, they are retained." *On the Holy Spirit*

Monday - Gaudentius of Brescia

By promising that the fullness of his teaching would be bestowed by the Holy Spirit, He desired that He should be believed equal with Himself in omnipotence. For in the Trinity there is no master and there is no servant; God and an angel; the Creator and the creature. There is that in which they differ, and that in which they are the same: they differ in Person, in Nature they are the same. And yet they are not Gods, but God; for the Oneness of God does not admit any division.

Lastly Christ says of the Holy Spirit in this same place: "Whom the Father will send in My name;" that is, in the Name of God, to proclaim God, namely, as the Son... And when He decreed that Baptism should be conferred in the Name of the Trinity, He did not say in the Names of, but in the Name of. For the Father is God, the Son is God, and the Holy Spirit is God... And so One is the Name of the Trinity, One is the power, and One the divinity, which shall endure forever and ever. Amen. *Sermon 20*

Tuesday: Augustine of Hippo

The Paraclete will give such testimony about Me, that He will make people who have not seen Me believe in Me. And because He will give testimony of Me, you also will give testimony. Hence: "And you shall give testimony;" He by inspiring your hearts, you by proclaiming Him with your voices. And so, because you have been with Me from the beginning, you will be enabled to proclaim what you know, which now you do not because you don't have the fullness of the Spirit within you. For the charity of God, which will be given to you and poured forth in your hearts by the Holy Spirit, will give you the courage to give testimony. He, giving testimony and forming steadfast witnesses, removes fear from the hearts of Christ's friends, and changes the hatred of enemies into love.

Tractate 92 on John

Wednesday: Agobard of Lyons

Let the believer beware that he not presume altogether or even in part on his own powers, but on God's help, to arrive at the culmination of goodness and to persevere in good works, as the Lord says, "Apart from me you can do nothing." The apostle also: "It is God who is at work in you, both to will and to accomplish for good favor." And again: "By grace you have been saved through faith, and that not of yourselves." Still further: "Not that we are able to consider anything by us as though from us, but our sufficiency is from God." The Lord says, "No one can come to me unless the Father who sent me shall draw him." God does in man many good things which man does not do; but man does no good things which God does not show man how to do. For truly men do their own will, not God's, when they perform that which displeases God. But when they do what they will so that they serve the divine will, it is his will by which what they will is foreseen and decreed although they do voluntarily what they do. God loves us as we shall be by his grace, not as we are by our own merit. God foresees, foreknows, assists, and rewards in us his own goodness. No one is good but God alone, who is not good with the goodness of another. Men, however, are good, not by their own goodness, but by the goodness of God, who is the fount and source of goodness; nay, rather, who is goodness, from whom comes all good, and without whom there is nothing good.

On the Truth of the Faith

Thursday: Bernard of Clairvaux

You are created, healed, saved. Which of these, O man, comes from you? Which is not impossible to free choice? You could neither create yourself, since you were not there to do so; nor, when in sin, could you restore yourself to grace; nor raise yourself from the dead, to say nothing of those other good things, which are either necessary to those who have to be healed, or laid up in store for those who are to be saved. This is obvious enough in the case of creation and salvation. Yet, no one doubts it even in regard to justification except the man who, being ignorant of the righteousness that comes from God and seeking to establish his own, does not submit himself to God's righteousness. For can it be that, while acknowledging the power of the Creator and the glory of the Savior, you are ignorant of the righteousness of the Healer? "Heal me," said the prophet, "and I shall be healed; save me, and I shall be saved; for You are my praise." He acknowledged the righteousness of God, and hoped at the same time both to be healed of his sin by Him and to be cut free from sorrow. Hence he rightly declared that God, not himself, was his praise. For this reason also, David cried out: "Not unto us, O Lord, not unto us, but to Your name give glory;" for it was from God that he was looking for both robes, that is to say, the robe of righteousness and the robe of glory.

On Grace and Free Choice

Friday: Basil the Great of Caesarea

Where is the source of Christ's perfect wisdom? "The Father has Himself given Me commandment, what to say and what to speak." Through these words He guides us to the knowledge of the Father. He directs our wonder at all that He has made so that "through Him" we may know the Father.

The work of the Father is not separate or distinct from the work of the Son; for whatever things He sees the Father doing, "the Son also does in like manner." The Father enjoys our wonder at all that proceeds from the glory of the Only Begotten. He rejoices in the doer Himself as well as in the greatness of the deeds, and exults in being acknowledged as the Father of our Lord Jesus Christ, "for whom and through whom all things exist." The Lord says, "All Mine are Thine," as though He were submitting the lordship over created things to the Father, and "Thine are Mine," to show that the creative command came to Him from the Father. The Son did not need help with His work, nor are we to think that each detail of the work had been dictated to Him; such a menial condition would be quite inadequate to His divine dignity. Rather the Word was full of His Father's grace; He shines forth from the Father, and does all things according to the likeness of Him that begot Him. For if He is in essence without variation, He is also without variation in power. And their power is equal, their works are also equal. Christ is the power of God, and the wisdom of God. All things were made through Him and all things were created through and for Him, not as if He were discharging a slavish service, but in the fulfilment of the Father's will as Creator.

When He says, "I have not spoken on My own," and again, "as the Father has told Me, so I speak," and "the word which you hear is not Mine but the Father's who sent Me," and in another place, "as the Father gave Me commandment, so I do," He employs this kind of language not because He is unable to exercise choice or lacks the ability to initiate, or because He has to wait for a prearranged signal. He wants to make it plain that His own will is connected in indissoluble union with the Father. We must not think that what He calls "commandment" is an imperious order delivered verbally, the Father giving orders to the Son as to a subordinate, giving orders concerning what He ought to do. Instead let us think in terms befitting the Godhead, and realize that there is a transmission of will, like the reflection of an object in a mirror, passing from Father to Son without passage of time. "For the Father loves the Son, and shows Him all things that He Himself does." All that the Father has belongs to the Son; He does not acquire it little by little, but all together and at once. *On the Holy Spirit*

Saturday: Hilary of Poitiers

Christ Himself gives evidence of the nature of our life in Him through the sacrament of the flesh and blood imparted to us, when He says ... "Since I live, you also will live; since I am in My Father, and you are in Me, and I am in you." If He means a unity merely of will, why did He describe a kind of order of ascent in the establishment of that unity? His purpose surely was that we should believe that He was in the Father by nature, as being divine; whereas we are in Him by virtue of His birth in the flesh, and He is in us through the mystery of the sacraments: and that thus we should have a doctrine of a unity consummated through the Mediator, since, while we abide in Him, He would abide in the Father, and thus abiding, should abide in us, and thus we should advance in unity with the Father.

On the Trinity

Collect

Almighty, everlasting God, make us always to have a devout will toward You and to serve Your Majesty with a pure heart, through Jesus Christ, Your Son, our Lord, who lives and reigns with You and the Holy Spirit, one God, now and forever. *Gelasian Sacramentary*

AT LAUDS

Psalmody

Sunday: 67, C1, 5	Wednesday: 64, C4, 65	Friday: 76, C5, 92
Monday: 63, C2, 36	Thursday: 88, C6, 90	Saturday: 143, C7, 148
Tuesday: 43, C3, 57		

Lesson

Sunday: I John 2:12-17   Wednesday: I John 4:17-21   Friday: II John
Monday: I John 3:1-9   Thursday: I John 5:6-13   Saturday: Jude 1-19
Tuesday: I John 4:1-6

Hymn and Verse *as at the Ascension, p.429*

Antiphon to the Benedictus - *Cum venerit Paraclitus*   *Tone 8G*

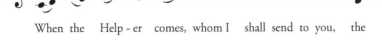

When the Help-er comes, whom I shall send to you, the

Spi-rit of truth who pro-ceeds from the Fa-ther, He

will test-i-fy of Me, al-le-lu-ia.   *John 15:26*

✠ BLESSÉD is the Lord God of / Israel; *
For He has visited and re- / deemed His people. etc.

Collect

Lamb of God, who takes away the sin of the world, look upon us and have mercy upon us; You, who are Yourself both Victim and Priest, Yourself both Reward and Redeemer; keep safe from all evils those whom You have redeemed, O Savior of the world, who lives and reigns with the Father and the Holy Spirit, one God, now and forever.

Gallican Sacramentary

AT TERCE, SEXT AND NONE

Chapter

Sunday, Monday and Tuesday: I Peter 4:8-11
Wednesday and Thursday: Hebrews 2:9-18
Friday: I Corinthians 7:17-24
Saturday: Acts 19:1-8

Responsories and Verses *As at the Ascension, p.431*

AT VESPERS

Psalmody

Sunday: 110, 111, 112, 113   Wednesday: 123, 124, 125   Friday: 129, 130, 131, 132
Monday: 114, 115, 116, 117   Thursday: 126, 127, 128   Saturday: 133, 135, 136a
Tuesday: 120, 121, 122

Lesson

Sunday: I John 2:18-29   Wednesday: I John 5:1-5   Friday: III John
Monday: I John 3:10-24   Thursday: I John 5:14-21   Saturday: Jude 20-25
Tuesday: I John 4:7-16

Hymn and Verse   *as at the Ascension, p.432*

Antiphon to the Magnificat - *Veni Sancte Spiritus, reple*   Tone 8G

Come, Ho - ly   Spi - rit,   fill the hearts of Your faith - ful

and kin - dle   in   them   the   fire   of   Your   love.   *Liturgical text*

✠ MY SOUL magnifies / the Lord, *
   And my spirit has rejoiced in / God my Savior. etc.

Collect

Lord God, heavenly Father, we give thanks to You, that through Your Holy Spirit You have appointed us to bear witness of Your dear Son, our Lord Jesus Christ: We beseech You, inasmuch as the world cannot endure such testimony, and persecutes us in every way, grant us courage and comfort, that we may not be offended because of the cross, but continue steadfastly in Your testimony, and be found always among those who know You and Your Son, until we obtain eternal salvation through the same, Your Son Jesus Christ, our Lord, who lives and reigns with You and the Holy Spirit, one true God, world without end. Amen.   *Veit Dietrich*

PENTECOST

AT MATINS

Invitatory - *Spiritus Domini replevit*   *Tone 6*

The Spi- rit of the Lord fills the whole world, O come, let us wor-ship Him!

Hymn - *Komm Heiliger Geist, Herre Gott*

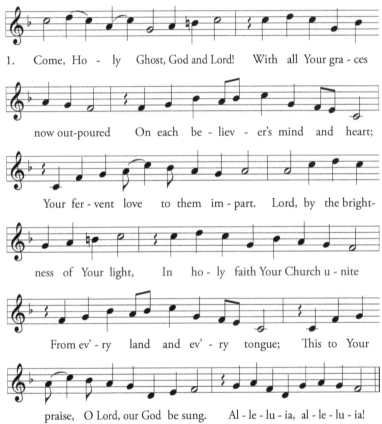

1. Come, Ho - ly Ghost, God and Lord! With all Your gra - ces
now out-poured On each be - liev - er's mind and heart;
Your fer - vent love to them im - part. Lord, by the brightness of Your light, In ho - ly faith Your Church u - nite
From ev' - ry land and ev' - ry tongue; This to Your
praise, O Lord, our God be sung. Al - le - lu - ia, al - le - lu - ia!

2. Come, holy Light, Guide Divine,
Now cause the Word of Life to shine!
Teach us to know our God aright
And call Him Father with delight.
From every error keep us free;
Let none but Christ our Master be
That we in living faith abide,
In Him, our Lord, with all our might confide.
Alleluia, alleluia!

3. Come, holy Fire, Comfort true,
Grant us the will Your work to do
And in Your service to abide;
Let trials turn us not aside.
Lord, by Your power prepare each heart
And to our weakness strength impart
That bravely here we may contend,
Through life and death to You, our Lord, ascend.
Alleluia, alleluia!

Martin Luther, 1524

Psalmody

Sunday: 42, 44, 45	Wednesday: 53, 55, 56	Friday: 61, 62, 66
Monday: 46, 47, 48	Thursday: 58, 59, 60	Saturday: 68a, 68b, 69a
Tuesday: 49, 50, 52		

Lesson

Sunday: John 14:22-31	Wednesday: John 6:44-51	Friday: Luke 5:17-26
Monday: John 3:16-21	Thursday: Luke 9:1-6	Saturday: Matthew 20:29-34
Tuesday: John 10:1-11		

Homily

Sunday - Aelred of Rievaulx

In His work of disposing all things the Spirit of the Lord has filled the whole world from the beginning, reaching from end to end of the earth in strength, and delicately disposing everything; but as sanctifier, the Spirit of the Lord has filled the whole world since Pentecost, for on this day the gracious Spirit Himself was sent by the Father and the Son on a new mission, in a new mode, by a new manifestation of His mighty power, for the sanctification of every creature. Before this day the Spirit had not been given, for Jesus was not yet glorified, but today He came forth from His heavenly throne to give Himself in all His abundant riches to the human race, so that the Divine outpouring might pervade the whole wide world and be manifested in a variety of spiritual endowments.

It is surely right that this overflowing delight should come down to us from heaven, since it was heaven that a few days earlier received from our fertile earth a fruit of wonderful sweetness. When has our land ever yielded a fruit more pleasant, sweeter, holier, or more delectable? Indeed, faithfulness has sprung up from the earth. A few days ago we sent Christ on ahead to the heavenly kingdom, so that in all fairness we might have in return whatever heaven held that should be sweet to our desire. The full sweetness of earth is Christ's humanity, the full sweetness of heaven Christ's Spirit. Thus a more profitable bargain was struck: Christ's human nature ascended from us to heaven, and on us today Christ's Spirit has come down. *Homily on Pentecost*

Monday - Johann Gerhard

The Lord Christ says: So much so God loved the world, that He gave His only born Son. With these words he describes the inexpressible love of God toward the human race. With the gift of His Son, he proved and demonstrated His love to the human race and therewith holds up before us three mysteriously incomprehensible things about the beloved Lord with a minimum of words. God the Lord is incomprehensible. His love is incomprehensible. His gift, which He bestowed out of love, is incomprehensible...

What God, then, has given out of love, we should accept through faith. As Christ says, God has given His Son to the world, so that all who believe in Him should not become lost, but rather have eternal life. God the Lord proffers the gift to the entire world, but only those become recipients of it who seize the gift with true faith.

How could God have given us stronger evidence of His compassion, and how could He have given us and established for us a more steadfast foundation for our faith than His Son?! Our faith seizes hold of Him and finds in Him God's grace and salvation. For faith establishes us in Christ and sees to it that Christ lives in us. Faith unites us with Christ, so that, just as Christ pleases God the Lord, we also are loved by God through this Loved One; so that just as Christ is holy and righteous, we also are made righteous through Him with the righteousness that avails before God; so that just as Christ achieved complete obedience of the Law and paid for our sin, so also justification unto life has come to us through His righteousness.

Homily for Pentecost Monday

Tuesday - Aphrahat of Persia

O pastors, be made like unto that diligent pastor, the chief of the whole flock, who cared so greatly for his flock. He brought near those who were afar off. He brought back the wanderers. He visited the sick. He strengthened the weak. He bound up the broken. He guarded the fatlings. He gave Himself up for the sake of the sheep. He chose and instructed excellent leaders, and committed the sheep into their hands, and gave them authority over all His flock. For He said to Simon Cephas: "Feed my sheep and my lambs and my ewes." So Simon fed His sheep; and he fulfilled all his time and handed over the flock to you, and departed. You also must feed and guide them well. For the pastor who cares for the sheep engages in no other pursuit along with that. He does not make a vineyard, or plant gardens, nor does he fall into the troubles of the world. Never have we seen a pastor who left the sheep in the wilderness and became a merchant, or one who left the flock to wander and became a farmer. But if he deserts the flock and does these things he thereby hands over the flock to the wolves.

Demonstrations

Wednesday - Prosper of Aquitaine

In the Gospel according to Matthew it is said that knowledge and understanding are gifts of God which He grants to whomsoever He pleases: "Then His disciples came and said to Him: 'Why speakest Thou to them in parables? But He answered and said to them: 'Because to you it is given to know the mysteries of the kingdom of heaven; but to them it is not given.'" John the Evangelist also proclaims that no man possess any good which he has not received from on high. "A man, he says, "cannot receive anything unless it be given him from heaven." In the same Gospel the Truth itself teaches that no one comes to the Son except drawn to Him by the Father, for it is God who bestows on any man that is to come to Him, both understanding and willingness. He says: "No man can come to me, except the Father, who hath sent me, draw him; and I will raise him up in the last day. For it is written in the Prophets: 'And they shall all be taught of God.' Every one that hath heard of the Father and hath learned, cometh to Me;" and further, "Therefore did I say to you that no man can come to me, unless it be given him by My Father."

The authority of Sacred Scripture confirms that a divine gift and a divine help is necessary for man to make progress in faith and good works and to persevere in them till the end. Thus the Apostle Paul, writing to the Philippians, says: "Being confident of this very thing: that He who hath begun a good work in you, will perfect it unto the day of Christ Jesus." Some one wanted to explain this text so as to prove from it his own perverse teaching; he wanted the text which reads, who hath begun in you," to be understood as though it read, who hath begun "from" you. Thus he attributed both the beginning and the completion of a work not to God but to man, whose will would be responsible for such a beginning and completion. But in the same epistle the great preacher of grace shatters this most insane pride, saying: "In nothing be ye terrified by the adversaries: which to them is a cause of perdition, but to you of salvation, and this from God. For unto you it is given for Christ, not only to believe in Him, but also to suffer for Him." And again he says: "For it is God who worketh in you, both to will and to work, according to His good will." Likewise in his First Epistle to the Thessalonians he teaches that the beginning, progress, and perfection of every virtue come from God, saying, "Now God Himself and our Father and the Lord Jesus direct our way unto you. And may the Lord multiply you and make you abound in every charity towards one another and towards all men, as we do also towards you. To confirm your hearts without blame, in holiness, before God and our Father, at the coming of our Lord Jesus Christ, with all His saints.

The Call of All Nations

Thursday - Atto of Verceil

The number fifty signifies remission, which we may gather from the Old Testament. For in the fiftieth year, which was called the year of jubilee, that is of remission, debts were remitted to all debtors, slavery was ended to those servants who desired freedom. Well, therefore, may this fiftieth day be called the day of Jubilee, because the Holy Ghost, descending on the Apostles, gave them the remission of all their sins, and freed them from the contagion of their former frailty.

This festival was also celebrated in the Old Testament, and in it, among the Jews, the first-offering was annually made of the new fruits. Mystically also in the Christian Church, on this day bread, made from the new corn, that is, the new virtues of the Holy Ghost, on which we are nourished, and by which we live, was first given by the Apostles to the Gentiles. Nor is it irrelevant to the matter that on the fiftieth day after the Lord had killed the firstborn of Egypt, and destroyed the power of its princes, and had set free the children of Israel from their servitude and from the depths of the Red Sea, He gave the law to Moses which was to be preached to the people; and in like manner on the fiftieth day... He declared by the Holy Ghost to His Apostles, how they themselves should act and teach others.

Eleventh Sermon for Pentecost

Friday - Peter Chrysologus

You see here, brothers, God does not look to the wishes of the foolish, nor see the faith of the ignorant, nor trouble with the foolish desires of the weak. But He will come to our aid because of another's faith, which He conferred by grace alone. For whatever comes from the Divine Will, He does not deny. And when, brothers, does a physician look to the wishes of the sick or heed their desires: since they always crave for and ask for things that may be harmful. Instead, he will now make use of steel, now of fire, now of a bitter drink, and apply them even to the unwilling, so that when they are well they will understand what was done for them, which they couldn't while ill. And if a man will ignore insults and be indifferent to abuse so that he may bring life and health to the diseased; how much the more will Christ the Physician, in His divine goodness, draw to salvation those who are sick from the wounds of sin, or suffering the delirium of unlawful vice; even the reluctant and unwilling?

O if we but chose, brethren, O if we but chose to look into every paralysis of our mind, and see our soul as it lies abandoned on its bed of sin; we would see ourselves as Christ sees; each day patiently observing our sinful desires, drawing us, urging us, even unwilling, towards His saving remedies!

Son, He says, your sins are forgiven you. Saying this, He shows that it is His will for men to know that He is God; though now as man still hidden to human eyes. Through His signs and wonders He was already compared with the prophets who, through Him, had also wrought signs and wonders. Now He began to implant in human hearts that He was God: for to forgive sin, since it is beyond human power, is the particular sign of divinity.

The envy of the Pharisees proves this: for when He said: Your sins are forgiven you, the Pharisees answered: He blasphemes. Who can forgive sins but God alone? O Pharisee! who knowing, does not know; who confessing, denies; who testifying, impugns! If it is God who forgives sins, why isn't Christ God to you, who by one act of forgiveness is proven to have taken away the sins of the whole world? "Behold," says Scripture, "the lamb of God who takes away the sins of the world." But that you may have yet greater proofs of His Divinity: listen to Him who pierced the secret of your breast. Look upon Him who reached into the hidden places of your thoughts. Understand Him who lays bare the secret counsels of your heart!

Sermon 50

Saturday - Peter of Blois

Tribulation hastens your journey to God. Each of the tribulations you bear is a message sent to you by God bidding you hasten to Him and not linger on the way. Observe how debased the considerations are which make the degenerate soul reluctant to hasten to God. Tribulation removes the delight and pleasure in transient things which prevent men from hastening to God; so Gregory says: "The evils which oppress us here force us to go to God." So do not underestimate the benefit of tribulation, which frees you from an oppressive prison and hastens your journey to the kingdom of Heaven.

Twelve Advantages of Tribulation

Collects

Sunday

O God, who at this time taught the hearts of Your faithful people by sending to them the light of Your Holy Spirit, grant us by the same Spirit to have a right judgment in all things and always to rejoice in His holy comfort, through Jesus Christ, Your Son, our Lord, who lives and reigns with You and the Holy Spirit, one God, now and forever. *Gelasian Sacramentary*

Monday

O God, who gave the Holy Spirit to Your apostles, grant to Your people the performance of their petitions, that as You have given them faith, You may also give them peace; through Jesus Christ, Your Son, our Lord, who lives and reigns with You and the Holy Spirit, one God, now and forever. *Gregorian Sacramentary*

Tuesday

Assist us, O Lord, we beseech You, with the power of Your Holy Spirit, that our hearts may be purified, according to Your mercy, and we may be defended from all adversities, through Jesus Christ, Your Son, our Lord, who lives and reigns with You and the Holy Spirit, one God, now and forever. *Leonine Sacramentary*

Wednesday

May the Spirit, the Paraclete, O Lord, who proceeds from You, illumine our minds, and, as Your Son has promised, lead us into all truth; through the same Jesus Christ, Your Son, our Lord, who lives and reigns with You and the Holy Spirit, one God, now and forever. *Gelasian Sacramentary*

Thursday

May the outpouring of Your Holy Spirit, O Lord, cleanse our hearts, and make them fruitful with its plentiful dew; through our Lord Jesus Christ who lives and reigns with You and the Holy Spirit, one God, now and forever. *Gelasian Sacramentary*

Friday

Let Your Holy Spirit, O Lord, come into our midst, and washing us with the pure water of repentance, prepare us always to be a living sacrifice to You, through Jesus Christ, Your Son, our Lord, who lives and reigns with You and the Holy Spirit, one God, now and forever. *Mozarabic Missal*

Saturday

Let Your mercy, O Lord, be upon us, and the brightness of Your Holy Spirit illumine our souls; that He may enkindle our cold hearts and light up our dark minds, who abides evermore with You and Your Son Jesus Christ, in glory now and forever. *Mozarabic Missal*

AT LAUDS

Psalmody

Lesson

Hymn - *Beata nobis gaudia*

1. Blest joys for migh-ty won-ders wrought The year's re- volv-
2. The quiv - 'ring fire their heads be-dewed In clo-ven tongues
3. In var - ying tongues the Lord they praised, The gath'-ring peo-

ing orb hath brought, What time the Ho - ly Ghost in flame
si - mi - li- tude, That el - o - quent their words might be,
ple stood a - mazed; And whom the Com - for - ter di - vine

Up-on the Lord's dis - cip - les came.
And fer-vid all their char - i - ty.
In-spired, they mocked as full of wine.

4. These things were done in type today,
When Eastertide had worn away,
The number told which once set free
The captive at the jubilee.

5. And now, O holy God, this day
Regard us, as we humbly pray,
And send us from thy heavenly seat
The blessings of the Paraclete.

6. Thou once in every holy breast
Didst bid indwelling grace to rest:
This day our sins, we pray, release,
And in our time, O Lord, give peace.

7. To God the Father, God the Son,
And God the Spirit, praise be done;
And Christ the Lord upon us pour
The Spirit's gift for evermore. Amen.

Attr. Hilary of Poitiers, 4th c.

Verse

℣: They were all filled with the Holy Spirit, allelu- / ia.
℟: And began to speak, allelu- / ia.

Acts 2:4

Antiphon to the Benedictus - *Ego sum panis*

Tone 8G

I am the liv-ing bread, says the Lord, which came down

from hea - ven. Al - le - lu - ia, al - le - lu - ia.

John 6:51

✠ BLESSÉD is the Lord God of / Israel; *
For He has visited and re- / deemed His people. etc.

Collect

May the Spirit, the Paraclete, O Lord, who proceeds from You, illumine our minds and, as Your Son has promised, lead us into all truth, through the same, Jesus Christ, our Lord, who lives and reigns with you and the Holy spirit, one God, now and forever.

Gelasian Sacramentary

AT TERCE, SEXT AND NONE

Chapter

Sunday: Acts 2:1-13	Wednesday: Acts 5:12-16	Friday: Acts 2:22-28
Monday: Acts 10:42-48a	Thursday: Acts 8:5-8	Saturday: Romans 5:1-5
Tuesday: Acts 8:4-17		

Responsory and Verse at Terce

℣: The Spi - rit of the Lord has filled the world. Al - le -
℟: The Spi - rit of the Lord has filled the world. Al - le -

lu - ia, al - le - lu - ia.
lu - ia, al - le - lu - ia.

℣: And He who con-tains all things has know-ledge of man's voice.

Al - le - lu - ia, al - le - lu - ia.
℟: The Spirit...

℣: Glo-ry be to the Fa-ther, and to the Son, and to the Ho-ly Spi - rit.
℟: The Spirit...

Wisdom 1:7

℣: The Helper, the Holy Spirit, allelu- / ia.
℟: Will teach you all things, allelu- / ia.

Responsory and Verse at Sext

℣: The Help-er, the Ho-ly Spi - rit. Al - le - lu - ia, al - le - lu - ia.
℟: The Help-er, the Ho-ly Spi-rit. Al - le - lu - ia, al - le - lu - ia.

℣: Will teach you all things. Al - le - lu - ia, al - le - lu - ia.
℟: The Helper...

℣: Glo-ry be to the Fa-ther, and to the Son, and to the Ho-ly Spi - rit.
℟: The Helper...

John 14:26

℣: They were all filled with the Holy Spirit, allelu- / ia.
℟: And began to speak, allelu- / ia.

Acts 2:4

Responsory and Verse at None

℣: They were all filled with the Ho - ly Spi - rit. Al - le -
℟: They were all filled with the Ho - ly Spi - rit. Al - le -

lu - ia, al - le - lu - ia.
lu - ia, al - le - lu - ia.

℣: And be - gan to speak. Al - le - lu - ia, al - le - lu - ia.
℟: They were...

℣: Glo-ry be to the Fa-ther, and to the Son, and to the Ho-ly Spi - rit.
℟: They were...

John 20:20

℣: The apostles were speaking in other tongues, allelu- / ia.
℟: The wonderful works of God, allelu- / ia.

Acts 2:11

AT VESPERS

Psalmody

Sunday: 136b, 137, 138	Wednesday: 9, 10, 11	Friday: 17, 147a, 147b
Monday: 140, 141, 142	Thursday: 12, 13, 14, 16	Saturday: 19, 54, 77
Tuesday: 144, 145, 7		

Lesson

Sunday: I Samuel 1:20-28	Wednesday: I Samuel 7:9-17	Friday: I Samuel 12:14-25
Monday: I Samuel 2:22-36	Thursday: I Samuel 8:10-22	Saturday: I Samuel 14:6-14
Tuesday: I Samuel 5:1-12		

Hymn - *Veni Creator Spiritus*

1. Come Ho - ly Ghost, Cre - a - tor blest, Vouch-safe with - in
2. To Thee, the Com - fort - er, we cry, To Thee, the gift
3. The sev'n- fold gifts of grace are Thine, O fin - ger of

our souls to rest; Come with Thy grace and heav'n-ly aid,
of God Most High; The Fount of life, the fire of love,
the Hand Di - vine; True Pro - mise of the Fa - ther Thou,

And fill the hearts which Thou hast made.
The soul's a - noint - ing from a - bove.
Who dost the tongue with speech en - dow.

4. Thy light to every thought impart
And shed Thy love in every heart;
The weakness of our mortal state
With deathless might invigorate.

5. Drive far away our wily foe
And Thine abiding peace bestow
if Thou be our protecting Guide,
No evil can our steps betide.

6. Make Thou to us the Father known,
Teach us th'e-ternal Son to own
And Thee, whose name we ever bless,
Of both the Spirit, to confess.

7. Praise we the Father and the Son
And Holy Spirit, with them One;
And may the Son on us bestow
The gifts that from the Spirit flow. Amen.

Rabanus Maurus, 9th c.

Verse

℣: They were all filled with the Holy Spirit, allelu- / ia.
℟: And began to speak, allelu- / ia.

Acts 2:4

Antiphon to the Magnificat - *Spiritus qui a Patre*

Tone 8G

The Spi - rit, who pro-ceeds from the Fa - ther, al - le - lu - ia,

He will tes - ti - fy of Me. Al - le - lu - ia, al - le - lu - ia. *John 15:26*

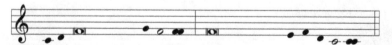

✠ MY SOUL magnifies / the Lord, *
And my spirit has rejoiced in / God my Savior. etc.

Collect

O Lord Jesus Christ, almighty Son of God: We beseech You, send Your Holy Spirit into our hearts, through Your word, that He may rule and govern us according to Your will, comfort us in every temptation and misfortune, and defend us by Your truth against every error, so that we may continue steadfast in the faith, increase in love and all good works, and firmly trusting in Your grace, which through death You have purchased for us, obtain eternal salvation, You who reigns, with the Father and the Holy Spirit, world without end. Amen.   *Veit Dietrich*

HOLY TRINITY WEEK

AT MATINS

Hymn - *Veni Creator Spiritus*

1. Come Ho - ly Ghost, Cre - a - tor blest, Vouch-safe with - in
2. To Thee, the Com - fort - er, we cry, To Thee, the gift
3. The sev'n- fold gifts of grace are Thine, O fin - ger of

our souls to rest; Come with Thy grace and heav'n-ly aid,
of God Most High; The Fount of life, the fire of love,
the Hand Di - vine; True Pro - mise of the Fa - ther Thou,

And fill the hearts which Thou hast made.
The soul's a - noint - ing from a - bove.
Who dost the tongue with speech en - dow.

4. Thy light to every thought impart
And shed Thy love in every heart;
The weakness of our mortal state
With deathless might invigorate.

5. Drive far away our wily foe
And Thine abiding peace bestow
if Thou be our protecting Guide,
No evil can our steps betide.

6. Make Thou to us the Father known,
Teach us th'e-ternal Son to own
And Thee, whose name we ever bless,
Of both the Spirit, to confess.

7. Praise we the Father and the Son
And Holy Spirit, with them One;
And may the Son on us bestow
The gifts that from the Spirit flow. Amen.

Rabanus Maurus, 9th c.

Psalmody

Sunday: 69b, 70, 71
Monday: 72, 73, 74
Tuesday: 78a, 78b, 78c

Wednesday: 75, 79, 80
Thursday: 81, 82, 83

Friday: 84, 86, 87, 93
Saturday: 85, 89a, 89b

Lesson

Sunday, Monday and Tuesday: John 3:1-15
Wednesday and Thursday: Luke 20:27-40
Thursday: Matthew 22:23-33 or Mark 12:18-27

Friday and Saturday: Luke 17:1-10
Saturday: Matthew 17:19-21

Homily

Sunday - Martin Luther

It is commanded that we do good works and be obedient to the Law, but we don't see the kingdom of God by doing so. If we want to see this we must become entirely different and new men. This doesn't happen through bodily birth but through water and the Spirit - these are the true father and mother of this new-born offspring.

The water is nothing other than Holy Baptism. For Christ says in Mark 16:16: "He who believes and is baptized will be saved." But water doesn't have this power naturally. Water is water. It's a created element which cannot of itself move or change the heart or wash away sins. You can clean clothes and dirt from your skin with water, but not your soul. But this water which our Lord speaks about and which we call Baptism is not just simple water. It's water in which God's Word, His command and promise, are contained. Here two things, water and Word, are joined together so completely that we can't separate the one from the other. If you take the Word away from the water you don't have Baptism. If you take the water away from the Word you also don't have Baptism. But if the water and the Word remain together, you have a water in which the Holy Spirit is present, and through which He wants to regenerate you to the Kingdom of God, that is, to forgive your sins and save you.

So we should diligently think about this passage, especially against that blind rabble of Anabaptists who reject infant baptism and call it useless. But how can this Baptism be useless? Here you are told that Christ has set apart water in order that by it the Holy Spirit might bring about regeneration. Now if children need to be born again or else cannot see the Kingdom of God, why would anyone deny them Baptism? Or why would anyone claim that water, comprehended in God's command and connected with God's Word, cannot be used to regenerate them? Don't the words of Christ insist that whoever is to be born again must be born of water? So, even though water without the Spirit can't do anything, the Holy Spirit doesn't want to do His work without water... Christ here orders it. And no one should dare to break such an order.

Second House Postil for Trinity Sunday

Monday - Gregory of Nazianzus

The Word of Scripture recognizes three births for us: one from the body, one from baptism, and one from resurrection. The first takes place at night and in slavery and in passions. The second takes place in the day and in freedom and releases from passions, cutting away all the veil that has surrounded us since birth and leading us back toward the life on high. The third is more fearful and more swift, assembling in a moment all that has been created and presenting it to the Creator to give an account of its servitude and way of life here, as to whether one has followed only the flesh, or risen up with the Spirit and respected the grace of the re-creation. It is manifest that my Christ has honored in Himself all these births, the first by breathing in the first and living breath, the second by His incarnation and the baptism with which He was baptized, the third by the resurrection that he offered as first fruits when He became firstborn among many brothers and thus deigned to become firstborn from the dead.

The [second birth is illumination and is] radiance of souls, transformation of life, engagement of the conscience toward God. Illumination is help for our weakness, illumination is renunciation of the flesh, following of the Spirit, communion in the Word, setting right of the creature, a flood overwhelming sin, participation in light, dissolution of darkness. Illumination is a vehicle leading toward God, departure with Christ, support of faith, perfection of mind, key to the kingdom of heaven, change of life, deliverance from slavery, release from bonds, transformation of our composite nature. Illumination [of Baptism]... is the most beautiful and most magnificent of the gifts of God...

Just at Christ, its giver, is called by many and diverse names, so also is His gift... We call it gift, grace, baptism, illumination, anointing, robe of incorruption, bath of rebirth, seal, everything honorable. It is a gift because no offering is given for it beforehand; and grace, as given even to debtors; and baptism, as burying sin in the water; and anointing, as priestly and royal, since they were the ones anointed; and illumination, as most radiant; and robe, as entirely covering shame; and bath, as washing clean, and seal, as a safeguard and a sign of authority. In this the heavens rejoice together, this the angels glorify because it is akin to their great radiance. This is an image of the blessedness to come. We desire to sing forth its praises, but we are not able to do so worthily.

Festal Oration 40 - On Baptism

Tuesday - Thomas Aquinas

It is impossible to attain to the knowledge of the Trinity by natural reason. For... man cannot obtain a knowledge of God by natural reason except from creatures. Now creatures lead us to the knowledge of God, as effects do to their cause. Accordingly, by natural reason we can know of God only that which belongs to Him as the cause of all things... Now the creative power of God is common to the whole Trinity; and hence it belongs to the unity of essence, and not to the distinction of persons. Therefore, by natural reason we can know what belongs to the unity of essence, but not what belongs to the distinction of persons.

Whoever, then, tries to prove the trinity of persons by natural reason, detracts from faith in two ways. First, as regards the dignity of faith itself, which consists in its being concerned with invisible things that exceed human reason; wherefore the Apostle says that faith is of things that appear not, and the same Apostle says also, we speak wisdom among the perfect, but not the wisdom of this world, or of the princes of this world; but we speak the wisdom of God in a mystery which is hidden. Secondly, as regards the utility of drawing others to faith. For when anyone in the endeavor to prove what belongs to faith brings forward arguments which are not cogent, he falls under the ridicule of the unbelievers: since they suppose that we base ourselves upon such arguments, and that we believe on their account.

Therefore, we must not attempt to prove what is of faith, except by authority alone, to those who receive the authority; while as regards others, it suffices to prove that what faith teaches is not impossible...

Summa Theologica

Wednesday - Justin Martyr

God calls even the body to resurrection, and promises it everlasting life. When He promises to save the man, He thereby makes His promise to the flesh; for what is man but a rational living being composed of soul and body? Is the soul by itself a man? No, it is but the soul of a man. Can the body be called a man? No, it can but be called the body of a man. If, then, neither of these is by itself a man, but that which is composed of the two together is called a man, and God has called man to life and resurrection, He has called not a part, but the whole, which is the soul and the body.

On the Resurrection

Thursday - Augustine of Hippo

If flesh and blood shall not gain possession of the kingdom of God, then it's all for nothing that we have believed that our Lord rose again from the dead in the body in which he was born and crucified, and that in it he ascended into heaven before the very eyes of his disciples... [But our Lord] didn't want them to remain with the ruinous assumption that they were going to do the same kind of things in the kingdom of God, in that eternal life, as they used to do in this life, occupied with the pleasures of eating and drinking, of marrying husbands and wives, and producing children according to the flesh. You see, it's the flesh's liability to decay that requires these activities, not the specific nature of flesh...

The Jews, you see, certainly believed in the resurrection of the flesh; but they thought it was going to be such that they would have the same kind of life in the resurrection as they led in this world. And so, with such fleshly, gross ideas about it they were unable to answer the Sadducees, when they put their problem about the resurrection; whose wife a woman would be whom seven brothers had had in turn, each of them wishing to raise up seed for his dead brother from his wife. The Sadducees, I mean, were a particular sect of the Jews which didn't believe in the resurrection. So when the Sadducees put this problem, the Jews were uncertain and hesitant, and couldn't really answer it, because they assumed that the kingdom of God could be possessed by flesh and blood, imperishability, that is, by what is perishable. Along comes Truth, he is questioned by the misguided and misguiding Sadducees, that problem is put to the Lord. And the Lord, who knew what he was saying, and who wished us to believe what we didn't know, gives an answer by his divine authority which we are to hold by faith. The apostle, for his part, explained it to the extent that it was granted him to; which we, as best we can, must try to understand.

So what did the Lord say to the Sadducees? You are mistaken, he said, not knowing the scriptures, nor the power of God. For in the resurrection they marry neither husbands nor wives; for neither do they start dying again, but they will be equal to the angels of God. Great is the power of God. Why do they not marry husbands or wives? Because they won't start dying again. It's where one generation departs, you see, that another is required to succeed it. So there will be no such liability to decay in that place. And the Lord himself passed through the usual stages of growth, from infancy to adult manhood, because he was bearing the substance of flesh that was still mortal; but after he has risen again at the age at which he was buried, are we to imagine that he is growing old in heaven? So, they will be, he says, equal to the angels of God. He eliminated the assumption of the Jews, refuted the objection of the Sadducees; because the Jews did indeed believe the dead would rise again, but they had gross, fleshly ideas about what activities they would rise again for.

Sermon on the Resurrection of the Dead

Friday - Cyril of Alexandria

If he who sins against you repents and acknowledges his fault, forgive him: and not only once, but very many times. For we must not show ourselves lacking in love and neglect mercy, because one is weak and again and again offends; but rather let us imitate those whose business it is to heal bodily ills, and who do not tend to a sick man only once or twice, but just as often as he happens to fall ill. For let us remember that we also are liable to infirmities, and overpowered by our passions; and this being the case, we pray that those whose duty it is to rebuke us and who possess the authority to punish us, may be kind to us and forgiving. It is our duty therefore, having compassion over our mutual infirmities, to bear one another's burdens; even so we shall fulfil the law of Christ.

Homily 114 on Luke's Gospel

Saturday - Baldwin of Forde

Faith is the mustard seed, the smallest of all seeds. But when it has grown it is the greatest of all herbs and becomes a tree, so that the birds of the air come and dwell in its branches. The seeds and herbs are the tenets of philosophers and the traditions of human beings - plants, that is, that the heavenly Father did not plant. Compared with these, the simplicity of faith seems contemptible, but when it has grown into the multitude of the faithful, then, through the mystery of the cross, it is raised on high as a tree, so that the righteous may dwell in its protection.

The Commendation of Faith

Collect

Almighty and everlasting God, who has given to us, Your servants, grace, by the confession of a true faith, to acknowledge the glory of the eternal Trinity and in the power of the Divine Majesty to worship the Unity, we implore You that You would keep us steadfast in this faith and evermore defend us from all adversities; who lives and reigns, Father, Son, and Holy Spirit, one God, now and forever.

Gregorian Sacramentary

AT LAUDS

Psalmody

Sunday: 67, C1, 5	Wednesday: 64, C4, 65	Friday: 76, C5, 92
Monday: 63, C2, 36	Thursday: 88, C6, 90	Saturday: 143, C7, 148
Tuesday: 43, C3, 57		

Lesson

Sunday: I Samuel 15:1-9	Wednesday: I Samuel 18:5-16	Friday: I Samuel 23:1-5
Monday: I Samuel 16:1-13	Thursday: I Samuel 21:10-15	Saturday: I Samuel 24:1-7
Tuesday: I Samuel 17:1-11		

Collect

O Lord, the Savior and Protector of all who fear You, turn away from us the false pleasures of worldly wisdom; that by the teaching of Your Spirit, we may find pleasure in the superior prophetic and apostolic decrees, rather than in words of philosophy; lest the vanity of falsehood deceive those whom truth enlightens, through Jesus Christ, Your Son, our Lord, who lives and reigns with You and the Holy Spirit, now and forever. Amen.

Gelasian Sacramentary

AT TERCE, SEXT AND NONE

Chapter

Sunday, Monday and Tuesday: Romans 11:33-36
Wednesday and Thursday: II Thessalonians 2:8-14
Friday and Saturday: Galatians 3:6-11

AT VESPERS

Psalmody

Sunday: 110, 111, 112, 113	Wednesday: 123, 124, 125	Friday: 129, 130, 131, 132
Monday: 114, 115, 116, 117	Thursday: 126, 127, 128	Saturday: 133, 135, 136a
Tuesday: 120, 121, 122		

Lesson

Sunday: I Samuel 15:10-23	Wednesday: I Samuel 21:1-9	Friday: I Samuel 23:14-18
Monday: I Samuel 16:14-23	Thursday: I Samuel 22:11-23	Saturday: I Samuel 24:16-22
Tuesday: I Samuel 17:31-54		

Collect

O Lord God, heavenly Father; we poor sinners confess that no good thing dwells in our flesh, and that left to ourselves, we die and perish in sin, since that which is born of the flesh is flesh and cannot see the kingdom of God. But we implore You: grant us Your grace and mercy, and for the sake of Your Son, Jesus Christ, send Your Holy Spirit into our hearts, that being regenerate, we may firmly believe the forgiveness of sins, according to Your promise in baptism; and that we may daily increase in brotherly love and in other good works, until we at last obtain eternal salvation, through the same, Your beloved Son, Jesus Christ, our Lord, who lives and reigns with You and the Holy Spirit, one true God, world without end. Amen.   *Veit Dietrich*

THE FIRST WEEK
AFTER TRINITY

AT MATINS

Hymn - *Nun bitten wir den Heiligen Geist*

1.   To God the Ho-ly   Spi - rit let us   pray For the   true faith need-

ed   on our way, That He may de-fend us when life is end-ing

And, from ex - ile home we are   wend - ing. Lord, have mer-cy!

2. O sweetest Love, Your grace on us bestow;
Set our hearts with sacred fire aglow
That with hearts united we love each other,
Every stranger, sister, and brother.
Lord, have mercy!

3. Transcendent Comfort in our every need,
Help us neither scorn nor death to heed
That we may not falter nor courage fail us
When the foe shall taunt and assail us.
Lord, have mercy!

4. Shine in our hearts, O Spirit, precious light;
Teach us Jesus Christ to know aright
That we may abide in the Lord who bought us,
Till to our true home He has brought us.
Lord, have mercy!

Martin Luther, 1524

Psalmody

Sunday: 89c, 94, 96   Wednesday: 104a, 104b, 104c   Friday: 106a, 106b, 107a
Monday: 97, 98, 99, 100   Thursday: 105a, 105b, 105c   Saturday: 107b, 108, 109
Tuesday: 101, 102, 103

Lesson

Sunday, Monday and Tuesday: Luke 16:19-31
Monday: Mark 10:23-31, Matthew 19:23-29
Tuesday: Luke 11:29-36

Wednesday and Thursday: Luke 12:11-21
Thursday: Luke 18:24-30

Friday and Saturday: Matthew 5:17-19
Saturday: Luke 16:16-18

Homily

Sunday - Aelfric of Eynsham

Truly the following sentence applies to the perishing soul, "On this day you dwell in peace, for the coming vengeance is now hidden from your eyes." The perverse soul is indeed dwelling in peace in its day, as it rejoices in fleeting time, is exalted with honors, is excessive in temporary pleasures, is dissolved in carnal lusts, and is not terrified of future punishment, but hides the future miseries from itself; lest worldly bliss be troubled by reflecting upon them. So it has peace in its day, when it will not temper today's mirth with any care about future unhappiness, but goes to the punishing fire with eyes closed. The soul which lives this way will be afflicted when the righteous rejoice; and all the perishable things, which it now counts as peace and bliss, will be turned into bitterness and strife; for it will have great contention with itself, asking why it had not, while living, cared about or foreseen the condemnation which it will then be suffering. Thus it is written, "Blessed is the man who fears the Lord... but truly the desire of the wicked shall perish." *Sermones Catholici*

Monday   Asterius of Amasea

It is also worthwhile to examine intelligently how each of these men when dead was carried forth. The poor man when he fell asleep had angels as his guards and attendants, who carried him, full of joyful expectation, to the place of rest; and the rich man, Christ says, died and was buried. It is not possible in any respect to improve the declaration of the Scriptures, since a single sentence adequately indicates the unhonored decease of the rich man. For truly the sinner when he dies is buried, being earthy in body and worldly in soul. He debases the spiritual within him to the material by yielding to the enticements of the flesh, leaving behind no good memorial of his life, but, dying the death of beasts, is wrapped in unhonored forgetfulness. For the grave holds the body, and Hades the soul - two gloomy prisons dividing between them the punishment of the wicked. And who would not blame the wretched man for his thoughtlessness? - since when he was on earth he prided himself, held his head high, exulted over all who lived about him and were of the same race, deeming those whom he happened to meet hardly better than ants and worms, and vainly boasting of his short-lived glory. But when he dies, and like a scourged slave is deprived of those usurped possessions of which in his folly he thought himself master, he is as deeply humiliated as he was previously highly exalted, and, wailing complaints like a mourning old woman, cries loudly and vainly on the patriarch, saying, "Father Abraham, have mercy on me, and send Lazarus, that he may dip the tip of his finger in water, and cool my tongue; for I am tormented in this flame." He seeks mercy, which he had not given when he had the power of helping another, and demands that Lazarus come down into the fire to him to help him. He prays that he may suck the finger of the leper slightly moistened in water. Such is the thoughtlessness of those who love the body. This is the end of those who love wealth and pleasure. It therefore becomes the wise man who is provident of the future, to consider the parable as a sort of medicine to prevent sickness; and to flee the experience of like evil, preferring the sympathetic and philanthropic disposition as the condition of the life to come. For the Scripture has presented the admonition to us dramatically in the persons of particular characters in order to impress upon us by a concrete and vivid example the law of good conduct, so that we may never think lightly of the precepts of the Scripture as terrifying in word only, without inflicting the threatened punishment. *On the Rich Man and Lazarus*

Tuesday - Ambrose of Milan

You rich, how far will you push your frenzied greed? Are you alone to dwell on the earth? Why do you cast out men who are fellow-creatures and claim all creation as your own? Earth at its beginning was for all in common. It was meant for rich and poor alike. What right have you to monopolize the soil? Nature knows nothing of the rich. All are poor when she brings them forth. Clothing and gold and silver, food and drink and covering - we are born without them all; naked she receives her children into the tomb, and no one can enclose his acres there. A little turf suffices for poor and rich, and the earth which proved too narrow for the appetites of the living is wide enough at last for the rich and all that is his.

Nature, impartial at our coming, is impartial at our going; she bears us all equal, and entombs us equal in her bosom. Who can tell class from class among the dead? Open the earth again and find your rich man if you may; excavate a tomb a short while after, and if you know the man that you see, prove by token that he was poor. The sole difference is that the rich has more to waste away with him; the silken garments and cloth of gold swathing his body are lost for the living without helping the dead. Being rich, he has perfumes lavished on him, but that does not stop the stench; he wastes the sweetness that might be used by others and is none the sweeter for it himself. And he leaves behind him heirs to bicker...

But in this lifetime even, why would he think he has everything in plenty? You, the rich man who call yourself rich, you do not know how needy you are, how truly necessitous you feel. The more you have, the more you want, and however much you win, in your own eyes you are poor still. Rapacity is not quenched by gain; it is fanned the more... Holy Scripture shows us how wretchedly poor a rich man may be, how abject a beggar he may be.   *On Naboth*

Wednesday - Augustine of Hippo

The redemption of a man's soul is his riches. How right God was to make fun of that silliest of rich men - He was warning us not to follow his example - the one whose land bore good crops, and the man was more worried about plenty than about poverty. You see, he thought to himself, saying, What shall I do, where shall I accumulate my crops? And after he'd sweated and fretted about his lack of space, he finally thought he had hit on a good plan. But it was a silly plan. It was a plan devised not by good sense but by greed. I will pull down, he says, my old barns, and put up new and larger ones, and I will fill them; and I will say to my soul, Soul, you have heaps of good things; take your fill, enjoy yourself. He said to him, Fool, precisely where you thought you were being clever, what's this foolish thing you've said. "I will say to my soul, You have heaps of good things; take your fill"? This night shall your soul be taken away. These things you have prepared, whose will they be? For what does it profit a man if he gains the whole world, but suffers the ruin of his own soul?

That's why the redemption of a man's soul is his riches. That kind of riches this silly fool of a man did not have. Obviously, he wasn't redeeming his soul by giving alms, he was hoarding perishable crops. I repeat, he was hoarding perishable crops, himself on the point of perishing because he had handed out nothing to the Lord before whom he had been due to appear. How will he know where to look at that trial, when he starts hearing the words, I was hungry and you did not give me to eat? He was planning to sate his soul with excessive and unnecessary feasting, and proudly disregarding all those empty bellies of the poor. He didn't realize that the bellies of the poor were much safer storerooms than his barns... if he stowed it away in the bellies of the poor, it would of course be digested on earth, but in heaven it would be kept all the more safely. So then, the redemption of a man's soul is his riches.
                                           Sermon 36

Thursday - Basil the Great of Caesarea

There are two kinds of temptations. There are afflictions which try the hearts of men like gold in the furnace, testing their metal by patience. But sometimes - and this is true of many - the very prosperities of life become a temptation. When things go ill it is hard not to be depressed; when they go too well, it is not less hard not to be puffed up with insolent pride. The first kind of temptation we see in Job, that great and invincible champion; the devil's violence bore down on him like a torrent, but he met it all with unshaken heart and firm purpose; the fiercer and closer his adversary's grip, the greater his triumph proved over his temptations.

Then there is temptation through prosperity, and among examples here is the rich man... He had wealth already. He hoped for more. God in his mercy did not doom him outright for his thanklessness; rather he added riches to riches, to make the man tire perhaps of plenty and to move his soul to generosity and the common sharing... Why was the land left to bring forth in plenty if the man was to put it to no good use? So that God's forbearance should be the more evident. Even to men such as this His goodness is imparted; "He makes His sun rise on the evil and on the good, and sends rain on the just and on the unjust." But this goodness of God brings greater punishment on the wicked. He sent His showers on the soil, though covetous hands tilled it. He gave His sun to warm the seed and multiply things - a fit soil, temperate weather, abundant seed, oxen to work with, and all that farming thrives on. And on the man's side what was there? Surliness, uncharitableness, selfishness; these were his answer to his Benefactor. He didn't stop to think that others were men as much as he; he did not consider it a duty to distribute his surplus to those in need. He didn't heed the commandment: "Do not refrain from doing good the needy" or "Let not alms and faithfulness forsake you;" or, "Break your bread for the hungry."

And all the prophets and teachers cried out. But they were not heard. His barns groaned with the press of stored harvests, but the miser's heart was not satisfied. He continually added new to old, swelled his plenty with yearly increase, and came at last to the hopeless pass where greed forbade him to let the old be brought out, yet he had no room to store the new. Thus his schemes are vain, his cares desperate. "What can I do?" Poor creature, what distress he is in - miserable in his prosperity, pitiable for his present wealth, more pitiable for the anticipated increase!... He complains as the poor do. Will not the destitute, the beggar, utter the very same words? "What can I do? Where can I find food and clothing?" These are the rich man's words too. He is broken-hearted, consumed with worries. What heartens others distresses the miser. It does not cheer him to have his granaries filled up. His heart is wrung by the overflow of wealth. He fears, after all, that it may reach the people outside and help relieve the destitute.

Homily on "I Will Pull Down My Barns"

Friday - Rabanus Maurus of Mainz

When we advise you, brothers, to have right faith and firm hope, we especially exhort you to take care to have love in you and show it by action in all things. For through it and in it you may know that you will have a true blessedness because without it no man will see God.

This quality is called greater than faith and hope by the apostle because when the others give way, it alone will remain. For hope follows faith, and blessedness hope, but there is no change for love, but perfection alone endures. This is the citadel of all virtues, this the promise of the Kingdom, this the reward of all the saints in heaven, because in eternal joy the saints have nothing more pleasing, nothing sweeter than the perfect love of God which, because they see it present, they love it more, and enjoy its good more sweetly...

This is why the Lord answers: "You shall love the Lord your God from your whole heart and from your whole soul and from your whole mind," and adds also a second like it, "You shall love your neighbor as yourself. On these two commandments hang all the law and the prophets." When he says, "from your whole heart and from your whole soul and from your whole mind," He means with all understanding and all will and with all memory God ought to be loved. The love of God, however, consists in the complete observance of His commandments, as elsewhere He says: "If any man love Me, let him keep My words." Of this the Truth Himself elsewhere says: "In this shall all men know that you are my disciples, if you have love for each other." Likewise the apostle: "The fullness of the law is love."

Sermon on Faith, Hope and Love

Saturday - Anselm of Canterbury

And now, O Lord Jesus, my Redeemer... help my imperfection. I bow down my whole self before the glorious insignia of Your Passion, with which You accomplished my salvation. In Your Name, O Christ, I adore the royal standard of Your victorious cross. The thorny crown; the nails glistening with Your Blood; the lance plunged into Your sacred side; Your wounds; Your blood; Your death; Your burial; Your triumphant resurrection, and Your glory, - O Christ, I suppliantly adore and glorify them. For the balm of life breathes forth on me from all of them. By their life-giving odor revive and raise my spirit from the death of sin. Shield me by their virtue from the crafts of Satan; and comfort me, O Lord, that the yoke of Your commandments may be sweet to me, and that the burden of the cross which You bid me to carry after You may be light and bearable to the shoulders of my soul.

For what courage have I for bearing up according to Your precepts against the so many and so manifold oppressions of the world? Are my feet like hart's feet, that I should be able to follow after You in Your fleet passage through the thorns and roughnesses of Your sufferings? But hear my voice, I pray You, and bend over Your servant Your sweet cross, which is a tree of life to all that lay hold on it; and then will I run with alacrity, even as I hope to do; then will I carry after You without fainting and unweariedly the cross Your enemies have given You.

Lay that most divine cross, I pray You, on my shoulders; whose breadth is love spreading over all creation; whose length, eternity; whose height, omnipotence; whose depth, unfathomable wisdom. And fasten my hands to it, and my feet; and clothe me from head to foot with the impression and the likeness of Your Passion. Grant me, I implore You, to abstain from deeds of the flesh, which You hate, and to do justice, which You love; and either way to seek Your glory. So shall I consider my left hand to have been fastened with the nail of temperance, and my right hand with the nail of justice, to that lofty cross of Yours. Let my mind meditate in Your law continually, and direct its every thought to You continually; and so by the nail of prudence fasten You my right foot to the same tree of life. Let not the joyless joy of this fleeting life dissipate the senses, which should only minister to the spirit, nor yet its jocund joylessness waste and diminish the rewards of the life eternal laid up in store for me; and so shall my left foot also be nailed to the cross by the nail of fortitude.

But, that some likeness may appear in me even to the thorns on Your Head, let the compunction of a saving repentance be impressed in my mind, and compassion for the miseries of others, and a penetrating zeal urging and goading me to what is right in Your eyes; and so shall I in my griefs be conformed to You, so shall the threefold wreath of thorn be fastened on me.

Meditation on the Humanity of Christ

Collect

O God, the Strength of all those who put their trust in You, mercifully accept our prayers; and because through the weakness of our mortal nature we can do no good thing, grant us the help of Your grace that in keeping Your commandments we may please You both in will and deed; through Jesus Christ, Your Son, our Lord, who lives and reigns with You and the Holy Spirit, one God, now and forever.

Galatian Sacramentary

AT LAUDS

Psalmody

Sunday: 3, C8, 51
Monday: 118a, C9, 118b
Tuesday: 1, C10, 2

Wednesday: 8, C11, 20
Thursday: 18a, C12, 18b

Friday: 146, C13, 5
Saturday: 149, C14, 150

Lesson

Sunday: I Samuel 26:1-2
Monday: I Samuel 27:1-7
Tuesday: I Samuel 29:1-11

Wednesday: I Samuel 30:16-25
Thursday: II Samuel 1:1-16

Friday: II Samuel 2:1-7
Saturday: II Samuel 3:6-11

Collect

We beseech You, O Lord, be gracious to Your people, that they, abhorring day by day the things which displease You, may be more and more filled with the love of Your commandments, and being supported by Your comfort in this mortal life, may advance to the full enjoyment of life immortal; through Jesus Christ, Your Son, our Lord, who lives and reigns with You and the Holy Spirit, one God, forever and ever. Amen. *Leonine Sacramentary*

AT TERCE, SEXT AND NONE

Chapter

Sunday, Monday and Tuesday: I John 4:16-21
Wednesday and Thursday: I Corinthians 15:12-23a
Friday and Saturday: Colossians 3:5-11

AT VESPERS

Psalmody

Sunday: 136b, 137, 138
Monday: 140, 141, 142
Tuesday: 144, 145, 7

Wednesday: 9, 10, 11
Thursday: 12, 13, 14, 16

Friday: 17, 147a, 147b
Saturday: 19, 54, 77

Lesson

Sunday: I Samuel 26:13-25
Monday: I Samuel 28:3-20
Tuesday: I Samuel 30:1-15

Wednesday: I Samuel 31:1-13
Thursday: II Samuel 1:17-27

Friday: II Samuel 2:8-17
Saturday: II Samuel 3:17-21

Collect

Lord God, heavenly Father, we beseech You so to rule and govern our hearts by Your Holy Spirit, that we may not, like the rich man, hear Your word in vain and become so devoted to temporal things as to forget eternal things; but that we readily and according to our ability minister to such as are in need, and not defile ourselves with luxury and pride; in trial and misfortune keep us from despair, and grant us to put our trust wholly in Your fatherly help and grace, so that in faith and Christian patience we may overcome all things, through Your Son, Jesus Christ, our Lord, who lives and reigns with You and the Holy Spirit, one God, now and forever. *Veit Dietrich*

THE SECOND WEEK
AFTER TRINITY

AT MATINS

Hymn - *Ach, Gott vom Himmel*

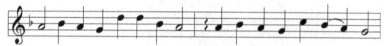

1. O, Lord look down from heav'n be-hold, And let Thy pi - ty wa - ken.

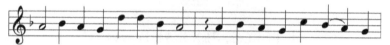

How few are we with-in Thy fold, Thy saints by men for - sak - en!

True faith seems quenched on ev - 'ry hand, Men suf - fer not

Thy Word to stand; Dark times have us o'er - tak - en.

2. With fraud which they themselves invent
Thy truth they have confounded;
Their hearts are not with one consent
On Thy pure doctrine grounded.
While they parade with outward show,
They lead the people to and fro,
In error's maze astounded.

3. May God root out all heresy
And of false teachers rid us
Who proudly say: "Now, where is he
That shall our speech forbid us?
By right or might we shall prevail;
What we determine cannot fail;
We own no lord and master."

4. Therefore saith God, "I must arise,
The poor My help are needing;
To Me ascend My people's cries,
And I have heard their pleading.
For them My saving Word shall fight
And fearlessly and sharply smite,
The poor with might defending."

5. As silver tried by fire is pure
From all adulteration,
So through God's Word shall men endure
Each trial and temptation.
Its light beams brighter through the cross,
And, purified from human dross,
It shines through every nation.

6. Thy truth defend, O God, and stay
This evil generation;
And from the error of their way
Keep Thine own congregation.
The wicked everywhere abound
And would Thy little flock confound;
But Thou art our Salvation.

Martin Luther, 1524

464

Psalmody

Sunday: 21, 22, 23

Wednesday: 30, 31, 32

Friday: 37a, 37b, 38

Monday: 24, 25, 26

Thursday: 33, 34, 35

Saturday: 39, 40, 41

Tuesday: 27, 28, 29

Lesson

Sunday, Monday and Tuesday: Luke 14:16-24

Wednesday and Thursday: Luke 9:12-17a

Thursday: Matthew 14:13-21

Friday and Saturday: Luke 8:41-56

Saturday: Mark 5:21-43

Homily

Sunday - Athanasius of Alexandria

This bread is the food of the righteous. Not only are the saints on earth nourished by such bread and such blood, but we also eat them in heaven. For the Lord is the food even of the exalted spirits, and of the angels. And He is the joy of all the heavenly host. He is everything to all, and He has pity upon all according to His loving-kindness. Already the Lord has given us angels' food. And He promises to those who continue with Him in His trials, saying, "And I promise to you a kingdom, just as My Father bestowed one upon Me, that you may eat and drink at My table in My kingdom, and sit on thrones judging the twelve tribes of Israel." O what a banquet is this, my brethren, and how great is the harmony and gladness of those who eat at this heavenly table! For they delight themselves not with that food which is cast out, but with that which produces life everlasting. Who then will be deemed worthy of that assembly? Who is so blessed as to be called, and accounted worthy of that divine feast? Truly, "Blessed is he who shall eat bread in Your kingdom." *Festal Easter Letter*

Monday - Gregory I of Rome

Bodily pleasures, when we do not possess them, arouse in us a great desire for them. But as soon as we do possess and devour them our satisfaction turns to distaste. Spiritual pleasures, on the other hand, seem distasteful when not possessed, but once we possess them we desire them. The more hungrily the one enjoying them seeks them, the more does the one hungering for them enjoy them. In the former the desire pleases, the realization displeases; in the latter as the desire is paltry, the realization is all the more pleasing. In the former desire produces satiety, and satiety distaste, but in the latter desire causes satiety and satiety desire.

Spiritual pleasures increase our inner longing even as they satisfy it, because the more we savor them, the more we perceive that there is something to be loved even more. But we can't love them when we don't possess them, because their taste is unknown. Who can love what he doesn't know? The psalmist counsels us, Taste and see that the Lord is good, meaning 'You will not get to know his goodness unless you taste it. Touch the food of life with the taste buds of your heart, so that trying it you be made able to love its sweetness.

Mankind lost these delights when it sinned in paradise. It went forth, its mouth shut to the food of eternal sweetness. We too are born amid the hardships of exile. We have come to this place with a sense of loathing. We do not know what we ought to desire. The more we separate ourselves from partaking of this sweetness, the more the disease of our loathing increases. Now we don't desire inner pleasures since for a long time we've been unaccustomed to tasting them. We are consumed with loathing, and are worn out by the long scourge of starvation. Because of our inner unwillingness to taste the sweetness that has been prepared for us, in our wretched state we have an outer love of our hunger.

But heavenly Constancy does not abandon us who have abandoned Him. He recalls to the eyes of our memory the delights we have rejected, and sets them before us again. By a promise He drives away our apathy. He invites us to rid ourselves of our loathing. A certain man gave a great dinner and invited many...

When you are unable to abandon everything of the world, outwardly conduct your external affairs well, but inwardly hasten to those that are eternal. Do not let anything stand in the way of your heart's desire. Do not be involved with any of this world's delights. If you love what is good, be delighted with better goods, heavenly ones. If you fear evil, bring eternal evils to mind. Then when you see that there is more to love, and more to fear, you may not remain altogether attached here. For this we have as our helper the Mediator between God and men. We shall more quickly obtain all things through Him if we are burning with true love for Him, who lives and reigns with the Father, in the unity of the Holy Spirit, God for ever and ever. Amen.

Homily 36

Tuesday - Prosper of Aquitaine

The earthly Adam was conquered and transmitted death to all men, for all are born of him and the condition of our sinful parent passes down to us. But a new Man was born from heaven in the womb of the holy virgin, and in His goodness He fashioned a fresh beginning for mortal men. He entered all men's flesh, and by sharing their nature delivered the dead, and by transforming life created the living. Just as grace embraced only those men of former times who beheld Christ in faith, so in our own time Christ renews only those in whose hearts He is welcomed.

Observe, man, what great power has been bestowed on you without cost. You can become the son of God if you wish; the almighty Spirit has formed and overshadowed you with the power of the Word. Do not now regard yourself as one born of the physical seed of your fathers; your enslaved beginning in the flesh must now be dissolved. Do not harness any of the old man to the new. This world, this life has not been bestowed on you; nothing here is yours, and you yourself are not your own. You have been purchased, and it is right to repay that price as best you can, so that by paying you may be richer, and so that the wealth which you bestow may accrue to you, so that the Redeemer himself may become your portion. *On Divine Providence*

Wednesday - Ambrose of Milan

We have a foretaste of the heavenly, because when the fifties are ordered to sit down, albeit with a distinct sacred number, the people of a more lasting Church are seen which lie down without definite number. There is also a mystery in that the people who eat are satisfied, and the Apostles minister to them. Here a sign is given of hunger satisfied forever, because one who has received the food of Christ will never hunger again. And the future distribution of the Lord's Body and Blood is announced in the ministry of the Apostles. Already there is the miracle of how five loaves abounded for five thousand people, for it is clear that the people were satisfied not with a little, but with an abundance of food. *Homily on Luke's Gospel*

Thursday - Aurelius Prudentius

Bring in twelve baskets the fragments left from the feast. The guests in their thousands are now amply filled with the eating of five loaves of bread and a pair of fishes. Thou art our meat and our bread, Thou our sweet savor that never fails; he can never hunger any more who partakes of Thy banquet, not filling a void in his belly but refreshing that by which he truly lives. The closed avenue of the ears, that knows no sound, clears away at Christ's bidding all its thick obstructions and gains the power to enjoy voices and give passage to whispers. Every sickness yields, every weakness is banished, the tongue speaks that had been tied in torpid silence, and the sick man carries his bed rejoicing through the city.

The Daily Round

Friday - Ambrose of Milan

It is clear, therefore that [Christ] loosed and vivified those who believe in Him as Abraham did, and did nothing contrary to the Law when He healed upon the Sabbath day. For the law did not prohibit men from being healed upon the Sabbaths; it even circumcised them upon that day, and gave command that the Offices should be performed by priests for the people; it did not forbid the healing even of mute animals… For the Law commanded them to abstain from every self-serving work, that is, from all grasping after wealth which is procured by trading and by other worldly business; but it exhorted them to attend to the exercises of the soul, which consist in reflection, and to doing beneficial works for their neighbors' benefit. And therefore the Lord reproved those who unjustly blamed Him for having healed upon the Sabbath days. For He did not make void, but fulfilled the law…

Homily on Luke's Gospel

Saturday - Ephrem the Syrian

"Who touched me? For I perceived power going out from Me." No such detail about our Physician is reported in any other place. This is because no where else did our Physician encounter an affliction such as this. This affliction was presented to many physicians, yet only one Physician encountered this affliction to heal it. Many physicians encountered and wearied her. Only one encountered her who was able to give her rest from the labors of many physicians. The healing art met a shameful affliction but added pain after pain to it. The more they tried, the worse the affliction got. The fringe of the Lord's cloak touched her and ripped this suffering out by its root. She perceived within herself that He healed her affliction.

Since the art of healing clothed with all our practical wisdom was reduced to silence, the divinity clothed with garments was proclaimed. He clothed Himself in the body and came down to humanity so that humanity might loot Him. He revealed His divinity through signs so that faith in His humanity alone could not be explained. He revealed His humanity that the higher beings might believe that He was a lower being. And He revealed His divinity so that the lower beings would accept that He was a higher being. He took on a human body so that humanity might be able to attain to divinity, and He revealed His divinity so that His humanity might not be trampled under foot.

Commentary on Tatian's Diatessaron

Collect

O Lord, who never fails to help and govern those whom You bring up in Your steadfast fear and love, make us to have a perpetual fear and love of Your holy name; through Jesus Christ, Your Son, our Lord, who lives and reigns with You and the Holy Spirit, one God, now and forever.

Gelasian Sacramentary

AT LAUDS

Psalmody

Sunday: 67, C1, 5	Wednesday: 64, C4, 65	Friday: 76, C5, 92
Monday: 63, C2, 36	Thursday: 88, C6, 90	Saturday: 143, C7, 148
Tuesday: 43, C3, 57		

Lesson

Sunday: II Samuel 3:22-30
Monday: II Samuel 5:1-12
Tuesday: II Samuel 6:12-17

Wednesday: II Samuel 7:12-29
Thursday: II Samuel 11:1-17

Friday: II Samuel 13:1-22
Saturday: II Samuel 15:1-14

Collect

We implore You, O Lord, let Your faithful people rejoice always in Your benefits, that being ordered by Your governance, they may please You in their lives, and happily obtain the good for which they pray; through Jesus Christ, our Lord, who lives and reigns with You and the Holy Spirit, one God, now and forever. *Leonine Sacramentary*

AT TERCE, SEXT AND NONE

Chapter

Sunday, Monday and Tuesday: I John 3:13-18
Wednesday and Thursday: Isaiah 44:1-3
Friday and Saturday: Joel 2:23-24, 26-27

AT VESPERS

Psalmody

Sunday: 110, 111, 112, 113
Monday: 114, 115, 116, 117
Tuesday: 120, 121, 122

Wednesday: 123, 124, 125
Thursday: 126, 127, 128

Friday: 129, 130, 131, 132
Saturday: 133, 135, 136a

Lesson

Sunday: II Samuel 4:1-12
Monday: II Samuel 6:1-11
Tuesday: II Samuel 7:1-11

Wednesday: II Samuel 9:1-8
Thursday: II Samuel 12:1-23

Friday: II Samuel 13:23-29
Saturday: II Samuel 18:1-8

Collect

Lord God, heavenly Father, we give thanks to You that through Your holy word You have called us to Your great supper, and we beseech You to quicken our hearts by Your Holy Spirit, that we may not hear Your word without fruit, but that we may prepare ourselves rightly for Your kingdom, and not allow ourselves to be hindered by any worldly care, through Your beloved Son, Jesus Christ, our Lord, who lives and reigns with You and the Holy Spirit, one true God, now and forever. Amen.

Veit Dietrich

THE THIRD WEEK
AFTER TRINITY

AT MATINS

Hymn - *Allein zu dir, Herr Jesu Christ*

1. In Thee a - lone, O Christ, my Lord, My hope on earth re-

main - eth; I know Thou wilt Thine aid af - ford

Naught else my soul sus - tain - eth. No strength of man, no

earth-ly stay, Can help me in the e - vil day; Thou on - ly

Thou can aid sup-ply. To Thee I cry; On Thee I bid

my heart re - ly.

2. My sins, O Lord, against me rise,
I mourn them with contrition;
Grant, through my death and sacrifice,
To me a full remission.
Lord, show before the Father's throne
That Thou didst for my sins atone;
So shall I from my load be freed.
Thy Word I plead;
Keep me, O Lord, each hour of need.

3. O Lord, in mercy stay my heart
On faith's most sure foundation
And to my inmost soul impart
Thy perfect consolation.
Fill all my life with love to Thee,
Toward all men grant me charity;
And at the last, when comes my end,
Thy succor send.
From satan's wiles my soul defend.

Johannes Schneesing, 1542

Psalmody

Lesson

Sunday, Monday and Tuesday: Luke 15:1-10
Monday: Matthew 18:12-14
Tuesday: Mark 6:14-29 or Matthew 14:1-12

Wednesday and Thursday: Matthew 5:25-30
Thursday: Luke 12:57-59

Friday and Saturday: Mark 11:11-24
Saturday: Matthew 21:18-22

Homily

Sunday - Maximus of Turin

How is God able to forget us, brethren - He who in the Gospel says that even the hairs of our head have been numbered? If He remembers our hairs, much more does He remember our souls. For we take numbering to mean care and solicitude in our regard, since no one numbers something unless he wants to be particularly attentive to it; no one numbers unless he is concerned that he might be defrauded because of not taking a count. A shepherd frequently numbers his flock in order to keep it safe. When one sheep out of a hundred sheep had gone astray, the Lord, who is the good shepherd, went over the number again and carried it back to the flock on His own shoulders. One who is numbered, then, is in such safekeeping that when he goes astray he is brought back on His own shoulders lest the number be diminished. Do not think, therefore, brethren, that God forgets even the least. He remembers everyone, recalls everyone...

Sermon 70

Monday - Cyril of Alexandria

The woman lit a lamp to search for that which had fallen. For we were found by the wisdom of God the Father, which is the Son, when the Divine light of holy wisdom shone upon us, when the sun rose, and the day star ascended, and the day dawned, according to the Scriptures. For God also said by the holy prophet of Christ the Savior of us all, "My righteousness approaches quickly and My mercy is revealed, and My salvation will burn as a lamp." And as He said of Himself at one time: "I am the Light of the world" and at another, "I have come as a Light into this world; he who follows me will not walk in darkness but have the light of life." By the light, therefore, that which was lost is saved. And there was rejoicing by the powers above. For they rejoice even in one sinner who repents, as He has taught us who knows all things.

Homily 106 on Luke

Tuesday - Gregory II of Rome

We directed you, reverent brother, in imitation of the Apostles commanded by the Lord: "Go and preach the gospel!" "Freely you have received, freely give," into the lands of the West, for the enlightenment of the people of Germany sitting in the shadow of death, expecting you to reap profit from them in the future, like that faithful servant in the Scripture in dealing with his talent. We have perceived the fragrance of the ministry of the Word arising from your gift of obedience and we have learned that through the broadcasting of your preaching, as you have reported, the unbelieving people are being converted. For this reason we give thanks to the power of the Lord and pray that He, from whom all good proceeds and whose will it is that all men should come to a knowledge of the truth, may work with you and may lead that people out of darkness into light by the inspiration of His might. We believe that a bountiful reward shall be recorded for you in heaven. If you persevere you will be able to say with the Apostle: "I have fought a good fight, I have finished my course, I have kept the faith."

But, to win the crown of your labor, keep at it! For God promises salvation to those who will endure unto the end. Let no threats alarm you, no fears cast you down, but holding fast to your faith in God, proclaim the word of truth. The completion shall come by divine aid, as long as the will to do the good work persists. How many you have turned from their errors we have learned from your written report, which we have carefully examined, and we give our deepest gratitude to God, rejoicing in this harvest of souls. *Letter to Boniface*

Wednesday - John Chrysostom

He did not simply say, "whosoever desires," since it's possible to desire even when one is sitting alone in the mountains; but, "whoever looks to lust;" that is to say, he who gathers in lust unto himself; he who, when nothing compels him, brings in the wild beast upon his thoughts when they are calm. For this comes no longer from nature, but from self-indulgence. This even the ancient Scripture corrects from the first, saying, "Do not look intently at beauty belonging to another." And then, lest any one should say, "what if I look but am not taken captive," He punishes the look, lest confiding in this security you should perhaps fall into sin. "What then," one may say, "if I should look, and really desire, but do no evil?" Even then you art set among the adulterers...

In truth the struggle is greater on looking, and not possessing the object of desire; nor is the pleasure as great which we get from the sight as the mischief we undergo from increasing this desire; thus giving our enemy strength, and giving broader scope to the devil, and no longer able to repulse him now that we have welcomed him into our innermost parts and have thrown our mind open unto him. Therefore He says, "commit no adultery with your eyes, and you will commit none with your mind."

For one may indeed look in another way, such as are the looks of the chaste; which is why He did not prohibit our seeing altogether, but only the seeing that is accompanied with desire. And if He had not meant this He would have simply said, "He who looks on a woman." But now He didn't say this, but, "He who looks to lust," "he who looks to please his eyes."

God didn't make the eyes for this reason, that you should thereby introduce adultery, but that, seeing His creatures, you should admire the Creator.

Just as one may randomly feel wrath, so also one may cast glances at random; that is, when you do it for lust. Rather, if you desire to look and find pleasure, look at your own wife, and love her continually; no law forbids that. But if you are to be curious about the beauties that belong to another you are injuring both your wife by letting your eyes wander elsewhere, and her on whom you have looked by touching her unlawfully. Although you have not touched her with the hand, yet you have caressed her with your eyes; for which reason this also is counted as adultery. And the penalty for this is not small, for then all within him is filled with discontent and turmoil, and great is the tempest, and most grievous the pain, and no captive nor person in chains can be worse off than a man in this state of mind. And often she who has shot the dart is long gone, while even so the wound remains. Or rather, it is not she who has shot the dart, but you yourself the fatal wound by your adulterous look.

And this I say to free modest women from the charge. But certainly if one decks herself out and invites towards herself the eyes all that come her way; even though she doesn't smite him who meets with her, she incurs the utmost penalty, for she mixed the poison, she prepared the hemlock, even though she didn't offer the cup. Or rather, she did offer the cup too, but no one was found to drink it. *Sermon 17 on Matthew*

471

Thursday - Martin Luther

We are not made for fleeing human company, but for living in society and sharing good and evil. As human beings we must help one another to bear all kinds of human misfortune and the curse that has come upon us. We must be ready to live among wicked people, and there everyone must be ready to prove his holiness instead of becoming impatient and running away. On earth we have to live amid thorns and thistles, in a situation full of temptation, hostility, and misfortune. Hence it does not help you at all to run away from other people, for within you are still carrying the same old scoundrel, the lust and evil appetite that clings to your flesh and blood. Even if you are all alone, with the door locked, you still cannot deny your father and mother; nor can you discard your flesh and blood and leave them on the ground. You have no call to pick up your feet and run away, but to stay put, to stand and battle against every kind of temptation like a knight, and with patience to see it through and to triumph.

Christ is a real Teacher, therefore. He does not teach you to run away from people, nor to move away, but to get hold of yourself and to discard the eye or the hand that offends you, that is, to get rid of the cause of your sin, the evil appetite and lust that clings to you and proceeds from your own heart. Once you are rid of this, it is easy to be in human society and to enjoy human company without sinning. Hence He says clearly, as we have heard: "If you look at a woman lustfully, you have committed adultery with her in your heart." He does not forbid looking at her; for He is talking to people who have to live in human society in the world, as the preaching in this chapter, both before and after, amply demonstrates. But He does want us to distinguish between looking and lusting. You may look at any woman or man, only be sure that you do not lust. That is why God has ordained for every person to have his own wife or husband, to control and channel his lust and his appetites. If you do not go any further than this, He approves it, He even pronounces His blessing upon it, and He is pleased with it as His ordinance and creature. But if you do go further, if you refuse to be content with what God has given you for your desires, and if you leer at others, you have already gone too far and have confused the two, so that your looking is corrupted by your lusting. *On the Sermon on the Mount*

Friday - Origen of Alexandria

Jesus was hungry, for He always wants to partake of the fruits of the Spirit which are in the righteous man; these figs are love, the first-fruits of the Spirit; joy, peace, etc. So long as we bear these, we will not be withered; but if we do not bear fruit when He comes and seeks it, it will be said to us, "Let no one eat fruit from you ever again..." Each of us is either a withered fig tree, or a tree bearing fruit, living and being cultivated so that it might bear more fruit...

Mark on this passage has added something which, taken literally, is discordant: "for it was not the season for figs." Then how did Jesus come hoping to find something on it, and how was it just for Him to say to it "Let no one eat fruit from you ever again"? The answer is that the fruits of the Spirit are sometimes rendered in their own season. But it is better yet if man, through the special help of the Word, is able to bear the fruits of the Spirit when the circumstances are opposed to bearing fruit.

For example, one of the fruits of the Spirit is love. The season for love is when it is not hard to bear fruit because one has been loved. But when someone by actions, schemes or character seems deserving of hatred and urges the believer to hate, but the righteous does not hate even such a person, but as a son of Him who makes the sun rise on the just and the unjust, loves him instead, giving the fruit of love even though it is not in season, he is blessed. So also with joy. It is not hard to bear the spiritual fruit of joy when there is nothing to cause grief or sadness or displeasure. But when a man, with the help of the Word, matures so that he can be pleased even in hard times and can rejoice in times of dishonor and scourging, and can remember in every time of disaster "Rejoice always," he would be blessed, bearing joy as a fruit even when it is "not the season for figs." *Commentary on Matthew*

Saturday - Meister Eckhart

Look! Those people are all businessmen who guard against serious sins, would like to be good people, and perform their good works for God's glory, such as fasting, vigils, praying, and whatever other good works there are. But they do them so that our Lord might give them something in return, or so that God might do something to please them. These are all businessmen. This can be seen to be something unrefined because they want to give one thing in return for another, and thus want to make a business deal with our Lord. But this business deal deludes them. For everything that they have and everything that they can accomplish-if they were to give all this for God's sake and do it completely for God's sake, God would still not be in the least obliged to give them anything or to do anything for them, if He did not want to do it willingly and freely. What they are, they are from God; and what they have, they have from God and not from themselves. Therefore God is not at all indebted to them for their works or for their giving, unless He freely and graciously wants to do something, but not because of their works or gifts because they are not giving what belongs to them nor are their works their own. Christ himself said: "Without me you can do nothing."

These are very foolish people who thus want to make business deals with our Lord. They don't know the truth very well or perhaps not at all. This is why our Lord struck them and drove them out of the temple. Light and darkness cannot exist side by side. God is the truth and a light in Himself. When then God comes into this temple, He drives out ignorance, which is darkness, and reveals himself in light and truth. Then the businessmen are gone insofar as the truth becomes known. Truth does not like business deals. God seeks nothing of His own. In all His works He is empty and free and works them out of genuine love. This is how the person acts who is united with God. He, too, is empty and free in all his works and he does them only for the glory of God, seeking nothing of his own, and it is God who is working this in him.

I will make a further claim. As long as a person in any of his works seeks anything at all of all that which God can or shall give, he is like these businessmen. If you want to be so completely free of making business deals that God permits you in this temple, you should do everything that you can in all your works purely to praise God, and you should be as empty as that nothing is empty which is neither here nor there. You should desire nothing at all for this. When you act this way, your works are spiritual and divine. Then the businessmen have been driven out of the temple completely, and God is alone within because this person has nothing but God as his intention. See, this is how the temple is free of businessmen. Look! The person who does not regard himself or anything else but God alone and God's honor is truly free and rid of all mercantilism in all his works and seeks nothing of his own, just as God is free and unencumbered in all his works and seeks nothing of his own.

Sermon on Matthew 21

Collect

O God, the Protector of all that trust in You, without whom nothing is strong, nothing is holy, increase and multiply upon us Your mercy that, You being our Ruler and Guide, we may so pass through things temporal that we finally lose not the things eternal; through Jesus Christ, Your Son, our Lord, who lives and reigns with You and the Holy Spirit, one God, now and forever.

Gregorian Sacramentary

AT LAUDS

Psalmody

Sunday: 3, C8, 51
Monday: 118a, C9, 118b
Tuesday: 1, C10, 2

Wednesday: 8, C11, 20
Thursday: 18a, C12, 18b

Friday: 146, C13, 5
Saturday: 149, C14, 150

Lesson

Sunday: II Samuel 18:9-15
Monday: II Samuel 19:1-8
Tuesday: II Samuel 20:14-22

Wednesday: II Samuel 24:1-17
Thursday: I Kings 1:1-14

Friday: I Kings 2:1-12
Saturday: I Kings 3:4-15

Collect

O Most Clement, who recalls the erring; Most Merciful, who does not despise sinners, we rely on Your own promise, O Lord, that You will give pardon to the penitent. May all who seek You, find You. *Gallican Sacramentary*

AT TERCE, SEXT AND NONE

Chapter

Sunday, Monday and Tuesday: I Peter 5:6-11
Wednesday and Thursday: Colossians 3:17-24a
Friday and Saturday: James 2:1-9a

AT VESPERS

Psalmody

Sunday: 136b, 137, 138
Monday: 140, 141, 142
Tuesday: 144, 145, 7

Wednesday: 9, 10, 11
Thursday: 12, 13, 14, 16

Friday: 17, 147a, 147b
Saturday: 19, 54, 77

Lesson

Sunday: II Samuel 18:24-33
Monday: II Samuel 20:1-13
Tuesday: II Samuel 23:1-7

Wednesday: II Samuel 24:18-25
Thursday: I Kings 1:32-40

Friday: I Kings 3:1-3
Saturday: I Kings 3:16-28

Collect

Lord God, heavenly Father, we all like sheep have gone astray, having suffered ourselves to be led away from the right path by Satan and our own sinful flesh: We beseech You graciously to forgive us all our sins for the sake of Your Son, Jesus Christ; and enliven our hearts by Your Holy Spirit, that we may abide in Your word, and in true repentance and a steadfast faith continue in Your Church unto the end, and obtain eternal salvation, through our Lord Jesus Christ, Your Son, who lives and reigns with You and the Holy Spirit, one God, now and forever. *Veit Dietrich*

THE FOURTH WEEK
AFTER TRINITY

AT MATINS

Hymn - *O Gott, Du Frommer Gott*

1. O God, my faith-ful God, True foun-tain ev - er flow - ing,
With-out whom no-thing is, All per-fect gifts be - stow-ing:
Give me a health-y frame, And may I have with - in
A con-science free from blame, A soul un-stained by sin.

2. Grant me the strength to do
With ready heart and willing
Whatever You command,
My calling here fulfilling;
That I do what I should
While trusting You to bless
The outcome for my good,
For You must give success.

3. Keep me from saying words
That later need recalling
Guard me lest idle speech
May from my lips be falling;
But when within my place
I must and ought to speak,
Then to my words give grace,
Lest I offend the weak.

4. If dangers gather round,
Still keep me calm and fearless;
Help me to bear the cross
When life is dark and cheerless;
And let me win my foe
With words and actions kind.
When counsel I would know,
Good counsel let me find.

5. And let me with all men,
When it is in my power
In peace and friendship live.
And if Your grace should shower
Great wealth and honor fair,
Then this refuse me not,
That naught be mingled there
Of goods unjustly got.

6. And if a longer life
You have on earth decreed me;
If then through many ills
Great age at length You give me,
Your patience on me shed
Avert all sin and shame
And crown my wizened head
With honor free from blame

7. Let me depart this life
Confiding in my Savior
By grace receive my soul
That it may live forever;
And let my body have
A quiet resting place
Within a Christian grave;
And let it sleep in peace.

475

8. And on that final day
   When all the dead are waking,
   Stretch out Your mighty hand,
   My deathly slumber breaking.
   Then let me hear Your voice,
   Redeem this earthly frame,
   And bid me to rejoice
   With those who love Your name. Amen.

Johann Heermann, 1630

Psalmody

Sunday: 69b, 70, 71	Wednesday: 75, 79, 80	Friday: 84, 86, 87, 93
Monday: 72, 73, 74	Thursday: 81, 82, 83	Saturday: 85, 89a, 89b
Tuesday: 78a, 78b, 78c		

Lesson

Sunday, Monday and Tuesday: Luke 6:36-42

Monday: Matthew 7:1-5
Tuesday: Luke 21:1-4

Wednesday and Thursday: Matthew 21:23-27

Thursday: Mark 11:27-33

Friday and Saturday: Matthew 17:10-18

Saturday: Mark 9:11-29

Homily

Sunday - Leo I of Rome

Be steady, Christian giver. Give what you receive, sow what you reap, scatter what you collect. Do not fear the cost. Don't long after questionable income. Your property increases by being well spent. Long for the just reward of mercy, and pursue the business of eternal profit. Your benefactor wants you to be beneficent, and He who gives so that you might have, entrusts it to you so that you might distribute it, saying "Give and it will be given to you"...

Those who love money and hope to increase their wealth with excessive growth, let them practice this holy investment instead and get rich by this art of usury. Don't lay hold of the necessities of working men or cause them to fall into the traps of impossible debts for the sake of deceitful gain. Instead, be creditors and the money-lenders to the One who said: "Give and it will be given to you," and, "the measure with which you measure, the same will be measured back to you."

Those are unfaithful and even unjust to themselves who don't want to have forever what they thought ought to be loved... If any would be benefactors to their own souls, they should entrust their goods to the One who is a suitable trustee of the poor and who pays a most generous interest.

Sermon 17

Monday - Augustine of Hippo

Our Lord is warning us against ignoring each other's sins; not that you should go poking and prying for things to find fault with, but that you should correct what you see. He was talking, of course, about the keen eye of the person who doesn't have a beam in his own eye, and so is sharp-sighted enough to remove the speck from his brother's eye... A speck in the eye is anger; a beam in the eye is hatred. So when someone who hates finds fault with someone else for being angry, he is wishing to remove a speck from his brother's eye, but he is hindered from doing so by the beam he is carrying around in his own eye. A speck is the beginning of a beam. I mean, when a beam is born, it's first a speck. Water the speck, and you are coaxing it up into a beam; feed your anger with evil suspicions, and you are coaxing it up into hatred.   *Sermon 82*

Tuesday - Eucherius of Lyons

It is clear then, that the eternal life is most blessed; for what other thing can be named, or thought about, that is more happy than everlasting life? As for this present short life, it is so very short, that it is throughout most miserable. It is pressed and assaulted on every side with surrounding, inevitable sorrows; it is distressed with many evil defects, and tossed to and fro with unknown and punishing accidents. For what is there in all the whole world that is so uncertain, so random, and so filled up with troubles, as the course of this life - which is full of labor, full of anguish, fraught with cares, and made ominous with dangers; which is distracted with violent and sudden changes, made unpleasant with bodily illness, afflicted with worry, and lies naked to all the whirlwinds of time and chance? What benefit then, yes, what reason have you to turn aside and run away from eternal joys, that you may pursue and follow after temporal miseries!

Do you not see... how every one that is prudent – even in this life – does, with plenty of all the necessities, furnish that cottage or field where he knows he will reside – and where he abides for but a short time, he provisions accordingly; where he intends a longer stay, he provides likewise a greater supply? Unto us also who in this present world... have but a very short time, are eternal ages reserved in the world which is to come; if it be that we competently provide for an eternal state, and for the present seek merely what is sufficient, not perversely bestowing the greatest care upon the shortest and smallest portion of time, and the smallest care on the time of greatest and endless extent.

And indeed I do not know which should sooner or most effectually incite us to a pious care of life eternal, either the blessings which are promised us in that state of glory, or the miseries which we feel in this present life. Those from above most lovingly invite and call to us; these below most rudely and unrelentingly would expel us hence. Seeing therefore that the continual evils of this life would bring us hence into a better, if we will not be induced by the good, let us then be compelled by the evil. Both the good and the bad agree to spur us on to the best, and though at odds with each other, yet both consent to make us happy. For while the one invites us, and the other compels us, both are solicitous for our good.   *On Contempt of the World*

Wednesday - John Chrysostom

But the boastful and arrogant Jews, wishing to interrupt His teaching, came to Him and asked, "By what authority are You doing these things?"... But what they mean is this: Have you received the teacher's chair? Have you been ordained a priest, that you display such authority? And yet He had done nothing implying arrogance, but had been careful for the good order of the temple, yet nevertheless having nothing to say, they object against this. And indeed when He cast them out, they did not dare to say anything, because of the miracles, but when He showed Himself, then they find fault with Him.

What does He say? He doesn't answer them directly, to show that if they had been willing to see His authority they could; but He questions them instead, saying, "The baptism of John— where was it from? From heaven or from men?"

And what sort of inference is this? The greatest to be sure. For if they had said from heaven, He would have said to them, why then did you not believe him? For if they had believed they would not have asked these things. For John said about Him, "I am not worthy to loose His sandal strap," and, "Behold! The Lamb of God who takes away the sin of the world!" and, "This is the Son of God," and, "He that comes from above is above all," and, "His winnowing fan is in His hand, and He will thoroughly clean out His threshing floor." So that if they had believed him, there was nothing to hinder them from knowing by what authority Christ does these things.

After this, because they were being crafty and said, "We do not know," He didn't say neither do I, but what? "Neither will I tell you." For if they had truly been ignorant it would have been necessary for them to be instructed; but since they were dealing craftily He answers them nothing and with good reason.

And why didn't they say that the baptism was from men? Because they "feared the multitude." Do you see a perverse heart? In every case they despise God and do everything for the sake of men. They feared John too, not honoring the saint, but because of men. And they were not willing to believe in Christ because of men; and all their evils were caused by this.   *Homily 67 on Matthew*

Thursday - Martin Luther

What irritates the pope, the cardinals, kings, and princes more than the fact that I, a beggar, give preference to the authority of God over their authority and in the name of the Lord reprove what deserves reproof? Even they themselves acknowledge that there are many things which are in need of a thoroughgoing reformation. But that a nobody, one who stepped out of a hidden nook into public life, should carry this out - this is something utterly unbearable for them. Therefore they oppose us with their authority and attempt to overwhelm us by means of it.

Indeed, no wrath in the entire world is more cruel than that of this bloodthirsty and hypocritical church. Where the government shows its wrath, there is still something left of human emotion. No bandit, however brutal he may be, is led to execution without people being touched by some compassion. But when that false and bloodthirsty church falls upon a son of the true church, it is not enough for it to have shed his blood; it also slanders him, curses him, declares him damned, and rages against his poor corpse. The Jews were not satisfied either when they had nailed Christ to the cross, from which they were not going to release Him until He was dead; but when He was thirsty, they gave Him vinegar and gall to drink and uttered blasphemies against Him when He was already at the point of death. Such violent passion is not encountered in the wrath of the government. Just so, the wrath and pharisaical fury of the false church is clearly a demonic rage.   *Lectures on Genesis*

Friday - William of St. Thierry

Our Lord did nothing by force, but everything by persuasion and instruction. The old slavery was truly past and a time of new freedom had dawned, and man for the sake of his salvation was being taught in a proper way how he had been created with a free will. Through miracles He who was Himself God promoted faith in God, and through His passion He elicited faith in the human nature which He bore. The people, devotees of pleasure, strove after riches to their ruin. He willed to be poor. They longed for honors and power. He refused to be king. They considered sons according to the flesh a great blessing. He spurned such wedlock and offspring. They were extremely proud and dreaded reproach. He endured every kind of insult. They thought injuries to be intolerable. What injury could be greater than that a just, innocent man be condemned? They cursed bodily pain. He was scourged and tortured. They feared death. He was punished with death. They thought the cross a humiliating kind of death. He was crucified. All the things we wanted to have when we did not live right He showed to be of no value by doing without them. All that we wanted to avoid and which caused us to turn away from zeal for godliness, He bore patiently and made powerless. No sin can be committed which does not involve seeking after what He despised or fleeing from what He endured. Thus His whole life on earth, through the humanity which He condescended to assume, was an instruction in living righteously. When these things are believed without hesitation and in faith are pondered in order to love what is believed and to see it as it is believed, what is this but the purification of the heart to see what is promised to the pure of heart? *The Enigma of Faith*

Saturday - Guerric of Igny

Truly the man who trusts in the Lord is blessed in the Lord, because whoever puts his trust in the Lord inserts himself into Him. The tree drinks in the sap of life and the waters of fertility from wherever its roots have penetrated. And surely he has sent out his roots to the waters who - I quote our master, Benedict - "has put his hope in God" and from the very Source of All Good drinks in the waters of life full of blessings and grace.

Through this loving and devoted confidence sins are forgiven, healing obtained for ills of the body and more importantly for ills of the soul, dangers averted, fears despised, the world overcome. All things are possible to the one who believes, there is no doubt about it. To those in sin Christ says: "Son, be of good cheer; your sins are forgiven you;" to those to whom He gives health of body or soul: "According to your faith let it be to you," and: "Your faith has made you well;" to those terrified and in danger of shipwreck: "Have faith in God," and: "Why are you fearful, O you of little faith?" to those whom He was arming against the cruelty of the world and the violence of the devil: "Be of good cheer, I have overcome the world."

And of course this is the victory that overcomes the world, our faith; but only if it is not lukewarm or fearful but confident, a faith unfeigned, a hope unshaken. Not only is the world overcome by it but heaven is won. By it man is established forever, is rooted and established in the Lord by charity. Those who trust in the Lord are like Mount Zion. Nor can he be moved forever who is rooted in the Eternal. For just as the Eternal cannot perish so neither can the man who unites himself with the Lord and so becomes one spirit with Him. Who has hoped in the Lord and been confounded? Who has continued in his commandments and been forsaken? If a man without faith should say: "He was forsaken because on the cross he cried: 'My God, my God, why have you forsaken me,'" I would say God did not really abandon him, for God was in Him reconciling the world to Himself. O what consolation to be thus forsaken, what love to be thus abandoned that you might deserve to be associated with the Only-begotten, Well-beloved of the Father in his sufferings. *Second Sermon for the Feast of Benedict*

Collect

Grant, O Lord, we implore You, that the course of this world may be so peaceably ordered by Your governance, that Your Church may joyfully serve You in all godly quietness; through Jesus Christ, Your Son, our Lord, who lives and reigns with You and the Holy Spirit, one God, now and forever. *Leonine Sacramentary*

AT LAUDS

Psalmody

Sunday: 67, C1, 5	Wednesday: 64, C4, 65	Friday: 76, C5, 92
Monday: 63, C2, 36	Thursday: 88, C6, 90	Saturday: 143, C7, 148
Tuesday: 43, C3, 57		

Lesson

Collect

O God of love, O Giver of concord, through Your only-begotten Son You have commanded that we should love one another even as You have loved us, the unworthy and the wandering, and gave Your beloved Son for our life and salvation; we pray, O Lord, give to us Your servants throughout the time of our earthly life, a mind forgetful of past ill-will, a pure conscience and sincere thoughts, and a heart to love our brethren, through Jesus Christ, Your Son, our Lord, who lives and reigns with You and the Holy Spirit, one God, now and forever.   *Coptic Liturgy of St. Cyril*

AT TERCE, SEXT AND NONE

Chapter

Sunday, Monday and Tuesday: Romans 8:18-23
Wednesday and Thursday: Ephesians 1: 15-21
Friday and Saturday: Jude 5-13

AT VESPERS

Psalmody

Lesson

Collect

Lord God, heavenly Father, You are merciful, and through Christ have promised us that You will neither judge nor condemn us but will graciously forgive us all our sins and abundantly provide for all our wants of body and soul: We pray You that by Your Holy Spirit You will establish in our hearts a confident faith in Your mercy, and will teach us also to be merciful to our neighbor, that we may not judge or condemn others, but will forgive all men; and that judging only ourselves, we may lead blessèd lives in Your fear, through Your dear Son, Jesus Christ our Lord, who lives and reigns with You and the Holy Spirit, one God, now and forever.

Veit Dietrich

THE FIFTH WEEK
AFTER TRINITY

AT MATINS

Hymn - *Mir nach! spricht Christus, unser Held*

1. Come fol-low Me, the Sav-ior spake, All in My way a - bid- ing;

De - ny your-selves, the world for-sake, O - bey My call and guid-ing.

O bear the cross, what-e'er be-tide, Take My ex-am-ple for your guide.

2. I am the Light, I light the way,
   A godly life displaying;
   I bid you walk as in the day,
   I keep your feet from straying.
   I am the Way, and well I show
   How you must sojourn here below.

3. My heart abounds in lowliness,
   My soul with love is glowing,
   And gracious words my lips express,
   With meekness overflowing.
   My heart, My mind, My strength, My all,
   To God I yield, on Him I call.

4. I teach you how to shun and flee
   What harms your soul's salvation,
   Your heart from every guile to free,
   From sin and its temptation.
   I am the Refuge of the soul
   And lead you to your heavenly goal.

5. But if too hot you find the fray,
   I, at your side, stand ready;
   I fight myself, I lead the way,
   At all times firm and steady.
   A coward he who will not heed
   When the chief Captain takes the lead.

6. Who seeks to find his soul's welfare
   Without Me, he shall lose it;
   But who to lose it may appear,
   In God shall introduce it.
   Who bears no cross nor follows hard
   Deserves not Me nor My reward.

7. Then let us follow Christ, our Lord,
   And take the cross appointed
   And, firmly clinging to His Word,
   In suffering be undaunted.
   For who bears not the battle's strain
   The crown of life shall not obtain.

Johann Scheffler, 1668

Psalmody

Sunday: 89c, 94, 96	Wednesday: 104a, 104b, 104c	Friday: 106a, 106b, 107a
Monday: 97, 98, 99, 100	Thursday: 105a, 105b, 105c	Saturday: 107b, 108, 109
Tuesday: 101, 102, 103		

Lesson

Sunday, Monday and Tuesday: Luke 5:1-11

Monday: John 1:35-51
Tuesday: John 21:15-19

Wednesday and Thursday: Luke 10:21-24

Friday and Saturday: Luke 18:15-17

Friday: Matthew 19:13-15
Saturday: John 7:1-13

Homily

Sunday - Hildebert of Tours

For what cause is Isaac, the beloved son, forbidden to take a wife from the daughters of Canaan, except that He of whom it is written, "This is My beloved Son, in Whom I am well pleased," will not be wed to a polluted soul? But the servant is commanded to take a wife for the son from his own kindred because the holy Church of the elect was alone to be joined to the Only-Begotten Son, and because Only-Begotten from His predestination and foreknowledge did not treat her as a stranger. And who is the servant that is sent to bring home the wife but the Prophets, and the Apostles, and all the Doctors, who, proclaiming the word to honest hearts, become the messengers for betrothing every Christian soul to the Only-Begotten Son? ... And this servant stood near the fountain and resolved, by a determination made beforehand, which maiden he should select; because holy preachers look at the fountains of sacred scripture, and collect from them what or to whom they should commit the word of their preaching, and from which hearers they may look for the certainty of faith. The servant seeks for something to drink, because every preacher thirsts after the soul of his hearers. It is Rebecca who gives the water, because it is the holy Church of the elect which satisfies the desire of its preachers, by the virtue of its faith; the Church which confesses the God of whom she hears, and offers to her instructor the water of refreshment, and satisfies his soul.   *Sermon on the Dedication of a Church*

Monday - John Chrysostom

For your part, for the time being hold on to what was said, remember it, and teach it to those who have not heard it. Let everyone meditate on it in church, in the marketplace and at home; nothing is sweeter than attention to the divine sayings. Listen, at any rate, to what the inspired author says of this, "Your sayings are like honey in my throat, better than honey and the honeycomb in my mouth." So place this honeycomb on your table at evening so as to fill it completely with spiritual sweetness. Have you not noticed how wealthy people bring in harpists and flute players after the meal? They turn their house into an auditorium; for your part turn your house into heaven, doing so not by altering the walls or changing the foundations, but by inviting the Lord of heaven to your table. God is not ashamed to be at such meals: in that setting there is spiritual teaching, there also sobriety, gravity and simplicity, there husband and wife and children, harmony and friendship, people linked by the bonds of virtue, there in the midst is Christ. It is not a roof of gold He looks for, in fact, nor gleaming columns, nor beautiful marble figures - rather, charm of soul, beauty of mind, a table groaning with righteousness and containing the fruits of almsgiving. If He sees such a table, He quickly joins the party and takes His place.   *Sermon 8 on Genesis*

Tuesday - Aphrarat of Persia

I implore you, pastors, that you do not set leaders over the flock who are foolish and stupid, or covetous and lovers of things. Everyone who feeds the flock will eat of their milk. And everyone who guides the yoke will be served from his labor. The priests have a right to partake of the altar, and the Levites will receive their tithes. Whoever eats of the milk, let his heart be upon the flock; and let each one who is ministered to from the labor of his yoke, take heed to his tillage. And let the priests who partake of the altar serve the altar with honor. And as for the Levites who receive the tithes, they have no portion in Israel. O pastors, disciples of our great Pastor, don't be like hirelings; for the hireling doesn't care for the sheep. Be like our sweet Pastor, whose life was not dearer to Him than His sheep. Train up the youths and raise up the maidens; and love the lambs and let them be reared in your bosoms; that when you come at last to the Chief Pastor, you may offer to Him all your sheep in completeness, and so He may give you what He has promised: "Where I am, you will be also." These things, brief as they are, will be sufficient for the good pastors and leaders.

Demonstrations

Wednesday - Athanasius of Alexandria

Because man sinned and fell, and all things are in confusion because of his fall: death prevailed from Adam to Moses, the earth was cursed, Hell was opened, Paradise shut, Heaven offended, mankind corrupted and dehumanized, while the devil was rejoicing against us. Then God, in His loving-kindness, not willing that man who was made in His own image should perish, said, "Whom shall I send, and who will go?" But while everyone else held their peace, the Son said, "Here am I, send Me." Then, saying "Go," He "delivered" man to Him, that the Word Himself might be made Flesh, and by taking the Flesh, restore it completely. For to Him, as to a physician, man "was delivered" to heal the bite of the serpent; as to life, to raise what was dead; as to light, to illumine the darkness; and, because He was Word, to renew the rational nature. Since then all things were delivered to Him, and He is made Man, at once all things were set right and perfected. Earth receives blessing instead of a curse, Paradise was opened to the robber, Hell cowered, the tombs were opened and the dead raised, the gates of Heaven were lifted up to await Him who "comes from Edom." The Saviour Himself clearly shows in what sense "all things were delivered" to Him, when He continues, as Matthew tells us: "Come to Me, all you who labor and are heavy laden, and I will give you rest." Yes, you were delivered to Me to give rest to those who had laboured, and life to the dead. And what is written in John's Gospel harmonizes with this: "The Father loves the Son, and has given all things into His hand." Given, in order that, just as all things were made by Him, so in Him all things might be renewed. For they were not delivered to Him, that being poor, He might be made rich, nor did He receive all things that He might receive power which previously He lacked. Perish the thought! Rather, they were delivered that as Saviour He might set all things right.

On Luke 10:22

Thursday - Clement of Alexandria

We also, repenting of our sins, renouncing our iniquities, purified by baptism, hurry back to the eternal light as children to the Father. Jesus therefore, rejoicing in the spirit, said: "I thank You, Father, Lord of heaven and earth, that You have hidden these things from the wise and prudent and revealed them to babes." The Master and Teacher applies the name babes to us who are more ready to embrace salvation than the wise of the world, who thinking themselves wise are puffed up with pride. And He exclaims in exultation and great joy, as if speaking with the children, "Even so, Father, for so it seemed good in Your sight." For this reason those things which have been concealed from the wise and prudent of this present world have been revealed to babes. We truly are the children of God, then, who have put off the old man, and stripped off the garment of wickedness, and put on the immortality of Christ; that we may become a new, holy people by regeneration, and may keep the new man undefiled.

The Instructor

Friday - Augustine of Hippo

So let the babies come, then, let them come; let the Lord be heard when He says, "Let the little children come to Me." Let the children come, the impoverished to the doctor. Let the lost come to the Redeemer. Let them come and don't let anyone forbid them. They have not yet committed anything in the branch, but they have already perished in the root. Let the Lord bless the little ones together with the great; let the doctor touch both the little ones and the great.

I entrust the cause of the little ones to the grown-ups. Speak for those who can't pray, for those who can only cry. If it's not for nothing you are their elders, be also their protectors. Look after the interests of those who cannot yet conduct their own case. Being lost was the common lot of us all. Let it also be our common lot to be found. We all got lost together. Let us all be found together in Christ. What we deserve is very different, but the grace we are offered is the same for us all. Infants have no evil in them but what they have contracted from the source. They have no evil but what they have contracted from their origin. Their elders, who have added many other sins to what they contracted, must not hold them back from salvation. Older in age means older too in wickedness. But the grace of God wipes out what you have contracted. It also wipes out what you have added. For where sin abounded, grace abounded all the more. *Sermon 115*

Saturday - Augustine of Hippo

Blood relatives of the virgin Mary were called the brothers of the Lord. For that was the custom of the Scriptures, to call any blood relatives and close kin brothers, but that is foreign to our way of speaking, not at all what we are used to. Who, in fact, would call his maternal uncle or his sister's son his brother? Yet scripture also calls these relatives brothers. Thus Abraham and Lot are called brothers, though Abraham was Lot's paternal uncle; and Laban and Jacob are called brothers, though Laban was Jacob's maternal uncle.

So then, when you hear the brothers of the Lord, think of Mary's relatives, not of her having any other children. You see, just as no dead person had been in the tomb where the Lord's body was placed, either before or after, so neither did Mary's womb carry any mortal child either before or after.

We have said who His brothers were; let us hear what they said: "Depart from here and go into Judea, that Your disciples also may see the works that You are doing." The works of the Lord did not escape the notice of the disciples, but they quite escaped the notice of these men. In fact, these brothers, that is, these blood relatives, may have had Christ as their relation, but they were hesitant about believing someone so near to them. That is what the gospel says. After all, we would not dare to express such an opinion on our own; you heard it just now. They go on to give Him advice: "No one does anything in secret while he himself seeks to be known openly. If You do these things, show Yourself to the world." And then: "For even His brothers did not believe in Him." Why could they not believe in Him? Because they were looking for human fame and glory. Even the advice His brothers seem to be giving Him refers only to His fame: "Perform miracles, get yourself known; in other words, show off to everybody, so that you can be praised by everyone." Flesh was talking to flesh; flesh without God was talking to flesh united to God. The prudence of the flesh was talking to the Word which was made flesh and dwelt among us. *Homily 28 on John*

Collect

O God, who has prepared for those that love You such good things as pass man's understanding, pour into our hearts such love toward You that we, loving You above all things, may obtain Your promises, which exceed all that we can desire; through Jesus Christ, Your Son, our Lord, who lives and reigns with You and the Holy Spirit, one God, now and forever. *Gelasian Sacramentary*

AT LAUDS

Psalmody

Sunday: 3, C8, 51	Wednesday: 8, C11, 20	Friday: 146, C13, 5
Monday: 118a, C9, 118b	Thursday: 18a, C12, 18b	Saturday: 149, C14, 150
Tuesday: 1, C10, 2		

Lesson

Sunday: I Kings 11:1-8	Wednesday: I Kings 12:25-33	Friday: I Kings 14:19-31
Monday: I Kings 11:26-43	Thursday: I Kings 13:11-34	Saturday: I Kings 15:16-34
Tuesday: I Kings 12:12-20		

Collect

Lord, I pray that You may be a lamp for me in the darkness. Touch my soul and kindle a fire within it, that it may burn brightly and give light to my life. Thus my body may truly become Your temple, lit by Your perpetual flame burning on the altar of my heart. And may the light within me shine on my brethren that it may drive away the darkness of ignorance and sin from them also, and thus together let us be lights to the world, manifesting the bright beauty of Your Gospel to all around us.

Columban

AT TERCE, SEXT AND NONE

Chapter

Sunday, Monday and Tuesday: I Peter 3:8-15
Wednesday and Thursday: I Timothy 2:1-7
Friday and Saturday: James 2:14-17

AT VESPERS

Psalmody

Sunday: 136b, 137, 138	Wednesday: 9, 10, 11	Friday: 17, 147a, 147b
Monday: 140, 141, 142	Thursday: 12, 13, 14, 16	Saturday: 19, 54, 77
Tuesday: 144, 145, 7		

Lesson

Sunday: I Kings 11:9-13	Wednesday: I Kings 13:1-10	Friday: I Kings 15:1-15
Monday: I Kings 12:1-11	Thursday: I Kings 14:1-16	Saturday: I Kings 16:1-14
Tuesday: I Kings 12:21-24		

Collect

O Jesus Christ, Son of the living God, who has given us Your holy word, and has bountifully provided for all our temporal wants, we confess that we are unworthy of all these mercies, and that we have rather deserved punishment: But we implore You, forgive us our sins, and prosper and bless us in our several callings, that by Your strength we may be sustained and defended, now and forever, and so praise and glorify You eternally, who lives and reigns with the Father and the Holy Spirit, one God, now and forever.

Veit Dietrich

THE SIXTH WEEK
AFTER TRINITY

AT MATINS

Hymn - *Ich bin getauft auf deinem Namen*

1. Bap-tized in - to Thy name most ho-ly, O Fa - ther, Son, and Ho-ly Ghost,

I claim a place, though weak and low-ly, A-mong Thy seed, Thy cho-sen host.

Bur-ied with Christ and dead to sin, Thy Spi-rit now shall live with - in.

2. My loving Father, Thou dost take me
To be henceforth Thy child and heir;
My faithful Savior, Thou dost make me
The fruit of all Thy sorrows share;
Thou, Holy Ghost, wilt comfort me
When darkest clouds around I see.

3. And I have vowed to love and fear Thee
And to obey Thee, Lord, alone;
Because the Holy Ghost did move me,
I dared to pledge myself Thine own,
Renouncing sin to keep the faith
And war with evil unto death.

4. My faithful God, Thou failest never,
Thy cov'nant surely will abide;
Oh, cast me not away forever
Should I transgress it on my side!
Though I have oft my soul defiled,
Do Thou forgive, restore, Thy child.

5. Yea, all I am and love most dearly
I offer now, O Lord, to Thee,
Oh, let me make my vows sincerely
And help me Thine own child to be!
Let naught within me, naught I own,
Serve any will but Thine alone.

6. Depart, depart, thou Prince of Darkness!
No more by thee I'll be enticed.
Mine is indeed a tarnished conscience,
But sprinkled with the blood of Christ.
Away, vain world! O sin, away!
Lo, I renounce you all this day.

7. And never let my purpose falter,
O Father, Son, and Holy Ghost,
But keep me faithful to Thine altar
Till Thou shalt call me from my post,
So unto Thee I live and die
And praise Thee evermore on high.

Johann Jacob Rambach, 1734

Psalmody

Sunday: 21, 22, 23	Wednesday: 30, 31, 32	Friday: 37a, 37b, 38
Monday: 24, 25, 26	Thursday: 33, 34, 35	Saturday: 39, 40, 41
Tuesday: 27, 28, 29		

Lesson

Sunday, Monday and Tuesday: Matthew 5:20-26

Tuesday: Luke 11:37-54

Wednesday and Thursday: Mark 10:17-21

Thursday: Luke 18:18-30 or Matthew 19:16-22

Friday and Saturday: Mark 5:1-20

Homily

Sunday - Martin Luther

Christ does not speak in generalities against plain people, but against the best people in the whole nation, the elite and the paragons of virtue, who shone like the sun in comparison with the others. In the whole nation no class was so highly praised and no titles so highly honored as that of the Pharisees and scribes. If you wanted to call a man holy, you would have to call him a Pharisee, just as among us the Carthusians or hermits have this reputation. Undoubtedly the disciples of Christ themselves supposed that there was no greater holiness to be found than the holiness of these men, and nothing was farther from their mind than that He would attack these people. He did not venture to call them by name right away. Instead of accusing certain individuals among them, He accused the entire class, condemning not particular vices or sins but all their righteousness and holy living. He goes so far as to exclude and reject them from the kingdom of heaven, to sentence them straight to hell-fire. It is as if He were to say of our time: "The priests and monks and those who are called 'spiritual,' all of them without exception, are damned to hell eternally, with all their works and ways, even when these are at their best." Who could hear or bear such a sermon?

Note first that while He concedes that they have a righteousness and that they lead an upstanding and honorable life, He so utterly rejects it that if it does not improve, it is already condemned and everything it can accomplish is lost. Note, secondly, that He is talking about people who would like to get to heaven and who take the other life seriously. This the great rude mass does not care about; they do not ask about God or the Word of God, and what we say about the Gospel is preached for nothing to them. But it is preached to the others, to teach them that such righteousness is a false righteousness that must be salted and corrected, a deception both to themselves and to others, and a road that leads away to hell.   *On the Sermon on the Mount*

Monday - Jerome of Jerusalem

"We know that a man is not justified by observing the Law, but by faith in Jesus Christ. We too have put our faith in Christ Jesus so that we may be justified by faith in Him and not by observing the Law." Some say that if Paul is right to assert that no one is justified by works of the Law but by faith in Jesus Christ, then the patriarchs, prophets, and saints who lived prior to Christ's advent were lacking in something... The saints who lived long ago, however, were justified by faith in Christ. Abraham foresaw the day of Christ and rejoiced. Moses regarded disgrace for the sake of Christ as of greater value than the treasures of Egypt, because he was looking ahead to his reward. Isaiah beheld the glory of Christ, as John the Evangelist notes. Jude speaks generally about all the saints of old: "Although you already know this, I want to remind you that Jesus delivered His people out of Egypt, but later destroyed those who did not believe."

Thus it is not so much the works of the Law that are condemned as those who are confident that they can be justified by them. The Savior says to His disciples, "Unless your righteousness surpasses that of the Pharisees and the teachers of the Law, you will not enter the kingdom of heaven." It is fitting to point out how many precepts the Law contains that no one is able to fulfill. It must also be said that some works of the Law are done by those who are ignorant of it. But doers of the Law are not justified because their deeds are done without faith in Christ.   *Commentary on Galatians*

Tuesday - Anselm of Canterbury

Where and what is the virtue and the strength of your salvation? Christ, Christ assuredly has raised you up again; He, the good Samaritan, has healed you; He, the good friend, has redeemed you with His life, and set you free. Christ, I say, Christ is He. And so the virtue of your salvation is the virtue of Christ. And where is it; where is this His virtue? Truly, "horns are in His hands, there is His strength hid." Yes, horns are in His Hands, for those hands are fastened to the arms of the Cross. But O, what strength is there in such weakness? What grandeur in such humility? What honor in such contempt? But because in weakness, it is a hidden thing; because in humility, it is veiled; because in contempt, it is concealed and covered up. O hidden strength! that Man fixed to a cross should transfix the eternal death that oppressed the race of man; that Man bound to a tree should unbind the world which had been fast bound by perpetual death! O veiled omnipotence! that Man condemned with thieves should save men condemned with demons. O virtue concealed and covered up! that one soul given up to torment should extricate innumerable souls from hell; should as man undergo the death of the body and destroy the death of souls.

Cur Deus Homo

Wednesday - Hilary of Poitiers

The young man became arrogant through the observance of the law. He did not recognize that the fulfillment of the law is Christ. He assumed he could be justified by works. He was not aware that Jesus had come for the lost sheep of the house of Israel and that the law could not save except through justifying faith. He questioned the Lord of the law and the only-begotten God as if He were an ordinary teacher of precepts that were written down in the law. Hence, the Lord rejected this declaration of a counterfeit faith, because the question was put to Him as if He were a mere teacher of the law. He replied: "Why do you call me good?" In order to make known how much He was to be recognized and acknowledged as good, He declared: "No one is good but God only." He would not have rejected the attribute of goodness if it had been attributed to him as God.

On the Trinity

Thursday - Clement of Alexandria

What was it that made the rich young man run away and made him abandon his teacher, and reject his plea, his hope, his life, and his past achievement? "Sell your possessions." But what does this mean? It is not, as some hastily interpret it, a command that he should throw away what he possesses and renounce his wealth. What he is told to banish from his soul are his notions about wealth, his attachment to it, his excessive desire for it, his morbid excitement over it, and his anxieties - those thorns of existence which choke the seed of true life.

There is nothing great or enviable about having no money, unless it is for the purpose of gaining true life. Otherwise it must be said that people with nothing at all, the destitutes who beg for daily bread in abject poverty by the roadside, even though they are "ignorant" of God and "of God's righteousness," would be the most blessed of men, the dearest to God, the sole possessors of eternal life, merely by virtue of their complete lack of any ways or means of livelihood and of their want of the smallest necessities. Again, there is nothing new in renouncing one's riches and giving them in charity to the poor or to one's fatherland. Many did this before the Savior's coming, some to have leisure for the pursuit of dead wisdom, others to gain empty fame and vainglory - men like Anaxagoras, Democritus and Crates.

Why then does He give this command which failed to bring salvation to men of old as if it were something new, divine, and uniquely life-giving? If there is something extraordinary that the new creation, the Son of God, reveals and teaches, then it cannot be the outward action that He is commanding; others have done that. It must be something else that is being indicated through it - something greater, more divine and more perfect. It is the stripping off of the passions from the soul itself and from its disposition; all that is alien must be uprooted and expelled from the mind. This is the appropriate lesson for the believer to learn, and the worthy doctrine for the Savior to teach...

Imagine a man who holds his possessions, his gold, silver and houses, as the gifts of God; who serves the God who gave them by using them for the welfare of mankind; who knows that he possesses them more for the sake of his brethren than his own; who is master of and not a slave of his possessions; who does not go about with his possessions in his heart or let himself be trapped by them; who is always engaged in some good and holy work; and who, should he be deprived of them, is able to bear their removal as cheerfully as their abundance. Such a man is the one whom the Lord calls "blessed" and "poor in spirit." He is worthy to inherit the kingdom of heaven; he is not the rich man who cannot obtain life.
Who is the Rich Man that is Saved?

Friday - Augustine of Hippo

The demons had much knowledge, but entirely lacked love. They dreaded receiving punishment from Him. They did not love the righteousness that was in Him. He made Himself known to them to the extent He willed; and He willed to be made known to the extent that was fitting. But He was not made known to them as He is known to the holy angels, who enjoy participation in His eternity, in that He is the Word of God. To the demons He is known as He had to be made known, by striking terror into them, for His purpose was to free from their tyrannical power all who were predestined for His kingdom and glory, which is eternally true and truly eternal.
The City of God

Saturday - Johannes Tauler

We are to be God's witnesses by confessing and intending Him in all our actions and endeavors, not only when all goes well, and when we are filled with the warmth of natural enthusiasm. People find it easy enough to confess God at such times. They know and love Him well enough until they are assailed by terrible trials. Then they seem to have forgotten what they had been about, and now that sufferings are upon them, they completely loose their moorings. They are not anchored in God but in their own feelings: a weak foundation indeed, and one built upon shifting sands.

Those, however, who are God's true witnesses are firmly anchored in Him, in love or in suffering, no matter what God may choose to give or take away. They do not set much store by their own methods; if they prove helpful to their spiritual life, well and good. But God, in His loving foresight, often shatters their foundations and thus they frequently find themselves thwarted. If they want to keep vigil, they are obliged to sleep; if they like to fast, they are made to eat; if they would like to keep silence and be at rest, they have to do otherwise. In this way, everything they cleave to crumbles, and they are brought face-to-face with their bare nothingness. Thus they are shown how total is their dependence upon God, and they learn to confess Him with a pure and simple faith, with no other support to sustain them.
Sermon 21

Collect

Lord of all power and might, the Author and Giver of all good things, graft into our hearts the love of Your name, increase in us true religion, nourish us with all goodness, and of Your great mercy keep us in the same; through Jesus Christ, Your Son, our Lord, who lives and reigns with You and the Holy Spirit, one God, now and forever.
Gelasian Sacramentary

AT LAUDS

Psalmody

Sunday: 67, C1, 5
Monday: 63, C2, 36
Tuesday: 43, C3, 57

Wednesday: 64, C4, 65
Thursday: 88, C6, 90

Friday: 76, C5, 92
Saturday: 143, C7, 148

Lesson

Sunday: I Kings 16:15-34
Monday: I Kings 17:8-16
Tuesday: I Kings 18:17-29

Wednesday: I Kings 19:1-8
Thursday: I Kings 21:1-16

Friday: I Kings 22:29-40
Saturday: II Kings 1:1-18

Collect

Almighty Lord God, give us righteous, true faith, and increase the same in us daily; give us also love and hope, in order that we may serve You and our neighbor according to Your will, through Jesus Christ, Your Son, our Lord, who lives and reigns with You and the Holy Spirit, one God, now and forever.   *Braunschweig-Lüneberg Kirchenordnung*

AT TERCE, SEXT AND NONE

Chapter

Sunday, Monday and Tuesday: Romans 6:3-11
Wednesday and Thursday: Hebrews 12:28b-13:8
Friday and Saturday: James 3:14-18

AT VESPERS

Psalmody

Sunday: 110, 111, 112, 113
Monday: 114, 115, 116, 117
Tuesday: 120, 121, 122

Wednesday: 123, 124, 125
Thursday: 126, 127, 128

Friday: 129, 130, 131, 132
Saturday: 133, 135, 136a

Lesson

Sunday: I Kings 17:1-7
Monday: I Kings 17:17-24
Tuesday: I Kings 18:30-40

Wednesday: I Kings 19:9-21
Thursday: I Kings 21:17-29

Friday: I Kings 29:41-53
Saturday: II Kings 2:1-15

Collect

Lord God, heavenly Father, we confess that we are poor, wretched sinners, and that there is no good in us, our hearts, flesh and blood being so corrupted by sin, that we never in this life can be without sinful lust and concupiscence; therefore we implore You, dear Father, forgive us these sins, and let Your Holy Spirit so cleanse our hearts that we may desire and love Your word, abide by it, and thus by Your grace be forever saved; through our Lord, Jesus Christ, Your Son, who lives and reigns with You and the Holy Spirit, one true God, now and forever. Amen.

Veit Dietrich

THE SEVENTH WEEK
AFTER TRINITY

AT MATINS

Hymn - *Sei Lob und Ehr' dem höchsten Gut*

1. Sing praise to God, the high-est good, The au-thor of cre - a - tion.

The God of love who un - der-stood Our need for His sal - va - tion.

With heal-ing balm our souls He fills And ev-'ry faith-less

mur - mur stills. To God all praise and glo - ry!

2. The angel host, O King of kings,
   Your praise is ever telling.
   In earth and sky, all living things
   Beneath Your shadow dwelling,
   Adore and praise their Maker's might,
   Whose wisdom orders all things right;
   To God all praise and glory!

3. What God's almighty pow'r has made,
   In mercy He is keeping.
   By morning glow or evening shade
   His eye is never sleeping.
   Within the kingdom of His might
   All things are just and good and right;
   To God all praise and glory!

4. We sought the Lord in our distress;
   O God, in mercy hear us.
   Our Savior saw our helplessness
   And came with peace to cheer us.
   For this we thank and praise the Lord,
   Who is by one and all adored;
   To God all praise and glory!

5. He never shall forsake His flock,
   His chosen generation;
   He is their refuge and their rock,
   Their peace and their salvation.
   As with a mother's tender hand,
   He leads His own, His chosen band;
   To God all praise and glory!

6. When earth can comfort us no more
   Nor human help avail us,
   Our Maker comes Himself, His store
   Of blessing does not fail us.
   And turns to us a Father's eye
   Whom earth all rest and hope denies;
   To God all praise and glory!

7. Thus all my pilgrim way along
   I'll sing aloud Your praises
   That men may hear the grateful song
   My voice unwearied raises;
   Be joyful in the Lord, my heart!
   Both soul and body, bear your part!
   To God all praise and glory!

8. All who confess Christ's holy name,
Give God the praise and glory.
Let all who know His pow'r proclaim
Aloud the wondrous story.
Cast ev'ry idol from its throne,
For God is God, and He alone;
To God all praise and glory!

9. Then come before His presence now
And banish fear and sadness;
To Your Redeemer pay your vow
And sing with joy and gladness;
Though great distress my soul befell,
The Lord my God did all things well;
To God all praise and glory!

Johann Jacob Schütz, 1675

Psalmody

Sunday: 42, 44, 45
Monday: 46, 47, 48
Tuesday: 49, 50, 52

Wednesday: 53, 55, 56
Thursday: 58, 59, 60

Friday: 61, 62, 66
Saturday: 68a, 68b, 69a

Lesson

Sunday, Monday and Tuesday: Mark 8:1-10
Tuesday: Matthew 15:32-39

Wednesday and Thursday: Matthew 16:1-12
Thursday: John 7:40-53

Friday and Saturday: Matthew 12:1-7
Friday: Mark 2:23-28
Saturday: John 8:31-36

Homily

Sunday - Bede the Venerable

Mystically, this miracle shows us that we cannot safely travel along the road of life unless the grace of the Redeemer nourishes us by the food of His Word... "And if I send them away hungry to their own houses, they will faint on the way..." The multitude had remained with the Lord to have their sick healed. So also each of the elect, with shining faith in the Holy Trinity, prays earnestly and without ceasing to the Lord that their soul be healed of its sickness, that is, for the forgiveness of their sins.

Moreover, the multitude remains for three days with the Lord when the faithful multitude depart from the sins they have committed through repentance and turn to the Lord in thought, word, and deed. The Lord will not send these to their homes hungry, lest they faint in the way; for those who are converted from sin faint on the road of life if they are sent away without the food of His holy teaching in their souls. Therefore lest they should grow weak on the journey of this earthly pilgrimage they must be fed with holy counsels. *Homily on Mark 8*

Monday - Maximus of Turin

Four thousand are fed. This signifies that all peoples - people from the four corners of the world - are filled with the sevenfold grace of the Spirit unto eternal life. And so, Beloved, we who believe in our Lord Jesus Christ, not through the Law but by faith, who are redeemed, not by its works but by grace itself; who are filled, not from the five loaves, that is, from the Five Books of Moses, but by the sevenfold grace of the Holy Spirit, as the blessed Isaias had prophesied, saying: "The Spirit of the Lord shall rest upon Him, the Spirit of wisdom and understanding, the Spirit of counsel and might, the Spirit of knowledge and of the fear of the Lord," let us continue in this grace of the Sevenfold Spirit, by which we were called. Let us be filled with the gift of the Holy Spirit through our Lord Jesus Christ, Who lives and reigns in the Unity of the Holy Spirit, God forever and ever. Amen. *Homily on the Loaves and Fishes*

Tuesday - Leo I of Rome

Use the Gospel story with faith, and note carefully, here with a spiritual mind and there with bodily sight, what things were visibly done by the Lord, as if you yourself were there together with the apostles. Credit to the man what as a child He took from a woman; credit to God the fact that His mother's virginity was in no way harmed by His conception nor by His birth. Recognize the form of a servant, wrapped in swaddling clothes and lying in a manger; but in the One announced by angels, declared by the heavens, worshipped by the wise men, confess the form of the Lord.

See Him as human when he did not decline the wedding feast, admit Him to be divine when He turned the water into wine. Let our own affections find their echo when He shed tears at the death of a friend, and feel the divine power when that same person, not a fetid corpse after the four days' burial, was raised alive by the power of His Word alone. To make mud of His spittle and the dust was the work of His body; but to open the blind man's eyes besmeared with this was certainly a work of that faculty which He had not given to the elements of nature because He had reserved it for the revelation of His glory. It is characteristic of the true man to relieve the tired body in quiet sleep; but of true God to restrain the force of raging storms by the rebuke of His command. It is the work of human kindness and a responsible spirit to provide food for the hungry; but to satisfy five thousand men, as well as their wives and children, with five loaves and two fish, who would dare to deny that this is the work of the divinity, which, these functions of true flesh cooperating with divinity, showed itself to be in man and man in itself? In no other way could the ancient wounds of original sin be healed in human nature but by the Word of God assuming flesh from the womb of the Virgin and, in one and same Person together, both being born as flesh and being the Word. *Sermon 47*

Wednesday - Jerome of Jerusalem

The Lord instructs the disciples to stay away from the yeast of the Pharisees. The Evangelist then clarifies this by adding that He was referring to the teaching of the Pharisees. What else is the teaching of the Pharisees but the observance of the Law according to the flesh? The sense of the passage is this: Do not think that the crafty plots of those few men coming from Judea who teach another gospel should be underestimated. An ember is tiny and almost invisible to the eye when you look at it, but if a small flame ignites the tinder, it devours city-walls, cities, vast forests, and whole provinces. Yeast... also seems like something small and inconsequential. But when it is mixed in with flour it spoils the entire batch by its vigorous activity, and everything in the mixture gives way to its forcefulness. Similarly, perverse doctrine begins with one person and at first finds a favorable audience of barely two or three people. But the cancer gradually festers in the body and, according to the familiar proverb, one sheep's disease pollutes the entire flock. Therefore, the ember must be extinguished as soon as it appears so that the house does not burn down. Yeast must be kept far from the batch of flour so that it does not spoil. Putrid flesh must be amputated so that the body does not rot. And the diseased animal must be sequestered from the sheepfolds so that the flocks do not die. Arius was one ember in Alexandria, but because he was not extinguished at once, his flame destroyed the entire city. *Commentary on Galatians*

Thursday - Peter of Blois

He who will not renounce all things that he possesses cannot be My disciple. He who does not hate father and mother, and even his own soul, is not worthy of Me. O good Jesus! Why have You dealt with us so? Moses laid a burden upon us which neither we nor our fathers were able to bear. We had hoped that You would come and lighten our burdens. And now Your hand is heavy upon us. Were not the hands of Moses heavy enough? Did You come to slay us with scorpions? You seek a reason to be angry against us and to destroy us. Are You not Jesus the Savior, and not the Destroyer? Why do You command what I cannot do, that is, to hate my father and my mother, and my own soul, and to love my enemy?

493

This is a hard speech. Who can hear it? I would go to other schools, and I would choose another master, but I hear Peter, answering both for himself and for others, Lord, to whom shall we go? You have the words of eternal life. If You pretend labor in Your precepts and hardness in Your discourse, yet I know how great the sweetness is which You have laid up for those who fear You. I will hope in You whose wisdom cannot be deceived, whose power cannot be overcome, whose kindness cannot be wearied, whose love cannot be lessened. If You scourge me, if You consume me, if You cut me asunder, if You slay me, I will hope in You, O Lord. Only help me and teach me to do Your will. But You are good to those that hope in You, to the soul that seeks You. *Sermon 53, "On Manifold Wisdom"*

Friday - Gregory of Nyssa

Do not despise men in their distress, do not think them of no account. Consider what they are and you will grasp their dignity. They have taken upon themselves the person of our Savior. For he, the compassionate one, has lent them his own person so as to shame the unmerciful and the haters of the poor... The poor are the treasurers of the good things that we hope for. They are the keepers of the gates of the kingdom, opening them to the merciful and shutting them on the harsh and stingy. They are the strongest of accusers, the best of defenders - not that they accuse or defend in words, but that the Lord sees what is done towards them, and every deed cries louder than a herald to Him who searches all hearts ...

You have been created rational beings, endowed with a mind to expound and interpret divine things. So don't be enticed by what is but transitory. Strive to win those things which never forsake those who possess them. Live with restraint. Don't think of everything as your own, but save a part for God's dear poor.

All things belong to God, the Father of us and of them. We are all of the same stock, all brothers. And when men are brothers, the best and fairest thing is that they should inherit in equal portions. The second best is that even if one or two take the greater part, the others should have at least their own share. But if one man should seek to be the absolute possessor of everything, refusing even a third or a fifth to his brothers, then he is a cruel tyrant. He is a savage with whom there can be no dealing, an insatiable beast gloatingly shutting its jaws over a meal that it will not share. No, he is more ruthless than any animal. Wolf does not drive wolf from the prey, and a pack of dogs will tear at the same carcass; but this man in his limitless greed will not admit one fellow creature to a share in his riches. *On Love of the Poor*

Saturday - Alcuin of York

Christ rejoiced when the world was completed and was joyful over the sons of men. And He promised to those, whoever they were, who would believe in it that they would have eternal life. Before He laid the foundations of the world, before He poured forth the seas, raised up the mountains, hung aloft the sky, established the earth beneath, this was promised by God, in whom there is no deceit - not that He can lie, nor does He will to do so, for He who is the Father of truth and Himself truthful cannot have deceit in Himself.

Let us discuss briefly why God is alone truthful, and every man is, in the apostle's word, called a liar? And, as He alone is said to possess immortality, although he has made the angels and many rational creatures to whom He has given immortality, so also He alone is said to be truthful, not because the other immortal creatures don't love the truth, but because He alone is immortal and true by nature. But let the others acquire immortality and truth from His gift. It is one thing to be true and to have it by nature and of oneself, another thing to be subject to the power of the one who gives you what you possess. And so we must not silently pass over how God, who does not lie, has promised eternal life endless ages ago. *Commentary on Titus*

Collect

O God, whose never-failing providence orders all things both in heaven and earth, we humbly implore You to put away from us all hurtful things and give to us those things that be profitable for us; through Jesus Christ, Your Son, our Lord, who lives and reigns with You and the Holy Spirit, one God, now and forever. *Gelasian Sacramentary*

AT LAUDS

Psalmody

Sunday: 3, C8, 51
Monday: 118a, C9, 118b
Tuesday: 1, C10, 2

Wednesday: 8, C11, 20
Thursday: 18a, C12, 18b

Friday: 146, C13, 5
Saturday: 149, C14, 150

Lesson

Sunday: II Kings 3:1-27
Monday: II Kings 4:18-37
Tuesday: II Kings 6:1-7

Wednesday: II Kings 8:7-15
Thursday: II Kings 9:1-13

Friday: II Kings 9:30-37
Saturday: II Kings 10:18-28

Collect

O God, who has forbidden us to be anxious about supplies for this life; grant, we pray You, that we may steadfastly pursue what belongs to You, and that all things salutary may be granted to us; through Jesus Christ, our Lord, who lives and reigns with You and the Holy Spirit, one God, now and forever. *Gelasian Sacramentary*

AT TERCE, SEXT AND NONE

Chapter

Sunday, Monday and Tuesday: Romans 6:19-23
Wednesday and Thursday: Romans 8:1-6
Friday and Saturday: James 4:7-10

AT VESPERS

Psalmody

Sunday: 136b, 137, 138
Monday: 140, 141, 142
Tuesday: 144, 145, 7

Wednesday: 9, 10, 11
Thursday: 12, 13, 14, 16

Friday: 17, 147a, 147b
Saturday: 19, 54, 77

Lesson

Sunday: II Kings 4:1-17
Monday: II Kings 5:1-14
Tuesday: II Kings 6:8-18

Wednesday: II Kings 8:16-27
Thursday: II Kings 9:14-29

Friday: II Kings 10:1-11
Saturday: II Kings 10:29-36

Collect

Lord God, heavenly Father, who, by Your Son, abundantly fed four thousand men besides women and children in the wilderness with seven loaves and a few small fishes: We pray You graciously abide among us with Your blessing and keep us from covetousness and the cares of this life, that we may seek first Your kingdom and Your righteousness, and experience Your ever-present help in all things needed for body and soul; through Your Son, our Lord Jesus Christ, who lives and reigns with You and the Holy Spirit, one true God, now and forever. Amen. *Veit Dietrich*

THE EIGHTH WEEK
AFTER TRINITY

AT MATINS

Hymn - *Wär' Gott nicht mit us diese Zeit*

1. If God had not been on our side And had not come to aid us,

The foes with all their pow'r and pride Would sure-ly have dis- mayed us;

For we, His flock, would have to fear The threat of men both

far and near Who rise in might a - gainst us.

2. Their furious wrath, did God permit,
Would surely have consumed us
And as a deep and yawning pit
Wisht life and limb entomed us.
Like men o'er whom dark waters roll
Their wrath would have engulfed our soul
And, like a flood, o'erwhelmed us.

3. Blest be the Lord, who foiled their threat
That they could not devour us;
Our souls, like birds, escaped their net,
They could not overpower us.
The snare is broken - we are free!
Our help is ever, Lord, in Thee,
Who madest earth and heaven.

Martin Luther, 1524

Psalmody

Sunday: 69b, 70, 71
Monday: 72, 73, 74
Tuesday: 78a, 78b, 78c

Wednesday: 75, 79, 80
Thursday: 81, 82, 83

Friday: 84, 86, 87, 93
Saturday: 85, 89a, 89b

Lesson

Sunday, Monday and Tuesday: Matthew 7:15-23
Monday: Luke 6:43-45
Tuesday: Matthew 12:43-50

Wednesday and Thursday: Mark 9:38-48
Thursday: Luke 9:49-50

Friday and Saturday: Matthew 23:13-23

Homily

Sunday - John Chrysostom

"Every tree that does not bear good fruit is cut down and thrown into the fire." In these words the Jews seem to be referred to, and because of this He reminds them of the words of John the Baptist, threatening them with punishment in these same words. For he had spoken in this way to them, warning them of the axe, and of the tree that shall be cut down, and of unquenchable fire.

If you consider this matter carefully you will see that there are two punishments threatened here: To be cut down, and to be cast into the fire; for he who is burned is also completely cast out of the kingdom, which is the more severe punishment. Many only fear hell. But I believe that the loss of glory is a torment more bitter than that of hell itself...

But may this never be the case with us, O Only-Begotten Son of God, nor that we ever experience this hopeless punishment. For how great an evil it is to fall from those good things I cannot accurately say...

Imagine a wonderful child, a virtuous child who also has dominion over the whole world, who is in all ways so virtuous that he is able to bring all men to yearn for His father's affection. What will the father not endure to see and delight in his most dear son? Let us think in the same way of that glory; for there is no son so sweet to a father as the peaceful rest from toil is to the just, and to depart and be with Christ. Intolerable indeed is the pain of hell. But were there ten thousand hells, such pain would be as nothing compared to falling from that blessed glory, and to be hated by Christ, to hear: "I do not know you," to be accused of not feeding Him when we saw Him hungry. Yes, it would certainly be better to endure a thousand thunder bolts than to see that face of gentleness turning away from us, and that eye of peace not able to stand the sight of us.

Homily 23 on Matthew

Monday - Martin Luther

All kinds of schismatics, fanatics, and heretics come into the church. They seem anxious to keep the Word and proclaim the truth, saying, "Here is God's Word; Here is Holy Scripture! We seek nothing for ourselves, only God's honor and the salvation of people's souls; we would gladly see God's Word and truth prosper, would gladly assist people," and so on. Thus they enter in with disarming deceit and sheep's clothing.

When poor sheep see this sheep's clothing they imagine that it is pure gold, grasp for it, and embrace it. For sheep's clothing easily fools a person when he hears God's Word and truth spoken of so highly. Who doesn't want to hear God's Word and know the truth? But Christians should remember that the devil can quote the truth and sing the praises of God's Word as well as any pious Christian. If you don't learn this, you'll be easily deceived and led astray, and then it is all over. For a man who allows himself to be deceived by sheep's clothing gets torn to pieces by the wolf.

That is why we need to say, I love to hear God's Word and truth; but before I trust what I hear completely, I'll check it against my catechism and the doctrine I've learned. Whoever is cautious and on guard and doesn't fall for everything, but searches the Word, will be safe and not be deceived. But whoever will not do this, is careless about his catechism and the doctrine he has previously learned, who only has ears for all of the crazy fanatics, such a person is doomed.

House Postil for the Eighth Sunday after Trinity

Tuesday - Bernard of Clairvaux

Is there anything you ought still to fear? Just one thing, something very serious, the sin of Judas, the sin of apostasy. It is a good thing that you have received wings like the dove and have flown away to be at rest. But on earth there will be no rest, only toil and trouble and affliction of spirit. For the soul that flies away what is there then to fear, if not that he may perhaps see a dead body or something of the sort on the ground, stretched out by these wicked hunters to stir his appetite, that he be captured in the snare they have set, and that the last state of that man be worse than the first. This, I tell you, is profoundly to be feared, lest someone by his heart alone, or even by his body, turn back to his own vomit. We read that the children of Israel in their hearts went back to Egypt. They could not return in body because they were prevented by the Red Sea closing in on their heels. This is what each one of us must fear to the core, that we somehow offend God to such an extent that we come to be manifestly repudiated and vomited up by him. And if shame prevents us from apostasizing in body, lukewarmness will gradually cause apostasy of the heart and the heart will live like a secular in religious habit and embrace whatever worldly consolations it can find. We are not holier than the apostle, who was afraid that, after having preached to others, he might himself become a castaway. And this is something to be afraid of until the snare is broken, until the soul has laid aside this body. The body itself is a kind of snare, which is why we read that the eye causes grief to the soul. It behooves a man therefore to feel secure when he carries his own snare about with him. But it is good to dwell in the aid of the Most High and so through him be capable of avoiding the snare.   *Third Sermon on Psalm 91*

Wednesday - Gregory of Nazianzus

Let us observe the supreme and first law of God, who rains on the just and the unjust and makes the sun rise on all equally. He spread out the earth for all the animals, with its fountains, rivers and forests; he gave air to winged animals, water to aquatic creatures, and to all the basic elements of life, not dominated by any power, not restricted by any law, not separated by any boundaries. No, all these necessities of life He has put at the disposal of all and abundantly, so that no one would lack anything. In this way He honors by equality of the gift the equality of nature and at the same time manifests the abundance of His goodness. But no sooner do men buy gold, or silver, or luxurious and unnecessary clothes, or glittering stones or any other thing for its style, than there are signs of war and mutiny and tyranny, and instantly eyebrows are raised with contempt and they deny mercy to the unfortunate people, even though they are their kinsmen. Nor do they try to help the needy, not even with their overabundance.

They should at least consider that poverty and wealth, freedom (as we call it) and slavery and other similar names were introduced quite late into the history of mankind, as a sort of common disease following the iniquity and its inventions. But, in the beginning, as the Gospel says, it was not so. He who created man at the beginning made him free and endowed him with freedom of choice, subjected only to his law, and made him rich in the delights of Paradise. The same things he desired for and the same grace he gave to the rest of mankind because they descend from the first and only man. Freedom and wealth were the only law; true poverty and slavery are its transgression.

But after life was infected by envy, contentiousness, and the astute tyranny of the serpent, men were more and more enticed by the bait of pleasure and the more powerful ones rose against the weaker; what was the same family broke away and split itself into a variety of groups; avarice suppressed what nobility there was in nature, making law an aid of power. You, however, look at the primitive equality, not at the later distinction, not at the law of the powerful, but at the law of the Creator. Help, as much as you can, nature; honor the primitive freedom; respect yourself; cover the dishonor of your family; assist those who are sick and aid those who are needy.

You, who are strong, help those who are weak; you, who are rich, assist those who are poor. You, who have not stumbled, raise up those who have fallen and are afflicted; you, who are full of spirit, comfort those who are discouraged; you, who enjoy prosperity, aid those who suffer adversities. Give thanks to God that you are among those who can do favors and not among those who need to receive them; that you need not look up to the hands of others, and that others look to yours. Do not be rich only in your wealth but also in your piety; not only in your gold but also in your virtue, or, better still, only in the latter.   *Discourse on Love for the Poor*

Thursday - Ivo of Chartres

The first Advent was in humility and meekness, the second will be with terror and majesty. In the first the Prophet says of Him to the Church, "Behold, your King comes to you, meek and humble." Of the terror of the second it is said in the Psalm: A fire shall go before Him, and a mighty tempest shall be stirred up all around Him, that this tempest may drive the wicked far away from the vision of His glory, but over them the fire shall burn. Of this tempest it is written: Let the wicked be taken away, that they may not see the glory of God. But of the fire to which the wicked will be given up, thus says the Lord by Moses: "A fire is kindled in My anger, And shall burn to the lowest hell." He Himself says that He will come to judgment with majesty: "When the Son of Man comes in His glory, all the nations will be gathered before Him." In the first Advent He came to justify the wicked, in the second He will come to condemn the wicked. In the first He came to call back those that had been snatched from Him, in the second He will come to glorify those that are converted to Him. In the first Advent Christ was betrayed for the wicked to a death which He did not deserve, in the second He will give up the wicked to a death which they do deserve. In the first Advent He came to re-form our hearts to the Image of God. But in the second, He will re-form our humble bodies to be made like His glorious body.

Seventh Sermon on Advent

Friday - Hilary of Poitiers

That they compass sea and land means that throughout the whole world they will be enemies of Christ's Gospel and will bring men under the yoke of the Law against the justification of faith. There were proselytes made into the Synagogue from among the Gentiles, the small number of whom is here noted by what is said "one proselyte." For after the preaching of Christ there was no faith left in their doctrine, but whoever was gained to the faith of the Jews became a child of hell... And he becomes the child of a twofold punishment, because he has not obtained remission of his Gentile sins, and because he has joined the company of those who persecuted Christ... For since Christ is come, reliance upon the Law is vain; for not Christ by the Law, but the Law by Christ, is sanctified, in whom it rests as on a seat or throne; so they are blind fools, who, overlooking the Sanctifier, pay honor to the things sanctified.

from the Catena Aurea of Thomas Aquinas

Saturday - Barnabus

The way of the Black One is crooked and full of cursing. For it is entirely a way of eternal death with punishment, in which lie the things which destroy men's souls - idolatry, pride, exaltation of power, hypocrisy, duplicity of heart, adultery, murder, robbery, conceit, transgression, treachery, malice, stubbornness, witchcraft, magic, covetousness, absence of the fear of God; persecutors of good men, hating truth, loving lies, not seeing the reward of righteousness, not clinging to the good nor to righteous judgment, paying no attention to the widow or the orphan, not alert to the fear of God but to that which is evil; men from whom gentleness and patience stand aloof and far off; loving worthless things, pursuing reward, not pitying the poor, not laboring for the oppressed, reckless with slanderous speech, not recognizing Him who made them, murderers of children, corrupters of God's creation, turning away from the needy, oppressing the afflicted, advocates of the rich, unjust judges of the poor, sinful throughout.

It is good therefore to learn the ordinances of the Lord, as many as have been written, and to walk in them. For he who chooses these things will be glorified in the kingdom of God; but he who chooses their opposites will perish together with his works. For this reason there is resurrection. For this reason there is recompense. I urge those of you who are in high position, if you will accept my good counsel, make sure that there are among you those to whom you may do good. Do not fail at this. The day is at hand in which everything will be destroyed together with the Evil One. The Lord is at hand and His reward. Again and again I beg you; be good lawgivers to one another; persevere as faithful counselors to yourselves; remove from yourselves all hypocrisy. And may God, who is Lord of the whole world, give you wisdom, judgment, learning, knowledge of His ordinances, patience.

Epistle of Barnabus

Collect

Grant to us, Lord, we implore You, the Spirit to think and do always such things as are right, that we, who cannot do anything that is good without You, may by You be enabled to live according to Your will; through Jesus Christ, Your Son, our Lord, who lives and reigns with You and the Holy Spirit, one God, now and forever.

Leonine Sacramentary

AT LAUDS

Psalmody

Sunday: 67, C1, 5	Wednesday: 64, C4, 65	Friday: 76, C5, 92
Monday: 63, C2, 36	Thursday: 88, C6, 90	Saturday: 143, C7, 148
Tuesday: 43, C3, 57		

Lesson

Sunday: II Kings 11:1-21	Wednesday: II Kings 16:1-20	Friday: II Kings 18:13-27
Monday: II Kings 12:17-21	Thursday: II Kings 17:24-33	Saturday: II Kings 19:20-37
Tuesday: II Kings 13:14-25		

Collect

Dissolve, O Christ, the schisms of heresy, which strive to corrupt the truth; that as You are acknowledged in heaven and on earth as one and the same Lord, so Your people, gathered from all nations, may serve You in unity of faith; through Jesus Christ, Your Son, our Lord, who lives and reigns with You and the Holy Spirit, one God, forever and ever. Amen.

Mozarabic Sacramentary

AT TERCE, SEXT AND NONE

Chapter

Sunday, Monday and Tuesday: Romans 8:12-17
Wednesday and Thursday: Romans 5:8-11a
Friday and Saturday: Hebrews 3:12-14

AT VESPERS

Psalmody

Sunday: 110, 111, 112, 113	Wednesday: 123, 124, 125	Friday: 129, 130, 131, 132
Monday: 114, 115, 116, 117	Thursday: 126, 127, 128	Saturday: 133, 135, 136a
Tuesday: 120, 121, 122		

Lesson

Sunday: II Kings 12:4-16	Wednesday: II Kings 17:1-23	Friday: II Kings 19:1-19
Monday: II Kings 13:1-9	Thursday: II Kings 18:1-8	Saturday: II Kings 20:1-11
Tuesday: II Kings 15:1-7		

Collect

Lord God, heavenly Father, we most heartily thank You that You have caused us to come to the knowledge of Your word. We pray You: graciously keep us steadfast in this knowledge until death, that we may obtain eternal life; send us now and always pious pastors, who faithfully preach Your word without offense or false doctrine, and grant them long life. Defend us from all false teachings, and frustrate the counsels of all who pervert Your word, who come to us in sheep's clothing, but are inwardly ravenous wolves, that Your true Church may always be established among us, and be defended and preserved from such false teachers, through Your Son, Jesus Christ, our Lord, who lives and reigns with You and the Holy Spirit, one God, now and forever. *Veit Dietrich*

THE NINTH WEEK
AFTER TRINITY

AT MATINS

Hymn - *Lobe den Heren, o meine Seele!*

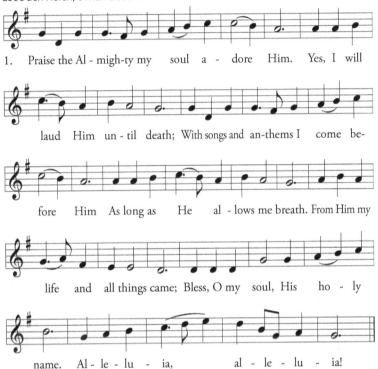

1. Praise the Al - migh-ty my soul a - dore Him. Yes, I will laud Him un - til death; With songs and an-thems I come be-fore Him As long as He al - lows me breath. From Him my life and all things came; Bless, O my soul, His ho - ly name. Al - le - lu - ia, al - le - lu - ia!

2. Trust not in princes; they are but mortal;
Earth-born they are and soon decay.
Vain are their counsels at life's last portal,
When the dark grave engulfs its prey.
Since mortals can no help afford,
Place all your trust in Christ, our Lord.
Alleluia, alleluia!

3. Blessèd, oh, blessèd are they forever
Whose help is from the Lord Most High,
Whom from salvation can nothing sever,
And who in hope to Christ draw nigh.
To all who trust in Him, our Lord
Will aid and consel now afford.
Alleluia, alleluia!

4. God the Almighty, the great Creator,
Ruler of sky and land and sea,
All things ordainèd, and sooner or later,
They come to pass unfailingly.
His rule is over rich and poor,
His promises ever stand sure.
Alleluia, alleluia!

5. Penitent sinners for mercy crying,
Pardon and peace from Him obtain;
Ever the wants of the poor supplying
Their faithful God He will remain.
He helps His children in distress,
The widows and the fatherless.
Alleluia, alleluia!

6. Praise, all you people, the name so holy
Of Him who does such wondrous things!
All that has being, to praise Him solely,
With happy heart its amen sings.
Children of God, with angel host
Praise Father, Son, and Holy Ghost!
Alleluia, alleluia!

Johann Daniel Herrnschmidt, 1714

Psalmody

Sunday: 21, 22, 23   Wednesday: 30, 31, 32   Friday: 37a, 37b, 38
Monday: 24, 25, 26   Thursday: 33, 34, 35   Saturday: 39, 40, 41
Tuesday: 27, 28, 29

Lesson

Sunday, Monday and Tuesday: Luke 16:1-9
Monday: Luke 16:10-15
Tuesday: Mark 12:38-44

Wednesday and Thursday: Luke 21:20-26
Wednesday: Mark 13:14-20
Thursday: Matthew 10:34-11:1

Friday and Saturday: Luke 21:34-36
Friday: Mark 4:21-23
Saturday: Luke 19:1-11

Homily

Sunday - Basil the Great of Caesarea

Remember your Benefactor, O Man! Be mindful of yourself, who you are, of what things have been placed in your charge, from Whom you receive them, and why you were favoured above others. You have been made a servant of the good God; an administrator for your fellow servant. Do not imagine that all these fruits were prepared for your stomach. Regard what you hold within your own hands as though it belonged to others. For a little while these things will give you pleasure; then slipping away from you they disappear, and then you must render a strict account of them. But you try with bolts and bars to keep them all hidden and sealed up, and you watch them anxiously. And you think within yourself, "What shall I do? What shall I do?"

Offhand I would say: "I will fill the souls of the hungry. I will open my barns, and I will send for all who are in need. I will be like Joseph in proclaiming the love of my fellow man. I will cry out with a mighty voice: 'Come to me all of you who lack bread; let each of you take, according to his need, from the abundance that divine love has given to me... '"

Imitate the earth, O Man, and bear fruit as it does, so that you may not be lower than the senseless creation. It nourishes its fruits to serve you, not for its own delight. Whenever you yield fruits of charity, you gather up for yourself; for the grace and reward of good works is returned to the giver. Have you given something to a person in need; what you have given becomes yours and is returned to you with interest. And as the wheat that falls to the earth brings increase to the one who has thrown it there, so the bread that you give to the hungry will later bring you a great gain. So let the end of your earthly tilling be the beginning of your heavenly sowing.

Homily on "I Will Pull Down My Barns"

Monday Asterius of Amasea

Know then, that each one of you is an administrator of what belongs to another; cast off then the pride of authority, and put on the humility and prudence of a steward, accountable for his acts. Always be waiting for your Lord, to whom with fear you must render a strict account. For you are a sojourner who has been privileged to receive merely a temporary and fleeting use of the things in your possession. And if you doubt this, look at what happens, and be taught by experience, that trustworthy teacher.

You have an estate, which you either inherited from your fathers, or obtained by some exchange. Recall and count up, if you can, all who have occupied it before you. And direct your mind also to the future, and think how many will occupy it after you. Then tell me who owns it, and to whom does it really belong; those who have had it, or those who now have it, or those who in the future will have it? For if some one should somehow or other call them all together, the owners would be found more numerous than the clods of dirt. And, furthermore, if you want to see exactly what our life is like, call to mind a time in summer while you were traveling and you saw a flourishing tree, tall and broad enough to shelter you with its shadow. You were glad to come under its shade, and there you remained as long as possible. And when it was necessary to move on, even as you were thinking of setting off again, another wayfarer appeared. And you picked up your luggage as he laid his down and appropriated all your conveniences, the bed of leaves, the fire, the shade of the tree, the water flowing by. And, while you resumed your walk, he began to recline and rest. He too enjoyed the place and then left it. And in a single day that one tree was the temporary lodging place for perhaps ten strangers. And that which was enjoyed by all belonged to only one owner. And so also the abundance of our life here delights and supports many, while it belongs to God alone, who has imperishable and indestructible life...

Such, brethren, is our life. If anything, it is still more transitory than the things I have mentioned. And I wonder at the way men say, "my estate," and "my house," and thus appropriate by an idle syllable things which are not theirs, and, with two deceptive letters, clutch things belonging to others. For as on the stage no one actor has exclusive right to play any given character, but any actor may assume the role, so is it in the case of the earth and its material things. Men, one after another, put them on and off like garments...

O man, nothing is your own. You are a slave and what is yours belongs to your Lord. For a slave has no property that is really his own...

You see, then, it has been made evident that you have received things which are not your own. Let us now further observe what is required of you, and what kind of control you have over them. Give to the hungry, clothe the naked, heal the afflicted, do not neglect the needy nor the outcast at the corners of the streets. Do not be anxious about yourself, nor stop to consider how you will live tomorrow. If you do these things the Scripture says that you will be honored by the Lawgiver. But if you do not heed the command, you will be severely punished.

Sermon on the Unjust Steward

Tuesday - Theodotus of Ancyra

The Lord of all comes in poverty as a slave. The hunter doesn't want to startle his prey. Choosing for His birthplace an unknown village in a remote province, He is born of a poor maiden and accepts all that poverty implies, for He hopes by stealth to ensnare and save us.

If He had been born in luxury to a high rank, unbelievers would have said the world had been transformed by wealth. If He had chosen the great city of Rome as his birthplace, they would have thought the transformation had been brought about by civil power. Suppose He had been the son of an emperor. They would have said: "How useful it is to be powerful!" Imagine Him the son of a senator. It would have been: "Look what can be accomplished by legislation!"

But what did He do? He chose surroundings that were poor and simple, so ordinary as to be almost unnoticed, so that people would know it was the Godhead alone that had changed the world. This was His reason for choosing His mother from among the poor of a very poor country, and for becoming poor Himself.

Let the manger teach you how poor the Lord was: He was laid in it because He had no bed to lie on. This lack of the necessaries of life was a most appropriate prophetic foreshadowing. He was laid in a manger to show that He would be the food even of the inarticulate. The Word of God drew to Himself both the rich and the poor, both the eloquent and the slow of speech as He lay in the manger in poverty.

Do you not see how His lack of worldly goods was a prophecy and how His poverty, accepted for our sake, showed His accessibility to all? No one was afraid to approach Christ, overawed by His immense wealth; no one was kept from coming to Him by the grandeur of His royal estate. No, He who was offering Himself for the salvation of the world came as an ordinary worker.

The Word of God in a human body was laid in a manger, so that both the eloquent and the slow of speech would have courage to share in the food of salvation. Perhaps this is what the prophet foretold when he said, speaking of the mystery of the manager: The ox knows its owner and the ass its master's manger, but Israel does not know Me; My people have not understood. He whose godhead made Him rich became poor for our sake, so as to put salvation within the reach of everyone. This was the teaching of Saint Paul when he said: He was rich, but for our sake He became poor, to make us rich through his poverty.

Homily 1 for Christmas

Wednesday - Aelfric of Eynsham

The commentator, Gregory, said that Jesus bewailed the overthrow of the city, which happened after His passion in vengeance of their crimes, because they would sinfully slay the Heavenly Prince. He spoke with weeping voice, not to the stones, nor to the buildings, but to the inhabitants, whom He bewailed with fatherly love, for He knew that their destruction would quickly take place. The mercy of God left the cruel citizens a space of forty years in which to repent of their crimes, but they did not care to repent. Rather they perpetrated greater crimes, so that they slew Stephen, the first martyr of God, with stones, and beheaded James, the brother of John. James the Just they also thrust from the temple, and slew, and raised persecution against the other apostles. The congregation of God which, after Christ's passion, was continuing in the city under James the Just went all together from the city to a village on the river Jordan; for God's command had come to them, that they should go from the wicked place before the vengeance came. God knew already that the Jews cared not for repentance, but more and more increased their crimes; He therefore sent the Romans to them and they brought ruin on them all...

Jesus showed for what reason this dispersion of the city happened when He said, "because you did not know the time of your visitation." He visited the inhabitants in His humanity, but they were not mindful of Him, neither by love nor by fear. Of that heedlessness the prophet spoke with lamenting voice: "The stork and the swallow observe the time of their coming. But My people do not know the doom of God." The Lord said to the city: "If you knew what was to befall you, then you would weep with me. Truly on this day you dwell in peace, for the vengeance to come is now hidden from your eyes." The inhabitants were dwelling in worldly peace, while they were carelessly serving fleshly lusts, with little thought of the miseries to come which were yet hidden from them. If they had foreseen that misery they could not have enjoyed with carefree minds the prosperity of the present life.

Sermon for the Eleventh Sunday after Pentecost

Thursday - Peter Damian

Listen to the counsel of your God, not only as One reigning with the Father, but as your most sweet friend, hanging upon the Cross; He cannot be deceived, because He is wisdom, nor does He want to deceive you, for whom He endured such disgrace and pain. He says "If anyone desires to come after Me, let him deny himself, and take up his cross daily, and follow Me." Hear a counsel, not a precept. For if it were such a precept that we must obey it whether we would or not, we might look for perpetual trouble; but when He says, If - if any man desires to follow Me, He has put it in our own power whether we will keep the same course or not. A mighty labor, indeed; but an incomparable reward. "After Me," He says. We must follow after Him, because He is the Truth, that we may not be deceived; through Him, because He is the Way, that we may not err; to Him, because He is the Life, that we may not die. "I," He says, "am the Way, the Truth, and the Life."

It follows, "Let him deny himself." Our first parent, when he had been fenced in by predetermined limits of obedience, roamed out into the open country of an evil liberty. He had been commanded to prefer the Will of his Creator to his own; but using, or rather abusing, his own will, when he wanted to make himself happy, he destroyed himself. Driven out of that happy inheritance, he got exile for a country, death for life, shame for glory. If you would return to your inheritance, deny your own will.

Sermon 47, on the Exaltation of the Cross

Friday - Theodulph of Orleans

The life of the righteous man is taught and equipped by reading, and by constantly reading a person is fortified against sin, according to him who said, "Your word I have hidden in my heart, that I might not sin against You." For these are the weapons, namely, reading and prayer, by which the devil is defeated; these are the means by which eternal blessedness is obtained; with these weapons vices are suppressed; upon these foods virtues are nourished.

But, also, if one is interrupted in reading, one should work with his hands, because "idleness is the enemy to the soul" and the ancient enemy easily carries off to vices the one whom he finds free from reading or praying. By the use of reading you will learn how you should live and how to teach others; by the use of prayer you will be able to be of value both to yourselves and to those united with you in love. By the work of the hands and the disciplining of the body, you will both deny nourishment to the vices and will supply your own needs, as well as have something to offer for the needs of sufferers.

Precepts to the Priests of His Diocese

Saturday - Gregory of Nazianzus

Let each one of us also speak this way... "I am not worthy that You should come under my roof." But when he will have looked on Jesus, though he be small in stature like Zacchaeus of old, and climb up on top of the sycamore tree by mortifying his members which are on the earth, and having risen above the body of humiliation, then he shall receive the Word, and it shall be said to him, "Today salvation has come to this house." Then let him lay hold on the salvation, and bring forth fruit more perfectly, scattering and pouring forth rightly that which as a publican he wrongly gathered.

Oration on the Holy Lights

Collect

Let Your merciful ears, O Lord, be open to the prayers of Your humble servants; and that they may obtain their petitions, make them to ask such things as shall please You; through Jesus Christ, Your Son, our Lord, who lives and reigns with You and the Holy Spirit, one God, now and forever.

Leonine Sacramentary

AT LAUDS

Psalmody

Sunday: 3, C8, 51
Monday: 118a, C9, 118b
Tuesday: 1, C10, 2

Wednesday: 8, C11, 20
Thursday: 18a, C12, 18b

Friday: 146, C13, 5
Saturday: 149, C14, 150

Lesson

Sunday: II Kings 20:12-21
Monday: II Kings 22:1-20
Tuesday: II Kings 24:1-9

Wednesday: II Kings 25:1-10
Thursday: I Chronicles 10:1-14

Friday: I Chronicles 12:16-22
Saturday: I Chronicles 14:1-7

Collect

O God, who leads us through things temporal to things eternal, stretch forth Your mercy to those who strive after Your heavenly promises, and as it is Your gift that we believe in You, so may all our life be Yours; through Jesus Christ, our Lord, who lives and reigns with You and the Holy Spirit, one God, now and forever.

Sarum Breviary

AT TERCE, SEXT AND NONE

Chapter

Sunday, Monday and Tuesday: I Corinthians 10:6-13
Wednesday and Thursday: Romans 6:16-18
Friday and Saturday: I Corinthians 9:19-22

AT VESPERS

Psalmody

Sunday: 136b, 137, 138
Monday: 140, 141, 142
Tuesday: 144, 145, 7

Wednesday: 9, 10, 11
Thursday: 12, 13, 14, 16

Friday: 17, 147a, 147b
Saturday: 19, 54, 77

Lesson

Sunday: II Kings 21:1-18
Monday: II Kings 23:26-37
Tuesday: II Kings 24:10-20

Wednesday: II Kings 25:11-30
Thursday: I Chronicles 11:1-9

Friday: I Chronicles 13:1-14
Saturday: I Chronicles 14:8-17

Collect

Lord God, heavenly Father, who has bountifully given us Your blessing and our daily bread: We implore You, preserve us from covetousness, and so quicken our hearts that we willingly share Your blessèd gifts with our needy brethren; that we may be found faithful stewards of Your gifts, and abide in Your grace when we are removed from our stewardship and come before Your judgment, through Your beloved Son, Jesus Christ, our Lord, who lives and reigns with You and the Holy Spirit, one true God, now and forever. Amen. *Veit Dietrich*

THE TENTH WEEK
AFTER TRINITY

AT MATINS

Hymn - *Gott der Vater wohn' uns bei*

1. God the Fa- ther, be our stay;
2. Je-sus Christ be Thou our stay; Oh let us per - ish nev - er!
3. Ho-ly Ghost be Thou our stay;

Cleanse us from our sins we pray, And grant us life for - ev - er.

Keep us from the ev - il one; Up-hold our faith most ho - ly And

let us trust Thee sole - ly With hum-ble hearts and low - ly.

Let us put God's ar-mor on With all true Chris-tians run - ning Our

heav'n-ly race and shun - ning The dev-il's wiles and cun - ning.

A-men, a-men! This be done; So sing we, "Al - le - lu - ia!"

Martin Luther, 1524

Psalmody

Sunday: 42, 44, 45
Monday: 46, 47, 48
Tuesday: 49, 50, 52

Wednesday: 53, 55, 56
Thursday: 58, 59, 60

Friday: 61, 62, 66
Saturday: 68a, 68b, 69a

Lesson

Sunday, Monday and Tuesday: Luke 19:41-48
Tuesday: Matthew 25:14-30

Wednesday and Thursday: Mark 6:30-44
Friday and Saturday: Matthew 11:20-24
Friday: Luke 10:10-20
Saturday: Luke 6:20-26

Homily

Sunday - Rupert of Deutz

Concerning the sacrament of Baptism we believe and know that it flowed from his death when he was presumed to have been devoured, that is, when he was already dead. For, says the Evangelist, "when they came to Jesus and saw that He was already dead, they did not break His legs. But one of the soldiers pierced His side with a spear, and immediately blood and water came out." Redeemed by that blood, we, Jews as well as Gentiles, are washed by that water, the Jews first, then the Gentiles - or rather, the dead first, then the living. For all believers who had died since the beginning of the world and who among the dead were awaiting the blessed hope were the first to receive the fruit of this salvation. They were like catechumens who had not yet participated at the heavenly altar... because the wall of hostility had not yet been removed. "And so," they say, "we too were by nature children of wrath, just as the others," and, "All our righteousnesses are like filthy rags."

Then, however, washed and made clean by that torrent, they entered God's sanctuary, God's Kingdom, which is entirely holy. Since the whole church of all past ages together was baptized at that time, this sacrament has been appointed as though at the door of the same church, so that whoever thereafter wishes to be incorporated in the church may be baptized on his own behalf, since the church was at once completely baptized in Christ's death. For the sacrament of Christ's death is present and effectual when water has been used and the word of the cross spoken, together with invocation of the Holy Spirit. Wherefore the apostle says, "All of us who have been baptized into Christ Jesus were baptized into His death."

On the Victory of God's Word

Monday - Gregory I of Rome

The errant soul which rejoices in fleeting time has here its own day. The things that make for its peace are present for it. When it enjoys temporal affairs, is overwhelmed with honors, relaxes in physical pleasure, feels no dread of coming punishment, it has peace in its own day. It will have a serious reason for offense, its condemnation on Another's day. Then when the righteous will rejoice, it will have to be miserable. Everything which makes not for its peace will be turned into bitter vexation; it will begin to be vexed with itself as to why it did not dread the condemnation it suffers, why it closed its inner eyes so as not to foresee the evils that would come after.

And so it is said, But now they are hidden from your eyes. An errant soul, given over to present affairs, and enfeebled by earthly pleasures, hides the coming evils from itself. It shrinks from anticipating future things which might disturb its present happiness. When it abandons itself to the delights of the present life, what else is it doing but rushing into the fire with its eyes closed?

Homily 39

Tuesday - Jerome of Jerusalem

The good judge will give to him who has faith and a good will in the Lord, even if, being human, he has something less in works; but he who does not have faith will lose even the other virtues that he seemed to possess by nature. And it is elegantly said: "what he seems to have will be taken from him." For whatever is apart from faith in Christ ought not be imputed to him who has badly abused it, but to him who gave the good nature even to the wicked servant. *Commentary on Matthew*

Wednesday - Ambrose of Milan

The cross of Christ gave back Paradise to us; this is the tree which the Lord showed to Adam when he pointed to the tree of life, which was in the middle of the garden, saying that it should be eaten, whereas the tree of the knowledge of good and evil should not be eaten. Adam erred, he did not keep the command, he tasted the forbidden fruit; we began to hunger for the tree which the flesh received as its food. That is why God united in Christ the flesh to the tree, so that the ancient hunger might cease, and that the life of grace might be restored. Blessed is the tree of the Lord, which crucified the sins of all; blessed is the flesh of the Lord, which nourished all. *Explanation of the Psalms*

Thursday - Aelfric of Eynsham

"Man shall not live by bread alone; but man lives by every word that proceeds from the mouth of the Lord." As man's body lives by bread, so shall his soul live by the words of God, that is, by God's doctrine, which, through wise men, he has set in books. If the body lacks food or cannot eat food, then it decays and dies; so likewise the soul. If it lacks the holy doctrine it will be perishable and powerless. By the holy doctrine it will be strong, and stimulated to God's will. *Homily for the First Sunday in Lent*

Friday - Bernard of Clairvaux

Perhaps one of you has been struck by this verse of the psalm: "The man who loves evil hates his soul." I would go on to say that he hates his flesh as well. Does a man not hate his soul when by his hard and impenitent heart he stores up wrath for himself on the day of wrath, trafficking today in hell's stocks? Moreover, it is not so much in the dispositions as in results that this hatred of body and soul is discovered. There is no doubt that a madman hates his body when he inflicts injury on himself in a frenzied delusion of mind. But is there any greater madness than that of the unrepentant heart and the obstinately sinful will? For now it is not the flesh which his hand attacks but the very mind which it tears and gnaws to pieces. If you have ever seen a man scratching at his hand and rubbing it until it bleeds, then you have a clear and distinct picture of a sinful soul. For craving gives way to suffering and mental itching yields to torment. And all the while he was scratching he was well aware that this would happen, but he pretended it would not. We tear our wretched souls to pieces the same way and make them sore with our own hands; only this is all the more serious in that our spiritual being is more precious and more difficult to heal. We act not so much out of a kind of obstinate enmity, as under a kind of numbness brought on by inner insensitivity. The mind sloshed out of itself does not feel the inward condemnation, for it is not at home, but probably in the belly, or still lower. Some minds dwell on stew-pans, others on purses. The Lord says, "Where your treasure is, there will your heart be also." Is it any wonder that the soul should feel her own wounds so little when she has forgotten who she is and is inwardly estranged from herself, having taken her journey into a far country? Yet there will be a time when, coming to herself, she will realize how cruelly she has mutilated herself just to get a miserable piece of game. But she was not able to feel that as long as she was burning to lay hands on some vile prey of flies, like a spider spinning its web out of its own viscera. *Sermon on Conversion*

Saturday - Baldwin of Forde

The voice of the poor and the glory of the poor is this: "Bow down Your ear, O Lord, hear me; for I am poor and needy." If a poor man comes up to someone vastly rich and powerful and says, "Incline your ear and hear me," who among his entourage will put up with this in patience? Will they not all drive him away with boos and hisses? Will he not be regarded as beneath contempt when the great man looks at him in his pride? Will he not order him thrown out of his house and expelled with insults? Who dares say to his lord, "Incline your ear?" Who, then, dares say it to the Lord of Lords? Who but the poor and the poor in spirit? This is his cry: "Rejoice the soul of Your servant, for to You, O Lord, I lift up my soul." If his mind is set on earthly things and not on those above, he cannot say, "to You, O Lord, I lift up my soul." It is the poor in spirit, therefore, who lift up their soul to God. They do not degrade themselves with worldly things, but desire and yearn and burn for those which are celestial. In God their life is hid with Christ; on him are fixed their eyes and their love; in him is their heart and their treasure.

O happy poverty, whose reward is to be not only in the kingdom of heaven, but the very kingdom of heaven itself! O happy poverty, honored by God, though despised by the world! For, "He will spare the poor and needy, and will save the souls of the needy." Their names will be honorable in his sight.

Tractate on the Beatitudes

Collect

O God, as You declare Your almighty power above all in showing mercy and pity, mercifully grant unto us such a measure of Your grace that we may obtain Your gracious promises and be made partakers of Your heavenly treasures; through Jesus Christ, Your Son, our Lord, who lives and reigns with You and the Holy Spirit, one God, now and forever.

Gelasian Sacramentary

AT LAUDS

Psalmody

Sunday: 67, C1, 5	Wednesday: 64, C4, 65	Friday: 76, C5, 92
Monday: 63, C2, 36	Thursday: 88, C6, 90	Saturday: 143, C7, 148
Tuesday: 43, C3, 57		

Lesson

Sunday: I Chronicles 15:25-29	Wednesday: I Chronicles 21:1-8	Friday: I Chronicles 28:1-10
Monday: I Chronicles 17:1-15	Thursday: I Chronicles 22:1-13	Saturday: I Chronicles 29:1-15
Tuesday: I Chronicles 19:1-15		

Collect

Hear our voice, O Lord, when we cry to You; let our heart seek Your face; that we, who now see through a glass dimly, may attain the blessedness of Your House and see You face to face; through Jesus Christ, Your Son, our Lord, who lives and reigns with You and the Holy Spirit, one God, now and forever.

Mozarabic Sacramentary

AT TERCE, SEXT AND NONE

Chapter

Sunday, Monday and Tuesday: I Corinthians 12:1-11
Wednesday and Thursday: I Corinthians 15:39-46
Friday and Saturday: I Corinthians 10:14-17

AT VESPERS

Psalmody

Sunday: 110, 111, 112, 113   Wednesday: 123, 124, 125   Friday: 129, 130, 131, 132
Monday: 114, 115, 116, 117   Thursday: 126, 127, 128   Saturday: 133, 135, 136a
Tuesday: 120, 121, 122

Lesson

Sunday: I Chronicles 16:1-6   Wednesday: I Chronicles 21:9-19   Friday: I Chronicles 28:11-21
Monday: I Chronicles 17:16-27   Thursday: I Chronicles 24:1-2, 24-32   Saturday: I Chronicles 29:16-30
Tuesday: I Chronicles 20:1-8

Collect

Almighty and everlasting God, who by Your Holy Spirit hast revealed the Gospel of Your Son, Jesus Christ, to us: we beg You so to enliven our hearts that we may sincerely receive Your word, and not make light of it, or hear it without bearing fruit, as did Your people, the unbelieving Jews, but that we may fear You and daily grow in faith in Your mercy, and finally obtain eternal salvation, through our Lord Jesus Christ, Your Son, who lives and reigns with You and the Holy Spirit, one God, now and forever.   *Veit Dietrich*

THE ELEVENTH WEEK
AFTER TRINITY

AT MATINS

Hymn - *Aus tiefer Not schrei' ich zu dir*

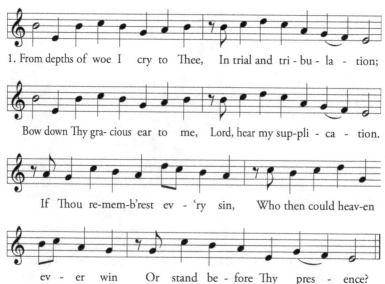

1. From depths of woe I cry to Thee, In trial and tri - bu - la - tion;

Bow down Thy gra- cious ear to me, Lord, hear my sup-pli - ca - tion.

If Thou re-mem-b'rest ev - 'ry sin, Who then could heav-en

ev - er win Or stand be - fore Thy pres - ence?

2. Thy love and grace alone avail
To blot out my transgressions;
The best and holiest deeds must fail
To break sin's dread oppression.
Before Thee none can boasting stand,
But all must fear Thy strict demand
And live alone by mercy.

3. Therefore my hope is in the Lord
And not in my own merit;
It rests upon His faithful Word
To them of contrite spirit
That He is merciful and just;
This is my comfort and my trust.
His help I wait with patience.

4. And though it tarry through the night
And till the morning waken,
My heart shall never doubt His might
Nor count itself forsaken.
O Israel, trust in God your Lord.
Born of the Spirit and the Word,
Now wait for His appearing.

5. Though great our sins, yet greater still
Is God's abundant favor;
His hand of mercy never will
Abandon us, nor waver.
Our shepherd good and true is He,
Who will at last His Israel free
From all their sin and sorrow.

Martin Luther, 1523

Psalmody

Sunday: 69b, 70, 71
Monday: 72, 73, 74
Tuesday: 78a, 78b, 78c

Wednesday: 75, 79, 80
Thursday: 81, 82, 83

Friday: 84, 86, 87, 93
Saturday: 85, 89a, 89b

Lesson

Sunday, Monday and Tuesday: Luke 18:9-14

Tuesday: Luke 10:38-42 or Luke 8:1-3

Wednesday and Thursday: Luke 7:31-35

Friday and Saturday: Matthew 15:29-31

Homily

Sunday - Paulinus of Nola

The Pharisee hymned his own works of justice in the temple, bringing them to the Lord's notice as if He were unaware of them. He did not pray to have his prayer heard, but demanded, so to speak, the reward due to his good works. Yes, his works were good, but still unwelcome to God because pride destroyed what justice had built. Nor did he make this demand silently, but in a loud voice, so that it became clear that he was not addressing the ears of God since he wished men to hear him as well. So since he was pleasing to himself he did not please God, for God has scattered the bones of men who are pleasing to themselves. "They have been put to shame," says the Psalmist, "because God has despised them," but He does not despise a humble and afflicted heart.

In brief, then, in the parable of the Gospel which compares the characters of the Pharisee and the publican, the Lord is clearly showing what He accepts and what He rejects in a man. As Scripture puts it: "God resists the proud, but gives grace to the humble;" so He proclaims that the publican left the temple more justified after confessing his sins than did the Pharisee after submitting his account for his just deeds. Now it was right that the one who praised himself left God's presence rejected, for though he boasted of his knowledge of the Law by his very name, he had forgotten what the Lord says through His prophet: "Over whom shall I dwell but over him who is poor and of a contrite spirit, and who trembles at My word?" But he that accuses himself with contrite heart is received and obtains pardon for the sins he confessed because of the grace of humility, and that holy Pharisee ("holy" in the sense that the Jews are holy) bears off the burden of his sins through boasting of his own holiness. *Letter 50, to Augustine*

Monday - Johannes Tauler

There is only a false peace for people who persist in their same old faults: be it pride, attachment to physical comforts, gratification afforded by the senses and other created things. They still make uncharitable judgments and at the slightest provocation they lash out in hatred against their neighbor. Their peace is a fraudulent one, for by keeping their own counsel they have not arisen and God cannot therefore work in them. They have to abandon their presumptions and arrogant ways and begin the strenuous work of self-denial, following the steps of Our Lord Jesus Christ in humility and love. By dying to self they have to learn what it means to truly arise.

On the other hand, we encounter noble souls so steeped in truth that it shines forth in them. They permit God to prepare the ground, leaving themselves entirely to Him. By this act of self-surrender they refuse to cling to anything of their own, be it their works, their special devotions, what they undertake and what they leave aside. They accept all things from God in humble awe and refer them back to Him in total detachment, bowing lowly to the divine Will. Whatever God may send, they are well pleased to accept it...

How different are these people who allow God to prepare the ground. They do not take matters into their own hands. Yet for all that, they, too, are prone to temptation, for no one is exempt from that. However, when tempted, through pride or carnal desire, through worldly attachments, anger, or whatever else, they immediately surrender it all to God and they allow themselves to fall into His loving arms. Such people do indeed rise up, for they go beyond themselves. They become a true Jerusalem; they dwell in peace in the midst of strife, and they possess joy in sorrow. Whatever God may ordain, they accept it with joy, and the whole world cannot deprive them of such serenity. If man and all the devils in hell had sworn to rob them of their peace, they could not do it. Their gaze is fixed unswervingly on God and they are truly filled with light, for God's light is pure and radiant everywhere, but nowhere does it shine brighter than in the deepest darkness. Ah, how glorious such men are! They are raised to a supernatural, a divine level, and none of their work is ever done without God. And if one may dare to utter it, they themselves no longer work, but God works in them. How blessed they are! They are the lofty pillars of the universe, on whom rests the weight of the whole world. To find oneself in such a state - what a glorious and joyful thing that would be.

The difference between the two kinds of people is this: The first want to prepare the depths of their souls themselves and will not leave it to God. Their faculties are imprisoned in their sins, from which they cannot free themselves. They may even delight in persisting in them of their own free will.

The others, however, those noble souls who allow God to do His work in them, those blessed men who have died to themselves and to the world, they are now lifted high above themselves. As soon as they are assailed by sin and become aware of it, they flee unto God and there can be no more trace of sin, for they now dwell in God's freedom.

Sermon for Epiphany

Tuesday - Eucherius of Lyons

Much physical curiosity, much care and many strict observations are placed upon the body; it undergoes much pain in hope of health; and does the soul not deserve medicine? If it is but fit and necessary that various helps and means of healing are sought for the body, for the recovering only of a temporal and transitory health, is it not unjust that the soul should be excluded and be suffered to languish and putrefy with deadly and spiritual diseases? Should the soul alone be a stranger to those proper and precious remedies ordained for it by the Physician? Rather, if so many things are provided for the body, let the provision for the soul be far more abundant. For if what is said by some is true, that this fleshy frame is the servant, and the soul is the mistress, would it then be wrong or harmful that the better part should receive the better attention? For with constant and intense diligence we should watch over that side where the greater dignity and our most precious treasure is laid up.

On Contempt for the World

Wednesday - Cyril of Alexandria

When some children are dancing and others are singing a dirge, their purpose does not agree. Both sides find fault with their friends for not being in harmony with them. So the Jews underwent such an experience when they accepted neither the gloominess of John the Baptist nor the freedom of Christ. They did not receive help one way or another. It was fitting for John as a lowly servant to deaden the passions of the body through very hardy training, and for Christ by the power of His Godhead freely to mortify the sensations of the body and the innate practice of the flesh, and to do so without reliance on strenuous ascetic labors. Nevertheless John, "while he was preaching the baptism of repentance," offered himself as a model for those who were obliged to lament, whereas the Lord, "who was preaching the kingdom of heaven," similarly displayed radiant freedom in himself. In this way Jesus outlined for the faithful indescribable joy and an untroubled life. The sweetness of the kingdom of heaven is like a flute. The pain of Gehenna is like a dirge.

Fragments

Thursday - Maximus of Turin

I have often thought to myself, brethren, that I should deprive you of the Sunday sermon and not dispense so frequently the sacraments of the heavenly words; for it is of no profit to offer food to someone who refuses it and to proffer a drink to someone who is not thirsty, since what you offer will not be drunk willingly but be given back with aversion as if it were turbid. And so it happens both that the purity of the cup is sullied and that the fastidious drinker discovers causes for offense. In the same way it is perhaps superfluous to present the preaching of the Lord's cup to your charity, since your soul, with bowels sealed, does not thirstily drain it but deceptively pours it out. For the one who does not hearken to it and whose heart does not embrace it pours out the Lord's commandment. The one who receives it, so to speak, on the outer part of his body and does not make it present within forgets what he has heard and spills out the words that have been preached, and so the person who had left church full returns home empty...

But I fear, brethren, that there may apply to many of you the Gospel reading which says: "We sang for you and you did not dance; we wailed and you did not weep." For we announce to you the joy of the heavenly kingdom and your hearts are not moved by eagerness. We preach the dour judgment and your feelings do not bring forth tears of repentance. It is a kind of lack of faith in divine things neither to rejoice in prosperous affairs nor to weep over difficult ones. Therefore the Lord demands dancing of us - not, to be sure, the light movement of a flexible body but the holiness of faith lifting itself up.   *Sermon 42*

Friday - Ignatius of Antioch

There are some who with wicked guile are accustomed to bear the Name but behave in ways unworthy of God. You must avoid them as wild beasts, for they are mad dogs, biting in secret; you must be on guard against them, for they are practically incurable. There is one Physician: both flesh and spirit, begotten and unbegotten, in man, God, in death, true life, both from Mary and from God, first passable and then impassible, Jesus Christ our Lord.   *Letter to the Ephesians*

Saturday - Gregory of Nazianzus

He saved me, stooping as a doctor over my foul-smelling passions. He was a man, but God. David's offspring, but Adam's Maker. A bearer of flesh, but, even so, beyond all body. From a mother, but she a virgin. Comprehensible, but immeasurable.

And a manger received him, while a star led the Magi, who so came bearing gifts, and fell on bended knee. As a man He entered the arena, but He prevailed, as indomitable, over the tempter in three bouts. Food was set before Him, but He fed thousands, and changed the water into wine. He got baptized, but He washed sins clean, but He was proclaimed by the Spirit, in a voice of thunder, to be the Son of the One Uncaused.

As a man He took rest, and as God he put to rest the sea. His knees were wearied, but He bolstered the strength and knees of the lame. He prayed, but who was it who heard the petitions of the feeble? He was the sacrifice, but the high priest: making an offering, but Himself God. He dedicated His blood to God, and cleansed the entire world.

And a cross carried him up, while the bolts nailed fast sin. But what's it for me to say these things? He had company with the dead, but He rose from the dead, and the dead, the bygone, he raised up.

So don't you dishonor His divinity on account of His humanity, but for the divine's sake, hold in renown the earthly form into which, thinking of you, He formed Himself, the incorruptible Son.   *On the Son*

Collect

Almighty and everlasting God, who are always more ready to hear than we to pray and give more than we either desire or deserve, pour down upon us the abundance of Your mercy, forgiving those things of which our conscience is afraid and giving us those good things that we are not worthy to ask, except through the merits and mediation of Jesus Christ, Your Son, our Lord, who lives and reigns with You and the Holy Spirit, one God, now and forever.   *Gelasian Sacramentary*

AT LAUDS

Psalmody

Sunday: 3, C8, 51
Monday: 118a, C9, 118b
Tuesday: 1, C10, 2

Wednesday: 8, C11, 20
Thursday: 18a, C12, 18b

Friday: 146, C13, 5
Saturday: 149, C14, 150

Lesson

Sunday: II Chronicles 1:1-12
Monday: II Chronicles 4:1-22
Tuesday: II Chronicles 6:1-21

Wednesday: II Chronicles 7:12-22
Thursday: II Chronicles 9:13-31

Friday: II Chronicles 11:1-17
Saturday: II Chronicles 13:1-22

Collect

O God, who are rich in forgiveness, and for this reason willed to assume our lowly flesh that You might leave us an example of humility and might make us steadfast in all manner of sufferings; grant that we may always hold fast the good things which we receive from You, and as often as we fall into sins, may be raised up by repentance through Your mercy; for You live and reign with the Father and the Holy Spirit, one God, now and forever. *Gothic Missal*

AT TERCE, SEXT AND NONE

Chapter

Sunday, Monday and Tuesday: I Corinthians 15:1-10
Wednesday and Thursday: I Corinthians 6:15-20a
Friday and Saturday: I Thessalonians 3:9-13

AT VESPERS

Psalmody

Sunday: 136b, 137, 138
Monday: 140, 141, 142
Tuesday: 144, 145, 7

Wednesday: 9, 10, 11
Thursday: 12, 13, 14, 16

Friday: 17, 147a, 147b
Saturday: 19, 54, 77

Lesson

Sunday: II Chronicles 3:1-17
Monday: II Chronicles 5:1-14
Tuesday: II Chronicles 6:41-7:11

Wednesday: II Chronicles 9:1-12
Thursday: II Chronicles 10:1-19

Friday: II Chronicles 12:1-12
Saturday: II Chronicles 14:1-15

Collect

Lord God, heavenly Father, we pray You so to guide and direct us by Your Holy Spirit that we may not forget our sins and be filled with pride, but continue in daily repentance and renewal, seeking our comfort only in the blessèd knowledge that You will be merciful to us, forgive us our sins, and grant us eternal life, through Your dear Son, Jesus Christ our Lord, who lives and reigns with You and the Holy Spirit, one God, now and forever. *Veit Dietrich*

THE TWELFTH WEEK
AFTER TRINITY

AT MATINS

Hymn - *Nun lob, mein' Seel', den Herren*

1. My soul, now praise your Mak - er! Let all with-in me bless His name

Who makes you full par - tak - er Of mer-cies more than you dare claim.

For - get Him not whose meek- ness Still bears with all your sin,

Who heals your ev- 'ry weak-ness, Re - news your life with - in;

Whose grace and care are end - less And saved you through the past;

Who leaves no suf-f'rer friend-less But rights the wronged at last.

2. He offers all His treasure,
Of justice, truth and righteousness,
His love beyond all measure,
His yearning pity o'er distress;
Nor treats us as we merit
But sets His anger by.
The poor and contrite spirit
Finds His compassion nigh;
And high as heav'n above us,
As dawn from close of day,
So far, since He has loved us,
He puts our sins away.

3. For as a tender father,
Has pity on his children here,
God in His arms will gather
All who are His in childlike fear.
He knows how frail our powers,
Who but from dust are made.
We flourish like the flowers,
And even so we fade;
The wind but through them passes,
And all their bloom is o'er.
We wither like the grasses;
Our place knows us no more.

519

4. His grace remains forever,
   And children's children yet shall prove
   That God forsakes them never
   Who in true fear shall seek His love.
   In heav'n is fixed His dwelling,
   His rule is over all;
   O hosts with might excelling,
   With praise before Him fall.
   Praise Him forever reigning,
   All you who hear His Word -
   Our life and all sustaining.
   My soul, O praise the Lord!   *Johann Gramann, 1525*

Psalmody

Sunday: 89c, 94, 96   Wednesday: 104a, 104b, 104c   Friday: 106a, 106b, 107a
Monday: 97, 98, 99, 100   Thursday: 105a, 105b, 105c   Saturday: 107b, 108, 109
Tuesday: 101, 102, 103

Lesson

Sunday, Monday and Tuesday: Mark 7:31-37
Tuesday: Matthew 9:32-38

Wednesday and Thursday: Matthew 11:25-30
Friday and Saturday: Luke 13:31-33
Saturday: John 5:16-23

Homily

Sunday - Bede the Venerable

Man became deaf, unable to hear the word of life after, puffed up against God, he listened to the serpent's deadly words; he was made mute and unable to declare the praises of his Maker from the time when he presumed to have a conversation with his seducer. Rightly did God close man's ears from hearing the praises of his Creator along with the angels - those ears which the unsuspected enemy by his speech had opened to hearing denunciation of this same Creator; rightly did God close man's mouth from proclaiming the praises of his Creator along with the angels - that mouth which the proud deceiver had filled with his lies about the forbidden food, in order, as the devil said, to improve upon the work of this same Creator. And alas, the unfortunate rebellion of the human race, which sprouted in a corrupt manner at the root, began to spread in a much more corrupt way in shoots from the branches, so that when our Lord came in the flesh, with the exception of a few of the faithful from among the Jews, almost the entire world, now deaf and mute, was wandering away from recognition and confession of the truth.

But where sin abounded, grace abounded all the more. Our Lord came to the Sea of Galilee, where He knew that there was a disabled person whom He would heal... Jesus took the disabled man at once aside from the crowd, put His fingers in his ears, and spitting, touched his tongue. He puts His fingers into the ears of the deaf person to make him hear when, through the gifts of spiritual grace, He converts to the hearing of His Word those who for a long while have not believed. Spitting He touches the tongue of a person who is mute to enable him to speak when, through the ministry of preaching, He endows him with the grasp of the faith he must confess... The spittle from our Lord's head and mouth is the Word of His Gospel, which He deigned to take from the hidden mystery of His divinity and administer visibly to the world, so that it could be healed.   *Homily for Holy Saturday*

Monday - Ambrose of Milan

Open your ears and enjoy the good odor of eternal life which has been breathed upon you by the grace of the Sacraments. This we pointed out to you as we celebrated the mystery of the opening [i.e. the rite of Baptism] and said "Ephphatha," that is, "be opened," so that everyone about to come to the table of grace might know what he was asked and remember the way he once responded. Christ celebrated this mystery in the Gospel, as we read, when He healed the one who was deaf and dumb.

On the Mysteries

Tuesday - Martin Luther

The world is crying and calling for such shepherds who can pasture. And the Lord Christ himself complains that He is lacking such shepherds—"The harvest is plentiful, but the laborers are few; pray therefore the Lord of the harvest to send out laborers into his harvest." Indeed, the whole world stands open, if only someone would want to pasture it, as St. Paul says, "If one aspires to the office of bishop, he desires a noble task." One must not compel, run after, and look for such shepherds; and one cannot find enough of them. For the burghers and peasants too say now, "Why should I let my son go on with his studies? He will be a beggar if he becomes a parson. I would rather let him learn a trade or become a merchant..." God the Father, Son, and Holy Spirit testify that pasturing the sheep was His dearest work, for which the Son became man and shed His blood, so that the people should be saved. He who does this work or helps in it shall be a great saint in heaven, with the patriarchs, prophets, apostles, martyrs, and all the saints. Does this mean nothing to you, and have you neither hope nor faith for it?

Against the Roman Papacy, an Institution of the Devil

Wednesday - Martin Luther

Christ here calls foolish, simple people "babes;" He is not speaking of actual infant children, nor of people who are childish in the eyes of the world. It could be a great doctor whom He here calls a babe, and on the other hand it could be a peasant whom He here calls wise and understanding. In the Psalter, David also calls them babes and children when he says, "Out of the mouth of babes and nursing infants You have ordained strength, because of Your enemies." These surely were not actually infant children by whom God established a power against his enemies and who were to praise and extol his glory in all the earth.

Here the Lord calls "babes" the people who count their own works as nothing, who attribute nothing to their own wisdom, and make nothing whatsoever of themselves, but consider only God to be wise and prudent. That is why they keep quiet and submit themselves completely to God and let themselves be taught by him alone. The others are too wise. They do not want to learn anything from God. Indeed, they even presume to raise trivial objections at God's doctrine and works. You can read about this in the first and second chapter of St. Paul's first letter to the Corinthians.

Therefore Christ says in Luke, "the sons of this world are more shrewd in their generation than the sons of light." But the foolish sons of light are more esteemed in the sight of God than the wise sons of the world. Concerning the babes the Lord says here in this Gospel: Now the wise must be foolish and the foolish wise. For this is just what was said: Father, You have hidden these things from the wise and understanding, but You have revealed them to babes, for the wise and understanding do not know them, but the babes and the fools do know them. Why is it that the wise do not know them? You have hidden them from them. But why do the babes know? You have revealed them to them.

But what He means by this saying must be understood in the light of what He has said previously, namely, that He had proclaimed the gospel of the kingdom of God in many places in Judea, such as Chorazin, Bethsaida, and in His own city Capernaum, and they had not accepted it because of their great wisdom, which prevented them from accepting the foolish, silly message of the gospel.

The gospel is a good, joyful message which teaches me how to know God, through which knowledge I obtain the forgiveness of sins and eternal life. As Christ says to His Father in John, "This is eternal life, that they may know You, the only true God, and Jesus Christ whom You have sent." He says the same things here in this Gospel: "No one knows the Son except the Father. Nor does anyone know the Father except the Son, and the one to whom the Son wills to reveal Him." He is speaking here of the knowledge of both the Father and of the Son. Now the one to whom this is revealed knows it, and he has eternal life. But this the Father has hidden from the wise and understanding, that they should know neither the Father nor the Son, and has revealed it to babes, that they might know the Father and the Son and thus have eternal life. *Sermon on St. Matthias' Day*

Thursday - Bruno of Segni

Dearly beloved, in everything that He did and said, our Lord Jesus Christ has left us a pattern of humility, and instruction in virtuous living, for He wished to teach us not only by words, but also by example. Hence it is written: Jesus began to do and to teach. As regards humility the Lord Himself said: Learn from Me, for I am meek and humble of heart.

Although He was the Almighty Lord, He chose to be poor for our sakes; He refused honors, freely submitted to sufferings, and even went so far as to pray for His persecutors. And He did all of this in order that we might not disdain to follow Him insofar as our frailty allows. If we fail to do so we are not true Christians, for anyone who says he loves Christ must tread the path He trod.

Because the Lord freely submitted to suffering and cross, He delivered us by His very death from the power of the devil. Moreover He prayed for sinners as He hung on the cross to give us an example. After all, if so much was willingly endured by the very Lord of the universe at the hands of slaves, by the just One at the hands of sinners, it behooves us to bear with the greatest patience wrongs done us by our own kith and kin.

And when we are in the midst of affliction, we too must pray earnestly... And we must also give alms, and do so in the right way. The right way of almsgiving consists in two things, namely, giving and forgiving. *Sermon 1 for Good Friday*

Friday - Meister Eckhart

I am as sure as I live that nothing is so near to me as God. God is nearer to me than I am to myself; my existence depends on the nearness and presence of God. He is also near things of wood and stone, but they know it not. If a piece of wood became as aware of the nearness of God as an archangel is, the piece of wood would be as happy as an archangel. For this reason man is happier than the inanimate wood, because he knows and understands how God is near him. His happiness increases and diminishes in proportion to the increase and diminution in his knowledge of this. His happiness does not arise from this, that God is near him, and in him, and that He possesses God; but from this, that he knows the nearness of God, and loves Him, and is aware that "the Kingdom of God is near." So, when I think on God's Kingdom, I am compelled to be silent because of its immensity, because God's Kingdom is none other than God Himself with all His riches. *On the Nearness of God*

Saturday - John Chrysostom

It is fitting that [we] believe in the God of the universe, the Father of our Lord, Jesus Christ, the cause of all things, the inexpressible, the incomprehensible, who can be explained neither by word nor by understanding, who has by His kindness and goodness created all things. And in Jesus Christ, His only-begotten Son, our Lord, who is in all ways like and equal to the Father with a likeness to Him that is unchangeable, consubstantial with the Father but known in His own Person; proceeding from the Father in a manner that cannot be expressed; who was before time began and is the Creator of all ages; who in later times, for our salvation, took the form of a slave and became man, dwelt with human nature, was crucified, and rose again on the third day.

You must have these articles of faith accurately fixed in your minds, that you may not be easily overwhelmed by the deceits of the devil. But if [someone wishes] to trip you up, you should know for sure that you must block up your ears to what they say. Answer them with confidence, and show them that the Son is like in substance to the Father. For it is the Son Himself who said: "As the Father raises up the dead and gives them life, even so the Son also gives life to whom He will," and in all things He shows that He has equal power with the Father. And if, from the other side [another] desires to destroy sound doctrines by glossing over the distinction of Persons, my beloved, wall up your ears against him too, and teach him that the substance of the Father, the Son, and the Holy Spirit is one, but that there are three Persons. For neither could the Father be called Son, nor the Son Father, nor could the Holy Spirit be called anything other than that. Each remains His own Person, but each possesses equal power. *Baptismal Catechesis*

Collect

Almighty and merciful God, whose gift it is that Your faithful possess all things pertaining to faith and life, we implore You that we may so faithfully cling to Your promises in this life that we fail not finally to attain to Your heavenly glory; through Jesus Christ, Your Son, our Lord, who lives and reigns with You and the Holy Spirit, one God, now and forever. *Leonine Sacramentary*

AT LAUDS

Psalmody

Sunday: 67, C1, 5	Wednesday: 64, C4, 65	Friday: 76, C5, 92
Monday: 63, C2, 36	Thursday: 88, C6, 90	Saturday: 143, C7, 148
Tuesday: 43, C3, 57		

Lesson

Sunday: II Chronicles 15:1-9	Wednesday: II Chronicles 25:1-16	Friday: II Chronicles 28:1-15
Monday: II Chronicles 20:1-24	Thursday: II Chronicles 26:1-23	Saturday: II Chronicles 29:1-19
Tuesday: II Chronicles 24:1-14		

Collect

Almighty, everlasting God, Lord, Heavenly Father, whose Word is a lamp to our feet and a light to our path; open and enlighten my mind that I may understand Your Word purely, clearly and devoutly, and fashion my life according to it, in order that I may never displease Your Majesty; through Jesus Christ, Your Son, our Lord, who lives and reigns with You and the Holy Spirit, one God, now and forever. *Johannes Bugenhagen*

AT TERCE, SEXT AND NONE

Chapter

Sunday, Monday and Tuesday: II Corinthians 3:4-11
Wednesday and Thursday: II Corinthians 4:5-11
Friday and Saturday: I Timothy 5:17-21

AT VESPERS

Psalmody

Sunday: 110, 111, 112, 113   Wednesday: 123, 124, 125   Friday: 129, 130, 131, 132
Monday: 114, 115, 116, 117   Thursday: 126, 127, 128   Saturday: 133, 135, 136a
Tuesday: 120, 121, 122

Lesson

Sunday: II Chronicles 17:1-13   Wednesday: II Chronicles 25:17-28   Friday: II Chronicles 28:16-27
Monday: II Chronicles 21:1-20   Thursday: II Chronicles 27:1-9   Saturday: II Chronicles 29:20-36
Tuesday: II Chronicles 24:15-25

Collect

Almighty and everlasting God, who has created all things: We thank You that You have given us sound bodies, and have graciously preserved our tongues and other members from the power of the adversary: We pray You, grant us Your grace, that we may rightly use our ears and tongues; help us to hear Your word diligently and devoutly, and with our tongues to praise and magnify Your grace, so that no one will be offended by our words, but that all may be edified thereby, through Jesus Christ, Your Son, our Lord, who lives and reigns with You and the Holy Spirit, one God, now and forever.

Veit Dietrich

THE THIRTEENTH WEEK
AFTER TRINITY

AT MATINS

Hymn - *Lord of Glory, Who Hast Bought Us*

1. Lord of glo - ry, Who hast bought us, with Thy life-blood as the price,

Nev-er grudg-ing for the lost ones That tre-men-dous sac - ri - fice;

And with that hast free-ly giv - en Bless-ings cout-less as the sand

To th'un-thank-ful and the e - vil With Thine own un-spar-ing hand;

2. Grant us hearts, dear Lord, to yield Thee
Gladly, freely, of Thine own;
With the sunshine of Thy goodness
Melt our thankless hearts of stone
Till our cold and selfish natures,
Warmed by Thee, at length believe
That more happy and more blessèd
'Tis to give than to receive.

3. Wondrous honor hast Thou given
To our humblest charity
In Thine own mysterious sentence,
"Ye have done it unto Me."
Can it be, O gracious Master,
Thou dost deign for alms to sue,
Saying by Thy poor and needy,
"Give as I have given to you"?

4. Yes, the sorrow and the sufferings
Which on every hand we see
Channels are for tithes and offerings
Due by solemn right to Thee;
Right of which we may not rob Thee,
Debt we may not choose but pay,
Lest that face of love and pity
Turn from us another day.

5. Lord of Glory, who hast bought us
With Thy life-blood as the price,
Never grudging for the lost ones
That tremendous sacrifice,
Give us faith to trust Thee boldly,
Hope, to stay our souls on Thee;
But, oh! best of all Thy graces,
Give us Thine own charity.

Eliza S. Alderson, 1864

Psalmody

Sunday: 21, 22, 23
Monday: 24, 25, 26
Tuesday: 27, 28, 29

Wednesday: 30, 31, 32
Thursday: 33, 34, 35

Friday: 37a, 37b, 38
Saturday: 39, 40, 41

Lesson

Sunday, Monday and Tuesday: Luke 10:23-37

Tuesday: Matthew 21:28-32

Wednesday and Thursday: Luke 13:22-30

Friday and Saturday: Mark 13:32-37

Homily

Sunday - Martin Luther

Let us learn what it means to love God. This Samaritan loves God, not that he had given anything to God, but by how he helps the poor wounded man as much as he can. The Lord says, If you want to love and serve Me, then love and serve your neighbor; He needs it. I don't. So our Samaritan serves the Lord God in heaven with his money, beast, oil and wine. It's not that God needs the help; he's not doing it for God, but for his neighbor. And yet, if we serve our neighbor, God will consider it to have been done to Him, because He has commanded it.

Other things that the world does, thinking that it serves God, are not commanded by Him, for example, that one should go on pilgrimage to the shrine of St. James or to Rome, construct churches, and such things. He wants us to serve and help one another. And you don't need to go to Rome to find Me, He says. You'll find Me right in your own home: in your wife, children, servants, magistrates and governors; also, in your neighbor's house, on the street, at the marketplace, and everywhere. There do your duty as required by love and friendship, and I will acknowledge it as having been done to Me.

House Postil for Trinity 13

Monday - Augustine of Hippo

You have something in yourself which you should be slapping, but you're sleeping. You observe your neighbor outside as someone to quarrel with, your partner, your companion, your joint owner. What you don't observe, don't see, is that other thing, that other law in your members, fighting back against the law of your mind, and taking you prisoner to the law of sin which is in your members. "But he's plundered me!" You're being dragged away prisoner, and you're angry with someone for plundering you!

Have you recognized yourself, have you seen where you really are? You've recognized your captor, show yourself a fighter, look for a redeemer. Just as that man himself, after saying "bringing me into captivity to the law of sin which is in my members," went on to say, "O wretched man that I am! Who will deliver me from this body of death? The grace of God, through Jesus Christ our Lord." But can you call upon grace if you don't see the punishment that's coming to you? So understand clearly, see where you are being dragged off to.

"But I take delight in justice." I know that you do; after all, you delight in the law of God according to the inner self. But you can see another law in your members. You take delight in the law of God; there's another law in your members; live by it and you'll die by it. Robbers have left you half-dead on the road; but you've been found lying there by the passing and kindly Samaritan. Wine and oil have been poured into you, you have received the sacrament of the Only-begotten Son; you have been lifted onto His mule, you have believed that Christ became flesh; you have been brought to the inn, you are being cured in the Church.

That's where and why I'm speaking; this is what I do, what all of us [preachers] are doing; we are performing the duties of the innkeeper. He was told, "If you spend any more, I will pay you back when I return." If only we spent at least as much as we have received! But however much we spend, brothers and sisters, it's the Lord's money. We are your fellow servants; we live on what we feed you with. Nobody should give us the credit for the benefits bestowed; we will be bad servants if we don't do it. But if we do it, we shouldn't arrogate any credit to ourselves, because we aren't doing it with our property. Let us all love Him, all esteem Him, and for His sake all love and esteem one another. We all have one King; may we all reach the one kingdom. *Sermon 179A*

Tuesday - Jerome of Jerusalem

The two sons are also described in a parable in Luke. One is temperate the other is luxurious. Zechariah the prophet says of them: "I took for myself two staffs: the one I called Beauty, and the other I called Bonds; and I fed the flock." First of all, through their knowledge of natural law, it is said to the people of the Gentiles: "Go and work in my vineyard," that is, What you do not want done to you, do not do to another. They responded haughtily: I will not; but afterward at the coming of the Savior they repented and worked in the vineyard of God. Thus they made up for the defiance of their words by means of labor. Now the second son is the people of the Jews who responded to Moses: "Everything that the Lord has said we will do." But they did not go into the vineyard. For when the son of the householder had been killed, they reckoned themselves to be the heir.

Now others think that the parable is not about Gentiles and Jews, but simply about sinners and the just, as the Lord Himself also explains what he later sets forth: "Assuredly, I say to you that tax collectors and harlots enter the kingdom of God before you." He says that because they who by their evil deeds had refused to serve God afterward received the baptism of repentance from John, whereas the Pharisees, who made a profession of justice and who were boasting that they were doing God's Law, did not do God's commands. For they held John's baptism in contempt.

Commentary on Matthew

Wednesday - Martin Luther

It is really a hard and tough life to be a Christian or a pious man, and it will not taste sweet to us. As that good girl said: "It takes a lot to be honorable." Indeed it does, and it takes a great deal more to lead a Christian life. Our dear Lord has in mind here that people may find it appealing and think to themselves: "I would like to live that way, but it takes a great deal." Christ says: "That is what I am saying, too. Therefore I am warning you to be on the lookout and not to let yourself be turned aside if it is a little sour and difficult, for it cannot be and will not be any other way in the world." A Christian has to know this and be armed against it, so that he does not let it trouble him or hinder him if the whole world lives otherwise. On no account dare he imitate the great mob, something Moses forbade already in Exodus 23:2: "You shall not follow the multitude to do evil;" as though he were saying: "You will always see the continuous activity of offense in the world." As Christ says here: "The way to destruction is broad, and those who walk upon it are many; the gate is very wide, to let the crowd pass through it."

That is the great offense that disconcerts a great many people and causes them to fall away from us... Christ wants to point this out and to warn His followers that in the world everyone should live as though he were alone and should consider His Word and preaching as the very greatest thing on earth, thinking this way to himself: "I see my neighbor and the whole city, yes, the whole world, living differently. All those who are great or noble or rich, the princes and the lords, are allied with it. Nevertheless I have an ally who is greater than all of them, namely, Christ and His Word. When I am all alone, therefore, I am still not alone. Because I have the Word of God, I have Christ with me, together with all the dear angels and all the saints since the beginning of the world. Actually there is a bigger crowd and a more glorious procession surrounding me than there could be in the whole world now. Only I cannot see it with my eyes, and I have to watch and bear the offense of having so many people forsake me or live and act in opposition to me." You must hold on to this if you want to endure. Otherwise this offense will overwhelm you when you see how other people live and believe.

Commentary on the Sermon on the Mount

Thursday - Leo I of Rome

The Word of Truth is fulfilled in everything by which we learn that it is a narrow and difficult road that leads to life, and though the wide road leading to death is crowded with great throngs, only here and there are the footsteps of the few entering the path of salvation. Why is the road on the left more populous than the right, unless the mass of people are given over to joys of the world and the good of the body? Although what they want is transitory and uncertain, they will undertake labor more willingly for the desire of pleasure than for the love of virtue. And, although unnumbered are those who long for things they can see, scarcely can any be found who put eternal things before temporal. The blessed apostle Paul says: "The things which are seen are temporary, but the things which are not seen are eternal," and the way of virtue lies in some ways hid and concealed, since "in hope we are saved," and true faith loves that above all which it reaches with no interference of the flesh.

It is a great labor and accomplishment to keep the unstable heart from all sin, and not to relax the vigor of the soul for any defilement though endless allurements of pleasure entice it from all sides. Whoever touch pitch, will they not also be defiled by it? Who is not weak in the flesh? Who is not soiled in the dust? Who indeed are of such great purity that they are not defiled by those very things in which life consists? The divine teaching commands us through the Apostle: "Those who have wives should be as though they had none, those who weep as though they did not weep, those who rejoice as though they did not rejoice, those who buy as though they did not possess, and those who use this world as not misusing it. For the form of this world is passing away." Blessed is the soul which runs the course of its journey in simple moderation and does not linger in those things through which it must walk, so that it is a steward, rather than an owner, of the things of the earth. Such a soul will not lack human affection but will rely on the divine promises.

Sermon 49

Friday - Gregory of Nazianzus

Can any fact be unknown to Wisdom, the world's Maker, who perfects, transforms, and limits things created, who knows the things of God just as man's spirit knows the things of man? What knowledge could be more perfect than that? How can He know distinctly what precedes the hour of the world's end, what, so to say, lies on its surface, and yet not know the hour itself? The thing is like a riddle - like saying a person has distinct knowledge of what is in front of a wall, but does not know the wall itself, or, that he distinctly knows the end of the day, but does not know the beginning of night. Knowledge of one thing here necessarily involves knowledge of the other. Surely everyone will see that if you separate the real from the apparent meaning of the passage it is saying that He does know as God, but that, as man, He does not. The absolute use of the title, "Son," here, without any relational qualification of the term telling you whose son, provides us with a deeper meaning, so that we interpret this ignorance in the most truly pious way by ascribing it not to the divine but to the human.

On God and Christ

Saturday - Evagrius of Pontus

The further the soul advances, the greater are the adversaries against which it must contend. Blessed are you if the struggle grows fierce against you at the time of prayer. Do not think that you have acquired any virtue before you have shed your blood in the struggle for it. Until death you must fight against sin, resisting it with all your strength. Do not allow your eyes to sleep or your eyelids to slumber until the hour of your death, but labor without ceasing, that you might enjoy life without end.

Compiled from The Praktikos and Chapters on Prayer

Collect

Almighty and everlasting God, give unto us the increase of faith, hope, and charity, and as we do obtain that which You promise, make us to love that which You command; through Jesus Christ, Your Son, our Lord, who lives and reigns with You and the Holy Spirit, one God, now and forever.

Leonine Sacramentary

AT LAUDS

Psalmody

Sunday: 3, C8, 51	Wednesday: 8, C11, 20	Friday: 146, C13, 5
Monday: 118a, C9, 118b	Thursday: 18a, C12, 18b	Saturday: 149, C14, 150
Tuesday: 1, C10, 2		

Lesson

Sunday: II Chronicles 30:1-27	Wednesday: II Chronicles 35:1-19	Friday: Proverbs 1:1-19
Monday: II Chronicles 32:1-23	Thursday: II Chronicles 36:1-10	Saturday: Proverbs 2:1-9
Tuesday: II Chronicles 33:1-25		

Collect

Grant, we implore You, almighty God, that we who amidst so many adversities have fainted through our own infirmity, may be relieved by the intervention of the Passion of Your only-begotten Son, who lives and reigns with You and the Holy Spirit, One God, now and forever. Amen.

Gregorian Sacramentary

AT TERCE, SEXT AND NONE

Chapter

Sunday, Monday and Tuesday: Galatians 3:15-22
Wednesday and Thursday: II Corinthians 5:1-11
Friday and Saturday: Hebrews 3:1-6

AT VESPERS

Psalmody

Sunday: 136b, 137, 138	Wednesday: 9, 10, 11	Friday: 17, 147a, 147b
Monday: 140, 141, 142	Thursday: 12, 13, 14, 16	Saturday: 19, 54, 77
Tuesday: 144, 145, 7		

Lesson

Sunday: II Chronicles 31:1-21	Wednesday: II Chronicles 35:20-27	Friday: Proverbs 1:20-33
Monday: II Chronicles 32:24-33	Thursday: II Chronicles 36:11-23	Saturday: Proverbs 2:10-22
Tuesday: II Chronicles 34:1-33		

Collect

Lord God, heavenly Father, we most heartily thank You that You have granted us to live in this accepted time, when we may hear Your holy gospel, know Your fatherly will, and behold Your Son, Jesus Christ! We pray You, most merciful Father: let the light of Your holy word remain with us, and so govern our hearts by Your Holy Spirit, that we may never forsake Your word, but remain steadfast in it, and finally obtain eternal salvation; through our Lord, Jesus Christ, Your Son, who lives and reigns with You and the Holy Spirit, one true God, now and forever. Amen.

Veit Dietrich

THE FOURTEENTH WEEK
AFTER TRINITY

AT MATINS

Hymn - *Von Gott will ich nicht lassen*

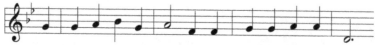

1. From God can no-thing move me; He   will not step a - side
2. When those whom I re - gard - ed As   trust-wor-thy and   sure
3. The   Lord my life ar - rang - es; Who   can His work de - stroy?

But   gent- ly will re - prove me And   be my con-stant   guide.
Have   long from me de - part - ed, God's   grace shall still en -   dure.
In   His good time He chang- es   All   sor - row in - to   joy.

He   stretch-es out His   hand   In   eve-ning and in   morn-ing,
He   res- cues me from   sin   And breaks the chains that bind me.
So   let me then be   still: My bo - dy, soul, and   spi - rit

My   life with grace a - dorn- ing; Wher- ev - er   I   may stand.
I   leave death's fear be- hind me; His   peace I   have with - in.
His   ten- der care in - her - it   Ac- cord- ing to His   will.

4. Each day at His good pleasure
God's gracious will is done.
He sent His greatest treasure
In Jesus Christ, His Son.
He every gift imparts.
The bread of earth and heaven
Are by His kindness given.
Praise Him with thankful hearts!

5. Praise God with acclamation
And in His grace rejoice.
Each day finds its vocation
Responding to His voice.
Soon years on earth are past;
But time we spend expressing
The love of God brings blessing
That will forever last!

6. Yet even though I suffer,
The world's unpleasantness,
And though the days grow rougher
And bring me great distress,
That day of bliss divine,
Which knows no end or measure,
And Christ, who is my pleasure,
Forever shall be mine.

7. For thus the Father willed it,
Who fashioned us from clay;
And His own Son fulfilled it
And brought eternal day.
The Spirit now has come,
To us true faith has given;
He leads us home to heaven.
O praise the Three in One!

Ludwig Hembold, c.1563

Psalmody

Sunday: 42, 44, 45   Wednesday: 53, 55, 56   Friday: 61, 62, 66
Monday: 46, 47, 48   Thursday: 58, 59, 60   Saturday: 68a, 68b, 69a
Tuesday: 49, 50, 52

Lesson

Sunday, Monday and Tuesday: Luke 17:11-19
Tuesday: Luke 12:1-10

Wednesday and Thursday: Matthew 12:14-21
Friday and Saturday: Matthew 24:40-41

Homily

Sunday - Bruno of Segni

What do these ten lepers stand for if not the sum total of all sinners? Not all men and women were leprous in body when Christ the Lord came, but in soul they were, and to have a soul full of leprosy is much worse than to have a leprous body.

But let us see what happened next. Standing a long way off they called out to him: "Jesus, Master, have mercy on us!" They stood a long way off because no one in their condition dared come too close. We stand a long way off too while we continue to sin. To be restored to health and cured of the leprosy of sin, we also must cry out: Jesus, master, have mercy on us. That cry, however, must come not from our lips but from our heart, for the cry of the heart is louder: it pierces the heavens, rising up to the very throne of God.

When Jesus saw the lepers he told them to go and show themselves to the priests. God has only to look at people to be filled with compassion. He pitied these lepers as soon as he saw them, and sent them to the priests not to be cleansed by them, but to be pronounced clean.

And as they went they were cleansed. Let all sinners listen to this and try to understand it. It is easy for the Lord to forgive sins. Sinners have often been forgiven before they came to a priest. In fact, their repentance and healing occur simultaneously: at the very moment of their conversion they pass from death to life. Let them understand, however, what this conversion means; let them heed the Lord's words: Return to me with all your heart, with fasting, weeping, and mourning; and rend your hearts and not your garments. To be really converted one must be converted inwardly, in one's heart, for a humbled, contrite heart God will not spurn.

One of them, when he saw that he was cured, went back again, praising God at the top of his voice. He threw himself at Jesus' feet and thanked Him. Now this man was a Samaritan. He stands for all those who, after their cleansing by the waters of baptism or healing by the sacrament of penance, renounce the devil and take Christ as their model, following him with praise, adoration, and thanksgiving, and nevermore abandoning his service.

And Jesus said to him: Stand up and go on your way. Your faith has saved you. Great, therefore, is the power of faith. Without it, as the apostle says, it is impossible to please God. Abraham believed God and because of this God regarded him as righteous. Faith saves, faith justifies, faith heals both body and soul.

Homily on Luke

Monday - An Anglo-Saxon Homily

The Lord Christ dwelt here in the world among men and revealed and performed before them many wonders and gently gave salvation to them and showed His mercy. Earlier, they were stony hearted and blind so that they could not perceive that which they saw there. But when the almighty Lord took away from them that wicked covering from their hearts and illuminated them with bright understanding, then they could perceive that and understand who descended into this world both as a help and as a salvation to them. Afterwards He revealed mercy to them, incited them to faith, uncovered to them His compassion, and made known His great love. Before we were made orphans; then we were kept away from that heavenly realm, and we were blotted out of that glorious document. Then we were written down for heavens. We were now afterwards marked down through the true Creator and through the living God and through that born Son, our Lord, for the joy of paradise. May the terrible fiend not hinder us from that journey, nor oppose us in that desired way, nor shut to us those gates that stand open to us, nor take away from us that fortress through his worthless deceits, nor keep us from that kingdom for which we have been shaped, nor lead us astray from that true faith in which we have been instructed.

Vercelli Homily 10

Tuesday - Ivo of Chartres

You know, beloved, that soldiers of this life, when about to receive temporal benefits from temporal lords, are first bound by soldiers' oaths and make profession that they will keep faith with their lords. How much more ought those about to fight for the eternal King and to receive eternal rewards, be bound by heavenly oaths and publicly profess the faith through which they are going to please him! For the apostle says, "Without faith it is impossible to please God."

He who examines the heart and innards recognizes this in our hearts, but for the sake of preserving the unity of the church... an oral confession is necessary along with the faith that is felt in the heart, because "with the heart one believes unto righteousness, and with the mouth confession is made unto salvation," not only of preachers but of hearers also. For there is no other way that a brother can be pleased with a brother, nor the peace of the church be preserved, nor can anyone teach another or learn from another the things necessary to salvation except he pass along what he has in his heart to the hearts of others by the use of words, as if they were his vehicles. Therefore, faith ought both to be preserved in the heart and expressed on the lips, for faith is the foundation of all good things, the beginning of man's salvation. Without this no one will be able to be counted among the sons of God, because without it neither does he acquire the grace of justification in this world nor will he possess eternal life in the future world. And if anyone does not walk by faith, he will not reach the place where he can see.

Sermon on the Apostles' Creed

Wednesday - John Chrysostom

Observe how He does not desist from His tender care of the infirm, and yet pacifies their envy. "And great multitudes followed Him, and He healed them all. Yet He warned them not to make Him known." Because, while the multitudes everywhere both admire and follow Him, [the pharisees] do not cease their wickedness.

Then, so that you aren't confounded by what is going on, and by their strange frenzy, He introduces the prophet also who foretold all this. For so great was the accuracy of the prophets, that they do not omit even these things, but foretell His very travels, and changes of locale, and the intent with which He acted; so that you might learn how they spoke everything by the Spirit. For if the secrets of men cannot in any way be known, how much more impossible is it to learn Christ's purpose, unless the Spirit revealed it.

What does the prophet say, then...? The prophet celebrates His meekness, and His unspeakable power, and opens to the Gentiles "a great and effectual door;" he also foretells the ills that will overtake the Jews, and signifies His unity with the Father. For "Behold," He says, "My Servant whom I have chosen, My Beloved in whom My soul is well pleased." Now if He chose Him, Christ set aside the law not as an adversary nor as an enemy of the lawgiver, but as one having the same mind with Him, and the same goals.

Then proclaiming His meekness, he says, "He will not quarrel nor cry out." For He indeed desired to heal in their presence; but since they thrust Him away, He didn't even contend against this.

And hinting at both His might and their weakness, he says, "A bruised reed He will not break." For indeed it would have been easy to break them all to pieces like a reed, and not merely as a reed, but one already bruised. "And smoking flax He will not quench." Here he sets forth both their anger that is kindled, and His might that is able to put down their anger and quench it with all ease; whereby His great mildness is signified.

Homily 40 on Matthew

Thursday - Martin Luther

"Friend, regard the righteousness of the laws and of the Pharisees as nothing, because I have not given them My Spirit, but My Spirit is in Him alone." Paul referred to this with his highest praise: "In whom are hid all the treasures," both physical and spiritual. Meanwhile He seems foolish, weak, and ridiculous, and therefore it is difficult to believe Him. For that reason He says, "To Him, to Him I have given the Spirit. No one ascends to heaven but He alone." Therefore cling to Him and take nothing to yourselves except what is in Christ, because apart from Him we do nothing and are nothing but heaps of sin. Here, however, He gives us the Treasure, who embraces all those things which He accomplishes publicly through works and plans, as well as all remaining sin. Therefore He commends this unique God to us, because the heavens and earth and demons must tremble.

Lecture on Isaiah 42

Friday - Hilary of Poitiers

Christ shows that a judgment is coming, since between two people in a field, one is taken up and one left behind. Between two grinding at the mill, one is chosen and one rejected. Between two lying in bed, one departs and one remains. This teaching means that the separation of the faithful from the unfaithful will consist in one being accepted and the other abandoned. For, like the prophet says, when the wrath of God rises, the saints will be hidden in God's chambers but the faithless will be left exposed to celestial fire. The two in the field therefore represent the faithful and the unfaithful, both of whom will be surprised by the day of the Lord in the midst of the world, in the course of their life's work. They will be separated, one taken and the other left. It will be the same for the two grinding at the mill, which represents the work of the law. For only some of the Jews, like Elijah, believed through the apostles that they must be justified by faith. One group will be taken up through the faith that produces good works, and the other group will be abandoned in the fruitless works of the law, grinding in vain at a mill that will never produce heavenly food. The two lying in bed are proclaiming the repose of the Lord after his Passion, which both Catholics and heretics confess alike. But because the truth of the Catholic faith preaches the unity of the Father and the Son, which we call their deity, whereas the false doctrine of heretics attacks this unity with many different insults, one of the two lying in bed will be taken up but the other will be left behind. For by accepting one and rejecting the other, God's judgment will prove the merit of each confession.

Homily on Matthew 26

Saturday - Paulinus of Nola

The two in the field are not two men but two peoples, as the Gentiles who believed and the Jews who remained behind show. The two women grinding at the mill, one of whom was taken as was one man from the field, portray in my opinion the synagogue and the Church. For in the entire course of Sacred Scripture the only allegorical representation is that of the distinction between believers and unbelievers throughout mankind, or that of the creation of the two forms of being in the nature of every man.

So, my brother, because we have always been close to each other in one heart as we are now in Christ, we have been either taken together or left together. We have been taken, however, not through our own merit, but through the grace of God, "whose gifts and calling are irrevocable." We have been taken not because our works gave us preference, but because of faith's good will...

The time is short and it is good for us to be without worry over pressing needs, as Paul says, so that we may be found ready, and when the Lord knocks we may not be afraid to open the door for fear of suffering deserved punishment, guiltily aware of our sleep or indifference. It will avail us nothing if... we prefer to serve a master other than our own and are caught red-handed intent on the world's business rather than Christ's, and so do not open to the Lord when He knocks, but rather are dragged unwilling to the Father. We are forewarned, then, to work and pray for our souls at a seasonable time. The seasonable time is now. *Letter 11, to Severus*

Collect

Keep, we implore You, O Lord, Your Church with Your perpetual mercy; and because the frailty of mankind without You cannot but fail, keep us ever by Your help from all things hurtful and lead us to all things profitable to our salvation; through Jesus Christ, Your Son, our Lord, who lives and reigns with You and Holy Spirit, one God, now and forever. *Gelasian Sacramentary*

AT LAUDS

Psalmody

Sunday: 67, C1, 5	Wednesday: 64, C4, 65	Friday: 76, C5, 92
Monday: 63, C2, 36	Thursday: 88, C6, 90	Saturday: 143, C7, 148
Tuesday: 43, C3, 57		

Lesson

Sunday: Proverbs 3:1-18	Wednesday: Proverbs 6:20-35	Friday: Proverbs 9:1-18
Monday: Proverbs 4:1-13	Thursday: Proverbs 8:1-21	Saturday: Proverbs 10:18-32
Tuesday: Proverbs 5:1-23		

Collect

May forgiveness, O Lord, we pray, proceed from the Most High. May it succor us in our misery; may it cleanse us from our offenses; may it be granted to penitents; may it plead for mourners; may it bring back those who wander from the faith; may it raise up those who are fallen into sins; may it reconcile us to the Father; may it confirm us with the grace of Christ; may it conform us to the Holy Spirit. Amen. *Mozarabic Breviary*

AT TERCE, SEXT AND NONE

Chapter

Sunday, Monday and Tuesday: Galatians 5:16-24
Wednesday and Thursday: II Corinthians 6:14-7:1
Friday and Saturday: Philippians 2:1-4

AT VESPERS

Psalmody

Sunday: 110, 111, 112, 113
Monday: 114, 115, 116, 117
Tuesday: 120, 121, 122

Wednesday: 123, 124, 125
Thursday: 126, 127, 128

Friday: 129, 130, 131, 132
Saturday: 133, 135, 136a

Lesson

Sunday: Proverbs 3:19-35
Monday: Proverbs 4:14-27
Tuesday: Proverbs 6:1-19

Wednesday: Proverbs 7:1-27
Thursday: Proverbs 8:22-36

Friday: Proverbs 10:1-17
Saturday: Proverbs 11:1-15

Collect

Lord God, heavenly Father, who by Your blessèd word and Your holy baptism has mercifully cleansed all who believe from the fearful leprosy of sin, and daily grants us Your gracious help in all our need: We implore You so to enlighten our hearts by Your Holy Spirit, that we may never forget these blessings, but always live in Your fear, and, trusting fully in Your grace, with thankful hearts continually praise and glorify You; through Your Son, our Lord Jesus Christ, who lives and reigns with You and the Holy Spirit, one true God, world without end. Amen. *Veit Dietrich*

THE FIFTEENTH WEEK
AFTER TRINITY

AT MATINS

Hymn - *Was Gott tut, das ist wohlgetan*

1. What God or-dains is al - ways good: His will is just and ho - ly.

As He di - rects my life for me, I fol-low meek and low- ly.

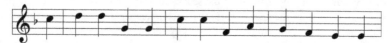

My God in - deed In ev - 'ry need Knows well how He will

shield me; To Him, then I will yield me.

2. What God ordains is always good:
He never will deceive me;
He leads me in His righteous way,
And never will He leave me.
I take content
What He has sent;
His hand that sends me sadness
Will turn my tears to gladness.

3. What God ordains is always good:
His loving thought attends me;
No poison can be in the cup
That my physician sends me.
My God is true;
Each morning new
I trust His grace unending,
My life to Him commending.

4. What God ordains is always good:
He is my friend and Father;
He suffers naught to do me harm
Though many storms may gather.
Now I may know
Both joy and woe;
Someday I shall see clearly
That He hath loved me dearly.

5. What God ordains is always good:
Though I the cup and drinking
Which savors now of bitterness,
I take it without shrinking.
For after grief
God gives relief,
My heart with comfort filling
And all my sorrow stilling.

6. What God ordains is always good:
This truth remains unshaken.
Though sorrow, need, or death be mine,
I shall not be forsaken.
I fear no harm,
For with His arm
He shall embrace and shield me;
So to my God I yield me.

Samuel Rodigast, 1675

Psalmody

Sunday: 69b, 70, 71 Wednesday: 75, 79, 80 Friday: 84, 86, 87, 93
Monday: 72, 73, 74 Thursday: 81, 82, 83 Saturday: 85, 89a, 89b
Tuesday: 78a, 78b, 78c

Lesson

Sunday, Monday and Tuesday: Matthew 6:24-34
Monday: Luke 12:22-34
Tuesday: John 6:22-29

Wednesday and Thursday: Matthew 6:7-15
Thursday: Luke 11:1-4

Friday and Saturday: Luke 20:1-8

Homily

Sunday - John Chrysostom

Though we hymn our common Lord for all sorts of reasons, we hymn Him particularly to give Him glory, since we stand astonished because of the cross and His death attended by curses. Does not Paul depict that death as a sign of His love for us? Christ dies for men like us. Paul refrains from speaking of sky, earth, sea and all that Christ committed to our use and recreation; he repeatedly returns to the cross with the words: "God demonstrates His own love toward us, in that while we were still sinners, Christ died for us." So Paul extends to us good hope when he says: "For if when we were enemies we were reconciled to God through the death of His Son, much more, having been reconciled, we shall be saved by His life." Is it not because of this in particular that Paul himself rejoices and glories and jumps and flutters for joy, telling the Galatians: "God forbid that I should boast except in the cross of our Lord Jesus Christ"? Why should you be surprised that he jumps and leaps and exults? He who endures these sufferings calls them his glory: "Father," He says, "the hour has come. Glorify Your Son."

The disciple who wrote this said: "for the Holy Spirit was not yet given, because Jesus was not yet glorified." He calls the cross a glory. When he wanted to demonstrate Christ's love, of what did he speak? His signs and wonders and marvels? No, he gives prominence to the cross, with the words: "God so loved the world that He gave His only begotten Son, that whoever believes in Him should not perish but have everlasting life." Paul too says: "He did not spare His own Son, but delivered Him up for us all, how shall He not with Him also freely give us all things?"

On Providence

Monday - Jerome of Jerusalem

Just as no one can serve two masters, so also it is difficult to keep both the shadow and the truth of the Law. The shadow is in the old Law until daytime draws near and the shadows dissipate. The truth is in the Gospel of Christ, "for grace and truth have come through Jesus Christ." If anyone thinks he is justified by observing the Law, he loses the grace of Christ and the Gospel which he possessed. When he loses grace, faith in Christ abandons him, and he stops doing the work of Christ.

Commentary on Galatians

Tuesday - Bernard of Clairvaux

What else could the enemy bring up to tempt you except that your life lies far ahead of you? And why should you be afraid if a great journey lies ahead, you who have received the food of the strong so you do not faint on the way? Elijah was served food by an angel, food which by human standards is the most common: bread and water. And yet he gathered so much strength from that food that he walked for forty days without feeling fatigue or hunger. Would you like the angels to minister this food to you? It will surprise me if you do not.

But if you long for this food, and seek it simply by an ambition more humble, and not in order to boast of angelic service, then listen to how it is written of the Lord that, when the devil tempted and coaxed him to change stones into loaves of bread, He resisted and said, "Man does not live by bread alone, but by every word that proceeds from the mouth of God." Then, once the temptation had been overcome and the tempter put to flight, angels came and ministered to him. So you, too, if you want to be served by angels, flee the consolations of this world and resist the temptations of the devil. Let your soul refuse to be comforted by other things if you want it to take pleasure in the remembrance of God. When you are hungry the devil urges you to run off for bread; but you ought instead to listen to Him who said, "Man does not live by bread alone." Apart from the sole necessity of sustaining the body, what other reason do you have to be so distracted by so many things that you look now for food, now for drink, and now for clothing or a bed, when you are able to find all that you need in a single thing: the word of God. This is the sweet and delicious smelling manna; it is a rest true and sincere, sweet and savory, joyful and holy.

Sermon 4 on Psalm 91

Wednesday - Cyril of Jerusalem

We say the prayer which the Savior delivered to His own disciples, with a pure conscience calling God our Father, and saying, "Our Father, who art in Heaven." O most surpassing loving-kindness of God! On those who revolted from Him and were in the very extreme of misery has He bestowed such complete forgiveness of their evil deeds, and so great a participation of grace, as that they should even call Him Father. 'Our Father, who art in Heaven'; these also, too, are a heaven who bear the image of the heavenly, in whom God is, dwelling and walking in them.

"Hallowed be Thy Name." The Name of God is in its own nature holy, whether we say so or not; but since it is sometimes profaned among sinners, according to the words, "the name of God is blasphemed among the Gentiles because of you," we pray that in us God's Name may be hallowed; not that it becomes holy from not being holy, but because it becomes holy in us when we become holy and do things worthy of holiness.

"Thy kingdom come." The clean soul can say with boldness, 'Thy kingdom come'; for he who has heard Paul saying, "do not let sin reign in your mortal body," but has cleansed himself in deed, thought, and word, will say to God, "Thy kingdom come."

"Thy will be done on earth as it is in heaven." The divine and blessed Angels do the will of God, as David in a Psalm has said, "Bless the Lord, you His angels, who excel in strength, who do His word." So then, you mean by your prayer, "as Your will is done by the Angels, so be it done on earth also by me, Lord."

"Give us this day our super-substantial bread." Common bread is not super-substantial bread, but the Holy Bread is super-substantial, that is, appointed for the substance of the soul. For this Bread does not go into the belly to be cast out into the sewer, but is diffused through all you are for the benefit of body and soul. But by this day, he means, "each day," as also Paul has said, "While it is called today."

"And forgive us our debts as we forgive our debtors." For we have many sins. We offend both in word and in thought, and we do very many things worthy of condemnation. And if we say that we have no sins we lie, as John says. Here we enter into a covenant with God, begging Him to pardon our sins, as we also forgive our neighbors their debts. Considering then what we receive and at what cost, let us not put off, nor delay to forgive one another. The offenses committed against us are slight and trivial, and easily settled; but those which we have committed against God are great, and call for mercy such as is His only. Take heed, therefore, lest for the sake of these small and inconsiderable sins against yourself, you bar yourself from forgiveness from God for your most grievous sins.

"And lead us not into temptation, O Lord." Does the Lord teach to pray that we may not be tempted at all? And how is it said elsewhere, "the man who is not tempted, is unproven;" and again,

"My brethren, count it all joy when you fall into various trials," or rather does not the entering into temptation mean the being overwhelmed by temptation? For the temptation is like a winter torrent difficult to cross. Some then, being most skillful swimmers, pass over, not being overwhelmed by temptations, nor swept downstream by them at all; while others who are not so skillful, entering into them sink in them. As for example, Judas entering into the temptation of covetousness, did not swim through it, but sinking beneath it was choked both in body and spirit. Peter entered into the temptation of the denial; but having entered it, he was not overwhelmed by it, but manfully swimming through it, he was delivered from the temptation. Listen again, in another place, to the company of unscathed saints, giving thanks for deliverance from temptation, "For You, O God, have tested us; You have refined us as silver is refined. You brought us into the net; You laid affliction on our backs. You have caused men to ride over our heads; we went through fire and through water; but You brought us out to rich fulfillment." You see them speaking boldly, because they passed through and were not pierced. But You brought us out into a wealthy place; now their coming into a wealthy place is their being delivered from temptation.

"But deliver us from the evil." If "Lead us not into temptation" had implied not being tempted at all, He would not have said, "But deliver us from the evil." Now the evil is the wicked spirit who is our adversary, from whom we pray to be delivered. Then, after completing the prayer, you say, "Amen;" by this Amen, which means "So be it," you set your seal to the petitions of this divinely taught prayer. *Mystagogical Catechesis*

Thursday - Augustine of Hippo

It is not wrong or useless also to pray for a long time when one is free, that is, when it does not interfere with other duties involving good and necessary actions. Even in them, though, one should always pray with holy desire. For praying for a longer time does not mean, as some suppose, praying with many words. A lot of talking is one thing; a lasting love is another. For scripture says even of the Lord himself that He spent the night in prayer and that He prayed at great length. In doing this what else did He do but offer us an example, insofar as He suitably offered prayers in time and, as eternal, heard them along with the Father? ...

We must have words by which we may be reminded and may consider what we ask for, not by which we believe that we should either instruct or persuade the Lord. When, therefore, we say, May Your name be made holy, we remind ourselves to desire that His name, which is always holy, may be also held holy among human beings, that is, that it may not be scorned. This is something that benefits human beings, not God. And when we say, May Your kingdom come, it will surely come whether we want it to or not, but we stir up our desire for that kingdom that it may come for us and that we may be found worthy to reign in it. When we say, May Your will also be done on earth as it is in heaven, we ask Him to give us obedience so that His will may be done in us as it is done in the heavens by the angels. When we say, Give us today our daily bread, the term "today" means at the time when we are asking for all we need, referring to the whole by its principal element, that is, by the term "bread," or referring to the sacrament of the faithful that is needed in this time, not for acquiring the happiness of this time but for acquiring that eternal happiness. When we say, Forgive us our debts as we also forgive our debtors, we remind ourselves of both what we should ask for and what we should do in order that we may be found worthy to receive it. When we say, Do not bring us into temptation, we remind ourselves to ask that we may not be abandoned by His help and consent to any temptation after being deceived, or yield to any temptation after being afflicted. When we say, Deliver us from evil, we remind ourselves to bear in mind that we are not yet in that good state in which we will suffer no evil. And this petition that is placed last in the Lord's Prayer is, of course, so widely applicable that, in whatever tribulation Christians may find themselves, they utter their groans in it, pour forth their tears in it, begin with it, linger over it, and bring their prayers to an end with it. For it was necessary that the truth itself be committed to our memory by these words.

For whatever other words we might say... we say nothing else but what is contained in that prayer of the Lord if we pray correctly and properly. But whoever says something that cannot belong to this prayer from the gospel, even if he does not pray in a way that is forbidden, prays in a carnal manner, something that I do not know how one can say is not forbidden, since it is fitting that those reborn of the Spirit pray only in a spiritual manner. *Letter to Proba*

Friday - Augustine of Hippo

God, you see, liked this arrangement, whereby a man of such great grace, that he could be thought to be the Christ, should bear witness to Christ. In a word, among those born of women, as Christ said himself, nobody has arisen greater than John the Baptist. If there was never a man greater than this man, the one who is greater than he is must be more than a man. Christ is thus bearing very weighty witness to himself - but to eyes that are bleary and weak the evidence that the day gives about itself is not very telling; weak eyes shrink from daylight, bear with lamp light. That is why the day that was to come sent a lamp ahead. But he sent the lamp ahead into the hearts of believers, in order to confound the hearts of unbelievers. I have prepared, he says, a lamp for my Christ; it's God the Father speaking through the prophet. I have prepared a lamp for my Christ; John, a herald for the Savior, a forerunner for the judge who is to come, a friend for the bridegroom to be. I have prepared, he says, a lamp for my Christ. Why have you prepared it? His enemies I will clothe with confusion; but upon him my sanctification shall blossom.

How were his enemies clothed with confusion by means of this lamp? Let's scrutinize the gospel. The Jews, to discredit him, said to the Lord, By what authority are you doing these things? If you are the Christ, tell us openly. They were looking for a pretext, not for faith; something to catch him out with, not something to be liberated by. Anyway, the one who could see their hearts, notice what answer he gave, to confound them with the lamp. I will ask you too, he said, one question: "tell me, John's baptism, where is it from? From heaven, or from men?" They were immediately sent staggering backward, and although the daylight was only shining gently, compelled to fumble and blink, since they were unable to gaze at that brilliance, and so they took refuge in the darkness of their hearts, and there they began to get very agitated among themselves, stumbling and falling about. "If we say," they said - this to themselves, where they were thinking, but where he could see - "If we say," they said, "It is from heaven, he will say to us, Why did you not believe him?" He, after all, had borne witness to Christ the Lord. "But if we say, From men, the people will stone us," because John was regarded as a great prophet. And they said, "We do not know." You don't know; you're in darkness, you're losing the light. How much better, after all, if darkness is occupying the human heart, to let the light in, not to lose it? When they said, "We do not know," the Lord said, "Neither do I tell you by what authority I am doing these things." You see, I know in what mind you said We don't know; not because you wish to be taught, but because you are afraid to confess. *Sermon 293*

Saturday - Cyril of Alexandria

They were not worthy to learn the truth and to see the pathway that leads directly to every good work. Christ answered them: "Neither will I tell you by what authority I do these things." So the Jews did not know the truth and were not taught of God, that is, of Christ. Christ reveals that knowledge to us who have believed in Him. We, receiving in mind and heart His divine and adorable mystery, or rather the knowledge of it, and being careful to fulfill those things which are pleasing to Him, shall reign with Him. *Homily 132 on Luke*

Collect

O Lord, we implore You, let Your continual pity cleanse and defend Your Church, and because she cannot continue in safety without Your help, preserve her evermore by Your help and goodness; through Jesus Christ, Your Son, our Lord, who lives and reigns with You and the Holy Spirit, one God, now and forever.   *Gelasian Sacramentary*

AT LAUDS

Psalmody

Sunday: 3, C8, 51
Monday: 118a, C9, 118b
Tuesday: 1, C10, 2

Wednesday: 8, C11, 20
Thursday: 18a, C12, 18b

Friday: 146, C13, 5
Saturday: 149, C14, 150

Lesson

Sunday: Proverbs 11:16-31
Monday: Proverbs 12:23-13:12
Tuesday: Proverbs 14:15-35

Wednesday: Proverbs 15:26-16:9
Thursday: Proverbs 17:1-17

Friday: Proverbs 18:10-24
Saturday: Proverbs 19:20-20:5

Collect

Grant us, O Lord, not to mind earthly things, but to love heavenly things; and even now, while we are placed among things that are passing away, to cleave to those that shall abide; through Jesus Christ, Your Son, our Lord, who lives and reigns with You and the Holy Spirit, one God, forever and ever. Amen.   *Leonine Sacramentary*

AT TERCE, SEXT AND NONE

Chapter

Sunday, Monday and Tuesday: Galatians 6:1-10
Wednesday and Thursday: Colossians 1:3-20
Friday and Saturday: James 5:7-10

AT VESPERS

Psalmody

Sunday: 136b, 137, 138
Monday: 140, 141, 142
Tuesday: 144, 145, 7

Wednesday: 9, 10, 11
Thursday: 12, 13, 14, 16

Friday: 17, 147a, 147b
Saturday: 19, 54, 77

Lesson

Sunday: Proverbs 12:1-22
Monday: Proverbs 13:13-14:14
Tuesday: Proverbs 15:1-25

Wednesday: Proverbs 16:10-33
Thursday: Proverbs 17:18-18:9

Friday: Proverbs 19:1-19
Saturday: Proverbs 20:6-30

Collect

Lord God, heavenly Father, we thank You for all Your benefits: that You have given us life and graciously sustained us unto this day: We implore You, take not Your blessing from us; preserve us from covetousness, that we may serve You only, love and abide in You, and not defile ourselves by idolatrous love of mammon, but hope and trust only in Your grace, through Jesus Christ, Your Son, our Lord, who lives and reigns with You and the Holy Spirit, one God, now and forever.

Veit Dietrich

THE SIXTEENTH WEEK
AFTER TRINITY

AT MATINS

Hymn - *Was mein Gott will, das g'scheh' allzeit*

1.   The will of God is   al-ways best. And shall be done for - ev - er;

And they who trust in Him are blest; He will for-sake them nev - er.

He   helps in- deed In   time of need; He   chas-tens with for- bear-ing

They who de-pend on God, their friend, Shall not be left de - spair - ing.

2. God is my comfort and my trust,
   My hope and life abiding;
   And to His counsel, wise and just,
   I yield to Him confiding.
   The very hairs,
   His Word declares,
   Upon my head He numbers.
   By night and day
   God is my stay;
   He never sleeps nor slumbers.

3. Lord, this I ask, O hear my plea,
   Deny me not this favor;
   When Satan sorely troubles me,
   Then do not let me waver.
   O guard me well,
   My fear dispel,
   Fufill Your faithful saying:
   All who believe
   By grace receive
   An answer to their praying.

4. When life's brief course on earth is run
   And I this world am leaving,
   Grant me to say, "Thy will be done,"
   Your faithful Word believing.
   My dearest Friend,
   I now commend
   My soul into Your keeping;
   From sin and hell,
   And death as well,
   By You the vict'ry reaping.

Albrecht von Brandenburg, 1554

Psalmody

Sunday: 89c, 94, 96 Wednesday: 104a, 104b, 104c   Friday: 106a, 106b, 107a
Monday: 97, 98, 99, 100   Thursday: 105a, 105b, 105c   Saturday: 107b, 108, 109
Tuesday: 101, 102, 103

Lesson

Sunday, Monday and Tuesday: Luke 7:11-17
Tuesday: Mark 3:1-5 or Luke 6:1-11

Wednesday and Thursday: Luke 5:27-32
Friday and Saturday: Matthew 19:3-12
Friday: Mark 10:1-16
Saturday: Matthew 5:31-42

Homily

Sunday - Peter Chrysologus

What is this trumpet that declares war against hell, rolls back the stone from the tomb, thunders forth life to the dead, and gives victory to all as they rise from their graves amid light everlasting? What is it? It is that to which our Lord referred: "The dead will hear the voice of the Son of God." This is not a trumpet of horn or wood or brass that sounds a mournful bellow, calling to war, but the Voice that comes from the heart of the Father, from the mouth of the Son - the call to life to all that are in heaven and in hell...

The same trumpet that in the beginning called the world from nothing will on the last day recall the world from death; and that which in the beginning raised man from the slime, the same at the end will recall him from the dust...

And if the Voice of God, the trumpet of Christ, through the cycle of days, months, seasons, and years, calls and recalls, leads forth and leads back, bids to be and bids not to be, gives to death and restores to life, why would He not perform in us one time what He does all the time in all other things? Does the divine power fail only with us, for whom alone the Divine Majesty of God has done all that we have been speaking about?

O man, if all that God has made returns from death to life for you, why shouldn't you also be brought to life from death through God? Or does God's creative power fail only in you? Every creature lives, moves, is changed, renewed for you. Brothers, I say this, not with any desire to belittle the power of the wonders of Christ, but so that I may exhort you, that by the example of this young man rising from the dead, we may be awakened to faith in the resurrection of all men. I do it so that you may believe that the Cross is the plough of our body, faith its seed, the grave its furrow, decomposition its bud, time its period of waiting; so that when the spring of the Lord's coming smiles on us, the full green of our bodies shall rise again in a life-giving harvest that will know no ending, no old age, that will not be bound into bundles, nor winnowed with a flail. For abandoning our old straw in death, our glorified bodies, like new fruit, will rise again in the harvest of eternal life. *Sermon 103*

Monday - Augustine of Hippo

There are those who have sin within their hearts but have not yet sinned in deed. Someone is inwardly shaken by lust. The Lord Himself said: "Whoever looks at a woman to lust for her has already committed adultery with her in his heart." He has not yet drawn near her in body, but already he has consented in his heart. He has within him a dead man, but has not yet carried him forth. And as often happens, as we know, and people experience this each day, should he at some

544

moment hear the word of God, hear as it were the voice of the Lord saying to him: "Arise," he will condemn his having consented to sin, and his soul will breathe in again saving health and righteousness. The man dead in his own house rises again; the heart revives within the secrecy of the soul. This resurrection of a dead soul has taken place within the secrecy of the conscience, as within the walls of a house.

Others, having inwardly consented to evil, proceed to the outward act; as though carrying forth the dead. What was hidden in secrecy, now appears for all to see. Are these who have come forth in outward deed now past hope? Far from it. Didn't Jesus say also to the young man: "I say to you, arise?" Didn't He restore him to his mother? So also he who has sinned in deed shall be restored to life, if he happens to have been warned and awakened by the word of truth, and will rise again at the voice of Christ. He could step forth on the way of sin, yet still not perish for ever.

But those who continue to do evil become bound up in evil habit, so that the very habit of evil will not let them see that it is evil. These become defenders of their own evil deeds. They rage when they are rebuked, like the Sodomites long ago, who said to the just man who rebuked them for their most evil inclination: You came to stay here, not to act as a judge. Their habit of abominable foulness became so dominant among them that wickedness now became justice; and one who opposed it, more to be censured than one who practised it. People like these, pressed down by malignant habit - it is as though they were buried. What am I saying, brothers? They are in fact so buried, that we may say that of them what was said of Lazarus: he now stinks. The hard power of habit is like a great stone laid upon the tomb; pressing down upon the soul, allowing it neither to breathe nor to rise again.

It was said of Lazarus: "he has been dead four days." The soul arrives at this state of habitual sin in four stages. In the first stage, there is a touch of pleasure in the heart. In the second, there is consent. In the third, there is deed. In the fourth, there is habit. There are some people who completely reject blatantly sinful things from their thoughts, so that they are not even tempted. There are some who are tempted, but do not consent to sin. Death is not found here; though it has begun. But when consent is added to the allurement of temptation, this is already damnation. After consent comes the act of sin. Act turns into habit; and then hope dies in the unhappy soul; so that we may say of him: By this time, he stinks; for he has been dead four days.

So then the Lord comes; and to Him all things are, of course, easy. But here He has some sense of difficulty. He groans in the spirit, and makes it clear that we need to cry out with a loud voice in rebuke to raise those who have become hardened in evil habits. Nevertheless, at the voice of the Lord crying out with a loud voice, the bonds that seemed inescapable are burst asunder. The dominion of hell trembled; and Lazarus is restored to the living. And the Lord also delivers from evil habits those who are four days dead. For, to Christ, who desires to revive him, even he who is four days dead is but sleeping.   *Sermon 98*

Tuesday - Gabriel Biel

Gabriel said to Joseph, "You will call His name Jesus for He will save His people from their sins." Truly He has already saved His people by preparing medicine. He continues to save them daily by driving out disease. He will save them ultimately by giving them perfect health and preserving them from every ill. The preparation of the medicine is the task of the human nature of Christ, the driving out of disease the task of the divine nature, and the perfect health the task of both natures.

He prepared the medicine when He instituted and commanded the medicinal sacraments. To heal the wounds inflicted by our sins, He, through the effusion of His blood, earned efficacy for the sacraments... Our Savior saves us daily by driving out disease, which is the task of His divine nature. Now it is obvious that this disease is sin, which He drives out when He forgives and ceases to impute to the sinner eternal punishment... He does not imperfectly heal the disease by merely driving it out, but He also gives health by the infusion of grace. For a man does not enjoy perfect health when, although without pain in his body, he is unable to use it for the tasks of life. But this capacity is a gift of grace. This is what Augustine meant when he said, "The Lamb takes away the sins both by forgiving what has been done and by helping the sinner not to sin again." This help is extended through grace.

No one removes sins except God alone, who is the lamb taking away the sins of the world, as Augustine said. For this reason, namely, that He forgives sins, the Jews accused Christ of blasphemy, since they did not believe Him to be God. Now no one confers grace except God. It is clear that grace comes into being only through God's creative action, since grace cannot be acquired through our works like other moral habits which, as Aristotle said, are naturally engendered in us by repetition of our own moral actions. The Apostle Paul said, "But if it is by grace, it is no longer on the basis of works, otherwise grace would no longer be grace." Because nature cannot make something out of nothing, that which is created comes from God alone. If grace could come from the creature, a grace which would suffice unto salvation, then any creature would be able to save himself by his own natural powers, that is, do what only grace can do. That is the error of Pelagius. Therefore, the prophet said, "The Lord will give grace and glory."

Sermon 2 on the Circumcision of Our Lord

Wednesday - Bede the Venerable

He who knew the hidden things of the heart is the one who came "to seek and to save that which was lost." He further strengthened in faith those He had already accepted as they repented. He stirred up to the grace of humility and piety those whom He put up with when they were still proud and wicked. There follows: "But Jesus hearing it said, 'Those who are well have no need of a physician, but those who are sick.'" By bearing witness that He came as a physician to those with a sickness, He increased the hope of obtaining healing and life for those who, having been roused from the illness of their sins, had already begun to follow the teaching of the Savior and Lifegiver. By saying that the healthy need no physician, He confuted the rashness of those who, counting upon their own righteousness, were scornful of seeking the help of heavenly grace. Who could be so just that he does not stand in need of divine aid, since John, whom none born of women was greater, said most clearly about himself, "A man can receive nothing unless it has been given to him from heaven"?

Lenten Homily on Matthew 9

Thursday - Ambrose of Milan

Jesus orders the tax collector to follow Him not by bodily steps, but by disposition of the mind. Thus, he who used to greedily take from sailors' hard-earned profits from labors and dangers, left that ignoble seat, and followed after the Lord with the whole footprint of his mind. He also makes preparation for a great feast; for he who receives Christ in his inner habitation feeds on the greatest delights of abundant pleasures. Thus, the Lord enters willingly and reclines in the disposition of one who has believed. But again, the envy of the unbelievers is kindled, and the appearance of future punishment prefigured; for when the faithful feast and recline in that Kingdom of the Heavens, hungry unbelief will be tormented. It is shown, at the same time, how great an abyss there is between the enemies of the Law and Grace, because those who follow the Law suffer the eternal hunger of a barren mind, but those who have received the word in the inner part of the soul, refreshed by the richness of heavenly food and drink, cannot hunger or thirst.

Exposition of the Holy Gospel According to Luke

Friday - John Chrysostom

A certain wise man, when enumerating which blessings are most important included "a wife and husband who live in harmony." In another place he emphasized this: "A friend or a companion never meets one amiss, but a wife with her husband is better than both." From the beginning

God in His providence has planned this union of man and woman, and has spoken of the two as one: "male and female He created them" and "there is neither male nor female, for you are all one in Christ Jesus." There is no relationship between human beings so close as that of husband and wife, if they are united as they ought to be. When blessed David was mourning for Jonathan, who was of one soul with him, what comparison did he use to describe the loftiness of their love? "Your love to me was wonderful, passing the love of women."

The power of this love is truly stronger than any passion; other desires may be strong, but this one alone never fades. This love (eros) is deeply planted within our inmost being. Unnoticed by us, it attracts the bodies of men and women to each other, because in the beginning woman came forth from man, and from man and woman other men and women proceed. Can you see now how close this union is, and how God providentially created it from a single nature? He permitted Adam to marry Eve, who was more than sister or daughter; she was his own flesh! God caused the entire human race to proceed from this one point of origin. He did not, on the one hand, fashion woman independently from man; otherwise man would think of her as essentially different from himself. Nor did He enable woman to bear children without man; if this were the case she would be self-sufficient. Instead, just as the branches of a tree proceed from a single trunk, He made the one man Adam to be the origin of all mankind, both male and female, and made it impossible for men and women to be self-sufficient. Later, He forbade men to marry their sisters or daughters, so that our love would not be limited to members of our families, and withdrawn from the rest of the human race. All of this is implied in Christ's words: "He who made them from the beginning made them male and female."

The love of husband and wife is the force that welds society together. Men will take up arms and even sacrifice their lives for the sake of this love. St. Paul would not speak so earnestly about this subject without serious reason; why else would he say, "Wives, be subject to your husbands, as to the Lord"? Because when harmony prevails, the children are raised well, the household is kept in order, and neighbors, friends and relatives praise the result. Great benefits, both for families and states, are thus produced. When it is otherwise, however, everything is thrown into confusion and turned upside-down.

Homily on Ephesians 5

Saturday - Theophilus of Antioch

And concerning chastity, the holy word not only teaches us not to sin in act, but not even in thought, not even in the heart to think of any evil, nor look on another man's wife with our eyes to lust after her. Solomon, who was a king and a prophet, said: "Let your eyes look straight ahead, and your eyelids look right before you. Make straight paths for your feet." And the voice of the Gospel teaches still more urgently concerning chastity, saying: "whoever looks at a woman to lust for her has already committed adultery with her in his heart." And the Gospel says: "whoever divorces his wife for any reason except sexual immorality causes her to commit adultery; and whoever marries a woman who is divorced commits adultery." Because Solomon says: "Can a man take fire to his bosom, and his clothes not be burned? Can one walk on hot coals, and his feet not be seared? So is he who goes in to his neighbor's wife; whoever touches her shall not be innocent."

To Autolycus

Collect

O Lord, we pray that Your grace may always go before and follow after us, that we may be continually given to all good works; through Jesus Christ, Your Son, our Lord, who lives and reigns with You and the Holy Spirit, one God, now and forever.

Gelasian Sacramentary

AT LAUDS

Psalmody

Sunday: 67, C1, 5	Wednesday: 64, C4, 65	Friday: 76, C5, 92
Monday: 63, C2, 36	Thursday: 88, C6, 90	Saturday: 143, C7, 148
Tuesday: 43, C3, 57		

Lesson

Sunday: Proverbs 21:1-20	Wednesday: Proverbs 25:1-28	Friday: Proverbs 29:1-27
Monday: Proverbs 22:11-29	Thursday: Proverbs 27:1-27	Saturday: Proverbs 31:1-9
Tuesday: Proverbs 23:29-24:22		

Collect

Everlasting God, who by Your Only-begotten Son, Jesus Christ, our Lord, has opened to us the portals of eternal life, sealed to us the bond of reconciliation, and by His joyful resurrection, has granted hope and salvation to the whole world; we implore You, awaken in us a desire for that beauteous eternity, that we, being released from the power of sin and death, may ever serve Your honor in newness of life, through the same Jesus Christ, our Lord, who lives and reigns with You and the Holy Spirit, one God, now and forever. *Wilhelm Löhe*

AT TERCE, SEXT AND NONE

Chapter

Sunday, Monday and Tuesday: Ephesians 3:13-21
Wednesday and Thursday: Colossians 2:8-13
Friday and Saturday: I Corinthians 6:9-11

AT VESPERS

Psalmody

Sunday: 110, 111, 112, 113	Wednesday: 123, 124, 125	Friday: 129, 130, 131, 132
Monday: 114, 115, 116, 117	Thursday: 126, 127, 128	Saturday: 133, 135, 136a
Tuesday: 120, 121, 122		

Lesson

Sunday: Proverbs 21:21-22:10	Wednesday: Proverbs 26:1-28	Friday: Proverbs 30:1-33
Monday: Proverbs 23:1-28	Thursday: Proverbs 28:1-28	Saturday: Proverbs 31:10-31
Tuesday: Proverbs 24:23-34		

Collect

Lord God, heavenly Father, who sent Your Son to be made flesh, that by His death He might atone for our sins and deliver us from eternal death: We pray You, confirm in our hearts the hope that our Lord Jesus Christ, who with but a word raised the widow's son, in like manner will raise us on the last day, and grant us eternal life: through Your beloved Son, Jesus Christ, our Lord, who lives and reigns with You and the Holy Spirit, one true God, now and forever. Amen.

Veit Dietrich

THE SEVENTEENTH WEEK
AFTER TRINITY

AT MATINS

Hymn - *The Church's One Foundation*

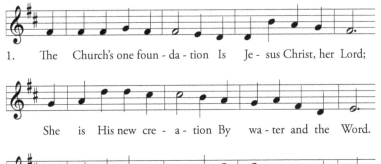

1. The Church's one foun - da - tion Is Je - sus Christ, her Lord;

She is His new cre - a - tion By wa - ter and the Word.

From heav'n He came and sought her To be His ho - ly Bride;

With His own blood He bought her, And for her life He died.

2. Elect from every nation,
   Yet one o'er all the earth;
   Her charter of salvation,
   One Lord, one faith, one birth;
   One holy name she blesses,
   Partakes one holy food,
   And to one hope she presses,
   With every grace endued.

3. Though with a scornful wonder
   Men see her sore oppressed,
   By schisms rent asunder,
   By heresies distressed,
   Yet saints their watch are keeping;
   Their cry goes up, "How long?"
   And soon the night of weeping
   Shall be the morn of song.

4. The Church shall never perish!
   Her dear Lord to defend,
   To guide, sustain, and cherish,
   Is with her to the end.
   Though there be those that hate her,
   False sons within her pale,
   Against both foe and traitor
   She ever shall prevail.

5. 'Mid toil and tribulation,
   And tumult of her war,
   She waits the consummation
   Of peace forevermore;
   Till, with the vision glorious,
   Her longing eyes are blest,
   And the great church victorious
   Shall be the church at rest.

6. Yet she on earth has union
   With God the Three in One,
   And mystic sweet communion
   With those whose rest is won.
   O blessèd heav'nly chorus!
   Lord, save us by Your grace
   That we, like saints before us,
   May see You face to face.   *Samuel J. Stone, 1866*

Psalmody

Sunday: 21, 22, 23	Wednesday: 30, 31, 32	Friday: 37a, 37b, 38
Monday: 24, 25, 26	Thursday: 33, 34, 35	Saturday: 39, 40, 41
Tuesday: 27, 28, 29		

Lesson

Sunday, Monday and Tuesday: Luke 14:1-11
Tuesday: Matthew 12:9-13

Wednesday and Thursday: Mark 9:17-29
Thursday: Luke 9:37-42

Friday: Luke 18:1-8a
Saturday: Luke 13:6-17

Homily

Sunday - Baldwin of Forde

The greater you are, the more you should humble yourself in all things. It is as if he said: The measure of your humility should be equal to the greatness of your dignity. Humility in honor is itself the honor of honor and the dignity of dignity. No dignity deserves the name of dignity if it scorns humility, for just as humility engenders honor, so, too, it preserves it. Every advancement in honor, when it takes place in [due and proper] order, begins with humility and ends with a high position, and he who humbles himself will be exalted - provided he does not humble himself in order to be exalted, but rather humbles himself so as not to be exalted. [Not to be exalted] in the world, I mean; in [the eyes of] God he is exalted. Someone who is truly humble does not strive for honor; when he receives honor, he does not snatch at it through ambition, but because of his humility he is himself snatched away to honor. Thus, he is not someone who plunders honor, but is like the plunder of honor itself. Humility without honor is sufficient in itself for honor, but honor without humility only brings upon itself confusion. Thus, just as humility justly precedes honor, it also justly preserves it. Those in [positions of] honor, therefore, should see that they show themselves humble in all things.   *Spiritual Tractates*

Monday - Leo I of Rome

Raise your faithful hearts, dearly beloved, to the shining beauty of eternal light. As you revere the mysteries devoted to human salvation, put your energy into all those things that have been done on your behalf. Love the purity of a chaste life, since Christ is the Son of a virgin. Abstain from carnal desires, since they wage war against the soul, as the apostle... encouraged us with his own words: "Be little children in respect to wickedness," because the Lord of glory conformed Himself to the infancy of mortals. Earnestly pursue humility, which the Son of God saw fit to teach His disciples.

Clothe yourselves in the virtue of patience, in which you can possess your souls since He who is the Redemption of all is also the Fortitude of all. Relish the things which are on high, not those things upon the earth. Walk steadily along the path of truth and of life. Do not let the things of earth hinder you, you for whom the things of heaven have been prepared, through Jesus Christ our Lord.

Sermon 32

Tuesday - Bernard of Clairvaux

If Christ submitted Himself to human misery so that He might not simply know of it, but experience it as well, how much more ought you not make any change in your condition, but pay attention to what you are, because you are truly full of misery. This is the only way, if you are to learn to be merciful. If you have eyes for the shortcomings of your neighbor and not for your own, no feeling of mercy will arise in you but rather indignation. You will be more ready to judge than to help, to crush in the spirit of anger than to instruct in the spirit of gentleness. "You who are spiritual, instruct such a one in the spirit of gentleness," says the Apostle. His counsel, or better, his precept, is that you should treat an ailing brother with the spirit of gentleness with which you would like to be treated yourself in your weakness. He shows then how to find out the right way to apply this spirit of gentleness: "Considering yourself lest you also be tempted."

It is worth noticing how closely the Disciple of Truth follows the order of his Master's thoughts. In the Beatitudes, just as the merciful come before the clean of heart, so the meek are spoken of before the merciful. When the Apostle tells the spiritually minded to instruct the earthly minded he adds: "In the spirit of meekness." The only ones who can instruct the brethren are those who are merciful, those who are meek or humble. In other words, one cannot really be merciful if he is not humble. Thus the Apostle clearly shows... that we must look for truth first in ourselves, and afterwards in our neighbor. "Considering yourself," he says, that is, considering how easily you are tempted and how prone to sin, you will become meek and ready to help others in the "spirit of gentleness." If the words of the Disciple do not impress you enough, perhaps you will take warning from the stern words of the Master: "Hypocrite! First remove the beam from your own eye, and then you will see clearly to remove the speck from your brother's." The heavy, thick beam in the eye is pride of heart. It is big but not strong, swollen, not solid. It blinds the eye of the mind and blots out the truth. While it is there you cannot see yourself as you really are, or even the ideal of what you could be, but what you would like to be, this you think you are or hope to be. For what else is pride but, as a saint has defined it, the love of one's own excellence. We may define humility as the opposite: contempt of one's own excellence.

The Steps of Humility and Pride

Wednesday - Augustine of Hippo

If faith falters, prayer perishes. I mean, who are going to pray to what they don't believe? Which is why the blessed apostle, in urging us to pray, said, "whoever calls on the name of the Lord shall be saved." And to show that faith is the fountainhead of prayer, and that the stream can't run when the head of water dries up, he went on to add, "How then shall they call on Him in whom they have not believed?" So in order to pray, let us believe; and in order that the very faith by which we pray may not fail, let us pray. Faith pours out prayer, prayer being poured out obtains firmness for faith. Indeed, it was to ensure that faith doesn't falter in the midst of temptations and trials that the Lord said, "Keep awake, and pray that you may not enter into temptation..." What can entering into temptation be, but going out from faith? Temptation succeeds, you see, to the extent that faith fails; and temptation fails to the extent that faith succeeds...

[Perfect faith] is indeed hard to find on earth... Look, here's God's church crammed full; who would come here if they had no faith at all? Who would fail to move mountains if their faith was complete? Think of the apostles themselves: they wouldn't have left everything they had, trampled on their worldly hopes and followed the Lord, unless they had had great faith; and yet if they had had complete faith, they wouldn't have said to the Lord, "Increase our faith." Look also at that man who admitted both things about himself (look at his faith, and his incomplete faith), who brought his son to the Lord to be cured of an evil demon, and on being questioned whether he believed, answered and said, "I believe, Lord, help my unbelief." I believe, he said, I believe, Lord, so there's faith there. But, help my unbelief, so faith is not complete.

Sermon 115

Thursday - Martin Luther

The devil occasionally assails the pious Christian hearts so hard with his fiery darts that they not only become oblivious to the exuberant glory of their filial relationship to God but also give way to the opposite ideas, as, for instance, that God has forgotten them or forsaken them, or has repudiated them and cast them from His sight. For that matter, St. Paul did not always leap for joy and glory unrestrainedly in his kinship with God, and then, in that knowledge, defy the devil and the evil world. This is borne out by the following and other statements: "And I was with you in weakness and in much fear and trembling." And in 2 Cor. 7:5 he speaks of "fighting without and fear within."

Thus our faith is still very feeble and cold. If it were as firm and stable as indeed it should be, we would almost die for sheer joy. But, God be praised, we know that even those of little faith are children of God. And Christ does not say in vain: "Fear not, little flock." But we should at all times sigh and pray with the apostle: "Lord, increase our faith!;" and with that man in Mark 9:24: "I believe; help my unbelief!"

This is our consolation, that the believer in Christ has been assured and guaranteed that he is an heir of God, not a servant or a maid but a son, who is an heir to all the possessions. To acquire this privilege we should be ready to crawl to the ends of the world on our knees, yes, on our bare feet.

Sixth Sermon on John 1

Friday - Clement of Rome

With prayers and supplications, let us earnestly entreat the Creator of the universe to preserve whole and entire the designated number of His elect throughout the entire world, for the sake of His beloved servant, Jesus Christ, our Lord. Through Him we have been called from darkness to light, from ignorance to the knowledge of the glory of His Name.

Thus, we are able to hope in Your Name, from which every creature has its origin.

You have opened the eyes of our heart, so that we may know You, who alone are the Most High in the heights of heaven, the Holy One among the holy.

You confound the arrogance of the haughty; bring to nothing the schemes of the nations; raise up the lowly and humble the proud; enrich and impoverish; take life away and bestow it.

You are the sole benefactor of the human mind and the God of all flesh.

You sound the deepest recesses and survey the actions of human beings.

You are the helper of all who are in danger and the savior of the hopeless.

You are the creator and the bishop of all spirits. You multiply the nations of the earth and from among them You have chosen, through Jesus Christ Your beloved servant, those who love You. Through this same Lord You have instructed, sanctified and honored us.

We beseech You then, Master, to be our helper and our protector. Save all of us who are in tribulation, uplift all who have fallen, be near to those in need; heal the sick, lead back those who have wandered far from Your flock; feed the hungry, liberate those who have been taken captive from out of our midst. Strengthen the weak, confirm the cowardly. Let all nations know that You are the only God, that Jesus Christ is Your servant, and that "we are Your people and the sheep of Your pasture."

Epistle to the Romans

Saturday - Origen of Alexandria

It is written in the Gospel that a woman was bowed over and could not in any way lift herself up. And when Jesus saw her and perceived why she was bowed over, He said, "ought not this woman, being a daughter of Abraham, whom Satan has bound - think of it - for eighteen years, be loosed from this bond on the Sabbath?" And how many others are still bowed down and bound by Satan, who hinders them from looking up at all? And he would have us to look down too! And no one can raise them up, except the Word that came by Jesus Christ, and that which came before, inspired the prophets. Jesus came to release those who were under the dominion of the devil.

Against Celsus, Book 8

Collect

Lord, we implore You, grant Your people grace to withstand the temptations of the devil and with pure hearts and minds to follow You, the only God; through Jesus Christ, Your Son, our Lord, who lives and reigns with You and the Holy Spirit, one God, now and forever. *Gelasian Sacramentary*

AT LAUDS

Psalmody

Sunday: 3, C8, 51	Wednesday: 8, C11, 20	Friday: 146, C13, 5
Monday: 118a, C9, 118b	Thursday: 18a, C12, 18b	Saturday: 149, C14, 150
Tuesday: 1, C10, 2		

Lesson

Sunday: Ecclesiastes 1:1-2:17	Wednesday: Ecclesiastes 10:1-11:10	Friday: Song of Solomon 4:1-16
Monday: Ecclesiastes 4:1-5:20	Thursday: Song of Solomon 1:1-2:7	Saturday: Song of Solomon 6:4-7:9
Tuesday: Ecclesiastes 7:15-8:15		

Collect

Almighty and Everlasting God, who resists the proud and gives grace to the humble; grant, we pray You, that we may not exalt ourselves and provoke Your indignation, but bow down and receive the gifts of Your mercy; through Jesus Christ, Your Son, our Lord, who lives and reigns with You and the Holy Spirit, one God, now and forever.

Leonine Sacramentary

AT TERCE, SEXT AND NONE

Chapter

Sunday, Monday and Tuesday: Ephesians 4:1-6
Wednesday and Thursday: Nehemiah 8:1-10 or Amos 9:13-15
Friday: Hosea 14:1-9
Saturday: Hebrews 9:2-12

AT VESPERS

Psalmody

Sunday: 136b, 137, 138   Wednesday: 9, 10, 11   Friday: 17, 147a, 147b
Monday: 140, 141, 142   Thursday: 12, 13, 14, 16   Saturday: 19, 54, 77
Tuesday: 144, 145, 7

Lesson

Sunday: Ecclesiastes 2:18-3:22   Wednesday: Ecclesiastes 12:1-14   Friday: Song of Solomon 5:1-6:3
Monday: Ecclesiastes 6:1-7:14   Thursday: Song of Solomon 2:8-3:11   Saturday: Song of Solomon 7:10-8:14
Tuesday: Ecclesiastes 8:16-9:18

Collect

Lord God, heavenly Father: We implore You so to guide and direct us by Your Holy Spirit, that we may not exalt ourselves, but humbly fear You, with our whole hearts hear and keep Your word, and hallow the Lord's day, that we also may be hallowed by Your word; help us, first, to place our hope and confidence in Your Son, Jesus Christ, who alone is our righteousness and Redeemer, and, then, so to amend and better our lives in accordance with Your word, that we may avoid all offenses and finally obtain eternal salvation, through Your grace in Christ, who lives and reigns with You and the Holy Spirit, one God, now and forever. *Veit Dietrich*

THE EIGHTEENTH WEEK
AFTER TRINITY

AT MATINS

Hymn - *Herzlich lieb hab' ich dich, o Herr*

1. Lord, Thee I love with all my heart; I pray Thee ne'er from me de- part, With ten-der mer - cy cheer me. Earth has no plea-sure I would share, Yea, heav'n it-self were void and bare If Thou, Lord wert not near me. And should my heart for sor-row break, My trust in Thee no one could shake. Thou art the Por - tion I have sought; Thy pre-cious blood my soul has bought. Lord Je - sus Christ, My God and Lord, my God and Lord, For-sake me not! I trust Thy Word.

2. Yea, Lord, 'twas Thy rich bounty gave
My body, soul, and all I have
In this poor life of labor.
Lord, grant that I in every place
May glorify Thy lavish grace
And serve and help my neighbor.
Let no false doctrine me beguile
And Satan not my soul defile.
Give strength and patience unto me
To bear my cross and follow Thee.
Lord Jesus Christ,
My God and Lord, my God and Lord,
In death Thy comfort still afford.

3. Lord, let at last Thine angels come,
To Abram's bosom bear me home,
That I may die unfearing;
And in its narrow chamber keep
My body safe in peaceful sleep
Until Thy reappearing.
And then from death awaken me
That these mine eyes with joy may see,
O Son of God, Thy glorious face,
My Savior and my Fount of grace,
Lord Jesus Christ,
My prayer attend, my prayer attend,
And I will praise Thee without end.

Martin Schalling, c.1567

Psalmody

Sunday: 42, 44, 45	Wednesday: 53, 55, 56	Friday: 61, 62, 66
Monday: 46, 47, 48	Thursday: 58, 59, 60	Saturday: 68a, 68b, 69a
Tuesday: 49, 50, 52		

Lesson

Sunday, Monday and Tuesday: Matthew 23:34-36

Monday: Luke 20:41-47 or Mark 12:35-37
Tuesday: John 5:30-47

Wednesday and Thursday: Luke 13:1-5
Friday and Saturday: Matthew 17:22-27

Homily

Sunday - Hugh of St. Victor

Man's heart, which had been kept secure by divine love, and one by loving One, afterward began to run here and there after earthly desires. For the mind which knows not to love its true good is never stable and never rests. Hence restlessness, and endless labor, and angst, until the man turns and clings to Him. The sick heart wavers and quakes. The cause of its disease is love of the world; the remedy, the love of God.

God dwells in the human heart in two ways: through knowledge and through love. Yet the dwelling is one, since every one who knows Him loves, and no one can love without knowing. Knowledge through cognizance of the faith builds the structure; love through virtue paints the building with color. *On the Morale of Noah's Ark*

Monday - Augustine of Hippo

In sacred scripture we find that David, King of Israel was pursued by King Saul. Many of you are familiar with the story, because you have had the scriptures in your hands, or have listened to them. David was persecuted by Saul. But David was very gentle, and Saul very ferocious, David meek and Saul jealous, the one patient and the other cruel, the one kind and the other ungrateful. David treated Saul with such leniency that when he had him in his power he did not lay a hand on him, did not harm him at all. The Lord God gave David an opportunity to kill Saul if he chose. But he chose to spare him. Yet Saul was not even by such kindness convinced to give up his persecution. So we see that in those days when Saul was persecuting David, there was a king already repudiated pursuing one who was destined to be king in the future, and that David fled from Saul into a cave.

What does this have to do with Christ…? In our Lord's passion the title "King of the Jews" was inscribed, a title calculated to rebuke the arrogance of those who dared lay hands on the king. In them Saul was present, and in Christ, David. As the apostolic gospel testifies, and as we know, as we confess, Christ was from David's line according to the flesh (Rom 1:3), but only according to the flesh, for in his divinity he is far above David, above heaven and earth, above all things visible and invisible; for, "All things were made through Him, and without Him nothing was made that was made." Yet when he came to us he deigned to become man from the lineage of David, for the Virgin Mary, who bore Christ, was of David's line, and so Christ was born into David's tribe.

So then, a title was inscribed: "King of the Jews." As we have said, Saul represented the Jewish people, as David stood for Christ. And there it was, the title, King of the Jews. The Jews were incensed at it, for they were ashamed to acknowledge as their king someone they had the power to crucify. They did not foresee that the cross to which they nailed him would one day adorn the brows of kings.

Explanation of Psalm 56

Tuesday - Johann von Staupitz

Since he has Christ the Christian lacks neither grace nor instruction. He has, then, everything necessary for salvation. For truly "He who did not spare His own Son, but delivered Him up for us all, how shall He not with Him also freely give us all things?"

The Christian has God for him. Who can be against him? There is no prosecutor any more. It is God Himself who justifies. There is no room for a judge to condemn, because the Christian has Christ to intercede for him. Therefore, he has unwavering love and a living hope. Although it is not by his own investigation that a man figures out whether "he is subject to the hate or love of God," he is able through the unfailing signs given for this purpose to have a sure hope and to cast off despair…

Through baptism hope overcomes tribulation… Through Holy Communion hope stills the hunger for eternal food. Through true Absolution hope reclothes the nakedness that results when righteousness is lacking…

Eternal Predestination and Its Execution in Time

Wednesday - Martin Luther

We must learn to distinguish well between Christ's rebukes and His threats, and know where to apply His words. For there are two classes of people on earth. Some are wicked and unruly; they pay no heed to God's Word and live as they see fit—smug, unashamed, and without fear. These must feel struck when He threatens: "Those eighteen on whom the tower in Siloam fell and killed them, do you think that they were worse sinners than all other men who dwelt in Jerusalem? I tell you, no; but unless you repent you will all likewise perish." The curse is aimed at the people to whom it is addressed and at no others, namely, at the obstinate, proud, and insolent characters who care nothing for Christ and His Word. These constitute a large multitude today, the great majority in all walks of life in the world. They go their way, let Christ preach to them as He pleases, and do what they want to do. Here one must unhesitatingly chide and threaten, and read texts such as the one containing Christ's pronouncement on the Day of Judgment: "Depart from Me, you cursed, into the everlasting fire."

The other small group addressed here by Christ strives to lead a pious, Christian life, has Baptism and Christ's Word, conducts itself to the best of its ability in such a way that it does not despise the Gospel, and, unlike the group just mentioned, abstains from greed, robbery, theft, lies, deceit, and wantonness. These are the ones whom the devil attacks as an enemy does, with all sorts of distress and misfortune, to frighten, sadden, and discourage them. Thus both groups are in trouble. Those who are fainthearted and timid to begin with the devil intimidates without any reason. This is what he did to the apostles after the Lords death, when he drove them to seek cover and made them afraid to appear in the open. But the others, the insolent and smug whom he should frighten and torment, he lets go their way; he flatters them and strengthens them in their wickedness. Thus the devil always plays a role directly opposed to that of Christ.

Therefore it is necessary to differentiate among people and to judge them as they are. Take, for example, a man who loves the Gospel and longs to believe and to live properly. He must learn to resist the devil, who frightens and saddens him, and to say: "You lie, you wicked devil, even though you appear in the guise of Christ my Lord and employ His words. I am baptized in His name, and I believe the Gospel. By the grace of God I am not one of the wicked and profligate who trample the Gospel underfoot and deliberately live contrary to it; but I act and I suffer in accord with it as well as I can. Would to God I could do more! Therefore such menacing and terrifying statements do not pertain to me. I must not and will not listen to them now. I will cling to the words Christ addresses to the poor, wretched little group which suffers persecution, misfortune, distress, and anxiety."

Sermon on John 14

Thursday - John Chrysostom

In the case of the Ninevites, remember, He strung the bow, unsheathed the sword, prepared the arrows, but did not attack. Doesn't it seem to you that the prophet's words are bow and arrow and sharpened sword when he says, "Yet forty days, and Nineveh shall be overthrown?"But he did not fire the arrow; it wasn't prepared for firing, after all, but for putting back in the quiver. You see, God doesn't act like soldiers who are armed for the purpose of meting out punishment. Instead, his goal is to bring us to our senses through fear and to stay the hand of retribution.

Don't be alarmed, therefore. The fear created by such words is an indication of deep lovingkindness. The harsher his words, the more these sayings come from great gentleness. For fathers, too, when they do not wish to punish their children, put on a show of anger. In a similar way God Himself, not wishing to punish, increases fear through His words. He says He is also preparing hell so as not to cast us into hell. This is also certainly the reason why many statements about retribution occur in the Gospels, more even than those about the kingdom. In the case of less perceptive people, you see, the promise of good things is not so conducive to virtue as is the fear of painful things, and less of a discouragement from evil. This is why he is given to dwelling on the latter and constantly cites it. So let us not get depressed by harsh words; they have much to offer us, after all. Instead, let us consider His longsuffering and righteous judgement and not give up hope of salvation - He is long-suffering, remember - and let us not lose heart - He is righteous, remember. Here below He gives evidence of great long-suffering, whereas there those who have not benefited from it He hands over to the experience of punishment.

Commentary on Psalm 7

Friday - Jerome of Jerusalem

Our Lord was the son of a king both according to the flesh and according to the Spirit, begotten both from the stock of David and from the Word of the Almighty Father. Therefore as the son of a king He did not owe tax, but as one who had assumed the humility of the flesh He had to fulfill all justice. We unfortunates, who are enrolled under Christ's name and do nothing worthy of such great majesty, for us He both underwent the cross and paid our tax. But we do not pay Him tribute in return for His honor and like the sons of a king we are immune from taxes.

Commentary on Matthew

Saturday - Origen of Alexandria

There are certain kings of the earth, and the sons of these kings do not pay toll or tribute. And there are others, who are not their sons but strangers from whom the kings of the earth receive tax or tribute. And among the kings of the earth, their sons are free as among fathers. But those who are strangers to them, while they are free in relation to things beyond the earth, are like slaves in respect to the kings who rule over them and keep them in bondage; as the Egyptians lorded it over the children of Israel, and greatly afflicted them and held them in violent bondage. It was for the sake of those who were in a bondage, like that of the Hebrews, that the Son of God took upon Himself the form of a slave, yet without doing work that was base or servile. As one having the form of that slave He pays tax and tribute no different from what His disciple paid. The same shekel sufficed, yes, the one coin which was paid for Jesus and His disciple. This coin, however, was not from the house of Jesus, but from the sea, and in the mouth of a fish of the sea...

Let him, then, who has the things of Caesar render them to Caesar, so that afterwards he may be able to render to God the things of God. But Jesus, who was "the image of the invisible God," didn't bear the image of Caesar, for "the ruler of this world has nothing in Him," so He takes the image of Caesar from its own place, from the sea, so that He might give it to the kings of the earth for Himself and His disciple, and so that those who receive the half-shekel might not imagine that Jesus was in their debt or in debt to the kings of the earth. He paid the debt, not having taken it up, nor having possessed it, nor having acquired it, nor at any time having made it His own possession, so that the image of Caesar might never be along with the image of the invisible God.

Commentary on Matthew

Collect

O God, forasmuch as without You we are not able to please You, mercifully grant that Your Holy Spirit may in all things direct and rule our hearts; through Jesus Christ, Your Son, our Lord, who lives and reigns with You and the Holy Spirit, one God, now and forever.

Gelasian Sacramentary

AT LAUDS

Psalmody

Sunday: 67, C1, 5	Wednesday: 64, C4, 65	Friday: 76, C5, 92
Monday: 63, C2, 36	Thursday: 88, C6, 90	Saturday: 143, C7, 148
Tuesday: 43, C3, 57		

Lesson

Sunday: Job 1:1-2:13	Wednesday: Job 13:1-14:22	Friday: Job 20:1-29
Monday: Job 4:1-5:27	Thursday: Job 16:1-17:16	Saturday: Job 22:1-30
Tuesday: Job 8:1-10:22		

Collect

Be gracious to hear our prayers, O merciful God, and guard Your people with loving protection; that we who confess Your Only-begotten Son as God born in our bodily flesh, may never be corrupted by the deceits of the devil; through the same Jesus Christ, Your Son, our Lord, who lives and reigns with You and the Holy Spirit, one God, now and forever.

Ambrosian Missal

AT TERCE, SEXT AND NONE

Chapter

Sunday, Monday and Tuesday: I Corinthians 1:4-9
Wednesday and Thursday: I Timothy 1:3-14
Friday and Saturday: I John 5:1-4a

AT VESPERS

Psalmody

Sunday: 110, 111, 112, 113   Wednesday: 123, 124, 125   Friday: 129, 130, 131, 132
Monday: 114, 115, 116, 117   Thursday: 126, 127, 128   Saturday: 133, 135, 136a
Tuesday: 120, 121, 122

Lesson

Sunday: Job 3:1-26   Wednesday: Job 15:1-35   Friday: Job 21:1-34
Monday: Job 6:1-7:21   Thursday: Job 18:1-19:29   Saturday: Job 23:1-24:25
Tuesday: Job 11:1-12:25

Collect

Lord God, heavenly Father: we are poor, miserable sinners; we know Your will, but cannot fulfill it because of the weakness of our flesh and blood, and because our enemy, the devil, will not leave us in peace. Therefore we implore You, shed Your Holy Spirit in our hearts, that, in steadfast faith, we may cling to Your Son Jesus Christ, find comfort in His passion and death, believe the forgiveness of sin through Him, and in willing obedience to Your will lead holy lives on earth, until by Your grace, through a blessed death, we depart from this world of sorrow, and obtain eternal life, through Jesus Christ, Your Son, our Lord, who lives and reigns with You and the Holy Spirit, one God, now and forever. *Veit Dietrich*

THE NINETEENTH WEEK
AFTER TRINITY

AT MATINS

Hymn - *Nun last uns gehn und tretan*

1. Now let us come be - fore Him, With song and prayer a - dore Him,

Who to our life hath giv - en All need-ed strength from heav- en.

2. The stream of years is flowing,
   And we are onward going,
   From old to new surviving
   And by His mercy thriving.

3. In woe we often languish
   And pass through times of anguish
   Of wars and trepidation
   Alarming every nation.

4. As mothers watch are keeping
   O'er children who are sleeping,
   Their fear and grief assuaging
   When angry storms are waging.

5. So God His own is shielding
   And help to them is yielding.
   When need and woe distress them,
   His loving arms caress them

6. O Thou Who dost not slumber,
   Remove what would encumber
   Our work, which prospers never
   Unless Thou bless it ever

7. Our song to Thee ascendeth,
   Who every day defendeth
   Us, and whose arm averteth
   The pain our hearts that hurteth.

8. O God of mercy, hear us;
   Our Father, be Thou near us;
   Mid crosses and in sadness
   Be Thou our Fount of gladness.

9. To all who bow before Thee
   And for Thy grace implore Thee,
   Oh, grant Thy benediction
   And patience in affliction.

10. Oh, close the gates of sorrow,
    And by a glorious morrow
    Of peace may places saddened
    By bloodshed dire be gladdened.

11. With richest blessings crown us,
    In all our days, Lord own us;
    Give grace, who grace bestowest,
    To all, e'en to the lowest.

12. Be Thou a Helper speedy
    To all the poor and needy,
    To all forlorn a Father;
    Thine erring children gather.

13. Be with the sick and ailing,
    Their Comforter unfailing;
    Dispelling grief and sadness,
    Oh, give them joy and gladness!

14. Above all else, Lord, send us
    Thy Spirit to attend us,
    Within our hearts abiding,
    To Heav'n our footsteps guiding.

15. All this Thy hand bestoweth,
    Thou Life, whence our life floweth.
    To all Thy Name confessing
    Grant, Lord, Thy daily blessing!

Paul Gerhardt, 1653

Psalmody

Sunday: 69b, 70, 71   Wednesday: 75, 79, 80   Friday: 84, 86, 87, 93
Monday: 72, 73, 74   Thursday: 81, 82, 83   Saturday: 85, 89a, 89b
Tuesday: 78a, 78b, 78c

Lesson

Sunday, Monday and Tuesday: Matthew 9:1-8

Monday: Mark 2:1-12
Tuesday: Matthew 7:24-29 or Luke 6:46-49

Wednesday and Thursday: Luke 5:33-39
Friday and Saturday: Matthew 16:21-23

Saturday: Mark 8:27-33

Homily

Sunday - Peter Chrysologus

Today's lesson makes clear to us that in His human actions Christ performed divine mysteries, and that in His visible works He had in mind invisible ends. Entering into a boat, it says, He passed over the water and came into His own city. Isn't this He who thrusting aside the waves of the sea laid bare its depths that the people of Israel might pass through the midst of the terrifying waves on dry ground as between mountains? Isn't this He who supported the feet of Peter on the crests of the waves, so that his watery path upon the sea stayed firm beneath his feet? And why does He deny Himself the service of the sea, and make the brief crossing of the lake in a hired boat? Entering into a boat, it says, he passed over the water.

And why should we wonder, brothers? Christ came to take upon Himself our infirmities, and to confer upon us His powers; to seek what is human, to give what is divine; to receive injuries, and return them with honors; to suffer affliction, and bring healing to others: for the physician who does not suffer infirmities does not know how to cure infirmities; and he who is not weak with the weak cannot bring health to the weak. Had He remained within His own powers, Christ would have had nothing in common with men; and unless He conformed to the way of life of our body, His taking of flesh would have been in vain. So He shared our necessities, that by these human needs He might be proven to be a true man.

Entering into a boat, it says. Christ enters the ship of His Church so that He may at all times calm the waves of the world; that He may transport those who believe in Him by a tranquil voyage to their heavenly country; and make those He had made sharers of His humanity, fellow citizens of His own city. It is not Christ therefore Who needs the ship, but the ship that needs Christ; for without its Heavenly pilot the ship of the Church would be unable to pass through the sea of the world, amid so many great hazards, and reach the heavenly harbor.   *Sermon 50*

Monday - Martin Luther

These two words, "grace" and "peace," contain a summary of all of Christianity. Grace contains the forgiveness of sins, a joyful peace, and a quiet conscience. But peace is impossible unless sin has first been forgiven, for the Law accuses and terrifies the conscience on account of sin. And the sin that the conscience feels cannot be removed by pilgrimages, vigils, labors, efforts, vows, or any other works; in fact, sin is increased by works. The more we work and sweat to extricate ourselves from sin, the worse off we are. For there is no way to remove sin except by grace. This deserves careful notice. For the words are easy; but in temptation it is the hardest thing possible to be surely persuaded in our hearts that we have the forgiveness of sins and peace with God by grace alone, entirely apart from any other means in heaven or on earth.

Because the world does not understand this doctrine, it neither can nor will tolerate it. It brags about free will, about our powers, about our works—all these as means by which to earn and attain grace and peace, that is, the forgiveness of sins and a joyful conscience. But the conscience cannot be quiet and joyful unless it has peace through this grace, that is, through the forgiveness of sins promised in Christ. Many have worked hard, inventing various religious orders and disciplines, to find peace and a quiet conscience; but instead they have plunged even more deeply into even greater misery, for such tactics are merely ways of multiplying doubt and despair. Therefore your bones and mine will know no rest until we hear the Word of grace and cling to it firmly and faithfully.

Lectures on Galatians

Tuesday - Bede the Venerable

Now this man building a house is the Mediator between God and men, the man Christ Jesus, who wanted to build and consecrate a lovely and holy house for Himself, namely the Church, in which to dwell forever. "He dug deep and laid the foundation on the rock," for He strove to completely root out whatever base desires He found in the hearts of His faithful, so that when the traces of earlier habits and unnecessary thoughts had been cast out, He could have a firm and unshakable dwelling place in them. He Himself is the rock upon which He laid the foundation for this sort of house. Just as in building a house nothing is more important than the rock on which the foundation is laid, so the holy Church has its rock, namely Christ, hidden in the depths of her heart. She puts nothing ahead of her faith and love of Him, because He did not hesitate to suffer even death for her.

Homily for the Dedication of a Church

Wednesday - Jerome of Jerusalem

Our Lord gave two examples: that of the garment and that of the old and new wineskins. We should understand the old as referring to the scribes and Pharisees. The cloth of the new garment and the new wine should be understood as the Gospel teachings which the Jews can't stand, lest a greater tear be made. Even the Galatians wanted to do something similar, when they wanted to mix the teachings of the Law with the Gospel and "put new wine into old wineskins." But the apostle says to them: "O foolish Galatians! Who has bewitched you that you should not obey the truth?" Therefore the words of the Gospel ought to be poured by the apostles, not by the scribes and Pharisees, who were corrupted by the traditions of the elders and weren't able to keep the pureness of the teachings of Christ.

Commentary on Matthew

Thursday - Martin Luther

Putting on Christ is understood in two ways: according to the Law and according to the Gospel. According to the Law, "Put on the Lord Jesus Christ; that is: Imitate the example and the virtues of Christ. Do and suffer what He did and suffered." So also 1 Peter 2:21: "Christ suffered for us, leaving us an example, that we should follow in His steps." In Christ we see the height of patience, gentleness, and love, and an admirable moderation in all things. We ought to put on this adornment of Christ, that is, imitate these virtues of His. In this sense we can imitate other saints as well.

But to put on Christ according to the Gospel is a matter, not of imitation but of a new birth and a new creation, namely, that I put on Christ Himself, that is, His innocence, righteousness, wisdom, power, salvation, life, and Spirit. We were dressed in the leather garment of Adam, which is a deadly garment and the clothing of sin. That is, we were all subjected and sold into the slavery of sin; horrible blindness, ignorance, and a contempt and hatred of God are present in us.

Besides, we are filled with evil lust, uncleanness, and greed. By propagation from Adam we have acquired this garment, that is, this corrupt and sinful nature, which Paul calls "the old man." He must be put off with all his activities, so that from sons of Adam we may be changed into sons of God. This does not happen by a change of clothing or by any laws or works; it happens by the rebirth and renewal that takes place in Baptism, as Paul says: "As many of you as were baptized have put on Christ." Titus 3:5: "He saved us, in virtue of His own mercy, by the washing of regeneration." For in those who have been baptized a new light and flame arise; new and devout emotions come into being, such as fear and trust in God and hope; and a new will emerges. This is what it means to put on Christ properly, truly, and according to the Gospel.

In Baptism, then, it is not the garment of the righteousness of the Law or of our own works that is given; but Christ becomes our garment. But He is not the Law, not a lawgiver, not a work; He is the divine and inestimable gift that the Father has given to us to be our Justifier, Lifegiver, and Redeemer. To put on Christ according to the Gospel, therefore, is to put on, not the Law or works but an inestimable gift, namely, the forgiveness of sins, righteousness, peace, comfort, joy in the Holy Spirit, salvation, life, and Christ Himself.

Lectures on Galatians

Friday - Rufinus of Aquileia

His cross was a triumph! It was a trophy of distinction! A triumph, however, is the token of having defeated an enemy. At His coming, then, Christ simultaneously brought three kingdoms under subjection. The apostle shows this with the words: "For at the name of Jesus every knee should bow, of those in heaven, and of those on earth, and of those under the earth." And by His death He vanquished all three. With this in mind, a manner of death was devised which symbolized this mystery. He was to be hoisted up in the air, thereby conquering the powers of the air and gaining victory over the heavenly rulers on high. His outstretched hands, according to the inspired prophet, He held out all day long to the people who were on the earth, testifying to the unbelievers and welcoming believers; while with the part of the cross buried in the earth He brought the underworld into subjection to Himself.

Commentary on the Apostles' Creed

Saturday - Augustine of Hippo

This Mediator between God and mankind, the man Christ Jesus, appeared between mortal sinners and the immortal and just God; mortal like man, just like God. Now the wage of justice is life and peace. Therefore by justice, in which He is joined with God, He cancelled out death for justified sinners, with whom He willed to have death in common. He was pointed out to saints of old that they might be saved through faith in His future passion, just as we are saved through faith in that passion now accomplished. Insofar as He was a man He is the Mediator. Insofar as He is the Word, He is not a mediator, for he is God's equal, God with God, and at the same time one God.

How you loved us, O good Father, who spared not even your only Son, but handed him over for us wicked men! How you loved us, for whose sake He who thought it no robbery to be Your equal was made subject to death, even to the death of the cross! He alone was free among the dead, for He had power to lay down his life and power to take it up again. For our sake He stood before You as both victor and victim, and victor because victim; for us He stood before you as priest and sacrifice, and priest because sacrifice, instead of slaves, making us Your sons, born of You to serve You. With good reason my hope is strong in Him, for You will heal all my infirmities through Him, who sits at Your right hand and intercedes for us; otherwise I would despair. Many and great are those infirmities, many and great; but greater is Your medicine. We might have despaired, thinking your Word remote from any conjunction with men, had He not become flesh and dwelt among us.

Confessions

Collect

O almighty and most merciful God, of Your bountiful goodness keep us, we implore You, from all things that may hurt us, that we, being ready, both in body and soul, may cheerfully accomplish those things that You would have done; through Jesus Christ, Your Son, our Lord, who lives and reigns with You and the Holy Spirit, one God, now and forever. *Gelasian Sacramentary*

AT LAUDS

Psalmody

Sunday: 3, C8, 51	Wednesday: 8, C11, 20	Friday: 146, C13, 5
Monday: 118a, C9, 118b	Thursday: 18a, C12, 18b	Saturday: 149, C14, 150
Tuesday: 1, C10, 2		

Lesson

Sunday: Job 25:1-26:14	Wednesday: Job 35:1-16	Friday: Job 39:1-30
Monday: Job 29:1-30:19	Thursday: Job 37:1-24	Saturday: Job 40:15-41:34
Tuesday: Job 32:1-33:33		

Collect

Almighty and everlasting God, slow to chide and swift to bless, whose pity is never-ending and whose mercy is infinite, attend to our supplications and incline Your merciful ears to our prayers, that, being strengthened by Your grace, we may be able to perform Your commands, through Jesus Christ, Your Son, our Lord, who lives and reigns with You and the Holy Spirit, one God, now and forever.

Ambrosian Manual

AT TERCE, SEXT AND NONE

Chapter

Sunday, Monday and Tuesday: Ephesians 4:22-28
Wednesday and Thursday: II Thessalonians 2:15-3:5
Friday and Saturday: I John 5:18-20

AT VESPERS

Psalmody

Sunday: 136b, 137, 138	Wednesday: 9, 10, 11	Friday: 17, 147a, 147b
Monday: 140, 141, 142	Thursday: 12, 13, 14, 16	Saturday: 19, 54, 77
Tuesday: 144, 145, 7		

Lesson

Collect

O mighty and everlasting God, who by Your Son Jesus Christ mercifully helped the palsied man both in body and soul: We implore You, for the sake of Your great mercy: Be gracious also to us; forgive us all our sins, and so govern us by Your Holy Spirit, that we may not ourselves be the cause of sickness and other afflictions; keep us in Your fear, and strengthen us by Your grace that we may escape temporal and eternal wrath and punishment, through Your Son, Jesus Christ, our Lord, who lives and reigns with the Father and the Holy Spirit, one God, now and forever.

Veit Dietrich

THE TWENTIETH WEEK
AFTER TRINITY

AT MATINS

Hymn - *Ach, Gott vom Himmel*

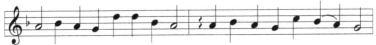

1. O, Lord look down from heav'n be-hold, And let Thy pi - ty wa - ken.

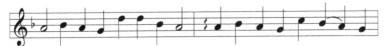

How few are we with-in Thy fold, Thy saints by men for - sak - en!

True faith seems quenched on ev - 'ry hand, Men suf - fer not

Thy Word to stand; Dark times have us o'er - tak - en.

2. With fraud which they themselves invent
Thy truth they have confounded;
Their hearts are not with one consent
On Thy pure doctrine grounded.
While they parade with outward show,
They lead the people to and fro,
In error's maze astounded.

3. May God root out all heresy
And of false teachers rid us
Who proudly say: "Now, where is he
That shall our speech forbid us?
By right or might we shall prevail;
What we determine cannot fail;
We own no lord and master."

4. Therefore saith God, "I must arise,
The poor My help are needing;
To Me ascend My people's cries,
And I have heard their pleading.
For them My saving Word shall fight
And fearlessly and sharply smite,
The poor with might defending."

5. As silver tried by fire is pure
From all adulteration,
So through God's Word shall men endure
Each trial and temptation.
Its light beams brighter through the cross,
And, purified from human dross,
It shines through every nation.

6. Thy truth defend, O God, and stay
This evil generation;
And from the error of their way
Keep Thine own congregation.
The wicked everywhere abound
And would Thy little flock confound;
But Thou art our Salvation.

Martin Luther, 1524

Psalmody

Lesson

Sunday, Monday and Tuesday: Matthew 22:1-14

Tuesday: Matthew 13:44-53

Wednesday and Thursday: Luke 14:12-15

Friday and Saturday: Matthew 13:31-35

Homily

Sunday - Hilary of Poitiers

We believe that the Word became flesh and that we receive His flesh in the Lord's Supper. How then can we not believe that He really dwells within us? When He became man He actually clothed Himself in our flesh, uniting it to Himself forever. In the sacrament of His body, He actually gives us His own flesh, which He has united to His divinity. This is why we are all one, because the Father is in Christ, and Christ is in us. He is in us through His flesh and we are in Him. With Him we form a unity which is in God. The manner of our indwelling in Him through the sacrament of His body and blood is evident from the Lord's own words: "the world will see Me no more, but you will see Me. Because I live, you will live also, for I am in My Father, and you in Me, and I in you." Were it merely a question of unity of will, why would He have given us this explanation of the steps by which it is achieved? He is in the Father by reason of His divine nature; we are in Him by reason of His human birth, and He is in us through the mystery of the sacraments. Surely this is what He wished us to believe; this is how He wanted us to understand the perfect unity that is achieved through our Mediator, who lives in the Father while we live in Him, and who, while living in the Father, lives also in us. This is how we attain to unity with the Father. Christ is in very truth in the Father by his eternal generation; we are in very truth in Christ, and He likewise is in us.

Christ Himself bore witness to the reality of this unity when He said: "He who eats My flesh and drinks My blood abides in Me, and I in him." No one will be in Christ unless Christ Himself has been in him; Christ will take to Himself only the flesh of those who have received His flesh. He had already explained the mystery of this perfect unity when He said: "As the living Father sent Me, and I live because of the Father, so he who feeds on Me will live because of Me." We draw life from His flesh just as He draws life from the Father... Christ is the well-spring of our life. Since we who are in the flesh have Christ dwelling in us through His flesh, we shall draw life from Him in the same way as he draws life from the Father.   *On the Trinity*

Monday - Leo I of Rome

The blessed Paul the apostle says, "For you have died, and your life is hidden with Christ in God. But, when Christ your life appears, then you also will appear with Him in glory." What is the participation with Christ for us except that we cease to be what we were? Or what is the likeness to the resurrection except the putting off of the old self? Consequently, those who understand the mystery of their restoration ought to divest themselves of the faults of the flesh and cast away all the filth of sin, so that when they go into the marriage feast they will shine in the garment of virtue.

Although the kindness of the bridegroom invites everyone to share the royal banquet, all who are called must be eager to prove themselves worthy of the honor of the sacred meal. Certain ones abuse the patience of God, and, though they are not undisturbed in conscience, they become secure because of the long impunity; although the punishment is delayed for this reason, that correction might be able to have its time. Let none, thinking they have not received what they deserve, delay to embrace the mercy of our God "by which He does not wish the death of sinners but only that they be converted and live."

Sermon 50

Tuesday - Gregory I of Rome

The kingdom of heaven is said to be like a net let down into the sea and gathering all kinds of fish. When full it is brought to shore, and the good fish are sorted into baskets, but the bad ones are thrown away. Our holy Church is compared to a net because it has been entrusted to fishermen and because all people are drawn up in it from the turbulent waters of the present age to the eternal kingdom, lest we drown in the depths of eternal death. This net gathers all kinds of fish because it calls to forgiveness of sins everyone, wise and foolish, free and slave, rich and poor, brave and weak. Hence the psalmist tells God: "To You all flesh will come." This net will be completely filled when it enfolds the entire number of the human race at the end of time.

The fishermen bring it in and sit down on the shore, because just as the sea signifies this present age, so the shore signifies its end. At the end of this present age the good fish are to be sorted into baskets, and the bad ones thrown away, because then all the elect will be received into eternal dwellings, and the condemned will be led away into external darkness, since they have lost the light of the kingdom within them. Now the net of the faith holds good and bad all together, like the different kinds of fish; but on the shore is revealed to the holy Church what she has been drawing in. The fish, when they have been caught, cannot be changed; but we, who are caught while we are wicked, can become good. Let us bear this in mind as we are in the process of being caught, lest we be thrown aside on shore.

Homily 9, on Matthew 13

Wednesday - Cyril of Alexandria

The lesson which He teaches us is love toward the poor, which is a precious thing in the sight of God. Do you take pleasure in being praised when you have some friends or relatives feasting with you? I'll tell you of something better. Angels will praise your bounty, and the rational powers above, and holy men too. And He who transcends all, who loves mercy and is kind, will accept it. Lend to Him fearing nothing, and you will receive with interest whatever you gave. "He who has pity on the poor lends to the Lord." And the Lord acknowledges the loan and promises repayment... The outlay, therefore, is not unfruitful. Rather compassion on the poor will make your wealth breathe forth a sweet smell.

Homily 103 on Luke

Thursday - Irenaeus of Lyons

Christ, when about to undergo His sufferings... after He had given thanks while holding the cup, and had drunk of it, and given it to the disciples, said to them: "Drink from it, all of you. For this is My blood of the new covenant, which is shed for many for the remission of sins. But I say to you, I will not drink of this fruit of the vine from now on until that day when I drink it new with you in My Father's kingdom." So then, He Himself will renew the inheritance of the earth, and will reorganize the mystery of the glory of the sons of God; as David says, "You renew the face of the earth." He promised to drink of the fruit of the vine with His disciples, indicating both these points: the inheritance of the earth in which the new fruit of the vine is drunk, and the resurrection of His disciples in the flesh. For the new flesh which rises again is the same which also received the new cup. And He cannot by any means be understood as drinking of the fruit of the vine when sitting down with His disciples above in a super-celestial place; nor again are those who drink it without flesh, for to drink of that which flows from the vine pertains to flesh, and not spirit.

And for this reason the Lord declared, "When you give a dinner or a supper, do not ask your friends, your brothers, your relatives, nor rich neighbors, lest they also invite you back, and you be repaid. But when you give a feast, invite the poor, the maimed, the lame, the blind. And you will be blessed, because they cannot repay you; for you shall be repaid at the resurrection of the just." And again He says, "Assuredly, I say to you, there is no one who has left house or parents or brothers or wife or children, for the sake of the kingdom of God, who shall not receive many times more in this present time, and in the age to come eternal life." For what are the hundredfold rewards in this world, the hospitality given to the poor, and the feasts for which a return is given? These will come in the time of the kingdom... [Then] they will not be engaged in any earthly occupation, but will have a table at hand prepared for them by God, supplying them with all sorts of dishes.

Against All Heresies

Friday - Ambrose of Milan

The Lord Himself is the grain of mustard seed. He was without injury; but the people were unaware of Him as a grain of mustard seed of which they took no notice. He chose to be bruised... He chose to be crushed... he chose to be planted in the earth, as a seed, "which a man took and sowed in his garden." For it was in a garden that Christ was taken prisoner, and likewise buried; He sprung up in a garden, where He also rose from the dead, and became a Tree...

You also then sow Christ in your garden - for a garden is a place that is full of flowers and various fruits - in which by virtue of your labor He may grow and breathe forth the multiple sweetness of His many virtues. There where fruit is, let Christ be found. Plant ye the Lord Jesus. He is a seed when "a man takes hold of Him;" He is a tree when He rises again, a tree that gives shade to the world; He is a seed when He is buried in the earth. He is a tree when raised to heaven.

Press close to Christ, and sow faith. We follow close and sow faith when we adore Christ crucified. Paul followed close in faith when he said: "And I, brethren, when I came to you, did not come with excellence of speech or of wisdom declaring to you the testimony of God. For I determined not to know anything among you except Jesus Christ and Him crucified" (I Corinthians 2:1-2).

We sow faith when from the prophetic and apostolic writings and from the Gospel we believe in the passion of the Lord. We therefore sow faith when we, as it were, bury it in the soft and tender soil of the Lord's flesh, so that from the embrace and warmth of the sacred Body, faith spreads itself abroad.

Homily on the Grain of Mustard Seed

Saturday - Maximus of Turin

As the leaven, when it is to be mixed in a heap of dough, is broken up and crushed into little pieces, and sprinkled through the mass until it is itself lost, so that it may bind together the scattered multitude of the grains of flour by its vigor, reducing to a solid mass what was inert and powerless when it was but powder, making this unity a potent whole of what had before seemed unprofitable, so the Lord Jesus Christ, since He is the Leaven of the whole world, was broken by manifold torments, was wounded and pierced, and His sap, which is His Precious Blood, poured out for our salvation, so that mingling with Him all mankind would be made into one body, they who before His passion were prostrate and divided.

So as to a Leaven we cling to Him; we who before were but dust of the Gentiles. We, I repeat, who before lay wholly scattered and broken in pieces, have by the power of His passion been kneaded into the Body of Christ, as the blessed Apostle says: "We are members of His body, of His flesh and of His bones." We therefore who were cast away like dust among the nations, by the sprinkling of the Blood of the Lord, are joined into the Body of His Oneness.

The woman who is said to hide the leaven in three measures of meal, who is she but the Holy Church, which each day strives to hide the doctrine of Christ in our hearts? She, I repeat, is the woman who in another place is said to be grinding at the mill... For the Holy Church grinds at the mill through her Law, through the Apostles, through the Prophets, when she makes catechumens, and when she breaks down the hardness of paganism, and grinds it into little pieces, and being ground, as flour. She makes them ready to be joined together by the Blood of the Lord.

Homily 3

Collect

Grant, we implore You, merciful Lord, to Your faithful people pardon and peace, that they may be cleansed from all their sins and serve You with a quiet mind; through Jesus Christ, Your Son, our Lord, who lives and reigns with You and the Holy Spirit, one God, now and forever.

Gelasian Sacramentary

AT LAUDS

Psalmody

Sunday: 67, C1, 5	Wednesday: 64, C4, 65	Friday: 76, C5, 92
Monday: 63, C2, 36	Thursday: 88, C6, 90	Saturday: 143, C7, 148
Tuesday: 43, C3, 57		

Lesson

Sunday: Ezra 1:1-11	Wednesday: Ezra 7:11-28	Friday: Nehemiah 1:1-11
Monday: Ezra 3:8-13	Thursday: Ezra 8:36-9:15	Saturday: Nehemiah 4:1-14
Tuesday: Ezra 5:1-6:12		

Collect

Lord Jesus Christ, Your flesh is true bread and Your blood the true cup. Grant us to have an earnest desire for Your feast. Feed us and give us to drink, O Lord. Abide in us that we may remain in You. Satisfy us early with Your comfort and fill us with Your treasures, that in You we may live, be satisfied, rejoice and be blessed.

Wilhelm Löhe

AT TERCE, SEXT AND NONE

Chapter

Sunday, Monday and Tuesday: Ephesians 5:15-21
Wednesday and Thursday: II Thessalonians 3:6-13
Friday and Saturday: Romans 5:14-17

AT VESPERS

Psalmody

Sunday: 110, 111, 112, 113   Wednesday: 123, 124, 125   Friday: 129, 130, 131, 132
Monday: 114, 115, 116, 117   Thursday: 126, 127, 128   Saturday: 133, 135, 136a
Tuesday: 120, 121, 122

Lesson

Sunday: Ezra 3:1-9   Wednesday: Ezra 8:21-35   Friday: Nehemiah 2:1-20
Monday: Ezra 4:1-24   Thursday: Ezra 10:1-17   Saturday: Nehemiah 4:15-23
Tuesday: Ezra 6:13-7:10

Collect

Lord God, heavenly Father: We thank You, that of Your great mercy You have called us by Your holy word to the blessèd marriage-feast of Your Son, and through Him forgive us all our sins; but, being daily beset by temptation, offense, and danger, and being weak in ourselves and given to sin, we implore You graciously to protect us by Your Holy Spirit, that we may not fall; and if we fall and defile our wedding-garment, with which Your Son has clothed us, graciously help us again and lead us to repentance, that we fall not forever; preserve in us a constant faith in Your grace, through our Lord, Jesus Christ, who lives and reigns with You and the Holy Spirit, one true God, now and forever. Amen.   *Veit Dietrich*

THE TWENTY-FIRST WEEK
AFTER TRINITY

AT MATINS

Hymn - *Erhalt uns, Herr, bei deinem Wort*

1.   Lord, keep us stead-fast in Your Word; Curb those who by de - ceit or sword

Would wrest the king-dom from Your Son And bring to naught all He has done!

2. Lord Jesus Christ, Your power make known,
For You are Lord of lords alone;
Defend Your Holy Church that we
May sing Your praise eternally.

3. O Comforter of priceless worth,
Send peace and unity on earth;
Support us in our final strife
And lead us out of death to life.

Martin Luther, 1541

Psalmody

Sunday: 21, 22, 23
Monday: 24, 25, 26
Tuesday: 27, 28, 29

Wednesday: 30, 31, 32
Thursday: 33, 34, 35

Friday: 37a, 37b, 38
Saturday: 39, 40, 41

Lesson

Sunday, Monday and Tuesday: John 4:46-54
Tuesday: John 6:30-43
Wednesday and Thursday: Matthew 8:14-17
Friday and Saturday: Matthew 13:10-15

Homily

Sunday - Cyril of Alexandria

The nobleman believed that Jesus needed to come. But Christ does not reject our lack of understanding. Rather, as God, He helps even the stumbling. What the man then should have been admired for doing is what Jesus teaches him even when he does not end up doing it. In this way Jesus is revealed both as the teacher of the most lovely things and the giver of good things in prayer. For, in "Go your way," there is faith. In "your son lives" there is the fulfillment of his longings, granted with both a generosity and an authority befitting God.   *Commentary on John*

Monday - Augustine of Hippo

Have mercy on me, O God, have mercy, for my soul trusts in you. Christ is praying in His passion, Have mercy on me, O God. God is saying to God, Have mercy on me. He who, together

573

with the Father, has mercy on you is crying out in you, Have mercy on me. Something in Him that belongs to you is crying out, Have mercy on me, something that He took from you; for He clothed Himself in flesh to set you free. Now this same flesh is pleading, Have mercy on me, O God, have mercy; the whole man is pleading, the man who is soul and flesh, for the Word assumed our entire humanity, the Word became a complete man.

True, the evangelist expresses it by saying, The Word was made flesh, and dwelt among us, but you must not take this to mean that He had no human soul. This is far from the truth. In the language of scripture, "flesh" means "human being." So scripture says elsewhere, All flesh will see the salvation of God. This does not mean that flesh alone will see it, and the soul will have no place, does it? Again, the Lord himself, referring to mankind, says, As you have given him power over all flesh. Surely He did not mean that His power extended over flesh only, and not, much more significantly, over souls? Was it not His main reason for coming, to set souls free? So in the case of our Lord Himself, the soul was there and the flesh was there; a whole man was there. This whole man was one with the Word, and the Word was one with this man; the man and the Word together were one single man, and the Word and the man together were one God.

Let Him say, then, Have mercy on me, O God, have mercy, and let us not be frightened when we hear the voice of one who both pleads for mercy and grants it. He pleads for it precisely because He also grants it, for He became man because He is merciful. He was born not by any necessity of His condition, but to set us free from our condition of necessity. Have mercy on me, O God, have mercy on me, for my soul trusts in you. You hear your Teacher praying, so learn to pray. He prayed for this very reason, to teach us to pray, just as He suffered to teach us to suffer, and rose from the dead to teach us to hope for resurrection.   *Explanation of Psalm 56*

Tuesday - Gaudentius of Brescia

Do not consider earthly what has been made heavenly by Him who has passed into it, and has made it His body and blood. For what we explained earlier in a general way about the eating of the flesh of the lamb is specifically to be observed in tasting these same mysteries of the Lord's Passion, lest you think, as did the Jew, that this is raw flesh, and raw blood and reject it saying: "How can this man give us His flesh to eat?" Nor should you, thinking it common and earthly, cook this sacrament in the pot of a carnal heart which is by nature subject to the whims of the body. Rather, you must believe that what has been declared to you has been accomplished through the fire of the divine Spirit, that what you receive is the body of that heavenly Bread and the blood of that sacred Vine. For when He gave the consecrated bread and wine to His disciples, He said: "This is my body, this is my blood." Let us believe, I pray you, the One whom we have believed. Truth does not lie. Therefore, when He was speaking about the eating of His body and the drinking of His blood to the crowds who wondered and murmured "This is a hard saying; who can understand it?" He added, in order that through heavenly fire He might wipe away those thoughts which I have said should be avoided: "It is the Spirit who gives life; the flesh profits nothing. The words that I speak to you are spirit, and they are life."

And for that reason we are commanded to eat the head of His divinity with the feet of His Incarnation, together with the inner mysteries, so that we may believe all things just as they have been handed down, not breaking that strongest bone of all, "This is my body, this is my blood."

Tractate 2 on Exodus

Wednesday - Athanasius of Alexandria

In ancient times He often came to the saints individually, and hallowed those who rightly received Him; but He had not yet become man when they were begotten, nor had He Himself yet suffered when they suffered. But at the end of the ages He came among us from Mary to abolish sin. For it pleased the Father to send His own Son "born of a woman, born under the Law." Thus it is said that He took flesh and became man, and in that flesh He suffered for us, as Peter says, "Christ suffered for us in the flesh." He did this to show, and so that all might believe, that while He has always been God, and sanctified those to whom He came, and ordered all things according to the Father's will, afterward He became man for our sakes. "Bodily," as the Apostle says, the Godhead dwelt in the flesh. This is to say, "Being God, He had His own body, and using this as an instrument, He became man for our sakes."

Because of this the properties of the flesh are said to be His, since He was in it, so as to hunger, to thirst, to suffer, to grow weary, and the like; things of which flesh is capable. On the other hand the works proper to the Word Himself, such as to raise the dead, to restore sight to the blind, and to cure the woman with an issue of blood, He did through His own body. And the Word bore the infirmities of the flesh, as His own, for the flesh was His; and the flesh served the works of the Godhead, because the Godhead was in it, for the body was God's. *3rd Discourse Against Arius*

Thursday - Hilary of Poitiers

The Lord was stricken, taking upon Himself our sins, and suffering for us. He was beaten down to the weakness of the cross and of death, so that we might receive health through His resurrection form the dead. He himself gave witness to His stricken state when He reminded His apostles of the prophecy, "I will strike the shepherd, and the sheep of the flock shall be scattered." But the Apostle equally confirmed its meaning when he wrote, "He (the Father) did not spare his beloved Son." Indeed He did not spare His beloved Son. He handed Him over to the vinedressers when He knew that they would kill Him. He had not spared the first Adam, fashioned from the slime of the earth. After his sin He cast him out of Paradise, lest he should touch the tree of Paradise and remain in an eternity of pain. So the second Adam from heaven assumed the nature of his body, and was smitten with the same death, so that He might call that nature back to eternal life, but without an eternity of pain. So it was that they persecuted the One smitten by God, adding the suffering of persecution to the pain of His wounds. For according to the prophet He suffered on our behalf, and we have thought of Him as one afflicted by suffering. *Commentary on Psalm 68*

Friday - Anonymous

If Jesus had said, "I will speak to them in parables so that seeing they may not see," it might be thought that it isn't the fault of those Jews who did not understand, but of Christ who spoke in such a way that they did not understand. But now He says, "This is why I speak to them in parables, because seeing they do not see." You must understand therefore it is not the fault of Christ who is unwilling to speak clearly but of those who while hearing are unwilling to hear. It was not because Christ was speaking in parables that they did not see but because of their way of seeing. Therefore Christ spoke to them in parables. Look, they saw the wonders of Moses. Did they not truly see? If they did truly see, they certainly would have also feared God the worker of miracles. Look, they heard the Teacher of the law. Did they not truly hear? If they did truly hear him, they certainly would have lived according to the law and believed in Him about whom the law prophesied. They saw also wonderful things, but seeing they did not really see. If they had seen them, they would also have profited by them. It is easier for those who see to know what they saw than for those who hear to understand what they heard. How did it happen that those who heard of the wonderful revelation of God did not see and know them? Because the Jews, seeing, were accustomed not to see, and hearing, not to hear; therefore God did not give them the eyes of faith to see Christ's divine miracles or to hear his living words. *Opus Imperfectum in Matthaeum*

Saturday - Maximus of Turin

It is not that He was not in the world before, since the world was made through Him, but that then for the first time God, who is Christ, shone in the hearts of believers by signs and wonders, and radiant faith came into people's darkened consciences. So although God is everywhere and maintains all things, yet since He was not seen before, He is said not to have appeared. But He appeared not so much for the eyes of human beings as for their salvation, for even though He was first seen by fleshly eyes when He was born of the virgin, still He did not appear because the eye of faith did not as yet recognize His power. Hence it is said to the Jews by the prophet: Seeing you will see and will not see; that is, the Savior whom they discerned with their fleshly eyes they did not see in a spiritual light. For after He manifested His divinity with miracles, appearing as it were freshly and unexpectedly to human minds, He filled the eyes of the heart, so to speak, so that the intellect might recognize what sight did not. Thus it happens that by faith we contemplate Christ, whom we have never seen, but the Jews, who gazed upon Him with their eyes and touched Him with their hands, today do not see Him.

Homily 101, 2nd Sermon for Epiphany

Collect

Lord, we implore You to keep Your household the Church in continual godliness, that through Your protection she may be free from all adversities and devoutly given to serve You in good works; through Jesus Christ, Your Son, our Lord, who lives and reigns with You and the Holy Spirit, one God, now and forever.

Gelasian Sacramentary

AT LAUDS

Psalmody

Sunday: 3, C8, 51	Wednesday: 8, C11, 20	Friday: 146, C13, 5
Monday: 118a, C9, 118b	Thursday: 18a, C12, 18b	Saturday: 149, C14, 150
Tuesday: 1, C10, 2		

Lesson

Sunday: Nehemiah 5:1-13	Wednesday: Nehemiah 8:13-9:4	Friday: Esther 5:1-6:13
Monday: Nehemiah 6:1-9	Thursday: Esther 1:1-2:18	Saturday: Esther 8:2-9:17
Tuesday: Nehemiah 7:1-6		

Collect

O God, who has forbidden us to be anxious about supplies for this life; grant, we pray You, that we may steadfastly pursue what belongs to You, and that all things salutary may be granted to us; through Jesus Christ, our Lord, who lives and reigns with You and the Holy Spirit, one God, now and forever.

Gelasian Sacramentary

AT TERCE, SEXT AND NONE

Chapter

Sunday, Monday and Tuesday: Ephesians 6:10-17
Wednesday and Thursday: I Timothy 6:7-14
Friday and Saturday: Ephesians 4:17-20

AT VESPERS

Psalmody

Sunday: 136b, 137, 138	Wednesday: 9, 10, 11	Friday: 17, 147a, 147b
Monday: 140, 141, 142	Thursday: 12, 13, 14, 16	Saturday: 19, 54, 77
Tuesday: 144, 145, 7		

Lesson

Sunday: Nehemiah 5:14-19	Wednesday: Nehemiah 13:1-13	Friday: Esther 6:14-8:2
Monday: Nehemiah 6:10-19	Thursday: Esther 2:19-4:17	Saturday: Esther 9:18-10:3
Tuesday: Nehemiah 8:1-12		

Collect

Almighty and everlasting God, who by Your Son has promised us the forgiveness of sins, righteousness, and everlasting life: We implore You, quicken our hearts by Your Holy Spirit that we in daily prayer may seek our help in Christ against all temptations, and, constantly believing His promise, obtain that for which we pray, and at last be saved, through Your Son Jesus Christ, who lives and reigns with You and the Holy Spirit, one true God, now and forever. Amen.

Veit Dietrich

THE TWENTY-SECOND WEEK
AFTER TRINITY

AT MATINS

Hymn - *Wir danken dir, o treuer Gott*

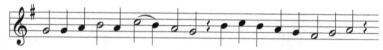

1.   O faith-ful God, thanks be   to Thee   Who dost for-give in - i - qui-ty.

Thou grant-est help in   sin's dis-tress, And soul and bo - dy dost Thou bless.

2. Thy servant now declares to me:
"Thy sins are all forgiven thee.
Depart in peace, but sin no more
And e'er My pardoning grace adore."

3. O Lord, we bless Thy gracious heart,
For Thou Thyself dost heal our smart
Through Christ, our Savior's precious blood,
Which for the sake of sinners flowed.

4. Give us Thy Spirit, peace afford
Now and forever, gracious Lord.
Preserve to us till life is spent
Thy holy Word and Sacrament.

Nicholaus Selnecker, 1572

Psalmody

Sunday: 42, 44, 45	Wednesday: 53, 55, 56	Friday: 61, 62, 66
Monday: 46, 47, 48	Thursday: 58, 59, 60	Saturday: 68a, 68b, 69a
Tuesday: 49, 50, 52		

Lesson

Sunday, Monday and Tuesday: Matthew 18:23-35
Tuesday: Luke 6:27-35

Wednesday and Thursday: Mark 3:6-15
Thursday: Luke 6:12-19

Friday and Saturday: Matthew 14:23b-36
Saturday: John 6:16-25

Homily

Sunday - Martin Luther

Christians who recognize their sins and have faith are comforted by the forgiveness of sins because they have been baptized, they hear the gospel, they have absolution, and the Holy Sacrament. And they trust the same word in each of these. For you see, God has put this treasure, the forgiveness of sins, in his Word and Sacrament and has commanded that we believe that Word. This is the reason that Christians don't come before God the way the wicked servant did, saying, "Have patience with me and I'll pay you everything I owe." But they don't minimize their sins either, but confess that they are very real and deplorable, and so they beg for forgiveness. Such people actually receive what they believe, that is, the forgiveness of sins. This kingdom of grace and forgiveness started for us in baptism and is still ours until we die. God established the preaching of the gospel, baptism, absolution and the Sacrament, so that our faith in the forgiveness of sins would be able to be constantly made stronger.

We should pay close attention, so that we will know how to dispose of sin, and that is in no other way than with the means shown in the third article of our Christian Creed: I believe in the forgiveness of sins. By this I mean that I confess and recognize my sins; I shiver and quail in terror because of them. But how can I be rid of them? I can dispose of them only by believing that even though sin is present and I feel it there, nevertheless, it is not sin, because it is forgiven.

House Postil for the Twenty-Second Sunday after Trinity

Monday - Guigo of Saint-Romain

Do not drive people away, but drive away from them what rightly offends you - that is to say, vice. And do this out of love for them - just as you want for yourself. It is not human nature that offends you, but the vices which impair it. Why probe the bleeding wounds of your own race, unless it is to heal them As you should your own?

You should be concerned not with what others do, but with what you do. For the person who is of value to all is the one who pays attention not so much to what others do as to what he makes of them and their deeds, whether good or evil. You can bring good from both, but much more particularly and notably from evil.

If you are going to reject evil people, begin with yourself. The good and the evil are raw material from which a just person can bring profit - rejoicing with the former, and having compassion on the latter.

Meditation 142

Tuesday - Walter Hilton

When love acts in the soul it does so wisely and gently, for it has great power to kill anger, envy, and all the passions of wrath and melancholy. And it brings into the soul the virtues of patience, gentleness, peaceableness, and friendliness to one's neighbor. People guided only by their own reason find it very hard to be patient, peaceful, sweet-tempered and charitable to their neighbors when they treat them badly and wrong them. But true lovers of Jesus have no great difficulty in enduring all this, because love fights for them and kills such movements of wrath and melancholy with amazing ease. Through the spiritual sight of Jesus it makes the souls of such people so much at ease and so peaceful, so ready to endure and so conformed to God, that if they are despised and disregarded by others, or suffer injustice or injury, shame or ill-treatment, they pay no attention. They are not greatly disturbed by these things and will not allow themselves to be, for then they would lose the comfort they feel in their souls, and that they are unwilling to do. They can more easily forget all the wrong that is done them than others can forgive it even when asked for forgiveness. They would rather forget than forgive, for that seems easier to them.

And it is love that does all this, for love opens the eye of the soul to the sight of Jesus, and confirms it in the pleasure and contentment of the love that comes from that sight. It comforts the soul so much that it is quite indifferent to what others do against it. The greatest harm that could befall such people would be to lose the spiritual sight of Jesus, and they would therefore suffer all other injuries than that one alone.

When true lovers of Jesus suffer harm from their neighbors, they are so strengthened by the grace of the Holy Spirit and are made so truly humble, so patient, and so peaceable, that they retain their humility no matter what harm or injury is inflicted on them. They do not despise their neighbors or judge them, but they pray for them in their hearts, and feel more pity and compassion for them than for others who never harmed them, and in fact they love them better, and more fervently desire their salvation, because they see that they will have so much spiritual profit from their neighbors' deeds, though this was never their intention. But this love and this humility, which are beyond human nature, come only from the Holy Spirit to those whom he makes true lovers of Jesus.

The Scale of Perfection

Wednesday - Augustine of Hippo

What can touching be, but believing? We touch Christ, you see, by faith. And it is better not to touch Him with the hand and to touch Him with faith, than to feel Him with the hand and not touch Him with faith. It wasn't a great matter to touch Christ. The Jews touched Him when they seized Him, they touched Him when they bound Him, touched Him when they hung Him up; they touched Him, and by touching Him in an evil way, they lost what they touched. By touching with faith, O catholic Church, faith saves you. Just see that you touch by faith only, that is, approach faithfully and firmly believe. If you have thought of Christ only as a man, you have touched Him on earth. If you have believed Christ is Lord, equal to the Father, then you have touched Him when He has ascended to the Father.

Sermon 246, for Thursday of Easter Week

Thursday - Bede the Venerable

Both therefore fell down before the Lord, those were plagued by bodily diseases, and those who were vexed by unclean spirits. The sick did this simply for the sake of obtaining health, but the demoniacs, or rather the devils within them, because under the mastery of a fear of God they were compelled not only to fall down before Him, but also to praise His majesty. And they cried out, saying, "You are the Son of God." And here we must wonder at the blindness of the Arians, who deny the Son of God after the glory of His resurrection, while the devils confess Him to be the Son of God while He is still clothed with human flesh.

There follows, "But He sternly warned them that they should not make Him known." For God said to the sinner, "What right have you to declare My statutes?" A sinner is forbidden to preach the Lord, lest anyone listening to his preaching should follow him in his error. The devil is an evil master, who always mingles falsehood with truth, that the veneer of truth may hide what is fraudulent. Not only devils, but people healed by Christ, and even Apostles, are ordered to be silent about Him before the Passion, lest by proclaiming the majesty of His Divinity, the working of His Passion be hindered.

But allegorically, in the Lord's coming out of the synagogue and then retreating to the sea, He prefigured the salvation of the Gentiles, to whom He willed to come on account of their faith, having abandoned the Jews on account of their treachery. For the nations, driven about in various paths of error, are properly compared to the unstable sea. Again, a great crowd from various provinces followed Him because He has graciously received many nations who came to Him through the preaching of the Apostles. And the ship which served the Lord in the sea is the Church, collected from amongst the nations; and He goes into it lest the crowd should crush Him. Fleeing from the troubled minds of carnal persons, He delights to come to and dwell within those who despise the glory of this world. Furthermore, there is a difference between thronging the Lord, and touching Him; for they throng Him when they by carnal thoughts and deeds trouble the peace in which truth dwells; but he touches Him, who by faith and love has received Him into his heart; for which reason those who touched Him are said to have been saved.

Commentary on Mark

Friday - Chromatius of Aquileia

Who was able to walk on the sea if not the Creator of the universe? He, indeed, about whom the Holy Spirit had spoken long ago through blessed Job: "Who alone spreads out the heavens, and treads on the waves of the sea." Solomon spoke about Him in the person of Wisdom: "I dwelt in high places, and my throne was in a pillar of cloud. Alone I have made the circuit of the vault of heaven and have walked on the waves of the sea." David likewise declared in his psalm: "God, Your way was in the sea, Your path in the great waters." So too Habakkuk noted, "The raging waters swept by. The deep uttered its voice."

What is more evident than this testimony, what is more clear? It points to Him walking on the water as well as on the ground. This is God's only begotten Son, who long ago according to the will of the Father stretched out the heavens and at the time of Moses in a pillar of cloud showed the people the way to follow. *Tractate 52 on Matthew*

Saturday - Anselm of Canterbury

This tumult of the waves, and the tottering or half-sinking of Peter, takes place in our time, according to the spiritual sense, even daily. For every man's own besetting sin is the tempest. You love God, you walk upon the sea and the swells of this world are under your feet. You love the world, it swallows you up. Its desire is to devour its lovers, not to bear them up. But when your heart wavers with the desire of sin, call on the Divinity of Christ so that you may conquer that desire. You think that the wind is contrary when the adversity of this world rises against you, and not also when its prosperity fawns upon you. For when wars, when tumults, when famine, when pestilence comes, when any private calamity happens even to individuals, then the wind is thought to be adverse. And then men think it time to call upon God; but when the world smiles with temporal happiness, then, truly, the wind is not contrary. Do not judge the tranquility of the time by such tokens as these, but judge it by your own temptations. See if you are tranquil within yourself. See if there isn't an internal tempest overwhelming you. It is a proof of great virtue to struggle with happiness, so that it will not seduce, corrupt, subvert. Learn to trample on this world. Remember to trust in Christ. And if your foot be moved, if you totter, if there are some temptations that you can't overcome, if you begin to sink, cry out to Jesus, "Lord, save me." *Sermon on Our Lord Walking on the Sea*

Collect

O God, our Refuge and Strength, the Author of all godliness, be ready, we implore You, to hear the devout prayers of Your Church, especially in times of persecution, and grant that those things which we ask faithfully we may obtain effectually; through Jesus Christ, Your Son, our Lord, who lives and reigns with You and the Holy Spirit, one God, now and forever. *Gelasian Sacramentary*

AT LAUDS

Psalmody

Sunday: 67, C1, 5	Wednesday: 64, C4, 65	Friday: 76, C5, 92
Monday: 63, C2, 36	Thursday: 88, C6, 90	Saturday: 143, C7, 148
Tuesday: 43, C3, 57		

Lesson

Sunday: Ezekiel 1:1-29
Monday: Ezekiel 3:16-27
Tuesday: Ezekiel 5:1-17

Wednesday: Ezekiel 8:1-18
Thursday: Ezekiel 10:1-11:12

Friday: Ezekiel 13:1-16
Saturday: Ezekiel 18:19-32

Collect

O God, who of Your great love to the world reconciled heaven and earth through Your Only-begotten Son; grant that we, who by the darkness of our sins are turned aside from brotherly love, may by Your light shed forth in our souls, be filled with Your own sweetness, and embrace our friends in You, and our enemies for Your sake, in a bond of mutual affection, through Jesus Christ, Your Son, our Lord, who lives and reigns with You and the Holy Spirit, one God, forever and ever. Amen.

Mozarabic Sacramentary

AT TERCE, SEXT AND NONE

Chapter

Sunday, Monday and Tuesday: Philippians 1:3-11
Wednesday and Thursday: I Timothy 1:5-12a
Friday and Saturday: Ephesians 5:10-14

AT VESPERS

Psalmody

Sunday: 110, 111, 112, 113
Monday: 114, 115, 116, 117
Tuesday: 120, 121, 122

Wednesday: 123, 124, 125
Thursday: 126, 127, 128

Friday: 129, 130, 131, 132
Saturday: 133, 135, 136a

Lesson

Sunday: Ezekiel 2:1-3:15
Monday: Ezekiel 4:1-17
Tuesday: Ezekiel 6:1-14

Wednesday: Ezekiel 9:1-11
Thursday: Ezekiel 11:14-25

Friday: Ezekiel 18:1-18
Saturday: Ezekiel 20:5-44

Collect

O almighty, eternal God: We confess that we are poor sinners and cannot answer one of a thousand, when You contend with us; but with all our hearts we thank You, that You have taken all our guilt from us and laid it upon Your dear Son Jesus Christ, and made Him to atone for it: We pray You graciously to sustain us in faith and so to govern us by Your Holy Spirit, that we may live according to Your will, in neighborly love, service, and helpfulness, and not give way to wrath or revenge, that we may not incur Your wrath, but always find in You a gracious Father, through Jesus Christ, our Lord, who lives and reigns with You and the Holy Spirit, one God, now and forever.

Veit Dietrich

THE TWENTY-THIRD WEEK
AFTER TRINITY

AT MATINS

Hymn - *Kirken den er et gammelt Hus*

1.   Built on the Rock the Church doth stand, E- ven when steep-les are fall - ing;

Crum-bled have spires in ev - 'ry land, Bells still are chim-ing and call - ing,

Call-ing the young and old to rest, But a - bove all the

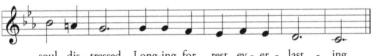

soul dis - tressed, Long-ing for rest ev - er - last - ing.

2. Surely in temples made with hands,
God, the Most High, is not dwelling;
High above earth His temple stands,
All earthly temples excelling.
Yet He whom heavens cannot contain
Chose to abide on earth with men,
Built in our bodies His temple.

3. We are God's house of living stones,
Builded for His habitation;
He through baptismal grace us owns
Heirs of His wondrous salvation.
Were we but two His name to tell,
Yet He would deign with us to dwell,
With all His grace and His favor.

4. Now we may gather with our King
E'en in the lowliest dwelling;
Praises to Him we there may bring,
His wondrous mercy forthtelling.
Jesus His grace to us accords;
Spirit and life are all His words;
His truth doth hallow the temple.

5. Still we our earthly temples rear
That we may herald His praises;
They are the homes where He draws near
And little children embraces.
Beautiful things in them are said;
God there with us His covenant made,
Making us heirs of His kingdom.

6. Here stands the font before our eyes
Telling how God did receive us;
The altar recalls Christ's sacrifice
And what His table doth give us;
Here sounds the Word that doth proclaim
Christ yesterday, today, the same,
Yea, and for aye our Redeemer.

7. Grant then, O God, where'er men roam,
That, when the church-bells are ringing,
Many in saving faith may come
Where Christ His message is bringing:
"I know Mine own, Mine own know Me;
Ye, not the world, My face shall see.
My peace I leave with you." Amen.

Nikolai Grundtvig, 1837

Psalmody

Sunday: 69b, 70, 71	Wednesday: 75, 79, 80	Friday: 84, 86, 87, 93
Monday: 72, 73, 74	Thursday: 81, 82, 83	Saturday: 85, 89a, 89b
Tuesday: 78a, 78b, 78c		

Lesson

Sunday, Monday and Tuesday: Matthew 22:15-22

Monday: Luke 20:20-26 or Mark 12:13-17
Tuesday: Matthew 23:1-12

Wednesday and Thursday: Matthew 10:1-15

Thursday: Matthew 10:16-25

Friday and Saturday: Matthew 10:26-33

Homily

Sunday - Leo I of Rome

Jewish wickedness bent over backwards to fabricate any pretext whatsoever for perpetrating crime against the Lord Jesus, dearly beloved, and the lies which false witnesses had brought forth in the service of unjust priests were producing nothing worthy of death. They found it to be something of an insurmountable task to frame Him, Lord of the world, with the stigma of having sought after a kingdom. Pilate wanted Jesus to be freed when he saw that their accusations were groundless. Whereupon they clamored falsely and menacingly in unison, "If you let this Man go, you are not Caesar's friend. Whoever makes himself a king speaks against Caesar."

O Pilate, you unwisely feared a ridiculous excuse. You would have had every reason to fear an unjust claim of royalty and would have been bound to put down an attempted revolution to protect the empire of Caesar if the stirrings of tyranny had exposed a plan to take power, if provisions for equipment, amassing of finances, or encampments of soldiers had been uncovered. Why did you allow him to be laden with the charge of striving after power when his teaching dealt mainly with humility? He did not speak out against Roman laws. He submitted to "assessment" and paid the tax. He did not hold back revenues, but taught that what belongs to God should be rendered unto God, and what belongs to Caesar rendered unto Caesar. He chose poverty, encouraged obedience, and preached peacefulness. Truly this does not constitute an attack upon Caesar, but a help to him.

Sermon 61

Monday - Boniface of Mainz

Give the tithes to the Church, because the Lord commands, saying, Render unto Caesar the things that are Caesar's, that is, taxes and tribute, and unto God the things which are God's, that is, tithes, and first-fruits, and all your vows, as the Lord commands, Whatsoever ye would that men should do unto you, do ye also unto them; and whatsoever ye would that men should not do unto you, do ye not unto them: for this is the law and the prophets. If ye accomplish this love one towards another, ye will fulfil all the commandments. Fear God alone everywhere, and honour the king, because, as it is written, There is no power but of God ; the powers that be are ordained of God. Whosoever, therefore, resisteth the power, resisteth the ordinance of God. Therefore, obey these pious commandments. Refuse not just tribute, as the Apostle enjoins, Tribute to whom tribute, custom to whom custom.

On Faith and Works of Love

Tuesday - Jerome of Jerusalem

No one should be called "teacher" or "father" except God the Father and our Lord Jesus Christ: Father, because from Him are all things; Teacher, because through Him are all things, or because by His dispensation in the flesh we have all been reconciled to God. It is asked why, in contradiction to this command, the apostle claims that he is the "teacher" of the Gentiles; or how it is that in common language... They call one another fathers... It is one thing to be a father or teacher by nature, something else to be one by tender feeling. If we call a man "father," we are conferring honor to his age; we are not pointing out the Creator of our life. One is called a "teacher," too, by one's association with the true Teacher. And lest I repeat things without end, just as the one God and the one Son by nature does not prejudice others from being called gods and sons by adoption, so also one Father and Teacher does not prejudice others from being called fathers and teachers though it is not proper to them.

Commentary on Matthew

Wednesday - John Chrysostom

Do you not know what the priest is? He is an angel of the Lord. Are they his own words that he speaks? If you despise him, you do not despise him, but God who ordained him. If God does not work through him, then there is no Baptism, nor Communion in the Mysteries, nor blessings; you are no longer Christians.

What then, you ask, does God ordain all, even the unworthy? God does not ordain all, but He works through all, though they themselves be unworthy, that the people may be saved. If, for the sake of the people, God spoke by an ass and by Balaam, a most wicked man, how much more will He speak by the mouth of the priest. What indeed will not God do or say for our salvation? By whom does He not act? For if He worked through Judas and through those others who "prophesied," people to whom He will say, "I never knew you; depart from me, you evildoers," and if others "cast out devils," will He not much more work through his priests?

Honor him, because every day he ministers to you, prays for you, and offers supplications for you. Do not say "he is unworthy." What does that matter? Does one who is worthy bestow these great benefits on you of himself? By no means. Everything comes about through your faith. Not even the righteous man can benefit you if you lack faith, nor the unrighteous harm you if you have faith... Is it the good life of the priest or his virtue which confers so much on you? The gifts that God bestows are not brought about by the power of the priest. Everything springs from grace. The priest has only to open his mouth, but it is God who works all things. The priest only performs the sign. The offering is the same whether it is offered by a common man or by Peter or Paul. Christ gave the same things to His disciples which the priests now administer. One is not less than the other, for it is not men who consecrate it, but Christ Himself who bestows sanctification. For as the words which God spoke are the same which the priest now utters, so is the offering the same.

This is the essence of the priesthood to my mind: preaching and proclaiming the Gospel... My purpose is not to achieve my own glory, nor that I may attain the splendor of honors and fame, but that... the souls of those taught by me may be acceptable. This mission has not been given to me in order to bring honor on myself, but to assure your welfare.   *On the Priesthood*

Thursday - Bruno of Segni

Behold, Christ flies, and flies by night: that flight, difficult in itself, may become more difficult through the obscurity of darkness. So if Christ fled from Herod, how much more should we flee from the devil and his members? Let us not be terrified by any difficulty of the journey; for it is better to be weary with hard labor than to be slain by the enemy. Straight and narrow is the way that leads to everlasting life. Yet we are not always to flee, neither always to resist. As time and place require we are sometimes to do the one, and sometimes the other. For the saints also fled sometimes, and sometimes resisted their enemies. Moreover our Savior Himself, who commanded, "When they persecute you in one city, flee to another," and who could have Himself fled, had He so willed it, at the time of His Passion, went forth of His own will to meet His enemies. Hence, therefore, if we flee from our enemies, whether visible or invisible, it is not to be from the fear of death, but from the fear of sinning.

Sermon for Holy Innocents

Friday - An Anglo-Saxon Homily

Behold, that will be a painful sorrow and a miserable separation of the body and the soul if that miserable inner evil, which is the accursed soul, who for having neglected the commands of God will be condemned, with the result that it then after the separation must slide into eternal hell-torments. There it will live with devils in crime and sin, in torment and sorrow, in woe and worms, among the dead and devils, in burning and bitterness, in foulness and in all those tortures which the devils prepared from the beginning, which they created for themselves, and which they themselves deserved.

But let us pay attention to the need of our souls. And let us work good while it is day and carry out good deeds. And let us forsake crime and sin and pride and envy and empty boasting and unrighteousness and adultery, fast-breaking, and drunkenness, and folly, and heretical deceits, avarice, and gluttony, lying and hypocrisy, slander and double speech, enmities, wickednesses, and miserliness, and all the customs which the devils created in themselves. And let us love our Lord with all mind and might, with all our heart and soul, with all truthfulness and wisdom. And let us love those nearest to us just as ourselves. And let us be merciful to poor men and foreigners and the sick, so that our Lord will honor us through that mercy. And still whoever of us sins against another in word or in deed, let him gently refrain, lest God with anger punish him for that, as He himself said, "Forgive, and you will be forgiven." May we suffer all for the love of our Lord, so that in exchange for the hardships here in the world we will there be granted the Lord's love.

Behold, we need to remember how much He suffered for us, after He took on a human body for the eternal salvation of mankind, and through that body saved us from the devil's slavery, and gave us a return to that eternal life, which before we forfeited, if we wish to gain it as the wise one said, "The Lord will save and keep those in the kingdom of heavens, who here in this world are humble to God and to men."

Lo, we hear that they who in this world are humble and kind will be blessed and rich before God. Behold, by that we can know and understand that they will be wretched and accursed before God who here in this world are proud and envious. Of all sins that is the most loathsome and displeasing to God, because mankind through that envy was first plunged into hell; and again, through mercy and humility [of Christ], they were released from the devil's thralldom.

Vercelli Homily 2

Saturday - Bernard of Clairvaux

He makes the will good, who made it free; and makes it good to this end, that we may be a kind of first fruits of His creatures; because it would have been better for us never to have existed than that we should remain always our own. For those who wished to belong to themselves, became indeed like gods, knowing good and evil; but then they were not merely their own, but the devil's. Hence, free will makes us our own; bad will, the devil's; and good will, God's... It is our own will that enslaves us to the devil, not his power; whereas, God's grace subjects us to God, not our own will. Our will, created good by the good God, shall nevertheless be perfect only when perfectly subjected to the Creator. This does not mean that we ascribe to it its own perfection, and to God, only its creation; since to be perfect is far more than to be made. The attributing to God of what is less excellent, and to us what is more, surely stands condemned in the very statement.

On Grace and Free Choice

Collect

Absolve, we implore You, O Lord, Your people from their offenses, that from the bonds of our sins which by reason of our frailty we have brought upon us we may be delivered by Your bountiful goodness; through Jesus Christ, Your Son, our Lord, who lives and reigns with You and the Holy Spirit, one God, now and forever.   *Gelasian Sacramentary*

AT LAUDS

Psalmody

Sunday: 3, C8, 51	Wednesday: 8, C11, 20	Friday: 146, C13, 5
Monday: 118a, C9, 118b	Thursday: 18a, C12, 18b	Saturday: 149, C14, 150
Tuesday: 1, C10, 2		

Lesson

Sunday: Ezekiel 28:1-10	Wednesday: Ezekiel 37:15-28	Friday: Ezekiel 47:1-12
Monday: Ezekiel 34:1-16	Thursday: Ezekiel 43:6-12	Saturday: Ezekiel 48:1-29
Tuesday: Ezekiel 36:16-28		

Collect

O God Almighty, the Father of Your Only-begotten Son; give me a body undefiled, a mind watchful, an unerring knowledge, the influence of the Holy Spirit for the obtaining and the assured enjoyment of the Truth; through Your Son, Christ, by whom glory be to You, in the Holy Spirit, unto the ages.   *Greek Liturgy of St. James*

AT TERCE, SEXT AND NONE

Chapter

Sunday, Monday and Tuesday: Philippians 3:17-21
Wednesday and Thursday: I Thessalonians 1:2-6
Friday and Saturday: I Thessalonians 4:9-12

AT VESPERS

Psalmody

Sunday: 136b, 137, 138	Wednesday: 9, 10, 11	Friday: 17, 147a, 147b
Monday: 140, 141, 142	Thursday: 12, 13, 14, 16	Saturday: 19, 54, 77
Tuesday: 144, 145, 7		

Lesson

Sunday: Ezekiel 33:1-20	Wednesday: Ezekiel 39:17-29	Friday: Ezekiel 47:13-23
Monday: Ezekiel 34:17-31	Thursday: Ezekiel 44:1-16	Saturday: Ezekiel 48:30-35
Tuesday: Ezekiel 37:1-14		

Collect

Lord God, heavenly Father: we thank You that You have until now granted us peace and graciously spared us from war and foreign dominion. We pray You, graciously let us continue to live in Your fear according to Your will, giving no cause for wars or other punishment; govern and direct our rulers, that they may not hinder the obedience due to You, but maintain righteousness, that we may enjoy happiness and blessing under their government, through our Lord Jesus Christ, who lives and reigns with You and the Holy Spirit, one true God, now and forever. Amen.

Veit Dietrich

THE TWENTY-FOURTH WEEK
AFTER TRINITY

AT MATINS

1. In the ver-y midst of life Snares of death sur-round us;
Who shall help us in the strife Lest the foe con-found us?
Thou on-ly, Lord, Thou on-ly! We mourn that we have great-ly
erred, That our sins Thy wrath have stirred. Ho-ly and right-eous God!
Ho-ly and migh-ty God! Ho-ly and all-mer-ci-ful
Sav-ior! E-ter-nal Lord God! Save us lest we per-ish.
In the bit-ter pangs of death. Have mer-cy, O Lord!

2. In the midst of death's dark vale
Pow'rs of hell o'ertake us.
Who will help when they assail,
Who secure will make us?
Thou only, Lord, Thou only!
Thy heart is moved with tenderness,
Pities us in our distress.
Holy and righteous God!
Holy and mighty God!
Holy and all-merciful Savior!
Eternal Lord God!
Save us from the terror
Of the fiery pit of hell.
Have mercy, O Lord!

3. In the midst of utter woe
When our sins oppress us,
Where shall we for refuge go,
Where for grace to bless us?
To Thee, Lord Jesus, only!
Thy precious blood was shed to win
Full atonement for our sin.
Holy and righteous God!
Holy and mighty God!
Holy and all-merciful Savior!
Eternal Lord God!
Lord, preserve and keep us
In the peace that faith can give.
Have mercy, O Lord!

Martin Luther, 1524

Psalmody

Sunday: 89c, 94, 96   Wednesday: 104a, 104b, 104c   Friday: 106a, 106b, 107a
Monday: 97, 98, 99, 100   Thursday: 105a, 105b, 105c   Saturday: 107b, 108, 109
Tuesday: 101, 102, 103

Lesson

Sunday, Monday and Tuesday: Matthew 9:18-26
Tuesday: Matthew 9:27-38

Wednesday and Thursday: Matthew 24:1-14
Friday: John 15:18-25
Saturday: Luke 14:25-35

Homily

Sunday - Odilo of Cluny

Christians are absolutely certain of the divine promise that the dead will rise again. Truth himself made the promise and Truth cannot lie. The promise given by Truth concerning the resurrection of the dead is reliable because, since Truth cannot lie, He must fulfill all He has promised. Moreover, to give us certain proof that bodies will rise again, the Lord himself deigned to demonstrate this to us in His own body. Christ rose so that Christians may not doubt that they too will rise: for what happened first in the head will happen later in the body.

Now we should realize, beloved, that there are two deaths and two resurrections: scripture speaks of a first death and a second death. The first, moreover, has two parts: in the one the guilty soul forsakes its Creator by sinning; in the other it is, by God's judgment, separated from its body as a penalty. The second death includes the death of the body and the everlasting punishment of the soul. The first death temporarily separates from their bodies the souls of good and bad alike. In the second death the wicked alone suffer torment in both body and soul forever.

In the past all were subject to both deaths, for original sin made everyone liable to punishment. But the immortal and righteous Son of God came and took mortal flesh from us in order to die for us. In that flesh He bore the punishment for sin, but without any guilt, for there could be no sin in Him. God's Son thus accepted on our behalf the second part of the first death, the death of the body alone, and by so doing rescued us from the control of sin and from the torment of everlasting punishment.

Sermon 5 on the Lord's Resurrection

Monday - Guerric of Igny

I know who it is who is gladdened by those good tidings. Without doubt it is he whom a holy heartfelt sorrow has previously brought low, sorrow over his pilgrim state and exile, sorrow over the bonds of death and the perils of hell; the man who grieves daily and laments that the snares of death have encompassed him and the perils of hell have found him. To this man today's message from heaven brings joy, this man receives with exultation the tidings of God's Son. To this man, I say, as he grieves and mourns that he is the prey of such evils surrounding him, the Liberator is not announced without gladness, the Liberator who is to give the oil of gladness for mourning, a mantle of praise for the spirit of grief, who will bring wretchedness to an end but give to the wretched happiness without end. Blessed therefore are they who mourn, for they shall be consoled. Blessed are they whom a holy heartfelt sorrow has brought low for they shall be gladdened by a good word.

A good word indeed and consoling is Your almighty Word, Lord, which today has come from a royal throne into the Virgin's womb. In it also He has made for Himself a royal throne in which , although He sits even now as a king in the heavens surrounded by a host of angels, He is nonetheless the comforter of those who grieve on earth.

First Sermon for the Annunciation

Tuesday - Antony of Egypt

Since the Lord made his sojourn with us, the enemy is fallen and his powers have diminished. For this reason, though he is able to do nothing, nevertheless like a tyrant fallen from power he does not remain quiet, but issues threats, even if they are only words. Let everyone of you consider this, and he will be empowered to treat the demons with contempt... They are evil, and they desire nothing so much as inflicting injury on those who love virtue and honor God. But because they have no power to act, they do nothing except issue threats...

To end our fear of them, we ought to ponder this: If the capability were theirs, they would not come in great mobs, nor create phantasms, nor would they work their fraud by being transfigured. It would suffice for only one to come and do what he can and wills - especially because everyone who actually possesses the power does not destroy with apparitions, nor arouse fear with large mobs, but exercises his might directly, as he wishes. The demons, however, unable to effect anything, play parts as if they were on stage, changing their forms and striking fear in children by the illusion of the hordes and their shapes. For these antics they deserve instead to be ridiculed as weaklings. The true angel of the Lord, at least, who was sent by the Lord to the Assyrians, had no need of hordes, nor of visible apparitions, nor of crashing sounds and rattling noises. He wielded his authority quietly, and at once destroyed a hundred and eighty-five thousand foes. But the demons, who lack the power to do anything, these are the sort who must try to frighten, even if through illusions.

Now if anyone considers the events of Job's life, and says: "Why then did the devil set forth and do all those things to him? Did he not strip him of his possessions, destroy his children and strike him with painful boils?" Let such a questioner know that the devil was not the one possessing strength, but it was God who turned over the testing of Job to him. It is clear that because he was capable of doing nothing, he asked this, and when he was granted his request, he acted. So on this ground also the enemy is to be condemned, that even when he desired it, he did not prevail against one righteous man. If he possessed strength, he would not have made the request. But in asking - not once, but twice - he showed himself weak and capable of nothing. It is not remarkable if he had no might against Job, when indeed destruction would not befall even the man's cattle unless God allowed it. In fact, the devil has no authority over swine, for, as it is written in the Gospel, they begged the Lord, saying, "Send us into the swine." But if they held no sway over the swine, how much less do they hold, over people made in the image of God!

Quoted in The Life of Antony *by Athanasius*

591

Wednesday - Cyprian of Carthage

When you see our people scattered and driven to flight through fear of persecution, none of you, dearly beloved brethren, has reason for feeling distressed at no longer finding your community assembled together, at no longer hearing your bishops preach. At such a time it is just not possible for everyone to be gathered in one place; they must needs be killed, even though they themselves may not kill. In those days, whenever any of our brothers happens to be parted from the flock temporarily, by force of circumstances, and finds himself separated from them in body, but not in spirit, let him not be dismayed at the terrors of his flight; as he looks for refuge and concealment, let him not be alarmed at the loneliness of his desert region. He is not alone who has Christ as his companion in flight; he is not alone who by dint of preserving his temple of God has God always with him wherever he may be.

And if, as he seeks flight among the lonely mountains, some brigand should overpower him, if some wild beast should attack him, if hunger, thirst, or cold should overcome him, or if, as he sails in desperate haste over the seas, storm and tempest should overwhelm him, Christ is there, watching over His soldier wherever the fighting may be. To all who die in persecution for the honor of His name, He presents the recompense which He promised He would give on the day of the resurrection. Nor is the glory of such a martyrdom any the less because a man may not have died in the public gaze, witnessed by many: to die for Christ's sake is still the reason for his dying. That one Witness who puts martyrs to the test and gives to them their crowns provides adequate testimony for his martyrdom.

Letter 58, to the Laity at Thibaris

Thursday - Cyprian of Carthage

Confession is a first step towards glory, not the final crown of merit; it is not the ultimate achievement but a beginning of greatness, and since it is written: "he who endures to the end will be saved," whatever comes before. The end is only a step in the climb to the heights of salvation, not the goal, which is the conquest of the peak's summit.

He is a confessor. But after his confession he is in all the greater danger because the Adversary has been the more provoked. He is a confessor. That only calls for the greater loyalty to Our Lord's Gospel, since it was by means of the Gospel that he came to deserve such an honor from Our Lord. "To whom much is given, much is required of him; and on whom greater dignity has been bestowed, of him greater service is demanded." Let none be lost through the example of a confessor; let none learn to be unjust, or arrogant, or unfaithful because of a confessor's behavior.

He is a confessor. Let him be humble and peaceful, let his actions show modesty and self-control, so that, as he is named a confessor of Christ, he may imitate the Christ whom he confesses. For if Christ said: "whoever exalts himself will be humbled, and he who humbles himself will be exalted," and if He Himself, the Word and the power and the wisdom of God His Father, was exalted by the Father because He humbled Himself on earth, how can ostentation appeal to Him who not only enjoined on us humility in His law, but was Himself rewarded for His humility by His Father with the most glorious of all names?

He is a confessor of Christ. Yes, provided that he does not later cause the majesty and good name of Christ to be blasphemed. Let not the tongue which has confessed Christ be spiteful or mischievous; let it not be clamorous with altercations and quarrels; after its glorious confession let it not hiss with serpent's venom against the brethren and the priests of God. If nevertheless he does afterwards become guilty and odious, if he fritters away his reputation as a confessor by the evil of his ways, if he stains his life with filth and infamy, and if, in consequence, he leaves the Church to which he owes his becoming a confessor, if he breaks up its harmony and unity, and so in place of loyalty to his first faith adopts unfaithfulness, he cannot flatter himself that his confession has predestined him to the reward of glory; on the contrary, it will only increase the retribution that awaits him.

On the Unity of the Catholic Church

Friday - Lactantius

Whatever wicked princes plan against us, God Himself permits to be done. And yet unjust persecutors, who reproached and mocked the name of God, must not think that they will escape with impunity, because they have been the ministers of His wrath against us. Those who have received power, but have abused it to an inhuman degree, and have even insulted God in their arrogance and trampled His eternal name under their wickedly impious feet, will be punished with the judgment of God. For this reason He promises that He will quickly take revenge upon them and wipe out the evil monsters from the earth. But He also commands us to wait patiently for the day of heavenly judgment, although He often avenges the persecutions of His people even in the present world, in which He Himself will honor or punish every man according to what he deserves. Therefore let not the souls of the sacrilegious expect that those whom they trample upon in this way will be despised and unavenged. Those ravenous and voracious wolves who have tormented just and innocent souls, who have not committed any crimes, will surely meet with their reward. Only let us labor, that nothing else in us may be punished by men but righteousness alone: let us strive with all our power that we may deserve from the hands of God both the avenging of our suffering and a reward.
Divine Institutes

Saturday - Eucherius of Lyons

If some eminent and powerful prince, having adopted you for his son and copartner, should forthwith send for you by his ambassador; you would (I believe) break through all difficulties, and the wearisome extent of sea and land, that you might appear before him and have your adoption ratified. God Almighty, the Maker and the Lord of Heaven and Earth, and all that is in them, calls you to this adoption and offers to you (if you will receive it) that precious title of "a son," by which He calls His Only Begotten, and your glorious Redeemer. And will you not be inflamed and ravished with His divine love? Will you not make haste and begin your journey towards Heaven, lest swift destruction come upon you, and the honors offered you be frustrated by a sad and sudden death?

And to obtain this adoption, you will not need to pass through the untraveled and dangerous deserts of the Earth, or to commit yourself to the wide and perilous sea: when you desire it, this adoption is within your reach, and abides with you. And shall this blessing, because it is as easy in the getting as it is great in the consequence, find you therefore reluctant or unwilling to attain it? How hard a matter to the lukewarm and the dissembler will the making sure of this adoption prove? For as to the faithful and obedient it is most easy, so to the hypocrite and the rebellious, it is most difficult.

Certainly, it is the love of life that has enslaved us so much to a enchantment with and doting for temporal things. Therefore do I now advise you, who are a lover of life, to love it more. It is the right way of persuading, when we do it for no other end but to obtain that from you, which of your own accord you desire to grant us. Now I am an ambassador for this life which you love: and entreat that this life which you love in its transient and momentary state, you would also love in the eternal. But I cannot see how or in what way you may be said to love this present life, unless you desire to have it made most excellent, perfect, and eternally permanent; for that which has the power to please you when it is but short and uncertain, will please you much more when it is made eternal and immutable; and that which you dearly love and value, though you have it but for a time, will be much more dear and precious to you, when you shall enjoy it without end. It is therefore but proper, that the temporal life should look still towards the eternal, that through the one, you may pass into the other. You must not rob yourself of the benefits of the life to come by a crooked and perverse use of the present. This life must not oppose itself, to the damage and hurt of the future: for it is very absurd and unnatural, that the love of life should cause the destruction and then death of life.
On Contempt for the World

Collect

Stir up, we implore You, O Lord, the wills of Your faithful people that they, plenteously bringing forth the fruit of good works, may of You be plenteously rewarded; through Jesus Christ, Your Son, our Lord, who lives and reigns with You and the Holy Spirit, one God, now and forever.

Gelasian Sacramentary

AT LAUDS

Psalmody

Sunday: 67, C1, 5	Wednesday: 64, C4, 65	Friday: 76, C5, 92
Monday: 63, C2, 36	Thursday: 88, C6, 90	Saturday: 143, C7, 148
Tuesday: 43, C3, 57		

Lesson

Sunday: Daniel 1:1-21	Wednesday: Daniel 6:1-28	Friday: Daniel 10:1-21
Monday: Daniel 2:17-49	Thursday: Daniel 8:1-27	Saturday: Daniel 12:1-13
Tuesday: Daniel 4:1-37		

Collect

Be present, O Lord, to hear our supplications; nor let Your merciful clemency be far away from Your servants. Heal our wounds, forgive our sins, that being severed from You by no iniquities, we may be able evermore to cleave to You our Lord, for You live and reign with the Father and the Holy Spirit, one God, now and forever.

Gelasian Sacramentary

AT TERCE, SEXT AND NONE

Chapter

Sunday, Monday and Tuesday: Colossians 1:9-14
Wednesday and Thursday: II Timothy 1:8-13
Friday and Saturday: Romans 11:25-32

AT VESPERS

Psalmody

Sunday: 110, 111, 112, 113	Wednesday: 123, 124, 125	Friday: 129, 130, 131, 132
Monday: 114, 115, 116, 117	Thursday: 126, 127, 128	Saturday: 133, 135, 136a
Tuesday: 120, 121, 122		

Lesson

Collect

O almighty and everlasting God, who by Your Son has promised us forgiveness of our sins and deliverance from eternal death: We pray that by Your Holy Spirit You will daily increase our faith in Your grace through Christ, and establish us in the certain hope that we shall not die, but peacefully sleep, and be raised again on the last day to eternal life and salvation; through our Lord Jesus Christ, Your Son, who lives and reigns with You and the Holy Spirit, one God, now and forever.

Veit Dietrich

THE TWENTY-FIFTH WEEK
AFTER TRINITY

AT MATINS

Hymn - *Urbs Sion aurea*

1. Je - ru - sa - lem the gold- en, With milk and hon- ey blest,

Be - neath thy con- tem - pla - tion Sink heart and voice op - pressed.

I know not, oh, I know not, What joys a - wait us there,

What ra - dian- cy of glo - ry, What bliss be - yond com- pare.

2. They stand, those halls of Zion,
   All jubilant with song
   And bright with many an angel
   And all the martyr throng.
   The Prince is ever in them;
   The daylight is serene;
   The pastures of the blessèd
   Are decked in glorious sheen.

3. There is the throne of David;
   And there, from care released,
   The shout of them that triumph,
   The song of them that feast;
   And they who with their Leader
   Have conquered in the fight
   Forever and forever
   Are clad in robes of white.

4. O sweet and blessèd country,
   The home of God's elect!
   O sweet and blessèd country
   That eager hearts expect!
   Jesus, in mercy bring us
   To that dear land of rest,
   Who art, with God the Father
   And Spirit, ever blest.

Bernard of Morlax, c.1140

Psalmody

Sunday: 21, 22, 23
Monday: 24, 25, 26
Tuesday: 27, 28, 29

Wednesday: 30, 31, 32
Thursday: 33, 34, 35

Friday: 37a, 37b, 38
Saturday: 39, 40, 41

Lesson

Sunday, Monday and Tuesday: Matthew 24:15-28
Tuesday: Luke 12:35-56

Wednesday and Thursday: Matthew 8:18-22
Thursday: Luke 9:57-62

Friday and Saturday: Mark 13:33-37

Homily

Sunday - Bede the Venerable

"Everyone who strikes out ahead and does not remain in the teaching of Christ does not have God; the one who remains in this teaching has both the Son and the Father." Note the distinction of words and embrace the truth of faith. He says that the one who does not remain in the teaching of Christ does not have God, but he says that the one who remains in His teaching has both the Son and the Father, so that he may show that the Father and the Son are the one true God and convict those of lying who maintain that the Son is either not God or posterior to or less than the Father.

"If anyone comes to you and does not bring forward this teaching, do not receive him in the house or speak a greeting to him; for the one who speaks a greeting to him shares in his malicious works." John put into practice also through his actions these things that he taught in words about abominable schismatics and heretics. For someone who heard him, the most holy and brave martyr Polycarp, bishop of the people of Smyrna, tells that at one time when he entered the baths at Ephesus to wash and saw Cerinthus there, he immediately leapt up and departed without washing, saying, "Let us flee from here, lest the very baths in which Cerinthus, the enemy of truth, is washing fall down."

When the same Polycarp had also on one occasion chanced to meet Marcion, who said to him, "Acknowledge me," he answered, "I acknowledge, I acknowledge the firstborn of Satan." The apostles and their disciples then used such great caution in religion that they would not allow anyone to have even the contact of a word with any of those who turned aside from the truth, just as Paul also says, "Reject a divisive man after the first and second admonition, knowing that such a person is warped and sinning, being self-condemned." *Commentary on 2nd John*

Monday - Origen of Alexandria

One abomination of desolation is mentioned; but He adds, as if of many, "False christs will rise." For Antichrist is generically one, but there are many species of him. It is as with falsehood. It is generically one, but because there are many false doctrines, there are many falsehoods... Just as the one true Christ had many holy prophets from the very beginning who foretold the sufferings of the Christ and the glories that were to follow, so every false christ has many false prophets... Those who teach the Word according to the Church are prophets of Christ. Those who preach the false word of Marcion (or any other) are prophets of the Antichrist which is according to him, that is, of the falsehood he introduced; so with the preachers of each heresy. All means of persuasion brought forth to defend the word of an Antichrist are signs and wonders of that Antichrist.

"If possible" is a case of hyperbole. He did not declare or say that even the elect would be thrown into error; rather He wants to show that the words of heretics are often exceedingly plausible and even have power to move those who hear them wisely.

Every word professing to be truth while not the truth, whether among the Gentiles or among the barbarians, is in a sense Antichrist. It seeks to mislead as if it were truth and to separate us from Him who said "I am the Truth." *Commentary on Matthew*

Tuesday - Gregory I of Rome

I consider, dearly beloved, how God's love has found a way through our obstinacy. We have no excuse now. We despise God, and He waits. He sees Himself rejected, and He calls us back. He accepts the insult of our rejection, and nevertheless He promises us a gift as often as we return. But let no one be neglectful because of His forbearance. The longer He extended His patience before the judgment the stricter will be the justice He demands there. That is why Paul said: "Do you not know that the goodness of God leads you to repentance? But in accordance with your hardness and your impenitent heart you are treasuring up for yourself wrath in the day of wrath and revelation of the righteous judgment of God;" and the psalmist: "God is a just judge, strong and forbearing." Before he called Him forbearing he said that He was just, so that you would know that the one you see bearing long and patiently with the sins of transgressors will finally judge them very severely. Hence there is said by a certain wise man: "God is patient in repaying." He is said to be patient in repaying because he repays the sins of men patiently; those whom He bears with for a long time that they may be converted are condemned more harshly when they are not...

Therefore, my friends, direct the eyes of your hearts toward your mortality. Make ready for the Judge who is coming to you by your daily weeping and sorrow. Certain death awaits everyone. Do not refuse to ponder the uncertainty of your knowledge of your temporal life. Do not burden yourself with care for earthly things. No matter the weight of gold and silver put on it, no matter the costly garments clothing your body, what else is it but a body? Do not pay attention then to what you have, but to what you are.

Homily 20, on Luke 12

Wednesday - Peter Damian

Let your mind be raised to those good things which are promised in our Country, that while in exile you may consider lightly whatever roughness annoys you in the Way. When we are expecting a weight of shining gold, the work of the journey is lightened. When a crown is proposed for the reward, the course of the race is cheerfully run. Think, therefore, how blessed is he, who, while such a multitude of the reprobate are shut out, himself is counted worthy to enter into the nuptial feast with the glorious company of the elect! Think of what dignity it is even to stand before the Creator of all things, to contemplate the beauty of most present truth; face to face, to behold God; to have a share in the choirs of the angels; where all are so filled with present joy as never to be anxious concerning future adversity; where, while the quiet mind enjoys the pleasantness of boundless light, it rejoices also transcendently in the reward of its fellow-citizens. There, while they thirst for, they drink - while they drink, they thirst for - the fountain of life; because there neither can cupidity beget passion, or satiety turn into disgust. And clearly they derive the whole strength of their blessedness for this reason: because they always stand in the presence of the Author of Life. Hence the eternal greenness of flourishing youth; hence the loveliness of beauty and the unwaning vigor of perfect health. It is from that fountain of eternity that they obtain the power of everlasting life and transcendent rejoicing: and, a thing far more excellent, of attaining to the perfect likeness of their Creator.

The Instruction of a Nun

Thursday - Martin Luther

The tree must come before the fruit, as Christ also says in Matthew 12:33: "Either make the tree good, and its fruit good;" as if He were to say, "You labor in vain over the fruit unless you first have a good tree." The condition and concern of the Pharisees was almost the same as what we see in our opponents today, who praise works at the top of their voice and are completely evil. How can it be that from an evil seed something good should be born? Those who wear cowls, who fast, pray, and keep vigils have nevertheless kept the old wickedness of the heart. As Horace says, "Those who cross the ocean change the climate but not their state of mind." So these people change their clothes, their manner of life, and their activities, but their state of mind remains the same.

In true theology, therefore, this is the first concern, that a man become good through the regeneration of the Spirit, who is a sure, holy, and courageous Spirit. Then it comes to pass that, as from a good tree, good fruits are also born... These are not the sort of works that the wicked papacy has counseled, like vowing to make pilgrimages or entering a monastery—a work which, in a supreme insult to Christ, they call a "second baptism"—but thanking God, who has been so kind and merciful, praising His gifts, and by them instructing other men in the same grace. So in the Gospel those who were healed by Christ, even though He forbade them, could not help preaching His blessings, praising Him, and calling others to this same hope.

These are the main works which testify that a tree has been changed from a barren tree to a fruitful one, from a dry tree to one that is succulent and flourishing. To this life Christ calls His disciple when He says: "Let the dead bury their own dead, but you follow Me." He means that other works are the works of the dead, but that those who live in Christ should acknowledge and proclaim the mercy of God so that others might learn to acknowledge it, too. This is the summary: Our whole life and salvation is placed in the mercy of God, which God reveals through the Word in this manner, that He orders sinners to trust in it for Christ's sake. This knowledge is righteousness, as Isaiah says : "And by His knowledge He shall justify many." Here there is no other work of ours but that we do not reject the offered mercy but accept it by faith. And even this is a gift of the Holy Spirit, because "not all have faith." After justification, when you believe the promise of the forgiveness of sins and eternal life and possess it by faith, then the next and continuing work is to give thanks to God and to preach these blessings of His. Because the world sets itself against this with all its force and Satan does not stop trying to take this proclamation away from us by throwing up various discomforts... *Commentary on Psalm 51*

Friday - Tertullian of Carthage

How useless is the advice of those simplistic moralists who teach that after death rewards and punishments fall with lighter weight! That is, if any judgment at all awaits the soul! Rather it ought to be assumed that judgment will be weightier at the end of life than during it. For nothing is more telling and complete than that which comes at the very end. So no judgment could be more complete than God's. Accordingly, God's judgment will be incomparably radical and comprehensive, because it will be pronounced at the very last, in an eternal irrevocable sentence, both of punishment and of consolation. Then souls will not conveniently dissolve into senselessness, but will return into their own proper bodies. All this occurs once for all, on "that day, too, of which the Father only knows," in order that a full trial be made of faith, and of faith's concerned sincerity which awaits in trembling expectation, keeping her gaze ever fixed on that day, in her perpetual ignorance of when it will arrive, daily trembling at that for which she yet daily hopes. *On the Soul*

Saturday - Augustine of Hippo

Who are the all to whom He says "Watch!" but His chosen and beloved ones who belong to His body, which is the Church? Hence He did not say this only to those who heard Him when he was speaking but also to those who came after them, before us and to us, and to those who will come after us up to His last coming. But is that day going to find all in this life, or is anyone going to say that the words, "Watch so that, when He comes suddenly, He does not find you sleeping," also apply to the dead? Why, then, does He say to all what pertains only to those who existed then except because it pertains to all in the way I said? For that day will come for each of us when the day comes for us to leave this life, as we will be when we are judged on the last day. And for this reason every Christian ought to watch so that the coming of the Lord does not find him unprepared. But that day will find him unprepared whom the last day of this life of his finds unprepared. Certainly it was clear at least to the apostles that the Lord was not going to come in their time, when they were still living in the flesh. Yet who would doubt that they were most watchful and observed what He said to all so that He would not come suddenly and find them unprepared?

Letter 199 to Hesychius

Collect

Almighty God, we implore You, show Your mercy unto Your humble servants, that we who put no trust in our own merits may not be dealt with after the severity of Your judgment, but according to Your mercy; through Jesus Christ, Your Son, our Lord, who lives and reigns with You and the Holy Spirit, one God, now and forever.

Gelasian Sacramentary

AT LAUDS

Psalmody

Sunday: 3, C8, 51	Wednesday: 8, C11, 20	Friday: 146, C13, 5
Monday: 118a, C9, 118b	Thursday: 18a, C12, 18b	Saturday: 149, C14, 150
Tuesday: 1, C10, 2		

Lesson

Sunday: Hosea 2:14-3:5	Wednesday: Hosea 14:1-9	Friday: Joel 3:1-21
Monday: Hosea 11:1-11	Thursday: Joel 2:1-20	Saturday: Amos 5:4-15
Tuesday: Hosea 12:11-13:8		

Collect

In that day of severe judgment, O Lord, exempt me from a harsh word, You who have protected me with Your assistance. May my sins remain hidden under the covering of Your grace and cast into the depths of the sea. May my little soul be bound up in the bundle of the Living God, so that with all the elect, I may reach the eternal fellowship of joy, through Jesus Christ, Your Son, our Lord, who lives and reigns with You and the Holy Spirit, one God, now and forever.

Johann Gerhard

AT TERCE, SEXT AND NONE

Chapter

Sunday, Monday and Tuesday: I Thessalonians 4:13-18
Wednesday and Thursday: I Thessalonians 1:2-6
Friday and Saturday: Hebrews 10:19-25

AT VESPERS

Psalmody

Sunday: 136b, 137, 138	Wednesday: 9, 10, 11	Friday: 17, 147a, 147b
Monday: 140, 141, 142	Thursday: 12, 13, 14, 16	Saturday: 19, 54, 77
Tuesday: 144, 145, 7		

Lesson

Sunday: Hosea 6:1-11	Wednesday: Joel 1:1-20	Friday: Amos 3:1-8
Monday: Hosea 11:12-12:10	Thursday: Joel 2:21-32	Saturday: Amos 5:18-6:7
Tuesday: Hosea 13:9-16		

Collect

Lord God, heavenly Father, we most heartily thank You that by Your word You have brought us out of the darkness of Papacy into the light of Your grace: We implore You, mercifully help us to walk in that light, guard us from all error and false doctrine, and grant that we may not, as the Jews, become ungrateful and despise and persecute Your word, but receive it with all our heart, govern our lives according to it, and put all our trust in Your grace through the merit of Your dear Son, our Lord Jesus Christ, who lives and reigns with You and the Holy Spirit, one God, now and forever.

Veit Dietrich

THE TWENTY-SIXTH WEEK
AFTER TRINITY

AT MATINS

Hymn - *Es ist gewisslich an der Zeit*

1. The day is sure-ly draw-ing near When Je- sus, God's a - noint-ed,

In all His pow-er shall ap - pear As judge whom God ap-point-ed.

Then fright shall ban - ish id - le mirth, And flames on

flames shall rav - age earth As Scrip-ture long has warned us.

2. The final trumpet then shall sound
And all the earth be shaken,
And all who rest beneath the ground
Shall from their sleep awaken.
But all who live will in that hour,
Bu God's almighty boundless power,
Be changed at His commanding.

3. The books are opened then to all,
A record truly telling
What each has done, both great and small,
When he on earth was dwelling,
And every heart be clearly seen,
And all be known as they have been
In thoughts and words and actions.

4. Then woe to those who scorned the Lord
And sought but carnal pleasures,
Who here despised His precious Word
And loved their earthly treasures!
With shame and trembling they will stand
And at the judge's stern command
To Satan be delivered.

5. My Savior paid the debt I owe
And for my sin was smitten;
Within the Book of Life I know
My name has now been written.
I will not doubt, for I am free,
And Satan cannot threaten me;
There is no condemnation.

6. May Christ our intercessor be
And through His blood and merit
Read from His Book that we are free
With all who life inherit.
Then we shall see Him face to face,
With all His saints in that blest place
Which He has purchased for us.

7. O Jesus Christ, do not delay,
But hasten our salvation;
We often tremble in the way
In fear and tribulation.
O hear and grant our fervent pleas;
Come, mighty judge, and set us free
From death and every evil.

Bartholomäus Rigwaldt, 1586

Psalmody

Sunday: 42, 44, 45	Wednesday: 53, 55, 56	Friday: 61, 62, 66
Monday: 46, 47, 48	Thursday: 58, 59, 60	Saturday: 68a, 68b, 69a
Tuesday: 49, 50, 52		

Lesson

Sunday, Monday and Tuesday: Matthew 25:31-46

Tuesday: John 8:37-45

Wednesday and Thursday: Mark 12:28-34

Thursday: John 8:31-36

Friday and Saturday: Mark 8:11-26

Saturday: Mark 13:1-13

Homily

Sunday - Origen of Alexandria

He could have said to the unrighteous, "I was sick, and you did not visit me; I was in prison, and you did not come to me." Instead he abbreviated his discourse and compressed both phrases into one, saying, "I was sick and in prison, and you did not visit me," for it was proper for a merciful judge to embellish the good deeds of people but to skim over their evil deeds. The righteous, however, dwell on each word, saying, "When did we see you hungry, and feed you; or thirsty, and give you drink?" And "when did we see you a stranger, and take you in; or naked, and clothe you?" Or "when did we see you sick or in prison, and come to you?" For it is characteristic of the righteous, out of humility, studiously to make light of each of their good deeds held up to them. It is as though to the Lord's words, "This, that and the other good thing you did to me," they disavowingly reply, "Neither this, that nor the other thing did we do to you." The unrighteous do not treat each item individually but are quick to say, "When did we see you hungry, or thirsty, or a stranger, or naked, or sick or in prison, and did not minister to you, for we ministered the word to you." They refer to everything they did and tend to play down their evil actions, which might appear worse if enumerated one by one, for it is characteristic of wicked people to mention their faults, by way of excuse, as being either nonexistent or few and far between.

Commentary on Matthew

Monday - An Anglo-Saxon Homily

So the Savior said to the proud one: Why were you so miserly of My goods that I gave and granted to you? Why did you neglect the gift which I gave to you? I, now, withdraw you from My gift that I earlier gave to you; henceforth, you will be destitute in the earthly kingdom. Why would you not recall that I will reward each good deed that a man does for My name? I will reward it as it is said in My gospel: "inasmuch as you did it to one of the least of these My brethren, you did it to Me," and I will give to you eternal joy in heavens. Why are you so unthankful to Me for My goods and My gifts? Behold, I formed and enlivened you, and everything which you have, I gave you. It is all Mine, and I withdraw yours from you. Live without me if you can.

I gave it to you with the intent that you share it with the needy... When they were begging you for My goods, you always refused to them even a tithe. Why did you not wish to consider it? If only you had shown mercy to them, then you would not have lost a whit of that which you gave them, nor have angered Me with what I had given you. Why did you feed only yourself from that which I made for both of you that you may enjoy happiness and preservation of life? Why did you keep for yourself and your children what could have sufficed for many men? It was not easy for you that you might secure it all, nor seal it all up. Do you fancy that all the earth brings forth should be yours? She who grows and blooms and brings forth life? I now withdraw all my help from you; have from your labor and for your toil that which you are able. I will withhold from you My rains so that they do not rain on your ground. And I will withdraw from you My mercy, and then the portion of your sorrows will at once be made known and manifested... If you have power, dispense rains over your land. If you are strong, give fruit to your land. I will encourage My sun and she will illuminate them. When she burns up all of your acres, then you will be destitute of My rain, and then your land will be worthless to you and useless.

My poor live by means of Me. Dwell without me if you can. My poor have Me always, and I will never abandon them. My poor love me, and they call Me their Lord and name Him frequently and love and hold Him in awe, as men must to their Lord. Thus, you rich, you do not love your Lord, nor will you have mercy from Him, nor may you, poor wretch, live for long at all.

Vercelli Homily 10

Tuesday - Bede the Venerable

He brought about the redemption of His people by giving us freedom, at the price of His own blood we who had been sold into the slavery of sin and were held bound to serving the ancient enemy. Hence the Apostle does well to exhort us, saying, "For you have been purchased at a great price; glorify and carry God in your bodies."

When Zechariah says, "for his people," he surely does not mean that He found them His people at His arrival, but that He made them His by visiting and redeeming them. Do you want to hear, my brothers, in what condition He found this people, and what He made of them? The end of this canticle clearly makes this evident by saying, "The daystar from on high has visited us, to enlighten those who sit in darkness and in the shadow of death, to guide our feet into the way of peace." He found us sitting in darkness and in the shadow of death, weighed down, that is, by the long-standing blindness of sins and ignorance, beguiled by the deception and besieged by the errors of the ancient enemy. He is rightly called death and a lie, just as on the contrary our Lord is called truth and life. Our Lord brought us the true light of recognition of Himself, and having taken away the darkness of errors, opened up for us a sure way to the heavenly fatherland. He guided the course of our works so that we may be able to advance in the way of truth, which He pointed out to us, and enter into the dwelling of perpetual peace, which He promised us.

Since we possess these gifts of the divine goodness, dearly beloved brothers, these promises of eternal goods, let us bless the Lord at all times, because He has visited and wrought redemption for His people. Let His praise be continually in our mouth; let us retain the memory of Him, and tell one another of the virtues of Him "who has called you out of darkness into His own wonderful light." Let us constantly plead for His help, that He may preserve the light of knowledge which He has conferred upon us and bring us all the way to perfect day. And that we may be worthy of being heard as we make our entreaty, let us cast off the works of darkness and clothe ourselves with the armor of light.

Homily on the Nativity of John the Baptist

Wednesday - Gregory of Nyssa

The way which God entered upon for you, do you enter upon for Him, proceeding with one body and one soul to the invitation from above, loving God and each other. For love and fear of the Lord are the first fulfillment of the law. It is indeed necessary for each of you to put into your souls fear and love as a kind of strong and firm foundation, and to refresh it with good deeds and sufficient prayer. Love of God does not come to us simply or automatically, but through many sufferings and great concern in cooperation with Christ, as Wisdom has said: "If you shall seek her like silver and like hidden treasures search her out: then will you understand the fear of the Lord: the knowledge of God you will find." But once you have found the knowledge of God and understanding fear, you will easily succeed in what follows, I mean loving your neighbor. For the first and the greater is obtained through suffering, and the second and the lesser follows upon the first with less toil. However, if the first is not there, clearly the second will not be present. For if one does not love God with all his heart and all his soul, how can he care wholesomely and guilelessly for the love of his brothers, since he is not fulfilling the love of the One on whose account he has a care for the love of his brothers? The person in this condition, who has not given his whole soul to God and has not participated in his love, the craftsman of evil finds disarmed and easily overpowers.

On the Christian Mode of Life

Thursday - Aelfric of Eynsham

Who is our neighbor? Let us ask Christ. Truly he says of all Christians, "You are all brothers, and have one Father, who is high-sitting in heaven." Now it is said to you by the true Christ, that you are brothers if you hold the bond of true brotherhood unbroken. But who is closer to me than my brother? I also love him, and he is my neighbor. John the apostle wrote in his epistle, and said that we know Christ's love for us, because He gave Himself for us, and we should give ourselves for our brothers. He who has riches and will not spend them for an indigent brother, does not have true love. If you yet can not accomplish so much as to die yourself for a brother's life, give your riches for his support. If you don't do so in peace for God's sake, how will you give yourself for him when facing the calamitous persecution of impious murderers? It is incumbent on us to do good in peace, with a gracious mind to our fellow creature, and again in persecution to give our life for the true God, or for a brother, as Jesus gave Himself for us. But the guileful fiend sows discord among mankind in many ways, and instigates one man by his possessions, and inflames the mind with great anger against another who would persecute us. Then we lose, on account of a little wealth, true love which is the best of wealth. Rather we should always shield that true love which leads us to the Living God, not the possessions which will eventually perish.

Homily on the Greater Litany

Friday - Jerome of Jerusalem

He does not cure the blind man in the village, but outside, for he cannot be healed of his blindness in the Law, but in the Gospel. If this very day, Jesus should enter Bethsaida, the synagogue of the Jews, if Jesus - I mean the Divine Word - should go into the synagogue of the Jews, into their council, as long as that blind man is in the synagogue, in the letter of the law, he cannot be healed unless he is led outside.

"He led him forth outside the village; and applying spittle to his eyes, He laid His hands upon him." Christ's spittle is medicine. "Applying spittle to his eyes, he laid his hands upon him, and asked him if he saw anything." Knowledge is always progressive. One cannot taste of perfect wisdom in an hour, however experienced he may be. One cannot arrive at perfect knowledge without expending a great deal of time in long pursuit of it. First, the dirt is removed; then, the blindness is lifted, and light comes. The Lord's spittle is the perfect doctrine that proceeds from His mouth to instruct perfectly. The Lord's spittle, if I may so speak, is knowledge as from His very essence, for just as the word that comes forth from His mouth is medicine, even so does His spittle seem to come forth from the very substance of God. This, then, is the meaning of our passage: with a penetrating contact, he wipes away the errors from his eyes... Spittle cures his eyes, hands are imposed upon the head; spittle drives out blindness, hands impart a blessing.

Homily 79

Saturday - Commodianus

By living doubtfully between faith and the world, thinking you are safe, you go on your way stripped of law and broken down by luxury. You are vainly looking forward to so many things. Why do you seek unjust things? And whatever you have done will there remain yours when dead. Consider, O foolish one, you once were not, and behold, now you are. You don't understand how you proceeded or how you are now preserved. You avoid the good and excellent God of your life, who is your Governor and who would rather see you live. In turning in on yourself you turn your back on God. You drown yourself in darkness while thinking that you are dwelling in light. Why do you run to the synagogue to the Pharisees, that He may become merciful to you, whom you of your own accord deny? You go abroad again from there, seeking what you think to be good things. You wish to live between both ways, but then you shall perish. Because you face punishment you say, "Who is He who has redeemed from death, that we may believe in Him?" Ah! But it will not be as you think it will, O evil man. For to him who has lived well there is advantage after death. You, however, when the day comes that you die, will be taken away to an evil place. But those who believe in Christ will be led into a good place and will delight in God's kind caress. But to you, the double minded, against you is punishment of the soul and your torment will stir you up to cry out against your brother.

The Instructions

Collect

O Lord, so rule and govern our hearts and minds by Your Holy Spirit that, being ever mindful of the end of all things and the day of Your just judgment, we may be stirred up to holiness of living here and dwell with You forever hereafter; through Jesus Christ, Your Son, our Lord, who lives and reigns with You and the Holy Spirit, one God, now and forever. *Swedish Evangeliebok, 1639*

AT LAUDS

Psalmody

Sunday: 67, C1, 5	Wednesday: 64, C4, 65	Friday: 76, C5, 92
Monday: 63, C2, 36	Thursday: 88, C6, 90	Saturday: 143, C7, 148
Tuesday: 43, C3, 57		

Lesson

Sunday: Amos 7:1-9	Wednesday: Micah 4:1-8	Friday: Nahum 1:15-2:13
Monday: Obadiah 1-21	Thursday: Micah 6:1-8	Saturday: Habakkuk 1:1-2:14
Tuesday: Jonah 3:1-4:11		

Collect

O King, glorious among Your saints, who are ever to be praised, yet never to be expressed; You, O Lord, are in the midst of us and Your Holy Name has been placed upon us. Leave us not, O our God; but in the day of Judgment deign to place us among Your saints and elect, O King most blessèd. *Sarum Breviary*

AT TERCE, SEXT AND NONE

Chapter: II Peter 3:3-14

AT VESPERS

Psalmody

Sunday: 110, 111, 112, 113	Wednesday: 123, 124, 125	Friday: 129, 130, 131, 132
Monday: 114, 115, 116, 117	Thursday: 126, 127, 128	Saturday: 133, 135, 136a
Tuesday: 120, 121, 122		

Lesson

Sunday: Amos 9:8-15	Wednesday: Micah 5:2-15	Friday: Nahum 3:1-19
Monday: Jonah 1:1-2:10	Thursday: Micah 7:8-20	Saturday: Habakkuk
Tuesday: Micah 2:1-13		2:15-3:19

Collect

O almighty, eternal and merciful God, who by Your beloved Son, our Lord and Savior Jesus Christ, has established the kingdom of grace for us that we might believe the forgiveness of our sins in Thy holy Church on earth, since You are a God who takes no pleasure in the death of the wicked, but that the wicked turn from his way and live: We implore You, graciously forgive us all our sins, through the same, Your Son Jesus Christ, who lives and reigns with You and the Holy Spirit, one God, now and forever.   *Veit Dietrich*

THE TWENTY-SEVENTH WEEK
AFTER TRINITY

AT MATINS

Hymn - *Wachet auf, ruft uns die Stimme*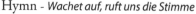

1. "Wake, a - wake, for night is fly - ing," The watch-men on the heights are cry - ing; "A - wake, Je - ru - sa - lem, a - rise!" Mid-night hears the wel-come voic - es And at the thrill-ing cry re - joic - es: "Oh, where are ye, ye vir - gins wise? The Bride-groom comes, a- wake! Your lamps with glad-ness take! Al - le - lu - ia! With brid - al care Your-selves pre - pare To meet the Bride - groom, who is near."

2. Zion hears the watchmen singing,
And all her heart with joy is springing,
She wakes, she rises from her gloom;
For her Lord comes down all-glorious,
The strong in grace, in truth victorious,
Her Star is ris'n, her Light is come.
Now come, Thou Blessèd One,
Lord Jesus, God's own Son,
Hail! Hosanna!
We enter all the wedding hall
To eat the Supper at Thy call.

3. Now let all the heav'ns adore Thee,
Let men and angels sing before Thee,
With harp and cymbal's clearest tone.
Of one pearl each shining portal,
Where, dwelling with the choir immortal,
We gather round Thy radiant throne.
No eye hath seen the light,
No ear hath heard the might,
Of Thy glory;
Therefore will we Eternally
Sing hymns of praise and joy to Thee!

Philip Nicolai, 1599

Psalmody

Lesson

Homily

Sunday - Gregory I of Rome

When the prophet saw this day, he said: That day will be a day of wrath, a day of distress and agony, a day of ruin and misery, a day of darkness and gloom, a day of clouds and hurricanes, a day of trumpet blast and uproar. Consider, my friend, how harsh for the hearts of the wicked the prophet saw that the day of judgment would be. He could not find enough words to describe it. But how great will be the happiness of the elect, those who will be found worthy to rejoice when they see him! At sight of him they observe all the elements trembling; and they are to enter marriage together with him. They rejoice at the bridegroom's marriage; and yet they themselves are the bride. In the bridal chamber of the eternal kingdom God is joined to our sight; and this sight will never be parted from the embraces of his love.

Then the door of the kingdom, which only today was open to those who repent, will be closed to those who wail. Even then there will be repentance, but it will be fruitless. No one will find pardon then, who squanders the time appropriate for it. Because of this Paul said: See, now is the acceptable time, see, now is the day of salvation; the prophet: Seek for the Lord while he can be found, call upon him while he is near.

Hence the Lord does not hear the same foolish virgins when they call upon him. Once the door of the kingdom has been shut, they have lost their chance to be near him. And then he added: Last of all the rest of the virgins also came, saying: "Lord, Lord, open to us." But he said in reply: "Truly I say to you, I do not know you." No one who was unwilling to listen to his precepts here will there be found worthy to receive what he asks for. It is in vain that one who has squandered the time suitable for repentance comes before the door of the kingdom with his entreaties.

Homily 10, on Matthew 25

Monday - An Anglo-Saxon Homily

It must happen that the sea will surge, a flood over the land. Life will have an end for each and all. Often may the one who wishes hold this truth in his own heart. Our Lord has set Himself an advent here on that proud day, highest of powerful kings. Then the King of humankind will kindle the land with fire. That will not be a little gathering to convene! Flame will be fueled once fire has grabbed the ends of the earth, the burning flame the bright creation. All this wide world will be filled with embers, cruel coals, since now grim-minded men rule, boastfully rebel against their Lord, do business with laughter, until the guardians of sin seduce them so they seek hell with a heap of the damned, fly away with the fiends. Fire will find them in troublesome torture. Day never shines there lightly in the sky, but it always stands locked once terror has taken hold of the soul. It is narrow above, and it is hot inside. It is not a grand house, but the greatest of horrors is there, not a hopeful home, but the abyss of hell is there, a terrible trip for the one who often mars the peace with his mouth. Nor does he know that murky creation: how eternally it stands without end for the one who is thrown there, a sacrifice for his sins, and there endures his fate forever. *On Judgement Day*

Tuesday - Paschasius Radbertus

Watch, for you do not know the day or the hour... The Last Day and the end of the world will come for each of us on the day we depart this present life. This means we must make sure we die in the state in which we wish to appear on the Day of Judgment. Bearing this in mind each of us should guard against being led astray and failing to keep watch, otherwise the day of the Lord's return may take us unawares. If the last day of our life finds us unprepared, then we shall be unprepared on that day also.

I do not for a moment believe the apostles expected the Lord to return in judgment during their own lifetime. All the same there can be no doubt that they took every care not to be drawn from the right path. They kept watch, observing the universal precepts their master had given to His disciples so as to be ready when He came again.

Consequently we must always be on the lookout for Christ's twofold coming, the one when we shall have to give an account of everything we have done, and the other when he comes day by day to stir our consciences. He comes to us now in order that his future coming may find us prepared. If my conscience is burdened with sin what good will it do me to know when the Day of Judgment will be? Unless the Lord comes to my soul beforehand and makes his home with me, unless Christ lives in me and speaks His word in my heart, it is useless for me to know if and when His coming will take place. Only if Christ is already living in me and I in Him will it go well with me when He comes in judgment. If I have already died to the world and am able to say, The world is crucified to me, and I to the world, then, in a sense, His final coming is already present to me. *Commentary on Matthew*

Wednesday - Gregory I of Rome

The Lord follows his preachers. Preaching comes first, and then the Lord comes to the dwelling places of our hearts; words of exhortation precede, and by means of them Truth is received by hearts. This is why Isaiah addresses preachers: Prepare the way of the Lord, make straight the pathways of our God! ...

Against all this we must consider that we are sent like lambs among wolves, so that we may preserve our awareness of innocence, and not have the sting of malice. A person who undertakes the office of preaching should not cause evils but rather suffer them. By his gentleness he may allay the anger of the violent, and being himself wounded by ill-treatment from others, he may heal the wounds of sinners. If his zeal for rectitude ever demands that he show anger against those subject to him, let his passion be the result of love and not of cruelty, then he may show proper regard for discipline externally, and love inwardly, with a father's devotion, toward those whom he reproves outwardly as if he were attacking them.

A leader shows this when he seeks nothing of the world, when he does not bend his neck under the burden of earthly desires. Hence the Lord says: "Carry no purse, no bag, no sandals; do not greet anyone on the road." A preacher should have such reliance on God that, even if he makes no provision for the needs of the present life, he may be certain that he will lack nothing. Otherwise, while his mind is engaged in temporal affairs, he may make less provision for the eternal good of others. Also he is not allowed to greet anyone on the road. This shows the great haste with which he ought to set out on the journey of his preaching. *Homily 19, on Luke 10*

Thursday - Cyril of Alexandria

Go, behold, I send you as sheep among wolves. What are You saying O Lord? How can sheep converse with wolves? When was a wild beast ever at peace with the sheep? Scarcely can the shepherds protect their flocks by gathering them into folds, and shutting them up in enclosures, and frightening the beasts of prey by the barking of dogs, yes, and even fighting themselves in their defense and running risks to protect the weaker members of their flock. How then does He command the holy Apostles, who are guileless men, and if we may so speak, sheep, to seek the company of wolves, and go to them of their own accord? Is not the danger manifest? Are they not set as an easy prey for their attacks? How can a sheep prevail over a wolf? How can one so peaceful vanquish the savageness of beasts of prey? Yes, He says, for they all have Me as their Shepherd; small and great; people and princes; teachers and taught. I will be with you and aid you, and deliver you from all evil. I will tame the savage beasts, I will change wolves into sheep.

Homily 61 on Luke

Friday - Bernard of Clairvaux

I reflect upon the fact that I am a human being - that is, I meditate upon the great privileges that God considered humanity worthy to receive. He set mankind over all earthly things, and while all other animals stoop forward toward the earth, "He gave each man an upturned face, so he could look up to heaven." "You crowned Him with glory and honor, Lord, and placed Him over what you have made." Animals He permitted only to taste earthly things, but on human beings He bestowed the capacity to enjoy eternal things of heaven. It is properly written that things which are visible last but for a time, while things which are invisible are eternal. Surely this represents a great honor given me by God! He gave me reason with which to judge myself and examine all my deeds, so that I will not be judged by anyone else. For as the apostle writes: "For if we would judge ourselves, we would not be judged." Brute beasts are not damned, therefore, because the power to judge themselves and to examine everything has not been given to them. It has been granted, however, to human beings.

The Sentences, Third Series

Saturday - Baldwin of Forde

Our Jesus therefore, is with us. Why should I not call him "ours" since He was given to us? "For unto us the Son is given." He who says, "As for me, I will rejoice in the Lord, and I will exult in God my Jesus," claims for himself a certain right to this Jesus. This Jesus of ours, with whom God has given us all things, cannot bear to be absent from us. He loves us so much that He who is the Wisdom of the Father says, "My delight is to be with the sons of men." He was with us in the flesh before He died for us; He was with us in death, insofar as His bodily presence was not yet lifted from the earth; after death, when He appeared to His disciples and gave them many proofs; and He is with us even now, even to the end of the world, until we shall be with Him, for we shall be always with the Lord. See how greatly Jesus loves us!

Neither death nor life can separate Him from us in the charity with which He loves us. For that reason, neither death nor life should separate us from His charity. Whom else should we love? Or rather whom should we love in the way that He is loved? For apart from all else, if we are not ungrateful and mean, it should be enough that He loves us. To someone who loves is owed above all an exchange of love. He who loves wants to be loved, and this is indeed right and proper. But if someone wants to be loved and does not want to love, it would be very strange if he judged himself and acquitted himself of being unjust. It is a true judgement that he who does not love the one that loves him is himself unworthy to be loved, and truly, he who does not love Jesus puts himself in great danger, worthy of the Apostle's execration and curse: "If anyone does not love our Lord Jesus Christ, let him be anathema, Maranatha!" Contrary to this is the same's prayer: "Grace be with all those who love our Lord Jesus Christ in sincerity." Jesus loved us first indeed, and lest we not love Him, He is with us even to the end of the world. "The Lord of hosts is with us, the God of Jacob is our refuge." *Tractate 1, on the Most Holy Sacrament of the Eucharist*

Collect

Absolve, we implore You, O Lord, Your people from their offenses, that from the bonds of our sins which by reason of our frailty we have brought upon us we may be delivered by Your bountiful goodness; through Jesus Christ, Your Son, our Lord, who lives and reigns with You and the Holy Spirit, one God, now and forever. *Gelasian Sacramentary*

AT LAUDS

Psalmody

Sunday: 3, C8, 51	Wednesday: 8, C11, 20	Friday: 146, C13, 5
Monday: 118a, C9, 118b	Thursday: 18a, C12, 18b	Saturday: 149, C14, 150
Tuesday: 1, C10, 2		

Lesson

Sunday: Zephaniah 1:14-2:3	Wednesday: Zechariah 6:9-15	Friday: Malachi 1:1-14
Monday: Haggai 1:1-2:9	Thursday: Zechariah 9:9-17	Saturday: Malachi 3:1-15
Tuesday: Zechariah 1:1-17		

Collect

Come now, High King of Heaven. Come to us in flesh and bone. Bring life to us who are weary with misery. Bring peace to us who are overcome with weeping, whose cheeks are covered with bitter salt tears. Seek us out, who are lost in the darkness of despair. Do not forget us, but show mercy on us. Impart to us your everlasting joy, so that we, who are fashioned by Your hands, may praise Your glory, for You live and reign with the Father and the Holy Spirit, One God, now and forever. Amen. *Exeter Book, c.950*

AT TERCE, SEXT AND NONE

Chapter

Sunday: I Thessalonians 5:1-11
Monday and Tuesday: II Corinthians 5:1-10
Wednesday and Thursday: I Thessalonians 1:1-10
Friday and Saturday: II Thessalonians 1:3-10

AT VESPERS

Psalmody

Sunday: 136b, 137, 138
Monday: 140, 141, 142
Tuesday: 144, 145, 7

Wednesday: 9, 10, 11
Thursday: 12, 13, 14, 16

Friday: 17, 147a, 147b
Saturday: 19, 54, 77

Lesson

Sunday: Zephaniah 3:5-20
Monday: Haggai 2:10-23
Tuesday: Zechariah 2:10-3:10:

Wednesday: Zechariah 8:1-23
Thursday: Zechariah 13:1-9

Friday: Malachi 2:1-17
Saturday: Malachi 3:16-4:6

Collect

O God, You are well-disposed to us; give us the strength of Your support. Give us encouragement, give the light that goes with it. Make us live by the dogmas of the Faith preached by Your holy apostles and the high teachings of the gospels of our Savior, Jesus Christ. Teach us to look upwards, to seek out and probe the heavenly, not the earthly. If that is our attitude and if You act in us, what glory for Your power, all-holy, omnipotent, praiseworthy; glory through Jesus Christ, Your beloved Son, with the Holy Spirit, now and forever. Amen.

An ancient papyrus, c.3rd-4th century

PROPERS FOR FEASTS
and Commemorations

The propers for all feasts and commemorations are intended for use at Matins but may be used at other hours as well.

November 30 - The Feast of St. Andrew, Apostle

Lesson: Matthew 4:18-25 or Mark 1:16-20

Homily - Gregory I

You have heard, dearly beloved, that at a single command Peter and Andrew left their nets and followed the Redeemer. They had at this time seen Him perform no miracles, they had heard nothing from Him about eternal retribution: and yet at a single command from the Lord they forgot everything they seemed to possess.

How many of His miracles do we see? How much suffering do we endure? How many harsh warnings threaten us? And yet we refuse to follow Him when he calls. He who counsels us about conversion is already seated in heaven; He has already subjected the necks of the Gentiles to the yoke of faith; He has already laid low the world's glory; in its mounting ruins He already declares the approaching day of His strict judgment: and yet our proud hearts do not desire willingly to abandon what they lose daily, whether they will or not. Dearly beloved, what are we going to say at His judgment, we who are not turned away from love of the present world by commands nor corrected by buffeting?

No one should say to himself, even when he regards others who have left a great deal behind, "I want to imitate those who despise this world, but I have nothing to leave behind." You leave a great deal behind, my friends, if you renounce your desires. Our external possessions, no matter how small, are enough for the Lord: He weighs the heart and not the substance, and does not measure the amount we sacrifice to Him but the effort with which we bring it. If we think only about the outward substance, we see that our holy traders purchased the everlasting life of angels when they gave up their nets and boat! The kingdom of God has no assessment value put on it, but it is worth everything you have. To Zacchaeus it was worth half his goods, because he kept the other half to restore fourfold what he had taken unjustly; to Peter and Andrew it was worth the nets and boat they gave up; to the widow it was worth two small coins, to another person it was worth a cup of cold water. The kingdom of God, as I said, is worth everything you have.

Homily 2, on Matthew 4

Collect

Almighty God, who gave such grace to your holy Apostle Saint Andrew that he readily obeyed the calling of Your Son Jesus Christ, and followed Him without delay; grant to us all, that we, being called by Your holy Word, may at once and obediently give up ourselves to fulfill Your holy commandments; through the same, Jesus Christ, Your Son, our Lord, who lives and reigns with You and the Holy Spirit, one God, now and forever.

December 4 - The Commemoration of John of Damascus, Bishop & Teacher

Confirm our minds, O Lord, in the mysteries of the true faith which have been set forth with power by your servant John of Damascus; that we, with him, confessing Jesus to be true God and true Man, and singing the praises of the risen Lord, may by the power of the resurrection attain to eternal joy; through Jesus Christ our Lord, who lives and reigns with you and the Holy Spirit, one God, now and for ever. Amen.

December 6 - The Commemoration of Nicholas of Myra, Bishop & Confessor

Almighty God, in your love you gave your servant Nicholas of Myra a perpetual name for deeds of kindness both on land and sea: Grant, we pray, that your Church may never cease to work for the happiness of children, the safety of sailors, the relief of the poor, and the help of those tossed by tempests of doubt or grief; through Jesus Christ our Lord, who lives and reigns with you and the Holy Spirit, one God, for ever and ever. Amen.

December 7 - The Commemoration of Ambrose of Milan, Bishop & Teacher

O God, you gave your servant Ambrose grace eloquently to proclaim your righteousness in the great congregation, and fearlessly to bear reproach for the honor of your Name: Mercifully grant to all bishops and pastors such excellence in preaching and faithfulness in ministering your Word, that your people may be partakers with them of the glory that shall be revealed; through Jesus Christ our Lord, who lives and reigns with you and the Holy Spirit, one God, now and for ever. Amen.

Lesser Feasts and Fasts

December 13 - The Commemoration of Lucia, Martyr

Loving God, for the salvation of all you gave Jesus Christ as light to a world in darkness: Illumine us, with your daughter Lucy, with the light of Christ, that by the merits of his passion we may be led to eternal life; through the same Jesus Christ, who with you and the Holy Spirit lives and reigns, one God, for ever and ever. Amen.

December 20 - The Commemoration of Sebastian, Martyr

O Lord, grant us courage by Your Spirit, that as you once strengthened Sebastian to suffer martyrdom in faithful witness of Christ, You would also strengthen us in the Faith, and teach us by his noble example to cherish Your law above human laws and to obey You rather than men, through Jesus Christ, Your Son, our Lord, who lives and reigns with You and the Holy Spirit, one God, now and forever. Amen.

December 21 - The Feast of St. Thomas, Apostle

Lesson: John 20:24-31

Homily - Baldwin of Forde

The word of God is plainly shown in all its strength and wisdom to those who seek out Christ, who is the word, the power and the wisdom of God. This word was with the Father in the beginning, and in its own time was revealed to the apostles, then preached by them and humbly received in faith by believers. So, the word is in the Father, as well as on our lips and in our hearts...

When this word is preached, in the very act of preaching it gives to its own voice which is heard outwardly a certain power which perceived inwardly, so much so that the dead are brought back to life and... the children of Abraham are raised from the dead. This word then is alive in the heart of the Father, on the lips of the preacher, and in the hearts of those who believe and love Him. Since this word is so truly alive, undoubtedly it is full of power.

It is powerful in creation, powerful in the government of the universe, powerful in the redemption of the world. For what is more powerful, more effective? Who shall speak of its power; who shall make its praises heard? It is powerful in what it accomplishes, powerful when it is preached. It does not come back empty; it bears fruit in all to whom it is sent.

It is powerful and "more piercing than any two-edged sword" when it is believed and loved. For what is impossible to the believer? What is difficult for the lover? When this word is spoken, its message pierces the heart like the sharp arrows of a strong archer, like nails driven deep; it enters so deeply that it penetrates to the innermost recess. This word is much more piercing than any two-edged sword, inasmuch as it is stronger than any courage or power, sharper than any shrewdness of human ingenuity, keener than all human wisdom, or the subtlety of learned argument.

Tractate 6, On the Word of God

Collect

Almighty and everliving God, who, for the greater confirmation of the Faith, suffered your holy Apostle Thomas to doubt Your Son's resurrection; grant to us believe perfectly and without any doubt in Your Son Jesus Christ, that our faith may never be reproved in Your sight. Hear us, O Lord, through the same, Jesus Christ, Your Son, our Lord, who lives and reigns with You and the Holy Spirit, one God, now and forever.

December 26 - The Feast of St. Stephen, Protomartyr

Collect

Grant us, O Lord, to learn to love our enemies by the example of Your martyr, St. Stephen, who prayed to You for his persecutors, who lives and reigns with the Father and the Holy Spirit, one God, now and forever.

December 27 - The Feast of St. John, Apostle & Evangelist

Collect

Merciful Lord, we implore You to cast the bright beams of Your light upon Your church, that, being illuminated by the doctrine of Your blessèd apostle and evangelist St. John, we may so walk in the light of Your truth, that we may at last come to the light of everlasting life, through Jesus Christ, Your Son, our Lord, who lives and reigns with You and the Holy Spirit, one God, now and forever.

December 28 - The Feast of Holy Innocents, Martyrs

Collect

O God, whose martyred innocents showed forth Your praise not by speaking but by dying, mortify all vices in us that our lives may indeed confess the Faith which our tongues speak, through Jesus Christ, Your Son, our Lord, who lives and reigns with You and the Holy Spirit, one God, now and forever.

December 31 - The Commemoration of Sylvester, Bishop

O Almighty Father, by the Word of Your Son, Jesus Christ, You guided your servant, Sylvester, in the way of truth; guide us also, we pray, by that same Word, that we may be preserved steadfast in our confession of the Faith, through the same, Jesus Christ, Your Son, our Lord, who lives and reigns with you and the Holy Spirit, one God, now and forever. Amen.

January 2 - The Commemoration of Wilhelm Löhe, Pastor

O Lord, our loving Father, You filled your servant Wilhelm with a love of Your Gospel and a zeal for the extension of Your Holy Church; grant us, we pray, to have the same evangelical zeal, that the preaching and teaching of the Gospel may be furthered among us and throughout the world, through the same, Jesus Christ, Your Son, our Lord, who lives and reigns with You and the Holy Spirit, one God, now and forever. Amen.

January 14 - The Commemoration of Hilary of Poitiers, Bishop & Teacher

O Lord our God, you raised up your servant Hilary to be a champion of the catholic faith: Keep us steadfast in that true faith which we professed at our baptism, that we may rejoice in having you for our Father, and may abide in your Son, in the fellowship of the Holy Spirit; who live and reign forever and ever. Amen.

January 17 - The Commemoration of Antony of Egypt, Abbot

O God, who by your Holy Spirit enabled your servant Antony to withstand the temptations of the world, the flesh, and the devil: Give us grace, with pure hearts and minds, to follow you, the only God; through Jesus Christ our Lord, who lives and reigns with you and the Holy Spirit, one God, for ever and ever. Amen.

January 18 - The Feast of the Confession of St. Peter

Lesson: Matthew 16:13-19   or Luke 9:18-27

Homily - Prosper of Aquitaine

In many men grace produces great fervor from its first stirrings and then it is quickly enriched with considerable increase. But in many also who advance slowly and hesitatingly, it hardly grows strong enough to reach the firmness that is necessary for perseverance. Our Lord indeed says, No man can come to me, except the Father, who has sent me, draw him. But Christ said this to teach us that faith, without which no one can come to Him, is a gift of the Father. This was shown in what He said to the Apostle Peter: Blessed art you, Simon Bar-Jonah; because flesh and blood hath not revealed it to you, but My Father who is in heaven. It is the Father who in the hearts of the men He wished to draw to Himself produced both the faith and the good will. Men who refuse the faith are neither drawn to Him nor do they come to Him. When they withhold their free consent, they do not come nearer, rather they go farther away from Him. It is love that leads to Him all those who come to Him. He loved them first and they returned His love. He sought them first and they in turn sought Him; and when God inspired their will with His own, they willingly followed Him.

The Call of All Nations

Collect

Heavenly Father, You revealed to Your holy apostle St. Peter the blessèd truth that Your Son Jesus is the Christ; strengthen us by the proclamation of this truth, that we may joyfully confess that there is salvation in no other; through the same Jesus Christ, Your Son, our Lord, who lives and reigns with You and the Holy Spirit, one God, now and forever.

January 24 - The Feast of St. Timothy, Bishop & Missionary

Lesson: John 21:15-17

Homily - John Chrysostom

For if a man "cannot enter into the kingdom of heaven except he be born again of water and the spirit," and if he that eats not the Lord's flesh and drinks not his blood is cast out of everlasting life, and all these things can happen through no other agency except their sacred hands (the priests', I mean), how can anyone, without their help, escape the fire of Gehenna or win his appointed crown? They are the ones-they and no others-who are in charge of spiritual travail and responsible for the birth that comes through baptism. Through them we put on Christ and are united with the Son of God and become limbs obedient to that blessed Head. So they should properly be not only more feared than rulers and kings, but more honored even than fathers. For our fathers begot us "of blood and the will of the flesh;" but they are responsible for our birth from God, that blessed second birth, our true emancipation, the adoption according to grace.

The priests of the Jews had authority to cure leprosy of the body, or rather, not to cure it, but only to certify the cure. And you know what rivalry there used to be for the priesthood then. But our priests have received authority not over leprosy of the body but over uncleanness of the soul, and not just to certify its cure, but actually to cure it. So people who look down on them are far more execrable than Dathan and his company and deserve more punishment. For although they claimed an office which did not belong to them, at least they had a marvellous opinion of it, as they showed by wanting it so much. But the people we are considering have done just the opposite at a time when the priesthood has been so embellished and enhanced. Their presumption, therefore, is far greater. In the assessment of contempt there is no comparison between coveting an honor which does not belong to you and making light of it. Between one and the other there is all the difference between admiration and disdain. Who could be so beggarly-minded as to make light of these great blessings? No one, I should say, except the victim of some demonic impulse.

On the Priesthood

Collect

Lord Jesus Christ, You have always given Your Church on earth faithful pastors to guide and feed Your flock; make all pastors to follow the good example of St. Timothy and to faithfully preach Your Holy Word and administer Your Holy Sacraments to Your people; and grant Your people wisdom to follow in the way that leads to eternal life, for You live and reign with the Father and the Holy Spirit, one God, now and forever.

January 25 - The Feast of the Conversion of St. Paul

Lesson: Matthew 19:27-30

Homily - Martin Luther

This is a doctrine different from all others. Moses does not reveal the Son of God; he discloses the Law, sin, the conscience, death, the wrath and judgment of God, and hell. These things are not the Son of God! Therefore only the Gospel reveals the Son of God. Oh, if only one could distinguish carefully here and not look for the Law in the Gospel but keep it as separate from the Law as heaven is distant from the earth! In itself the difference is easy and clear, but to us it is difficult and well-nigh incomprehensible. For it is easy to say that the Gospel is nothing but the revelation of the Son of God or the knowledge of Jesus Christ and not the revelation or knowledge of the Law. But in the conflict of conscience and in practice it is difficult even for those who have had a lot of experience to hold to this for certain.

Now if the Gospel is the revelation of the Son of God, as it really is, then it certainly does not demand works, threaten death, or terrify the conscience. But it shows the Son of God, who is neither the Law nor a work. But this simply cannot persuade the papists. Therefore they make a "Law of charity" of the Gospel. But Christ is the subject of the Gospel. What the Gospel teaches and shows me is a divine work given to me by sheer grace; neither human reason nor wisdom nor even the Law of God teaches this. And I accept this gift by faith alone.

This sort of doctrine, which reveals the Son of God, is not taught, learned, or judged by any human wisdom or by the Law itself; it is revealed by God, first by the external Word and then inwardly through the Spirit. Therefore the Gospel is a divine Word that came down from heaven and is revealed by the Holy Spirit, who was sent for this very purpose. Yet this happens in such a way that the external Word must come first. For Paul himself did not have an inward revelation until he had heard the outward Word from heaven, namely, "Saul, Saul, why do you persecute Me?" Thus he heard the outward Word first; only then did there follow revelations, the knowledge of the Word, faith, and the gifts of the Spirit.

Lectures on Galatians

Collect

O God, who through the preaching of Your blessèd Apostle St. Paul has caused the light of Your Gospel to shine to the Gentile world, give us grace to always rejoice in the saving light of Your Gospel and to spread it to the uttermost parts of the earth; through Jesus Christ, Your Son, our Lord, who lives and reigns with You and the Holy Spirit, one God, now and forever.

January 26 - The Feast of St. Titus, Bishop

Lesson: Matthew 24:42-47

Homily - Jerome of Jerusalem

It is not expedient for the apostles to know [the day of judgment]. Thus they will always believe that He is coming with the uncertainty of an imminent expectation. For they do not know when He will come... And he introduces the example of the householder, that is, Himself, and of the faithful servants, that is, the Apostles, as an encouragement to solicitous minds. With the expectation of receiving rewards, they are to serve their fellow servants the food of doctrines at the proper time.

Just as a solicitous servant and one who is always expecting the coming of his master gives food to his fellow servants at the proper time, and afterward he is appointed over all the goods of the householder, so on the contrary he who does not think that his master will come soon becomes rather secure and he takes it easy with feasting and luxury... [Such a one] will encounter in the householder not leniency but a most severe judge. The master of that servant will come on a day that he does not expect and at an hour he does not know, and he will separate him and put his share with the hypocrites. He teaches the same thing, that they might know that the lord is going to come at a time when he is not being thought of. He admonishes the stewards to vigilance and solicitude.

Commentary on Matthew

Collect

Almighty God, You called St. Titus to the work of bishop and teacher; make all shepherds of Your flock diligent in the preaching of Your Holy Word, that the entire world may know the boundless riches of our Savior, Jesus Christ, who lives and reigns with You and the Holy Spirit, one God, now and forever.

January 27 - The Commemoration of John Chrysostom, Bishop & Teacher

O God, you gave your servant John Chrysostom grace eloquently to proclaim your righteousness in the great congregation of Constantinople, and fearlessly to bear reproach for the honor of your Name: Mercifully grant to all bishops and pastors such excellence in preaching, and faithfulness in ministering your Word, that your people may be partakers with them of the glory that shall be revealed; through Jesus Christ our Lord, who lives and reigns with you and the Holy Spirit, one God, forever and ever.

January 28 - The Commemoration of Charlemagne, Holy Roman Emperor

Grant unto us, O Lord, faithful and zealous rulers who will uphold and further Your Gospel in our lands; that the work of Your Church may not be hindered but supported, and that those in the darkness of unbelief and error may be brought to the grace of Holy Baptism and joined to her holy fellowship; through Jesus Christ, Your Son, our Lord, who lives and reigns with You and the Holy Spirit, now and forever. Amen.

February 2 - The Feast of the Presentation of Our Lord

Lesson: Luke 2:22-32

Homily - Amphilochius of Iconium

Do you not see that the blessing of marriage, and what is said of all, is fulfilled only in the Lord? Namely that "Every male who opens the womb shall be called holy to the Lord." This refers to the Lord alone, and not to any others, though spoken of all who are firstborn. For with anyone who is a virgin, the way of nature is that the womb be opened by intercourse with a man. But it was not so with our Savior. Rather He Himself opened the womb of the virgin without intercourse and came forth in a transcendent manner. So these words "Every male who opens the womb shall be called holy to the Lord," refer to the Lord alone.

Was Cain holy, who laid violent hands on life, and who was the first of all to come forth from the maternal womb? Was Esau holy, the wild man, whose inheritance was the sword, since he also came first from the womb of his mother? Was Ruben holy, who violated his father's bed, and provoked a curse? He too came first from the fertile womb of Leah. Not one of these was holy, but all were given to chastisement. By this it is shown that this refers only to the Lord...

And he is merely being argumentative who says that if this refers to the Lord... then the Virgin did not remain a virgin. For the Scripture clearly says: "Every male opening the womb," and the virgin's womb, then, was truly opened if this refers to the Lord. But listen intelligently. In the Virgin Birth the virginal gates were not opened in any way. This is according to God's will, who was conceived there, and according to the words spoken concerning Him: "This gate shall be shut. It shall not be opened, and no man shall pass through it, because the Lord God of Israel has entered by it; therefore it shall be shut." In regard to that which pertains to the nature of the virgin, the virginal gates were not in any way opened; but in regard to that which pertains to the power of the Master who was born, nothing is shut to the Lord, but all things are open to Him. Nothing stands in His way. Nothing impedes Him. For all things are open to the Lord. And so the powers of heaven command the powers beneath: "Lift up the gates, O you rulers, and be lifted up you everlasting doors. And the King of Glory shall enter." *In Praise of Virginity, Marriage and Widowhood*

Collect

Almighty and everlasting God, we humbly implore Your Majesty, that as Your Only-begotten Son was this day presented in the Temple in the substance of our flesh, so we may be presented to You with pure and clean hearts by the same, Jesus Christ, Your Son, our Lord, who lives and reigns with You and the Holy Spirit, one God, now and forever.

February 14 - The Commemoration of Valentine, Martyr

Almighty and merciful Lord, deliver us, we pray, from the many dangers that beset us, and as You gave Your servant Valentine the grace of wisdom and of love, grant us the same also, that we may, like him, speak with the truth in love to all in need of counsel, even to our enemies; through Jesus Christ, Your Son, our Lord, who lives and reigns with You and the Holy Spirit, now and forever.

February 18 - The Commemoration of Martin Luther, Pastor & Teacher

O God, our refuge and our strength: You raised up your servant Martin Luther to reform and renew your Church in the light of your word. Defend and purify the Church in our own day and grant that, through faith, we may boldly proclaim the riches of your grace, which you have made known in Jesus Christ our Savior, who with you and the Holy Spirit, lives and reigns, one God, now and forever.

February 23 - The Commemoration of Polycarp of Smyrna, Bishop & Martyr

O God, the maker of heaven and earth, you gave your venerable servant, the holy and gentle Polycarp, boldness to confess Jesus Christ as King and Saviour, and steadfastness to die for his faith: Give us grace, following his example, to share the cup of Christ and rise to eternal life; through Jesus Christ our Lord, who lives and reigns with you and the Holy Spirit, one God, now and forever.

February 24 - The Feast of St. Matthias, Apostle

Lesson: Matthew 11:25-30

Homily - Bernard of Clairvaux

To will lies in our power indeed as a result of free choice, but not to carry out what we will. I am not saying to will the good or to will the bad, but simply to will. For to will the good indicates an achievement; and to will the bad, a defect; whereas simply to will denotes the subject itself which does either the achieving or the failing. To this subject, however, creating grace gives existence. Saving grace gives it the achievement. But when it fails, it is to blame for its own failure. Free choice, accordingly, constitutes us willers; grace, willers of the good. Because of our willing faculty, we are able to will; but because of grace, to will the good. Just as, simply to fear is one thing, and to fear God, another; to love, one thing, and to love God, another, - since to fear and to love, on their own signify affections, but coupled with the additional word "God," virtues - so also to will is one thing, and to will the good, another. For mere affections live naturally in us, as of us, but those additional acts, as of grace. This means only that grace sets in order what creation has given, so that virtues are nothing else than ordered affections. *On Grace and Free Choice*

Collect

O almighty God, who in place of the traitor Judas chose Your faithful servant Matthias to be of the number of the twelve Apostles, grant that Your Church, being always preserved from false apostles, may be ordered and guided by faithful and true pastors; through Jesus Christ, Your Son, our Lord, who lives and reigns with You and the Holy Spirit, one God, now and forever.

March 7 - The Commemoration of Perpetua & Felicitas, Martyrs

O God the King of saints, you strengthened your servants Perpetua and Felicitas and their companions to make a good confession, staunchly resisting, for the cause of Christ, the claims of human affection, and encouraging one another in their time of trial: Grant that we who cherish their blessèd memory may share their pure and steadfast faith, and win with them the palm of victory; through Jesus Christ our Lord, who lives and reigns with you and the Holy Spirit, one God, forever and ever.

March 12 - The Commemoration of Gregory I, Bishop & Teacher

Almighty and merciful God, you raised up Gregory of Rome to be a servant of the servants of God, and inspired him to send missionaries to preach the Gospel to the English people: Preserve in your Church the catholic and apostolic faith they taught, that your people, being fruitful in every good work, may receive the crown of glory that never fades away; through Jesus Christ our Lord, who lives and reigns with you and the Holy Spirit, one God, forever and ever.

March 17 - The Commemoration of Patrick of Ireland, Bishop & Missionary

Almighty God, in your providence you chose your servant Patrick to be the apostle of the Irish people, to bring those who were wandering in darkness and error to the true light and knowledge of you: Grant us so to walk in that light, that we may come at last to the light of everlasting life; through Jesus Christ our Lord, who lives and reigns with you and the Holy Spirit, one God, forever and ever.

March 18 - The Commemoration of Cyril of Jerusalem, Bishop & Teacher

Strengthen, O Lord, the bishops of your Church in their special calling to be teachers and ministers of the Sacraments, so that they, like your servant Cyril of Jerusalem, may effectively instruct your people in Christian faith and practice; and that we, taught by them, may enter more fully into celebration of the Paschal mystery; through Jesus Christ our Lord, who lives and reigns with you and the Holy Spirit, one God, now and forever.

March 19 - The Feast of St. Joseph, Guardian of Our Lord

Lesson: Matthew 1:18-25

Homily - Aelfric of Eynsheim

Of Abraham's race came the great king David; and of that royal race came the holy Mary; and of Mary Christ was born; and through Christ all mankind is blessed, those who rightly believe. Again the prophet Jeremiah said of Jesus: "This is our God, and there is none other accounted with Him. He has raised and established direction and discipline to His people Israel. He was afterwards seen upon earth, and with men He dwelt." Again, another prophet, Micah, prophesied concerning Christ's advent, saying: "There shall peace be on earth, when our Lord comes to our land, and when He goes into our houses." Again, Isaiah wrote in his prophecy, and said: "Behold a virgin shall conceive, and bear a Son, and He shall be named Emmanuel," which is interpreted, "God is with us." Again, Ezekiel prophesied of the city of Jerusalem and of Christ, saying, "Your King comes to you humble, and shall reestablish you." Daniel the prophet set forth in his prophecy that the archangel Gabriel came to him flying and said to him: "I am come to you, Daniel, in order to teach you, and do you understand my speech, and understand this vision. Four hundred and ninety years are reckoned from this day over you, and over your people, and over the city of Jerusalem; and then shall the old transgression be ended, and sin shall have an end, and unrighteousness shall be rooted out, and everlasting righteousness shall be brought, and vision and prophesies shall be fulfilled, and the Holy of all Holies shall be anointed." All these things are fulfilled through Christ's humanity.

After that space and term, which the archangel Gabriel announced to Daniel, Adam's transgression and his sin are ended through Christ; and Christ has rooted out every unrighteousness, and established everlasting righteousness, and He fulfilled all prophecies through Himself, and He is the Holy of Holies, for He is the head of all holy men. How is he anointed? A king is anointed with hallowed oil when he is hallowed to be king; and in every ordination, in deaconhood as well as in priesthood or bishophood, he who is invested in it is invested with hallowed oil. But Christ is Bishop of all bishops, and King of all kings. He is not anointed with earthly oil, but with the sevenfold grace of the Holy Spirit; for in Christ dwells bodily the perfection of the Godhead.

Homily for the Nativity of Our Lord

Collect

O God, who from the family of your servant David raised up Joseph to be the guardian of your incarnate Son and the spouse of his virgin mother: Give us grace to imitate his uprightness of life and his obedience to your commands; through Jesus Christ our Lord, who lives and reigns with you and the Holy Spirit, one God, forever and ever.

March 21 - The Commemoration of Benedict of Nursia, Abbot

Almighty and everlasting God, whose precepts are the wisdom of a loving Father: Give us grace, following the teaching and example of your servant Benedict, to walk with loving and willing hearts in the school of the Lord's service; let your ears be open to our prayers; and prosper with your blessing the work of our hands; through Jesus Christ our Lord, who lives and reigns with you and the Holy Spirit, one God, forever and ever.

March 25 - The Feast of the Annunciation of the Blessed Virgin Mary

Lesson: Luke 1:26-38

Homily - Sophrinus of Jerusalem

Hail, full of grace, the Lord is with you. Truly blessed are you among women, for you have changed the curse of Eve into a blessing and caused Adam, once accursed, to be blessed through you. Truly blessed are you among women, for it was through you that the Father's blessing dawned on humankind and freed it from the ancient curse. Truly blessed are you among women, for through you your ancestors will be saved, since you are going to bear the Savior who will gain them God's salvation. Truly blessed are you among women, for without seed you produced the fruit that brings blessing to all the earth, releasing it from the curse that made it bear thorns. Truly blessed are you among women, for though by nature you are a woman, you will in very truth become the mother of God: if He who is to be born of you is truly God incarnate, then, since you will be giving birth to God, you will with perfect justice be called the mother of God.

Do not be afraid, Mary, for you have found favor with God that can never be lost. You have won from God a most glorious favor, a grace long desired, a grace of great splendor, a saving grace, an unfailing grace, a grace that will last for ever. Many before you have been holy, but no one has been as favored as you, no one as blessed as you, no one as perfectly sanctified as you, no one as highly praised as you. No one else has like you been possessed from the first by purifying grace, no one else has been enlightened like you, or exalted like you, for no one has approached so close to God as you, or been enriched with such divine gifts, or endowed with such heavenly grace.

You surpass all human desire; you surpass all the gifts given by God to the whole human race, for God's dwelling within you has made you richer than all others. No one else has been able to contain God as you do; no one else has been capable of receiving God as you have; no one else has deserved to be so enlightened by God. And therefore you have not only received God, the Creator and Lord of the universe, but He has in an unheard-of way taken flesh from you; you bear Him in your womb, and will later give birth to Him who will redeem humankind from the Father's sentence, and confer on it eternal salvation. *Homily 2*

Collect

We implore You, O Lord, pour Your grace into our hearts; that as we have known the Incarnation of Your Son Jesus Christ by the message of an angel, so by His cross and passion we may be brought to the glory of His resurrection; through the same Jesus Christ our Lord, who lives and reigns with you and the Holy Spirit, one God, now and forever.

April 4 - The Commemoration of Isidore of Seville, Bishop & Teacher

Grant us, O Lord, faithful pastors like your servant Isidore, that we may be strengthened by their teaching in Your sacred truths, and that many may be converted to You through their preaching; through Jesus Christ, Your Son, our Lord, who lives and reigns with You and the Holy Spirit, one God, now and forever.

April 6 - The Commemoration of Martin Chemnitz, Teacher & Confessor

O Merciful and Everlasting Father, by Your grace You led Your servant Martin to promote peace and concord in Your Church; grant us such unity and peace in our time and in our many congregations, that the peace of Your Son, Jesus Christ, may be known in them and fill our hearts and minds, for He lives and reigns with You and the Holy Spirit, one God, now and forever.

April 11 - The Commemoration of Leo I of Rome, Bishop & Teacher

O Lord our God, grant that your Church, following the teaching of your servant Leo of Rome, may hold fast the great mystery of our redemption, and adore the one Christ, true God and true Man, neither divided from our human nature nor separate from your divine Being; through Jesus Christ our Lord, who lives and reigns with you and the Holy Spirit, one God, now and forever.

April 20 - The Commemoration of Johannes Bugenhagen, Pastor

O Lord, through Your servant Johannes, You guided Your Church in the true worship of Your Son; grant to us faithful pastors who will lead us to receive His gifts and to worship You in Spirit and truth, through the same, Jesus Christ, Your Son, our Lord, who lives and reigns with you and the Holy Spirit, one God, now and forever. Amen.

April 21 - The Commemoration of Anselm of Canterbury, Bishop & Teacher

Almighty God, you raised up your servant Anselm to teach the Church of his day to understand its faith in your eternal Being, perfect justice, and saving mercy: Provide your Church in every age with devout and learned scholars and teachers, that we may be able to give a reason for the hope that is in us; through Jesus Christ our Lord, who lives and reigns with you and the Holy Spirit, one God, forever and ever.

April 24 - The Commemoration of Johann Walter, Kantor

O Lord, You have given Your people the gift of music, that with it we may sing and proclaim Your praises on earth as in heaven; grant to us faithful musicians like your servant Johann, that the song of your Church may ring forth in our congregations and in our homes; through Jesus Christ our Lord, who lives and reigns with you and the Holy Spirit, one God, now and forever.

April 25 - The Feast of St. Mark, Evangelist

Lesson: Luke 10:1-9

Homily - Cyril of Alexandria

Just as brave soldiers when they go out to battle carry only the equipment necessary for war, so also for those who were sent out by Christ to bring aid to the world and to wage war against the world-rulers of this darkness, yes, and against Satan himself, on behalf of all who were in danger, it was proper that they should be free from the distractions of this world and from all worldly cares; that being tightly girded and clad in spiritual armor, they might contend mightily with those who resisted the glory of Christ, and who had made prey of all beneath the heavens. For they had caused its inhabitants to worship the creature instead of the Creator, and to offer religious service to the elements of the world. Armed, therefore, with the shield of faith, the breastplate of righteousness, and the sword of the Spirit, which is the Word of God, they must prove themselves invincible antagonists to their enemies. So they don't drag after them a heavy load of things that bring blame and condemnation, such as are the love of wealth and hoards of possessions, or the eagerness for such; for these things turn the mind of man away from what pleases God. These things prevent the mind from mounting upward to Him, and rather draw it downward to a desire for that which is but earthly and dust.

In enjoining them, therefore, to take neither provision nor purse, nor even to trouble themselves about shoes, He clearly teaches them that His commandment requires them to abandon all carnal wealth, and that His wish is that they should be free from every impediment in entering upon the duty to which they were especially called - namely, of preaching His mystery to men everywhere, and of winning to salvation those who were entangled in the nets of destruction.

Commentary on Luke

Collect

O Almighty God, who has instructed Your Holy Church with the heavenly doctrine of Your evangelist St. Mark, give us grace that being not like children carried away with every blast of vain doctrine, we may be established in the truth of Your Holy Gospel; through Jesus Christ, Your Son, our Lord, who lives and reigns with you and the Holy Spirit, one God, now and forever.

May 1 - The Feast of Sts. Philip & James, Apostles

Lesson: John 14:1-14

Homily - Augustine of Hippo

The disciples, in fact, were still assuming that the Father was something greater than the Son, when, seeing His flesh and not understanding His divinity, they said to the Son, Lord, show us the Father, and that will satisfy us. It is as if they were saying, "We already know You, and we bless You because we know You; yes, we are most grateful to You for having shown Yourself to us. But we do not know the Father yet; that is why our heart is on fire, is bursting with a holy eagerness to see Your Father who sent You. Show Him to us, and we will desire nothing more from You; for we shall be completely satisfied when we are shown the One than whom there can be none greater."

A good eagerness, a good desire, but little understanding. The Lord Jesus Himself, you see, on observing these little ones wanting and seeking great things, and aware of himself as being great among little ones - and little among little ones - answered Philip, one of the disciples who had spoken, Have I been with you for such a long time, and you have not come to know Me, Philip? Philip could have answered at this point, "We certainly do know You; but we did not say, did we, 'Show us Yourself?' We know You already, but we are still wanting the Father." So Jesus added straightaway, Anyone that has seen Me has seen the Father.

So then, if He was sent as the Father's equal, let us not form our assessment of Him from the frailty of the flesh, but let us fix our thoughts on the grandeur that was clothed in the flesh and not weighed down by the flesh. Abiding as God with the Father, He became a man among us, so that through Him you, for whose sake He became man, might become such a one as can grasp God. A human being, indeed, was unable to grasp God; He was able to see a human being, unable to grasp God. Why could a human being not grasp God? Because he did not have that eye of the heart needed to grasp Him. So something inside was sick, something outside was healthy; the eyes of the body were healthy, the eyes of the heart were ill. Christ was made man for the eyes of the body to see, so that by believing in Him who could be seen in a bodily way, you might be cured for seeing the same "Him" that you had not been able to see in a spiritual way.

Have I been with you for such a long time, and you have not come to know Me, Philip? Anyone that has seen Me has seen the Father. Why were they not seeing Him? Look, they were seeing Him, and were not seeing the Father; they were seeing the flesh, but the divine grandeur was hidden. What the disciples who loved Him were seeing was also being seen by the Jews who crucified Him. So within that flesh was the whole of Him, and in such a way within the flesh that He remained with the Father; He did not, after all, forsake the Father when He came to the flesh.

Homily 14 on John

Collect

O Almighty God, whom to know is everlasting life; grant us perfectly to know Your Son Jesus Christ to be the Way, the Truth and the Life, that following His steps we may steadfastly walk in the way that leads to eternal life; through the same Jesus Christ, Your Son, our Lord, who lives and reigns with you and the Holy Spirit, one God, now and forever.

May 2 - The Commemoration of Athanasius of Alexandria, Bishop & Teacher

Uphold your Church, O God of truth, as you upheld your servant Athanasius, to maintain and proclaim boldly the catholic faith against all opposition, trusting solely in the grace of your eternal Word, who took upon himself our humanity that we might share his divinity; who lives and reigns with you and the Holy Spirit, one God, now and forever.

May 5 - The Commemoration of Frederick the Wise of Saxony, Prince & Confessor

O Almighty God, as You have raised up men and rulers to protect Your Church in times of danger and persecution, raise up faithful men like Frederick, in our time, that the preaching of Your Gospel may be promoted and protected in all the places You would send it; through Jesus Christ our Lord, who lives and reigns with you and the Holy Spirit, one God, now and forever.

May 7 - The Commemoration of C.F.W. Walther, Pastor & Teacher

O Lord, our Heavenly Father, hear us, we pray, and grant to us purity of doctrine and orthodoxy of practice, that we may not be deceived or led astray by the winds of error that blow hard against us; through Jesus Christ our Lord, who lives and reigns with you and the Holy Spirit, one God, now and forever.

May 9 - The Commemoration of Gregory of Nazianzus, Bishop & Teacher

Almighty God, you have revealed to your Church your eternal Being of glorious majesty and perfect love as one God in Trinity of Persons: Give us grace that, like your bishop Gregory of Nazianzus, we may continue steadfast in the confession of this faith, and constant in our worship of you, Father, Son and Holy Spirit; for you live and reign forever and ever.

May 11 - The Commemoration of Cyril & Methodius, Missionaries

Almighty and everlasting God, by the power of the Holy Spirit you moved your servant Cyril and his brother Methodius to bring the light of the Gospel to a hostile and divided people: Overcome all bitterness and strife among us by the love of Christ, and make us one united family under the banner of the Prince of Peace; who lives and reigns with you and the Holy Spirit, one God, now and forever.

May 21 - The Commemoration of Constantine the Great, Emperor

God, who enlightened the Slavic peoples through the brothers Saints Cyril and Methodius, grant that our hearts may grasp the words of your teaching, and perfect us as a people of one accord in true faith and right confession; through Jesus Christ our Lord, who lives and reigns with you and the Holy Spirit, one God, now and forever.

May 25 - The Commemoration of Bede the Venerable, Teacher

Heavenly Father, you called your servant Bede, while still a child, to devote his life to your service in the disciplines of religion and scholarship: Grant that as he labored in the Spirit to bring the riches of your truth to his generation, so we, in our various vocations, may strive to make you known in all the world; through Jesus Christ our Lord, who lives and reigns with you and the Holy Spirit, one God, forever and ever.

May 27 - The Commemoration of Augustine of Canterbury, Bishop & Missionary

O Lord our God, who by your Son Jesus Christ called your apostles and sent them forth to preach the Gospel to the nations: We bless your holy name for your servant Augustine, first Archbishop of Canterbury, whose labors in propagating your Church among the English people we commemorate today; and we pray that all whom you call and send may do your will, and bide your time, and see your glory; through Jesus Christ our Lord, who lives and reigns with you and the Holy Spirit, one God, forever and ever.

May 31 - The Feast of the Visitation of the Blessed Virgin Mary

This feast may be kept instead on its original date, July 2

Lesson: Luke 1:39-56

Homily - Martin Luther

Just as a book title indicates what is the contents of the book, so this word "magnifies" is used by Mary to indicate what her hymn of praise is to be about, namely, the great works and deeds of God, for the strengthening of our faith, for the comforting of all those of low degree, and for the terrifying of all the mighty ones of earth. We are to let the hymn serve this threefold purpose; for she sang it not for herself alone but for us all, to sing it after her. Now, these great works of God will neither terrify nor comfort anyone unless he believes that God has not only the power and the knowledge but also the willingness and hearty desire to do such great things. In fact, it is not even enough to believe that He is willing to do them for others but not for you. This would be to put yourself beyond the pale of these works of God, as is done by those who, because of their strength, do not fear Him, and by those of little faith who, because of their tribulations, fall into despair.

That sort of faith is nothing; it is dead; it is like an idea learned from a fairy tale. You must rather, without any wavering or doubt, realize His will toward you and firmly believe that He will do great things also to you, and is willing to do so. Such a faith has life and being; it pervades and changes the whole man; it constrains you to fear if you are mighty, and to take comfort if you are of low degree. And the mightier you are, the more must you fear; the lowlier you are, the more must you take comfort.   *Commentary on the Magnificat*

Collect

Almighty God, who has dealt wonderfully with Your handmaiden, the Virgin Mary, and has chosen her to be the mother of Your Son, and has graciously made known that You regard the poor and the lowly and the despised; grant us grace in all humility and meekness to receive the Word with hearty faith, and so to be made one with your dear Son, who lives and reigns with you and the Holy Spirit, one God, now and forever.

June 1 - The Commemoration of Justin, Martyr

Almighty and everlasting God, you found your martyr Justin wandering from teacher to teacher, seeking the true God, and you revealed to him the sublime wisdom of your eternal Word: Grant that all who seek you, or a deeper knowledge of you, may find and be found by you; through Jesus Christ our Lord, who lives and reigns with you and the Holy Spirit, one God, forever and ever.

June 5 - The Commemoration of Boniface of Mainz, Bishop & Missionary

Almighty God, you called your faithful servant Boniface to be a witness and martyr in the lands of Germany and Friesland, and by his labor and suffering raised up a people for your own possession: Pour out your Holy Spirit upon your Church in every land, that by the service and sacrifice of many your holy Name may be glorified and your kingdom enlarged; through Jesus Christ our Lord, who lives and reigns with you and the Holy Spirit, one God, forever and ever.

June 9 - The Commemoration of Columba (Colm Cille), Missionary & Abbot

O God, by the preaching of your blessèd servant Columba you caused the light of the Gospel to shine in Scotland: Grant, we pray, that, having his life and labors in remembrance, we may show our thankfulness to you by following the example of his zeal and patience; through Jesus Christ our Lord, who lives and reigns with you and the Holy Spirit, one God, forever and ever.

June 11 - The Feast of St. Barnabas, Missionary

Lesson: Mark 6:7-13

Homily - Hugh of St. Victor

Since a time of repentance had been granted, man was set in this world in a place of repentance, so that he might correct evil things and recover good things. The purpose of this was that, when man, after he has been corrected, comes at last to the judgment, he might receive, not the penalty for sin, but the glory prepared for him as a reward for righteousness. It remains, then, that while there is time he should seek advice and ask for help for his correction and liberation. But as man is found to be sufficient of himself for neither, it is necessary that God, who by His grace delays the judgment, should by the same grace meanwhile supply advice for the escape and after the advice bestow help. So, then, it is fitting that He should, for the time being, lay aside the role of the judge, and first take on Himself the role of an adviser, and afterward that of a helper. He must act in such a way, at least, as at first to leave man entirely to himself, so that man himself may both experience his own ignorance and understand that he needs advice, and thereafter may feel his weakness and recognize that he needs help. *On the Sacraments of the Christian Faith*

Collect

Grant, O God, that we may follow the example of your faithful servant Barnabas, who, seeking not his own renown but the well-being of your Church, gave generously of his life and substance for the relief of the poor and the spread of the Gospel; through Jesus Christ our Lord, who lives and reigns with you and the Holy Spirit, one God, forever and ever.

June 14 - The Commemoration of Basil the Great of Caesarea, Bishop & Teacher

Almighty God, you have revealed to your Church your eternal Being of glorious majesty and perfect love as one God in Trinity of Persons: Give us grace that, like your bishop Basil of Caesarea, we may continue steadfast in the confession of this faith, and constant in our worship of you, Father, Son, and Holy Spirit; who live and reign forever and ever.

June 18 - The Commemoration of Ephrem the Syrian, Bishop & Poet

Pour out on us, O Lord, that same Spirit by which your deacon Ephrem rejoiced to proclaim in sacred song the mysteries of faith; and so gladden our hearts that we, like him, may be devoted to you alone; through Jesus Christ our Lord, who lives and reigns with you and the Holy Spirit, one God, forever and ever.

June 24 - The Nativity of St. John the Baptist, Prophet

Lesson: Luke 1:57-80

Homily - Aelred of Rievaulx

But what shall we say about him or how shall we praise someone who was praised by angelic authority before he was born and who in the womb, into which he came by the way infected with sin, was by an inexpressible grace made a most worthy dwelling place of Holy Spirit? Nor should we overlook that a priest was chosen to be his father, the temple chosen to be the place where his birth was foretold, the name to be conferred on him conferred by an angel. Not even the hour at which this happened should be overlooked. For it was at the hour of the incense offering.

Would that we, too, my brothers, might be among those priests to whom the apostle Peter says, "You are a chosen generation, a royal priesthood." Would that our hearts might become the temple of God, as the Apostle says, "The temple of God is holy, which temple you are." Perhaps at the hour of the incense offering, the hour of salutary compunction, when our prayer rises like incense in the sight of the Lord, an angel, a messenger of divine grace, will appear to us. For "John" means "the grace of God." And this name is aptly conferred at the command of an angel to him who, while still in his mother's womb, recognized that inexpressible grace by which the Word was made flesh. Afterwards with his finger he pointed out that same Word made flesh. He was the wonderful preacher of God's grace. By his words he opened the doors of the kingdom of heaven even to publicans and harlots...   *Sermon 14, for the Nativity of St. John the Baptist*

Collect

Almighty God, by whose providence your servant John the Baptist was wonderfully born, and sent to prepare the way of your Son our Savior by preaching repentance: Make us so to follow his teaching and holy life, that we may truly repent according to his preaching; and, following his example, constantly speak the truth, boldly rebuke vice, and patiently suffer for the truth's sake; through Jesus Christ your Son our Lord, who lives and reigns with you and the Holy Spirit, one God, forever and ever.

June 25 - The Commemoration of The Presentation of the Augsburg Confession

Lesson: John 15:1-11

Homily - Augustine of Hippo

The Savior, speaking to His disciples, commends still more and more the grace by which we are saved when He says, "By this My Father is glorified, that you bear much fruit; so you will be My disciples..." I have thought it worth while to mention this, because the apostle says, "if Abraham was justified by works, he has something to boast about, but not before God." For this is the glory before God, whereby God, and not man, is glorified, when he is justified, not by works, but by faith, so that even his doing well is imparted to him by God; just as the branch cannot bear fruit of itself. For f God the Father is glorified by this, that we bear much fruit and be made the disciples of Christ, let us not take credit for our own glory as if we had it from ourselves. For this grace is from of Him, and so the glory is not ours, but His. So also, in another passage, after saying, "Let your light so shine before men, that they may see your good works," to keep them from thinking that such good works were of themselves, He immediately added, "and may glorify your Father in heaven." For by this the Father is glorified: that we bear much fruit and be made the disciples of Christ. And by whom are we so made, but by Him whose mercy has gone before us? For we are His workmanship, created in Christ Jesus unto good works.

"As the Father loved me," He says, "I also have loved you; abide in My love." Here, you see, is the source of our good works. For how should we have them, if not that faith works by love? And how should we love, were we not first loved? With striking clearness this is declared by the same evangelist in his epistle: "We love God because He first loved us." But when He says, "As the Father loved me, so also have I loved you," He does not indicate that our nature is equal to His as His is to the Father's, but the grace by which the Mediator between God and men is the man Christ Jesus. For He is pointed out as Mediator when He says, "The Father—me, and I—you." For the Father also truly loves us, but in Him; for by this the Father is glorified, that we bear fruit in the vine, that is, in the Son, and so be made His disciples. *Tractate 82 on John*

Collect

Almighty God, our Heavenly Father, You have, of Your tender mercies toward us sinners, given us Your Son, that believing on Him we may have everlasting life; grant us, we pray, Your Holy Spirit, that we may continue steadfast in this faith to the end, and may receive that life everlasting, through Jesus Christ our Lord, who lives and reigns with you and the Holy Spirit, one God, forever and ever.

June 27 - The Commemoration of Cyril of Alexandria, Bishop & Teacher

O God, who made Your servant, Cyril, an invincible champion of the divine motherhood of the most Blessèd Virgin Mary, grant, we pray, that we who believe she is truly the Mother of God may be saved through the Incarnation of Christ your Son, who lives and reigns with you in the unity of the Holy Spirit, one God, forever and ever.

June 28 - The Commemoration of Irenaeus of Lyons, Bishop & Teacher

Almighty God, you upheld your servant Irenaeus with strength to maintain the truth against every blast of vain doctrine: Keep us, we pray, steadfast in your true religion, that in constancy and peace we may walk in the way that leads to eternal life; through Jesus Christ our Lord, who lives and reigns with you and the Holy Spirit, one God, forever and ever.

June 29 - The Feast of Sts. Peter & Paul, Apostles

Lesson: Matthew 16:13-20

Homily - Peter Abelard

There are diseases of the soul just as there are of the body; and therefore the Divine mercy has provided physicians for both beforehand. Our Lord Jesus Christ says, I came not to call the righteous, but sinners to repentance. His pastors now hold His place in the Church, to whom, as to physicians of the soul, we ought to confess our sins, that we may receive from them the medicine of salvation. He who fears the death of the body, in whatever part of the body he may suffer, however much he may be ashamed of the disease does not delay to reveal his disease to his doctor, and sets it forth so that it may be cured. However rough, however hard the remedy may be he does not avoid it so that he may escape death. Whatever prized possession he has, he doesn't hesitate to give it, if only for a little while he may put off the death of the body. What, then, should we do for the death of the soul? For this, however terrible, may be prevented forever without such hard labor and without such great expense. The Lord seeks us, not what we own. He doesn't need our wealth who bestows all things. For it is He to whom it is said, My goods are nothing to You. With Him, a man is by so much the greater, as, in his own judgment, he is less; with Him, a man is as much the more righteous, as in his own opinion he is the more the guilty. In His eyes we hide our faults all the more, the more that by confession we reveal them.   *Sermon on the Resurrection of Lazarus*

Collect

Merciful and eternal God, Your holy apostles, St. Peter and St. Paul received grace and strength to suffer martyrdom for the sake of Your Son, strengthen us, we implore You, by your Holy Spirit that we may confess Your truth faithfully and at all times be ready to lay down our lives for Him who laid down His life for us, even Jesus Christ, our Lord, who lives and reigns with You and the Holy Spirit, one God, now and forever.

July 19 - The Commemoration of Macrina the Younger, Virgin

Merciful God, who called your servant Macrina to reveal in her life and her piety the riches of your grace and truth: Mercifully grant that we, following her example, may seek after your wisdom and live according to her way; through Jesus Christ our Savior, who lives and reigns with you and the Holy Spirit, one God, forever and ever.

July 22 - The Feast of St. Mary Magdalene, Holy Woman

Lesson: Luke 7:36-50

Homily - Gregory I of Rome

When I think of Mary's repentance I am more disposed to weep than to speak. Whose heart is so stony that this sinful woman's tears wouldn't soften it with her example of repentance? Out of consideration for what she had done, she refused to moderate what she was doing. She came in while people were dining; she came uninvited; she poured out her tears while a feast was going on. Tell me what was the grief that consumed her that she wasn't ashamed to weep even during a feast?

This woman, whom Luke calls a sinner, John names Mary. I believe that she is the same Mary of whom Mark says that seven demons had been cast out. How should we interpret the seven demons except as the totality of vices? Since all time is comprehended in seven days, we correctly take the number seven to signify totality. Mary had seven demons since she was filled with the totality of vices. But you see that because she was aware of the stains of her disgrace she ran to the fountain of mercy to be washed clean. She was not ashamed before those who were dining. Since she felt such great shame inwardly, she did not believe that there was anything to be bashful about outwardly.

What astonishes us, my friends, Mary's coming, or the Lord's receiving her? Should I say that he received her, or that he drew her to himself? I had better say that he drew her and received her. Surely he drew her inwardly by his mercy, and received her outwardly by his gentleness.

                    Homily 33, on Luke 7

Collect

Almighty God, whose blessèd Son restored Mary Magdalene to health of body and of mind, and called her to be a witness of his resurrection: Mercifully grant that by your grace we may be healed from all our infirmities and know you in the power of his unending life; who with you and the Holy Spirit lives and reigns, one God, now and forever.

July 25 - The Feast of St. James the Elder, Apostle

Lesson: Matthew 20:20-28

Homily - Martin Luther

Take care to avoid sinning wantonly and to remain with your dear Lord. If you sin out of weakness, take comfort from the Lord's example here. He does not rage or act in an unfriendly way toward His people now, even as He did not before. For if He were not so friendly, we would get on poorly. We are the same kind of people as the disciples here. We also have a nice big blot on us and often ask for things just as foolish as they ask for here. Consequently, God often has to say, "If I gave you what you asked for, I would be a fool, just as you are." We often make such requests, even when we are praying the Our Father, but our dear Lord is so friendly, so good, that He does not think any the worse of us for our foolishness, even as He did not think any the worse of His apostles and other saints, who were of the same flesh and blood as we are. Thus the dear saints are a comfort to us, not as the monks portray their Francis as being entirely pure and unblemished, so that they make of him a chunk of wood, stone, or iron. This does not mean, however, that we should learn from the saints to sin - rather, that from their example we should take comfort in tribulation. As their sins were forgiven them by grace, they will also be forgiven us, if only we remain under this master of the house, who is called Christ and remain in His house. If only this occurs, then our weakness and errors pose no danger. *Homily on John*

Collect

O gracious God, Your servant and apostle St. James was first among the Twelve to suffer martyrdom for the Name of Jesus Christ; we pray You to pour out upon the pastors of Your Church that spirit of self-denying service that they may forsake all false and passing allurements and follow Christ alone; who lives and reigns with you and the Holy Spirit, one God, now and forever.

July 28 - The Commemoration of Johann Sebastian Bach, Kantor

Almighty God, beautiful in majesty and majestic in holiness, You teach us in Holy Scripture to sing Your praises and gave Your musician, Johann Sebastian Bach, grace to show forth Your glory in his music: be with all those who write or make music for Your people, that we on earth may glimpse Your beauty and know the inexhaustible riches of Your new creation in Jesus Christ our Savior; who lives and reigns with you and the Holy Spirit, one God, forever and ever.

July 31 - The Commemoration of Peter Chrysologus, Bishop & Teacher

O God, who made Peter Chrysologus an outstanding preacher of your incarnate Word, grant that we may receive the preaching of Your Gospel faithfully, and may constantly ponder in our hearts the mysteries of your salvation and faithfully express them in what we do, through Jesus Christ our Lord, who lives and reigns with you and the Holy Spirit, one God, forever and ever.

August 10 - The Commemoration of Lawrence of Rome, Deacon & Martyr

Lesson: Matthew 5:1-12

Homily - Origen of Alexandria

By His example, Jesus confirms all the beatitudes that he speaks in the Gospel. By his own witness, he confirms what he teaches. "Blessed are the meek," he says. He says something similar to this of himself: "Learn from me, for I am meek." "Blessed are the peacemakers.'" And what other man brought as much peace as my Lord Jesus, who "is our peace," who "dissolves enmity," and "destroys it in his own flesh"? "Blessed are they who suffer persecution on account of justice." No one suffered such persecution on account of justice as the Lord Jesus did, who was crucified for our sins. Thus, the Lord exhibited all the beatitudes in himself. For the sake of this likeness, he himself wept, because of what he had said: "Blessed are those who weep," to lay the foundations for this beatitude, too. He wept for Jerusalem "and said, 'If only you had known on that day what meant peace for you! But now it is hidden from your eyes,'" and the rest, up to the point where he says, "Because you did not know the time of your visitation." *Homily 38 on Luke*

Collect

O Lord God, giver of all good things, grant to us who have received great and abundant mercy, true charity toward the poor, and eyes to see in them the likeness of Your Son, and thus to follow the example of Your faithful servant, Lawrence; through Jesus Christ our Lord, who lives and reigns with you and the Holy Spirit, one God, forever and ever.

August 15 - The Feast of the Blessed Virgin Mary, Mother of Our Lord

Lesson: Luke 1:46-55

Homily - Bede the Venerable

"My soul proclaims the greatness of the Lord, and my spirit rejoices in God my Savior." With these words Mary first acknowledges the special gifts she has been given. Then she recalls God's universal favors, bestowed unceasingly on the human race.

When a man devotes all his thoughts to the praise and service of the Lord, he proclaims God's greatness. His observance of God's commands, moreover, shows that he has God's power and greatness always at heart. His spirit rejoices in God his saviour and delights in the mere recollection of his creator who gives him hope for eternal salvation.

These words are often for all God's creations, but especially for the Mother of God. She alone was chosen, and she burned with spiritual love for the son she so joyously conceived. Above all other saints, she alone could truly rejoice in Jesus, her Savior, for she knew that He who was the source of eternal salvation would be born in time in her body, in one person both her own son and her Lord.

For the Almighty has done great things for me, and holy is His name. Mary attributes nothing to her own merits. She refers all her greatness to the gift of the one whose essence is power and whose nature is greatness, for He fills with greatness and strength the small and the weak who believe in Him.

She did well to add: and holy is His name, to warn those who heard, and indeed all who would receive His words, that they must believe and call upon His name. For they too could share in everlasting holiness and true salvation according to the words of the prophet: and it will come to pass, that everyone who calls on the name of the Lord will be saved. This is the name she spoke of earlier: and my spirit rejoices in God my Savior.

Therefore it is an excellent and fruitful custom of holy Church that we should sing Mary's hymn at the time of evening prayer. By meditating upon the incarnation, our devotion is kindled, and by remembering the example of God's Mother, we are encouraged to lead a life of virtue. Such virtues are best achieved in the evening. We are weary after the day's work and worn out by our distractions. The time for rest is near, and our minds are ready for contemplation. *Homily on the Visitation*

Collect

O God, You chose the Blessèd Virgin Mary to be the mother of Your incarnate Son: Grant that we, who have been redeemed by His blood, may share with her the glory of Your eternal kingdom; through Jesus Christ our Lord, who lives and reigns with You, in the unity of the Holy Spirit, one God, now and forever.

August 17 - The Commemoration of Johann Gerhard, Teacher & Confessor

Almighty and Most Merciful God, You preserved Your servant Johann through times of hardship and tragedy and gave Him strength to teach and to sing Your praise; grant us such strength in our times of adversity, we pray, that we may not turn from Your gracious presence, but embrace You more fervently; through Jesus Christ, Your Son, our Lord, who lives and reigns with You and the Holy Spirit, one God, now and forever.

August 19 - The Commemoration of Bernard of Clairvaux, Abbot & Teacher

O God, by whose grace your servant Bernard of Clairvaux, kindled with the flame of your love, became a burning and a shining light in your Church: Grant that we also may be aflame with the spirit of love and discipline, and walk before you as children of light; through Jesus Christ our Lord, who lives and reigns with you, in the unity of the Holy Spirit, one God, now and forever.

August 24 - The Feast of St. Bartholomew, Apostle

Lesson: Luke 22:24-30

Homily - Anonymous 2nd Century Author

My child, him who proclaims to you the word of God, remember day and night, and honor him as the Lord. For wherever the kingship is proclaimed, the Lord is there. And seek out daily the company of the saints so that you might find refreshment in their words. Do not cause divisions, but make peace between disputants. Judge justly. Do not show partiality in reproving transgressions. Do not be of two minds whether or not something should be. Do not be one who stretches out his hands to receive, but holds them back when it comes to giving. *The Didache*

Collect

Almighty and everlasting God, who gave to Your apostle St. Bartholomew grace truly to believe and to preach Your Word: Grant that Your Church may love what he believed and preach what he taught; through Jesus Christ our Lord, who lives and reigns with You and the Holy Spirit, one God, forever and ever.

August 27 - The Commemoration of Monica, Widow

O Lord, our heavenly Father, we give You thanks for Your servant Monica and countless other mothers whom You have given to teach Your Word and grace to their children; grant us always to heed the faithful voice of our mother, Your Holy Church, that being fed and nourished by her, we may grow in faith and in the love of Your Son, our Lord, Jesus Christ, who lives and reigns with You and the Holy Spirit, now and forever.

August 28 - The Commemoration of Augustine of Hippo, Bishop & Teacher

Lord God, the light of the minds that know You, the life of the souls that love You, and the strength of the hearts that serve You: Help us, following the example of your servant Augustine of Hippo, so to know you that we may truly love You, and so to love You that we may fully serve You, whom to serve is perfect freedom; through Jesus Christ our Lord, who lives and reigns with you and the Holy Spirit, one God, now and forever.

August 29 - The Commemoration of The Beheading of St. John the Baptist, Prophet & Martyr

O Lord God, Heavenly Father, through Your servant, John the Baptist, You bore witness that Jesus Christ is the Lamb of God who takes away the sin of the world, and that all who believe in Him shall inherit eternal life; we humbly pray You to enlighten us by Your Holy Spirit, that we may at all times find comfort and joy in this witness, continue steadfast in the true faith, and at last with all believers attain unto eternal life; through the same, Jesus Christ, Your Son, our Lord, who lives and reigns with you and the Holy Spirit, one God, forever and ever.

August 31 - The Commemoration of Aidan & Cuthbert of Lindisfarne, Missionary & Bishops

Everliving God, You called Your servants Aidan and Cuthbert to proclaim the Gospel in northern England and gave them loving hearts and gentle spirits: Grant us grace to live as they did, in simplicity, humility and love for the poor; through Jesus Christ, who came among us as one who serves, and who lives and reigns with You and the Holy Spirit, one God, now and forever.

September 14 - The Feast of the Holy Cross

Lesson: John 12:20-33

Homily - Peter Damian

But why do we endeavour to collect into one the types of the Cross which are contained in Holy Scripture, when every page is subservient - the Holy Ghost so ordering it to this terrible sign? This is the Mercy-seat to which the two cherubim look with their faces turned towards each other: because the two Testaments, the Old and the New, concordantly, and without any difference, point to Him Who hung upon the Cross. For John saith, And He is the Propitiation for our sins; and Peter, speaking of the ancient Fathers, affirms, By the grace of Christ we trust that we shall be saved, even as they. The Cross, then, is the concord of Scriptures, and, as it were, the boundary and the border-land of old and new things. The Cross confederates heaven and earth; the Cross rejoins men and angels in the unanimity of their ancient concord. The Cross is the death of vice, and the

ountain and life of all virtue. The Cross is the path of the unwise, the high-road of them that are
:arnest in the race; the rest of those that have attained the goal. The Cross is the earnest for those
hat are enlisted; the strength of those that are engaged in war; the reward of those that have been
lischarged from service. The Cross is the courage of those that are fighting bravely; the recovery of
hose that are fallen; the crown of those that are victorious. The Cross subjects us to a momentary
leath, and recompenses us with eternal life. The Cross strips us of earthly goods, that it may enrich
us with heavenly possessions; teaches us to hunger, that it may satisfy us; inures us to humility, that
it may exalt us; accustoms us to patience, that it may crown us. The Cross is the rule to those that
ive in Christ; is the perfect pattern of righteousness; is the example of all good practices. The Cross
errifies the Devil, and he flies; invites good angels, and they enter; represses the vain fantasies of our
houghts, and introduces the Holy Ghost to chaste and pure hearts. The Cross refreshes the weary;
:trengthens the weak; and comforts those who have already begun to despair.

And what shall I more say? It was by the Cross that the King of Glory delivered us from the
etters of the cruel tyrant, and penetrated by His might into the dungeons of hell. He absolved all
His elect from the chains of their ancient condemnation; whom also He raised with Himself by the
glory of His Resurrection.   *Sermon 48*

Collect

Almighty God, whose Son our Savior Jesus Christ was lifted high upon the cross that He might draw
the whole world to Himself: Mercifully grant that we, who glory in the mystery of our redemption,
may have grace to take up our cross and follow Him; who lives and reigns with You and the Holy
Spirit, one God, in glory everlasting.

September 16 - The Commemoration of Cyprian of Carthage, Bishop & Martyr

Almighty God, who gave to Your servant Cyprian boldness to confess the Name of our Savior Jesus
Christ before the rulers of this world, and courage to die for this faith: Grant that we may always be
'eady to give a reason for the hope that is in us, and to suffer gladly for the sake of our Lord Jesus
Christ; who lives and reigns with you and the Holy Spirit, one God, forever and ever.

September 21 - The Feast of St. Matthew, Apostle & Evangelist

Lesson: Matthew 9:9-13

Homily - Bede the Venerable

When the Lord cures the more serious illnesses of the sinners among His chosen ones, He
demonstrates to all the more ample power of His healing grace. We have heard in the Gospel
'eading that Jesus felt compassion for Matthew as he sat at the tax-collector's place intent upon
:emporal concerns, and suddenly called him. He made a just man of a publican, a disciple of a tax-
collector. As he progressively increased in grace, Jesus promoted him from the ordinary group of
disciples to the rank of an apostle, and not only committed to him the ministry of preaching, but
also that of writing a gospel, so that he who had ceased to be an administrator of terrestrial business
might start to be an administrator of heavenly currency. Doubtlessly the reason why heavenly
providence arranged for this to happen was so that neither the enormity of one's wicked deeds nor
:heir great number should dissuade anyone from hoping for pardon, since one could look at this
man [Matthew], who had been freed from such bonds of the world and made heavenly in order to
become, in fact and in name, an evangelist, sharing this name with the angelic spirits.

Homily on John

Collect

O Almighty God, who by Your blessèd Son called St. Matthew from the receipt of taxes to be an Apostle and Evangelist; grant us grace to forsake all covetous desires and inordinate love of riches, and to follow Your Son, Jesus Christ, our Lord, who lives and reigns with You and the Holy Spirit, one God, now and forever.

September 29 - The Feast of St. Michael & All Angels

Lesson: Matthew 18:1-11

Homily - Bernard of Clairvaux

But if you should say an angel can be present within us, I do not deny it. I remember it is written, "An angel who spoke in me..." Nevertheless, there is a difference and it is this: the angel is within a man suggesting the good, not effecting it; he is in us urging us toward the good, not creating it. God is present in a man in such a way that He causes an effect, so that He infuses or rather is infused and partaken of; this occurs in such a way that someone need not fear to say that God is one spirit with our spirit, even if He is not one person or one substance with us. Indeed, you have the statement, "He who is joined to the Lord is one spirit with Him." Therefore, the angel is with the soul; God is in the soul. The angel is in the soul as its companion, God as its life.

Thus, just as the soul sees with its eyes, hears with its ears, smells with its nose, tastes with its mouth, touches with the rest of its body, so God accomplishes different ends through different spirits; for example, in some He shows Himself loving, in others perceiving, in others, doing other things, just as the manifestation of the Spirit is given to each for his own good. Who is this who is so common in our speech but in reality is so distant? How do we speak of Him in our conversations when hidden in His majesty He completely avoids our sight and our affections? Hear what He says to men, "as the heavens are higher than the earth, so are My ways higher than your ways, and My thoughts than your thoughts." We are said to love, and so is God; we are said to know, and so is God; and many more things of this kind. But God loves as charity, He knows as truth, He sits in judgment as justice, He rules as majesty, He governs as a principle, He protects as salvation, He operates as strength, He reveals as light, He assists as piety. And all of this the angels also do, and so do we, but in a far inferior manner; not indeed because of the good which we are but by the good in which we share.

Five Books on Consideration

Collect

O Everlasting God, You have ordained and constituted the service of angels and men in a wonderful order; mercifully grant that as Your holy angels always serve You in Heaven, so by your appointment they may help and defend us on earth; through Jesus Christ, Your Son, our Lord, who lives and reigns with You and the Holy Spirit, one God, now and forever.

September 30 - The Commemoration of Jerome of Jerusalem, Bishop & Teacher

O Lord, O God of truth, your Word is a lamp to our feet and a light to our path: We give you thanks for your servant Jerome, and those who, following in his steps, have labored to render the Holy Scriptures in the language of the people; and we pray that your Holy Spirit will overshadow us as we read the written Word, and that Christ, the living Word, will transform us according to your righteous will; through Jesus Christ our Lord, who lives and reigns with you and the Holy Spirit, one God, forever and ever.

October 1 - The Commemoration of Remigius of Rheims, Bishop & Confessor

O God, by the teaching of your faithful servant and bishop Remigius you turned the nation of the Franks from vain idolatry to the worship of you, the true and living God, in the fullness of the catholic faith: Grant that we who glory in the name of Christian may show forth our faith in worthy deeds; through Jesus Christ our Lord, who lives and reigns with you and the Holy Spirit, one God, forever and ever.

October 17 - The Commemoration of Ignatius of Antioch, Bishop & Martyr

Almighty God, we praise your Name for your bishop and martyr Ignatius of Antioch, who offered himself as grain to be ground by the teeth of wild beasts that he might present to you the pure bread of sacrifice. Accept, we pray, the willing tribute of our lives, and give us a share in the pure and spotless offering of your Son Jesus Christ; who lives and reigns with you and the Holy Spirit, one God, forever and ever.

October 18 - The Feast of St. Luke, Evangelist

Lesson: Luke 10:1-9

Homily - Baldwin of Forde

God opposed the schemes of the devil's malice in a more effective way, and in order to destroy the wickedness of his impiety and strengthen faith by a true prediction of the future, He inspired the prophets. He sent them ahead into the world before He Himself came in order to announce in advance His coming and provide a testimony for the works He would do in the world. Then, when He Himself came into the world, He chose apostles, the successors of the prophets, who would announce the fulfillment of what the prophets had earlier foretold.

Since the one Spirit filled the prophets and the apostles, who are witnesses to Christ, the word of faith rightly stands firm in their mouth, as it is written: "In the mouth of two or three witnesses, every word stands firm." He says, "in the mouth" as if there were but one mouth. Those who speak with one mouth are those who speak in agreement, and who agree with the truth as well as among themselves. Otherwise, if they feel different things and propose different things, they do not know the truth and are therefore not true witnesses. *The Commendation of Faith*

Collect

Almighty God, You inspired Your servant, St. Luke the Physician, to set forth in the Gospel the love and healing power of Your Son; manifest in Your Church the same power and love, to the healing of our bodies and souls; through the same Jesus Christ, Your Son, our Lord, who lives and reigns with You and the Holy Spirit, one God, now and forever.

October 23 - The Feast of St. James the Just, Bishop & Martyr

Lesson: Matthew 13:54-58

Homily - John Chrysostom

Do you see that Nazareth was where He was discoursing? "Are not his brothers," it is said, "such a one, and such a one?" And what of this? Why, by this especially you ought to have been led on to faith. But envy, you see, is a poor base thing, and often falls foul of itself. For what things were strange and marvellous, and enough to have gained them over, these offended them.

What then does Christ say to them? "A prophet," He says, "is not without honor, save in his own country, and in his own house: and He did not," it is said, "many mighty works, because of their unbelief." But Luke says, "And He did not there many miracles." And yet it was to be expected He should have done them. For if the feeling of wonder towards Him was gaining ground (for indeed even there He was marvelled at), why did He not do them? Because He looked not to the display of Himself, but to their profit. Therefore when this did not succeed, He overlooked what concerned Himself, in order not to aggravate their punishment.

And yet see after how long a time He came to them, and after how great a display of miracles: but even so they did not endure it, but were inflamed again with envy.

Why then did He yet do a few miracles? That they might not say, "Physician, heal thyself." That they might not say, "He is a foe and an enemy to us, and overlooks His own." That they might not say, "If miracles had been wrought, we also would have believed." Therefore He both did them, and restrained from doing them: the one, that He might fulfill His own part; the other, that He might not condemn them even more.

And consider the power of His words, herein at least, that, possessed as they were by envy, they yet admired. And concerning His works, they do not find fault with what is done, but feign causes which have no existence, saying, "By Beelzebub He casts out the devils;" even so here too, they find no fault with the teaching, but take refuge in the meanness of His race.

But mark, I pray you, the Master's gentleness, how He does not revile them, but with great mildness says, "A prophet is not without honor, save in his own country." And neither did He stop here, but added, "And in his own house." To me it appears that He made this addition with covert reference to His very own relatives.

Homily 48 on Matthew

Collect

Grant, O God, that, following the example of your servant James the Just, brother of our Lord, your Church may give itself continually to prayer and to the reconciliation of all who are at variance and enmity; through Jesus Christ our Lord, who lives and reigns with you and the Holy Spirit, one God, now and forever.

October 26 - The Commemoration of Alfred the Great, Monarch

O Sovereign Lord, you brought your servant Alfred to a troubled throne that he might establish peace in a ravaged land and revive learning and the arts among the people: Awake in us also a keen desire to increase our understanding while we are in this world, and an eager longing to reach that endless life where all will be made clear; through Jesus Christ our Lord, who lives and reigns with you and the Holy Spirit, one God, forever and ever.

October 28 - The Feast of Sts. Simon & Jude, Apostles

Lesson: John 15:17-21

Homily - Ignatius of Antioch

I exhort you: be eager to do everything in God's harmony, with the bishop presiding in the place of God and the presbyters in the place of the council of the apostles and the deacons, most sweet to me, entrusted with the service of Jesus Christ - who before the ages was with the Father and was made manifest at the end. All of you, then, having received a divine agreement in your convictions, admonish one another, and let no one view his neighbor in a merely human way; but constantly love one another in Jesus Christ. Let there be nothing in you that can divide you, but be united with the bishop and with those who preside, for an example and lesson of imperishability.

As, then, the Lord did nothing apart from the Father, either by Himself or through the apostles, since He was united with Him, so you must do nothing apart from the bishop and the presbyters. Do not try to make anything appear praiseworthy by yourselves, but let there be in common one prayer, one petition, one mind, one hope in love, in blameless joy - which is Jesus Christ, than whom nothing is better. All of you must run together as to one temple of God, as to one sanctuary, to one Jesus Christ, who proceeded from the Father and is with the One and departed to the One.

Letter to the Magnesians

Collect

O God, we thank you for the glorious company of the apostles, and especially on this day for Simon and Jude; and we pray that, as they were faithful and zealous in their mission, so we may with ardent devotion make known the love and mercy of our Lord and Savior Jesus Christ; who lives and reigns with you and the Holy Spirit, one God, forever and ever.

October 31 - The Feast of the Reformation

Lesson: Matthew 20:20-28

Homily - Martin Luther

A wonderful kingdom this! The others are set up by force of arms in such a way that the nations are subjugated against their will. This kingdom, however, is not established by force, and here men are not compelled against their will. But because it will be raised up, they will flow to it; that is, the virtues of the church will attract the nations so that they come of their own free will. The kingdom of Christ has been put in progress because it is placed in public view with its powers and gifts. Here one sees truth, pure doctrine, safety, peace; the Gospel is heard, and nothing can give greater joy. For it promises an abundance of things and salvation both here and hereafter, and a man stands safe in this Word against everything that opposes him, even against the gates of hell. Behold, these virtues should influence the nations to make them come. They are proclaimed through the Word, namely, that Christ is the King of mercy and of peace. Moses preaches the Law and is the minister of sin and death. Nobody runs to him. On the contrary, they are terrified. Christ, on the other hand, is the Minister of righteousness, of life, and of peace. Therefore the people flow to Him just as water flows by its own effort and needs no one to push it. This is what Christ says in Matt. 11:12: "The kingdom of heaven suffers violence."

Homily on Isaiah 2

Collect

O Lord God, Heavenly Father, pour out, we implore You, Your Holy Spirit upon Your faithful people, keep them steadfast in Your grace and truth, protect and comfort them in all temptation, defend them against all enemies of Your Word, and bestow upon Christ's Church militant Your saving peace, through the same Jesus Christ, Your Son, our Lord, who lives and reigns with You and the Holy Spirit, one God, now and forever.

November 1 - The Feast of All Saints

Lesson: Matthew 5:1-12

Homily - Bernard of Clairvaux

The soul sees that it is itself contaminated and that the source of this contamination springs not from outside, but from its own body, and not from elsewhere but from itself. It is something in the soul: as the memory, which is tainted, as the very will which injects it. For, in fact, the soul itself is nothing but reason, memory, and will. Now, however, the reason, greatly reduced and, as it were, blind (for so far it has failed to see this state of affairs) is acutely sick; it has come to recognize its malady but finds no remedy; it discovers that the memory is both foul and fetid, and that the will is sick and festering with terrible sores. And so that his whole humanity should be taken, the body itself rebels: the members become like so many windows by which death enters into the soul and confusion springs up like weeds.

Let the soul which is in this state harken to the divine voice, and to its own amazement and wonder it will hear it say, "Blessed are the poor in spirit, for theirs is the kingdom of heaven." Who is poorer in spirit than the man whose spirit finds no rest and who has nowhere to lay his head? This also is a counsel of devotion, that the man who is displeasing to himself is pleasing to God, and he who hates his own house, that is to say a house full of filth and wretchedness, is invited to the house of glory, a house not made with hands, eternal in the heavens. It is no wonder if he trembles with awe at the greatness of this honor, and finds it hard to believe what he has heard, if he starts in astonishment and says, "Is it possible for such wretchedness to make a man happy?" Whoever you are, if you are in this frame of mind, do not despair: it is mercy, not misery, that makes a man happy, but mercy's natural home is misery. Indeed it happens that misery becomes the source of man's happiness when humiliation turns into humility and necessity becomes a virtue. As it is written, "Rain in abundance, O God, you shed abroad; you restored your heritage as it languished." Sickness has real utility when it leads us to the doctor's hands, and he whom God restores to health gains by having been ill.

On Conversion

Collect

O Almighty God, who has knit together Your elect in one communion and fellowship in the mystical body of Your Son, Christ our Lord; Grant us grace so to follow Your blessed saints in all virtuous and godly living that we may come to those unspeakable joys which You have prepared for those who truly love You; through Jesus Christ, Your Son, our Lord, who lives and reigns with You and the Holy Spirit, one God, now and forever.

November 2 - The Commemoration of the Faithful Departed

Lesson: John 5:24-29

Homily - Guerric of Igny

If there are tombs in a garden surely there are not gardens in tombs? Yet perhaps there are, but in the tombs of the just. There indeed a certain most agreeable pleasantness which belongs to gardens will flourish as in spring, the springtime, that is, of their resurrection when their flesh will blossom again. Not only the bones of the just man will sprout like grass but also the whole of the just man will sprout like a lily and bloom forever before the Lord. Not so the godless, not so. They are buried with the burial of an ass. Without any hope of a better resurrection, they are subject to corruption, as a foretaste of their future fate. Concerning their tombs I had begun to say that as great as is the difference between their filth and the beauty of gardens in flower incomparably greater is the difference between the delight of spiritual men and the pleasure of carnal joys.

It is you, then, if I am not mistaken, who dwell in gardens, you who meditate on the law of the Lord day and night and walk about in as many gardens as you read books, pick as many apples as you select fine thoughts. And blessed are you for whom all the apples, both old and new, are kept, that is, for whom the words of the prophets, evangelists and apostles are laid up, so that to each of you those words of the Bride to the Bridegroom seem to be said: "All the apples, new and old, my Beloved, I have kept for you."

Search the Scriptures then. For you are not mistaken in thinking that in them you find life, you who seek nothing else in them but Christ, to whom the Scriptures bear witness. Blessed indeed are they who search His testimonies, who seek them out with all their heart.

Sermon 54, A Sermon for Arousing Devotion at Psalmody

Collect

Almighty God, in whose glorious presence live all who die in the Lord and before whom all the souls of the faithful, having been delivered from the burden of the flesh, live in joy and faithfulness, we give you hearty thanks for Your grace to all Your servants who have finished their course of faith and now rest from their labors, and we humbly implore Your mercy that we, with them, may have our perfect consummation and bliss, in body and soul, in Your eternal and everlasting glory; through Jesus Christ, Your Son, our Lord, who lives and reigns with You and the Holy Spirit, one God, now and forever.

November 11 - The Commemoration of Martin of Tours, Bishop & Confessor

Lord God of hosts, you clothed your servant Martin the soldier with the spirit of sacrifice, and set him as a bishop in your Church to be a defender of the catholic faith: Give us grace to follow in his holy steps, that at the last we may be found clothed with righteousness in the dwellings of peace; through Jesus Christ our Lord, who lives and reigns with you and the Holy Spirit, one God, now and forever.

November 17 - The Commemoration of Gregory Thaumaturgas, Bishop & Confessor

O Lord, our Heavenly Father, You once caused Your servant, Gregory, to be vigilant in prayer and constant in works of mercy; grant us, we pray, grace to follow his example, and through prayer and almsgiving, to bear the fruits of the faith You have given us in Your Son, Jesus Christ, our Lord, who lives and reigns with You and the Holy Spirit, one God, now and forever.

November 22 - The Commemoration of Cecilia, Martyr

Most gracious God, Your servant, Cecilia, sang in her heart to strengthen her confession of you; we give you thanks for Your gift of psalms, hymns and spiritual songs; and we pray that we may chant Your praises until, with Cecilia and all your saints, we come at the last to share in the song of those redeemed by our Savior Jesus Christ; who with you and the Holy Spirit lives and reigns, one God, in glory everlasting.

November 23 - The Commemoration of Clement of Rome, Bishop & Martyr

Almighty God, you chose your servant Clement of Rome to recall the Church in Corinth to obedience and stability: Grant that your Church may be grounded and settled in your truth by the indwelling of the Holy Spirit; reveal to it what is not yet known; fill up what is lacking; and keep it blameless in your service; through Jesus Christ our Lord, who lives and reigns with you and the Holy Spirit, one God, now and forever.

THE LITANY

To be said in place of the Kyrie at Lauds and Vespers on Rogation and Ember Days

℣: O Lord,

℣: O Christ,

℣: O Lord,

℟: Have mer - cy.

℟: Have mer - cy.

℟: Have mer - cy.

℣: O Christ,

℟: Hear us.

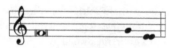

℣: God the Father in / heaven,

℣: God the Son, Re-deemer of / the world,

℣: God the Ho-ly / Spirit,

℟: Have mer - cy on us.

℟: Have mer - cy on us.

℟: Have mer - cy on us.

℣: Be gra - cious to us.

℣: Be gra - cious to us.

℟: Spare us, good Lord.

℟: Help us, good Lord.

℣: From all sin, from all
   error, / from all evil;

℣: From the crafts and
   assaults / of the devil;

℣: Form sudden / and evil death;

℣: From pesti- / lence and famine;

℣: From / war and bloodshed;

℣: From sedition and / from rebellion;

℣: From light- /ning and tempest;

℣: From all calamity by / fire and water;

℣: From ev- / erlasting death;

℣: By the mystery of Your
   holy / incarnation;

℟: De- liv- er us, O Lord.

℟: De- liv- er us, O Lord.

℟: De- liv- er us, O Lord.

℟: De- liv- er us, O Lord.

℟: De- liv- er us, O Lord.

℟: De- liv- er us, O Lord.

℟: De- liv- er us, O Lord.

℟: De- liv- er us, O Lord.

℟: De- liv- er us, O Lord.

℟: De- liv- er us, O Lord.

℣: By Your holy / nativity;   ℟: De- liv- er us, O Lord.

℣: By Your baptism,
fasting / and temptation;   ℟: De- liv- er us, O Lord.

℣: By Your agony / and bloody sweat;   ℟: De- liv- er us, O Lord.

℣: By Your / cross and passion;   ℟: De- liv- er us, O Lord.

℣: By Your precious death / and burial;   ℟: De- liv- er us, O Lord.

℣: By Your glorious
resurrection / and ascension;   ℟: De- liv- er us, O Lord.

℣: And by the coming of the
Holy Spirit, / the Comforter: ℟: De- liv- er us, O Lord.

℣: In all time / of tribulation;   ℟: De- liv- er us, O Lord.

℣: In all time of our / prosperity;   ℟: De- liv- er us, O Lord.

℣: In / the hour of death;   ℟: De- liv- er us, O Lord.

℣: And in the / day of judgment: ℟: De- liv- er us, O Lord.

℣:   We poor sin - ners   ℟: Im-plore You to hear us.

℣: To rule and govern Your
ho- / ly Christian Church;

℣: To preserve all pastors and ministers
of Your Church in the true
knowledge and understanding
of Your wholesome Word and to
sustain them in / holy living;   ℟: We im-plore You to hear us.

℣: To put an end to all schisms
and caus- / es of offense;   ℟: We im-plore You to hear us.

℣: To bring into the way of truth
all who have erred / and are
deceived;   ℟: We im-plore You to hear us.

℣: To beat down Satan / under our feet;   ℟: We im-plore You to hear us.

℣: To send faithful laborers in- / to
Your harvest;   ℟: We im-plore You to hear us.

℣: To accompany Your Word
with Your / grace and Spirit: ℟: We im-plore You to hear us.

℣: To raise those who fall and to
strength- / en those who stand;   ℟: We im-plore You to hear us.

℣: To comfort and help the
weakhearted / and the distressed: ℟: We im-plore You to hear us.

℣: To give to all peoples / concord and peace;   ℟: We im-plore You to hear us.

℣: To preserve our land from / discord and strife;   ℟: We im-plore You to hear us.

℣: To give our country Your protection in ev'- / ry time of need;   ℟: We im-plore You to hear us.

℣: To direct and defend our president and all in / authority;   ℟: We im-plore You to hear us.

℣: To bless and protect our magistrates and / all our people;   ℟: We im-plore You to hear us.

℣: To watch over and help all who are in danger, necessity, and / tribulation;   ℟: We im-plore You to hear us.

℣: To protect and guide / all who travel;   ℟: We im-plore You to hear us.

℣: To grant all women with child, and all mothers with infant children, increasing happiness / in their blessings;   ℟: We im-plore You to hear us.

℣: To defend all orphans and widows and to / provide for them;   ℟: We im-plore You to hear us.

℣: To strengthen and keep all sick persons / and young children;   ℟: We im-plore You to hear us.

℣: To free / those in bondage;   ℟: We im-plore You to hear us.

℣: And to have mer- / cy on us all: ℟: We im-plore You to hear us.

℣: To forgive our enemies, persecutors, and slanderers and / to turn their hearts;   ℟: We im-plore You to hear us.

℣: To give and preserve to our use the kindly / fruits of the earth;   ℟: We im-plore You to hear us.

℣: And graciously / to hear our prayers: ℟: We im-plore You to hear us.

℣: Lord Jesus / Christ, Son of God: ℟: We im-plore You to hear us.

℣: O, Lamb of God, who takes a-way the sin of the world,

℟: Spare us, O Lord.

℣: O, Lamb of God, who takes a-way the sin of the world,

R︀⁄: Hear us, O Lord.

℣: O, Lamb of God, who takes a - way the sin of the world,

R︀⁄: Have mer-cy on us, O Lord.

℣: O Christ,

R︀⁄: Hear us.

℣: O Lord,
℣: O Christ,

R︀⁄: Have mer - cy.
R︀⁄: Have mer - cy.

℣: O Lord,

R︀⁄: Have mer - cy.

℣: O Lord,

℣: O Christ,

℣: O Lord,

℟: Have mer - cy.

℟: Have mer - cy.

℟: Have mer - cy.

℣: O Christ,

℟: Hear us.

℣: God the Fa- ther in heav - en,

℟: Have mer-cy on us.

℣: God the Son, Re-deem-er of the world,

℟: Have mer-cy on us.

℣: God the Ho - ly Spi - rit,

℟: Have mer-cy on us.

℣: Be gra - cious to us.

℣: Be gra - cious to us.

℟: Spare us, good Lord.

℟: Help us, good Lord.

℣: From all sin, from all error, from all evil;
From the crafts and assaults of the devil;
Form sudden and evil death;
From pestilence and famine;
From war and bloodshed;
From sedition and from rebellion;
From lighting and tempest;
From all calamity by fire and water;
And from ev- / erlasting death;

℟: Good Lord, de-liv-er us.

℣: By the mystery of Your holy incarnation;
By Your holy nativity;
By Your baptism, fasting and temptation;
By Your agony and bloody sweat;
By Your cross and passion;
By Your precious death and burial;
By Your glorious resurrection and ascension;
And by the coming of the Holy Spirit, / the Comforter:

℟: Help us, good Lord.

℣: In all time of tribulation;
In all time of our prosperity,
In the hour of death;
And in the / day of judgment:

℟: Help us, good Lord.

℣: We poor sin- / ners implore You

℟: To hear us, O Lord.

℣: To rule and govern Your holy Christian Church;
To preserve all pastors and ministers of Your Church in the true knowledge
and understanding of Your wholesome Word and to sustain them in holy
living;
To put an end to all schisms and causes of offense;
To bring into the way of truth all who have erred and are deceived;
To beat down Satan under our feet;
To send faithful laborers into Your harvest;
And to accompany Your Word with Your / grace and Spi-rit:

℟: We im-plore You to hear us, good Lord.

℣: To raise those who fall and to strengthen those who stand;
And to comfort and help the weakhearted / and the dis-tressed:

℟: We im-plore You to hear us, good Lord.

℣: To give to all peoples concord and peace;
To preserve our land from discord and strife;
To give our country Your protection in every time of need;
To direct and defend our president and all in authority;
To bless and protect our magistrates and all our people;
To watch over and help all who are in danger, necessity, and tribulation;
To protect and guide all who travel;
To grant all women with child, and all mothers with infant children, increas-
ing happiness in their blessings;
To defend all orphans and widows and to provide for them;
To strengthen and keep all sick persons and young children;
To free those in bondage;
And to have mer- / cy on us all:

℟: We im-plore You to hear us, good Lord.

℣: To forgive our enemies, persecutors, and slanderers and to turn their hearts;
To give and preserve to our use the kindly fruits of the earth;
And graciously / to hear our prayers:

℟: We im-plore You to hear us, good Lord.

℣: Lord Jesus / Christ, Son of God:

R℣: We im - plore You to hear us.

℣: Christ, the Lamb of God, who takes a - way the sin of the world,

R℣: Have mer - cy.

℣: Christ, the Lamb of God, who takes a - way the sin of the world,

R℣: Have mer - cy.

℣: Christ, the Lamb of God, who takes a - way the sin of the world,

R℣: Grant us Your peace.

℣: O Christ,

R℣: Hear us.

℣: O Lord,
℣: O Christ,

R℣: Have mer - cy.
R℣: Have mer - cy.

℣: O Lord,

R℣: Have mer - cy. A - men.

651

ADDITIONAL MORNING AND EVENING HYMNS

These hymns may be used at Matins, Lauds and Vepsers in place of the Office Hymn given.
They are arranged according to their traditional use during the week.

Sunday at Matins - *Iam nunc, paterna claritas*

1. O Fa - ther of un - cloud-ed light! We pray Thee, kneel-
2. That this our bo - dy's mor- tal frame May know no sin
3. Re - deem-er of the world, we pray That Thou wouldst wash

ing in Thy sight, From all de - file - ment to be freed,
and fear no shame, Nor fire here - af - ter be our end
our sins a - way, And give us, of Thy bound-less grace,

And ev' - ry sin - ful act and deed.
Of pas - sions which our bo - soms rend.
The bless - ings of the heav'n-ly place.

4. That we, thence exiled by our sin,
Hereafter may be welcomed in;
That blessèd time awaiting now,
With hymns of glory here we bow.

5. O Father, this we ask be done,
Through Jesus Christ, Thine only Son,
Who, with the Holy Ghost and Thee,
Doth live and reign eternally. Amen.

Gregory I

Sunday at Lauds - *Aeterne rerum Conditor*

1. E - ter - nal Ma - ker of the worlds, Who day and night
2. The light which puts dark- ness to flight, Which seg - re - gates
3. Light-bring-ing sun is thus a - roused, And hea - ven frees

in turn un - furls; And time and sea - sons change You give,
each night from night; The day's her - ald is sound-ing forth,
from its dark shroud, That all the er - rant, wav'- ring throng,

Your crea- tures te - dium to re - lieve;
Call - ing that bright and shin - ing orb.
De - sert the way of sin and wrong.

4. At morn the sailor courage finds
And raging seas grow mild, subside
Simon the Church's rock was then
At rooster's-crow pardoned from sin.

5. Let us at once therefore arise.
The morn opens our sleepy eyes,
And slothful ones it chastens now,
And puts to shame those lying 'round.

6. At cock's crow hope returns again,
The ill find health restored to them,
The robber puts his sword away,
And lapsing souls return to faith.

7. Look, Jesu, on Your frail elect,
And by Your gaze our faults correct
And with Your look, remove our sin
And in our tears ease guilt within.

8. O Light, shine brightly on our minds;
Dispel the evil dreams of night;
May our first words be praises true
In prayers and vows we chant to You.

9. To God the Father glory be,
And praise eternal Son to You
Whom with the Spirit Paraclete
Does live and reign all ages through. Amen.

Ambrose of Milan

Sunday at Vespers - *Lucis Creator optime* As indicated in the Ordinary of Vespers

Monday at Matins - *Somno refectis artubus*

1. Our limbs re - freshed with slum - ber now, And sloth cast off
2. To Thee our ear - liest morn - ing song, To Thee our hearts'
3. As shades at morn - ing fly a - way, And night be - fore

in prayer we bow; And while we sing Thy prais - es dear,
full pow'rs be - long, And Thou, O Ho - ly One, pre - cede
the star of day; So each trans- gres- sion of the night

O Fa - ther, be Thou pre- sent here.
Each foll'- wing ac - tion, word and deed.
Be purged by Thee, cel - es - tial Light!

653

4. Cut off, we pray Thee, each offense,
And ev'ry lust of thought and sense;
That by their lips who Thee adore
Thou may'st be praised forevermore.

5. Grant this, O Father, ever One
With Christ Thy sole-begotten Son,
And Holy Ghost, whom all adore,
Reigning and blest forevermore. Amen

Ambrose of Milan

Monday at Lauds - *Splendor paternae gloria* As indicated in the Ordinary of Lauds

Monday at Vespers - *Immense caeli Conditor*

1. O great Cre - a - tor of the sky, Who would-est not
2. The floods a - bove Thou didst or - dain; The floods be - low
3. Up - on our souls, good Lord, be - stow Thy gift of grace

the floods on high With earth - ly wa - ters to con-found,
Thou didst re - strain; That mois- ture might at - tem - per heat,
in end - less flow; Lest some re - newed de - ceit or wile

But made the firm - a - ment their bound;
Lest the parched earth should ru - in meet.
Of for - mer sin should us be - guile.

4. Let faith discover heav'nly light;
So shall its rays direct us right;
And let this faith each error chase
And never give to falsehood place.

5. Grant this, O Father, ever One
With Christ, Thy sole-begotten Son,
And Holy Ghost, whom all adore,
Reigning and blest forevermore. Amen.

Gregory I

Tuesday at Matins - *Consors paterni luminis*

1. O Light of light, O Day-spring bright, Co - e - qual in
2. All dark - ness from our minds dis - pel, And turn to flight
3. O Christ, Thy par - don, full and free, Be - stow on us

654

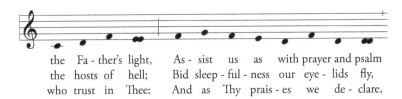

the Fa - ther's light,   As - sist   us   as   with prayer and psalm
the hosts of   hell;   Bid sleep - ful - ness our eye - lids fly,
who trust in   Thee: And as   Thy prais - es   we   de - clare,

Thy ser - vants break the night-time's calm.
Lest ov - er - come in sloth we   lie.
O   with   ac - cep - tance hear our prayer.

4. O Father this we ask be done,
Through Jesus Christ, Thine only Son;
Who, with the Holy Ghost and Thee,
Doth live and reign eternally. Amen.

Ambrose of Milan

Tuesday at Lauds - *Ales diei nuntius*

1.   Day's her - ald   bird, with des- cant clear   Pro - claims the   morn-
2.   "Take up   your beds" the Sav - ior cries, "From dull and   life-
3.   Sup-pliant, on   Je - sus' name we call,   Be - fore   His   throne

ing   light   is near; And Christ who wakes the   souls   of   men,
less   ease   a - rise;   In sob - er char - i - ty   and fear,
re - pent - ant fall; Each con-trite heart doth vig - il   keep,

In - vites us   un - to   life a - gain.
Watch ye,   for   I   the   Lord am near.
A - roused from dead and   earth- ly sleep.

4. O Christ, our sinful slumbers wake
Night's cold and slavish fetters break;
Thy freedom to our souls restore,
New light on ev'ry sense outpour.

5. Glory to God the Father be,
Like glory, only Son, to Thee;
And to the Spirit Paraclete,
Now and through ages infinate. Amen.

Aurelius Prudentius

Tuesday at Vespers - *Telluris ingens Conditor*

1. Thou fram - er of this earth - ly sphere, Whose e - dict made
2. That so the soil its herb might yield And flow - ers fair
3. The wounds of sin which parch the soul, With Thy re - fresh-

    the land ap - pear; Th'en-cum-b'ring wat - ers drove a - side,
    to deck the field, And gold - en fruit and har - vests bear,
    ing grace make whole; From guilt and shame our hearts re - lease,

    And fixed the ground un - moved for aye;
    And pleas - ant food for man pre - pare.
    And calm our pas - sions in - to peace.

4. Let us Thy holy will obey,
    Turn us from ev'ry evil way
    That we Thy flock from peril freed
    May on Thy choicest bounties feed.

5. Most gracious Father, hear our prayer;
    Coequal only Son, give ear;
    Who with Thee, Spirit, Paraclete
    Reign throughout ages, infinite. Amen.

Gregory

Wednesday at Matins - *Rerum Creator optime*

1. Cre - a - tor of the earth and skies, Our bless - ed guide,
2. Dear Christ, to Thee we come for aid, Look not up - on
3. We lift our hearts and hands to Thee, As pro - phet bade

    we call on Thee, Look down up - on our mis - er - ies,
    our faults, we pray; To Thee our grate - ful thanks are paid
    and Paul hath shown; While dark-ness flees from land and sea

    From sin and sor - row make us free.
    Now that the night has passed a - way.
    We seek Thee; hear our earn - est groan.

4. Thou see'st the evil we have done,
Each deed before Thee open lies;
Thy pardon send, O Holy One!
In pity heed our prayers and cries.

5. To God the Father glory be,
All praise eternal Son to Thee
Whom with the Spirit Paraclete
Doth live and reign eternally. Amen.

Gregory I

Wednesday at Lauds - *Nox et tenebrae et nubila*

1. Ye gloom of night, ye clouds and shade, O'er earth in dark
2. Earth's dus - ky veil is rent a - way, Pierced by the spark-
3. O Christ, to Thee our heav'n-ward gaze, With pure and ear-

con - fus - ion spread, The light is here! Be- hold the dawn!
ling sol - ar ray; Bright hues o'er na-ture's face re - turn,
nest hearts we raise; Now to our prayers and hymns give ear,

Christ com - eth, haste ye and be gone,
Waked by the quick-'ning glance of morn.
And with Thy- self our sen - ses cheer.

4. Our souls with cares and sins o'ergrown,
Are cleansed by Thy sweet light alone;
Thou Eastern Star of heav'nly sheen
Illume us with Thine eye serene.

5. Lord, Holy, Virgin born, to Thee,
Eternal praise and glory be;
With Father and with Holy Ghost
Long as eternity shall last. Amen.

Aurelius Prudentius

Wednesday at Vespers - *Caeli Deus sanctissime*

1. Most ho - ly God, the Lord of Heav'n, Who this Thy glo-
2. The fourth great day, who bright and clear Didst form the sun's
3. There- by of dark-ness and of light To fix the bound-

rious, light hast giv'n To deck with glow - ing tints on high
re - ful - gent sphere; And with the chang- ing moon or - dain
a - ries a - right, And give each month a not - ed sign

The shin - ing   zen - ith of the sky;
The cour - ses   of the star - ry train;
To mark its   or - i - gin di - vine;

4. With all Thy light our souls illume,
O chase away our mental gloom
From error's chain our hearts release,
And give the burdened conscience peace.

5. Most gracious Father, hear our prayer;
Coequal only Son, give ear;
Who with Thee, Spirit, Paraclete
Reign throughout ages, infinite. Amen.

Gregory I

Thursday at Matins - *Nox atra rerum contegit*

1. The dus - ky veil of   night hath laid   The var - ied hues
2. Take far   a - way our   load of   sin,   Our guilt-stained minds
3. For lo! our minds are dull and cold, En - ven - omed by ,

of   earth in   shade;   Be- fore Thee, right- eous Judge of all,
make clean with - in;   Thy pre-cious grace, O Christ, im-part,
sin's dead - ly   hold;   They dark-ness now would glad - ly flee

We con - trite in   con - fess - ion fall.
From all of - fence to guard our hearts.
And seek, Re - deem - er, un - to   Thee.

4. Far from them drive the shades of night
The in-most darkness put to flight;
Til in the daylight of the Blest
They joy to find themselves at rest.

5. O Father, this we ask be done
Through Jesus Christ, Thine only Son;
Who with the Holy Ghost and Thee
Doth live and reign eternally! Amen.

Gregory I

Thursday at Lauds - *Lux ecce surgit aurea*

1. Be - hold the gold - en morn a - rise! The pal - ing night
2. Out-pour Thy gifts, se - ren - est Light! And make us fault-
3. So may the day speed on; our tongue No false- hood know,

for - sakes   the   skies,   The   mis - ty   sha - dows melt   a - way
less   in   Thy   sight; Ne'er may we   ut - ter   words of   guile,
our hands   no   wrong; Our eyes from   e - vil   gaze   re - frain

Which led   our   err - ing   sense   a - stray.
Dark thoughts our bo - soms ne'er   de - file.
No   guilt our guard- ed   bod - ies   stain.

4. Behold th'Allseeing from on high
   Surveys us with a watchful eye;
   Each day our every act He knows
   From early dawn to evening's close.

5. Glory to God the Father be!
   Like glory, Only Son, to Thee;
   And to the Spirit Paraclete
   Now, and through ages infinite! Amen.

Aurelius Prudentius

Thursday at Vespers - *Magnae Deus potentiae*

1.   Al - migh- ty   God, whose sov'-reign will   Bade liv - ing   forms
2.   O'er some out-spread the   seas;   the   rest   With dew and   rain
3.   O   grant that in   the   cleans-ing   flood   Bap-tized   of   Thine

the   wa - ters   fill;   To   part   as - signed   a   dwell - ing   there,
from Heav'n re-freshed;   So   from one Migh - ty   Par - ent   born,
a - ton - ing   Blood,   We,   set   from death and   sor - row   free,

And   part   up - lift - ed   to   the   air;
Each   its   own   sta - tion   might a - dorn;
Hence-forth may   not   de - part   from   Thee!

4. O ne'er may crime the conscience grieve,
   Nor pride th'uplifted soul deceive
   The contrite keep Thou from despair
   The proud from endless ruin spare.

5. Kind Father, hear from Heav'n on high,
   Coequal Only Son, our cry;
   And Thou, Blest Spirit Paraclete
   Who reign through ages infinite! Amen.

Gregory I

Friday at Matins - *Tu Trinitatis Unitas*

1. Thou Trin - i - ty in un - i - ty, Who rul - est all
2. Now joy - ful from our beds we rise, While morn-ing breaks
3. If an - y sin this night de - filed The soul, by Sa-

things might-i - ly, Bow down to hear the songs of praise
up - on the skies; O make our mor - tal fail - ings whole,
tan's arts be - guiled, Re - gard from Heav'n, Thy dwell-ing place

Which we, Thy wake - ful ser - vants raise.
Thou great Phy - si - cian of the soul.
And cleanse it by Thy glor- ious grace.

4. Let pureness ev'ry frame possess,
Nor sloth-ful-ness our hearts oppress,
Nor sin's cold leprosy with ill
The fervor of our spirits chill.

5. Redeemer, in Thy saving might
Illume us with Thy saving light;
That in our walk from day to day
From Thee we never more may stray.

6. O Father, this we ask be done
Through Jesus Christ, Thine only Son;
Who with the Holy Ghost and Thee,
Doth live and reign eternally. Amen.

Gregory I

Friday at Lauds - *Aeterna Caeli Gloria*

1. O Christ, whose glo - ry fills the heav'n, Our on - ly hope
2. Grant us Thine aid, Thy praise to sing, As op - 'ning days
3. The morn - ing star fades from the sky, The sun breaks forth;

in mer - cy giv'n, Child of a vir - gin, meek and pure;
new dut - ies bring; That with the light our life may be
night's sha - dows fly: O Thou, true Light, up - on us shine:

Son of the High-est ev - er - more:
Re - newed and sanc - ti - fied by Thee.
Our dark - ness turn to light di - vine.

4. Within us grant Thy light to dwell:
And from our souls dark sins expel;
Cleanse Thou our minds from stain of ill,
And with Thy peace our bosoms fill.

5. To us strong faith forever give,
With joyous hope, in Thee to live;
That life's rough way may ever be
Made strong and pure by charity.

6. All laud to God the Father be;
All praise, Eternal Son, to Thee;
All glory, as is ever meet,
To God the Holy Paraclete. Amen.

Anonymous, 5th cent.

Friday at Vespers - *Plasmator hominis Deus*

1. Mak - er of man who from Thy throne Dost or - der all
2. The migh - ty forms that fill the land, In - stinct with life
3. From all Thy ser - vants drive a - way What-e'er of thought

things, God a - lone; By whose de - cree the teem- ing earth
at Thy com-mand, Are giv'n sub- dued to hu - man-kind
im - pure to - day Hath been with op - en ac - tion blent,

To rep - tile and to beast gave birth:
For ser - vice in their rank as - signed.
Or ming- led with the heart's in - tent.

4. In heaven Thine endless joys bestow,
And grant Thy gifts of grace below;
From chains of strife our souls release,
Bind fast the gentle bands of peace.

5. Grant this, O Father, ever One
With Christ, Thy sole-begotten Son,
Whom, with the Spirit we adore,
One God, both now and evermore. Amen.

Gregory I

Saturday at Matins - *Summae Parens clementiae*

1. Fa - ther of heav'n-ly clem - en - cy,   And ru - ler of
2. O Lord of all the roll - ing spheres,   We send our cries
3. Our bod - ies and our minds re - fine   In fires of love;

cre - a - tion's frame,   In sub-stance one, in per - sons three,
and prayers to Thee;   In mer - cy mark the prayers and tears,
dear Sav - ior, be   Our strength, and give us grace di - vine,

We praise and bless Thy ho - ly name.
And keep our souls from e - vil free.
To keep our wills a - loft with Thee.

4. Now as our anthems, upward borne,
Awake the silence of the morn,
Enrich us with Thy gifts of grace,
From heav'n, Thy blissful dwelling place.

5. O Father, this we ask be done
Through Jesus Christ, Thine only Son,
Who with the Holy Ghost and Thee
Doth live and reign eternally. Amen.

Ambrosian, 7th century

Saturday at Lauds - *Aurora jam spargit polum*

1. Dawn sprink-les all the east with light;   Day o'er the earth
2. Each phan-tom of the night de - part,   Each thought of guilt
3. So that last morn - ing, dread and great,   Which we with tremb-

is glid - ing bright; Morn's glitt- 'ring rays their course be - gin;
for - sake the heart; Let ev' - ry ill that dark-ness brought
ling hope a - wait, With bless - ed light for us shall glow,

Fare- well to dark - ness and to sin.
Be - neath its shade now come to nought.
Who chant the song we sang be - low:

4. All laud to God the Father be,
All laud, Eternal Son, to Thee;
All laud, as is forever meet,
To God the Holy Paraclete. Amen.   *Anonymous, 4th-5th century*

Saturday at Vespers - *O Lux beata Trinitas*

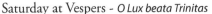

1. O Tri - ni - ty of bless - ed light, O U - ni - ty
2. To Thee our morn-ing song of praise, To Thee our eve-
3. All laud to God the Fa - ther be; All praise, E - ter-

of sov'- reign might, As now the fi - 'ry sun de - parts,
ning prayer we raise, Thee may our glo - ry ev - er - more
nal Son to Thee, All glo - ry as is ev - er meet,

Shed Thou Thy beams with - in our hearts.
In low - ly rev - er - ance a - dore.
To God the Ho - ly Par - a - clete.   A - men.

Ambrose of Milan

ST. PATRICK'S BREASTPLATE

This prayer may be said at Matins or Lauds as an extended collect, o responsively as a litany..

I arise today
  through a mighty strength,
    the invocation of the Trinity,
  through belief in the threeness
  through confession of the oneness
  of the Creator of creation.

I arise today
  through the strength of Christ
    and His baptism,
  through the strength of His
    crucifixion and burial,
  through the strength of
    His resurrection and ascension,
  through the strength of His descent
    for the judgment of doom.

I arise today
  through the strength
    of the love of Cherubim,
  in the obedience of angels,
  in the service of archangels,
  in hope of resurrection
    to meet with reward,
  in the prayers of Patriarchs,
  in the predictions of Prophets,
  in the preachings of Apostles,
  in the faith of Confessors,
  in the innocence of holy Virgins,
  in the deeds of righteous men.

I arise today
  through the strength of Heaven:
  light of sun,
  brilliance of moon,
  splendor of fire,
  speed of lightning,
  swiftness of wind,
  depth of sea,
  stability of earth,
  firmness of rock.

I arise today
  through God's strength to pilot me,
  God's might to uphold me,
  God's wisdom to guide me,
  God's eye to look before me,

God's ear to hear me,
God's word to speak for me,
God's hand to guard me,
God's way to lie before me,
God's shield to protect me,
God's host to secure me -
  against snares of devils,
  against temptations of vices,
  against inclinations of nature,
  against everyone who shall wish me ill,
    afar and near,
    alone and in a multitude.

I summon today all those powers
  between me (and these evils) -
  against every cruel and merciless power
    that may oppose my body and soul,
  against incantations of false prophets,
  against black laws of the heathen,
  against false laws of heretics,
  against craft of idolatry,
  against spells of women and
    smiths and wizards,
  against every knowledge that
    endangers man's body and soul.

Christ to protect me today
  against poison, against burning,
  against drowning, against wounding,
  so that there may come to me
  an abundance of reward.

Christ with me, Christ before me,
  Christ behind me.
Christ in me, Christ beneath me,
  Christ above me,
Christ on my right, Christ on my left,
Christ where I lie, Christ where I sit,
  Christ where I arise,
Christ in the heart of every man
  who thinks of me,
Christ in the mouth of every man
  who speaks of me,
Christ in every eye that sees me,
Christ in every ear that hears me.

I arise today
 through a mighty strength,
  the invocation of the Trinity,
 through belief in the threeness
 through confession of the oneness
 of the Creator of creation.

Salvation is of the Lord.
Salvation is of the Lord.
Salvation is of Christ.
May Thy salvation, O Lord, be ever with us.

TONE FOR THE LESSONS AND CHAPTERS

The readings in each liturgy may be chanted. As with the Psalm tones, the tone for the readings consist of various parts. The reading is always preceded by an introduction, stating from which book the reading is taken. Each sentence of the reading is divided into an even number of parts, in each pair, the first part ends with a flex (at a comma or natural pause), the second with either a metrum (at a colon or period within the verse, but not at the end of the verse), interrogation (question mark), or punctum (end of verse). The reading is followed by the Conclusion which consists of a versicle and response.

Introduction

From the Acts of the A- / post-les.   From St. Paul's epistle to the / Ro-mans.

flex   *metrum*

Lesson

flex   *punctum*

flex   *interrogativum*

Conclusion

℣: O Lord, have mercy up- / on us.   ℟: Thanks be to   God.

TONE FOR THE COLLECTS

The collects and prayers may be chanted. Like the tones for the readings, prayer tones are composed of flexes, metrums and punctums. The elements correspond, however, not to punctuation marks, but to the elements of the prayer being chanted. Each prayer is made up of specific parts:

The Address, which identifies to whom one is praying;

The Description, which states something about God or something that He has done or said that forms the basis for the request;

The Request, which states the need of the one praying;

The Reason, which states the desired outcome; and

The Conclusion, which gathers the entire prayer together in the name of Jesus and is usually doxological and Trinitarian.

This formula is the basis for all Collects (and a good pattern for one's private prayers, whether ex corde or composed). The Tones below are meant to highlight this pattern as well as each element in prayer.

The first metrum signals the end of the Description.

The first flex signals the end of the Request.

The second flex is at the name of Jesus in the doxological ending.

The second metrum is at the name of the Holy Spirit.

The punctum completes the prayer.

Festive Tone   *To be used at Matins, Lauds and Vespers on Sundays and feasts.*

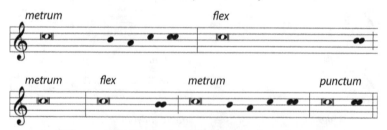

Ferial Tone   *To be used at Terce, Sext, None, and Compline, and at Matins, Lauds and Vespers on ferial days. The ferial tone is sung on the same note (C) throughout, with only a slight pause where the flex or metrum would fall. This tone may be lowered by a fifth.*

THE NINE PSALM TONES

including the flex and the various terminations

Tone 3a

Tone 3b

Tone 3g

Tone 3g²

Tone 4A

Tone 4g

Tone 5

Tone 6

Tone 7a

Intonation Tenor   Flex   Tenor   Mediation   Tenor   Termination

Tone 7b

Intonation Tenor   Flex   Tenor   Mediation   Tenor   Termination

Tone 7c

Intonation Tenor   Flex   Tenor   Mediation   Tenor   Termination

Tone 7c²

Intonation Tenor   Flex   Tenor   Mediation   Tenor   Termination

Tone 7d

Intonation Tenor   Flex   Tenor   Mediation   Tenor   Termination

Tone 8G

Intonation Tenor   Flex   Tenor   Mediation   Tenor   Termination

Tone 8c

Intonation Tenor   Flex   Tenor   Mediation   Tenor   Termination

Tonus Peregrinus

Intonation Tenor   Flex   Tenor   Mediation   Tenor   Termination

SCHEDULE FOR READING THE BIBLE
OVER THE COURSE OF THE YEAR

The readings at Lauds and Vespers are designed so that the chief parts of the entire Bible will be read over the course of the year. This traditional schedule, listed by season of the church year, is given below for the benefit of those who wish to adapt the readings to their own particular devotional pattern. The Gospels and the Psalms are not included. Certain apocryphal readings (italicized) are also included here for those who wish to read them.

Advent	Isaiah
Christmas	Romans, I Corinthians
Epiphany	II Corinthians, Galatians, Ephesians, Philippians, Colossians, I & II Thessalonians, I & II Timothy, Titus, Philemon, Hebrews
Prelent	Genesis
Lent	Exodus, Leviticus, Numbers, Deuteronomy, Joshua, Judges, Ruth
Passiontide	Jeremiah
Triduum	Lamentations
Easter	Acts of the Apostles, Revelation, James, I & II Peter, I, II & III John, Jude
Pentecost - July	I & II Samuel, I & II Kings, I & II Chronicles
August	Proverbs, Ecclesiastes, Song of Solomon *Wisdom of Solomon, Ecclesiasticus*
September	Job, Esther, *Apocryphal Esther*, Ezra, Nehemiah *Tobit, Judith*
October	Ezekiel, Daniel
November	The 12 Minor Prophets, *I & II Macabees*

SCHEDULE FOR PRAYING
THE WEEKLY PSALTER

The rubrics within the liturgies of this book are based on a schedule that ensures the entire Psalter is prayed each month, with certain Psalms prayed more frequently. It is recognized that some will desire to pray the entire Psalter in a week rather than in a month. The following schedule, based upon the pattern given by Benedict of Nursia in his monastic Rule is offered for such use. The following is an approximation of Benedict's use, as It is not entirely clear from his monastic rule just how the longer Psalms were to be divided, exactly which Psalms were said at each day's Matins, or which Canticles were said at Lauds.

	Sunday	Monday	Tuesday	Wednesday	Thursday	Friday	Saturday
Matins	3	3	3	3	3	3	3
	95	95	95	95	95	95	95
	21-32	33-35	44-50	56	71-75	81-87	98-109
		37-42*	52-55*	58-62	77-80*	89	
				66		93-94	
				68-70*		96-97	
Lauds	67	67	67	67	67	67	67
	51	51	51	51	51	51	51
	118	5	43	64-65	88	76	143
	63	36	57	Cant.	90	92	Cant.
	Cant.	Cant.	Cant.	148-150	Cant.	Cant.	148-150
	148-150	148-150	148-150		148-150	148-150	
Terce	119	1-2	7-9	10-11	12-14	15-17	18-20
	(1-32)	6					
Sext	119	119	120-124	120-124	120-124	120-124	120-124
	(33-64)	(97-144)					
None	119	119	125-128	125-128	125-128	125-128	125-128
	(65-96)	(145-176)					
Vespers	110-113	114-117	129-132	133	138-140*	141-142	144b-147
				135-137		144a*	
Compline	4	4	4	4	4	4	4
	91	91	91	91	91	91	91
	134	134	134	134	134	134	134

* Psalms 33, 37, 40, 44, 68, 69, 73, 74, 78, 139, 143, 144 are each divided as if two separate psalms

SOURCES AND ACKNOWLEDGMENTS

The vast majority of the homilies have been taken from sources in the public domain, most of them having been edited using updated language for the sake of readability. Among these the following are the most important:

The Sunday Sermons of the Great Fathers (4 Volumes) by M.F. Toal, 1957-1960
The Catena Aurea of St. Thomas Aquinas (4 Volumes) translated by John Henry Parker, 1841
The Ante-Nicene Fathers (10 Volumes) by Alexander Roberts and James Donaldson, 1885
The Nicene and Post-Nicene Fathers, First Series (14 Volumes) by Philip Schaff, 1886
The Nicene and Post-Nicene Fathers, Second Series (14 Volumes) by Philip Schaff, 1890
Ante-Nicene Exegesis of the Gospels (4 Volumes) by Harold Smith, 1925
Medieval Preachers and Medieval Preaching by J. M. Neale, 1855
Sermons of Dr. Martin Luther (8 Volumes) by John Nicholas Lenker, 1906
Dr. Martin Luther's House Postil (3 Volumes) by M. Loy, 1884-1887

Many selections were also taken from works under copyright. Acknowledgement is gratefully given for the following homiletical selections (listed in alphabetical order by patristic author):

Excerpt from Aelred of Rievaulx, "Sermon 14 for the Nativity of St. John Baptist" in *Liturgical Sermons* translated by Theodore Berkeley, Cistercian Fathers Series #58 (Collegeville, MN: Cistercian Publications, © 2001) p.218-219. Used by permission of Liturgical Press. All rights reserved.

Excerpt from Aelred of Rievaulx, "Homily on Pentecost" in *Journey with the Fathers: Commentaries on the Sunday Gospels, Year B*, edited by Edith Barnecut © 1993 New City Press. Used by permission.

Excerpt from Agobard of Lyons, "The Truth of the Faith," *Early Medieval Theology, Library of Christian Classics, Volume IX*, edited by George E McCracken. © 1957 Westminster John Knox Press.

Excerpt from Alcuin of York, "Commentary on Titus," *Early Medieval Theology, Library of Christian Classics, Volume IX*, edited by George E McCracken. © 1957 Westminster John Knox Press.

Excerpt from Ambrose of Milan, "Exposition of the Gospel of St. Luke" in *Luke*, Ancient Christian Commentary on Scripture, New Testament, No. 3, © 2003 IVP Academic Press. Used by permission.

Excerpt from Ambrose of Milan, "Explanation of the Psalms" in *Grace and the Human Condition, Message of the Fathers of the Church Series #15*, by Peter C. Phan, © 1993 Liturgical Press. Reprinted with permission.

Excerpt from Andrew of Crete, "Sermon 9 for Palmarum" in *Readings for the Daily Office*, translated and edited by J. Robert Wright © 2000 Church Publishing Incorporated

Excerpt from *Anglo-Saxon Spirituality*, Classics of Western Spirituality Series, edited by Robert Boenig, © 2001 Paulist Press; used by permission.

Excerpt from Antony of Egypt in *The Life of Antony and the Letter to Mercellinus* by St. Athanasius, Classics of Western Spirituality Series, edited by Robert C. Gregg, © 1979 Paulist Press; used by permission.

Excerpt from Aphrahat of Persia, "Demonstrations" in *The Pastor: Readings from the Patristic Period* edited by Philip L. Culbertson & Arthur Bradford Shippee, © 1979 Fortress Press; used by permission.

Excerpt from Thomas Aquinas, "Summa Theologica" in *The Basic Writings of St. Thomas Aquinas* edited by Anton C. Pegis © 1945 Hackett Publishing Company, Inc. Used by permission.

Excerpt from Augustine of Hippo, "Sermon 382" in *The Works of Augustine: A Translation for the 21st Century. Volume III/10.* © 1995 New City Press. Used by permission.

Excerpt from Augustine of Hippo, "Sermon 22 on Matthew 8" in *Luke*, Ancient Christian Commentary on Scripture, New Testament, No. 3, © 2003 IVP Academic Press. Used by permission.

Excerpt from Augustine of Hippo, "Sermon 94" in *Luke*, Ancient Christian Commentary on Scripture, New Testament, No. 3, © 2003 IVP Academic Press. Used by permission.

Excerpt from Augustine of Hippo, "Sermon on the Resurrection of the Dead" in *The Works of Augustine: A Translation for the 21st Century. Volume III/10.* © 1995 New City Press. Used by permission.

Excerpt from Augustine of Hippo, "Sermon 36" in *The Works of Augustine: A Translation for the 21st Century. Volume III/2.* © 1991 New City Press. Used by permission.

Excerpt from Augustine of Hippo, "Sermon 82" in *The Works of Augustine: A Translation for the 21st Century. Volume III/3.* © 1991 New City Press. Used by permission.

Excerpts from Augustine of Hippo, "Sermon 115" in *The Works of Augustine: A Translation for the 21st Century. Volume III/4.* © 1992 New City Press. Used by permission.

Excerpt from Augustine of Hippo, "Homily 28 on John" in *The Works of Augustine: A Translation for the 21st Century. Volume III/12.* © 2009 New City Press. Used by permission.

+ *Soli Deo gloria* +

Printed in the USA
CPSIA information can be obtained
at www.ICGtesting.com
LVHW091919040923
757140LV00021B/87/J